Lecture Notes in Computer Science   12728

More information about this subseries at http://www.springer.com/series/7407

Bradford L. Chamberlain ·
Ana-Lucia Varbanescu · Hatem Ltaief ·
Piotr Luszczek (Eds.)

High Performance Computing

36th International Conference, ISC High Performance 2021
Virtual Event, June 24 – July 2, 2021
Proceedings

Springer

Editors
Bradford L. Chamberlain ⓘ
Hewlett Packard Enterprise
Seattle, WA, USA

Paul G. Allen School of Computer Science
& Engineering
University of Washington
Seattle, WA, USA

Hatem Ltaief ⓘ
Extreme Computing Research Center
Thuwal Jeddah, Saudi Arabia

Ana-Lucia Varbanescu ⓘ
University of Amsterdam
Amsterdam, The Netherlands

Piotr Luszczek ⓘ
The University of Tennessee, Knoxville
Knoxville, TN, USA

ISSN 0302-9743 ISSN 1611-3349 (electronic)
Lecture Notes in Computer Science
ISBN 978-3-030-78712-7 ISBN 978-3-030-78713-4 (eBook)
https://doi.org/10.1007/978-3-030-78713-4

LNCS Sublibrary: SL1 – Theoretical Computer Science and General Issues

This Springer imprint is published by the registered company Springer Nature Switzerland AG
The registered company address is: Gewerbestrasse 11, 6330 Cham, Switzerland

Preface

ISC High Performance—formerly known as the International Supercomputing Conference—was founded in 1986 as the Supercomputer Seminar. Originally organized by Hans Meuer, Professor of Computer Science at the University of Mannheim, and former director of its computer center, the seminar brought together a group of 81 scientists and industrial partners who shared an interest in high-performance computing (HPC). Since then, the annual conference has become a major international event within the HPC community, causing it to outgrow Mannheim and move to its current location of Frankfurt by way of Heidelberg, Dresden, Hamburg, and Leipzig over the years. Recent years have seen a general increase in both the number of high-quality research papers submitted to the conference and the number of conference attendees. Unfortunately, the ongoing coronavirus pandemic seems to have resulted in a slight dip in the number of paper submissions this year, while also requiring ISC-HPC 2021 to be held as a virtual event rather than the in-person conference in Frankfurt that we had originally hoped for.

The ISC-HPC 2021 call for papers was published in September 2020, inviting scientists and engineers to submit manuscripts describing their latest research results for potential publication at the conference. In all, 74 papers were submitted from authors all over the world. The ISC-HPC 2021 Research Papers Program Committee consisted of 75 members representing more than 60 institutions and 17 countries from around the world. After initial reviews were completed, a rebuttal process gave authors the opportunity to respond to reviewers' questions and help clarify points of confusion. Final consensus about the papers' outcomes was reached through in-depth discussions at per-track virtual Program Committee meetings, followed by a cross-track virtual meeting where decisions were finalized. In the end, the Program Committee selected 24 papers for publication at this year's conference.

For the past several years, the ISC-HPC conference has sponsored an award to encourage outstanding research in high-performance computing and to honor the best overall research paper submitted to the conference. Three years ago, this annual award was renamed in memory of the late Dr. Hans Meuer, who served as the general chair for ISC from 1986 through 2014, and who was a co-founder of the TOP500 benchmark project. This year, from all of the submitted research papers, the Program Committee selected the best paper based on a combination of its technical depth, realization, impact to the ISC-HPC community, and novelty. On this basis, the ISC-HPC~2021 Hans Meuer Award was awarded to *A Performance Analysis of Modern Parallel Programming Models Using a Compute-Bound Application* by Andrei Poenaru, Wei-Chen Lin, and Simon McIntosh-Smith from the University of Bristol. This paper presents an in-depth performance analysis of a compute-bound application using six portable programming models—OpenMP, OpenCL, CUDA, OpenACC, Kokkos, and SYCL. The paper's reviewers and the members of the Best Paper Committee appreciated the breadth of the study in terms of spanning representative programming models, compilers, and hardware platforms. The Best Paper Committee also considered the analysis to be timely and very relevant to the ISC community. Overall, the paper is an interesting read and provides a model to follow when comparing portable programming models via a case study.

As the chairs of the Research Papers Program Committee, we would like to express our gratitude to everyone who submitted papers to ISC-HPC. We also wish to thank our diligent track chairs and conflict chairs, the members of the Best Paper Committee, and all of our colleagues who served on the Research Papers Program Committee as reviewers and referees. We hope that you remain safe during the coming year, and hope to see you in person in Frankfurt for ISC-HPC 2022.

June 2021   Bradford L. Chamberlain
                                                              Ana Lucia Varbanescu

Organization

Program Chair

Martin Schulz   TU Munich, Germany

Program Deputy Chair

Keren Bergman   Columbia University, USA

Research Papers Program Committee

Research Paper Chairs

Bradford L. Chamberlain (Chair)	Hewlett Packard Enterprise, USA
Ana Lucia Varbanescu (Deputy Chair)	University of Amsterdam, Netherlands

Architecture, Networks, and Storage

Ron Brightwell (Chair)	Sandia National Laboratories, USA
Nectarios Koziris	National Technical University of Athens, Greece
Michael Kuhn	Otto von Guericke University Magdeburg, Germany
Jay Lofstead	Sandia National Laboratories, USA
Preeti Malakar	Indian Institute of Technology Kanpur, India
Kathryn Mohror	Lawrence Livermore National Laboratory, USA
Dhabaleswar Panda	Ohio State University, USA
Maria S. Perez	Universidad Politecnica de Madrid, Spain
John Shalf	Lawrence Berkeley National Laboratory, USA
Tor Skeie	Simula Research Laboratory, Norway
Guangming Tan	Institute of Computing Technology, China
Osamu Tatebe	University of Tsukuba, Japan
Carsten Trinitis	Technical University of Munich, Germany
Venkatram Vishwanath	Argonne National Laboratory, USA

HPC Algorithms and Applications

Florina Ciorba (Chair)	University of Basel, Switzerland
Stratos (Efstratios) Dimopoulos	UCSB and Apple, USA
Pierre Fortin	University of Lille, France
Lin Gan	Tsinghua University and National Supercomputing Center in Wuxi, China
Georgios Goumas	National Technical University of Athens, Greece
Kamer Kaya	Sabancı University, Turkey
Julian Kunkel	University of Reading, UK
Hatem Ltaief	KAUST, Saudi Arabia
Diana Moise	Cray, Switzerland
Gabriel Noaje	NVIDIA, Singapore
Tapasya Patki	Lawrence Livermore National Laboratory, USA
Olga Pearce	Lawrence Livermore National Laboratory, USA
Dirk Pleiter	KTH, Sweden
Filippo Spiga	NVIDIA, UK
Estela Suarez	Forschungszentrum Jülich, Germany
Hongyang Sun	Vanderbilt University, USA
Daniele Tafani	Fujitsu, Germany
Samuel Thibault	University of Bordeaux, France

Machine Learning, AI, and Emerging Technologies

Aparna Chandramowlishwaran (Chair)	UCI, USA
Yufei Ding	University of California, Santa Barbara, USA
Amir Gholami	University of California, Berkeley, USA
Gurbinder Gill	Katana Graph Inc., USA
Jiajia Li	Pacific Northwest National Laboratory, USA
Maryam Mehri Dehnavi	University of Toronto, Canada
Bogdan Nicolae	Argonne National Laboratory, USA
Mostofa Patwary	NVIDIA, USA
Edgar Solomonik	University of Illinois at Urbana-Champaign, USA
Sofia Vallecorsa	CERN, Switzerland
Abhinav Vishnu	AMD, USA
Rio Yokota	Tokyo Institute of Technology, Japan
Yang You	National University of Singapore, Singapore

Performance Modeling, Evaluation, and Analysis

Simon McIntosh-Smith (Chair)	University of Bristol, UK
Sudheer Chunduri	Argonne Leadership Computing Facility, USA
Tom Deakin	University of Bristol, UK
Georg Hager	University of Erlangen-Nuremberg, Germany
Jeff Hammond	Intel, USA
Simon Hammond	Sandia National Laboratories, USA
Guillaume Mercier	Bordeaux INP, France
Ali Mohammed	University of Basel, Switzerland
Bernd Mohr	Forschungszentrum Jülich, Germany
Gihan Mudalige	University of Warwick, UK
Michele Weiland	University of Edinburgh, UK
Charlene Yang	Lawrence Berkeley National Laboratory, USA
Jidong Zhai	Tsinghua University, China

Programming Environments and Systems Software

Christian Terboven (Chair)	RWTH Aachen University, Germany
Alexandru Calotoiu	ETH Zürich, Germany
Sunita Chandrasekaran	University of Delaware, USA
Huimin Cui	Institute of Computing Technology, China
Marta Garcia	BSC, Spain
Brice Goglin	Inria, France
Bilel Hadri	KAUST Supercomputing Laboratory, Saudi Arabia
Christian Iwainsky	TU Darmstadt, Germany
Michael Klemm	AMD and OpenMP ARB, Germany
Dhabaleswar Panda	Ohio State University, USA
Christian Plessl	Paderborn University, Germany
Swaroop S. Pophale	ORNL, USA
Dirk Schmidl	Atos, Germany
Sven-Bodo Scholz	Radboud University, Netherlands
Thomas R. W. Scogland	Lawrence Livermore National Laboratory, USA
Christian Terboven	RWTH Aachen University, Germany
Miwako Tsuji	RIKEN, Japan

BoFs Committee

Masha Sosonkina (Chair)	Old Dominion University, USA
Roman Wyrzykowski (Deputy Chair)	Czestochowa University of Technology, Poland
Marc Baboulin	Université Paris-Saclay, France
Claudia Blaas-Schenner	TU Wien, Austria

Joshua Booth	University of Alabama in Huntsville, USA
Nahid Emad	University of Versailles, France
Dominik Göddeke	University of Stuttgart, Germany
Mozhgan Kabiri Chimeh	NVIDIA, UK
Carola Kruse	Centre Européen de Recherche et de Formation Avancée en Calcul Scientifique, France
Harald Köstler	FAU Erlangen-Nuremberg, Germany
Simon McIntosh-Smith	University of Bristol, UK
Iosif Meyerov	Lobachevsky State University of Nizhni Novogorod, Russia
Lubomir Riha	Technical University of Ostrava, Czech Republic
Marie-Christine Sawley	Intel, France
Masha Sosonkina	Old Dominion University, USA
Vladimir Stegailov	Higher School of Economics and JIHT RAS, Russia
Dave Turner	Kansas State University, USA
Roman Wyrzykowski	Czestochowa University of Technology, Poland

PhD Forum Committee

Olga Pearce (Chair)	Lawrence Livermore National Laboratory, USA
Abhinav Bhatele (Deputy Chair)	University of Maryland, USA
Eishi Arima	University of Tokyo, Japan
Hans-Joachim Bungartz	Technical University of Munich, Germany
Florina Ciorba	University of Basel, Switzerland
Christian Engelmann	Oak Ridge National Laboratory, USA
Georgios Goumas	National Technical University of Athens, Greece
Katherine Isaacs	University of Arizona, USA
Tanzima Islam	Texas State University, USA
Stefan Lankes	RWTH Aachen University, Germany
Laercio Lima Pilla	CNRS and LRI, France
Shinobu Miwa	University of Electro-Communications, Japan
Cosmin E. Oancea	University of Copenhagen, Denmark
Amanda Randles	Duke University, USA
Bettina Schnor	University of Potsdam, Germany

Project Posters Committee

Erwan Raffin (Chair)	Atos, France
Christian Perez (Deputy Chair)	Inria, France
Jean-Thomas Acquaviva	Data Direct Networks, France
Marco Aldinucci	University of Torino, Italy

Bartosz Bosak	Poznan Supercomputing and Networking Center, Poland
Nick Brown	University of Edinburgh, UK
Are Magnus Bruaset	Simula Research Laboratory, Norway
Theodoros Christoudias	The Cyprus Institute, Cyprus
Andrew Ensor	Auckland University of Technology, New Zealand
Claudia Frauen	DKRZ, Germany
Ana Gainaru	Oak Ridge National Laboratory, USA
Andra Hugo	Apple, France
Francesc Lordan Gomis	Barcelona Supercomputing Center, Spain
Hatem Ltaief	KAUST, Saudi Arabia
Bogdan Nicolae	Argonne National Laboratory, USA
Eric Petit	Intel, France
Phil Ridley	Arm, UK
Hiroyuki Takizawa	Tohoku University, Japan
Ben van Werkhoven	Netherlands eScience Center, Netherlands
Andreas Wicenec	University of Western Australia, Australia
Francieli Zanon Boito	Inria, France
Ameli Chi Zhou	Shenzhen University, China
Philipp Neumann	Helmut Schmidt University, Germany
Christian Perez	Inria, France
Erwan Raffin	Atos, France

Research Posters Committee

Keita Teranishi (Chair)	Sandia National Laboratories, USA
Aparna Chandramowlishwaran (Deputy Chair)	UCI, USA
Sridutt Bhalachandra	Lawrence Berkeley National Laboratory, USA
Marc Casas	Barcelona Supercomputing Center, Spain
Irina Demeshko	Los Alamos National Laboratory, USA
Christian Engelmann	Oak Ridge National Laboratory, USA
Patrick Flick	Google, USA
Kei-ichiro Fukazawa	Kyoto University, Japan
Ana Gainaru	Oak Ridge National Laboratory, USA
Lin Gan	Tsinghua University and National Supercomputing Center in Wuxi, China
Wilfried Gansterer	University of Vienna, Austria
José Gracia	University of Stuttgart, Germany
Ryan E. Grant	Sandia National Laboratories, University of New Mexico, USA
Hui Guan	University of Massachusetts Amherst, USA
Toshihiro Hanawa	The University of Tokyo, Japan
Chirag Jain	Indian Institute of Science, India

Oguz Kaya	Université Paris-Saclay, France
Kazuhiko Komatsu	Tohoku University, Japan
Ignacio Laguna	Lawerence Livermore National Laboratory, USA
Seyong Lee	ORNL, USA
Jiajia Li	Pacific Northwest National Laboratory, USA
Israt Nisa	Lawrence Berkeley National Laboratory, USA
Swaroop S. Pophale	ORNL, USA
Kento Sato	RIKEN, Japan
Jesmin Jahan Tithi	Intel, USA
Vadim Voevodin	RCC MSU, Russia
Jeffrey Young	Georgia Institute of Technology, USA
Rohit Zambre	AMD Research, USA

Tutorials Committee

Kevin Huck (Chair)	University of Oreagon, USA
Kathryn Mohror (Deputy Chair)	Lawrence Livermore National Laboratory, USA
Damian Alvarez	Forschungszentrum Jülich, Germany
Katie Antypas	Lawrence Berkeley National Laboratory, USA
Rosa M. Badia	Barcelona Supercomputing Center, Spain
Pavan Balaji	Argonne National Laboratory, USA
Jong Choi	Oak Ridge National Laboratory, USA
Dan Ellsworth	Colorado College, USA
Mozhgan Kabiri Chimeh	NVIDIA, UK
Michael O. Lam	James Madison University and Lawrence Livermore National Laboratory, USA
David Lecomber	Arm, UK
Kelvin Li	IBM, Canada
Simon McIntosh-Smith	University of Bristol, UK
C. J. Newburn	NVIDIA, USA
Dhabaleswar Panda	Ohio State University, USA
Ojas Parekh	SNL, USA
Olga Pearce	Lawrence Livermore National Laboratory, USA
Christian Plessl	Paderborn University, Germany
Harald Servat	Intel, Spain
Michela Taufer	University of Delaware, USA

Workshops Committee

Heike Jagode (Chair)	University of Tennessee Knoxville, USA
Hartwig Anzt (Deputy Chair)	Karlsruhe Institute of Technology, Germany
Emmanuel Agullo	Inria, France

Richard Barrett	Sandia National Laboratories, USA
Roy Campbell	Department of Defense, USA
Florina Ciorba	University of Basel, Switzerland
Anthony Danalis	University of Tennessee Knoxville, USA
Manuel F. Dolz	Universitat Jaume I, Spain
Nick Forrington	Arm, USA
Judit Gimenez Lucas	Barcelona Supercomputing Center, Spain
Thomas Gruber	University of Erlangen-Nuremberg, Germany
Joachim Hein	Lund University, Sweden
David Henty	University of Edinburgh, UK
Marc-Andre Hermanns	RWTH Aachen University, Germany
Kevin Huck	University of Oregon, USA
Sascha Hunold	TU Wien, Austria
Fuerlinger Karl	Ludwig Maximilian University Munich, Germany
Eileen Kühn	Karlsruhe Institute of Technology, Germany
Diana Moise	Cray, Switzerland
Tapasya Patki	Lawrence Livermore National Laboratory, USA
Jelena Pjesivac-Grbovic	Verily Life Sciences and Google, USA
Philip Roth	Oak Ridge National Laboratory, USA
Ana Lucia Varbanescu	University of Amsterdam, Netherlands

Proceedings Chairs

Hatem Ltaief (Chair)	KAUST, Saudi Arabia
Piotr Luszczek (Deputy Chair)	Innovative Computing Laboratory, USA

Contents

HPC Algorithms and Applications

Performance Modeling, Evaluation, and Analysis

Architecture, Networks, and Storage

Microarchitecture of a Configurable High-Radix Router for the Post-Moore Era

Yi Dai[✉], Kai Lu[✉], Junsheng Chang, Xingyun Qi, Jijun Cao,
and Jianmin Zhang

National University of Defense Technology, Changsha 410073, Hunan, China
{daiyi,Kailu,Changjunsheng,qi_xingyun,caojijun,jmZhang}@nudt.edu.cn

Abstract. With *Moore's* law approaching its physical limitations, the exponential growth of pin density and clock frequency on an integrated circuit has ended. The microprocessor clock frequencies have almost ceased to grow since 2014, instead of doubling every 36 months before 2005. Based on this observation, we propose a novel architecture to implement a configurable high-radix router with wider internal ports but lower arbitration radices. With some special features of our proprietary communication stack which can dynamically bind available physical lanes to provide robust data transmission to the upper network layer, our Pisces router can flexibly operate at radix-24/48/96 mode with different bandwidth per port. The simulation results demonstrate Pisces switch achieves stable high throughput under all traffic models. Furthermore, due to the relieved port contention and burst-tolerance attributes, Pisces router reduces the packet delay by over 59% compared to MBTR or YARC, under unbalanced traffic models at full load.

Keywords: High-radix routers · Configurable radix · Aggregated buffer.

1 Introduction

The interconnection network, which mainly dominates the communication bandwidth and latency, is increasingly becoming the bottleneck of system performance due to the ever-increasing volume of transferred data and variety of communication patterns. One of the most critical barriers toward realizing exascale computing is the data movement and bandwidth challenges [1]. The high-radix routers used to construct high-radix networks [2–4] mainly determine the communication latency, throughput, and network cost. By lowering the network diameter while providing path diversity, high-radix routers can effectively decrease network latency and power [5]. However, with Moore's law approaching its physical limitations, the I/O pin count and clock frequency have barely increased since 2014. Increasing the router radix will in turn, reduce per-port bandwidth under a fixed number of I/O pins. Besides, the arbitration complexity that mainly determines the operation frequency of the router scales with the

© Springer Nature Switzerland AG 2021
B. L. Chamberlain et al. (Eds.): ISC High Performance 2021, LNCS 12728, pp. 3–17, 2021.
https://doi.org/10.1007/978-3-030-78713-4_1

port number, which makes it more challenging to implement a high-radix router with high switching capacity but narrow ports [6].

In this paper, we propose a novel microarchitecture of a high-radix router with configurable communication stacks and multi-port shared buffers to enable resilient packet processing. Attributed to some special features of our self-developed communication stack which provides transparent packet delivery between the variable number of physical ports and the network layer fabric, a low-radix internal switch with wider ports is implemented to provide a high aggregated switching capacity with reduced hardware complexity. Our Pisces router can flexibly support radix-24/48/96 switch mode with a variable number of ports running at the configurable bandwidth.

The OPA (Omni-Path Architecture) switch developed by Intel adopts a hierarchical crossbar to implement a 48-port switch by integrating four physical ports as one Mport [7]. Hence up to 12 Mports are interconnected by a central crossbar and a local Mport crossbar is used to connect physical ports to the central crossbar. Although this hierarchical switch architecture can effectively reduce the arbitration complexity by splitting a high-radix switch into a two-level crossbars. The router radix and port bandwidth is unconfigurable and still constrained by pin density.

The contributions of this paper include:

- We propose a novel design approach based on configurable communication stack to build a scalable and flexible high-radix router with reduced hardware cost while maintaining very high throughput under all traffic models.
- We propose a new implementation method for a cost-efficient DAMQ (Dynamically Allocated Multi-Queue) buffer, composed of control DAMQ and data DAMQ. This type of DAMQ is designed explicitly for the low-latency packet scheduling with continuous read, write, and concurrency of read-write. By maximizing the logic reuse of the control DAMQ and data DAMQ, our scheme implements a combined DAMQ with 48% less logic overhead while maintaining high throughput and low latency.
- We systematically present the microarchitecture of the Pisces internal switch and Pisces design highlights for network error tolerance and congestion control in detail. Notably, we implemented a hierarchical arbitration structure that can complete a 256-to-1 arbitration within one clock cycle. The simulation results demonstrate Pisces internal switch considerably reduces the packet delay by over 59% compared to MBTR [8] and YARC [9], under unbalanced traffic models.

We organize the paper as follows. In Sect. 2, the microarchitecture of Pisces router is presented in detail. Besides, we also present the optimization strategies and trade-off we made to optimize the architecture and performance, including the communication stack with configurable physical and link transport layer; the multi-port shared DAMQ with minimum hardware cost; the hierarchical arbitration mechanism; network exception handling, and congestion control. We use cycle-accurate simulation to evaluate throughput and delay in Sect. 3. Finally, we conclude in Sect. 4.

2   Pisces Router Microarchitecture

The virtual channels (VCs) split a physical link into multiple independent channels and allocate a dedicated buffer to each of them at each port (of switches, routers, and end-nodes). Most flow control mechanisms use VCs to provide quality of service (QoS) or process deadlock [10]. Generally, four VCs are used for the protocol-level deadlock avoidance. After providing an escape VC for each adaptive VC to implement fully adaptive routing based on Duato's theory [11], the ultimate VC number should be 8. As a result, the arbitration complexity of Pisces 96-radix switch, will be 768×768 with 8 VCs per port, which is infeasible for high-frequency circuit implementation. High-radix routers with narrow ports have been widely used to reduce the network diameter and cost. Since the total bandwidth of the router is determined by the number of differential IO pins, more ports mean less bandwidth per port.

On the other hand, the complexity of arbitration logic scales quadratically with the number of ports which makes it more difficulty to improve the clock frequency [6]. Consequently, processing wider data within one clock cycle might be the best way to catch up with the ever-increasing bandwidth, however, which contradicts with more narrow ports for high-radix routers. So we wonder if we could implement an internal switch operating with wider flits to provide a scalable processing capacity for configurable number of ports with different bandwidths. In this way, the arbiter complexity of a 96-radix switch can be considerably reduced, since the internal switch radix is only 24 with each internal port binding four ports. Also, a configurable communication stack is used to delivery aggregated flits from the link transport layer to the internal switch in a transparent way.

2.1   The Configurable Communication Stack with Enhanced Link Error Tolerance

We implement a proprietary communication stack to provide configurable and reliable packet transportation to the upper network layer. Hence Pisces router can be configured to different switch mode with variable number of ports running at a wide range of bandwidth with 96 to 24 physical ports. The hardware communication stack includes PMA (Physical Media Attachment) layer, PCS layer, and LLP (Logical Link Protocol) layer. LLP with packet retransmission implemented in hardware provides reliable point-to-point data transport to the upper network layer. Generally, the physical-link layers are implemented for certain specific bandwidth binding fixed number of lanes. Besides, the basic data unit of link transfer typically varies with port bandwidth as well. As a result, it is very difficult to reuse functional components for different port configuration. However, due to some special features of our proprietary communication stack, which not only automatically adapt the wide-port to narrow-port transportation but enhance the link fault tolerance, the hardware cost for configurable data delivery is effectively reduced. The block diagram of the communication stack of Pisces router is shown in Fig. 1.

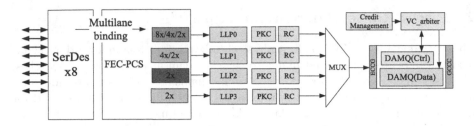

Fig. 1. Configurable communication stack design.

The SerDes (Serializer/Deserializer) macro is commonly used in high-speed serial communication to provide a PMA layer over a single physical lane. Each SerDes composed of a pair of functional blocks converting data between serial and parallel interfaces in each direction. A differential pair transmit the serial data to minimize the number of I/O pins. The link bit error rate (BER) has increased by several orders of magnitude with the increase of SerDes signaling rate ranging form 14 Gbps to 25 Gbps. The forward error correction (FEC) technique is used to correct bit and avoid link-level retransmission. As long as the pre-FEC BER is below the FEC limit, all bit errors can be successfully identified and corrected to avoid packet loss [12]. So we integrate FEC into the PCS layer denoted as FEC-PCS shown in Fig. 1.

On the other hand, lane degrade tolerance becomes indispensable for high-speed differential signaling. When lane failure occurs, the PCS layer can automatically distribute and collect data to and from remaining good lanes. In essence, once a lane failure is detected, PCS will request a connection renegotiation to restart a handshake process with the other side PCS, thus both sides operating at the proper lane modes. For example, 8x-lane PCS can automatically degrade to 6x-lane operation mode when two lanes fail. This feature, along with point-to-point packet retransmission, avoids application suspension due to the poor link quality. The OPA switch supports a similar functionality called dynamic lane scaling, which enables data transmission with one or more lane failures [7]. To the best of our knowledge, most commercial PCS with FEC could barely support lane failures. Pisces FEC-PCS supports both FEC protection and dynamic lane failures against packet loss for highly reliable communication.

The FEC-PCS can provide flexible bandwidth and data width to the LLP layer by dynamically binding different number of lanes. LLP layer is used to provide reliable point-to-point packet delivery for each port. As shown in Fig. 1, four FEC-PCS modules, namely one 8× FEC-PCS, one 4× FEC-PCS, and the other two 2× FEC-PCS, are set for every 8× SerDes to support radix-24/48/96 switch modes by adapting wide FEC-PCS to narrow FEC-PCS. For example, the radix-96 switch mode with four narrow ports per 8× SerDes can be configured by degrading the FEC-PCS with 8× and 4× lanes to 2× lanes. On the other hand, for the radix-24 switch mode with 8× lanes per port, all 8× SerDes are assigned to the 8× FEC-PCS, bypassing other FEC-PCS modules.

The LLP layer provides reliable packet transmission for each port based on a sliding window go-back-to-N protocol. For Pisces router, LLP's basic data unit for packet organization and credit management is fixed to 64bits. As a result, LLP's flit size is independent of the transfer and fabric layers. LLP can operate at flexible bandwidth with configured flit width. Four LLP components is set to implement configurable data transmission, that could be attributed to the following two features. Firstly, flexible interface width to LLP can be provided by FEC-PCS with different gearbox configuration. Secondly, LLP can be easily configured to support different bandwidths while operating with fixed data unit to reduce hardware cost.

Before the packet entering the internal switch, the packet check, route computation, and fabric-flit encapsulation are performed. The packet Check module (PKC) ensures the integrity of each arriving packet. For example, when some fatal errors happen at the link layer, LLP has to empty the buffer to recover the link. There might be corrupted packets entering the switch core. PKC module will insert the body and tail flits for the incomplete packet. Thereby the virtual cut-through (VCT) switching would not be stalled or suspended by illegal packets. The Route Computation (RC) module lookups the routeing table configured by the network management software for adaptive routing and network error tolerance. According to the lookup results and the busy status of available output ports, the RC module will select a less congested route for the corresponding packet and decode the internal routing information, including the row number, column number, aggregated port number, and group number to the packet head's control field. Finally, LLP data will be assembled and encapsulated as a wider fabric flit processed by the internal switch. At the egress, fabric flits will be segmented into multiple LLP data units before sending them to the destined ports.

The internal switch uses the dynamically allocated multi-queue (DAMQ) to store packets of different VCs. DAMQ maintains a FIFO queue for each VC and dynamically allocates memory for each arriving packet. As shown in Fig. 1, each DAMQ is coupled with a VC arbiter to grant a packet from multiple VC requests then forward it to the destined row buffer of the internal switch. To provide data path protection, the error correction code (ECC) is generated by the ECCG module for each fabric flit. When the flit is read out from the DAMQ, the ECCC module checks the corresponding ECC field for 1-bit error correction and 2-bit error detection.

2.2   Multi-port Shared DAMQ with Data Prefetch

Although DAMQ involves more complicated logic, it has been widely used to support multi-VC design with minimum memory overhead by dynamically allocating VC buffers on traffic demand. Our team has been implementing high performance DAMQ with continuous read and write, and concurrency of read-write to achieve low delay and high throughput [15]. Besides, with a fair credit management that can efficiently assign memory on demand among bursty or uneven VCs, our DAMQ achieves microburst absorption, thus effectively improving memory utilization and throughput.

For Pisces router, the DAMQ implementation becomes more complicated as it is shared by multiple ports to support flexible switch mode. All packets delivered by LLP with different port configuration will be written into a shared input DAMQ before entering the internal switch. For radix-96 switch mode with 8 VCs per port, up to 32 independent VC queues from four ports need to be maintained in a DAMQ. Generally, packet data and control info are separately stored in data DAMQ and control DAMQ to provide independent data and control path for more efficient packet processing. Due to the increase of VC number and data width, the data DAMQ could hardly close the timing of a high frequency processing while providing zero-delay read and concurrent read-write operation. In this section, we combine data and control DAMQs to largely eliminate the hardware cost of control logic of data DAMQ. By reusing linked VC lists and prefetch logic of control DAMQ, our scheme can effectively reduce the hardware complexity, while maintaining high throughput and low latency.

As discussed in Ref. [15], the control data, including routing and QoS (Quality of Service) related information, are extracted from the packet head and stored in a control DAMQ. The control data is always read out in advance to initiate the head parsing. However, the corresponding packet might remain in the data DAMQ until the arbiter grants it. In this way, the control and data path are processed in parallel, hiding packet buffering and reading latency. Due to the tripled data width, the high-frequency data DAMQ is much more challenging to implement. In contrast, the control 32-VC DAMQ with tens of bits width is more feasible to meet a high frequency's timing constraints.

The control DAMQ is essentially a partial copy of the data DAMQ. For any flit stored in the data DAMQ, there must be a corresponding control data stored exactly in the same address as this flit. Based on this observation, we analyze the processing flow of both the control DAMQ and the data DAMQ when they work together to schedule a packet. Then we found that most logical process of them is the same. Therefore, we take a radical scheme to remove most data DAMQ's functional modules but remain the full functionalities of the control DAMQ by treating the data DAMQ as the mirror memory of the control DAMQ. The implementation of data and control DAMQ can be integrated together as shown in Fig. 2.

The DAMQ implementation mainly includes the following functional modules:

- **Shared buffer management**: contain the read/write access control for shared memory and multiple read requests arbitration.
- **Linked list management**: include the head and tail maintenance for each VC and the idle list of the free buffers.
- **Data prefetch module**: include bypass and prefetch logic coupled with each VC and the idle buffer list, to implement continuous read and concurrent read-write.

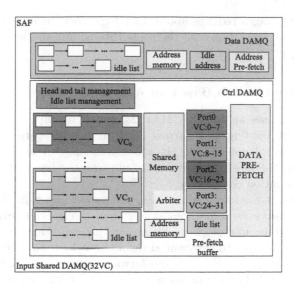

Fig. 2. The integration of control DAMQ and data DAMQ.

Consequently, the data DAMQ removes most functional modules but maintains the idle list associated functions, including the address memory storing the idle buffer addresses, the head and tail management for the idle list, and the idle address prefetch logic. Since the flit stored in the data DAMQ might not be read out synchronously with its control data stored in the control DAMQ, their idle memory status is different from each other. Hence the data DAMQ needs to maintain an idle list of its own. Fortunately, due to the small volume of the address memory, the timing requirements of 1GHz can be easily satisfied by the data DAMQ. However, the control DAMQ maintains complete DAMQ functions including up to 32 FIFO queues, which costs 32 head and tail management modules, plus an idle list management module, as shown in Fig. 2. It is worth noting that for the lower radix switch mode, such as 48 or 24, the corresponding VC number should be 16 or 8 with two ports or one port aggregated in one input DAMQ. The maximum VC number reaches 32 when the radix-96 switch mode is configured.

When the control data is read out in advance to initiate the arbitration request, the corresponding data in data DAMQ might not be synchronously read out until the arbiter finally grants the request. Due to the lack of addresses maintenance in the data DAMQ, the arbiter has to temporarily register the address of the control data when receiving an arbitration request. This address will be returned to the data DAMQ when the associated packet is scheduled from the data DAMQ in a VCT manner. With this minor modification of the arbitration logic, our scheme achieves all merits of the previous DAMQ design [15] but effectively reduce the hardware cost by pruning most functional modules of the data DAMQ. The synthesis and simulation results demonstrate this combined DAMQ design reduces about 48% logic cost, including combination logic and sequential logic, but with the same throughput and latency compared with the DAMQ proposed in Ref [15].

2.3 The Internal Switch Based on Aggregated Tiles

The Pisces router uses an internal 24 × 24 switch to implement an external 96 × 96 switch by binding four narrow ports to an aggregated wide port. As we analyzed in Sect. 1 considering the clock frequency ceases to grow, wider data processing is the most efficient way to improve the bandwidth, meanwhile reducing the arbitration complexity.

When running at the low-speed modes, the packet injection or arriving rate from the LLP is two even four times slower than the internal switching bandwidth. There must be idle clock cycles under this condition during the VCT packet scheduling, leading to substantial throughput loss. To address this issue, the input DAMQ adopts SAF (store-and-forward) flow control to make sure the packet can be scheduled in a continuous manner [17] without any null cycles.

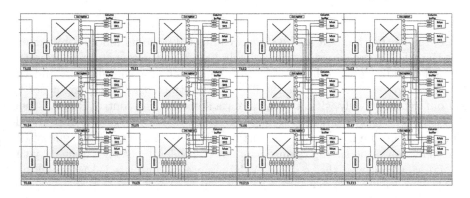

Fig. 3. The microarchitecture of the internal switch arranged as a 3 × 4 tile matrix ($R = 3$, $C = 4$).

Another reason for the SAF flow control is once the packet from the lower speed port is granted, other packets might be blocked because of the delay of the whole packet transmission. Although the SAF flow control increases the schedule delay of a specific packet. This delay can be hidden by processing multiple packets from four LLPs in an alternative manner. Since the total bandwidth of the communication stack matches the Aport bandwidth, no throughput is lost.

To further reduce the memory and wire overhead, the internal switch is organized as a MBTR architecture [8]. There are some options to implement radix-24 switch with different MBTR parameters [8]. Figure 3 shows the microarchitecture of the internal switch. MBTR can build a radix-N switch with (N/A) tiles, which can be flexibly organized as a $R \times C$ tile matrix, where A is the number of switch ports handled in each tile, R is the number of row tiles and C is the number of column tiles. Besides, the number of row and column buffers of the subswitch at each tile is AC and AR, respectively. If we use $A = 3$, which means binding three ports per tile. The radix-24 switch can be organized as 4×2 or 2×4 tile array. The total number of column buses of the 4×2 tile matrix reaches 96 which is four times more than that of row buses. For another option of 2×4, although the column buses can be reduced to 48, the 12×6 subswitch might intensify output competition resulting in poor performance under unbalanced traffic. None of them is a good choice. Then we figure out a MBTR structure of $A = 2$ based on aggregated tiles shown in Fig. 3. To reach a better balance between performance and hardware cost, an ideal option for the radix-24 internal switch organization is a 3×4 matrix of tiles with fewer wire and memory consumption.

The routing information used by the internal switch is encapsulated in each packet head. An arbiter associated with each Aport schedules the packets from the input DAMQ to their destined row buffers. As shown in Fig. 3, each Aport has a dedicated row buffer at different tiles of the same row. The packet is sent to different row buffers according to the routing information of column number, via a dedicated row bus. There are 8 Aports in the same row. Consequently, 8 row buffers each for one Aport are set at each subswitch. The subswitch schedules the packet to their destined column buffers according to the routing information of row number. As shown in Fig. 3, the subswitch's outputs connect to all 6 Aports of the same column in a point-to-point manner. As a result, there are 3 column buffers integrated at each Aport egress, each connecting to one tile of each row. Hence, 6 column buses connect subswitch's outputs to each Aport of the same column. In sum, there are 8 row buffers and 6 column buffers for the tiles binding two Aports. So we implement 8×6 subswitches. The total number of row and column buffers of Pisces router is 24 and 72. Each buffer is implemented by a combined DAMQ.

According to the throughput equation for an asymmetrical $p \times q$ IQ switch [8], the throughput of the subswitch 8×6 can be calculated by $\rho_0 = (r+1) - \sqrt{r^2 + 1}$ where $r = p/q$. So the throughput should be 67% with $p = 8, q = 6$. Under random traffic the traffic from each Aport is distributed evenly to four row buffers. Hence the packet injection rate of the subswitch is 25%. As a result, the non-saturated relative 100% throughput can be achieved by each subswitch. Moreover, the sufficient and necessary condition of 100% throughput can also be established by Pisces router with a relative speed up of 1.7, according to the theoretical analysis of the MBTR throughput in Ref. [8].

Although the radix of the internal switch is considerably reduced by aggregating multi-port into a wider internal Aport. The number of VCs is increased by four times to bind four ports for radix-96 switch mode. As a result, for the subswitch 8×6, the packet scheduler needs to perform up to 256-to-1 arbitration for the eight row buffers, each with 32 VC requests. When we adopt the same arbitration structure of MBTR for the subswitch 8×6. There should be a 32×1 VC arbiter associated with each row buffer to choose one VC request to participate in its destined port arbitration. As a result, eight 32×1 VC arbiters fully connect with five 8×1 port arbiters to schedule packets to the column buffer. However, this arbitration structure cannot meet the timing requirements of a high frequency. To address this issue, we propose a hierarchical arbitration structure by splitting the 32-to-1 VC arbiter into four 8×1 arbiters, coupled with a 4×1 group arbiter that sends the ultimate VC requests to the final port arbiters. This third-level arbitration structure can considerably reduce the critical path delay by 40%, completing the whole arbitration within one 1GHz clock cycle. Only if the VC request is granted simultaneously by the group arbiter and the port arbiter. The corresponding packet can be scheduled from the row buffer to the destined column buffer. The entire packet scheduling starts with the VC arbiter at the input DAMQ that sends the packet to the destined column by writing it into a dedicated row buffer. This first stage arbitration is called column routing. The second stage VC arbiter associated with each row buffer forwards the packet to the column buffer at the final destination Aport.

Another challenge of the internal wide flit arbitration is the successive single-flit scheduling in a full pipelined way. The minimum packet size is generally composed of two flits, which provides more timing margin for the arbitration logic design. However, the full pipelined scheduling of the single flit packet requires the request generation, VC arbitration, port arbitration and priority updating to be completed within one clock cycle. The simulation and synthesis results demonstrate this challenge can be satisfied by the remarkable performance of our hierarchical arbitration mechanism, which ensures no pipeline stall or throughout loss when scheduling successive single-flit packets from all 32 VCs.

2.4   Packet Exception Process and Congestion Control

The packets destined to the same Aport but from different tiles of the same column will be stored in the column buffers at the destined Aport. As shown in Fig. 4, the DAMQ$_{ip0,op0}$ denote the column buffer of the 0th Aport storing the packets from the 0th row tile. Hence there are three column buffers at the Aport egress, each connecting to one tile of each row. The Aport egress performs some critical functionalities such as packet discarding, congestion control, and VC mapping, which improves network error tolerance and enables QoS and deadlock avoidance [18].

The hierarchical arbitration structure from the column buffers to Aport is similar to the subswitch arbitration. The 32×1 VC arbiter each associated with one column buffer is composed of four 8×1 VC arbiters coupled with one 4×1 group arbiter. A 3×1 port arbiter chooses a VC request from three 32×1 VC arbiters. The packet granted by the port arbiter might not be validated and sent to the downstream router under some exception conditions. The packet exception handling module maintains 32 timers each for a specific VC of the downstream input DAMQ. The timer monitors the credit-available signal of the corresponding VC. If the credit timer expires, it indicates that this VC's packet has not been scheduled in a long time due to the lack of credits and the router must prevent the error from propagating throughout the network.

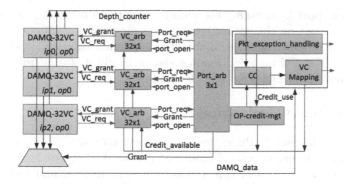

Fig. 4. Block diagram of column buffer output logic.

This credit timeout exception could happen when the attached computer node stops processing the requests from some VC, thereby no credits released to the upstream router. Once packets are blocked in a router for a long time, this blockage will backpressure to another router then to the whole network. Once detecting a timeout of credit unavailability of a specific VC, the Pisces router will start discarding packets of the VC which incurred the timeout. Another exception of link disability will also trigger unconditional packet discarding to prevent the port failure from propagating. More importantly, these exceptions will be periodically feedback to the route selection module at the ingress to mask blocked or failed ports, thus ensuring the seamless integrity of a running computation without route recalculation.

Congestion Control (CC) module is set for each Aport egress to detect network congestion by monitoring the buffer occupancy of local buffers and the credit status of the downstream buffer. As shown in Fig. 4, these congestion related status are respectively collected from the three column buffers and the credit management module of the outgoing port. CC module recognizes congestion based on each VC. When the buffer depth of some VC exceeds the preset threshold, meanwhile the credit for the downstream buffer access accumulates very slowly. The packets will be stuck in the local buffers, which means the congestion source locates at the downstream router that has no enough space for the packet progress. Thereby, this blocked local port should be regarded as a victim port. If the output credit is available, but local buffer depth reaches the congestion threshold, the local port is recognized as a congestion root. In this case, the CC module will tag the corresponding packets with the FECN (Forward Explicit Congestion Notification) bit [19] at a configured ratio. When the packets with FECN tags arrived at the destination NIC (Network Interface Control), the CNP (Congestion Notification Packet) packets with BECN (Backward Explicit Congestion Notification) bit go back to the source NIC to throttle the injection rate to relieve the congestion. Especially, Pisces router itself can fix the local instant congestion by feedbacking the victim port to the route computation modules. Therefore, the packet destined to the victim port will be routed to another idle port by masking the victim output. As network congestion has a significant impact on the packet latency and network throughput, congestion management is indispensable to improve the communication efficiency and network fairness. The VC mapping module shown in Fig. 4 is used to convert the traffic VC number for QoS or deadlock avoidance [18].

3   Performance Evaluation

As we analyzed in Sect. 2, Pisces router supports radix-24/48/96 switch mode by configuring different operating modes of PCS and LLP. For radix-24 switch mode, the number of VCs of row and column buffers is 8, and just one port binds to an Aport. Similarly, the VC number and aggregated port number are respectively 16VCs, and 2 ports/Aport for radix-48 switch mode. At last, 32VCs, and 4 ports/Aport configurations is set for radix-96 switch mode.

We implement Pisces router in register transfer level (RTL) and conduct cycle-accurate simulations to evaluate the delay and throughput of the internal switch under both uniform and unbalanced traffic. We also build a radix-36 YARC and MBTR router in RTL for comparing Pisces router with them. YARC is made of 36 6 × 6 subswitches arranged as a 6 × 6 array. MBTR consists of 12 tiles organized as a 3 × 4 matrix, each tile binding three ports and integrating a 12 × 9 subswitch [8]. Moreover, all implementation schemes for YARC and MBTR, including credit flow control, combined DAMQ, and arbitration implementation are the same as the Pisces router for a fair comparison. Because of the architectural difference, Pisces router has four times VC number for each DAMQ, two times wider flit of the internal switch, and two times shorter packet length, compared to YARC and MBTR.

A packet's delay is calculated from the time that the first flit arrives at an input Aport until the time that the last flit departs from an output Aport. For Pisces router, both the row and column DAMQ supports up to 32VCs, credit-based flow control is used for lossless packet switching. Each Aport under test is connected to a communication stack model that generates traffic to the switch and mimics the behavior of the PCS layer, LLP layer, and packet assembling and multiplexing. We generate uniform traffic by allocating destination ports evenly among injected packets. With hotspot traffic, half of traffic load goes to one-third of the output ports. For exponential and Poisson traffic, the packet destinations follow an exponential and Poisson distribution, respectively. As the method for synthetic traffic generation is just the same as we used for MBTR-36 evaluation in Ref. [8], we compare the Pisces router with our previous MBTR-36 router in terms of throughput and delay.

For all simulation experiments, we evaluate the performance by configuring the packet injection rate with 10%, 30%, 50%, 70%, 90%, 100%, corresponding to six points on each curve. Due to the credit-based flow control, when the input load exceeds the saturated throughput. The backpressure from the flow control will, in turn, reduce the packet injection rate to make it approximate to the throughput. The lines labeled as Pisces-4×, Pisces-2×, and Pisces-1× respectively denote the Pisces switch with the configuration of radix-96/48/24 modes.

As we discussed above, the number of ports and traffic rate per port are different for each switch mode. The number of VCs is 32, 16, and 8, respectively, for radix-96/48/24 switch mode. Since DAMQ provides dynamic VC allocation on traffic demand, we generate configurable unbalanced VC for each traffic model. For example, 25% of the VCs can be assigned to transmit 80% of the traffic. As analyzed in Ref. [8], an idea credit management for multiple shared VCs can effectively eliminate the negative effect of uneven and bursty VCs on buffer utilization. The simulation results suggest that the throughput and delay under unbalance VC configurations maintain almost the same as that under random VC distribution when applying combined DAMQ to all router models in comparison. This also verifies that the combined DAMQ achieves comparable burst tolerance capacity to our prior DAMQs [15] but with less hardware cost.

We carry out cycle-accurate evaluation experiments, each running 250us. The communication stack model built with SystemVerilog mimics the behavior of link transport, flit assembling, and port arbitration for different switch configurations. For the radix-96 configuration, there are four low-speed ports participating in the injection arbitration. Once an injection port is granted, its assembled packet will be forwarded to the destined row buffer. For the radix-48 and radix-24 modes, the packet injection behavior is similar to that of radix-96, but with different number of injection ports.

We can see from Fig. 5 that all router models have identical throughput under low traffic load. Although their throughputs both reach 98% under uniform traffic. The throughput of YARC and MBTR decreases by about 30% and 50% under hotspot and exponential traffic, respectively, due to the HoL (Head of Line) blocking. However, the Pisces switch shows stable high throughput under all traffic models. Surprisingly, Pisces-4×, Pisces-2×, and Pisces-1× even get a little bit better throughput under unbalanced traffic like Exponential and Hotspot than relatively balanced Poisson traffic. This phenomenon might be attributed to the multi-port shared DAMQ that provides more flexible and burst-tolerant packet buffering for unbalanced and burst traffic. On the other hand, the port contention is considerably reduced by aggregating multiple lower-speed ports into one wide internal port.

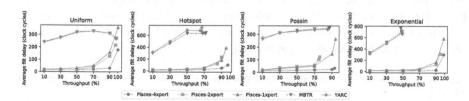

Fig. 5. Throughput and average flit delay of pisces, MBTR and YARC under uniform, hotspot, poisson and exponential traffic models.

MBTR achieves indistinguishable delay and throughput from YARC, as shown in Fig. 5. However, Pisces switch outperforms them by a large margin almost under all traffic models. Although YARC and MBTR demonstrate more stable performance under heavy load, Pisces-2x considerably reduces the average flit delay of them by 21%, 64%, 65%, and 59%, respectively under uniform, Hotspot, Poisson, and Exponential traffic models. It seems like the unbalanced traffic has limited impact on the Pisces switch due to the relieved port contention and burst-tolerance shared buffers.

As shown in Fig. 5, Pisces-4× switch achieves the lowest latency among all three switch modes. For the high-radix switch mode with narrow ports such as Pisces-4×, the HoL blocking can be considerably mitigated by more shared buffering queues and several times higher processing capacity. Although the aggregated bandwidth of narrow ports matches the internal Aport bandwidth, the alternative packet scheduling and memory sharing among multiple ports make the traffic injection to Pisces internal switch more smooth and stable than direct injection in YARC and MBTR. This also explains why Pisces-1× becomes unstable under high traffic load and suggests the poorest delay performance.

4   Conclusion

We propose a scalable and flexible high-radix router microarchitecture with configurable port number and bandwidth. Attributed to the enhanced features of our customized communication stack that can dynamically bind available physical lanes and automatically adapt the wide-port to narrow-port, Pisces router implements flexible switch modes for radix 24, 48 and 96 with minimum hardware cost. In this paper, Pisces router implementation challenges and the corresponding solutions are presented in detail, such as multi-port shared DAMQ with high throughput and low latency, scalable switching architecture based on aggregated tiles, and hierarchical arbitration for single-cycle arbiters. Due to more smooth packet injection, reduced port contention, and burst-tolerance buffers, the simulation results demonstrate Pisces switch achieves very high throughput under all traffic models and reduces the packet delay by over 59% compared to MBTR under unbalanced traffic models. Moreover, many enhanced new features of Pisces router, such as link fault tolerance, load balancing, congestion control, and adaptive routing make Pisces router well qualified for highly reliable large-scale interconnects of exascale computing systems.

Acknowledgment. This research was supported by the key technology R&D program (2018YFB0204300).

References

1. Top Ten Exascale Research Challenges. DOE ASCAC Subcommittee Report (2014)
2. Scott,, S., Abts, D., Kim, J., Dally, W.J.: The black widow high-radix clos network. In: ISCA, Boston, MA (2006)

3. Alverson, R., Roweth, D., Kaplan, L.: The gemini system interconnect. In: HOTI, pp. 83–87 (2010)
4. Faanes, G., et al.: Cray cascade: a scalable HPC system based on a Dragonfly network. In: Proceedings of the International Conference on High Performance Computing, Networking, Storage and Analysis (SC): Los Alamitos, p. 103. CA, USA, Article (2012)
5. Kim, J., Dally, W.J., Towles, B., Gupta, A.K.: Microarchitecture of a high-radix router. ACM SIGARCH Comput. Architecture News **33**(2), 420–431 (2005)
6. Ahn, J.H., Choo, S., Kim J.: Network within a network approach to create a scalable high-radix router microarchitecture. In: HPCA, pp. 1–12 (2012)
7. Chari, S., Pamidi, M.R.: The intel omni-path architecture (OPA) for machine learning. white paper (2017)
8. Dai, Y., Lu, K., Xiao, L.Q., Su, J.S.: A cost-efficient router architecture for HPC inter-connection networks: design and implementation. IEEE Trans. Parallel Distrib. Syst. **30**(4), 738–753 (2019)
9. Brick, S.: BlackWidow hardware system overview. In: CUG, Lugano, Switzerland (2006)
10. Duato, J.: A new theory of deadlock-free adaptive routing in wormhole networks. IEEE Trans. Parallel Distrib. Syst. **4**(12), 1320–1331 (1993)
11. Duato, J., Pinkston, T.: A general theory for deadlock-free adaptive routing using a mixed set of resources. IEEE Trans. Parallel Distrib. Syst. **12**(12), 1219–1235 (2001)
12. Mizuochi T.: Next generation FEC for optical communication. In: Optical Fiber Communication Conference (p. OTuE5). Optical Society of America (2008)
13. 25G Ethernet Consortium. Low-Latency FEC Specification. https://25gethernet. org/ll-fec-specification
14. Top 500 organization. http://www.top500.org. Accessed 4 Nov 2020
15. Zhang, H.Y., Wang, K.F., Zhang, J.M., Wu, N., Dai, Y.: A fast and fair shared buffer for high-radix router. J. Circ. Syst. Comput. **23**(01), 1450012 (2014)
16. Wang, K.F., Fang, M., Chen, S.Q.: Design of a tile-based high-radix switch with high throughput. In: IPCSIT, vol. 17, IACSIT Press, Singapore (2011)
17. Dally, W.: Virtual-channel flow control. In: ISCA (1990)
18. Chen, L., Pinkston, T.M.: Worm-bubble flow control. In: HPCA, Shenzhen, China, pp. 1–12 (2013)
19. Liu, Q., Russell, R.D., Gran, E.G.: Improvements to the infiniBand congestion control mechanism. In: HOTI, pp. 27–36 (2016)

BluesMPI: Efficient MPI Non-blocking Alltoall Offloading Designs on Modern BlueField Smart NICs

Mohammadreza Bayatpour$^{(\boxtimes)}$, Nick Sarkauskas, Hari Subramoni, Jahanzeb Maqbool Hashmi, and Dhabaleswar K. Panda

The Ohio State University, Columbus, USA
{bayatpour.1,sarkauskas.1,subramoni.1,hashmi.29,panda.2}@osu.edu

Abstract. In the state-of-the-art production quality MPI (Message Passing Interface) libraries, communication progress is either performed by the main thread or a separate communication progress thread. Taking advantage of separate communication threads can lead to a higher overlap of communication and computation as well as reduced total application execution time. However, such an approach can also lead to contention for CPU resources leading to sub-par application performance as the application itself has less number of available cores for computation. Recently, Mellanox has introduced the BlueField series of adapters which combine the advanced capabilities of traditional ASIC based network adapters with an array of ARM processors. In this paper, we propose BluesMPI, a high performance MPI non-blocking Alltoall design that can be used to offload MPI_Ialltoall collective operations from the host CPU to the Smart NIC. BluesMPI guarantees the full overlap of communication and computation for Alltoall collective operations while providing on-par pure communication latency to CPU based on-loading designs. We explore several designs to achieve the best pure communication latency for MPI_Ialltoall. Our experiments show that BluesMPI can improve the total execution time of the OSU Micro Benchmark for MPI_Ialltoall and P3DFFT application up to 44% and 30%, respectively. To the best of our knowledge, this is the first design that efficiently takes advantage of modern BlueField Smart NICs in deriving the MPI Alltoall collective operation to get peak overlap of communication and computation.

Keywords: BlueField · SmartNIC · MPI · Alltoall · Offload

1 Introduction

The rapid growth in the scale of supercomputing systems over the last decade has been driven by the multi-/many-core architectures, and RDMA-enabled,

This research is supported in part by National Science Foundation grants #1818253, #1854828, #1931537, #2007991, #2018627, and XRAC grant #NCR-130002.

© Springer Nature Switzerland AG 2021
B. L. Chamberlain et al. (Eds.): ISC High Performance 2021, LNCS 12728, pp. 18–37, 2021.
https://doi.org/10.1007/978-3-030-78713-4_2

high-performance interconnects such as InfiniBand [8] (IB). The Message Passing Interface (MPI) [4] has been extensively used for implementing high-performance parallel applications and it offers various primitives such as point-to-point, collective, and Remote Memory Access operations. An MPI library that supports highly efficient communication primitives will be essential to the performance of HPC and parallel deep learning applications.

Overlap of communication and computation is critical for increasing resource utilization and performance. MPI provides non-blocking point-to-point and collective primitives that are used to achieve communication and computation overlap. In MPI, communication must be progressed, either by the main thread by calling MPI_Test or an extra offload entity such as a separate thread, or a hardware feature inside the network. If none of these exist, the amount of overlap will be limited as the main process thread must context switch from the application computation to progress the communication inside the MPI library. This also greatly depends on the application developer on how frequently they explicitly call MPI_Test. The application developer can either call MPI_Test or there may be an asynchronous communication thread in MPI. Both scenarios, however, can lead to sub-par performance as the main application has less CPU resources for useful application-level computation. Therefore, network offload mechanisms are gaining attraction as they have the potential to completely offload the communication of MPI primitives into the network, maximizing the overlap of communication and computation. However, the area of network offloading of MPI primitives is still nascent and cannot be used as a universal solution.

Table 1. Designs and features to support efficient non-blocking collectives in representative MPI libraries. C#1: computation and communication overlap, C#2: communication latency, challenge #3: network scalability, C#4: availability of cores for compute, C#5: hardware contexts for multiple communicators

| | Features of representative MPI libraries | | | | | | |
	No offload	Core [16]-Direct	SHARP [15]	HW tag [6] matching	RDMA-aware [17]	MPICH [7] Async Thrd	MVAPICH2 Async [11]	Proposed
C#1	Poor	Good	Fair	Fair	Fair	Good	Fair	Good
C#2	Good	Good	Good	Good	Poor	Fair	Good	Good
C#3	Good	Fair	Good	Fair	Fair	Good	Good	Good
C#4	Poor	Good	Good	Fair	Good	Poor	Fair	Good
C#5	Good	Poor	Fair	Fair	Good	Good	Good	Good

Table 1 summarizes the different hardware offloading approaches. Among the most recent schemes in networking technologies, SHARP collective offload mechanism [15] only supports Barrier and Allreduce operations and it supports a few number of application level communicators as the Switch contexts are limited. Due to the limitation of SHARP contexts inside each switch, MPI libraries have to allow only one process per node (also known as the leader process) to use the

SHARP feature. Therefore, all the processes inside the same node must use host CPU resources to conduct the intra-node operations before using SHARP. This can limit the overlap opportunities of SHARP. Hardware Tag Matching for MPI point-to-point operations [5,6] is another state-of-the-art network offloading feature for MPI. Even though this mechanism can improve the overlap of communication and computation of large Rendezvous messages, when this point-to-point mechanism is used in dense collectives such as Alltoall, its overlap potential hugely degrades as the scale goes higher. This is due to a limited number of outstanding tags in this architecture [6]. On the other hand, in recent years, Smart NICs are able to bring more compute resources into the network and a high performance middleware such as MPI must take advantage of these additional resources to fill in the limitations of other in-network technologies. Smart NICs can act as a brand new host on the network by setting them to "separated host" mode. Therefore, instead of using them as a packet processing engine where all packets go through the processors inside the Smart NIC, these Smart NICs have the potential for any in-network offloading purpose.

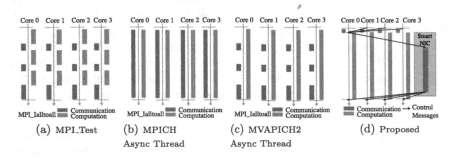

Fig. 1. Timeline of various designs for MPI non-blocking collectives

1.1 Challenges

In this paper, our goal is to efficiently take advantage of modern Smart NICs in separated host mode to propose novel MPI non-blocking Alltoall designs for large messages that 1) Achieves maximum overlap of communication and computation without requiring any changes inside the upper-level application, 2) Leaves the entire host processor for the useful application computation with minimal context-switching, and 3) Minimizes the overhead involved in offloading to the Smart NIC and provides good communication latency. In other words, we are envisioning communication offload, as outlined in Fig. 1. To achieve our goal, we are considering additional compute capabilities that are available in modern high performance interconnects, such as Smart NICs. One of the latest developments of such interconnects is the BlueField adapter that is based on the ConnectX-6 series of Infiniband Mellanox models. This adapter is equipped with an array of cache-coherent 1999 MHz ARM cores and they can be used as a general-purpose system [3]. It also provides support for dual-port Remote Direct

Memory Access (RDMA). These developments lead to the following broad challenge: **How can existing production-quality HPC middleware such as MPI be enhanced to take advantage of emerging networking technologies to deliver the best performance for HPC and DL applications on emerging dense many-core CPU/GPU systems?**

We break down this broad challenge into the following questions: **1)** What shortcomings regarding MPI exist in current state-of-the-art in-network technologies? **2)** Can we use additional compute resources provided by modern Smart NICs to accelerate MPI collective primitives? **3)** What are the challenges regarding exploiting these modern Smart NICs for offloading non-blocking Alltoall operations? **4)** Can we propose efficient designs to take advantage of Smart NICs capabilities without requiring the upper-level application changes? **5)** How to minimize pure communication latency of non-blocking Alltoall collective operations designed using BlueField Smart NICs?, and **6)** What are the performance overheads of each component of the framework and what is the impact of the proposed design at the microbenchmark level as well as the application-level?

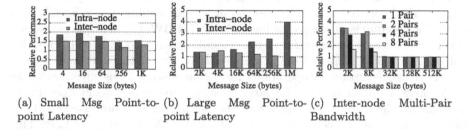

(a) Small Msg Point-to-point Latency (b) Large Msg Point-to-point Latency (c) Inter-node Multi-Pair Bandwidth

Fig. 2. Comparison of point-to-point latency and bandwidth of the processes on Blue-Field smart NIC versus processes on the host. Latency Relative Performance (speedup) is calculated by BF-latency/Host-latency, and bandwidth speedup is calculated by Host-bw/BF-bw. We can observe that as message size increases, the inter-node performance of ARM cores of BlueField (BF) smart NIC converges to the performance of XEON cores.

1.2 Motivation and Characterization

As an initial step to answering our broad challenge, we need to identify opportunities provided by Smart NICs and thoroughly characterize a system enabled with BlueField adapters. Based on this characterization, we conclude which MPI operations have the potential for offloading to the ARM cores of the BlueField and provide insights for our proposed Smart NIC-aware MPI library. To do so, we compare the latency and bandwidth of communication between MPI processes on the host cores versus MPI processes running on the ARM cores of the BlueField adapters using OSU Micro Benchmarks [1]. Please refer to Sect. 1.5 for detailed experimental setup information. For each test, we launch all the processes on the XEON cores of hosts and measure the latency and bandwidth.

Then, we perform a similar test by launching all the processes on the ARM cores of the BlueField Smart NIC and calculate the speedup of host tests versus Smart NIC tests. The speedup is calculated by ARM-latency/host-latency.

Figures 2(a) and (b) shows that for intra-node operations, as the message size increases, the performance of intra-node operations diverges from the host processes. This is in line with our expectations as for the intra-node operations, CPU is in charge of the copy operations, and having a faster CPU has a significant impact on point-to-point performance. Therefore, in our BluesMPI framework, we avoid going through the CPU based intra-node operations for BluesMPI worker processes on the Smart NIC. On the other hand, Fig. 2(b) shows an opposite trend. Here **as the message size increases, inter-node latency of Smart NIC worker processes and host processes converge.** This is because the HCA is in charge of operations and for medium and large messages (large than 16 KB) where the rendezvous protocol is used for point-to-point operations. In this protocol, there are no copy operations involved. Therefore, as message size increases, the network overheads will have more share of the total latency.

Figure 2(c) illustrates the bandwidth comparison between the process running on ARM core of Smart NIC and the processes running on the host XEON cores. The speedup is calculated by host-BW/ARM-BW. For multiple pair bandwidth tests, we used osu_mbw_mr [1] that calculates the aggregate bandwidth for multiple pairs of processes. Here experimental results of the inter-node operation are shown as intra-node operations are not interesting for us anymore. These results show a similar trend as for large message inter-node latency operations. Here also as the message size increases, the performance of processes on ARM cores of Smart NIC converges to the performance of XEON cores of host. This trend is consistent as the number of pairs increases as well. **This shows that processes on Smart NIC have the potential to handle dense communication for large messages using RDMA.**

Based on this characterization, our proposed BluesMPI framework is purely based on RDMA operations and the focus is to provide maximum overlap of communication and computation with low communication latency for dense nonblocking Alltoall collectives with medium and large messages.

1.3   Contributions

In this paper, we characterize various MPI point-to-point operations and identify the aspects of the MPI library that can be efficiently driven by the additional compute resources on the modern Smart NICs. Then based on our characterization, we propose BluesMPI, an adaptive MPI non-blocking Alltoall collective offload design on modern Smart NICs. We propose various designs on the top of BlueField for MPI_Ialltoall operations. Our experimental results show that BluesMPI can successfully take advantage of the available Smart NICs SoC on the network and lower the execution time of OSU Micro Benchmark by 44% and P3DFFT application by 30% on 1024 processes. To the best of our knowledge, this is the first design that efficiently takes advantage of modern BlueField

Smart NICs in deriving the MPI collective operations to get the peak overlap of communication and computation.

To summarize, this paper makes the following contributions:

- In-depth analysis and characterization of MPI operations running on the available compute resources of Smart NICs.
- Proposing novel designs for non-blocking Alltoall operations that provide full overlap of communication and computation and low pure communication latency.
- Performing a thorough characterization of different components of the proposed BluesMPI framework.
- Performance evaluations of the proposed designs at the micro benchmark level and application level.

1.4   Overview of BlueField Smart NICs

Within each of the products in the BlueField family is the BlueField Data Processing Unit (DPU). This is a system-on-chip containing 64-bit ARMv8 A72 cores connected in a mesh, DDR4 memory controllers, a ConnectX network controller, and an integrated PCIe switch. The DPU is sold as part of products in different lines of the BlueField family. These include BlueField Smart NICs, Blue-Field storage controllers, and the BlueField Reference Platform. Figure 3 depicts a schematic overview of the BlueField Smart NIC architecture. The BlueField Smart NIC has two modes of operation: Separated Host mode (default) and Embedded CPU Function Ownership (Smart NIC) mode. Each physical port on the Smart NIC can be independently configured to either mode [3]. In separated host mode, the ARM cores can appear on the network as any other host and the main CPU (i.e. ×86) is exposed through a PCIe function for direct connectivity to the ConnectX. The ARM cores are exposed through a symmetric (to the host) PCIe function for their own connectivity to the ConnectX network adapter. Bandwidth is shared between the two functions. In our experiments, we use this mode. Embedded CPU Function Ownership (Smart NIC) mode places several restrictions on the host. In Smart NIC mode, all network controller resources

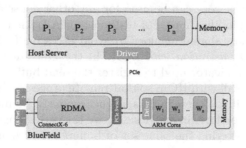

Fig. 3. BlueField smart NIC architecture

are controlled by the ARM cores via the Embedded CPU Physical Function (ECPF). The ECPF in this mode will own the embedded switch (e-switch) as well. In order to pass traffic to the host, either the e-switch must be set up with forwarding rules, or kernel netdev representors (Open vSwitch virtual ports) must be configured on the ARM cores [3].

1.5 Experimental Setup

We used the HPC Advisory Council High-Performance Center (HPCAC) [2] cluster for our evaluation. HPCAC has 32 nodes that contain the BlueField-2 network adapters. These adapters have an array of 8 ARM cores operating at 1999 MHz with 16 GB RAM. Each BlueField adapter is equipped with Mellanox MT41686 HDR ConnectX-6 HCAs (100 Gbps data rate) with PCI-Ex Gen3 interfaces [3]. The host is equipped with the Broadwell series of Xeon dual-socket, 16-core processors operating at 2.60 GHz with 128 GB RAM.

2 BluesMPI Designs

In this section, we provide the details of various components of the proposed BluesMPI framework. In Sect. 2.1, we discuss the overall design of the framework and explain each step that is required for non-blocking Alltoall collective operations to be offloaded onto the Smart NIC. In Sect. 2.2, we describe the details of various novel designs for non-blocking Alltoall operations.

2.1 BluesMPI Non-blocking Alltoall Collective Offload Framework

In BluesMPI, non-blocking Alltoall collective operations are offloaded to a set of the Worker processes which have been spawned in the MPI_Init to the Smart NICs that are in the separated host mode. Therefore, all that application's host processes have to do is to prepare a set of metadata and provide it to the Worker processes. Once the collective operations are completed, Worker processes notify the host processes. BluesMPI framework goes over a set of steps in order to prepare the non-blocking Alltoall collective operations to be offloaded to the Worker processes on the Smart NIC. Although these steps are described for nonblocking Alltoall, a similar framework can be used for any other dense collective communication, with a few modifications. For instance, for Allgather, some of the steps can be done in the host shared memory to avoid excessive IB link utilization.

Step 0) *Buffers Registration with HCA:* In the first step, all the processes inside the host communicator need to register the send buffer and receive buffer of the MPI collective call with HCA, so that remote processes are able to perform RDMA Read and Write on these buffers, asynchronously. Memory registration is a costly operation, therefore, in our designs, we take advantage of a registration cache to avoid re-registering the same set of buffers more than once.

Step 1) *Metadata Aggregation to the Host Communicator Leader Process:*
Once a process in the host communicator registers its send and receive buffers,
it creates a collective info object that includes RDMA buffer addresses and
keys. It also includes this process's rank in MPI_COMM_WORLD as well as the
count and datatype of this collective call. This information is the Metadata for
the collective call from this host process. The host communicator leader (which
is rank 0 in our design) gathers the Metadata from all the processes in the
communicator.

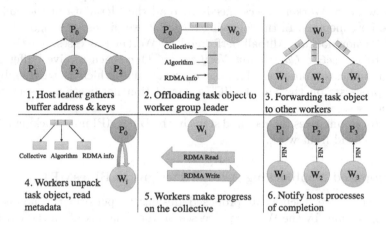

Fig. 4. BluesMPI procedure to offload non-blocking Alltoall collective operation to the
worker processes on the Smart NIC. Step 0 is not included in this figure.

Step 2) *Metadata Registration with HCA and Offloading the Task Object to
Leader of the Workers Group:* Once the host communicator leader generates the
array of Metadata, it has to register this array with HCA so that all the Worker
process on the Smart NIC can read whatever information that they require at
any time during progressing the collective. Once the registration is done, the host
communicator leader creates a new task object and sends it to the Workers group
leader. This task object has the information about the type of the collective and
the algorithm which must be performed by the Worker processes on the Smart
NIC. It also has the RDMA information of the Metadata array and the host
communicator size.

From now, the host processes are free to perform useful application computation. In the meantime, the leader of the Worker group on Smart NIC waits
for the incoming task objects from the leaders of the host communicators. Since
the application could have several sub-communicators, the leader of the Workers group on Smart NIC can receive several task objects at the same time. It
is also possible that even for a single host communicator, several back-to-back
nonblocking collective calls are issued before going into the MPI_Wait. In order

to handle all these scenarios, the leader of the Worker group on the Smart NIC creates a FIFO queue and pushes all the new task objects into this queue.

Step 3) *Picking up a Task from Queue of Offloaded Tasks and Forward it to the Non-leader Workers:* The leader of the Smart NIC Worker group picks a task from the head of the tasks queue and broadcasts this object task to all the processes in the Workers group.

Step 4 and 5) *Progress the Collective on Behalf of the Host Communicators:* Once every Worker process on the Smart NIC receives a task object, it unpacks the object and based on the task type, it performs the appropriate operations on it. Now every Worker process needs to read the Metadata of the collective from the host memory. In the following Sect. 2.2, we discuss the algorithm that we used for nonblocking Alltoall performed by Worker processes.

Step 6) *Collective Completion Notification:* Once each receive buffer of the host communicator processes has the correct value which is written by the Worker processes on the Smart NIC, a completion notification is sent to the host processes.

Figure 4 summarizes the required steps in the BluesMPI non-blocking Alltoall collective offload framework.

2.2 Proposed Nonblocking Alltoall Designs in BluesMPI

In this section, we discuss our proposed designs to perform the nonblocking Alltoall operations by the Worker processes on the Smart NIC. In these designs, we consider balanced Workers per node, meaning that the number of the Workers per node is the same between all the nodes. As the first step to perform the nonblocking Alltoall, Worker processes must receive a task object regarding this operation. This is done by the steps performed by the BluesMPI framework discussed in Sect. 2.1. Once each Worker process has access to this task object and its Metadata, it has full read and write access to every buffer of every process in the host communicator.

In a perfect scenario, it is expected that the Worker processes issue RDMA read and write operations to HCA on behalf of the host communicator processes. This is because once the non-blocking collective is issued by the host process, this process starts working on the application computations and it is not inside MPI, progressing the communication. Therefore, in order to have a complete overlap of communication and computation for the non-blocking collective operation, and assuming that there is no extra communication progress thread running on the host CPU, Worker processes should be able to progress the HCA on behalf of the host processes. However, modern interconnects do not have this support. This means that even if a remote Worker process on the Smart NIC has the RDMA address and key of a local memory of host processes, it cannot directly issue RDMA read or write from the host local memory to the destination memory of another host process. Therefore, in our proposed non-blocking Alltoall designs, data is staged in the main memory of the Smart NIC, and then it is forwarded to the destination. Figure 5(a) depicts a single transfer in our proposed designs. Scatter destination algorithm works best for medium and large messages [11], thus our proposed designs are based on this algorithm. In the scatter destination algorithm for Alltoall, there is a loop with communicator-size iterations and in each iteration, an exclusive piece of send buffer is sent to the destination receive buffer of the remote process.

Once the Worker processes running on the ARM cores of the Smart NIC have the collective Metadata, they share the collective progression among themselves in a balanced manner. Therefore, if there are PPN number of the processes of the host communicator in the same node and there are WPN number of Worker processes per node, each Worker process is responsible for the PPN/WPN number of the host processes. Depending on how Worker processes on the Smart NIC take advantage of the staging based message transfer mechanism depicted in Fig. 5(a), we explore three designs: 1) Direct Design, 2) Message Chunking Design, and 3) Message Pipelining Design. All of these designs in nature are scatter destination Alltoall designs.

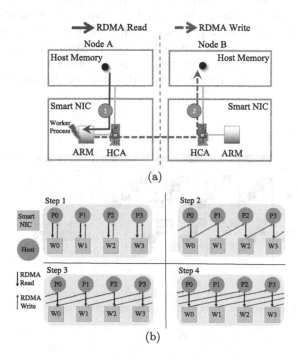

Fig. 5. (a) A single message transfer from a host communicator process in node A to another host process on node B in our proposed Alltoall designs. (b) The Proposed Direct Design in BluesMPI for Ialltoall for 1 PPN, 1 WPN, and 4 nodes scenario.

Direct Design. In this design, each Worker process starts from the first host process which is assigned to it and then delivers each exclusive piece of data from the local memory of the host process to all other host processes in the host communicator. If there are N processes in the host communicator, since we are performing an Alltoall operation, the send buffer of each host process will have N exclusive data each with a size that depends on the count and datatype inputs of MPI_Ialltoall. Each of these N elements is sent to the appropriate index of the receive buffer of another process in the host communicator. Therefore, if a Worker process is responsible for the H number of host processes, it has to perform N × H number of message transfers on behalf of those H number of host processes that offloaded their collective communication on this Worker process. Each of these individual back-to-back staging based transfers uses the mechanism illustrated in Fig. 5(a) in an asynchronous manner while the host process is performing the application compute and it is outside of the MPI library. Figure 6 shows the Direct Design for the first four message transfers of a Worker process. To further optimize this algorithm, we propose a link efficient load-balanced staging technique. To achieve load balancing, in this design, we need to make sure that at any point during the Direct Design, only one Worker process is writing to receive buffer of a host process. Therefore, instead of allowing each Worker process to start writing to the destination processes with rank 0, each Worker process sets its initial destination process to the same host process that is assigned to it. An example is provided in Fig. 5(b). Figure 7(a) shows that we can achieve 38% in pure communication latency by taking advantage of this link load-balancing mechanism.

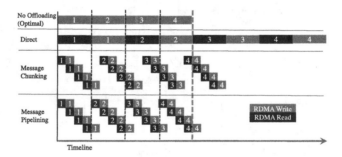

Fig. 6. Timeline of the proposed staging based Alltoall designs for large messages. For No Offloading scenario, scatter destination algorithm used in blocking Alltoall is considered.

Message Chunking Design. One of the major bottlenecks in the Direct Design is that it suffers from the overheads of the message staging in the Smart NIC. This is because due to the staging operation, the number of the RDMA operations doubles compared to the No Offloading CPU driven scatter destination scenario. Although in the Direct Design, there is a full overlap of communication and computation, still, in order to get noticeable benefit in total application time, we need to further reduce the pure communication time of Direct Design. In order to do so, in Message Chunking Design, we break down

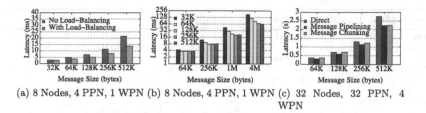

(a) 8 Nodes, 4 PPN, 1 WPN (b) 8 Nodes, 4 PPN, 1 WPN (c) 32 Nodes, 32 PPN, 4
                                                         WPN

Fig. 7. (a) Impact of load-balancing, (b) Impact of chunking, (c) Performance comparison of different proposed designs. In these figures, pure communication latency of MPI_Ialltoall is reported.

a single message size of msg_size to multiple chunks. Then in each iteration, we try to overlap the RDMA write of the current chunk with the RDMA read of the next chunk. Figure 6 illustrates the Message Chunking Design. Infiniband links are bi-directional, therefore, RDMA Write and Read can happen at the same time without any extra cost. The base of this algorithm is indeed the Direct Design, however, in the Message Chunking Design, we replace each staging based transfer of size msg_size with an another primitive that chunks the message to $chunk\_size$ equivalent pieces and overlaps the RDMA read and writes of back to back chunks for this specific message. In this design, chunk size plays a major role in the pure communication performance. Figure 7(b) shows the impact of the chunk size compared to Direct Design. All of our experiments are conducted on the HPCAC cluster which is introduced in Sect. 1.5.

Message Pipelining Design. Message Chunking Design is able to further reduce the impact of the staging to Smart NIC. However, due to the nature of this design that it considers each message transfer in an isolated manner, there are still multiple chunks of the messages that are not taking advantage of the overlapping between RDMA read and write. This is due to the fact that for each message transfer, the first RDMA read and last RDMA write are not getting overlapped with any other operations. This is also depicted in Fig. 6. Although by increasing the number of the chunks, we can reduce this impact, but on the other hand, choosing too small chunks can have a negative impact on IB links as they are able to fill up the bandwidth and get the best performance. In order to reduce the number of chunks which have not been overlapped, in Message Pipelining Design, we take advantage of pipelining the back to back transfers. In this design, RDMA write from Smart NIC to host memory of the current message transfer of size msg_size is overlapped with RDMA read of the next message from host memory to Smart NIC. In this design, there will be only two messages which have not been overlapped: the RDMA read of the first message transfer and the RDMA write of the last message transfer. As the communicator size N increases, the negative impact of staging to Smart NIC also decreases, as the total number of transfers increases by a factor of N while the number of messages which have not been overlapped remains 2. On a small scale and

---

Algorithm 1: Message Pipelining Design (Design-3)

Input	:	$rdma\_info$ — Array of Send/Recv/FIN Buffers RDMA Info
Input	:	$world\_ranks$ — Array of Host processes ranks in MPI_COMM_WORLD
Input	:	$host\_comm\_size$ — Host communicator size
Input	:	$worker\_comm\_size$ — Workers communicator size
Input	:	$worker\_rank$ — Rank of this worker process in Workers communicator
Input	:	$count$ — Count
Input	:	$datatype\_size$ — Datatype size of a single element
Input	:	$chunk\_size$ — Chunk size to be used for data staging procedure
Output:		mpi_errno

1 **begin**
2   customers_list_size =
3      $host\_comm\_size$ / $worker\_comm\_size$
4   **for** $i \leftarrow 0$ **to** $customers\_list\_size$ **do**
5   Find the host processes that this worker is responsible for
6   customers_list[i] =
7   customers_list_size × $worker\_rank$ + i
8   **end**
9   chunk_num = msg_size / $chunk\_size$
10   total_msgs = $host\_comm\_size$ × customers_list_size × chunk_num
11   **for** $msg \leftarrow -1$ **to** $total\_msgs$ **do**
12   Prepare for RDMA Read for a single chunk
13   i = (msg +1) / chunk_num
14   **if** $msg = total\_msgs - 1$ **then**
15   Skip RDMA Read, set read completion flag for this chunk and jump to skip_read
16   **end**
17   src_rank = customers_list[i / $host\_comm\_size$]
18   src_world_rank = world_ranks[src_rank]
19   sendbuf = rdma_info[src_rank].sendbuf.buf_addr
20   src_key = rdma_info[src_rank].sendbuf.rkey
21   dst_rank = ((i % $host\_comm\_size$) + src_rank) % $host\_comm\_size$
22   src_buf = sendbuf + dst_rank × msg_size + $chunk\_size$ × ((msg + 1) % chunk_num)
23   Initiate an RDMA Read for a single chunk
24   staging_tmp_buf_read = staging_tmp_buf + msg_size × ((msg + 1) %2)
25   NonBlockingRdmaRead(staging_tmp_buf_read,
26   src_key, src_buf, src_world_rank, $chunk\_size$)
27   Prepare for RDMA Write for a single chunk
28   skip_read:
29   i = msg / chunk_num
30   **if** $msg = -1$ **then**
31   Skip RDMA Write, set write completion flag for this chunk and jump to skip_write
32   **end**
33   src_rank = customers_list[i / $host\_comm\_size$]
34   dst_rank = ((i % $host\_comm\_size$) + src_rank) % $host\_comm\_size$
35   dst_world_rank = world_ranks[dst_rank]
36   recvbuf = rdma_info[dst_rank].recvbuf.buf_addr
37   dst_key = rdma_info[dst_rank].sendbuf.rkey
38   dst_buf = recvbuf + src_rank × msg_size + $chunk\_size$ × (msg % chunk_num)
39   staging_tmp_buf_write = staging_tmp_buf + msg_size × (msg %2)
40   NonBlockingRdmaWrite(staging_tmp_buf_write,
41   dst_key, dst_buf, dst_world_rank, $chunk\_size$)
42   skip_write:
43   BlockingWaitRdmaReadWrite()
44   **end**
45   Barrier(worker_comm)
46   Notify all the host processes in the customers_list
47 **end**

especially for large messages, this design is combined with Message Chunking Design. Therefore, each message is chunked into multiple pieces, and the RDMA write of the last chunk of each message is overlapped with the RDMA read of the first chunk of the next message. Algorithm 1 provides further details about the procedure that worker processes perform to implement this algorithm. Figure 6 compare the pipelining opportunities of all the Direct, Message Chunking, and Message Pipelining designs. Figure 7(c) compares their performance against each other.

Once each Worker process is done with the task assigned to it, it goes into a barrier, and it waits for all other Worker processes in the same group to finish their task. Once every Worker process is done, they notify thehost processes which are assigned to them. They do so by issuing an RDMA write to the FIN flag on the local memory of each host process which was provided to Worker processes. After this step, each Worker process goes into a broadcast operation, and they wait for the leader of the Workers group to assign them a new collective offloading task.

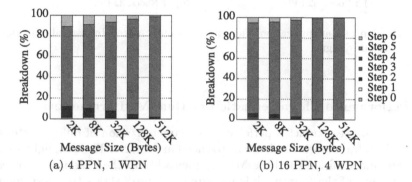

(a) 4 PPN, 1 WPN   (b) 16 PPN, 4 WPN

Fig. 8. Performance breakdown of pure communication latency of MPI_Ialltoall directly followed by MPI_Wait for different steps of the BluesMPI framework discussed in Sect. 2.1. These tests run on 8 nodes using Message Pipelining design.

3 Results

In this section, we discuss the experimental analysis of MPI collective primitives using OSU Micro Benchmarks [1] and a modified P3DFFT [12] application with nonblocking Alltoall support that is proposed by Kandalla et al. [9]. We provide a performance breakdown of different steps of BluesMPI framework. BluesMPI is designed on the top of the MVAPICH2 v2.3 MPI library. Comparisons with HPCX 2.7.0 with HCOLL NBC flag enabled, MVAPICH2-X v2.3 with MPICH asynchronous thread enabled, as well as optimized asynchronous thread enabled are also provided. All the reported numbers are an average of three runs and micro-benchmark evaluations ran for 1,000 iterations for each message size and an average of three experiments is reported. The standard deviation between these iterations is kept under 2%.

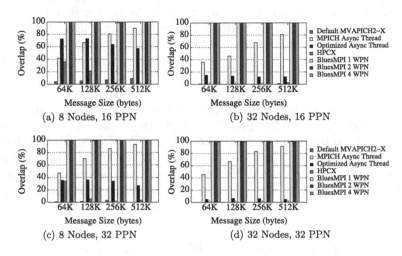

Fig. 9. Overlap of communication and computation reported by osu_ialltoall benchmark for various designs.

3.1   Performance Characterization of BluesMPI Framework

In this section, we conduct a performance characterization of different steps of the BluesMPI framework which are introduced in Sect. 2.1. To do so, light-weight timers are added inside the BluesMPI framework and the time taken for each of the six steps of the framework is measured. Figure 8 shows this performance breakdown of pure communication of MPI_alltoall for two tests with 8 nodes. As we can see here, for smaller message sizes, the overheads of BluesMPI are more visible compared to larger messages. This is because the overheads of BluesMPI, which are the steps of 1 to 4 and step 6 (considering step 5 as the useful collective time) are not dependant on the message size and they only depend on the Workers group size and host communicator size. This means that if the Workers group size and host communicator size do not change, the overhead remains constant, regardless of the message size. Therefore, only step 5 is dependant on the job size and message size of MPI_Ialltoall. Figure 8 shows the same trend. For a single job size, as the message size increases, step 5 latency increases, and since other steps remain constant, the percentage overhead compared to step 5 decrease. After step 5, steps 4 and 6 have the highest overhead compared to other steps. This is because these two steps run on the slower ARM cores of the BlueField and therefore, compared to host-related overhead (steps 0, 1, and 2), they are more signified.

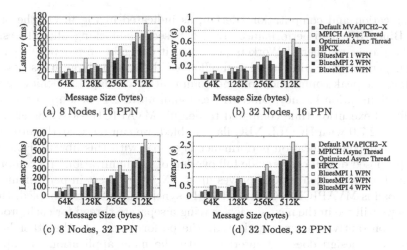

Fig. 10. Pure communication time of MPI_Ialltoall (time of MPI_Ialltoall followed by MPI_Wait) for various designs.

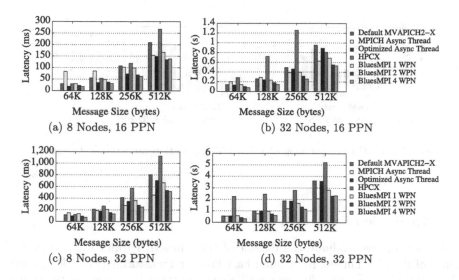

Fig. 11. Total execution time of osu_ialltoall benchmark for various designs.

3.2 Performance of MPI Collective Operations

In this section, we compare the performance of MPI_Ialltoall using the osu_ialltoall benchmark from the OSU Micro Benchmark suite. Figures 9, 10, and 11 show the impact of our proposed BluesMPI collective offloading framework on the InfiniBand based BlueField Smart NICs. For these tests, we used our most optimized algorithm which is Message Pipelining Design discussed in Sect. 2.2. As we can see here, our proposed design can guarantee the peak communication and computation overlap, as indicated in Fig. 9. On the other hand, BluesMPI high-performance staging based nonblocking alltoall design, with the proper number of Workers per node, it can gain on-par pure communication performance with tuned non-offloaded designs for large messages. By providing the peak communication and computation overlap and achieving low pure communication latency, BluesMPI can gain up to 2X speedup in the total osu_ialltoall execution time compared to default MVAPICH2-X. Comparing to the HPCX 2.7.0 with HCOLL NBC flag enabled, we can see that the proposed design's pure communication performance is on-par with this library. However, as the proposed design can provide full overlap of communication and computation, the total execution time improves up to 2X. The closest in performance of osu_ialltoall is MVAPICH2-X with MPICH asynchronous thread enabled. However, as we will see in the next section, having a separate thread for each process running constantly can severely degrade the performance. On the other hand, our proposed design does not interfere with the main application's compute, and therefore, can provide full overlap of communication and computation in a transparent manner, showing its benefits at the application level.

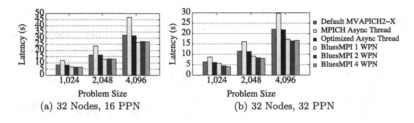

Fig. 12. CPU time per loop of P3DFFT application for various designs.

3.3 Application Evaluations

In this section, we evaluate the impact of the BluesMPI framework on performance of Parallel Three-Dimensional Fast Fourier Transforms (P3DFFT) application. This library uses a 2D, or pencil, decomposition and increases the degree of parallelism and scalability of FFT libraries. The data grid during each iteration is transformed using nonblocking Alltoall collectives [9]. Figure 12 shows the impact of the proposed BluesMPI designs with various number of Workers per node and various scales. For these tests, we used the Message Pipelining Design discussed in Sect. 2.2. The program that we used is test_sine.x and we set x and y grids to 2048. On x-axis, we run the tests for different values of z. As we can see here, as the scale of the application increases, the benefits of the BluesMPI also become more visible, gaining up to 30% improvement in the execution time of this application at 32 PPN 32 Nodes of the BlueField-enabled thor nodes of HPCAC cluster. It can be seen from this figure that even having a single Worker on each Smart NIC is having benefit. This is because even with a single Worker per node BluesMPI can achieve close to full overlap and communication and computation and if an application can provide enough computation to be overlapped with the communication time of the collective, it can see benefit with a single Worker per Smart NIC as well. On the other hand, MVAPICH2-X with MPICH asynchronous thread is showing the worst performance. This is because this thread is constantly running and it interferes with the main application's compute resources.

4   Related Work

There have been some recent research efforts that offload networking functions onto FPGA-based SmartNICs. There are also studies on offloading tasks to SmartNICs in distributed applications. Floem [13] proposed a dataflow programming system aimed at easing the programming effort. Liu et al. [10] built an "actor" based prototype (called ipipe) and developed several applications using it. The evaluation showed that by offloading computation to a SmartNIC, considerable host CPU and latency savings is achievable. Researchers have also explored various ways of offloading the progression of communication to NICs for MPI point-to-point and collective operations. Sur et al. [18] discuss different mechanisms for better computation/communication overlap on InfiniBand clusters. These mechanisms exploit RDMA Read and selective interrupt-based asynchronous progress and achieves nearly complete computation/communication overlap. Potluri et al. [14] studied novel proxy-based designs to optimize the internode point to-point and collective MPI primitives for Intel Xeon Phi based cluster systems connected using InfiniBand network.

5   Conclusion and Future Work

In this paper, we characterized the performance impact of the smart NICs on MPI and we found out the potential MPI primitives that can be offloaded into the Smart NICs. Based on our observations, we proposed BluesMPI, an adaptive non-blocking Alltoall collective offload framework that can be used on modern Smart NICs. Furthermore, we proposed efficient offloading designs for non-blocking Alltoall operations on the top of the BlueField Smart NIC. Our experimental evaluations showed that using the proposed methods, we are able to efficiently take advantage of the additional compute resource of Smart NICs in the network and accelerate the performance of OSU Micro Benchmarks and P3DFFT by a factor of 44% and 30%, respectively. To the best of our knowledge, this is the first design that efficiently takes advantage of modern BlueField Smart NICs in deriving the MPI collective operations to get the peak overlap of communication and computation. Our future work is to provide similar designs for other dense collective operations as well.

References

1. http://mvapich.cse.ohio-state.edu/benchmarks
2. High-Performance Center Overview. https://www.hpcadvisorycouncil.com/cluster_center.php
3. Mellanox BlueField. https://docs.mellanox.com/x/iQO3
4. Panda, D.K., Subramoni, H., Chu, C.H., Bayatpour, M.: The MVAPICH project: Transforming research into high-performance MPI library for HPC community. J. Comput. Sci. 101208 (2020)
5. Bayatpour, M., et al.: Communication-aware hardware-assisted MPI overlap engine. In: Sadayappan, P., Chamberlain, B.L., Juckeland, G., Ltaief, H. (eds.) ISC High Performance 2020. LNCS, vol. 12151, pp. 517–535. Springer, Cham (2020). https://doi.org/10.1007/978-3-030-50743-5_26
6. Bayatpour, M., Ghazimirsaeed, S.M., Xu, S., Subramoni, H., Panda, D.K.: Design and characterization of infiniband hardware tag matching in MPI. In: 20th Annual IEEE/ACM CCGRID (2020)
7. Gropp, W., Lusk, E., Doss, N., Skjellum, A.: A high-performance, portable implementation of the MPI, message passing interface standard. Technical report, Argonne National Laboratory and Mississippi State University
8. InfiniBand Trade Association (2017). http://www.infinibandta.com
9. Kandalla, K., Subramoni, H., Tomko, K., Pekurovsky, D., Sur, S., Panda, D.K.: High-performance and scalable non-blocking all-to-all with collective offload on infiniband clusters: a study with parallel 3D FFT. Comput. Sci. **26**, 237–246 (2011)
10. Liu, M., Cui, T., Schuh, H., Krishnamurthy, A., Peter, S., Gupta, K.: iPipe: a framework for building distributed applications on SmartNICs. In: SIGCOMM 2019: Proceedings of the ACM Special Interest Group on Data Communication, pp. 318–333 (2019). https://doi.org/10.1145/3341302.3342079
11. Network-Based Computing Laboratory: MVAPICH2-X (Unified MPI+PGAS Communication Runtime over OpenFabrics/Gen2 for Exascale Systems). http://mvapich.cse.ohio-state.edu/overview/mvapich2x/
12. Pekurovsky, D.: P3DFFT library (2006–2009). www.sdsc.edu/us/resources/p3dfft/
13. Phothilimthana, P.M., Liu, M., Kaufmann, A., Simon Peter, R.B., Anderson, T.: Floem: a programming system for NIC-accelerated network applications. In: Proceedings of the 2010 IEEE 26th Symposium on Mass Storage Systems and Technologies (MSST). 13th USENIX Symposium on Operating Systems Design and Implementation (2018)
14. Potluri, S., et al.: MVAPICH-PRISM: a proxy-based communication framework using InfiniBand and SCIF for Intel MIC clusters. In: Proceedings of SC 2013, SC 2013, pp. 54:1–54:11 (2013)
15. Scalable hierarchical aggregation protocol: scalable hierarchical aggregation protocol. https://www.mellanox.com/products/sharp
16. Subramoni, H., Kandalla, K., Sur, S., Panda, D.K.: Design and evaluation of generalized collective communication primitives with overlap using ConnectX-2 offload engine. In: Internationall Symposium on Hot Interconnects (HotI), August 2010 (2010)

17. Subramoni, H., et al.: Designing non-blocking personalized collectives with near perfect overlap for RDMA-enabled clusters. In: Kunkel, J.M., Ludwig, T. (eds.) ISC High Performance 2015. LNCS, vol. 9137, pp. 434–453. Springer, Cham (2015). https://doi.org/10.1007/978-3-319-20119-1_31
18. Sur, S., Jin, H.W., Chai, L., Panda, D.K.: RDMA read based rendezvous protocol for MPI over infiniband: design alternatives and benefits. In: Proceedings of the Eleventh ACM SIGPLAN Symposium on Principles and Practice of Parallel Programming, PPoPP 2006 (2006)

Lessons Learned from Accelerating Quicksilver on Programmable Integrated Unified Memory Architecture (PIUMA) and How That's Different from CPU

Jesmin Jahan Tithi[1]([✉]), Fabrizio Petrini[1], and David F. Richards[2]

[1] Parallel Computing Labs, Intel Corporation, 3600 Juliette Ln,
Santa Clara, CA 95054, USA
{jesmin.jahan.tithi,fabrizio.petrini}@intel.com
[2] Lawrence Livermore National Laboratory, Livermore, CA 94550, USA
richards12@llnl.gov

Abstract. Quicksilver represents key elements of the Mercury Monte Carlo Particle Transport simulation software developed at Lawrence Livermore National Laboratory (LLNL). Mercury is one of the applications used in the Department of Energy (DOE) for nuclear security and nuclear reactor simulations. Thus Quicksilver, as a Mercury proxy, influences DOE's hardware procurement and co-design activities. Quicksilver has a complicated implementation and performance profile: its performance is dominated by latency-bound table look-ups and control flow divergence that limit SIMD/SIMT parallelization opportunities. Therefore, obtaining high performance for Quicksilver is quite challenging.

This paper shows how to improve Quicksilver's performance on Intel Xeon CPUs by 1.8× compared to its original version by selectively replicating conflict-prone data structures. It also shows how to efficiently port Quicksilver on the new Intel Programmable Integrated Unified Memory Architecture (PIUMA). Preliminary analysis shows that a PIUMA die (8 cores) is about 2× faster than an Intel Xeon 8280 socket (28 cores) and provides better strong scaling efficiency.

Keywords: Dynamic particle simulation · History-based simulation · Mercury · Monte-Carlo simulation · Particle transport · PIUMA · Quicksilver

1 Introduction

Quicksilver [1,13] is a proxy application representing the memory access patterns, communication patterns, and branch divergence of the Mercury Monte Carlo Particle Transport code [3] developed at Lawrence Livermore National Laboratory (LLNL). Quicksilver models Mercury by solving a simplified particle transport problem and is used to facilitate novel architecture co-design.

Quicksilver's performance is dominated by latency bound table look-ups and branch divergence. The code uses template classes containing objects, vectors,

B. L. Chamberlain et al. (Eds.): ISC High Performance 2021, LNCS 12728, pp. 38–56, 2021.
https://doi.org/10.1007/978-3-030-78713-4_3

queues, arrays, enums, and pointers to user-defined complex data types. Most of these data structures are accessed randomly and require multiple levels of indirection and non-unit strides for lookup. The code's control flow is dominated by branch divergence and allows few SIMD/SMT opportunities. Due to its irregular and sparse nature, getting high performance for Quicksilver is challenging. State-of-the-art GPUs have been reported to do only marginally well compared to general-purpose CPUs [13].

Intel's Programmable Integrated Unified Memory Architecture (PIUMA) is a new architecture optimized for irregular and sparse workloads and developed under the DARPA HIVE [5] program. PIUMA consists of many multi-threaded cores and natively supports fine-grained memory and network accesses, a globally shared address space, and powerful offload engines. PIUMA uses limited caching and small granularity memory accesses to efficiently deal with the memory behavior of sparse workload. At the same time, PIUMA uses single-issue in-order pipelines with many threads to hide memory latency and avoid speculation. PIUMA supports in-network collectives, near-memory compute and remote atomics in hardware [5]. These characteristics of PIUMA are a good match for Quicksilver because of its unique application properties—latency bound random accesses, inefficient caching, and use of atomics. In this paper we show how to accelerate Quicksilver on PIUMA.

Contributions. This paper makes the following contributions:

- Shows a detailed performance analysis of Quicksilver on Intel Xeon CPUs.
- Improves Quicksilver performance on Xeon by 1.8× compared to baseline.
- Discusses how to port Quicksilver to the Intel PIUMA Architecture.
- Discusses optimizations to obtain 2× speedup and better scaling on PIUMA compared to Xeon.
- Discusses what additional changes are needed in the Quicksilver/Mercury code to scale to thousands of threads.

2   Background

2.1   Mercury and Quicksilver

The particle transport problem asks how particles interact with materials or structures. The Monte Carlo method solves the particle transport problem by tracking the paths of sample particles through a structure and using pseudo-random numbers to sample probability distributions of various reactions (scattering, fission, absorption, etc.) that may occur when particles collide with atoms in a material. Mercury uses distributed memory (MPI-based) particle streaming as well as domain replication to scale across nodes. It implements threads using OpenMP with thread-private tally storage and these tallies are the primary method for collecting data from Monte Carlo transport simulations to record different stats/events throughout the simulation [13].

Quicksilver is designed to model Mercury's call tree and memory usage patterns. Quicksilver tracks particles through a 3-dimensional, hexahedral problem domain with either vacuum or reflective boundary conditions. It implements a 3D polyhedral mesh where each mesh element consists of 24 triangular facets. Particles are tracked as they move through mesh elements and facets until the particles reach census (the end of the time step), are absorbed, or escape the problem domain.

A reaction is by far the most expensive event a particle can perform and induces a significant amount of divergent behavior. Each reaction has an associated cross-section table that stores the probabilities of such reaction occurring. During a reaction event, particles must search the cross-section table to determine which reaction they will experience and then perform that reaction.

2.2 PIUMA

This section gives an overview of the Programmable Integrated Unified Memory Architecture (PIUMA) and is adapted from article [5]. The PIUMA [5,10,12] architecture consists of a collection of highly multi-threaded cores (MTC) and single-threaded cores (STC) as shown in Fig. 1. The MTCs are round-robin (interleaved) multi-threaded to address the lack of instruction-level parallelism in most sparse workloads and incorporate latency hiding through thread-level parallelism as opposed to aggressive out-of-order speculative execution models. Each thread can have only one in-flight instruction. This simplifies the core design and has better energy efficiency. The STCs are in-order stall-on-use cores that can exploit some instruction and memory-level parallelism but avoid aggressive out-of-order pipelines to minimize power consumption. While the MTCs are used as the data-parallel engines in PIUMA, the STCs are used for single-threaded performance-sensitive tasks, such as memory and thread management.

MTCs and STCs are grouped into blocks. Each block has a large local scratchpad (SPAD) for low latency storage. PIUMA blocks are organized into dies and each die consists of 8 blocks. Each block's offload region contains a direct memory access (DMA) engine that executes gather, scatter, copy, initialization, reduction, and broadcast operations. The DMA engine supports executing atomic operations at the remote destinations.

All MTCs and STCs in PIUMA have a local instruction cache (I\$), data cache (D\$), and register file (RF). PIUMA supports selective data caching. Whether

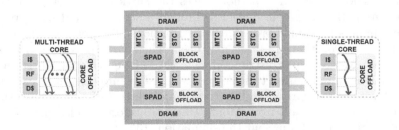

Fig. 1. High-level diagram of PIUMA architecture (adapted from [5]).

data is cached is determined by a programmable unique bit in the address. In general, no global variable is cached by default. Caches are not coherent across the whole system which helps scalability. Programmers are responsible to choose what memory accesses to cache (e.g., read-only global variables or local stack), what to put on SPAD (e.g., frequently reused read-write data structures) or what to store in the global address space. There are no prefetchers to avoid unnecessary data fetches and limit power consumption. Instead, the offload engines are used to efficiently fetch large chunks of data if needed.

PIUMA implements a distributed global address space (DGAS) in hardware and with DGAS, each core can uniformly access memory across the full system (containing multiple PIUMA nodes) using simple load/store operations. This simplifies programming because there is no implementation difference between accessing local and remote memory. This also eliminates the overhead of setting up communication for remote accesses. There is one memory controller per block and it supports native 8-byte accesses while supporting standard cache line accesses as well.

PIUMA also includes ISA-supported remote atomic operations to all memory locations in the system. Locking, ordering, and compute is managed by hardware at the remote memory interface to allow fast execution. With high-performing atomic operations, the programmer can implement efficient synchronization and dynamic load balancing.

PIUMA uses a low-diameter, high-radix HyperX topology network containing all-to-all connections on each level. Each link is optimized for 8-byte messages to avoid the software and hardware inefficiencies of message aggregation and large buffers prevalent in traditional systems. PIUMA utilizes a small-granularity interface with concurrent transactions to achieve similar aggregate bandwidths as traditional implementations. By design, the network bandwidth exceeds local DRAM bandwidth in PIUMA to support higher remote traffic common in many sparse workloads.

3   Quicksilver

Because Mercury is not publicly available, we used its proxy, Quicksilver, to model how the control flow and memory access patterns observed in Monte Carlo transport map to the PIUMA architecture. Quicksilver's simplified structure and smaller code size are also more suitable for the cycle-accurate simulator that is used to model PIUMA.

The core kernel of Quicksilver has multiple potential execution paths. The code uses dynamic data structures and multiple levels of indirection for data lookups. Its small and random memory loads/stores are difficult to cache or coalesce and frequent branching reduces vectorization opportunities. All these properties make Quicksilver a challenging code for GPUs. Previous work comparing Quicksilver's performance on an Nvidia P100 GPU [4] vs. an IBM Power9 processor highlighted the impact of divergence on GPU performance [13]. For simulations dominated by collision or facet crossing (i.e., when a specific code branch is taken more frequently and predictably), P100 is 30% faster than Power9. However, when the events are balanced (branches are taken with equal probabilities at random), P100 is slower by nearly a factor of two.

3.1   High-Level Algorithm

Pseudo-code for Quicksilver is shown in Algorithm 1.1. The program can be divided into three sections: cycle_init(), cycle_tracking() and cycle_finalize(). Simulations run for multiple time steps and each of these functions is called once per time step. The cycle_init() function initializes the particle tracking and builds the target number of particles at the start of each time step. The cycle_finalize() function handles bookkeeping at the end of the time step and computes global reductions on all tallies. The majority of the computational work of Quicksilver occurs in cycle_tracking() and the time spent in that section is used to compute the performance metric or Figure of Merit (FOM).

The cycle_tracking() function contains a parallel loop over all particles. For each particle, three distances are computed: distance to census, distance to crossing a mesh facet, and distance to the next reaction. Distance to census is merely the distance the particle will travel at its current velocity before the end of the time step. Distance to facet is a ray-tracing problem. Distance to reaction considers the probabilities of all possible reactions, determines the mean free path, and multiplies that mean free path by a random factor. Once these three distances are computed, the particle executes the segment with the shortest distance. Moving to census is trivial: it simply updates a tally that counts the number of census events. Moving to the next facet may involve entering a new material or possibly moving particles to a different spatial domain handled by a different MPI process. In the case of a reaction segment, a random reaction is selected, and control flow branches to the code that handles that reaction.

```
Quicksilver(...){                              cycle_tracking(...){
  //pre-processing and initialization            for all particles {
  cycle_init(...){                                 do{
    source particles                                 //select segment with the shortest distance
    perform population control                       segmentOutcome=segment_outcome(...)
    initialize tallies                               //executed selected event and update tallies
  }                                                  if(segmentOutcome == facet){
  //core-kernel, particle tracking                     facet_crossing_event(...)
  cycle_tracking(...){                                  increment tallies
    for all particles {                              }
      do{                                            if(segmentOutcome == collision){
        compute distance to census                     collision_event(...)
        compute distance to facet                      increment tallies
        compute distance to collision                }
        execute segment with shortest distance       if(segmentOutcome == census){
        increment tallies                              census_event(...)
      } while(!absorbed or                             increment tallies
            !incensus or                             }
            !escaped)                              } while(!absorbed or
    }                                                    !incensus or
  }                                                      !escaped)
  //post-processing                                }
  cycle_finalize(...){                           }
    reduce all tallies
  }
}
```

Algorithm 1.1. Pseudocode for the original Quicksilver code.

Once the selected segment is complete, tallies are incremented and the three distances are recomputed to repeat the process until all the particles either reach census (the end of the time step), are absorbed, or escape.

3.2   A Deeper Analysis of cycle_tracking

The cycle_tracking() function can be further sub-divided into two computationally expensive sub-modules which account for more than 95% of total runtime for the Coral2_P1*.inp input files that come with the proxy app [1]. The first sub-module (MCT_Segment_outcome) computes distances to census, facet_crossing, and reaction. The second sub-module (CollisionEvent) executes reaction events. Preliminary analysis shows that for the Coral2_P1_1.inp input file, Collision-Event takes 53.3% of the total time and MC_segment_outcome takes 44.6% of the total time on an Intel® Xeon Socket with 28 cores.

Both of these functions have low arithmetic intensities. Intel Advisor's profiling shows that the most expensive loop inside CollisionEvent has an arithmetic intensity of 0.002, and its performance is bounded by the L2 bandwidth. The function MCT_Nearest_facet called inside MCT_Segment_outcome has an arithmetic intensity of 0.005 and is bounded by the L3 bandwidth. Other functions called by CollisionEvent and MCT_Nearest_Segment are bounded by scalar L1 bandwidth, usable cache bandwidth, inter-loop data dependency, and the speed of latency bound look-ups. Arithmetic intensities range from 0.002 to 1.3.

The CollisionEvent function presents additional challenges as it is very irregular and branchy. In Mercury, many thousands of lines code are reachable by CollisionEvent due to the large number of possible reactions. Furthermore, the function is write-heavy and calls math functions such as sqrt, log, sin, cos, and inv. Write-heaviness is linked to frequent object creation (malloc and memcpy) that can be inefficient in highly threaded code and math functions are typically slow for in-order single-issue pipeline threads unless supported in the hardware.

Another interesting feature of cycle_tracking() is that the time spent in the parallel loop over particles varies widely from particle to particle. This behavior arises not only because each particle experiences an effectively random number of events, but also from the fact that different events require different amounts of compute time. Figure 2 shows a histogram of the run time for 6,400 particles, $4 \times 4 \times 4$ mesh, $1 \times 1 \times 1$ domain. The slowest particle takes $2\times$ more time than the median. This suggests cycle tracking will likely benefit from some form of load balancing.

4   CPU Optimizations

This section discusses different optimizations that can improve Quicksilver's performance on Xeon over $1.8\times$ compared to its original version.

The baseline code was taken from https://github.com/LLNL/Quicksilver, commit id 320d271cf68dafd92667cad08531a1caa744a834, updated on July

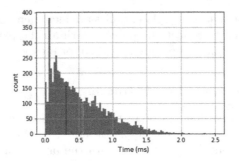

Fig. 2. Variation in runtime for each particle in cycle-tracking (in milliseconds).

2nd 2020. We have used the CTS2 Benchmark's CTS2_1.inp with 40,960 particles and the Coral2_Benchmark's CORAL2_P1_1.inp [2] with 163,840 particles and the following platform to guide the Xeon optimizations:

- CPU Name: Intel® Xeon® Platinum 8280 CPU @ 2.70GHz, Turbo boost on by default (CLX 8280)
- Memory: 196 GiB (DRAM), 39.4 MiB (L3) 1 MiB (L2), 32 KiB (L1)
- Number of Sockets: 1, 28 cores, 28 threads
- Parallelism: shared-memory thread parallel
- Compiler in Xeon: Intel® 64 Version: 19.0.2.187 Build 20190117

The following compiler flags "-O3 -xCORE-AVX512 -ipo -ansi-alias -finline - restrict -qopenmp -mP2OPT_hpo_omp_inline_atomic=2" are used to compile the code. The KMP_AFFINITY has been set to "verbose,granularity=fine,proclist = [0,1,2,3,4,5,6,7,8,9,10,11,12,13,14,15,16,17,18,19,20,21,22,23,24,25,26,27], explicit".

4.1 Engineering Optimizations

Because of the large variation in per-particle time observed in Sect. 3 we chose to focus first on load balancing. Replacing static thread scheduling (`#pragma omp parallel schedule (static,1)`) with dynamic thread scheduling (`#pragma omp parallel for schedule (dynamic,1)`) improved performance by 1.2× on one socket (28 cores) of Xeon CLX 8280 running 28 threads.

Next, we focused on the data access patterns in the CollisionEvent function. The most heavily used data structure in CollisionEvent is NuclearData. The size of NuclearData is in the order of $\mathcal{O}(N_{\text{reactions}} \times N_{\text{isotopes}} \times N_{\text{groups}} \times N_{\text{matterials}})$ and for the CORAL2_P1_1.inp input, it occupies around 331 KiB of storage space. This data is accessed randomly and is a potential source of conflict according to Intel Advisor. Making NuclearData private for each thread could potentially improve performance by reducing access/queuing delays. Hence, we made the instances of NuclearData thread private by using the storage specifier `static __thread` and making sure that each thread called the appropriate allocation and

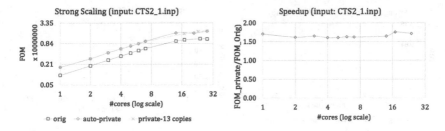

Fig. 3. Original vs. Optimized on the CTS2_1.inp input (40,960 particles). The Figure of Merit (FOM) is segments per second.

initialization functions. With this change, the compiler creates a unique instance of the variable for each thread that uses it and destroys that instance when the thread terminates. This simple change improves performance by 1.72× over the original. We call this approach automatic or compiler-assisted privatization.

We also tried some basic inlining of function calls, inlining atomic tally updates (tally is the data structure that keeps track of different events) inside the CollisionEvent, and MC_segment_outcome functions, and caching read-only pointers and variables independently. This improved performance by 1.1× without any prior optimizations.

Adding all three optimizations together gives an 1.82× aggregate speedup over the original code. The **keys to this speedup** are NuclearData privatization and dynamic thread scheduling. Other optimizations contributed very little.

Because of the significant memory penalty imposed by privatizing large data structures, we wanted to determine whether it is possible to get a similar performance gain using fewer copies of NuclearData than one per thread. We manually replicated NuclearData N_R times and assigned each thread to access the $(id\%N_R)$-th replica of NuclearData. This improved the runtime from the baseline version by 1.85×. However, manual privatization requires much more code changes (40 lines) than the compiler assisted data privatization (6 lines) and thus one may prefer the latter option.

Figure 3 shows the performance difference between the optimized version vs. the original code from GitHub on one socket of CLX 8280 on the CTS2_1.inp Input. In the figure, 'private-13-copies' stands for manual privatization with 13 copies of NuclearData created by the first 13 threads and then shared by the rest using the modulo operation, and 'auto-private' refers to compiler-assisted privatization. Regardless of the privatization method, the optimized code is 1.8× faster than the original.

Figure 4 shows the performance difference between the optimized version and the original code on the CORAL2_P1_1.inp. In this case, too, the optimized code performs 1.8× better than the original.

To summarize, by selectively privatizing a conflict prone data structure and adding dynamic load-balancing, we were able to obtain around 1.8× speedup.

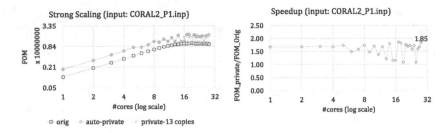

Fig. 4. Original vs. Optimized on the CORAL2_P1_1.inp Input (163,840 particles). The Figure of Merit (FOM) is segments per second.

4.2 Algorithmic Optimizations

The above optimizations are mainly engineering optimizations. There are algorithmic optimization opportunities that can improve performance, too. For example, it is possible to change the NuclearData data structure to be a structure of arrays rather than an array of structures and then compute the prefix sum of reaction probabilities instead of individual probabilities. That way, it is possible to replace the $\mathcal{O}(N_{\text{reactions}} \times N_{\text{isotopes}})$ cost linear scan through the reaction tables with a $\mathcal{O}(\log(N_{\text{reactions}} \times N_{\text{isotopes}}))$ cost binary search providing a 2× gain over the original [14]. However, this requires major changes in multiple data structures which might not be easy to adapt in Mercury. Significant algorithmic changes are outside the scope of this paper since the goal is to make minimal changes while porting Quicksilver to PIUMA.

5   Quicksilver on PIUMA

PIUMA has been designed with programmability in mind. It supports C and many features of C++. It has its own OpenMP style programming extensions to exploit both Single Program Multiple Data (SPMD) and task-based parallelization schemes. PIUMA hardware is not yet available, so a Sniper based cycle-accurate simulator [9] has been used to model and validate multi-die PIUMA configurations. In addition, an FPGA-based RTL system has been used to model up to 1 PIUMA die. The two systems, Sniper and RTL, provide performance estimates that are within 5% of each other [5].

5.1   Initial Porting Effort

It's fairly easy to port any OpenMP or pthread style shared-memory code to PIUMA since any memory location can be read/written by simple load/store operations (thanks to DGAS).

To port the shared-memory version of Quicksilver to PIUMA, we made the following changes in the code:

- Overloaded the 'new' and 'delete' operators to allow specification of where to allocate memory (main memory, scratchpad, private or shared).
- Changed the memory allocation calls to match the memory allocation library of PIUMA which are specialized for DGAS allocations.
- Replaced rand48() with Piuma_rand().
- Replaced atomics and synchronizations/barriers with PIUMA versions.
- Removed file I/O operations unsupported by the simulator.
- Found and fixed some memory leaks in the original code.

We also changed the main program to include PIUMA library header files and the Makefile to support PIUMA runtime. We used the STCs for memory allocations and initialization and the MTCs to simulate the particles. STCs are only used in the initialization phase.

Since PIUMA supports a variety of memory allocation options, the porting process involved deciding how to allocate various data structures in memory. By default, PIUMA uses an interleaved/striped memory allocation. For a program running on M cores with M memory controllers, any memory allocation will be striped in round-robin chunks across those memory controllers. This ensures even access pressure across the memory controllers and reduces queuing latency and conflicts for randomly accessed data. PIUMA also allows allocation to a particular core's local memory controller or scratchpad (SPAD). When a core allocates any data on SPAD, it gets allocated to its local SPAD by default. PIUMA also allows a program to selectively cache data by turning on a given bit in the address of that data. We initially chose to cache function parameters, global pointers, and variables used in the most time consuming functions (CollisionEvent and MCT_Nearest_Facet).

5.2   Comparing PIUMA to Xeon

In addition to the porting changes just described, we also added a few optimizations intended to make the comparison between PIUMA and Xeon as fair as possible. These included:

- Conversion of repeated division operation to one division followed by repeated multiplications, because divisions are costlier than multiplication.
- Replacing software transcendental functions with hardware versions, since hardware versions are faster.
- Function inlining for most heavily used functions to reduce calling overheads.
- Selective caching for frequently accessed read-only global variables because cached accesses are faster.
- Use of builtin relaxed atomics whenever feasible since relaxed atomics are faster than the standard ones.

Since PIUMA does not cache data by default and that PIUMA's cache is not as large as Xeon's, we used the SPAD as a substitute for the cache. SPAD is faster than the main memory but slower than cache. We know from our Xeon analysis that NuclearData is a performance-critical data structure so we allocated the

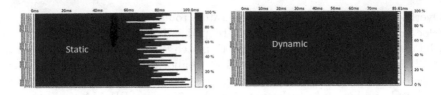

Fig. 5. Static vs. dynamic scheduling of particles on PIUMA. Input: 10,240 particles, 4 × 4 × 4 mesh, 1024 particles per MTC.

most heavily used arrays of NuclearData in the SPAD. We allocated certain tally data (that tracks counts of different events) in the SPAD as well because Quicksilver does frequent atomic updates on tallies and SPAD atomics are faster than atomics on main memory.

As we ran Quicksilver on the PIUMA simulator we quickly realized that the load-imbalance due to static scheduling of the particle loop in cycle_tracking was much worse on PIUMA than Xeon. This is not surprising considering PIUMA's much larger number of threads per core. Therefore, we implemented a dynamic load-balancing technique where each MTC thread atomically updates a shared global *next_particle* variable by a chunk size and works on that chunk of particles. Figure 5 shows the thread timeline plots for static and dynamic scheduling. The thread timelines clearly show that the load imbalance with static partitioning is almost completely eliminated by dynamic scheduling.

With these changes, the PIUMA implementation of Quicksilver is quite similar to the Xeon implementation from Sect. 4 with data privatization optimizations removed. We refer to this implementation as the baseline version.

Figure 6 compares performance between the PIUMA baseline implementation and a Xeon version without NuclearData privatization for the Coral2_P1_1.inp input with 20,480 particles, 4×4×4 mesh, 1×1×1 domain, and 1 iteration of tracking. (We are limited to only one iteration of cycle_tracking because the cycle-accurate simulator used to simulate the PIUMA system is significantly slower than running on actual hardware.) The figure shows that while 1 PIUMA core performs similarly to 1 Xeon core, PIUMA wins on strong scaling and 16 cores of PIUMA (1,024 MTC threads) are 2× faster than 16 cores of Xeon CLX 8280. PIUMA's strong scaling efficiency is 56%, and CLX's efficiency is 27%. Admittedly, making this comparison with a small number of particles (about 8× fewer than we used in Sect. 4) disadvantages Xeon. However, as shown in Fig. 4, Xeon performance flattens rapidly beyond 8 threads for large problems too. Even if Xeon were to scale as in Fig. 4, PIUMA would be substantially faster at 16 cores.

The **key takeaway** here is that without data privatization, a single PIUMA core runs as fast as a single Xeon core, but when we strong scale to 16 cores, PIUMA performs 2× better than Xeon—thanks to its lightweight threads and latency hiding capability.

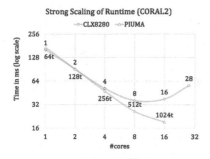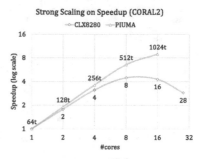

Fig. 6. Performance of Quicksilver on CLX and PIUMA, without data privatization

5.3 PIUMA Optimized Version

Next, we set out to optimize the PIUMA version of Quicksilver by addressing hotspots highlighted by the PIUMA simulator. We also wanted to test Nuclear-Data privatization since that change provided 1.7× speedup on Xeon. Based on these objectives, we made the following changes:

– In MC_nearest_facet, fused the loop over 24 facets to compute the distance to facets with the loop that finds their minimum. This removes temporary arrays and reduces repeated object creation.
– Moved tallies to main memory from SPAD and inlined the most expensive scalar flux update.
– Removed NuclearData from SPAD and created a private copy in each core's local main memory.
– Allocated parts of the Domain (node, plane, and points) in the SPAD.
– Cached mesh, node, plane, and points in the MC_nearest_facet function.

We call this version the optimized version on PIUMA.

Figure 7 shows the performance difference between the optimized version of Quicksilver on PIUMA and the Xeon code with data privatization on the Coral2_P1_1.inp input with 20,480 particles, 4×4×4 mesh, 1×1×1 domain. At 16 cores, the PIUMA optimized version is 1.65× faster than its own baseline. This is slightly less than the 1.7× speedup we obtained on Xeon from data privatization, but the scalability gap remains. With data-privatization optimization on Xeon, PIUMA is slower than Xeon up to 4 cores, performs similar to Xeon at 8 cores, and around 2× faster at 16 cores. PIUMA shows better strong scaling at 16 cores where each MTC thread is processing 20 particles and each Xeon thread is processing 1,280 particles; PIUMA's strong scaling efficiency is 77% whereas Xeon's efficiency is only 24%. Nevertheless, Xeon benefits more than PIUMA from data privatization, especially at smaller core counts.

Note that, moving NuclearData from SPAD to main memory does not degrade performance at 16 cores. In fact, the PIUMA performance on 16 cores improved slightly from 19.22 ms (see Fig. 6) to 19.02 ms by reducing the contention in accessing a single SPAD. As detailed in the next subsection, it also

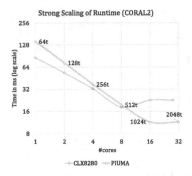 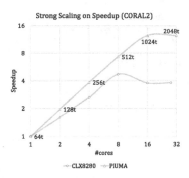

Fig. 7. Performance of Quicksilver on CLX and PIUMA, with data privatization

matters little whether NuclearData is privatized to each core or distributed. The major portion of the speedup of the optimized PIUMA version comes from loop fusion, removal of temporaries, and the inlined tally update. In contrast, when we tested the loop fusion optimization by itself on Xeon, we obtained very little speedup; only about 2%. This is consistent with the fact that the MTC threads are very lightweight and significantly slower at temporary object creation compared to a thread running on an out-of-order Xeon core. (It also explains why Xeon sees relatively little benefit from the same optimization.)

5.4 Exploring Memory Allocation Options on PIUMA

One obvious disadvantage of data privatization optimizations is the extra storage space required for the private copies. Fortunately, PIUMA's DGAS architecture provides a way to avoid that cost. PIUMA provides Malloc_at_core(id) that allocates data at a memory controller close to the core with a given id but striped across multiple ports if available. This style of allocation is similar to the default allocation technique on Xeon and is usually good for data accessed using unit strides. We used this allocation option in the previous subsection to create core-private copies of NuclearData. However, PIUMA can also do distributed memory allocation. The default malloc on PIUMA allocates data in chunks of B bytes across all cores' memory controllers. This stripes data across both memory controllers and ports which is good for randomly accessed data because it distributes access pressure across all controllers evenly.

To understand benefits of private vs. distributed allocations we tested Quicksilver with two allocation options:

- Private: Each core has its own copy of NuclearData.
- Distributed: A single copy of NuclearData is distributed across all memory controllers in a stripped/interleaved manner.

As shown in Table 1, the performance of these two options is very similar. With 20,480 particles, on 8 cores (512 MTCs), the distributed allocation (1 copy) version took 20.64 ms whereas the private allocation (8 copies) version

Table 1. Distributed vs. private allocation on PIUMA. MC = Memory Controller.

Memory Policy	Time (ms)
1 copy interleaved across all MC	20.64
8 copies at 8 MCs	19.35

Table 2. Impact of data replication on PIUMA

# Copies	Time (ms)	Cores per copy
1	35.44	8 cores access a single copy
2	23.27	4 cores access each copy
4	20.33	2 cores access each copy
8	19.35	Each core has own copy

took 19.35 ms. Thus, the benefits of private vs. distributed copies for randomly accessed data (e.g., NuclearData) is minimal on PIUMA.

To further understand the difference between private and distributed allocation, we varied the total number of private copies of NuclearData from 1 to 8. Note that any PIUMA core can access data stored at any other PIUMA core so the allocations are private only in the sense of locality and do not restrict access. As shown in Table 2, if only one copy of NuclearData is allocated on just one core's local memory, performance suffers badly for 8 cores and 20,480 particles. The speedup as the number of copies increases is reminiscent of our data privatization trials on Xeon. It is probably not a coincidence that the speedup for a single copy vs. one copy per core is roughly 1.8× on both Xeon and PIUMA.

The clear lesson here is that it is vitally important to reduce or eliminate data access conflicts for heavily-used and randomly-accessed data structures like NuclearData. PIUMA with distributed allocations provides a distinct advantage since it reduces conflict without the need for multiple copies of the data.

5.5   A Closer Look at Strong Scaling

Although it isn't very noticeable in Fig. 7, there is a fairly large drop in strong scaling efficiency from 8 to 16 PIUMA cores on the CORAL_2 input with 20,480 particles. Because a PIUMA die consists of 8 cores, the 16 core simulation requires 2 dies and it is worth asking whether the break in scaling is due to penalties associated with running on multiple dies.

To understand PIUMA's scaling, we first examined dynamic scheduling. With only 20 particles per thread at 16 cores there is reason to be concerned that some of the efficiency loss could be due to load imbalance. Table 3 compares the time to finish for the first and last threads as the number of cores increases. It is immediately apparent that the gap between the first and last thread is growing relative to the time to finish. For 1 core, the 1.5 ms difference is just 1% of the runtime. Hence, thread imbalance is insignificant. For 16 cores, the

Table 3. Strong Scaling efficiency with 20,480 particles.

	Last thread finish time			First thread finish time		
#cores	Time (ms)	speedup	%efficiency	Time (ms)	speedup	%efficiency
1	143.6	1	100	142.1	1	100
2	72.62	2	98.9	71.7	2	99.1
4	37	3.9	97	35.8	4	99.2
8	19.41	7.4	92.5	18.4	7.7	96.5
16	11.62	12.4	77.2	10.4	13.7	85.4

Table 4. Performance on 16 PIUMA cores chosen from various numbers of dies.

dies	cores per die	total cores	Distributed time (ms)	Private time (ms)
2	8	16	11.63	11.83
4	4	16	12.23	12.05
8	2	16	12.68	12.02
16	1	16	12.61	12.17

last thread is 1.2 ms behind the first, but this makes the last thread roughly 10% slower than the first since the runtime is only 11.6 ms. This increase in thread imbalance contributes to the decline in scaling efficiency. Hence, at least some of the breakdown in scaling is due to load imbalance. But even using the first-thread finish time as an idealized model for a perfectly balanced simulation, there is still a significant decrease in scaling efficiency from 96.5% to 85.4% as we engage a second die.

To further characterize the effect of running on multiple dies we ran simulations using cores from multiple dies instead of picking them from a minimum number of dies. The results in Table 4 show that for runs with 16 total cores, it hardly matters how many dies are used. This is true regardless of whether the NuclearData is distributed across memory controllers or private to each core. Even when we pick 16 cores from 16 different dies, slowdown is minimal compared to the minimum 2 dies. This result seems very surprising at first, but can be explained by the fact that in PIUMA, network bandwidth exceeds local DRAM bandwidth. In contrast, conventional architectures are designed to accommodate higher local traffic than remote traffic. It is clear from this analysis that the loss of scaling efficiency is due to a variety of causes and not solely to the addition of a second die.

Table 5. Performance bottlenecks at 2,048 threads on PIUMA.

%Cycles	Source
26.14%	$\_\_builtin\_piuma\_fence(FENCE\_DMA, FENCE\_BLOCKING)$;
25.97%	$pos = \_\_atomic\_fetch\_add(\&\_size, 1, \_ATOMIC\_RELAXED)$;
7.58%	$return\_data[index]$;
5.21%	$currentCrossSection- = mcs * \_rections[reactIndex].\_crossSection[...]$
3.96%	$start = \_\_atomic\_fetch\_add(next\_particle CHUNK ...\_RELAXED)$;
3.56%	$\_\_builtin\_piuma\_barrier\_wait(cid)$;
1.80%	$for(intreactIndex = 0; reactIndex < numReacts; reactIndex + +)$
1.49%	$\_\_atomic\_fetch\_add(\&(....\_tallies.\_balanceTask[tally\_index].\_numSegments), 1, ...$
1.03%	$double\ A = plane.A, B = plane.B, C = plane.C, D = plane.D$;

5.6   Hitting the Scaling Limit on PIUMA

If we continue strong scaling the CORAL_2 input by running on 2,048 threads (i.e., 32 PIUMA cores on 4 dies), Quicksilver stops scaling (see Fig. 7). With only 10 particles per thread it is tempting to conclude that the amount work per thread has become too small in comparison to various overheads. However, a careful analysis reveals a more subtle explanation.

Table 5 shows the lines of code that consume the most compute cycles at 2,048 threads. Starting with the second line of the table, we see that an atomic fetch_add in the ParticleVault uses over 25% of the simulation time. Because this atomic is called whenever a particle is added to the vault, we would expect the time spent in this atomic to scale with the number of particles. Why is this atomic a problem at 2,048 threads but not at smaller thread counts? The answer is that frequent atomics on a single variable do not scale to 2,048 threads. There is too much contention. Thus, the strong scaling breakdown is caused not by the work per thread decreasing compared to a fixed overhead cost, but rather because the overhead cost has substantially increased at higher thread counts.

The $\_\_builtin\_piuma\_fence$ shown in line 1 of Table 5 is related to memcpy and the explanation for it is similar. Quicksilver uses two different classes to represent particles: MC_Particle and MC_Base_particle. The purpose of MC_Base_particle is to reduce data size when transferring particles using MPI calls or even transferring to the GPU memory. Converting between particle representations generates memcpy calls which are invoked indirectly via copy constructors (i.e., malloc followed by a memcpy). Although these conversions are obviously inefficient, they become a performance problem only at high thread counts.

In PIUMA, memcpy calls are internally converted to DMA calls which need a fence to indicate completion. Hence, the appearance of __builtin_fence in Table 5. When an MTC thread encounters a DMA_FENCE, it waits until the DMA operation is completed. During this process, the threads need to access some common properties of the ParticleVault (e.g., size, capacity) and some other shared global variables regarding thread state that are not read-only (cannot be cached). This overwhelms the single memory controller that stores that data

Table 6. Performance Bottleneck With Only One Type of Particle

%Cycles	Source
33.22%	$pos = $ _ _$atomic_fetch_add(\&_size, 1, $ _ _$ATOMIC\_RELAXED)$;
12.65%	$start = $ _ _$atomic\_fetch\_add(next\_particle\,CHUNK$ _ _$ATOMIC\_RELAXED)$;
8.55%	$return\_data[index]$;
5.62%	$currentCrossSection- = mcs * \_rections[reactIndex].\_crossSection[...]$;
5.04%	$index = $ _ _$atomic\_fetch\_add(\&this- > \_extraVaultIndex, 1, ...RELAXED)$;
1.94%	_ _$atomic\_fetch\_add(\&(...\_tallies.\_balanceTask[tally\_index].\_numSegments), 1, ...$
1.92%	$for(int\;reactIndex = 0; reactIndex < numReacts; reactIndex + +)$
1.74%	_ _atomic_fetch_add_fp(& (...tallies._sFD[particle.domain]._task[_tally_idx]._cell[particle.cell]._grou
1.09%	$double\;A = plane.A, B = plane.B, C = plane.C, D = plane.D$;

when simultaneously accessed by 2,048 threads. Once again, we see that the strong scaling is limited because overheads increase at higher thread counts.

There are other atomic operations that appear in Table 5 such as the atomics on the variable used for dynamic load-balancing (*next_particle* on line 5) and atomics used in scale flux tally update (line 8). Essentially, anything that is a single point of frequent access by all threads becomes problematic at scale.

Fortunately, it is relatively easy to resolve these scaling problems by decreasing the pressure on any single point of access. For example, we could avoid frequent memcpys by using only a single particle type. Avoiding contention on the ParticleVault can be done by giving each die (8 cores, 512 threads) its own vault. We tested the first option using a version of Quicksilver that had only a single particle class. Table 6 shows that this change indeed removes the memcpy from the list of bottlenecks. With this change, the atomic operation moves up to the topmost position in the bottleneck and overall runtime improves very little.

We believe that we can push the scalability beyond $1, 024$ threads, and it will require replicating data structures that require single points of frequent atomics. Replicating them at a die (or two dies) level, gathering updates locally, and then reducing/merging globally should solve the current scalability issue.

We have learned from the above exploration that a shared-memory style implementation with atomics accessing a single copy of a variable is not feasible when the number of threads crosses a threshold. Similarly, MPI-style programming with private data per core can lead to unnecessary data replication. MPI+X style programming where X is OpenMP, CilkPlus, Pthreads, or another shared-memory programming paradigm, can help avoid replicating data on different ranks on the same node. However, good performance can be obtained only when the "+X" can effectively parallelize a large fraction of the code. PIUMA's DGAS memory model allows programmers to easily find a sweet spot by choosing between a single distributed copy for data accessed at random or replicated data when necessary to avoid choking a single memory controller.

6   Related Work

While there is considerable prior work to optimize Monte Carlo Transport applications and proxies for GPUs [6–8,11], there is little published work on Quicksilver beyond the original paper [1,13] that compared performance of the power8 CPU and P100 GPU concluding minimal benefit of the GPU. A recent poster [14] suggests changes in some key data structures and algorithms in the CollisionEvent function can reduce the search cost in the reaction table from linear to logarithmic. This work is orthogonal to our work since our goal is model Mercury rather than change its algorithms or internal data structures.

PIUMA is a recently proposed architecture, and work to date has focused mainly on graph algorithms and related kernels (e.g., SpMV, Graph500, Triangle Counting, BFS, k-truss, Louvain, Nerstrand) [5]. These are different (and relatively simpler) than Quicksilver. Therefore, this is the first research work that gives us some intuition on the performance of a Monte Carlo transport application on a PIUMA-like DGAS architecture.

7   Conclusion

We have described our experiences optimizing the Quicksilver proxy app on both Xeon and a new Programmable Integrated Unified Memory Architecture (PIUMA). On Xeon, we achieved over 1.8× speedup compared to the original, mainly from selective data replication of randomly accessed data. In contrast, data replication provided little benefit to PIUMA's specialized memory architecture. Instead, PIUMA performance was significantly improved by loop fusion and elimination of temporary object creation. Comparing our best versions on each platform PIUMA is 2× faster than Xeon and scales better.

Although we focus on Quicksilver, the lessons learned should be universal and applicable to a broad class of applications running on PIUMA. We learned:

- For randomly accessed data, contiguous allocation on one memory controller is inefficient.
- Any data that is allocated in a single memory controller and is accessed frequently by all threads is a bottleneck. Placing variables accessed by atomics on SPAD improves performance. Ideally, any single point of atomics should be avoided. Instead, privatizing the data and reducing it at the end (with/without atomics) should help.
- Selectively using SPAD and caching improves performance.
- If there is low caching efficiency for a particular data structure, do not cache, especially, if that takes away space from other cacheable data. Cache those data that have some spatial and (possibly) temporal locality.
- Dynamic allocation and frequent memcpy called by MTC threads during computation are slow in PIUMA. Allocating ahead of time and reusing them during an actual run is the way to go.

Acknowledgments. This research was, in part, funded by the U.S. Government. The views and conclusions contained in this document are those of the authors and should not be interpreted as representing the official policies, either expressed or implied, of the U.S. Government. Prepared by LLNL under Contract DE-AC52-07NA27344. LLNL-CONF-817842. Thanks to Marcin Lisowski and Joanna Gagatko from Intel for their initial help with Quicksilver on PIUMA. We would also like to thank Sebastian Szkoda, Vincent Cave and Wim Heirman from Intel for their help with PIUMA runtime.

References

1. Co-design at Lawrence Livermore National Laboratory: Quicksilver, Lawrence Livermore National Laboratory (LLNL), Livermore, CA, United States. https://computing.llnl.gov/projects/co-design/quicksilver, https://github.com/LLNL/Quicksilver
2. "Coral2". https://asc.llnl.gov/coral-2-benchmarks/
3. "Mercury". https://wci.llnl.gov/simulation/computer-codes/mercury
4. Nvidia P100. https://www.nvidia.com/en-us/data-center/tesla-p100/
5. Aananthakrishnan, S., et al.: PIUMA: programmable integrated unified memory architecture. arXiv preprint arXiv:2010.06277 (2020)
6. Bergmann, R.M., Vujić, J.L.: Algorithmic choices in WARP-A framework for continuous energy Monte Carlo neutron transport in general 3D geometries on GPUs. Ann. Nucl. Energy **77**, 176–193 (2015)
7. Bleile, R., Brantley, P., O'Brien, M., Childs, H.: Algorithmic improvements for portable event-based Monte Carlo transport using the nvidia thrust library. Tech. rep., Lawrence Livermore National Lab. (LLNL), Livermore, CA, USA (2016)
8. Brown, F.B., Martin, W.R.: Monte Carlo methods for radiation transport analysis on vector computers. Progress Nucl. Energy **14**(3), 269–299 (1984)
9. Carlson, T.E., Heirman, W., Eyerman, S., Hur, I., Eeckhout, L.: An evaluation of high-level mechanistic core models. ACM Trans. Archit. Code Optim. 11(3), 1–25 (2014). https://doi.org/10.1145/2629677
10. David, S.: DARPA ERI: HIVE and intel PUMA graph processor. WikiChip Fuse (2019). https://fuse.wikichip.org/news/2611/darpa-eri-hive-and-intel-puma-graph-processor/
11. Hamilton, S.P., Slattery, S.R., Evans, T.M.: Multigroup monte carlo on GPUs: comparison of history-and event-based algorithms. Ann. Nucl. Energy **113**, 506–518 (2018)
12. McCreary, D.: Intel's incredible PIUMA graph analytics hardware. Medium (2020). https://dmccreary.medium.com/intels-incredible-piuma-graph-analytics-hardware-a2e9c3daf8d8
13. Richards, D.F., Bleile, R.C., Brantley, P.S., Dawson, S.A., McKinley, M.S., O'Brien, M.J.: Quicksilver: a proxy app for the Monte Carlo transport code mercury. In: CLUSTER, pp. 866–873. IEEE (2017)
14. Tithi, J.J., Liu, X., Petrini, F.: Accelerating quicksilver-a Monte Carlo proxy app on multicores. https://www.youtube.com/watch?v=ARrymLNiL7M

A Hierarchical Task Scheduler
for Heterogeneous Computing

Narasinga Rao Miniskar[1]($\boxtimes$)(iD), Frank Liu[1](iD), Aaron R. Young[1](iD),
Dwaipayan Chakraborty[2](iD), and Jeffrey S. Vetter[1](iD)

[1] Advanced Computing Systems Research Section, Oak Ridge National Laboratory,
Oak Ridge, TN 37831, USA
{miniskarnr,liufy,youngar,vetter}@ornl.gov
[2] Rowan University, 201 Mullica Hill Road, Glassboro, NJ 08028, USA

Abstract. Heterogeneous computing is one of the future directions of HPC. Task scheduling in heterogeneous computing must balance the challenge of optimizing the application performance and the need for an intuitive interface with the programming run-time to maintain programming portability. The challenge is further compounded by the varying data communication time between tasks. This paper proposes RANGER, a hardware-assisted task-scheduling framework. By integrating RISC-V cores with accelerators, the RANGER scheduling framework divides scheduling into global and local levels. At the local level, RANGER further partitions each task into fine-grained subtasks to reduce the overall makespan. At the global level, RANGER maintains the coarse granularity of the task specification, thereby maintaining programming portability. The extensive experimental results demonstrate that RANGER achieves a 12.7× performance improvement on average, while only requires 2.7% of area overhead.

Keywords: Extreme heterogeneity · Accelerators · HPC system
architecture · Challenges in programming for massive scale

1 Introduction

As technology scaling comes to a standstill, heterogeneous computing has become a viable solution for ensuring the continuous performance improvement of high-performance computing (HPC). One specific notion of heterogeneous computing is the future of "extreme" heterogeneity [35], which is when the general-purpose

This manuscript has been co-authored by UT-Battelle, LLC under Contract No. DE-AC05-00OR22725 with the U.S. Department of Energy. The United States Government retains and the publisher, by accepting the article for publication, acknowledges that the United States Government retains a non-exclusive, paid-up, irrevocable, worldwide license to publish or reproduce the published form of this manuscript, or allow others to do so, for United States Government purposes. The Department of Energy will provide public access to these results of federally sponsored research in accordance with the DOE Public Access Plan.

B. L. Chamberlain et al. (Eds.): ISC High Performance 2021, LNCS 12728, pp. 57–76, 2021.
https://doi.org/10.1007/978-3-030-78713-4_4

microprocessors are augmented by diverse types of accelerators in vastly different architectures (e.g., general purpose GPUs, FPGAs, neuromorphic arrays and
special-purpose accelerator ASICs). These accelerators can have diverse functionalities (e.g., different computational kernels in machine learning) but are
also spatially distributed. To fully materialize the potential of heterogeneous
accelerators, it is crucial to maintain and improve the programming portability
and productivity of the applications and to intelligently manage the resources
presented by the heterogeneous accelerators.

Task parallelism is a highly effective parallel programming model for achieving programming portability and productivity. It allows the run-time to automatically schedule atomic computing tasks on the available resources while honoring
the data dependencies between tasks. Task parallelism is widely used in many
programming systems as either a direct abstraction available to the user or in
the underlying implementation (e.g., OpenMP [23], OpenACC [22], CUDA [21],
Charm++ [14], Cilk [6], OpenCL [16]). In task parallelism, the dependencies
among different tasks can be represented by a directed acyclic graph (DAG),
which contains information such as task computation time on different devices
(i.e., CPUs or accelerators) represented by the nodes or vertices of the DAG, the
data dependencies among the tasks represented by the directed edges, and the
amount of data that must be communicated between different tasks represented
as an edge property of the DAG. Even for homogeneous devices, task scheduling
is NP-complete [34]. Hence, many research activities are focused on developing
heuristics to ensure good completion times (i.e., makespans). Task scheduling
in a heterogeneous computing environment is a much more challenging problem
not only due to the different execution times of the heterogeneous devices but
also due to varying data communication latency between devices.

With its many diverse accelerators, extremely heterogeneous computing
poses some unique challenges for task scheduling. First, as the accelerators
become more diverse, one-size-fits-all, cookie-cutter-style device management
might not be optimal. Each kernel accelerator has a unique data access pattern and requirement for the hardware resources (e.g., sustained bandwidth to
the global memory, size of the scratchpad memory). It is difficult to balance the
needs of all kernel accelerators by a generic, centralized scheduler. Second, as
more kernel accelerators with diverse capabilities become available, it becomes
necessary to ensure that a larger pool of tasks is present to ensure application
scalability. Performing task scheduling for many tasks for an increasing number
of devices will require substantial computing resources. Finally, a larger pool
of tasks poses a widening dichotomy between the optimal management of the
resources and the need to ensure programming portability.

This work proposes RANGER, a hierarchical task scheduler, to address these
challenges. From an algorithm perspective, RANGER performs task scheduling
at two levels. At the top (i.e., global) level, RANGER considers the scheduling
decision of the current task and its immediate child tasks on the decision tree
to ensure global optimality. At the lower (i.e., local) level, RANGER deploys an
accelerator-specific scheduler to further partition the task into subtasks while

considering the nature of the computational kernel, its computational density, and the available hardware resources, such as the scratchpad memory module. Because the local schedulers have direct control over the interconnect switching fabric and other available hardware resources (e.g., accelerators, DMAs), they are capable of making optimal control decisions. In regard to implementation, instead of burdening the top-level global task scheduler with many subtasks, which are substantially more in quantity, each kernel accelerator is augmented with a customized RISC-V core to off-load the computational overhead of low-level scheduling and resource management. The most notable benefit of the hierarchical scheduling approach is that it bridges the dichotomy of coarse-grained scheduling desired by interfacing with programming models with the need for fine-grained, kernel/accelerator-dependent local task scheduling to ensure the overall optimality. Through extensive experimentation, we demonstrated that RANGER achieves a 12.7× makespan improvement on average compared with an equivalent centralized scheduler, while only requires a 2.74% area overhead. The experiments also demonstrated the excellent scalability of the RANGER architecture with respect to the number of parallel applications

The main contributions of this work are as follows.

1. We propose RANGER, a hierarchical task-scheduling framework for extremely heterogeneous computing.
2. We design and implement the overall RANGER architecture, as well as customized RISC-V cores and related logic in the GEM5 simulator[5].
3. We design and implement local Accelerator-Specific Command Schedulers (ASCS).
4. We conduct thorough experimentation to demonstrate the effectiveness of RANGER and to provide quantitative area and computational overhead.

The remainder of this paper is organized as follows. Section 2 discusses the background of task scheduling and related work. Section 3 describes the details of RANGER and its implementations. Section 4 presents experimental evaluations, followed by conclusions and future work in Sect. 5.

2   Background and Related Work

Task scheduling is a well-studied topic in disciplines such as computer architecture, programming languages, embedded systems, and real-time computing. A list of representative related works [1,6,7,9,11,15,17,19,20,24,29,34] cover diverse topics, such as static (i.e., offline) and dynamic (i.e., online) scheduling, scheduling with hard deadlines, and hardware-enabled scheduling policies.

In this paper, we assume that the dependencies among tasks are either fully or partially known. A widely accepted formalism to describe task dependencies is based on graphs [1,33]. An example is shown in Fig. 1 in which an application is represented by a DAG, defined by the tuple $G = (V, E)$, and a companion computation cost matrix (CCM). The vertex set V of size v represents the tasks in the application, and the edge set E of size e represents the data dependencies between the tasks. If there is an edge (e_{ij}) from task T_i to T_j, it means that task T_j has a data dependency to task T_i. Hence, task T_j cannot start until task T_i is completed. The CCM of size $v \times p$ represents the execution time of each task on each processing device, where p is the size of the processor set P. Each edge also contains a weight, which represents the communication cost between the tasks. Theoretically, the communication time depends not only on the tasks but also on which device the communication is originated and on which device it is terminated. However, one common approximation is to estimate the communication time based on the amount of data that must be transferred and the average communication bandwidth, as well as the average starting latency. This common approximation is defined as follows [33]:

$$\overline{c}_{(i,j)} = \overline{L} + \frac{data_{(i,j)}}{\overline{B}}, \tag{1}$$

where $\overline{B}$ is the average communication bandwidth between computing devices, and $data_{(i,j)}$ reflects the amount of data that must be transferred from task i to task j. $\overline{L}$ represents the average latency before any bulk data communication can be started. Generally, $\overline{L}$ could include hardware latency, such as the signal hand-shaking time for interconnects, and software latency, such as the time needed for context switching by the operating systems. With this approximation, the average communication time between tasks can be determined as shown by the edge weights in Fig. 1.

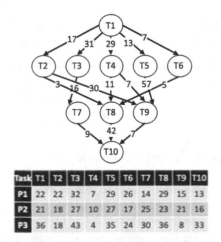

Fig. 1. DAG of an application with 10 tasks and the CCM for each task on three devices.

Task	T1	T2	T3	T4	T5	T6	T7	T8	T9	T10
P1	22	22	32	7	29	26	14	29	15	13
P2	21	18	27	10	27	17	25	23	21	16
P3	36	18	43	4	35	24	30	36	8	33

The objective of task scheduling is to minimize the overall execution time of the application or makespan. Because the task scheduling problem is NP-complete [34], many existing methods are based on heuristics. Among static task schedulers, Predict Earliest Finish Time (PEFT) [1] has a good trade-off between accuracy and computational complexity. Based on the Heterogeneous Earliest Finish Time (HEFT) [33] scheduler, PEFT considers the impact that the current scheduling decision has on all subsequent scheduling decisions within the decision tree. To estimate the potential impact of a scheduling decision, it uses a clever method to compute an optimal cost table, thereby avoiding the costly operation of fully traversing the whole decision tree.

The concept of *a task* is the atomic unit for data transferring and computation. Implicitly, it is assumed that the data needed for each task have been readily transferred to the local scratchpad memory on each device before the computation can start. For each application, the task specifications can be given at different levels. For example, tasks can be further partitioned into finer subtasks by inspecting the computation kernels and the dependencies between more fine-grained subcomponents. The granularity of the task specification has significant practical implications. On one hand, coarse-grained task specifications are more acceptable and have better programming portability in the programming models. They also imply fewer number data transfers and better data transferring efficiency. However, a higher computational density in each task also means that larger amounts of data must be transferred and stored on the local memory, which requires a larger local scratchpad memory module on each device. On the other hand, partitioning tasks into finer granularity has the benefit of requiring smaller scratchpad memory on each accelerator device. The larger number of tasks also gives the scheduler the opportunity to fully leverage all available devices, thus potentially achieving better scalability. However, because there are many more data transferring jobs, data transferring becomes less efficient due to the larger number of starting latency.

The biggest hurdle of fine-grained tasks specification is the severe loss of the programming portability. As shown later in this paper, the need to specify many tasks in the programming systems makes it difficult to interface with the programming models. This constraint was investigated in a recent study [31] by analyzing applications' performance and their efficiency via a proposed metric called *minimum effective task granularity*. The paper concluded that the cost of sending data reflected as part of hardware latency and dispatching tasks reflected in the software latency impose a floor on the granularity.

Another body of closely related work is off-loading scheduling tasks to hardware. The concept was explored in several studies [3, 8, 26, 30]. In a more recent study [20], a Rocket Chip [4]-based hardware scheduler demonstrated impressive performance improvements when compared with a pure software implementation of the same scheduling method.

In this paper, we propose RANGER, a hierarchical scheduler, to address the conflicting dichotomy between programming portability and the requirements for better resource management in heterogeneous computing. At the top (i.e., global) level, RANGER maintains the task specifications at a coarse granularity. Hence, it is easy for RANGER to interface with existing task dependency specification mechanisms implemented in various programming models. At the lower level, RANGER uses Accelerator-Specific Command Scheduler (ASCS), which are specifically designed for each device to interface with the top-level scheduler and global memory. Based on the characteristics of the computational kernel and available resources, ASCS partitions each task into subtasks and manages them. In the RANGER architecture, the ASCS is executed on a customized RISC-V [36] processor core embedded in each accelerator to off-load the computations of task scheduling from the central host. The fine-grained subtask specifications and local ASCS schedulers ensure better use of the local hardware resources, such as the local scratchpad memory. The amortized data communication latency also makes it possible for the global coarse-grained scheduler to better use available accelerator devices. Unlike other hardware off-loading of task scheduling work—such as in Arnold et al. [3] and Morais et al. [20]—the main novelty of RANGER is the combination of two techniques by developing hardware-assisted hierarchical scheduling to address the conflicting dichotomy between programming portability and the resource requirement.

3   RANGER Architecture and Implementation

This section describes the RANGER architecture design, accelerator devices, and overall hierarchical task-scheduling method.

3.1   Baseline Accelerator Architecture

The baseline heterogeneous computing platform is a heterogeneous computing platform, as shown in Fig. 2. The host, an array of heterogeneous accelerator devices, and the main memory are connected by a shared bus. A top-level runtime runs on the host, which is responsible for communicating with the applications, determining the task schedules and assignments, and dispatching the scheduling decisions to each device. Once a task is dispatched to a device, each device would communicate with the global memory through its DMA channel, fetch the needed data from global memory to scratchpad memory on the device, launch the computation, and transfer the results back to global main memory after the task has completed. The global main memory usually has the characteristics of higher density and lower cost per gigabyte but longer access time (e.g., DRAM memory). On the other hand, the local scratchpad memory has much faster access time but at a lower density (e.g., SRAM memory). First-in-first-out (FIFO) logic circuits are inserted at various interfaces. The global bus can be implemented with different switching fabrics. This study uses the AXI bus [2], the industry standard for on-chip interconnect, although it is also possible to use various network-on-chip (NoC) switching fabrics.

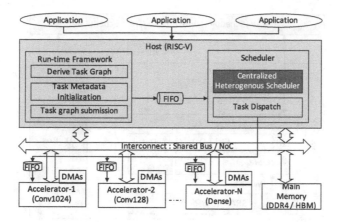

Fig. 2. Baseline architecture design of the heterogeneous accelerator platform.

3.2 RANGER Architecture and Memory-Mapped IO Interface

The RANGER architecture is shown in Fig. 3. Compared with the baseline architecture design shown in Fig. 2, each device is augmented with a RISC-V processor, which takes control of the interface to the global bus, as well as the scratchpad memory and accelerator.

A more detailed view of each device is shown in Fig. 4. The accelerator on each device interfaces with the RISC-V core through memory-mapped I/O. This is facilitated by the added MEMCTRL logic, which can determine whether the requested memory operation (LOAD/STORE) is intended for the accelerator, the DMA-In or DMA-Out channel to the local scratchpad memory, or the main

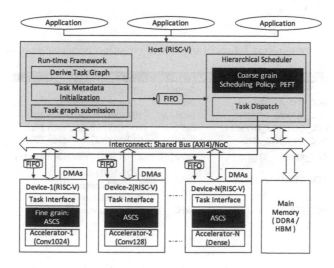

Fig. 3. RANGER architecture design of the heterogeneous accelerator platform.

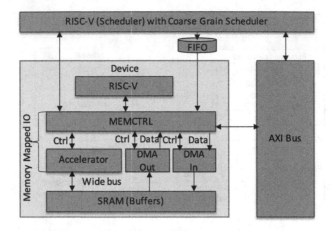

Fig. 4. RANGER Device: RISC-V, accelerator and DMA channels with memory-mapped I/O.

memory (DRAM). Furthermore, each DMA channel and the accelerator on the device also have their own unique memory-mapped registers.

As an illustration, a memory-mapped register for a convolution accelerator (CONV) is shown in Table 1. The DMA memory-mapped I/O configuration enables the transferring of any tile representing a 3D array in the DRAM memory to the local scratchpad SRAM by specifying offsets in the (x, y, z) plane. The number of banks in the SRAM is designed to be twice the number of inputs and outputs required for the accelerator to ensure that the SRAM design is equivalent to a bank conflict-free design. The assignment of the SRAM bank to the input buffer is determined by the controller kernel, which runs on the embedded RISC-V core.

Table 1. Memory-mapped IO registers of a convolution accelerator in RANGER

Register	MEMIO Offset	Range of Values
ACC_SRC_ADDR	0x00	32-bit SRAM address
ACC_DST_ADDR	0x04	32-bit SRAM address
ACC_IN_XYZ_OFFSET	0x08	3D-(X,Y,Z) offsets, each 20bit
ACC_OUT_XYZ_OFFSET	0x10	3D-(X,Y,Z) offsets, each 20bit
ACC_OUT_XYZ_SIZE	0x18	64-bit (X,Y,Z) size, each 20bit
ACC_KERNEL_STRIDE	0x20	32-bit (Kernel-size, Stride-size)
ACC_CTRL	0xF8	0: DO NOTHING 1: START Computation
ACC_STATUS	0xFC	Returns status 0: Busy Running 1: Free

3.3 Top-Level Scheduler

The top-level, coarse-grained global scheduler runs on the host shown in Fig. 3. Theoretically, any task scheduler from a rich body of research can be used as the top-level scheduler. In this study, PEFT [1] was implemented as the global scheduler to make it easier to compare RANGER performance with other solutions. To populate the required CCM of PEFT, each device—RISC-V, the added control logic, the DMA interface, and the accelerator—was implemented in GEM5. Each task was profiled to generate the corresponding entry in the CCM. It is also possible to use other performance prediction techniques, such as Johnston et al. [13] or Liu et al. [18]. The run-time range of each task in this study is on the order of milliseconds. Hence, extra effort was taken to optimize the coarse-grained scheduler to ensure that each scheduling decision can be completed within 1 ms on the customized RISC-V core. The computed scheduling decisions are formatted as the mapping of tasks to the available devices in which each task specification contains a set of commands and input/output memory locations. These commands are pushed into the FIFO queue of the corresponding device, as shown in Fig. 3.

3.4 Low-Level Scheduler

The low-level scheduler is responsible for further partitioning the given task into finer granularity. The partitioning and sequencing of the subtasks and their dependencies can vary from one kernel accelerator to the other. For example, a convolution kernel requires two sets of input and generates one set of output, whereas a batch normalization (BN) kernel has only one set of input and one set of output. Furthermore, each of these two kernels has different computational density. To maintain the flexibility and ensure the optimality, the authors developed ASCS. Based on the sizes of the inputs and outputs of a given task, its computational density, and the amount of available scratchpad SRAM memory, an ASCS scheduler generates subtasks, each of which also contains the instructions on how to configure the accelerator/DMA-channel-specific memory-mapped addresses. By doing so, ASCS provides more fine-grained control of the DMA channels and its interface to the global DRAM.

Because of their application-specific nature, the ASCS schedulers are specially tailored for each kernel accelerator as a part of the accelerator development process. They are also parameterized so that when the accelerator hardware specification (e.g., the size of the accelerator, the amount of scratchpad memory) changes, the ASCS schedulers can be easily updated.

For example, a high-level description of the ASCS scheduler for the convolution accelerator is shown in Algorithm 1. The functionality of a convolution operation is to compute a stream of output by convoluting a stream of input with a set of given weights. The convolution is carried out by the unit of "tile." Depending on the available scratchpad memory, different tile size configurations can lead to different decisions on whether to leverage weight reuse, input reuse, or output reuse. In Algorithm 1, the subtasks pipeline is created and initialized in lines 1 and 2. Depending on the tile configuration, single or double buffers are allocated, as shown in line 3. After initialization, the four nested loops shown from lines 4 to 7 iterate in order of tile height, tile weight, the channels, and the inputs. The pipelined subtasks are identified by their individual timestamps and maintained in a circular queue.

Within the innermost loop, the DMA process to fetch the weights, inputs, and outputs will be activated, as required, based on the data reuse leveraged by the kernel. Lines 11, 13, and 16 indicate the configuration of DMA channels for the weights, input, and output tiles. Line 17 is the computation of the scheduled subtask. Line 18 performs the configuration of the DMA channels and accelerator for the next subtask in the queue. All three routines are nonblocking and thus are executed concurrently.

The ASCS routines are designed and developed to be lightweight and are executed on the RISC-V processor on each accelerator device. Combined with the added peripheral logic, they provide configurability and flexibility to the accelerator. By considering the available computational resources (e.g., the number of Multiplier-Accumulator or MAC units), computational density of the kernel, and size of the available scratchpad memory, the ASCS schedulers in RANGER ensure that the optimal tile size is used so that the execution time of the subtasks, DMA transferring time, and computation time of the subtasks are balanced to achieve maximal throughput for the given task, as illustrated in Fig. 5.

3.5   Implementation Details of Accelerator Kernels

This study implemented three types of accelerators: 2D CONV, BN, and fully connected dense layer (DENSE). Multiple flavors of each type are implemented by changing the number of MAC units and the scratchpad memory size. For example, five flavors of CONV accelerator were implemented: CONV1024, CONV512, CONV256, CONV128, and CONV64. Generally speaking, the bigger accelerators have higher performance but also require larger area. The accelerator statistics are listed in Table 2. The BN accelerator requires less scratchpad memory because the nature of the kernel is similar to the inner product operation in the numerical linear algebra. The area estimates are based on the data extracted from various designs fabricated on a TSMC 16 nm CMOS technology [27].

```
    // Input feature map: (OH, OW, OD),    Output feature map: (IH, IW, ID)
    // Weights : (OD, ID, KH, KW)
    // Input Tile: (oth, otw, otd),          Output Tile: (ith, itw, itd)

1:   (weights_task, ifmap_task, kernel_task, ofmap_task) = CreateSubTasksForCommands(task);
2:   pipeline = new Pipeline ( [weights_task, ifmap_task, kernel_task, ofmap_task ] )
3:   AllocateStreamDoubleBuffers(pipeline)
4:   for oh: 0 to OH  step  oth  do
5:     for ow: 0 to OW  step  otw  do
6:       for od: 0 to OD  step  otd  do
7:         for id: 0 to ID. step  itd   do
8:           ts = pipeline->GetCurrentTimeStamp();
9:           next_ts = pipeline->GetNextTimeStamp();
10:          if weight_dma_to_be_activated:
11:            pipeline->ConfigureDMA(next_ts, weights_task, dram_weights_address, sram_weights_address)
12:          if input_fmap_to_be_activated:
13:            pipeline->ConfigureDMA(next_ts, ifmap_task, dram_ifmap_address, sram_ifmap_address)
14:          pipeline->ConfigureKernel(next_ts+1, kernel_task, sram_weights_address, sram_ifmap_address,
                                            sram_ofmap_address)
15:          if output_fmap_to_be_activated:
16:            pipeline->ConfigureDMA(next_ts+2, ofmap_task, sram_ofmap_address, dram_ofmap_address)
17:          pipeline->RunCurrentTimeStampTasks()
18:          pipeline->ConfigureNextTimeStampTasks()
19:          pipeline->WaitForTasks()
20:        end
21:      end
22:    end
23:  end
24:  pipeline->RunAllPrologTasks()
```

Algorithm 1: High-level description of ASCS scheduling algorithm for the convolution kernel.

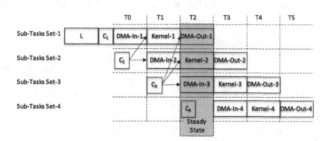

Fig. 5. Illustration of ASCS subtask execution pipeline. The "C" blocks include the configuration of DMA channels and accelerators for each subtask. Starting from the second subtask, they are concurrently executed with the DMA transfer of the previous subtask.

Using these kernel accelerators, we implemented multiple heterogeneous designs of the RANGER architecture, as shown in Table 3. The cycle-accurate GEM5 simulator was extended [5] to include the accelerators, memory-mapped I/O logic, and DMA components. The DMA component was implemented from scratch with the support of tiled 3D data transfer and burst mode use of the DMA channels. For each heterogeneous design, we also implemented a baseline version with only the accelerators and without the RISC-V core and extra control logic. Overall, the implementation is realized by ~1,800 lines of C++ code and ~700 lines of Python code for configuration. The statistics and characteristics of these RANGER and baseline designs are tabulated in Table 3.

Table 2. List of kernel accelerators and their area estimations in a TSMC 16 nm technology.

	Accelerator	Functionality	MAC Units	SRAM Size (KB)	Area (mm^2)
1	CONV1024	2D Convolution	1024	256.0	1.81
2	CONV512	2D Convolution	512	256.0	1.28
3	CONV256	2D Convolution	256	256.0	1.01
4	CONV128	2D Convolution	128	256.0	0.88
5	CONV64	2D Convolution	64	128.0	0.59
6	BN1024	Batch Normilization	1024	8.0	1.09
7	BN512	Batch Normilization	512	4.0	0.55
8	BN256	Batch Normilization	256	2.0	0.28
9	BN128	Batch Normilization	128	1.0	0.14
10	BN64	Batch Normilization	64	0.5	0.08
11	DENSE1024	Dense	1024	128.0	1.30
12	DENSE512	Dense	512	128.0	0.76
13	DENSE256	Dense	256	128.0	0.50
14	DENSE128	Dense	128	128.0	0.37
15	DENSE64	Dense	64	128.0	0.30

Table 3. Various heterogeneous designs, the number of kernel accelerators, and the estimated area. Design A and B are the aliases of Design 1 and 2, respectively.

| Design | Accelerators | | | | | | | | | | | | | | | | Area mm^2 | | |
| | 2D Convolution | | | | | Batch Normilization | | | | | Dense | | | | | Total | | | |
	1024	512	256	128	64	1024	512	256	128	64	1024	512	256	128	64		RANGER	Baseline	Overhead
Design 1	1	1	1	1	1	1	1	1	1	1	1	1	1	1	1	15	11.290	10.945	3.15 %
Design 2	2	2	2	2	2	2	2	2	2	2	2	2	2	2	2	30	22.581	21.891	3.15 %
Design 3	3	3	3	3	3	2	2	2	2	2	2	2	2	2	2	35	28.266	27.461	2.93 %
Design 4	4	4	4	4	4	2	2	2	2	2	2	2	2	2	2	40	33.951	33.031	2.79 %
Design 5	5	5	5	5	5	2	2	2	2	2	2	2	2	2	2	45	39.636	38.601	2.68 %
Design 6	6	6	6	6	6	2	2	2	2	2	2	2	2	2	2	50	45.321	44.171	2.60 %
Design 7	7	7	7	7	7	2	2	2	2	2	2	2	2	2	2	55	51.006	49.741	2.54 %
Design 8	8	8	8	8	8	2	2	2	2	2	2	2	2	2	2	60	56.691	55.311	2.49 %
Design 9	9	9	9	9	9	2	2	2	2	2	2	2	2	2	2	65	62.376	60.881	2.46 %
Design 10	10	10	10	10	10	2	2	2	2	2	2	2	2	2	2	70	68.061	66.451	2.42 %
Design A	1	1	1	1	1	1	1	1	1	1	1	1	1	1	1	15	11.290	10.945	3.15 %
Design B	2	2	2	2	2	2	2	2	2	2	2	2	2	2	2	30	22.581	21.891	3.15 %
Design C	3	3	3	3	3	3	3	3	3	3	3	3	3	3	3	45	33.871	32.836	3.15 %
Design D	4	4	4	4	4	4	4	4	4	4	4	4	4	4	4	60	45.161	43.781	3.15 %
Design E	5	5	5	5	5	5	5	5	5	5	5	5	5	5	5	75	56.452	54.727	3.15 %
Design F	6	6	6	6	6	6	6	6	6	6	6	6	6	6	6	90	67.742	65.672	3.15 %
Design G	7	7	7	7	7	7	7	7	7	7	7	7	7	7	7	105	79.032	76.617	3.15 %
Design H	8	8	8	8	8	8	8	8	8	8	8	8	8	8	8	120	90.323	87.563	3.15 %
Average																			2.74 %

The area of each RISC-V core is estimated to be $0.023\,\text{mm}^2$ [37] in the TSMC 16 nm technology. Table 3 shows that the RANGER architecture only requires ~2.74% of area overhead compared with the corresponding baseline designs. The largest RANGER core has an estimate area of $90\,\text{mm}^2$. As a comparison, a quad-core Intel Coffee Lake processor has the die area of $126\,\text{mm}^2$ in a comparable technology [12].

4   Experimental Evaluation

To evaluate the performance of RANGER, the authors used a run-time frame-work running on the host RISC-V core shown in Fig. 3. The task descriptions are specified in JSON format, which is the output of a Python-based converter. Values of CCM of the top-level scheduler are the profiling results of the individual kernels in GEM5. The makespans of tasks and applications are extracted from the performance counters of DMAs from GEM5.

4.1   Application Benchmarks

The inference phase of four widely used deep neural networks (DNNs) were used as the benchmarks: InceptionV3 [32], ResNet-50 [10], UNet [25], and Vgg16 [28]. We would like to point out that RANGER is a general-purpose scheduler and can handle any DAG tasks. In this study DNNs inference applications were the chosen simply because their DAGs are readily available, and they represent increasingly important workloads. The details of these four DNNs are omitted due to space limitation. Each inference application comprises three types of computational kernels: CONV, BN, and fully connected DENSE. For example, InceptionV3 is represented by 189 tasks—94 CONV, 94 BN, and one DENSE—with its task DAG shown in Fig. 6.

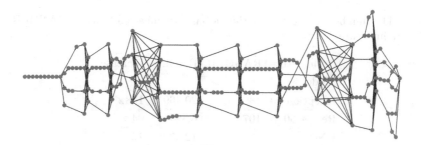

Fig. 6. Task DAG of Inception-v3. The left-most node is the source node of the DAG, and the sink node is at the extreme right.

The execution time of each application is measured by the cycle counts reported by GEM5. For comparison, the same set of applications was also run on

Table 4. Comparison of makespans for various RANGER and baseline designs. On average, RANGER achieves a 12.7× speedup.

Model	Makespan											
	Inception-v3			Resnet-50			VGG16			UNet		
Architecture design	RANGER	Baseline	Speedup	RANGER	Baseline	Speedup	RANGER	Baseline	Speedup	RANGER	Baseline	Speedup
Design 1	94,788,333	762,320,311	8.04×	88,346,488	504,482,689	5.71×	389,202,487	3,193,921,550	8.21×	336,496,490	1,233,341,834	3.67×
Design 2	53,422,061	752,853,720	14.09×	57,531,844	500,829,541	8.71×	209,315,117	3,149,123,579	15.04×	201,002,387	1,177,865,323	5.86×
Design 3	41,881,254	752,544,223	17.97×	52,782,400	500,433,710	9.48×	191,533,321	3,147,951,787	16.44×	173,986,414	1,171,882,097	6.74×
Design 4	38,749,897	752,450,123	19.42×	52,195,186	500,340,314	9.59×	181,632,752	3,147,767,996	17.33×	157,652,345	1,169,892,512	7.42×
Design 5	37,999,017	752,407,810	19.80×	52,191,088	500,295,143	9.59×	180,193,518	3,147,649,984	17.47×	150,250,684	1,169,590,055	7.78×
Design 6	37,988,551	752,393,040	19.81×	52,191,088	500,288,595	9.59×	180,193,518	3,147,724,843	17.47×	150,250,684	1,169,578,215	7.78×
Design 7	37,914,589	752,387,551	19.84×	52,190,081	500,282,221	9.59×	180,193,518	3,147,642,459	17.47×	150,250,684	1,169,575,296	7.78×
Design 8	37,898,912	752,382,660	19.85×	52,190,081	500,275,555	9.59×	180,193,518	3,147,724,163	17.47×	150,250,684	1,169,574,480	7.78×
Design 9	37,891,335	752,382,660	19.86×	52,190,081	500,272,549	9.59×	180,193,518	3,147,669,094	17.47×	150,250,684	1,169,574,480	7.78×
Design 10	37,618,903	752,367,084	20.00×	52,190,081	500,264,005	9.59×	178,630,640	3,147,724,117	17.62×	147,870,807	1,169,574,480	7.91×
Design A	94,788,333	762,320,311	8.04×	88,346,488	504,482,689	5.71×	389,202,487	3,193,921,550	8.21×	336,496,490	1,233,341,834	3.67×
Design B	53,422,061	752,853,720	14.09×	57,531,844	500,829,541	8.71×	209,315,117	3,149,123,579	15.04×	201,002,387	1,177,865,323	5.86×
Design C	42,241,318	752,541,894	17.82×	52,447,643	500,420,375	9.54×	174,801,184	3,144,474,922	17.99×	173,986,414	1,171,816,637	6.74×
Design D	38,570,566	752,444,207	19.51×	51,672,158	500,332,941	9.68×	155,344,163	3,144,196,072	20.24×	157,652,123	1,169,797,015	7.42×
Design E	37,793,805	752,406,134	19.91×	51,362,009	500,254,081	9.74×	153,596,950	3,144,134,148	20.47×	150,247,240	1,169,471,954	7.78×
Design F	37,793,452	752,401,577	19.91×	51,162,596	500,254,081	9.78×	153,596,950	3,144,134,148	20.47×	150,247,240	1,169,470,736	7.78×
Design G	37,708,203	752,386,686	19.95×	51,162,596	500,254,081	9.78×	153,596,950	3,144,134,148	20.47×	150,247,240	1,169,468,346	7.78×
Design H	37,704,900	752,386,686	19.95×	51,161,299	500,254,081	9.78×	153,596,950	3,144,134,148	20.47×	150,247,240	1,169,468,346	7.78×
Average			17.66×			9.10×			16.96×			6.96×

the baseline design shown in Fig. 2 with the detailed design specs tabulated in Table 3. The results are tabulated in Table 4. As shown in the table, across multiple design points, the average speedup of Inception-v3, ResNet, VGG16, and UNet achieved by RANGER are 17.66×, 9.10×, 16.96×, and 6.96× respectively, with the average speedup of 12.7× across all four applications.

To execute the benchmarks on the accelerator cores by using the baseline architecture, the tasks in each application must be further partitioned based on the amount of scratchpad memory available. The numbers of the fine-grained subtasks are shown in Table 5, which also includes the corresponding RANGER task numbers as a comparison. In this case, scheduling these subtasks is computed by the host. Figure 7 shows RANGER scheduling decisions of 10 Inception-v3 applications running in parallel on Design 1 from Table 3.

Table 5. The numbers of tasks that the global host must consider in RANGER and baseline architecture.

Architecture Model	RANGER	Baseline	Increase
Inception-v3	189	20,469	108×
Resnet-50	107	6,824	64×
UNet	17	12,372	728×
VGG16	16	38,064	2,379×

4.2 Scalability Study

This section further investigates the scalability of the RANGER architecture. To saturate the many kernel accelerators in the designs, we increased the repetition of the applications to 10 (i.e., during each experiment,10 identical but independent applications were issued on a given RANGER design). The results are plotted with respect to various RANGER designs in Fig. 8. This study is similar to the strong-scaling study in the traditional HPC applications. The plot clearly shows that the speedup is plateaued to ~2× at Design 3, which has 35 kernel accelerators.

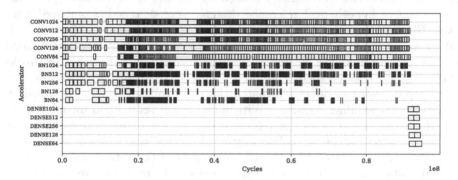

Fig. 7. Scheduling decisions of 10 parallel instances of Inception-v3 computed by RANGER on Design 1. Each box represents a task being scheduled on a particular device.

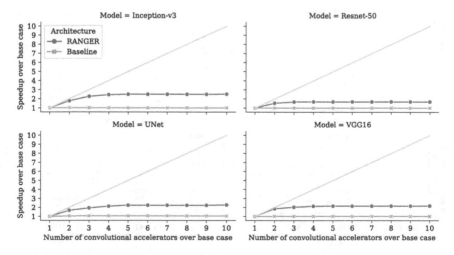

Fig. 8. Measured speedup of RANGER by running 10 parallel instances of each application with respect to Designs 1–10, which contain an increasing number of kernel accelerators. The speedup plateaus at Design 3 due to an insufficient number of tasks for the available kernel accelerators.

In the second study, the experiment was repeated by varying the application repetitions, which is similar to the weak-scaling study of HPC workloads. The results are shown in Fig. 9. With repetition set to 100, the RANGER architecture demonstrates good scalability from Design A, which has 15 kernel accelerators, to Design H, which contains 120 kernel accelerators.

4.3 Overhead of the Local Schedulers

The speedups achieved by RANGER are contributions of the top-level hierarchical scheduling scheme and the implementation of the low-level ASCS. To investigate the performance inefficiency caused by the two-level scheduling scheme, a collection of hypothetical reference designs were designed. Compared with RANGER designs, each reference design has an identical number of kernel accelerators as its RANGER counterpart but with a sufficiently large scratchpad memory to accommodate all needed data. Hence, there is no need to invoke local schedulers because there is no need to further partition each task. Instead, the host processor can directly dispatch the tasks to the accelerators based on the top-level scheduling decisions. With much larger scratchpad memory modules, the estimated areas of the reference designs are listed in Table 6. These reference designs cannot be realistically implemented due to their large areas. For instance, nine out of 10 reference designs have the estimate area of over $200 \, mm^2$, which makes them extremely expensive to manufacture. As a reference point, an octa-core Intel Coffee Lake processor on a comparable technology only has a die area of $174 \, mm^2$ [12].

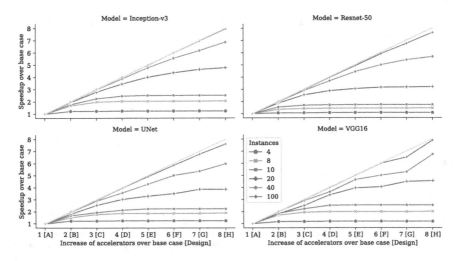

Fig. 9. Measured speedup of RANGER by running an increasing number of instances of the same application on Designs A–H. RANGER demonstrates excellent scalability with 100 instances of application running in parallel.

Table 6. Area estimate of reference designs compared with their RANGER counterparts. Designs of these sizes are extremely expensive to manufacture.

Model	Area mm^2		
Architecture design	RANGER	Reference	Difference
Design 1	11	165	14.61×
Design 2	23	275	12.18×
Design 3	28	337	11.93×
Design 4	34	440	12.96×
Design 5	40	445	11.23×
Design 6	45	484	10.67×
Design 7	51	512	10.04×
Design 8	57	546	9.63×
Design 9	62	603	9.67×
Design 10	68	662	9.73×

Table 7. Comparison of makespans for RANGER and reference. On average, RANGER shows only 10.88% of penalty, which is the measurement of performance overhead of the local ASCS.

Model	Makespan											
	Inception-v3			Resnet-50			VGG16			UNet		
Architecture design	RANGER	Reference	Difference	RANGER	Reference	Difference	RANGER	Reference	Difference	RANGER	Reference	Difference
Design 1	94,788,333	95,707,644	−0.96%	88,346,488	88,621,038	-0.31%	389,202,487	214,684,328	81.29%	336,496,490	216,796,889	55.21%
Design 2	53,422,061	56,538,771	−5.51%	57,531,844	63,717,300	−9.71%	209,315,117	165,634,098	26.37%	201,002,387	156,806,696	28.18%
Design 3	41,881,254	45,388,469	−7.73%	52,782,400	58,538,562	−9.83%	191,533,321	150,559,308	27.21%	173,986,414	145,184,318	19.84%
Design 4	38,749,897	40,891,867	−5.24%	52,195,186	56,076,426	−6.92%	181,632,752	144,136,809	26.01%	157,652,345	134,955,240	16.82%
Design 5	37,999,017	39,601,255	−4.05%	52,191,088	55,193,132	−5.44%	180,193,518	141,111,694	27.70%	150,250,684	129,117,096	16.37%
Design 6	37,988,551	38,921,698	−2.40%	52,191,088	54,871,507	−4.88%	180,193,518	139,536,510	29.14%	150,250,684	128,893,489	16.57%
Design 7	37,914,589	38,412,723	−1.30%	52,190,081	54,847,500	−4.85%	180,193,518	138,354,082	30.24%	150,250,684	127,945,051	17.43%
Design 8	37,898,912	38,260,460	−0.94%	52,190,081	54,561,879	−4.35%	180,193,518	137,473,689	31.07%	150,250,684	127,915,851	17.46%
Design 9	37,891,335	38,260,436	−0.96%	52,190,081	54,561,879	−4.35%	180,193,518	137,473,689	31.07%	150,250,684	127,915,851	17.46%
Design 10	37,618,903	37,782,552	−0.43%	52,190,081	53,711,730	−2.83%	178,630,640	134,278,895	33.03%	147,870,807	121,184,411	22.02%
Average			−2.95%			−5.06%			31.01%			20.53%

The comparison on the RANGER design makespans and the reference designs are tabulated in Table 7. For Inception-v3 and ResNet, RANGER designs clearly have similar makespans with small but consistent improvements. For VGG16 and UNet, RANGER designs show a 31–21% degradation of the makespans. Across all four applications, RANGER shows an average of 10.88% on makespan penalties. The host runs the identical top-level scheduler with identical DAG specifications in both RANGER and reference studies. Therefore, the measured penalty directly indicates the performance overhead of the low-level ASCS scheduler. However, given the impracticality of the reference designs, the authors believe that this magnitude of overhead is completely acceptable.

5   Conclusion

This paper presents RANGER, a framework and architecture design for hierarchical task scheduling in extremely heterogeneous computing. As a framework, one crucial benefit of hierarchical scheduling is that it only requires coarse-grained task dependency specifications at the top level, whereas more fine-grained, accelerator-specific scheduling can be performed at the lower level. The coarse-grained task specifications make it much easier to maintain programming portability and productivity in heterogeneous computing. Introducing localized low-level schedulers enables the deployment of more sophisticated, accelerator-specific scheduling solutions to better utilize hardware resources. From an architecture perspective, RANGER uses customized RISC-V cores to mitigate the computational overhead of task scheduling. Through extensive experimentation, we demonstrated that RANGER architecture achieves 12.7× performance gains on average in terms of makespan with only a 2.7% area overhead in a 16 nm technology.

In future work, we plan to further improve the global and local schedulers in RANGER. They also plan to integrate RANGER with contemporary parallel run-times to further explore its potential.

Acknowledgments. This material is based upon work supported by the US Department of Energy (DOE) Office of Science, Office of Advanced Scientific Computing Research under contract number DE-AC05-00OR22725.

This research was supported in part by the DOE Advanced Scientific Computing Research Program Sawtooth Project and the Laboratory Directed Research and Development Program of Oak Ridge National Laboratory, managed by UT-Battelle LLC for DOE.

References

1. Arabnejad, H., Barbosa, J.G.: List scheduling algorithm for heterogeneous systems by an optimistic cost table. IEEE Trans. Parallel Distrib. Syst. **25**(3), 682–694 (2013)
2. ARM Corp.: AMBA: the standard for on-chip communication. https://www.arm.com/products/silicon-ip-system/embedded-system-design/amba-specifications. Accessed 10 Dec 2020
3. Arnold, O., Noethen, B., Fettweis, G.: Instruction set architecture extensions for a dynamic task scheduling unit. In: 2012 IEEE Computer Society Annual Symposium on VLSI, pp. 249–254. IEEE (2012)
4. Asanovic, K., et al.: The Rocket chip generator. EECS Department, University of California, Berkeley, Technical report UCB/EECS-2016-17 (2016)
5. Binkert, N., et al.: The GEM5 simulator. ACM SIGARCH Comput. Archit. News **39**(2), 1–7 (2011)
6. Blumofe, R.D., Joerg, C.F., Kuszmaul, B.C., Leiserson, C.E., Randall, K.H., Zhou, Y.: Cilk: an efficient multithreaded runtime system. J. Parallel Distrib. Comput. **37**(1), 55–69 (1996)
7. Canon, L.C., Marchal, L., Simon, B., Vivien, F.: Online scheduling of task graphs on heterogeneous platforms. IEEE Trans. Parallel Distrib. Syst. **31**, 721–732 (2019)

8. Dallou, T., Engelhardt, N., Elhossini, A., Juurlink, B.: Nexus#: a distributed hardware task manager for task-based programming models. In: 2015 IEEE International Parallel and Distributed Processing Symposium, pp. 1129–1138. IEEE (2015)
9. Frigo, M., Leiserson, C.E., Randall, K.H.: The implementation of the Cilk-5 multithreaded language. In: Proceedings of the ACM SIGPLAN 1998 Conference on Programming Language Design and Implementation, pp. 212–223 (1998)
10. He, K., Zhang, X., Ren, S., Sun, J.: Deep residual learning for image recognition. In: Proceedings of the IEEE Conference on Computer Vision and Pattern Recognition, pp. 770–778 (2016)
11. Huang, T.W., Lin, C.X., Guo, G., Wong, M.: Cpp-Taskflow: fast task-based parallel programming using modern C++. In: 2019 IEEE International Parallel and Distributed Processing Symposium (IPDPS), pp. 974–983. IEEE (2019)
12. Intel Corp.: Coffee lake - microarchitecture - intel. https://en.wikichip.org/wiki/intel/microarchitectures/coffee_lake. Accessed 10 Dec 2020
13. Johnston, B., Milthorpe, J.: AIWC: OpenCL-based architecture-independent workload characterization. In: 2018 IEEE/ACM 5th Workshop on the LLVM Compiler Infrastructure in HPC (LLVM-HPC), pp. 81–91. IEEE (2018)
14. Kale, L.V., Krishnan, S.: Charm++: parallel programming with message-driven objects. In: Wilson, G.V., Lu, P. (eds.) Parallel Programming Using C++, vol. 1, pp. 175–213. MIT Press, Cambridge (1996)
15. Kaleem, R., Barik, R., Shpeisman, T., Hu, C., Lewis, B.T., Pingali, K.: Adaptive heterogeneous scheduling for integrated GPUs. In: 2014 23rd International Conference on Parallel Architecture and Compilation Techniques (PACT), pp. 151–162. IEEE (2014)
16. Khronos Group: OpenCL: the open standard for parallel programming of heterogeneous systems (2019)
17. Kukanov, A., Voss, M.J.: The foundations for scalable multi-core software in Intel Threading Building Blocks. Intel Technol. J. **11**(4) (2007)
18. Liu, F., Miniskar, N.R., Chakraborty, D., Vetter, J.S.: DEFFE: a data-efficient framework for performance characterization in domain-specific computing. In: Proceedings of the 17th ACM International Conference on Computing Frontiers, pp. 182–191 (2020)
19. Ma, Z., Catthoor, F., Vounckx, J.: Hierarchical task scheduler for interleaving subtasks on heterogeneous multiprocessor platforms. In: Proceedings of the 2005 Asia and South Pacific Design Automation Conference, pp. 952–955 (2005)
20. Morais, L., et al.: Adding tightly-integrated task scheduling acceleration to a RISC-V multi-core processor. In: Proceedings of the 52nd Annual IEEE/ACM International Symposium on Microarchitecture, pp. 861–872 (2019)
21. Nickolls, J., Buck, I.: NVIDIA CUDA software and GPU parallel computing architecture. In: Microprocessor Forum (2007)
22. OpenACC: OpenACC: directives for accelerators (2015)
23. OpenMP: OpenMP reference (1999)
24. Robison, A.D.: Composable parallel patterns with Intel Cilk Plus. Comput. Sci. Eng. **15**(2), 66–71 (2013)
25. Ronneberger, O., Fischer, P., Brox, T.: U-Net: convolutional networks for biomedical image segmentation. In: Navab, N., Hornegger, J., Wells, W.M., Frangi, A.F. (eds.) MICCAI 2015. LNCS, vol. 9351, pp. 234–241. Springer, Cham (2015). https://doi.org/10.1007/978-3-319-24574-4_28

26. Shao, Y.S., Xi, S.L., Srinivasan, V., Wei, G.Y., Brooks, D.: Co-designing accelerators and SoC interfaces using gem5-Aladdin. In: 2016 49th Annual IEEE/ACM International Symposium on Microarchitecture (MICRO), pp. 1–12. IEEE (2016)
27. Sijstermans, F.: The NVIDIA deep learning accelerator. In: Proceedings Hot Chips: A Symposium on High Performance Chips, August 2018
28. Simonyan, K., Zisserman, A.: Very deep convolutional networks for large-scale image recognition. arXiv preprint arXiv:1409.1556 (2014)
29. Sinnen, O.: Task Scheduling for Parallel Systems, vol. 60. Wiley, Hoboken (2007)
30. Själander, M., Terechko, A., Duranton, M.: A look-ahead task management unit for embedded multi-core architectures. In: 2008 11th EUROMICRO Conference on Digital System Design Architectures, Methods and Tools, pp. 149–157. IEEE (2008)
31. Slaughter, E., et al.: Task bench: a parameterized benchmark for evaluating parallel runtime performance, pp. 1–30 (2020)
32. Szegedy, C., Vanhoucke, V., Ioffe, S., Shlens, J., Wojna, Z.: Rethinking the inception architecture for computer vision. In: Proceedings of the IEEE Conference on Computer Vision and Pattern Recognition, pp. 2818–2826 (2016)
33. Topcuoglu, H., Hariri, S., Wu, M.Y.: Performance-effective and low-complexity task scheduling for heterogeneous computing. IEEE Trans. Parallel Distrib. Syst. **13**(3), 260–274 (2002)
34. Ullman, J.D.: NP-complete scheduling problems. J. Comput. Syst. Sci. **10**(3), 384–393 (1975)
35. Vetter, J.S., Brightwell, R., et al.: Extreme heterogeneity 2018: DOE ASCR basic research needs workshop on extreme heterogeneity (2018). https://doi.org/10.2172/1473756
36. Waterman, A., Lee, Y., Avizienis, R., Cook, H., Patterson, D.A., Asanovic, K.: The RISC-V instruction set. In: Hot Chips Symposium, p. 1 (2013)
37. Western Digital Corp.: RISC-V: accelerating next-generation compute requirements. https://www.westerndigital.com/company/innovations/risc-v. Accessed 10 Dec 2020

Machine Learning, AI, and Emerging Technologies

Auto-Precision Scaling for Distributed Deep Learning

Ruobing Han[1($\boxtimes$)], James Demmel[2], and Yang You[3]

[1] Georgia Institute of Technology, Atlanta, GA, USA
hanruobing@gatech.edu
[2] University of California, Berkeley, CA, USA
demmel@berkeley.edu
[3] National University of Singapore, Singapore, Singapore
youy@comp.nus.edu.sg

Abstract. It has been reported that the communication cost for synchronizing gradients can be a bottleneck, which limits the scalability of distributed deep learning. Using low-precision gradients is a promising technique for reducing the bandwidth requirement. In this work, we propose Auto Precision Scaling (APS), an algorithm that can improve the accuracy when we communicate gradients by low-precision floating-point values. APS can improve the accuracy for all precisions with a trivial communication cost. Our experimental results show that for many applications, APS can train state-of-the-art models by 8-bit gradients with no or only a tiny accuracy loss ($<0.05\%$). Furthermore, we can avoid any accuracy loss by designing a hybrid-precision technique. Finally, we propose a performance model to evaluate the proposed method. Our experimental results show that APS can get a significant speedup over state-of-the-art methods. To make it available to researchers and developers, we design and implement CPD (Customized-Precision Deep Learning) system, which can simulate the training process using an arbitrary low-precision customized floating-point format. We integrate CPD into PyTorch and make it open-source (https://github.com/drcut/CPD).

Keywords: Low precision · Distributed deep learning · Scalability

1 Introduction

State-of-the-art deep learning models are becoming deeper and larger, which take an extremely long time to train. As a result, distributed memory systems are becoming popular to train these huge models. Most researchers are using synchronous SGD for data-parallel training [10,14,24,26]. However, we can not always improve the training speed by just using more processors, as the communication cost is a non-trivial overhead for distributed systems and multi-GPU systems. For example, communication can take 40% of wall-clock time for BERT training on a 8 NVIDIA GTX1080Ti GPU server. A potential solution is to use

© Springer Nature Switzerland AG 2021
B. L. Chamberlain et al. (Eds.): ISC High Performance 2021, LNCS 12728, pp. 79–97, 2021.
https://doi.org/10.1007/978-3-030-78713-4_5

low-precision gradients [14,20]. However, for IEEE floating point system, previous methods can only use 16-bit for communicating gradients. One reason is that current communication systems only support half/single/double-precision formats. To solve this problem, we build a system that allows researchers to use an arbitrary low precision format (<32 bits) to communicate gradients. We refer to it as CPD: A High-Performance System for Customized-Precision Deep Learning. We integrate CPD into PyTorch for public usage.

We find that directly using low-precision gradients can easily hurt testing accuracy and even make the training diverge. One reason is that the values in gradients may easily underflow or overflow as the numerical range of the low precision is quite narrow compared to that of the high precision. So there are lots of zeros and INF values, which can make the training process diverge. To solve this problem, we propose the APS (Auto-Precision-Scaling) algorithm, which is a layer-wise adaptive scheme for efficient gradients communication. With APS, we can make the distributed training converge with only 8 bits or even 4 bits totally for the sign, exponent (exp) and mantissa (man). In our experiments, APS can improve the accuracy for any precision with a minor overhead. Compared to previous methods, the main contributions of our paper include:

- we propose APS, a layer-wise adaptive scheme, that can improve the accuracy for arbitrary low-precision formats;
- we are able to use several 8-bit floating point formats to train state-of-the-art classification models and segmentation models on distributed systems;
- we are able to use 8-bit floating point formats for gradients to train ResNet-50 on a 256-node distributed system;
- we build a system that can use arbitrarily customized low-precision floating-point operations and make it open-source to the public.

2   Related Work

[Gradient Sparsification]. A large DNN model typically has millions of elements in parameters and gradients. Researchers found that some values in gradients are much more important than others [8]: larger values in gradients will have a greater impact on the parameter updating and the training process. Based on this finding, some works only synchronize a part of gradients at each iteration. There are several methods to choose the threshold and accumulate the stale gradients with new gradients [8,17,20]. For example, [17] proposed DGC, which communicates a fraction of the gradients each iteration and store the remaining gradients locally with momentum correction to maintain the accuracy. While in [22], some layer's gradients will be randomly dropped out in each iteration to reduce the communication cost. All of these methods depend on gradients' magnitude rather than gradients' precision used during communication, so our method is orthogonal to these methods: we can use the above algorithms to select the gradients and use APS to communicate them with low precision.

[Gradient Quantization]. Researchers can use half-precision floating-point to communicate gradients in AlexNet/ResNet training with 100+ nodes [14,19,20]. The underflow/overflow issue is a serious problem in low-precision computation. To solve this problem, [19] suggests researchers should carefully select a constant scalar to scale the loss value, which in turn will scale the gradient value. The constant scalars typically are different for different models and precisions. Instead of using low-precision floating point for gradients, some researchers [4,23] proposed algorithms that quantize the gradients. Both QSGD [4] and TernGrad [23] use the same idea: they encode the gradients to unbiased estimate gradients represented by fewer bits and communicate these gradients with some extra information, and finally decode these communicated results into the normal gradients.

Although these two algorithms also use fewer bits to represent gradients, APS is significantly different from them. Instead of using a customized data structure to represent gradients with fewer bits, APS uses floating-point format to communicate gradients. APS is able to mitigate the round-off error so that we can have numerical values close to the original precision. APS is transparent for high level users, which means they can use the same hyper-parameters and training strategies but with less time spent on communication. For large scale distributed systems, it is extremely expensive to fine-tune the hyper-parameters as it will require lots of computing resources. Thus, it is highly necessary to maintain the same hyper-parameter set. Although QSGD can also maintain the hyper-parameter set, it introduces an extra hyper-parameter, the bucket size, which may significantly affect the accuracy. Ternary can not maintain the same hyper-parameter set because it asks users to decrease dropout ratio to keep more neurons, use smaller weight decay and disable ternarizing in the last classification layer while training on distributed systems. Besides, compared to training on small-scale distributed systems, training on large-scale distributed systems will require lots of accumulation operations, which requires a high numerical precision. Otherwise, the results will be significantly different due to the accumulative effect. The validation of Ternary is only verified on small distributed systems with no more than eight nodes. QSGD is verified on a distributed system that has only 16 nodes. APS does not require any additional hyper-parameters, and it can maintain the hyper-parameter set used for FP32. Besides, we have

Table 1. The difference between APS and other methods.

Methods	Same hyper parameter as FP32	Communication cost with gradient size L	Extra hyper parameter
APS	Yes	Allreduce (8 bits) + Allreduce (8L bits)	No
Loss scaling [19]	Yes	Allreduce (L * 16 bits)	Scaling factor
TernGrad [23]	No	Uses special distributed system	No
QSGD [4]	No	Depends on coding algorithm	Bucket size
Flex16+5 [16]	Yes	Single node. Gradients: (16L+5) bits	No

verified the validation of APS on a large scale distributed system (256 nodes) with state-of-the-art deep learning models. Table 1 summarizes the difference between APS and other methods.

[Low-Precision for Deep Learning]. There are several papers that explored the possibility of using a lower precision for DNN. However, most of them were focused on the inference stage. Recently, [19] used the half-precision format (IEEE 754 16-bit) in DNN training. With the help of loss-scaling (the scale factor is a manually-tuned hyper-parameter), they achieve a similar accuracy as the FP32 format. After that, [21] used 8 bits in DNN training (16 bits for parts of the data) and achieve a comparable accuracy as the baseline. The specific design of 8 bits and 16 bits are based on the information of data distributions. [15] looked into older representations of FP to produce faster silicon. Different from floating-point, some researchers tried using fixed-point and its variants. [6] used a dynamical fixed point (DFXP) format for parameters, activations and gradients. DFXP will change the scaling factor if overflow occurs during training. Instead of changing the scaling factor after overflow happens, [6] designed a predictor to change the scaling factor in advance to avoid overflow. However, the previous low precision (<16 bits) DNN training studies are mainly focused on single node (i.e. small-batch training). If we want to finish the training in a short time, we need distributed training on clusters. Although some works use low precision gradient [19,21], they do not communicate these low precision gradient. Low precision gradient synchronization will result in round-off error dilemma and hurt the accuracy (Sect. 4.2). In addition to saving bandwidth for synchronization, APS can be used as an algorithm to improve the accuracy for any given precision. We believe this is an important property as many new floating point formats have been proposed [21]. Please see Table 2 for more details.

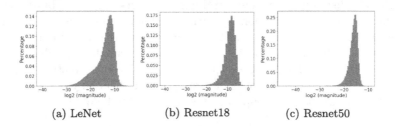

(a) LeNet   (b) Resnet18   (c) Resnet50

Fig. 1. Gradients distributions for different Neural Networks.

[Customized-Precision System]. Most state-of-the-art systems only support a fixed number of bits in a floating-point format. For example, CUDA only supports floating-point formats with 16, 32, and 64 bits for fixed exponent/mantissa bits. QPyTorch [27] is a recent system that allows users to assign customized number of bits to exponent/mantissa in DNN training. However, QPyTorch has several limitations for real-world applications. When users design a format with only a few bits for exponent, the cast results from IEEE FP32 to the low precision format are numerically incorrect, which leads to a serious bug. Besides, it only supports IEEE 754 single-precision for all-reduce operations, which are being used at each iteration for distributed training. To solve these problems, we develop the CPD (Customized-Precision Distributed Deep Learning) system.

3   APS: Auto-Precision-Scaling

3.1   The Limitation of the Loss Scaling Algorithm

The loss scaling algorithm is being used in recent large-scale systems [14,19,20]. The key idea of loss scaling is: as the ranges that can be presented by low precision and high precision are different, users can scale all layers' gradients with a factor to potentially solve the overflow/underflow problem. According to the properties of derivative, users can easily scale all gradients by multiplying the loss value with this factor (see Fig. 3(b)). The loss scaling algorithm requires researchers to find a suitable loss scaling factor for each model, as the gradient distributions for different models are quite different in real-world applications (Fig. 1). Besides, there are several widely used precision formats [15,21]. For different formats, the representation ranges are also different (Table 2). Therefore, even for the same model, the suitable loss scaling factors are different when training with different precisions. To make things more complicated, even within a single model, the distributions of different layers are quite different (Fig. 2). Previous researchers also reported the gradient distribution for a single layer also changes in training process [6,16]. These inconsistencies may make the loss scaling algorithm extremely unreliable in real-world applications.

Table 2. Different floating-point formats have different representation ranges.

Format	Exp bits	Man bits	Range
IEEE 754 FP32	8	23	$[2^{-149}, 2^{127}]$
IEEE 754 FP16	5	10	$[2^{-24}, 2^{15}]$
BFloat16	8	7	$[2^{-133}, 2^{127}]$
FP16 in [21]	6	9	$[2^{-39}, 2^{31}]$
FP8 in [21]	5	2	$[2^{-16}, 2^{15}]$

3.2   Layer-Wise Precision for Scaling the Gradients

To solve these problems, we propose Auto Precision Scaling algorithm (APS), which uses a layer-wise scheme to scale the gradients. Let us refer to the layer ID as i and the gradient of this layer as $grad_i$. Then the algorithm computes the exponent values of $|grad_i|$ as $grad\_exp_i$. Assume the model has n layers, the algorithm stores a vector $E = \{grad\_exp_1, grad\_exp_2, ..., grad\_exp_i, ..., grad\_exp_n\}$ in the memory and does an all-reduce operation for this vector

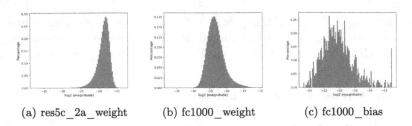

(a) res5c_2a_weight   (b) fc1000_weight   (c) fc1000_bias

Fig. 2. Gradients distributions of different layers in ResNet50 with 8K batch size.

to get the maximum value in the whole system. Then the algorithm shifts the gradients of each layer based on the information of vector E and cast them to a lower precision. After finishing an all-reduce operation for these low precision gradients, the algorithm casts them to a higher precision and then shifts them to the original exponent. For more details, please see Algorithm 1. Besides, we can synchronize the gradients for several consecutive layers as a whole tensor, which can speed up communication process by reducing the latency.

Algorithm 1. Auto Precision scaling algorithm

Input: *Gradient*: gradient (high precision)
Input: *exp_bit*: bits of low precision exponent
Input: *man_bit*: bits of low precision mantissa
Input: *N*: numbers of distributed nodes
1: $upper\_bound\_exp \leftarrow 2^{exp\_bits-1} - 1$
2: **for all** $g \in Gradient$ **do**
3:    $max\_grad\_exp \leftarrow$ FindMaxExp($g * N$)
4:    $\tilde{f} \leftarrow upper\_bound\_exp$ - AllReduce(max_grad_exp, MAX)
5:    $g \leftarrow g * 2^{\tilde{f}}$
6:    $low\_g \leftarrow$ Cast(g, exp_bit, man_bit)   ▷ cast to low precision
7:    $low\_g \leftarrow$ AllReduce(low_g, SUM)
8:    $g \leftarrow$ Cast($low\_g, 8, 23$)   ▷ cast back to high precision (exp: 8, man: 23)
9:    $g \leftarrow g / 2^{\tilde{f}}$
10: **end for**
11:
12: **function** FindMaxExp($Tensor$)
13:    $max\_exp \leftarrow -INF$
14:    **for all** $i \in Tensor$ **do**
15:       **if** $i! = 0$ **then**
16:          $tmp\_exp \leftarrow$ Ceil(Log2(Abs(i)))
17:          **if** $tmp\_exp > max\_exp$ **then**
18:             $max\_exp \leftarrow tmp\_exp$
19:          **end if**
20:       **end if**
21:    **end for**
22:    **return** max_exp
23: **end function**
24:

Figure 3 shows the comparison between the loss scaling algorithm and APS algorithm. When we use 8 bits (exp: 5 bits, man: 2 bits), we can only represent values with exponents in $[-16, 15]$, shown as the area between the two black lines. Values greater than 2^{15} will overflow and cast to INF, while values smaller than 2^{-16} will underflow and cast to 0. The blue curve and green curve represent the gradients' distribution of two layers separately. The loss scaling algorithm will scale all layers' gradients with a given constant number, which is carefully selected by hand to avoid the overflow for the maximum gradients. In this case, the loss scaling algorithm will scale all gradients by 2^{-5}. The scaled gradients are represented by dashed curves (Fig. 3(b)). Although it can avoid overflow, it will cause some small values to underflow, which will be cast to 0. APS algorithm will scale each layer with a different constant. In other words, the algorithm will automatically scale each layer's gradient with the greatest factor that does not cause overflow. As for the situation the figure shows, we will scale the blue layer by 2^{10}, and the green layer by 2^{-5} (Fig. 3(c)). We highlight the difference between APS and other widely-used techniques in Table 1.

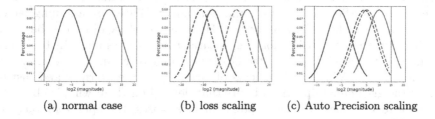

(a) normal case   (b) loss scaling   (c) Auto Precision scaling

Fig. 3. These figures show the comparison between loss scaling and APS. When we use 8 bits (exp: 5 bits, man: 2 bits), we can only represent values with exponents in $[-16, 15]$, shown as the area between the two black lines. The gradient distributions of two layers are represented by blue/green curves separately. Values greater than 2^{15} will overflow and cast to INF, while values smaller than 2^{-16} will underflow and cast to 0. The dashed curves represent the data distributions after scaled. (Color figure online)

3.3 Technical Details for APS

Using the Power of 2 as Scaling Factors. For loss scaling [19], users can choose arbitrary values as scaling factors. However, in APS, the algorithm will only choose a scaling factor that is the power of two. This choice can take advantage of the properties of the floating-point numbers. By doing so, we can minimize the round-off error. For example, Fig. 4 shows an example of using value 10 or 8 for the scaling factor. We use 8 bits precision (exp: 5 bits, man: 2 bits). The gray box denotes the sign bit, the yellow box denotes the exponent bit, and green box denotes the mantissa bit. For a normal floating-point format, when multiplied by 8 (a value that is the power of 2), only the exponent part will be changed, and the mantissa part will remain the same. So after it is multiplied and divided by 8, the output value is still the same as the input value. While using 10 as the scaling factor, both the exponent and mantissa part will be changed, which may truncate the numerical value. Either multiplied by 10 or divided by 10 will cause a round-off error.

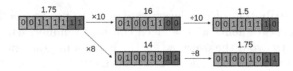

Fig. 4. It is necessary to use the power of 2 as scaling factor.

Trade-Off Between Underflow and Overflow. In most cases, numbers represented by high precision formats are out of the ranges low precision formats can represent. So the scaling technique can be a trade-off between underflow and overflow. An example is shown in Fig. 5. The original distribution is shown in the green curve, it has both an underflow part and an overflow part. Using a scaling factor larger than 1 will move the green curve to the red curve, which is affected by overflow. In contrast, the blue curve, shifted by a scaling factor smaller than 1, is affected by underflow. However, overflow often can be much more harmful than underflow for deep neural networks training. In backward propagation, the gradients of latter layers are used to calculate the gradients of previous layers. When the gradients of latter layers are overflow and cast to INF, all the gradients in previous layers that depend on them will also be INF. According to the rules of floating point, in most cases, the operators' outputs will be INF if there is an INF for operand. And this domino effect will make the training process diverge as we will lose lots of important information. Therefore, our experiments and analysis indicate that we should choose a scaling factor that can avoid overflow. Among all these working values, we choose the largest one, which makes the smallest fraction fall into the underflow range.

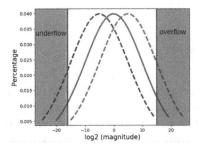

Fig. 5. The green curve is the original data distribution. The blue/red dashed curves are distributions scaled by factors smaller/greater than 1.0, which leads to different underflow/overflow fractions. (Color figure online)

Find the Maximum Scaling Factor. The above section suggests that we should choose the maximum scaling factor which does not incur overflow. This condition is described by Eq. (1), we have to find the maximum value that meets this condition. In this section, we define g as gradients, f as the scaling factor,

$\hat{p}$ as the upper bound of the required floating point precision, N as the number of nodes in the system, $\hat{g}$ as the maximum element of the gradients, and $\tilde{f}$ as $\log_2 factor$. Thus, we have the summation over all the distributed nodes:

$$\left| \sum_{i=1}^{N} (g_i \times f) \right| \leq \hat{p} \tag{1}$$

However, as each node only knows its local gradients, it is hard to exactly get the maximum factor with negligible communication cost. So in APS, we use a heuristic algorithm to find a suitable scaling factor. We relax the bound in Eq. (1) as Eq. (2).

$$\left| \sum_{i=1}^{N} (g_i \times f) \right| = f \times \left| \sum_{i=1}^{N} g_i \right| \leq f \times \sum_{i=1}^{N} |g_i| \leq f \times N \times |\hat{g}| \tag{2}$$

A straightforward approach is to just communicate each node's largest gradient to get the global maximum gradient and then calculate the factor. On top of that, we want to do further optimizations to speed up the communication process. The condition can be written as Eq. (3):

$$f \leq \frac{\hat{p}}{|N \times \hat{g}|} \tag{3}$$

As Sect. 3.3 suggests that we should use only the power of 2 as the scaling factor, we can further transform Eq. (3) ($f = 2^{\tilde{f}}$ and $\tilde{f}$ is an integer):

$$\tilde{f} < \lceil \log_2(\frac{\hat{p}}{|N \times \hat{g}|}) \rceil = \lceil \log_2(\hat{p}) - \log_2(|N \times \hat{g}|) \rceil \tag{4}$$

So we will assign $\tilde{f} = \log_2(\hat{p}) - \lceil \log_2(|N \times \hat{g}|) \rceil$ to meet the requirements. For a given floating-point number, the logarithm is exactly equal to the exponent part. So instead of communicating $|N \times \hat{g}|$, we only communicate $\lceil \log_2(|N \times \hat{g}|) \rceil$. If we use IEEE 754 floating-point precision and communicate the former value, we have to communicate 32-bit floating point numbers. While using the latter one, we only need to communicate 8 bits, as IEEE 754 floating-point format has 8 bits for exponent.

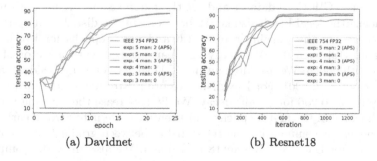

(a) Davidnet   (b) Resnet18

Fig. 6. 4K batch size for CIFAR10 on 8 nodes

4   Experiments

It is hardware friendly to use a power of 2 as the number of bits. This is efficient for both memory access and computational operations. So we tried using 4 and 8 bits for gradients in distributed training. We provide an emulator of CPD implementation to make sure our experiments can be reproduced on any device. The major concern for using mixed precision is the casting from high precision to low precision. The standard IEEE floating-point format uses the rounding-to-nearest method, while some researchers prefer stochastic rounding [4,21,23] which can get an unbiased estimate for high precision values. Although stochastic rounding has nice mathematical properties, its randomness makes it hard to reproduce. Also, in some situations, it is slower than the rounding-to-nearest method. So in the following experiments, we use round-to-nearest even method, which is a special case of the round-to-nearest method. We fix the number of epochs as the same for all precisions for a given model. As mentioned before, we not only focus on reducing the communication cost, but also want to make APS algorithm transparent for users, which means APS will not change the training process. Therefore, unless otherwise noted, the low precision training will use the same hyper-parameter as IEEE FP32. All hyper-parameters are referenced from previous related work [1–3,10], we didn't try to fine-tune the hyper-parameters. We use IEEE FP32 for parameters and activations.

Besides, we also compare the training curves between APS and the baseline. In this way, we are able to show that using APS does not affect the training process. Most importantly, we also compare the training curves and accuracies with/without APS, to show that APS can improve the accuracy for a given precision. In our experiments, the machines on all distributed systems run the same software environment: 64-bit Ubuntu 16.04 with CUDA toolkit 9.0, cuDNN7.6 and PyTorch1.3.1.

4.1   Training on Small-Scale Distributed Systems

In this section, we pick state-of-the-art deep learning models (DavidNet and Resnet18 for classification and FCN for segmentation) and train them on an 8-node distributed system, and each node has a NVIDIA V100 GPU. We use ring all-reduce [9] for all experiments in this distributed system. For classification models, we use CIFAR10 dataset and set the batch size as 4K for both models, which means the local batch size is 512 per node in the distributed system. For ResNet18, we set the learning rate as 1.6 and use 5 epochs for learning rate warming up [10] from 0.1. We decay the learning rate with a factor of 0.1 at 40th and 80th epoch. We use Momentum SGD with 0.9 for m. Besides, we use a weight decay γ of 0.0001. For DavidNet, we use Nesterov momentum with m of 0.9 and set γ as 0.256 for weight decay. We first increase the learning rate from 0 to 0.4 linearly in the first 5 epochs and then decrease it to zero linearly in the last 20 epochs. We summarize the relationship between gradient precisions and the accuracy for DavidNet/ResNet18 in Table 4. We also show the comparison for the training curves of different precisions in Fig. 6. These results show that APS can make a significant difference in low-precision learning.

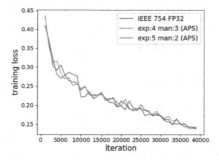

Fig. 7. Training FCN on cityscapes dataset with batch size 16 on 8 nodes. Using 8 bits with APS, we can have a similar training curve as IEEE FP32

Table 3. FCN model on cityscapes with batch size 16 on 8 nodes. APS can achieve even higher accuracy with low precision (exp: 4 man: 3) compared to FP32.

Precision (exp, man)	Using APS	MIOU	MAcc
(8, 23): 32 bits	/	75.16	82.84
(4, 3): 8 bits	Yes	75.88	84.34
	No	74.60	82.55
(5, 2): 8 bits	Yes	74.76	82.62
	No	74.41	82.30

In addition to the classification models, we also select a state-of-the-art segmentation model, FCN [18] (with pre-trained ResNet50 for backbone), for experiments. We use cityscape [5] for dataset. We do our experiments on MMSegmentation [2] and use its hyper-parameter. In the training, we set crop size as 769 × 769 and train 40K iterations. The experimental results in Table 3 and Fig. 7 show that we can use 8 bits (exp: 4 man: 3) to maintain the testing accuracy by APS.[1] LARS [25] is a state-of-the-art method being widely used for distributed training which can significantly improve the testing accuracy. As LARS will set the local learning rate for each layer separately based on gradients, we want to study the relationship between LARS and low-precision gradients. We suspect LARS maybe sensitive to gradients. So we try using LARS with low precision gradients to see if the round-off error caused by the low precision communication hurts the accuracy or not. We train ResNet18 on CIFAR10 dataset with 8K batch size using 8 nodes and find low precision will hurt the accuracy. On the other hand, by using APS, we can maintain the same accuracy and even improve accuracy. The results are shown in Table 5 and Fig. 8. Perhaps surprisingly, the

---

[1] mIOU: Mean Intersection-Over-Union, the average IOU over each semantic class. mAcc: (pixels in the detected area that match the ground truth)/total number of pixels in the ground truth. The higher the two metricses, the better the quality.

Table 4. Models are trained on CIFAR10 dataset with 4K batch size by 8 nodes. For all precisions, even by 4 bits, APS can make the training processes converge with little or no accuracy loss.

Model	Precision (exp, man)	Using APS	Accuracy
DavidNet	(8, 23): 32 bits	/	88.2
	(5, 2): 8 bits	Yes	88.4
		No	88.3
	(4, 3): 8 bits	Yes	88.6
		No	10.0
	(3, 0): 4 bits	Yes	81.3
		No	10.0
ResNet18	(8, 23): 32 bits	/	91.4
	(5, 2): 8 bits	Yes	91.4
		No	90.1
	(4, 3): 8 bits	Yes	91.6
		No	90.4
	(3, 0): 4 bits	Yes	86.7
		No	10.0

models' qualities training with low precision are close or even slightly higher than these model trained with high precision, This phenomenon is also reported in [17,19]. This may be due to the fact that low precision can relieve overfitting, like L1 normalization.

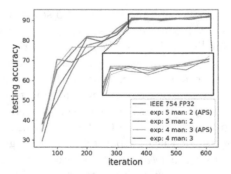

Fig. 8. ResNet18 on CIFAR10 with 8K batch size by LARS. APS allows LARS to maintain the same accuracy as 32 bits while using low-precision communication.

4.2   Training on Large-Scale Distributed Systems

We train ResNet50 [12] on a 256-node distributed system. Instead of ring all-reduce used in Sect. 4.1, we use the Hierarchical all-reduce [14,20]: we partition the nodes into 16 groups, and assign a *master* node for each group. Each all-reduce operation will finish 3 steps: (1) within each group, all worker nodes send their local gradients to the master node; (2) we conduct the ring all-reduce across all the master nodes; (3) within each group, the master node broadcasts the global gradients to all the worker nodes. There are two reasons why we use the hierarchical all-reduce approach:

Table 5. ResNet18 with LARS. APS can improve the accuracy for both (exp: 5, man: 2) and (exp: 4, man: 3). It can even get a higher accuracy than 32-bit precision.

Precision (exp, man)	Using APS	Testing accuracy
(8, 23): 32 bits	/	92.072
(4,3): 8 bits	Yes	92.44
	No	92.036
(5,2): 8 bits	Yes	92.015
	No	91.737

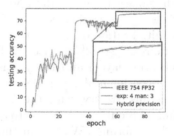

Fig. 9. Training ResNet50 with 32 bits, 8 bits, and hybrid precision.

- **Performance**: the ring all-reduce with p nodes need to finish $2(p-1)$ steps (each step transfers the same amount of data). The hierarchical all-reduce with a group size of k only needs $4(k-1)+2(p/k-1)$ steps. In our experiments with 256 nodes and a group size of 16, we only need to finish 74 steps, instead of 510 steps for using ring all-reduce.
- **Round-off error**: when we use a low precision floating point to add a small number with a large number, the smaller number may be truncated and cast as zero in this addition operation. This situation is common in all-reduce process. To avoid this problem, we should try to minimize the number of large-and-small additions. If we use ring all-reduce, we have to add a local gradient with the summation of all other nodes' local gradients in the last step. The summation may be 255x larger than this local gradient if we have 256 nodes. When we use the hierarchical all-reduce, we have only 16 nodes for

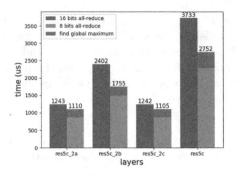

Fig. 10. The time of communication on 32 nodes.

intra-group reduction. In this situation, the last step will add a local gradient with a 15x larger gradient. The situation is the same as inter-group all-reduce among 16 master nodes.

Taking the above two factors into account, we choose to use the hierarchical all-reduce with a group size of 16. In the following section, we prove that this group size can minimize the round-off error. We use 8K batch size to train ResNet50 on ImageNet dataset [7]. As APS does not require us to modify the hyper-parameters, we use the same setting and data preprocessing as [10], except the learnable scaling coefficient γ is initialized as 1 for all BN layers in our experiments. We adopt the initialization of [11] for the 1000-way fully-connected layer. Based on the suggestions of [21,23], we use IEEE FP32 for the gradient of the last layer (i.e. classification layer) and low precision for all other layers' gradient. We also have the experimental results of using low precision for all layers, please see Fig. 9 for details. We try using the APS algorithm on different precisions (Table 6), and find APS only needs 8 bits to achieve roughly the same accuracy as the standard 32-bit format. We can further improve the accuracy by hybrid precision: using FP32 for the first 30 epochs and 8 bits for the last

Table 6. We use APS to train ResNet50 with 8K batch size (256 nodes). APS can improve the accuracy for 8-bit gradient. With APS, we can use 8-bit gradient for the whole training process, with only a tiny loss in testing accuracy (<0.05%).

Precision (exp, man)	With APS	Top-1 accuracy
(8, 23): 32 bits	/	76.02
(5,2): 8 bits	Yes	75.98
	No	71.00
(4,3): 8 bits	Yes	75.93
	No	0.1
(8, 23) + (4, 3)	Yes	76.09

Table 7. Training ResNet50 with APS by low precision for different layers. We can improve the accuracy by using high precision for the last classification layer.

Precision for other layers	Precision for the last classification layer	Top-1 accuracy
(5, 2)	(5,2)	75.08
	FP32	75.98
(4, 3)	(4, 3)	75.46
	FP32	75.93

60 epochs. This method can help us maintain the same accuracy as IEEE FP32 (Table 7).

We also have a comparison between different group sizes and present the results in Table 8. To further explain the difference between different group sizes, we compare the average round-off error for the gradient of the first convolutional layer's weight using 8 bits (exp: 5, man: 2) and present the result in Table 9. The average round-off error is described by Eq. 5 (the gradients got by the high/low precision communication are denoted as $grad\_h$ and $grad\_l$ separately and we assume there are N elements in the gradient tensor). It shows using the hierarchical all-reduce can decrease the round-off error compared to ring-allreduce. It also shows that 16 is the most suitable group size for a 256-node distributed system.

$$average\_round\_off\_error = \frac{\sum_{i=0}^{N} \left| \frac{grad\_h_i - grad\_l_i}{grad\_h_i} \right|}{N} \tag{5}$$

Table 8. For ResNet-50 on a 256-node system, using a group size of 16 can improve the accuracy compared to a group size of 32 for 8 bits, as it can reduce the round-off error. We use low precision gradients for all layers

Precision (exp, man)	Group size	Top-1 accuracy
(4, 3): 8bits	32	74.95
	16	75.46
(5, 2): 8bits	32	74.91
	16	75.08

4.3 Performance Analysis

In this section, we analyze the performance of APS on a distributed system with 32 V100 GPUs. In detail, there are 4 servers, each servers is installed with

Table 9. The average round-off error for the first convolutional layer's weight of ResNet-50 using 8 bits (exponent: 5 bits, mantissa: 2 bits) on a 256-node cluster.

Group size	4	8	16	32	64	256 (ring all reduce)
Round-off error	55%	44.21%	41.83%	49.62%	58.21%	85.22%

8 GPUs. All servers are connected by InfiniBand and share a distributed file system.

[Layer-Wise Performance Analysis]. Figure 10 shows the time cost for synchronizing gradients of some layers in ResNet50 (gradient shape of each layer: res5c_branch2a: 2048 * 512, res5c_branch2b: 512 * 512 * 3 * 3, res5c_branch2c: 512 * 2048). The blue bars denote the time cost by using half precision without APS. The bars on the right set of each blue bars show the total time for using APS to communicate the same gradient. The gray bars denote the time cost to get the global maximum gradient. The orange bars denote the time cost to communicate gradients using 8 bits. For all layers, APS with 8 bits can speed up the communication process. Our experiments show that merging short messages into a single one can reduce the overall communication time. Here, res5c_2a, res5c_2b, res5c_2c are three consecutive layers in ResNet50. We synchronize them as a whole, and present the result on the rightmost column in Fig. 10. We can achieve a 1.36× speedup over half-precision.

[End-to-End Performance Analysis]. We also analyze the end to end performance for using 8 bits gradients with APS algorithm. We record the time for each iteration. Half-precision training [14, 20] (using half-precision for both computation and communication) is used for baseline. The baseline's time (t_base) includes two parts: (1) the gradients all-reduce operation and (2) the computation and data processing time. APS's communication time (t_aps) includes the time for three parts: (1) gradients all-reduce operation, (2) reducing the global maximum value for each gradient, and (3) the computation and data processing time. In Fig. 11, we show the time cost for iterations with different batch size for different models. For ResNet-50, with batch size 32, t_base = 137.67ms and t_aps = 122.95ms per iteration. The speedup is 1.12x. While for batch size 8, the speedup is 1.18x. For ResNet-18 with batch size 256, the speedup is 1.35x. Even for DavidNet that has relative few parameters, we can also achieve 1.15x speed up with batch size 16. Considering ResNet and DavidNet have been well optimized by industry vendors, we think this level of speedup is very good. As the communication cost will increase with a larger number of nodes, we believe APS can achieve a higher speedup for larger systems. We are also designing a new computer architecture with a startup company for APS. We believe APS will get a higher speedup on specialized hardware. The speedup will also be higher in the federated learning situation where the computation is done on mobile devices and the communication is conducted over the internet.

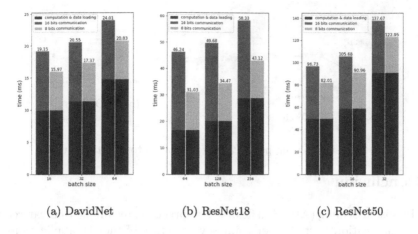

(a) DavidNet   (b) ResNet18   (c) ResNet50

Fig. 11. Time cost per iteration (8 bits by APS is consistently faster).

5   CPD: Customized-Precision Deep Learning

Because of the limitations in QPyTorch, we built CPD to emulate the low-precision training for our experiments. CPD has the following functions, which are not supported by any previous systems: (1) arbitrary low-precision, with number of exponent bits $<= 8$ and number of mantissa bits $<= 23$; (2) various accumulation strategies (e.g. Kahan summation algorithm [13]); (3) using any low-precision accumulator for GEMM and reduce/all-reduce function.

Accumulation is a common operation in Deep Learning (e.g. GEMM and all-reduce). During accumulation, a number maybe added by a much larger number. In this case, the smaller number may be truncated to zero and does not affect the accumulation. To avoid losing the information of small values during accumulation, we can use a higher precision to store the accumulator. Although higher precision accumulators can maintain accuracy, they will cost more energy and hurt the performance. So the precision of the accumulator is a key factor for low precision computation. To the best of our knowledge, existing systems only support using IEEE FP32 for the accumulator, while CPD allows users to apply arbitrary low precision (≤ 32 bits) for the accumulator. This feature is significantly helpful for hardware designers. An example of 3-bit accumulator is shown in Fig. 12.

We can also use different accumulation strategies to maintain accuracy. CPD supports not only default sequential summation, but also the Kahan summation algorithm. It also allows users to implement their own strategies.

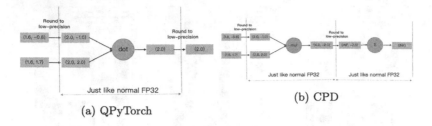

Just like normal FP32

(a) QPyTorch

(b) CPD

Fig. 12. 3-bit floating point (2-bit exp) for vector multiplication.

6   Conclusion

Auto Precision Scaling (APS) is a flexible low-precision technique that can reduce the communication cost. It can train several state-of-the-art applications by 8 bits for gradient communication without losing accuracy. APS can save the bandwidth and improve the accuracy for any given low-precision with almost no cost. For low-precision formats in our experiments, APS can improve the accuracy for all of them. Besides, we can train ResNet-50 by a hybrid precision to get the same accuracy as the baseline with the same number of epochs on 256 nodes. We analyze the time of APS for gradient communication and find that the saving in time is larger than the additional cost in compute. Furthermore, we built the CPD system that allows users to simulate any arbitrary low-precision format. We integrate CPD into PyTorch and make it open source to the public.

References

1. Davidnet. https://github.com/davidcpage/cifar10-fast
2. Mmsegmentation. https://github.com/open-mmlab/mmsegmentation
3. torchvision. https://github.com/pytorch/vision
4. Alistarh, D., Grubic, D., Li, J., Tomioka, R., Vojnovic, M.: QSGD: communication-efficient SGD via gradient quantization and encoding. In: Advances in Neural Information Processing Systems, pp. 1709–1720 (2017)
5. Cordts, M., et al.: The cityscapes dataset for semantic urban scene understanding. In: Proceedings of the IEEE Conference on Computer Vision and Pattern Recognition, pp. 3213–3223 (2016)
6. Courbariaux, M., Bengio, Y., David, J.P.: Training deep neural networks with low precision multiplications. arXiv preprint arXiv:1412.7024 (2014)
7. Deng, J., Dong, W., Socher, R., Li, L.J., Li, K., Fei-Fei, L.: ImageNet: a large-scale hierarchical image database. In: 2009 IEEE Conference on Computer Vision and Pattern Recognition, pp. 248–255. IEEE (2009)
8. Dryden, N., Moon, T., Jacobs, S.A., Van Essen, B.: Communication quantization for data-parallel training of deep neural networks. In: 2016 2nd Workshop on Machine Learning in HPC Environments (MLHPC), pp. 1–8. IEEE (2016)
9. Gibiansky, A.: Bringing HPC techniques to deep learning. Technical report, Baidu Research (2017)
10. Goyal, P., et al.: Accurate, large minibatch SGD: training ImageNet in 1 hour. arXiv preprint arXiv:1706.02677 (2017)

11. He, K., Zhang, X., Ren, S., Sun, J.: Delving deep into rectifiers: surpassing human-level performance on ImageNet classification. In: The IEEE International Conference on Computer Vision (ICCV), December 2015
12. He, K., Zhang, X., Ren, S., Sun, J.: Deep residual learning for image recognition. In: Proceedings of the IEEE Conference on Computer Vision and Pattern Recognition, pp. 770–778 (2016)
13. Higham, N.J.: Accuracy and Stability of Numerical Algorithms, vol. 80. SIAM (2002)
14. Jia, X., et al.: Highly scalable deep learning training system with mixed-precision: training ImageNet in four minutes. arXiv preprint arXiv:1807.11205 (2018)
15. Johnson, J.: Rethinking floating point for deep learning. arXiv preprint arXiv:1811.01721 (2018)
16. Köster, U., et al.: Flexpoint: an adaptive numerical format for efficient training of deep neural networks. In: Advances in Neural Information Processing Systems, pp. 1742–1752 (2017)
17. Lin, Y., Han, S., Mao, H., Wang, Y., Dally, W.J.: Deep gradient compression: reducing the communication bandwidth for distributed training. arXiv preprint arXiv:1712.01887 (2017)
18. Long, J., Shelhamer, E., Darrell, T.: Fully convolutional networks for semantic segmentation. In: Proceedings of the IEEE Conference on Computer Vision and Pattern Recognition (CVPR), June 2015
19. Micikevicius, P., et al.: Mixed precision training. arXiv preprint arXiv:1710.03740 (2017)
20. Sun, P., Wen, Y., Han, R., Feng, W., Yan, S.: GradientFlow: optimizing network performance for large-scale distributed DNN training. IEEE Trans. Big Data (2019)
21. Wang, N., Choi, J., Brand, D., Chen, C.Y., Gopalakrishnan, K.: Training deep neural networks with 8-bit floating point numbers. In: Advances in Neural Information Processing Systems, pp. 7675–7684 (2018)
22. Wangni, J., Wang, J., Liu, J., Zhang, T.: Gradient sparsification for communication-efficient distributed optimization. arXiv preprint arXiv:1710.09854 (2017)
23. Wen, W., Xu, C., Yan, F., Wu, C., Wang, Y., Chen, Y., Li, H.: TernGrad: ternary gradients to reduce communication in distributed deep learning. In: Advances in Neural Information Processing Systems, pp. 1509–1519 (2017)
24. Ying, C., Kumar, S., Chen, D., Wang, T., Cheng, Y.: Image classification at super-computer scale. arXiv preprint arXiv:1811.06992 (2018)
25. You, Y., Gitman, I., Ginsburg, B.: Scaling SGD batch size to 32k for ImageNet training. arXiv preprint arXiv:1708.03888, 6 2017
26. You, Y., Zhang, Z., Hsieh, C.J., Demmel, J., Keutzer, K.: ImageNet training in minutes. In: Proceedings of the 47th International Conference on Parallel Processing, p. 1. ACM (2018)
27. Zhang, T., Lin, Z., Yang, G., Sa, C.D.: QPyTorch: a low-precision arithmetic simulation framework (2019)

FPGA Acceleration of Number Theoretic Transform

·Tian Ye[1]([⊠]), Yang Yang[2], Sanmukh R. Kuppannagari[2], Rajgopal Kannan[3], and Viktor K. Prasanna[2]

[1] Department of Computer Science, University of Southern California, Los Angeles, CA 90089, USA
tye69227@usc.edu
[2] Ming Hsieh Department of Electrical and Computer Engineering, University of Southern California, Los Angeles, CA 90089, USA
{yyang172,kuppanna,prasanna}@usc.edu
[3] US Army Research Lab, Playa Vista, CA 90094, USA
rajgopal.kannan.civ@mail.mil

Abstract. Fully Homomorphic Encryption (FHE) is a technique that enables arbitrary computations on encrypted data directly. Number Theoretic Transform (NTT) is a fundamental component in FHE computations as it allows faster polynomial multiplication. However, it is computationally intensive and requires acceleration for practical deployment of FHE. The latency and throughput of existing NTT hardware designs are limited by the complex data communication pattern between adjacent NTT stages and the modular arithmetic operations. In this paper, we propose a parameterized architecture for NTT on FPGA. The architecture can be configured for a given polynomial degree, modulus and target hardware in order to optimize the latency and/or throughput. We develop a novel low latency fully pipelined modular arithmetic logic to implement the NTT core, the key computational unit of NTT. Streaming permutation network is used to reduce the data communication complexity between NTT stages. We implement the proposed architecture for various polynomial degrees, moduli, and data parallelism on state-of-the-art FPGAs. Experimental results show that our architecture configured to perform 4096 polynomial degree NTT achieves up to $1.29\times$ and $4.32\times$ improvement in latency and throughput respectively over state-of-the-art designs on FPGA.

Keywords: Number theoretic transform · Parallel computing · FPGA

1 Introduction

Fully Homomorphic Encryption (FHE) provides a solution to utilize cloud platforms in a trusted and secure manner by directly performing computations on

---

T. Ye and Y. Yang—Equal contribution.

© Springer Nature Switzerland AG 2021
B. L. Chamberlain et al. (Eds.): ISC High Performance 2021, LNCS 12728, pp. 98–117, 2021.
https://doi.org/10.1007/978-3-030-78713-4_6

encrypted data [17]. Polynomial multiplication is one of the most time-consuming operations in FHE applications [28]. Naive implementation of polynomial multiplication results in $O(N^2)$ time complexity, where N is the degree of the polynomial. Number Theoretic Transform (NTT) has been proposed to reduce the complexity to $O(N \log N)$. Profiling results from [28] show that NTT is a primary bottleneck in FHE based applications such as FHE-Convolutional Neural Networks accounting for 55.2% of the execution time. Therefore, high performance implementation of NTT will have a critical impact of FHE based applications.

FPGAs have gained a lot of traction due to their immense flexibility and high energy efficiency. They are being widely adopted in cloud platforms where they are attached to the data center nodes to design highly customized, domain specific accelerators [13,27]. The logic density and compute throughput of state-of-the-art FPGAs have increased dramatically in recent years [18,35]. They also provide fine-grained memory access to high bandwidth on-chip SRAMs and external DRAMs. These features make them a logical choice for accelerating compute intensive applications such as NTT.

However, it is non-trivial to efficiently utilize the abundant FPGA resources for NTT to achieve low latency and high throughput. First, NTT requires complex data communication between computation stages due to loop-dependent permutation stride[1] in the algorithm [14]. Previous FPGA implementations have used all-to-all connections to facilitate communications [22,29,32]. The routing complexity increases quadratically with the data processing rate per cycle [31]. The design in [24] fully unrolls all the computation stages and uses fixed-function switch to reduce complexity. The wiring length as well as the interconnect area doubles from stage i to stage $i + 1$. In addition, due to the high polynomial degree in FHE applications [2], input coefficients often are not available concurrently. This adds an extra layer of complexity as the communication pattern also changes for different input data beats in the same computation stage. Second, designing low latency NTT cores to execute the key computation operation of NTT is challenging due to high resource requirements of modular arithmetic. Arbitrary modular arithmetic requires division operations that are expensive in FPGAs. Although division avoiding reduction algorithms [6,23] for arbitrary fixed modulus have been developed, they require additional multiplications, thereby incurring high latency. Lastly, based on the application, we may seek to minimize the resource consumption, maximize performance, or optimize some weighted combination of these. Thus, a parameterized design is desirable.

In this paper, we design an FPGA-based fully pipelined high performance NTT architecture. The architecture is parameterized and can be configured to support a wide range of polynomial degrees, moduli, and data parallelism. We use data parallelism, parallel input and output coefficients per cycle, to control the required I/O bandwidth for a given implementation. These parameters can be chosen at design time to meet latency and throughput requirements as well as the device resource constraints. To improve throughput, our design fully unrolls all the NTT computation stages. We employ streaming permutation net-

---

[1] Given a stride S, a permutation stride is defined as reordering an m-element data vector such that elements with distance of S are shifted into adjacent locations.

work (SPN) to reduce the routing complexity between NTT stages [10]. SPN reduces routing complexity by trading expensive long wires and switches with more pipeline stages. It can scale to large data parallelism with lower cost in terms of wiring and interconnect area compared to other types of interconnect such as crossbar. To obtain low latency NTT core with modular multiplication, our design supports any prime modulus q that is produced by choosing positive integers i and j to satisfy the property $2^j \equiv 2^i - 1 \pmod{q}$ (henceforth referred to as the *modulus property*). For such a modulus q, the modulo operation can be replaced by repeated additions, subtractions and shift operations (Sect. 3.3). As a result, an NTT core with low latency and low resource requirements can be realized. Note that the algorithm proposed in [37] is designed only for $q = 2^{14} - 2^{12} + 1$. In this work, we generalize the algorithm to support any q that satisfies the modulus property.

The key contributions of this paper are:

- We design a parameterized NTT architecture on FPGA that can support a wide-range of polynomial degrees, moduli, and data parallelism. Given the polynomial degree and the hardware resource constraints, our architecture can be configured to obtain high throughput and low latency.
- We utilize streaming permutation network to support various data parallelism and to reduce the data communication complexity between NTT stages. This technique enables our architecture to be fully unrolled and pipelined for all the NTT stages, which leads to high throughput.
- To obtain low latency, we develop a compact NTT core that can perform modular arithmetic operations without any multiplication. Our NTT core design can be used to generate a collection of algorithms for different moduli as required by the given application.
- We implement our architecture for various polynomial degrees, moduli and data parallelism on state-of-the-art FPGAs. It can be configured to perform 512, 1024, 2048 and 4096 polynomial degree NTT in less than 0.57 μs, 0.76 μs, 1.03 μs and 1.99 μs respectively. By further increasing data parallelism, throughput of 43.0, 20.6, 9.2 and 1.7 million transforms per second is achieved for 512, 1024, 2048 and 4096 polynomial degree NTT respectively.
- Our design achieves superior throughput while also improving the latency compared with state-of-the-art designs on the same hardware. We improve the latency up to 1.29× and the throughput up to 4.32×.

2   Related Work

NTT Acceleration: Recent work [22,29,32] focus on optimizing memory layout to enable parallel and conflict-free memory access between NTT stages. However, in these designs require all-to-all connection between NTT cores and intermediate data memory, which limits the scalability. Throughput is also reduced due to reusing the same set of NTT cores across all the stages. A systolic array approach for NTT acceleration is presented in [25]. This architecture fully unrolls all the NTT stages. However, data parallelism in NTT is not explored and computation in each NTT stage is serialized. The NTT hardware proposed in [5,26] is limited to a specific setting. Nejatollahi et al. use processing-in-memory technology to accelerate NTT [24]. The design unrolls all the NTT computation stages and all the input coefficients to improve parallelism, but latency and throughput are affected by the long computation cycles in Processing In-Memory (PIM) technology. [3,19,20,30] use CPU or GPU to accelerate NTT, but the optimizations in these designs cannot be applied due to the differences in the underlying architecture. The work in [19] executes several NTTs concurrently to exploit massive GPU parallelism. In such a design, reducing the batch size does not lead to reduced latency. Thus, this design is not suitable for our scenario where in addition to throughput, latency for a single NTT computation needs to be minimized.

Modular Multiplication: This is one of the key operations of NTT and many works have focused on its efficient implementation. In [21], the modulo algorithm allows the output to be slightly greater than the modulus q. This optimization avoids division operations, but still requires additional large-latency multiplications. [22] implemented an iterative modulo operation based on Montgomery reduction [23]. This can be resource-consuming as each iteration has a multiplication. In [29], modular multiplication is based on Barrett reduction [6]. It requires pre-computations depending on the twiddle factors. This consumes more on-chip storage. Also, their algorithm requires two additional multiplications. [37] designed an architecture for $q = 2^{14} - 2^{12} + 1$ that avoids any multiplication in the modular reduction. This results in low latency and reduced resource requirements. However, many applications of NTT have large coefficients, and thus need larger q. Therefore, our work extends this design for any prime q that satisfies $2^j \equiv 2^i - 1 \pmod{q}$ for some positive integers i and j. Please Sects. 3.3 and 4.2 for details.

To the best of our knowledge, existing work on FPGAs does not account for the performance impact of the interstage data. As a result, the scalability and achievable performance are limited. In contrast, we use streaming permutation network to enable a fully unrolled and pipelined architecture with variable data parallelism. We further develop low latency modular arithmetic unit that supports arbitrary modulus q satisfying the modulus property.

3   Background

3.1   Fully Homomorphic Encryption (FHE)

Homomorphic encryption is a practical approach for privacy-preserving computation using lattice-based cryptography [17]. It allows direct computations, including addition, scaling and multiplication, on ciphertext without access to the original data. There are a variety of encryption schemes, e.g., BGV [8], BFV [16] and CKKS [12]. For all these encryption schemes, both the plaintext and the ciphertext are high-degree polynomials, typically ranging from 2^{10} to

2^{15} [2]. The security level is quantified by two parameters, the degree of polynomials and the width of the selected modulus. Both are critical to the performance of homomorphic computations. Typical parameters for different security levels can be found in [2].

3.2 Number Theoretic Transform (NTT)

Polynomial multiplication is one of the most computationally expensive operation of homomorphic encrypted computations [28]. The complexity of multiplying two polynomials of degree N is $O(N^2)$. To reduce the complexity to $O(N \log N)$, number-theoretic transform (NTT) is used [1].[2] This simplifies the polynomial multiplication into N coefficient-wise multiplications.

Algorithm 1: Number Theoretic Transform

Input: Coefficients $A = (A[0], A[1], ..., A[n-1])$ and twiddle factors in bit-reversed order $\phi = (\phi[0], \phi[1], ..., \phi[n-1])$

Output: $A \leftarrow \text{NTT}(A)$ in bit-reversed order

1   **for** $(m \leftarrow n/2; m \geq 1; m \leftarrow m/2)$ **do**
2   **for** $(i \leftarrow 0; i < \frac{n}{2m}; i \leftarrow i+1)$ **do**
3         $S \leftarrow \phi[\frac{n}{2m} + i]$
4   **for** $(j \leftarrow 0; j < m; j \leftarrow j+1)$ **do**
5            $U \leftarrow A[2m \cdot i + j]$
6            $V \leftarrow S \cdot A[2m \cdot i + j + m] \bmod q$
7            $A[2m \cdot i + j] \leftarrow U + V \bmod q$
8            $A[2m \cdot i + j + m] \leftarrow U - V \bmod q$
9   **end**
10   **end**
11 **end**

In Algorithm 1, each iteration of the outer loop is called a stage. The algorithm has $\log N$ sequential stages as the outer loop in Line 1, and each stage has $N/2$ independent instances of Line 5–8 that can be computed in parallel. Each instance of Line 5–8 takes two coefficients as input, performs modular arithmetic and updates the two coefficients. Modular arithmetic includes modular multiplication, addition and subtraction. Note that the computational pattern of the NTT algorithm is similar to that of the FFT algorithm. However, NTT performs modular arithmetic on integer coefficients as opposed to FFT which performs arithmetic on complex numbers. As performing modular arithmetic is computationally expensive, existing FFT implementations such as [11,36] cannot be trivially extended to accelerate NTT.

3.3 Modular Reduction

As NTT limits the coefficients to be in a finite ring of integers, modular computations are required in the algorithm. Modular addition and subtraction are

---

[2] All logs in this paper are to base 2.

trivial, which require only one more addition or subtraction. In contrast, it is non-trivial to design an efficient modular multiplication, as division and modulo operations are expensive on FPGAs. Typical modular reduction algorithms, e.g., Barrett reduction [6] and Montgomery reduction [23], replace the expensive division operation with multiplication operation when the modulus is preconfigured. A recent work [21] proposes a relaxation that allows the output to be slightly longer than the modulus, which speeds up the reduction. However, they still require resource-consuming multiplication operation. Instead, we utilize the design proposed in [37] that has additions and subtractions only. We generalize it from $q = 12289$ to any q that satisfies $2^j \equiv 2^i - 1 \pmod{q}$. Algorithm 2 is an example of the reduction algorithm for $q = 2^{28} - 2^{16} + 1$ that avoids additional multiplications. The algorithm is hardcoded for a specific value of q. We also provide designs similar to Algorithm 2 for a collection of different q values. One of them can be selected and embedded into NTT cores at design time.

Algorithm 2: Reduction for $q = 2^{28} - 2^{16} + 1$

Input: 56-bit integer $z[55:0]$
Output: $y = z \bmod q$
1 $c \leftarrow z[55:52] + z[51:40] + z[39:28]$
2 $d \leftarrow z[55:52] + z[55:40] + z[55:28]$
3 $e \leftarrow c[13:12] + c[11:0]$
4 $f \leftarrow ((e[12] + e[11:0]) << 16) - (e[12] + c[13:12])$
5 $y \leftarrow f + z[27:0]$
6 **if** $y \geq q$ **then**
7 $\quad | \quad y \leftarrow y - q$
8 **end**
9 $y \leftarrow y - d$
10 **if** $y < 0$ **then**
11 $\quad | \quad y \leftarrow y + q$
12 **end**

3.4   Challenges in Accelerating NTT

The two main challenges in NTT are the implementation of the NTT core and the interstage connection network. The key component of the NTT core is modular multiplication which is usually resource-consuming and slow, as discussed in Sect. 3.3. An efficient design for the NTT core, especially modular multiplication, is necessary to reduce the latency and resource consumption. Our design of the low-latency NTT core is described in Sect. 4.2. The interconnection between the NTT stages is a butterfly network, which has high complexity in terms of wiring length and area. For a naïve butterfly network, the wiring length and the interconnect area doubles from stage i to stage $i + 1$ [33]. This is prohibitively large. Existing works proposed several ways to address the challenge. The designs proposed in [22,29] fold all the NTT stages and reuse the same set of NTT cores for all the stages. They simplify the interconnection by data reading and writing in the on-chip memory. However, this method results in low throughput due to the folding of all the stages. In this paper, we support a fully unrolled and pipelined design. We use a streaming permutation network [10] as interconnection with a low resource requirement.

4   Accelerator Design

4.1   Design Methodology

Key NTT parameters such as the degree of polynomial and the modulus width are often chosen by considering not only the level of security, but also the latency, throughput, and hardware resource constraints. As a result, these parameters can differ considerably across homomorphic encrypted (HE) applications [3,4,15]. It is desirable to design the hardware architecture such that it can be configured to run NTT with different settings easily. In addition, due to the high polynomial degree in HE-based applications [2], processing all the input coefficients concurrently requires high hardware resource and I/O bandwidth. Common loop tiling technique is often used to fold input coefficients into smaller groups. Each group is then processed in a streaming manner. This technique reduces I/O bandwidth and hardware resources, but permuting streaming data is challenging as data elements need to be moved across both spatial and temporal dimensions. The design in [25] only processes two coefficients per cycle in each NTT computation. This greatly simplifies the data permutation but leads to inefficient utilization of the available bandwidth. Other NTT hardware implementations on FPGA use carefully designed intermediate data layout in on-chip SRAM to reduce memory access conflicts [22,29]. Complex routing and arbitration logic are needed to permute data in each NTT computation stage. As a result, the number of NTT cores is limited in these designs, which impacts the NTT latency and throughput.

Our NTT hardware architecture is constructed by fully unrolling and pipelining all the NTT computations stages. NTT input and output are folded and processed in a streaming fashion to satisfy I/O bandwidth constraint and to reduce resource consumption. Key NTT algorithmic and architecture settings are exposed as parameters, allowing hardware re-configuration to support various NTT use cases. We define the following parameters that can be specified at design time to customize our architecture:

- Polynomial Degree (N): Application parameter. It determines the polynomial degree for number theoretic transform. Our architecture supports any polynomial degree. For HE-based computation, N is typically a power-of-two number and between 2^{10} to 2^{15} [2,12].
- Modulus (q): Application parameter. Modulus used in Algorithm 1. We support prime modulus q that is produced by choosing positive integers i and j to satisfy the property $2^j \equiv 2^i - 1 \pmod{q}$. i and j determine the bit width of the modulus and the polynomial coefficients.
- Data Parallelism (p): Architecture parameter. It determines the number of coefficients being processed per cycle in each NTT computation stage ($2 \leq p \leq N$). Higher data parallelism improves latency and throughput but requires more I/O bandwidth and FPGA resources. To reduce design complexity, p is restricted to be a power-of-two number.

– Pipeline Parallelism: Architecture parameter. It determines the unrolled NTT computation stages in the NTT hardware. In this paper, we fix this parameter to $\log N$.

The proposed architecture receives p input coefficients per cycle. After a fixed delay, it starts to produce p output coefficients per cycle. Our design does not have restriction on the location of the input and output data. They can be from external DRAM or other IP blocks inside the FPGA. We utilize direction connection permutation (when permutation stride is less than p) and streaming permutation network (SPN) [10] (when permutation stride is greater than or equal to p) to facilitate data communication between NTT stages (Sect. 4.3). Given parameter N and p, our architecture instantiates $\log N$ computation stages, and each stage contains $p/2$ NTT cores. Figure 1 and 2 present the top-level architecture of 16-point NTT with $p = 4$ and $p = 8$ respectively. There are 4 NTT computation stages, and 3 permutation networks are needed in the design.

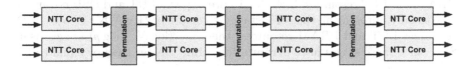

Fig. 1. Top level architecture of 16-point NTT with $p = 4$.

In contrast to prior work, SPN avoids the complex routing and arbitration logic between NTT computation stages by trading expensive long wires and switches with multi-stage parallel routing networks. The highly scalable and extensible SPN can be configured to realize arbitrary stride permutation between its input and output. To reduce the modular arithmetic latency, customized NTT core is developed to replace costly multiplications in modulo operations with additions, subtractions, and shift operations (Sect. 4.2). The utilization of streaming permutation network and low latency NTT core allows us to fully unroll and pipeline all the NTT computation stages to obtain low latency and high throughput.

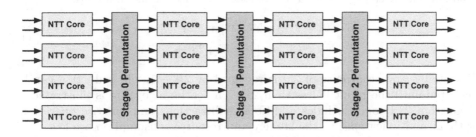

Fig. 2. Top level architecture of 16-point NTT with $p = 8$.

The parameterized architecture opens up design space trade-offs concerning latency, throughput, I/O bandwidth constraint, resource consumption, and application requirement. Applications need to consider N and q accordingly in order to achieve certain level of security [2,12]. For example, with $N = 1024$, it is recommended to use 27-bit modulus q in order to achieve 128-bit security [2]. Larger polynomial degree (N) needs more NTT computation stages, thereby increasing the latency. Higher data parallelism (p) can speed up the NTT latency and throughput, but it has implications on routing resources and I/O bandwidth requirements. Given application parameters N and q, the largest data parallelism (p) can be determined by considering the following constraints:

- I/O Bandwidth: Each input and output coefficient is of size $\lceil \log q \rceil$ bits. Given available input and output bandwidth BW, p can be chosen such that $2 \times p \times \lceil \log q \rceil \times Fmax = BW$, where $Fmax$ is the FPGA design frequency and a factor of 2 is to account for both input and output.
- FPGA Resources: The architecture is implemented under limited LUT, BRAM and DSP resources. Each NTT core requires LUT and DSP resources. Due to fully unrolling all the NTT stages, there are $p/2 \log N$ NTT cores. SPN consumes LUT and BRAM resources, there are $(\log N - \log p)$ stages using SPN since those stages have permutation stride greater than or equal to p.

Our parameterized architecture provides users with the flexibility to configure N, p, and q with a variety of options.

4.2   NTT Core

The NTT core is used to perform the inner loop body of the NTT algorithm that receives two coefficients as inputs and generates two coefficients as outputs. The key component of the NTT core is the module for modular multiplication. To perform the modulo q operation efficiently, we use a design similar to the one proposed in [37]. Moreover, we generalize it by providing designs for a collection of prime q values. Those q are produced by choosing positive integers i and j to satisfy the property $2^j \equiv 2^i - 1 \pmod{q}$. To illustrate the algorithm, we use $q = 2^{28} - 2^{16} + 1$ as an example. In this example, all coefficients are 28 bits, and thus the multiplication result is up to 56 bits. Denote the 56-bit number as $z[55:0]$, and it can be reduced in the following way for the first step:

$$
\begin{aligned}
z[55:0] &= 2^{28} \cdot z[55:28] + z[27:0] \\
&= (2^{16} - 1) \cdot z[55:28] + z[27:0]
\end{aligned}
\tag{1}
$$

Essentially, any occurrence of 2^{28} is replaced by $2^{16} - 1$. The reduction can be repeated until the result is less than 2^{28}. The entire algorithm is illustrated in Algorithm 2. It only includes additions, subtractions and bit-wise operations without multiplications, so the latency and resource consumption are low.

Although the algorithm is highly dependent on the value of q, different values of q have similar algorithms. Specifically, the algorithms for other q still have the same kinds of operations as Algorithm 2, but they have different numbers of inputs in Line 1–2 and bit widths of the inputs in Line 1–5. For a given q, by customizing the number of inputs and bit widths, we can obtain low latency NTT cores using Algorithm 2. The latency and resource utilization for various q are evaluated in Sect. 5.4.

Note that only supporting q values with the modulus property does not make the NTT design less applicable. From the perspective of polynomial multiplications, the modulus q only needs to be a prime greater than the maximum coefficient of the input polynomial. There are many eligible prime q satisfying the property. For example, it can be verified that there are over 100 such q ranging from 14 bits to 60 bits. Therefore, for any given polynomial, we can easily choose the smallest q greater than all the coefficients.

4.3   Permutation Network

Parallel input data is required to be permuted before being processed by the subsequent NTT cores, since each computation stage has a different stride (S). As described in Algorithm 1, S can be formulated as $S_i = 2^{\log N - i - 1}$, where i is the computation stage and satisfies $0 \leq i < \log N$. The last stage has stride equal to 1, so no permutation is needed.

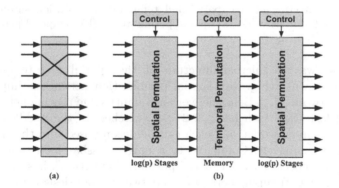

Fig. 3. Permutation network of the 16-point NTT with $p = 8$. (a) Direct connection permutation with $S = 2$. (b) Streaming permutation network.

Due to the fully unrolled design, each stage has a fixed permutation pattern and does not require dynamic re-configuration. Our architecture employs two types of permutation modules, as shown in Fig. 3. With $S < p$, later stages of the NTT computation, only spatial permutation is needed—shuffling data within the p inputs in the same cycle. We use a direct connection permutation with fixed wiring for these stages. This type of permutation module achieves low latency but cannot permute data in the time dimension across different input beats. For earlier stages, with $S \geq p$, streaming permutation network in [10] is used to re-arrange input data from different cycles in a streaming fashion. As shown in

Fig. 3(b), the datapath consists of two p-to-p spatial permutation networks and one temporal permutation network. Spatial permutation, reordering within the p data inputs in the same cycle, is realized using the classic Benes network [7]. In the middle, temporal permutation uses on-chip SRAM to rearrange data across different cycles. The control logic, which includes routing information and memory read/write addresses, are generated statically at IP core configuration time.

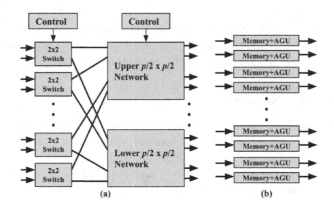

Fig. 4. Microarchitecture of the spatial and temporal permutation sub-network in streaming permutation network. (a) Spatial permutation. (b) Temporal permutation.

Figure 4 shows the microarchitecture of the spatial and temporal sub-networks. As shown in Fig. 4(a), spatial permutation network is implemented using Benes network [7]. A Benes network is a multi-stage routing network, with the first and last stage each has $p/2$ 2×2 switches. In the middle, there are two $p/2 \times p/2$ sub-networks, and each can be decomposed into the three-stage Benes network recursively. Compared to a naive crossbar interconnect, which requires $O(p^2)$ connections, each spatial permutation network has $(p/2) \cdot \log p$ 2 $\times$ 2 switches. Thus, streaming permutation network in our design asymptotically has lower complexity. Moreover, wiring length in the network does not change with permutation stride [9]. Each 2×2 switch has one control bit to route inputs to the upper or lower sub-networks respectively.

Figure 4(b) illustrates the design of temporal permutation network. It has p dual-port memory blocks and p address generation units (AGU). AGU produces the control signals and addresses to the memory block it connects to. Each AGU issues memory read and write addresses independently, thereby achieving temporal permutation across data received in different cycles.

As N data points stream through the interconnect with p per cycle, they are first permuted spatially by the first spatial permutation network, then the data are written into the p memory blocks. Finally, p data points with stride S_i are read out per cycle and permuted again by the second spatial permutation network. Since the architecture parameters – N and p – are fixed at run-time, the configurations for all the 2×2 switches and the AGUs can be determined offline and remain valid as long as N and p don't change. We store this information in FPGA's on-chip memory. More details about the routing algorithm can be found in [10].

5   Experiments and Results

5.1   Experimental Setup

In this section, we present a detailed evaluation of the proposed NTT architecture. All the designs are implemented using SystemVerilog on Virtex-7 XC7VX690 and XC7VX980 FPGA. The XC7VX690 device has 433,200 LUTs, 866,400 Flip-Flops and 1,470 BRAMs; the XC7VX980 device has 612,000 LUTs, 1,224,000 Flip-Flops and 1,500 BRAMs. Both devices have 3,600 DSPs. We use Xilinx Vivado 2020 to perform synthesis, place and route.

Our flexible and scalable architecture gives users a wide range of design options based on the application requirement and resource availability. We evaluated the performance and resource utilization of our designs by varying the polynomial degree (N) and data parallelism (p). We use $\langle x, y \rangle$ to denote a design with $N = x$ and $p = y$. Based on the widely used NTT parameters [2,3], we conducted experiments with NTT polynomial degree $N = 512, 1024, 2048$. We conducted a sweep over a range of available bandwidth to our designs by choosing p from 32 to 128. The metrics for performance analysis are NTT latency in μs and throughput in *polynomials transformed per second*. The performance metrics were measured by running post place and route simulations. The resource utilization is reported in terms of usage of LUTs, Flip-flops, BRAMs, and DSPs.

5.2   Performance Evaluation

Table 1 shows the measured NTT performance for various polynomial degrees (N) and data parallelism (p) on XC7VX980 FPGA. In this set of experiments, we fixed the modulus and the polynomial coefficients to 28 bits, which is commonly used by prior work [3,22]. Note that our architecture can easily support modulus with different bit width as described in Sect. 4.2. End-to-end latency from receiving the first input data to producing the last output coefficient is in the range of 0.57 μs to 1.29 μs. Higher polynomial degree incurs higher latency due to the additional NTT computation stages and also due to increased I/O time for a given p. Our architecture can achieve a high operating frequency between 210 MHz and 220 MHz for $p = 32$ and $p = 64$ designs. For a given N, $p = 128$ design consumes the least number of clock cycles. Due to the increased parallelism in each stage, majority of the NTT stages in $p = 128$ design uses fixed direct connection instead of streaming permutation network (Sect. 4.3), which reduces the latency in terms of clock cycles. However, $p = 128$ has many more NTT cores than $p = 32$ and $p = 64$ designs. It increases the resource consumption significantly and poses challenge during the place and route phase.

Table 1. Measured performance and resource utilization of complete NTT designs on XC7VX980 FPGA

Design	Latency	Throughput	LUT	FF	BRAM	DSP
$\langle 512, 32 \rangle$	0.66	13,750,000	82,498	89,688	64	576
$\langle 512, 64 \rangle$	0.57	26,625,000	161,703	171,472	96	1,152
$\langle 512, 128 \rangle$	0.60	43,000,000	303,040	316,920	156	2,304
$\langle 1024, 32 \rangle$	0.91	6,781,250	94,394	104,846	80	640
$\langle 1024, 64 \rangle$	0.76	13,125,000	187,283	204,162	128	1,280
$\langle 1024, 128 \rangle$	0.82	20,625,000	360,765	391,945	234	2,560
$\langle 2048, 32 \rangle$	1.29	3,390,625	107,293	120,718	96	704
$\langle 2048, 64 \rangle$	1.03	6,468,750	212,835	237,719	160	1408
$\langle 2048, 128 \rangle$	1.18	9,250,000	418,214	468,230	312	2,816

As a result, we observe that the frequency drops to 150 MHz - 170 MHz, and the overall latency for $p = 128$ is higher than $p = 64$ for the same value of N.

Sustained throughput in terms of *polynomials transformed per second* is also shown in Table 1. Different from the latency results, $p = 128$ designs perform the best from throughput perspective. Although frequency of the designs with $p = 128$ drops almost 25% compared with the other designs, $p = 128$ has 2× and 4× the processing rate compared to $p = 64$ and $p = 32$ respectively. The processing rate increase helps offset the frequency drop in this case. In the best-case scenario ($N = 512$), our architecture can transform more than 40 million *polynomials per second* in a streaming fashion.

The results on latency and throughput verify the scalability and flexibility of our architecture. Since our architecture is fully pipelined and can process p inputs per cycle, different data parallelism (p) requires different bandwidth to stream the input and the output coefficients. Table 2 shows the required I/O bandwidth in order to fully utilize the hardware pipeline when performing $N = 1024$ NTT on VX980 FPGA. p is the primary factor that influences the required bandwidth. Since p also means the design generates p output coefficients per cycle, the same amount of input bandwidth is needed on the output side. For $p = 128$, our design requires a sustained total bandwidth of 170 GB/s. This bandwidth can be made available if the polynomials are stored in on-chip SRAM (i.e., produced by other IP cores within the FPGA) or in high bandwidth external memory such as DDR4 or HBM. When adopting our architecture for different applications, p is an important parameter for bandwidth allocation.

5.3   Resource Utilization

The resource utilization of our implementations is reported in Table 1. Since each stage requires $p/2$ NTT cores, and there are $\log N$ stages in total, higher data parallelism (p) demands more hardware resources. On the other hand, with more parallel inputs per cycle, fewer stages need streaming permutation network

Table 2. I/O bandwidth required to fully utilize the proposed NTT accelerator with $N = 1024$, 28-bit input and output coefficients

Device	Data parallelism (p)	Input bandwidth [GB/s]	Output bandwidth [GB/s]
VX980	32	27.8	27.8
VX980	64	53.8	53.8
VX980	128	84.5	84.5

(Sect. 4.3), which helps reduce the resource consumption. We observe that the reduction in streaming permutation network is less than the increase in the resource demand with more NTT cores.

Overall, Table 1 shows that optimizing different metrics can lead to different design configurations. Given a polynomial degree N, one may choose to use $p = 64$ as the latency optimized design, $p = 128$ as the throughput optimized design, and $p = 32$ as the design that requires the least hardware resources (Sect. 5.2). An optimal design should be obtained by having a holistic view on the system requirements in terms of latency, throughput, resource availability and application requirements.

5.4   Evaluation of NTT Core and Streaming Permutation Network

NTT Core: As the modulus q affects the modulo algorithm in the NTT cores, we evaluate how the resource utilization and achieved frequency for NTT cores vary for various q. We performed experiments on a standalone NTT core for $\lceil \log q \rceil = 16, 27, 28$ and 32. The results are shown in Table 3.

Note that this experiment is performed on a single NTT core instead of the entire architecture, so the frequency shown in Table 3 are higher than the ones in the integrated experiments. Except for the 27-bit case, smaller q values consume less resources in terms of LUTs and FFs and achieve higher frequency. Note that $q = 2^{27} - 2^{21} + 1$ utilizes more resources than $q = 2^{28} - 2^{16} + 1$; this is because it needs to sum up 5 inputs for the first two steps, in contrast to the 3 inputs for the 28-bit case as shown in Line 1–2 of Algorithm 2. Due to the same reason, the 27-bit case has a lower frequency. However, the variance of the frequency for all the cases is not significant. Also, all of them have the same latency of 5 cycles, so the impact of q on the overall performance is minimal.

Streaming Permutation Network: We evaluate the latency and resource consumption of the streaming permutation network by synthesis, place and route each streaming permutation network in $\langle 1024, 32 \rangle$, $\langle 1024, 64 \rangle$, and $\langle 1024, 128 \rangle$ designs as a standalone module on VX980 FPGA. Input and output coefficients are 28-bit wide. Each streaming permutation network has two spatial permutation sub-networks, which has $\log p$ stages, and one temporal permutation sub-network. Figure 5 shows the resource utilization of streaming permutation network for $p = 32, 64, 128$ with permutation stride $S = 512$. For a given p, the

Table 3. FPGA resource utilization on VX690 for NTT core with various moduli

Modulus q	LUT	FF	DSP	Latency	Frequency
16 bits ($2^{16} - 2^{12} + 1$)	246	206	1	5 cycles	281 MHz
27 bits ($2^{27} - 2^{21} + 1$)	485	424	4	5 cycles	262 MHz
28 bits ($2^{28} - 2^{16} + 1$)	458	376	4	5 cycles	274 MHz
32 bits ($2^{32} - 2^{20} + 1$)	534	479	4	5 cycles	270 MHz

resource consumption is very similar for different S, therefore we omit the details for other strides in the interest of space. We observe close to linear increase in resource consumption with the increase in data parallelism. The majority of BRAM resources consumed by the streaming permutation network is due to the temporal permutation network. It requires p independent memory blocks, each of which is mapped to 1 BRAM18 resource configured as simple dual-port mode. Each BRAM18 memory stores at most $1024/p$ data inputs. The BRAM resource reported in the Fig. 5 is based on BRAM36 resource, each BRAM36 contains 2 BRAM18 blocks. As p increases to 128, BRAMs are also used to store the configuration tables in the spatial permutation sub-networks. As a result, it requires 14 extra BRAMs. LUTs are mainly used by configuration tables and the AGUs.

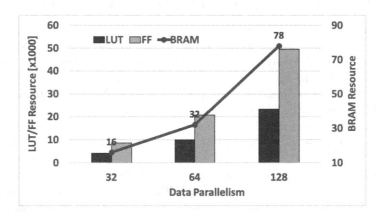

Fig. 5. Resource utilization for streaming permutation network $S = 512$ in $\langle 1024, 32 \rangle$, $\langle 1024, 64 \rangle$, and $\langle 1024, 128 \rangle$ designs. 28-bit per input and output coefficients are used.

Figure 6 shows the latency in cycles and frequency in MHz for each streaming permutation network, measured from the time the first input is received to the time the first output is produced. Latency is between 15 cycles to 30 cycles, depending on the values of p and S. The latency of spatial permutation subnetwork only grows logarithmically, as there are $\log p$ stages in each spatial permutation sub-network. For a given p, as S varies, the spatial permutation latency does not change. Temporal permutation latency increases with S because the hardware needs to wait for more data inputs before it can generate the first output. But temporal permutation resource consumption does not change much with different S. Good scalability is also observed with regard to frequency, we observe 340 MHz for $p = 32,64$ designs and 315 MHz for $p = 128$.

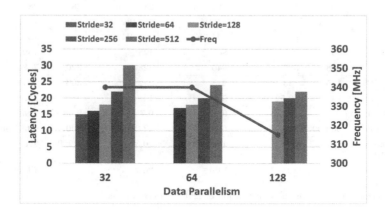

Fig. 6. Latency of streaming permutation network in $\langle 1024, 32 \rangle$ design. 28-bit per input and output coefficients are used.

5.5   Comparison with Prior Work

We compare our design with existing implementations on FPGA [22,25,29] in terms of the consumed resources, latency and throughput. Recall that the latency is the duration between receiving of the first input at an input port and generating of the last output at an output port. The throughput is the number of transformed polynomials per second. We use our performance results obtained on XC7VX690 FPGA, which is the same device used in [22]. Table 4 shows the comparison.

Both designs in [22,29] fold all the stages and reuse the same set of processing elements for all the stages. Without unrolling all the stages, this leads to much lower throughput than ours. Complex routing and arbitration logic is needed between NTT cores and intermediate data buffer. For modulo arithmetic, their designs offer more flexibility than ours by supporting all moduli with a general modular multiplication design. However, this design choice requires more DSPs per NTT core and has higher latency.

In [29], the authors only reported resources and performance for $N = 4096$ and $\lceil \log q \rceil = 52$ with at most 32 NTT cores on Intel FPGAs. For a fair comparison, we compute the utilization of Xilinx DSPs for their NTT core for $\lceil \log q \rceil = 28$. According to Algorithm 1 in [29], their NTT core includes three 30×30 partial multiplications, two of which only output lower 30 bits and one of which outputs higher 30 bits. The former can be implemented by three 15×15 multiplications and the latter needs four 15×15 multiplications. Thus, the entire

Table 4. Comparison with prior work

Design	[22]	[25]	This paper $p = 32$	This paper $p = 64$	[29][a]	This paper $p = 32$
Platform	VX690	Zynq UltraScale+	VX690	VX690	VX690	VX690
N	1024	1024	1024	1024	4096	4096
$\lceil \log q \rceil$	28	16	28	28	28	28
LUT	132K	3K	94.4K	187.2K	–	117.3K
FF	59K	3K	104.5K	205.5K	–	135.2K
BRAM	96	29	80	128	–	189
DSP	448	58	640	1280	320	768
Freq. [MHz]	125	183	215	212	300	224
Energy [μJ]	–	12.52	9.4	14	–	22.9
Latency [μs]	2	101.84	0.92	0.75	2.56	1.99
Throughput	500,000	98,193	6,718,750	13,250,000	390,625	1,687,500
Throughput per DSP	1,116	1,693	10,498	10,352	1,220	2,197
Throughput per LUT	3.78	32.7	71.17	70.77	–	14.38

[a] The performance and resource utilization of [29] are extrapolated.

NTT core includes ten 15×15 multiplications, which needs 10 DSPs according to [34]. We also verified this by actually implementing their NTT core on Xilinx VX690. We choose the largest design with 32 NTT cores from [29]. We assume that their design can still achieve 300 MHz frequency as they reported, which is an optimistic upper bound. The estimated latency, throughput and throughput per DSP are shown in the last two columns of Table 4. Our design for $N = 4096$ with $p = 32$ achieves 4.32× improvement in throughput, 1.80× improvement in throughput per DSP and 1.29× improvement in latency compared with the design in [29].

The design in [22] has the same N and $\lceil \log q \rceil$ as our sample design, and they also use VX690 FPGA as the target platform. Even though our architecture fully unrolls all the NTT stages, our design with $p = 32$ still has similar hardware cost compared with theirs. This is mainly due to the resource-efficient NTT cores in our architecture. We can achieve superior performance due to increased FPGA frequency and fully pipelined design. Our design with $p = 32$ achieves 2.17× improvement in latency and 9.41× in throughput per DSP compared with the design in [22].

The design in [25] fully unrolls and pipelines all the $\log N$ stages. We calculate their throughput assuming their systolic array is fully pipelined. Note that this gives an upper bound on their throughput. Different from our approach, data communication complexity is greatly simplified in their design as each systolic processing element only processes two coefficients per cycle in each NTT stage. This can also lead to under-utilization of I/O bandwidth. Their design can be mapped to our architecture by setting $p = 2$. The performance of their design is reduced significantly as the amount of parallelism is small. However, their design consumes very small amount of resources, which is beneficial for devices with limited resources or power constraints.

In addition to the prior work shown in Table 4, a ReRAM-based ASIC architecture is proposed in [24] to accelerate NTT. It performs fine-grained computations using the PIM technology. The architecture consumes very low energy [24]. The simulated design runs at 910 MHz. This requires a sustained I/O bandwidth of 2.3 GB/s for $N = 1024$. However, the arithmetic operation in each stage requires $O(\log^2 q)$ cycles. In the VLSI model [33], the time complexity (latency) is $O(\log N \log^2 q)$ and the area is $O(N \log N \log q + N^2)$. The second term of the area is for the interconnection between stages. For $N = 1024$ and $\lceil \log q \rceil = 16$, the design simulation in [24] shows latency of 83.12 µs and throughput of 553 thousand transforms per second. Note that for $N = 1024$ and $\lceil \log q \rceil = 28$, our design with $p = 32$ has latency of 0.92 µs and throughput of 6.7 million transforms per second.

6   Conclusion

In this paper, we designed an FPGA architecture for NTT with configurable parameters including polynomial degree, modulus and data parallelism. We utilized streaming permutation network as interconnection between each stage to reduce complexity. We also developed a low-latency design for modulo operations. The experiments for polynomials of degree 4096 showed that our design achieves 4.32× throughput compared with the state-of-the-art design on FPGA while also improving the latency by 1.29×. Thus, our design can be used to implement both high throughput NTT intensive workloads as well as low latency NTT inference workloads such as privacy preserving ML inference.

In the future, we will make our design more flexible by allowing reconfiguration of polynomials with variable degrees and moduli at runtime. Also, we will develop a design space exploration tool for trade-off analysis on performance, resource consumption and application requirements.

Acknowledgement. This work has been sponsored by the U.S. National Science Foundation under grant numbers OAC-1911229 and CNS-2009057. Equipment grant by Xilinx is greatly appreciated.

References

1. Aho, A.V., Hopcroft, J.E.: The Design and Analysis of Computer Algorithms. Pearson Education India (1974)
2. Albrecht, M., et al.: Homomorphic encryption security standard. Tech. rep. (2018)
3. Alkim, E., Barreto, P.S.L.M., Bindel, N., Kramer, J., Longa, P., Ricardini, J.E.: The lattice-based digital signature scheme qTESLA. In: ACNS (2020)
4. Alkim, E., Ducas, L., Pöppelmann, T., Schwabe, P.: Post-quantum key exchange: a new hope. In: USENIX SEC (2016)
5. Banerjee, U., Ukyab, T.S., Chandrakasan, A.P.: Sapphire: a configurable crypto-processor for post-quantum lattice-based protocols. In: TCHES (2019)

6. Barrett, P.: Implementing the Rivest Shamir and Adleman public key encryption algorithm on a standard digital signal processor. In: CRYPTO 1986 (1987)
7. Beneš, V.E.: Optimal rearrangeable multistage connecting networks. Bell Syst. Tech. J. **43**(4), 1641–1656 (1964)
8. Brakerski, Z., Gentry, C., Vaikuntanathan, V.: (Leveled) fully homomorphic encryption without bootstrapping. In: ITCS (2012)
9. Chen, R., Park, N., Prasanna, V.K.: High throughput energy efficient parallel FFT architecture on FPGAs. In: HPEC (2013)
10. Chen, R., Prasanna, V.K.: Automatic generation of high throughput energy efficient streaming architectures for arbitrary fixed permutations. In: FPL (2015)
11. Chen, R., Le, H., Prasanna, V.K.: Energy efficient parameterized fft architecture. In: 23rd International Conference on Field programmable Logic and Applications, pp. 1–7. IEEE (2013)
12. Cheon, J.H., Han, K., Kim, A., Kim, M., Song, Y.: A full RNS variant of approximate homomorphic encryption. In: Selected Areas in Cryptography - SAC (2018)
13. Chiou, D.: The microsoft catapult project. In: IISWC (2017)
14. Cooley, J.W., Tukey, J.W.: An algorithm for the machine calculation of complex Fourier series. Math. Comput. **19**, 297–301 (1965)
15. Dowlin, N., Gilad-Bachrach, R., Laine, K., Lauter, K., Naehrig, M., Wernsing, J.: CryptoNets: applying neural networks to encrypted data with high throughput and accuracy. Tech. Rep. MSR-TR-2016-3 (2016)
16. Fan, J., Vercauteren, F.: Somewhat practical fully homomorphic encryption. Cryptology ePrint Archive, Report 2012/144 (2012)
17. Gentry, C.: Fully homomorphic encryption using ideal lattices. In: STOC (2009)
18. Intel: Stratix 10 MX FPGAs. https://www.intel.com/content/www/us/en/products/programmable/sip/stratix-10-mx.html
19. Kim, S., Jung, W., Park, J., Ahn, J.: Accelerating number theoretic transformations for bootstrappable homomorphic encryption on GPUS. In: IEEE International Symposium on Workload Characterization (IISWC), pp. 264–275. IEEE Computer Society, Los Alamitos (2020)
20. Lee, W.K., Akleylek, S., Yap, W.S., Goi, B.M.: Accelerating number theoretic transform in GPU platform for qTESLA scheme. In: ISPEC (2019)
21. Longa, P., Naehrig, M.: Speeding up the number theoretic transform for faster ideal lattice-based cryptography. In: Cryptology and Network Security (2016)
22. Mert, A.C., Karabulut, E., Öztürk, E., Savaş, E., Becchi, M., Aysu, A.: A flexible and scalable NTT hardware: applications from homomorphically encrypted deep learning to post-quantum cryptography. In: DATE (2020)
23. Montgomery, P.L.: Modular multiplication without trial division. Math. Comput. **44**, 519–521 (1985)
24. Nejatollahi, H., Gupta, S., Imani, M., Rosing, T.S., Cammarota, R., Dutt, N.: CryptoPIM: in-memory acceleration for lattice-based cryptographic hardware. In: DAC (2020)
25. Nejatollahi, H., Shahhosseini, S., Cammarota, R., Dutt, N.: Exploring energy efficient quantum-resistant signal processing using array processors. In: ICASSP (2020)
26. Nguyen, D.T., Dang, V.B., Gaj, K.: A high-level synthesis approach to the software/hardware codesign of NTT-based post-quantum cryptography algorithms. In: ICFPT (2019)
27. Putnam, A., et al.: A reconfigurable fabric for accelerating large-scale datacenter services. In: ISCA (2014)

28. Reagen, B., et al.: Cheetah: optimizing and accelerating homomorphic encryption for private inference. In: IEEE International Symposium on High-Performance Computer Architecture (HPCA), pp. 26–39. IEEE (2020)
29. Riazi, M.S., Laine, K., Pelton, B., Dai, W.: HEAX: an architecture for computing on encrypted data. In: ASPLOS (2020)
30. Seiler, G.: Faster AVX2 optimized NTT multiplication for Ring-LWE lattice cryptography. report 2018/039 (2018)
31. Serpanos, D.N., Wolf, T.: Architecture of Network Systems (2011)
32. Sinha Roy, S., Turan, F., Jarvinen, K., Vercauteren, F., Verbauwhede, I.: Fpga-based high-performance parallel architecture for homomorphic computing on encrypted data. In: HPCA (2019)
33. Ullma, J.D.: Computational Aspects of VLSI (1984)
34. Xilinx: 7 Series FPGAs Data Sheet: Overview. https://www.xilinx.com/support/documentation/data_sheets/ds180_7Series_Overview.pdf
35. Xilinx: Xilinx UltraScale+ HBM FPGAs. https://www.xilinx.com/products/silicon-devices/fpga/virtex-ultrascale-plus-hbm.html
36. Yu, C.L., Kim, J.S., Deng, L., Kestur, S., Narayanan, V., Chakrabarti, C.: FPGA architecture for 2D discrete fourier transform based on 2d decomposition for large-sized data. J. Signal Process. Syst. **64**(1), 109–122 (2011)
37. Zhang, N., Yang, B., Chen, C., Yin, S., Wei, S., Liu, L.: Highly efficient architecture of NewHope-NIST on FPGA using low-complexity NTT/INTT. In: TCHES (2020)

Designing a ROCm-Aware MPI Library for AMD GPUs: Early Experiences

Kawthar Shafie Khorassani, Jahanzeb Hashmi^(✉), Ching-Hsiang Chu^(✉), Chen-Chun Chen^(✉), Hari Subramoni^(✉), and Dhabaleswar K. Panda^(✉)

The Ohio State University, Columbus, OH 43210, USA
{shafiekhorassani.1,hashmi.29,chu.368,chen.10252}@osu.edu,
{subramon,panda}@cse.ohio-state.edu

Abstract. Due to the emergence of AMD GPUs and their adoption in upcoming exascale systems (e.g. Frontier), it is pertinent to have scientific applications and communication middlewares ported and optimized for these systems. Radeon Open Compute (ROCm) platform is an open-source suite of libraries tailored towards writing high-performance software for AMD GPUs. GPU-aware MPI, has been the de-facto standard for accelerating HPC applications on GPU clusters. The state-of-the-art GPU-aware MPI libraries have evolved over the years to support NVIDIA CUDA platforms. Due to the recent emergence of AMD GPUs, it is equally important to add support for AMD ROCm platforms. Existing MPI libraries do not have native support for ROCm-aware communication. In this paper, we take up the challenge of designing a ROCm-aware MPI runtime within the MVAPICH2-GDR library. We design an abstract communication layer to interface with CUDA and ROCm runtimes. We exploit hardware features such as PeerDirect, ROCm IPC, and large-BAR mapped memory to orchestrate efficient GPU-based communication. We further augment these mechanisms by designing software-based schemes yielding optimized communication performance. We evaluate the performance of MPI-level point-to-point and collective operations with our proposed ROCm-aware MPI Library and Open MPI with UCX on a cluster of AMD GPUs. We demonstrate 3–6× and 2× higher bandwidth for intra- and inter-node communication, respectively. With the rocHPCG application, we demonstrate approximately 2.2× higher GFLOPs/s. To the best of our knowledge, this is the first research work that studies the tradeoffs involved in designing a ROCm-aware MPI library for AMD GPUs.

Keywords: ROCm · AMD GPUs · MPI

1 Introduction

Modern High-Performance Computing (HPC) systems are equipped with state-of-the-art accelerators including Graphics Processing Units (GPUs).

This research is supported in part by NSF grants #1818253, #1854828, #1931537, #2007991, #2018627, and XRAC grant #NCR-130002.

ⓒ Springer Nature Switzerland AG 2021
B. L. Chamberlain et al. (Eds.): ISC High Performance 2021, LNCS 12728, pp. 118–136, 2021.
https://doi.org/10.1007/978-3-030-78713-4_7

Such systems are currently fueling the next generation of Artificial Intelligence (AI) and scientific applications. This trend is timely to avert the challenges presented by the end of Moore's law [15], which sustained performance growth for the last several decades. The use of GPUs is prevalent in many modern HPC and cloud systems for driving scientific applications and Machine Learning workloads. However, it is important to innovate further by evolving and expanding the support provided by GPUs to meet the ever-increasing computational requirements of next-generation applications.

The landscape of accelerator-based computing is currently dominated by NVIDIA GPUs. However, other alternatives like Radeon Instinct devices (GPUs) from AMD and Xe GPU from Intel have recently started emerging. In particular, AMD GPUs offer a promising platform that has been adopted by upcoming next-generation exascale systems such as Frontier [3] and El Capitan [6]. In addition to these up-and-coming systems, a current compute platform, the Corona cluster at Lawrence Livermore National Laboratory [2], is also equipped with 291 nodes consisting of AMD Mi50 and AMD Mi60 GPUs. Of these nodes, 123 of them are equipped with AMD EPYC 7002 series CPU nodes, with each node consisting of 8 AMD Radeon Instinct MI50 GPU accelerators.

Prior to the emergence of AMD GPUs, NVIDIA GPU platforms have been the *defacto* standard for exploiting GPUs within applications for communication and computation tasks. NVIDIA GPUs rely on NVIDIAs in-house toolkit called Compute Unified Device Architecture (CUDA) to support GPU-accelerated high-performance applications. In the past, applications wanting to use AMD GPUs often had to rely on the OpenCL library, which made it difficult to port applications while CUDA as a programming system was much more developed. Recent efforts by AMD has resulted in Radeon Open Compute (ROCm) software stacks that offer seamless support for high-performance libraries required for efficient computation and communication on modern AMD GPU hardware. ROCm is an open-source toolkit provided by AMD consisting of libraries, profilers, and APIs used in the development of high-performance software for AMD GPUs. An important feature offered by ROCm is HIP [14]—a C++ Runtime API and kernel language that allows developers to create portable applications for AMD and NVIDIA GPUs. In most cases, HIP offers one-to-one mappings of API calls between CUDA and ROCm and provides tools for automatic translation from CUDA to HIP code. This source-to-source translation, also referred to as *hipification*, has helped in seamlessly porting application codes to AMD hardware.

The Message Passing Interface (MPI) standard, is considered a *defacto* API for writing parallel programs on modern HPC systems. In order to accelerate large-scale high-performance applications on GPU clusters, GPU-aware MPI has been the widely adopted programming model in use. The state-of-the-art MPI libraries have evolved over the years to incorporate GPU-aware communication support at the MPI layer. This is also referred to as CUDA-aware MPI as it entails support for NVIDIA CUDA platforms due to the dominance of NVIDIA GPUs in the hardware configuration of GPU-enhanced clusters. The emergence of AMD GPUs and their adoption in upcoming exascale systems makes it important to have support for AMD ROCm platforms in modern MPI libraries. Current MPI implementations do not have native support for direct communication between device resident data on AMD GPUs or ROCm-aware communication. In order to accelerate scientific applications, Machine Learning workloads, and to have parallel applications ready to scale on next-generation exascale systems with AMD GPU hardware configurations, it is crucial to have the appropriate support at the middleware level by designing a ROCm-aware MPI runtime.

In this paper, our goal is to design a ROCM-aware MPI runtime which brings about the following challenges: 1) How can we design an abstract and extensible communication layer for MPI libraries that interfaces with both the CUDA and the ROCm run-times? **2)** Can we appropriately make use of the various features supported by ROCm including ROCm IPC, ROCm-RDMA (PeerDirect), etc., and identify the ranges in which each of these features is optimal for data transfer? **3)** How can we utilize unified memory and AMD's Large Bar mapped memory feature to optimize the performance of MPI operations?

1.1   Contributions

In this paper, we design a ROCm-aware implementation of MPI developed over MVAPICH2-GDR by delving into the details and challenges of utilizing existing hardware and software. The challenge here is to properly extend the native support within the MPI library to run with ROCm on AMD GPUs. We design a communication layer that is able to interface with both CUDA for NVIDIA GPUs and ROCm for AMD GPUs and derive MPI operations seamlessly. We evaluate the proposed ROCm-aware MPI implementation against Open MPI with UCX as the ROCm-aware communication backed on the Corona Cluster at the benchmark-level and with ROCm-enabled applications. In summary, the paper incorporates the following contributions:

- Design an abstract and extensible communication layer in the MPI runtime to interface with both CUDA and ROCm run-times to drive MPI communication.
- Identify challenges with utilizing existing hardware and software configurations for enabling ROCm-aware MPI communication.
- Propose new designs in the MPI library to exploit AMD GPUs using ROCm libraries and features e.g., ROCm PeerDirect, ROCm IPC, and unified memory.
- Incorporate tuning based selection of ROCm designs for MPI protocols (e.g., eager vs. rendezvous) for appropriate message ranges.
- Comprehensive evaluation of MPI point-to-point and collective operations for GPU resident data and comparing our proposed ROCm-aware MPI implementation against state-of-the-art communication libraries (Open MPI + UCX).

– Evaluate the efficacy of our proposed ROCm-aware MPI using various applications such as a 3DStencil, and HPCG and compare the performance against
Open MPI + UCX on the LLNL Corona cluster.

**To the best of our knowledge, this is the first research work that
studies and analyzes the tradeoffs involved in designing a ROCm-
aware MPI library for AMD GPUs.**

2 Background

2.1 Radeon Open Compute (ROCm)

ROCm [5] is an open-source software platform tailored towards high-performance
computing and Machine Learning on AMD GPUs. It consists of tools for development on GPUs, APIs, and drivers that support AMD GPUs. ROCm also has
support for various programming models such as OpenMP, OpenCL, and HIP.
It has recently been integrated with many scientific applications such as HPCG,
NAMD, GRID, and GROMACS and Machine Learning frameworks including
TensorFlow, Pytorch, RAJA, and Kokkos.

2.2 ROCm Remote Direct Memory Access (RDMA)

ROCm RDMA enables third-party devices such as the Mellanox Infiniband HCA
device to have a direct peer-to-peer data path with GPU memory. This removes
CPU intervention from communications between GPUs across the network, further enhancing communication latency between GPU-GPU transfers.

2.3 Inter-Process Communication (IPC)

IPC is used to address overheads associated with data transfer between GPUs
within a node. The ROCm platform has support for the IPC interface allowing a
process to expose its GPU buffer to a remote process, optimizing the movement
of data between GPUs. This allows for directly implementing an MPI call over
GPU device memory. A remote process could directly call *deviceMemCpy* on the
exposed IPC handle from the sender process leading to optimized data transfer
between GPUs.

2.4 Message Passing Interface (MPI)

The Message Passing Interface (MPI) is a programming paradigm used to enable
communication amongst processes for parallel applications. There are multiple
communication primitives within MPI including one-sided, point-to-point, and
collective operations. One-sided communication, also referred to as remote memory access (RMA), involves one process communicating with another without
any intervention from the remote process. A process sends data to a receiving process without requiring synchronization, eliminating this step from the

data transfer process. Point-to-point operations involve direct communication between a sender process and a receiver process, and unlike the non-blocking nature of one-sided communication, it requires some synchronization between the two processes involved. Collective communication refers to multiple processes communicating with one or many processes.

In this work, we focus on point-to-point and collective communication and what factors to consider when making these operations ROCm-aware. Through CUDA-aware MPI functionality in various MPI libraries such as MVAPICH2-GDR [16] and Open MPI [11], these operations can be run on NVIDIA GPUs. They utilize various schemes to optimize and enhance the GPU-based communication through GPUDirect RDMA and IPC. In order to extend these operations to run on AMD GPUs, we require a ROCm-aware implementation of MPI. We evaluate Open MPI + Unified Communication X (UCX) [7] against our proposed development, where UCX is used as the ROCm-aware communication backend to support AMD GPU runs since Open MPI is not a stand-alone ROCm-aware MPI library.

2.5   Protocols for High-Performance Communication in MPI

Figures 1(b) and 1(b) depict how the eager and rendezvous protocol respectively are typically implemented. The eager protocol consists of four steps—1) copying the data from the application buffer to buffers internal to the MPI library, 2) initiating the data transfer to the remote process, 3) detecting the reception of data in buffers internal to the MPI library and, 4) copying the data back to the application buffer. With most high-performance networks like InfiniBand, the network itself takes care of the actual data transfer. Thus, initiating the data transfer at the sender and detecting the reception of the data at the receiver are low overhead tasks. So, apart from the time to transfer data over the network, the main costs involved in an eager transfer are the memory copies at the sender/receiver. Note that steps #1 and #2 happen inside the send function call itself. With a rendezvous protocol on the other hand (Fig. 1(b)), MPI designers take advantage of the RDMA feature that high-performance interconnects like InfiniBand offers and transfers data directly from the source application buffer to the target application buffer (with the appropriate exchange of control information), thereby avoiding the extra large memory copies from the application buffer to internal communication buffers within the library.

3   Designing and Implementation of ROCm-Aware MPI

3.1   Overview of Technologies Offered by NVIDIA and AMD for GPU Based Communication

As discussed earlier, the state-of-the-art GPU-aware MPI libraries have supported NVIDIA GPUs and hence, the communication designs employed by these MPI libraries were highly CUDA specific. For example, two popular GPU-aware

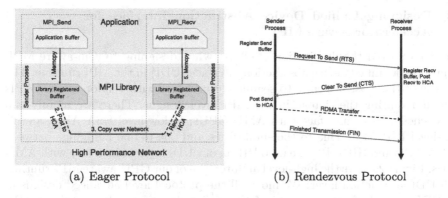

(a) Eager Protocol   (b) Rendezvous Protocol

Fig. 1. Point-to-point communication protocols in MPI

MPI libraries MVAPICH2-GDR and Open MPI supported NVIDIA's GPUDirect technology for communicating GPU resident data over RDMA networks. However, with the newer AMD GPU and ROCm stacks offering similar technologies, the MPI libraries have to go through the same route by evaluating various technologies offered by ROCm. We summarize the key communication technologies offered by both the vendors and their similarities/differences in Table 1 below:

Table 1. Similarities and differences between CUDA and ROCm communication features used by GPU-aware MPI libraries

	Technology		Dependency	
	NVIDIA	AMD	NVIDIA	AMD
RDMA Support	GPUDirect RDMA	ROCmRDMA (PeerDirect)	nv_peer_mem Kernel Module	ROCm Driver (no kernel module)
Peer-to-peer	CUDA IPC	ROCm IPC	CUDA Runtime	ROCr Runtime
Mapped Copy	GDRCopy BAR1	Large BAR Feature	GDRCopy Kernel Module	ROCm Driver (no kernel module)

As demonstrated, most of the features provided by AMD are integrated into the ROCm driver or the ROCr runtime while NVIDIA often requires separate modules to enable features like GDRCopy and GPUDirect RDMA. The unified package offered by AMD is advantageous since most HPC centric clusters often do not install separate kernel modules due to security concerns.

3.2   Designing Unified Device Abstraction Interface for Accelerator-Aware MPI

In order to avoid the duplication of efforts when designing ROCm-aware MPI, we propose a unified device abstraction interface (UDI) in the MPI runtime. The purpose of this abstraction is to seamlessly interface with vendor-specific APIs without requiring the change in the MPI level designs. There are mainly two approaches used to interface with AMD GPUs; 1) low-level HSA APIs, and 2) high-level HIP APIs. Due to the similarities and one-to-one mappings between CUDA APIs and HIP APIs, we used HIP in our UDI layer to interface with AMD GPUs. Figure 2 shows the high-level architecture of our GPU-aware MPI runtime with UDI abstraction layer. We move all the protocol level advanced designs in the UDI layer. For instance, one of the major designs employed by our MPI library for peer-to-peer IPC transfers is to amortize the overheads of registering handles by caching the registered handles for subsequent communications. By moving this design to UDI, we avoid redundancy and the same designs are used for both CUDA IPC as well as ROCm IPC. As later shown in Fig. 4 these designs lead to significant performance improvement for both CUDA-aware and ROCm-aware MPI communication.

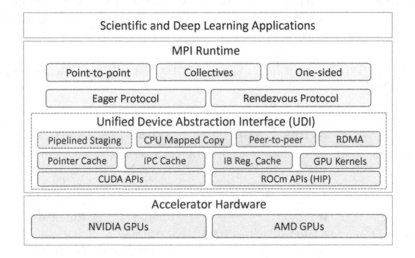

Fig. 2. A high-level overview of the proposed designs in accelerator-aware MPI. We propose a Unified Device abstraction Interface (UDI) layer in MPI that abstracts the common operations in a GPU-aware MPI runtime. The modular design makes it easy to interface with vendor-specific backend implementations such as CUDA or ROCm (HIP) APIs.

3.3   PeerDirect

Network adapters can directly access device-resident data through ROCm-RDMA, enabling direct memory access for 3rd party PCIe devices. For AMD

GPUs, ROCmRDMA, or PeerDirect support, is available through the ROCm driver. AMD GPUs large-bar configuration allows for the entire GPU memory to be exposed, enabling peer-to-peer DMA access. The ROCm-aware PeerDirect approach in the proposed ROCm-aware MPI library works with the rendezvous protocol for data transfer. The source process and the remote process exchange the addresses of their buffers. An RDMA operation is then used to issue the data transfer. A registration cache is used here to keep a record of the reused buffers to reduce the overhead of repeated registration of GPU memory.

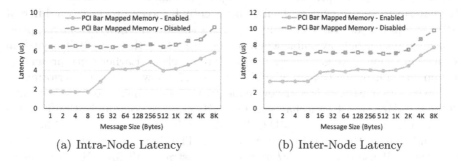

(a) Intra-Node Latency   (b) Inter-Node Latency

Fig. 3. Utilizing PCI bar mapped memory for small message inter-node and intra-node communication

3.4   CPU-Driven GPU Mapped Memory Copy Based Design

In order to enhance small message performance on NVIDIA GPUs, GDRCOPY, a low-overhead CPU driven copy that allows for the CPU to map the GPU memory, is used. It utilizes a specific API and the GDRCopy kernel module to pin the device buffer using PCI BAR1 memory. The host CPU treats this mapped memory just like any other host memory and derives the communication. On AMD GPUs, no such kernel module is required, and instead, it offers support for Large BAR (Base Address Register) feature that maps entire GPU memory to host address space. We exploit large Bar features to provide similar small message performance enhancements. In Fig. 3, we see the impact of utilizing the mapped copy through the Large BAR feature of AMD GPUs by evaluating the performance difference when it is enabled compared to when it is disabled. In the small message range where these designs would have the most impact between the range of 1B to 8 KB, we see up to 3× lower latency in utilizing the PCI Bar Mapped Memory copy for intra-node point-to-point communication and up to 2× better performance for inter-node communication. We evaluate the impact of the added PCI Bar Mapped Memory copy on intra-node and inter-node point-to-point performance in Fig. 5(a) and Fig. 6(a), respectively.

3.5   ROCm IPC Based Design

The simplest approach to designing a rendezvous based transfer for large message sizes between GPUs on a node would be to implement a staging based design where the data transfer involves staging to the host memory. The source would copy data from the device to the shared host memory region between the two processes, and the destination would then copy from the host to its device memory. This would incur an added cost for large message sizes where the performance would be impacted by the overhead of these additional copies. Inter-Process Communication (IPC) provides a peer-to-peer mechanism that allows for direct MPI calls over device memory, facilitating a copy between processes on different GPUs within a node, while entirely bypassing the host memory. However, peer-to-peer support is only available when two devices share the same PCIe switch in the system topology (e.g., devices are the same socket). Earlier work presenting the benefits of utilizing IPC on NVIDIA GPUs [17] shows enhanced performance in allowing direct MPI calls over device memory for large message sizes. We apply IPC-based data transfer mechanisms for ROCm-aware communication through enabling direct access to the AMD GPU memory between processes on the same node and sharing the same PCI root complex. The design is detailed as follows: A process will use $deviceIPCMemHandle$ (abstract call in UDI) to generate an IPC handle on its device buffer and send this handle to the remote process. This will expose its device buffer, allowing for it to be mapped by the remote process into its own address space and then directly issue a $deviceMemCpy$ call on the addressable buffer. In utilizing ROCm IPC with the rendezvous protocol, this exchange happens during the handshake between the source process and the remote process. When the source is sending a Request to Send (RTS) message, it will also exchange the IPC handle generated. The remote process will map this handle and directly copy from the device memory of the source.

Historically, IPC usage has shown overhead due to generating and exchanging IPC handles repeatedly. This added cost makes the performance gain, that would be obtained through bypassing host memory, negligible. In order to eliminate this added overhead and to demonstrate benefit from the IPC designs, we utilize an IPC Cache in the proposed ROCm-aware MPI. This implements caching of IPC handles at the source and destination, allowing for direct data movement whenever a cache hit is encountered on the handle. This IPC cache exists in the UDI layer where it is utilized for the ROCm run-time in order to have the handles cached for subsequent communication. Figure 4(a) demonstrates the difference in latency for large message intra-node point-to-point communication between 128 KB and 4 MB with IPC cache enabled compared to IPC cache disabled. We see 2–3× lower latency when IPC cache is enabled and approximately 10× higher bandwidth (Fig. 4(b)).

We integrate the ROCm-IPC design into the proposed ROCm-aware MPI library to improve intra-node performance for data transfer between GPUs on the same node. We evaluate designs for large message ranges to determine the appropriate range of use on AMD GPUs. We present intra-node latency, bandwidth, and bi-directional bandwidth with ROCm-IPC being used for message sizes > 8 KB in Fig. 5.

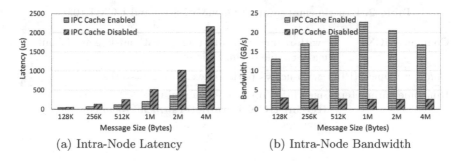

(a) Intra-Node Latency   (b) Intra-Node Bandwidth

Fig. 4. Utilizing IPC cache for large message intra-node communication

4 Performance Evaluation

In this section, we detail the hardware and software configurations of the compute platform used for the evaluation. We also present a detailed evaluation of the proposed ROCm-aware MPI implementation against Open MPI 4.1.0 + UCX 1.10.0 (details of the configuration provided in Table 2). We report a comparison of latency, bandwidth, and bi-directional bandwidth for MPI point-to-point operations and MPI collective operations. We then delve into the application level benchmarks by evaluating hipified versions of 3D Stencil, and HPCG (rocHPCG) with ROCm support.

4.1 Experimental Setup

The evaluation was conducted on the **Corona Cluster**, deployed at Lawrence Livermore National Laboratory [2]. It consists of 291 AMD EPYC 7002 series CPU nodes: 82 nodes are equipped with 4 MI50 AMD GPUs per node, 82 nodes have 4 MI60 AMD GPUs per node, and 123 nodes consisting of 8 MI50 AMD GPUs per node. The MI50 AMD GPUs have 32 GB HBM, with single-precision peak theoretical floating-point performance of up 13.3 teraFLOPS.

Each node is equipped with dual-socket Mellanox IB HDR-200, with AMD EPYC 7402 24-Core Processor running Mellanox OFED 5.0, and ROCm version 4.1.0. In our evaluation, we utilized the nodes with 8 MI50 GPUs per node to evaluate the performance of dense GPU nodes.

Peak Achievable Performance of Interconnects–To evaluate the performance of the proposed ROCm-aware MPI and OpenMPI + UCX compared to the peak achievable performance, we utilized the following tests:

- rocm_bandwidth_test: We utilized this test to evaluate the performance between two GPUs on a node (displays the peak achievable bandwidth by performing a uni/bi-directional copy involving the two devices [1]).
- Infiniband Perftest: We utilized the *ib_read_bw* and *ib_read_lat* provided by the Infiniband Perftest package to measure the peak achievable bandwidth and minimum achievable latency of communicating data across two nodes [4].

Table 2. Experimental setup of OpenMPI 4.1.0 and UCX 1.10.0

Configure UCX	–with-rocm=<path-to-rocm>–without-knem–without-cuda–enable-optimizations
Configure OpenMPI	–with-ucx=<path-to-ucx>–without-verbs
Run-time parameters	-mca btl "^openib" -mca pml ucx **ROCm UCX Parameters:** rocm, rocm_copy, rocm_ipc

4.2   Micro-Benchmark Evaluation

In order to develop a comprehensive evaluation of various point-to-point and collective MPI operations, we utilized the OSU Micro-Benchmarks (OMB) suite version 5.7 that has support for AMD GPUs via the HIP interface. These micro-benchmarks are used in evaluating MPI operations across different MPI libraries on the CPU and support for CUDA-aware operations on the GPU for point-to-point, one-sided, and collective communication. The metrics reported represent measures of latency, bandwidth, or bi-directional bandwidth. We utilize OMB with added support for ROCm-aware MPI operations (through HIP) to evaluate our proposed ROCm-aware MPI implementation against Open MPI + UCX.

Intra-Node Point-to-Point—We evaluate the most common configuration for binding MPI processes to GPUs for an MPI+GPU run where one MPI process utilizes a single GPU. We evaluate intra-node point-to-point communication with two processes bound to two GPUs on the same node. Figure 5 depicts the results of evaluating this on MI50 GPUs on the Corona system for latency, bandwidth, and bi-directional bandwidth performance. Two GPUs on the same socket within the node (i.e. GPU 0 and GPU 1) share the same PCIe switch and can have peer-to-peer access enabled. The proposed ROCm-aware MPI demonstrates as low as 1.74 μs latency (Fig. 4(a)) for 8 Bytes. For small message intra-node communication, we utilize the PCI Bar Mapped Memory approach proposed in Sect. 3.4 in order to obtain the latency presented. As demonstrated in Fig. 3(a), within the range of 1 B to 8 KB we see between 16–66% benefit based on message size by enabling PCI Bar Mapped Memory for this range as opposed to disabling it. This PCI Bar Mapped Memory approach improves the latency of the proposed ROCm-aware MPI from ~6.54 μs to ~1.80 μs within the range of 1 B to 16 Bytes. Within the range of 128 Bytes to 8 KB, we see a vast performance difference between the proposed ROCm-aware MPI and Open MPI + UCX. This gap in performance between the two MPI libraries can be attributed to the use of Loopback designs in conjunction with the PCI Bar Mapped Memory in the proposed designs. The loopback design utilizes ROCm RDMA and the PCI Bar Mapped Memory to avoid expensive copy operations by relying on IB verbs to initiate the transfer between the host and device [20]. In Fig. 5(c), we see that the bandwidth of the proposed ROCm-aware MPI is about 3× higher than that of Open MPI + UCX and between 3–6× higher for bi-directional bandwidth. In this range, the proposed ROCm-aware MPI utilizes the ROCm-IPC cache proposed in Sect. 3.5 to deliver 23.8 GB/s bandwidth,

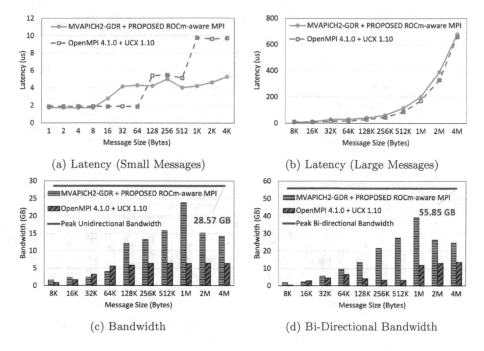

(a) Latency (Small Messages)   (b) Latency (Large Messages)

(c) Bandwidth   (d) Bi-Directional Bandwidth

Fig. 5. Comparison of intra-node MPI point-to-point operations between proposed ROCm-aware MPI Library and Open MPI + UCX on the Corona system

and 39.2 GB/s bi-directional bandwidth at 1 MB message transfer. As depicted in Fig. 5(b), enabling the IPC cache designs improves the bandwidth by over 4X. We see similar trends as Fig. 4(b) in this comparison between the proposed ROCm-aware MPI library and OpenMPI + UCX, with the proposed designs performing about 3× higher than Open MPI + UCX.

Inter-Node Point-to-Point—Device-resident data is typically sent over the network in order to achieve higher scalability and enhanced performance for HPC applications. We evaluated the performance of MPI communication of GPU resident data across the InfiniBand network (IB HDR 200 Gbps) by using point-to-point latency, bandwidth, and bi-directional bandwidth benchmarks. Figure 6 shows the result of inter-node device-to-device communication between two MPI processes each bound to a GPU on different nodes.

We see similar trends in latency between the proposed ROCm-aware MPI and OpenMPI + UCX, achieving 3.5 μs and 4.01 μs minimum latency, respectively. This is in comparison to the minimum achievable latency of 2.8 μs for this configuration of communication. The proposed ROCm-aware MPI utilizes the PCI Bar Mapped memory for small message size communication demonstrated in Fig. 3(b) to achieve low latency between the range of 1 B to 8 KB. In terms of the figbandwidth evaluation, shown in Fig. 6(c), the peak achievable bandwidth is 11.71 GB/s. The proposed ROCm-aware MPI is able to achieve close to peak performance with 11.57 GB/s bandwidth compared to OpenMPI + UCX at 6.67

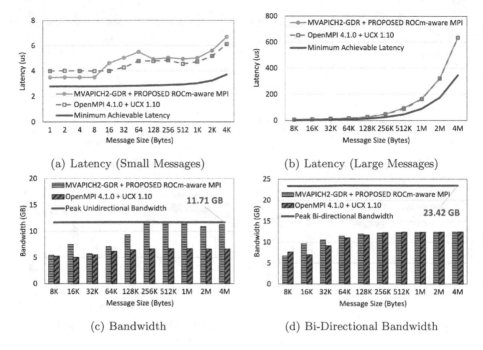

(a) Latency (Small Messages)   (b) Latency (Large Messages)

(c) Bandwidth   (d) Bi-Directional Bandwidth

Fig. 6. Comparison of inter-node MPI point-to-point operations between proposed ROCm-aware MPI Library and Open MPI + UCX on the Corona system

GB/s bandwidth. This communication across the nodes is critical for scalability and important to analyze in order to understand how well the bandwidth provided by the Infiniband networks is saturated by the MPI libraries.

MPI Collective Operations—We evaluate the performance of the proposed ROCm-aware MPI and Open MPI + UCX on 128 GPUs (16 nodes, 8 GPUs per node) on the Corona system for MPI Collective operations including broadcast, reduce, gather, allgather, alltoall, and allreduce using ROCm-aware OMB. In Fig. 7, we evaluate small message collective operations ranging from 4 B to 4 KB. For broadcast operations, the proposed ROCm-aware MPI shows 9.03 μs compared to 18.04 μs for Open MPI + UCX. In Fig. 7(b), we see 3.13 μs compared to 4.34 μs in the lower range at 4 B for reduce operations. We see 2.07 μs compared to 4.81 us for our proposed ROCm-aware MPI and Open MPI + UCX, respectively for gather operations in Fig. 7(c). In Figs. 7(d), 7(e), and 7(f), we see a larger difference between the proposed ROCm-aware MPI and Open MPI + UCX for dense collectives, with the former having 2-5X lower latency in this message range. In Fig. 8, we evaluate large message collective operations with the message size ranging from 8 KB to 1 MB. Due to node failures with scaling Open MPI + UCX to multiple nodes with 8 processes per node where the run crashes after outputting results for 512 Bytes, Fig. 7(d) and Fig. 8(d) are missing values for the Allgather comparison.

The performance gain demonstrated in collective operations is reliant on optimized point-to-point primitives detailed above when evaluating point-to-point benchmarks and optimized collective algorithms within the MPI library. The protocol level advanced designs in the UDI layer are utilized for point-to-point and collective operations. In addition to the optimized protocol level designs in the UDI layer, the library has been tuned on the system in order to adaptively select optimized GPU-based collective algorithms for different message ranges. The various collectives evaluated have been optimized for GPU-based communication to account for and utilize interconnects between GPUs, node density (number of GPUs within a node), and scalability to yield enhanced performance.

4.3   Application-Level Evaluation

In this section, we evaluate the performance of the proposed ROCm-aware MPI implementation against Open MPI + UCX using various application kernels including ROCm-aware HPCG and 3D Stencil benchmark. Several applications are in the early stages of adding support for ROCm to run on AMD GPUs with experimental versions released to the public.

3D Stencil—3D Stencil is a communication kernel that mimics the communication pattern of stencils and halo-exchanges in scientific applications. The kernel creates a 3D cartesian grid of MPI processes and runs the benchmark for n iterations. In each iteration, a given MPI rank performs a 7-point stencil and communicates k messages with each of its peers. We demonstrate the latency of 3D stencil for 16 (Fig. 9(a)), 32 (Fig. 9(b)), and 64 (Fig. 9(c)) GPUs. We encountered runtime failures when running the 3D Stencil kernel with Open MPI. We found that Open MPI failed during MPI_Cart_create due to an implementation bug. Due to this failure, we are not able to present a comparison with Open MPI for this application.

RocHPCG—High-Performance Conjugate Gradients (HPCG) benchmark is proposed to complement LINPACK (HPL) and used to rank modern HPC systems [10]. The computational and data-access patterns employed by the benchmark are representative of a variety of scientific codes. The numerical methods contain different communication patterns involving MPI point-to-point and collective operations. The rocHPCG is a ROCm-aware port of the HPCG benchmark intended for AMD GPUs. In Fig. 10(a) we evaluate the proposed ROCm-aware MPI against Open MPI + UCX on 16 GPUs across 16 nodes on the Corona cluster. We demonstrate the performance of each of the phases in rocHPCG: DDOT (dot products), WAXPBY (vector update phase), SpMV (sparse matrix-vector multiplication), and MG (multi-grid). Likewise, we demonstrate the performance of the proposed ROCm-aware MPI on 32 GPUs (Fig. 10(b) and 64 GPUs (Fig. 10(c)). We used per-process grid dimensions of (nx, ny, nz) = (104, 104, 104). On 16 GPUs, we see a final 633.3 GFLOPs/s for all the phases combined with our proposed ROCm-aware MPI compared to 585.9 GFLOPS/s for Open MPI + UCX. On 32 GPUs, we see a vaster difference with 1056.9 GFLOPs/s compared to 565.5 GFLOPs, and on 64 GPUs we demonstrate 1673.4

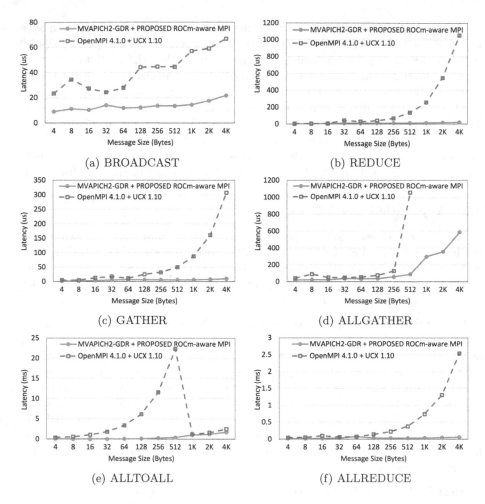

Fig. 7. Comparison of small message MPI collective operations between proposed ROCm-aware MPI Library and Open MPI + UCX on 128 GPUs (16 nodes, 8 GPUs per node) on the Corona system

GFLOPs/s compared to 740.4 GFLOPs/s with our proposed ROCm-aware MPI and Open MPI + UCX, respectively.

5   Related Work

Over the last few years, GPU devices have been widely used on modern clusters to provide higher computing power. Hence, communication between GPUs has become a critical bottleneck. Wang et al. [23] proposed early research using standard MPI libraries to transfer data between GPUs in InfiniBand clusters. The communication excluded the involvement of the CPU, so it prevented the CPU/GPU buffer management and data movement issues. Potluri et

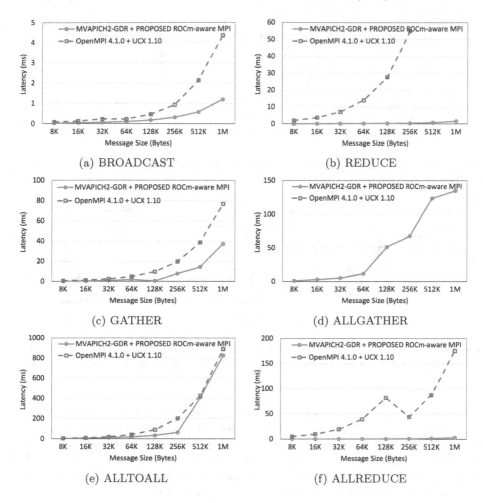

Fig. 8. Comparison of large message MPI Collective operations between proposed ROCm-aware MPI Library and Open MPI + UCX on 128 GPUs (16 nodes, 8 GPUs per node) on the Corona system

al. [18] aimed to deal with inter-node GPU-to-GPU MPI communication using GPUDirect RDMA. They studied the limitations of the system architectures and proposed a hybrid solution from the existing host-based pipeline and new GPUDirect-based designs. Based on the previous work on GPU-Aware MPI using GPUDirect RDMA, Shi et al. [20] further optimized the communications for small message sizes between inter-node GPUs. It supported using the eager protocol at not only sender but receiver sides as well. A new data path design was also proposed that allowed low-latency data movements between host and remote GPU memories. Recent works [9,12] identified and addressed the limitations in efficient processing on MPI derived datatypes for GPU resident data. They demonstrated significant performance improvements through novel CUDA

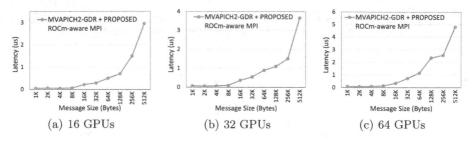

(a) 16 GPUs   (b) 32 GPUs   (c) 64 GPUs

Fig. 9. Evaluation of 3D Stencil Code with the proposed ROCm-aware MPI Library on the Corona system

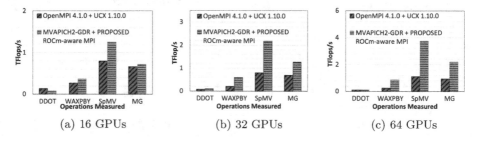

(a) 16 GPUs   (b) 32 GPUs   (c) 64 GPUs

Fig. 10. Comparison of rocHPCG between proposed ROCm-aware MPI Library and Open MPI + UCX on the Corona system [Per-process grid size (nx, ny, nz) = (104, 104, 104)]

kernel-based packing/unpacking and kernel fusion designs for non-contiguous data transfer. Subramoni et al. [21] addressed the trade-off between communication protocols in point-to-point data transfer. They proposed designs to identify the communication characteristics of processes at runtime and dynamically adapt to them. The fully in-band design allowed the transition from one eager-threshold to another without sacrificing the throughput.

Sharkawi et al. [19] discussed the techniques used in Spectrum-MPI on modern clusters equipped with IBM POWER9 CPUs. Kawthar et al. [13] evaluated the performance of existing CUDA-aware MPI libraries on OpenPOWER GPU-enabled systems by comparing benchmark-level point-to-point performance of Spectrum MPI, Open MPI+UCX, and MVAPICH2-GDR. Much of the work done using GPU-resident data transfer and communication has been heavily focused on NVIDIA GPUs due to the heavy deployment of NVIDIA GPUs across platforms. In the context of AMD GPUs, Kuznetsov et al. [14] investigated the ROCm platform and evaluated whether it is comparable to CUDA. They also focused on the programmers' experience of porting classical molecular dynamics algorithms from CUDA to ROCm and the performance benchmarking with these modern architectures. In addition, Tsai et al. [22] discussed the experience of porting the functionality in a CUDA-focused library to the HIP ecosystem. They demonstrated the porting workflow of linear algebra kernels and some techniques from CUDA to HIP in detail. Cai et al. [8] introduced the Synthesized Collective Communication

Library (SCCL), which is a latency-optimal and bandwidth-optimal implementation of collective communication algorithms.

6 Conclusion

As next-generation HPC systems such as Frontier and El Capitan adopt AMD GPUs, it is important to ensure that scientific applications and the communication middleware such as MPI are supported and enhanced for these systems. In order to add support for AMD GPUs, ROCm is used as the high-performance software development platform on AMD GPUs. Over the years, the state-of-the-art GPU-aware MPI libraries evolved with enhanced support for device resident data transfer. These implementations heavily rely on the CUDA toolkit to exploit NVIDIA GPUs. With the recent trend of AMD GPU usage, it is pertinent to have a ROCm-aware MPI library with support and optimizations for AMD GPU-resident data transfer. In this work, we took up the challenge of designing a ROCm-aware MPI runtime through designing an abstract communication layer that interfaces with the CUDA and the ROCm runtimes. We utilized the various features available through ROCm such as PeerDirect, ROCm IPC, and large-BAR mapped memory to generate GPU-based communication for AMD GPUs. We evaluated the performance of MPI-level point-to-point and collective operations with our proposed ROCm-aware MPI Library built over MVAPICH2-GDR and Open MPI with UCX as the ROCm-aware communication backend on the Corona cluster. We demonstrated 3–6× higher bandwidth for intra-node communication and 2× higher bandwidth for inter-node communication, respectively. With the rocH-PCG application, we demonstrate approximately 2.2× higher GFLOPs/s with MVAPICH2-GDR + our proposed ROCM-aware MPI compared to OpenMPI with UCX. To the best of our knowledge, this is the first research work that studies the tradeoffs involved in designing a ROCm-aware MPI library for AMD GPUs.

References

1. Bandwidth test for ROCm. https://github.com/RadeonOpenCompute/
2. Corona. https://hpc.llnl.gov/hardware/platforms/corona
3. Frontier: ORNL's exascale supercomputer designed to deliver world-leading performance in 2021. https://www.olcf.ornl.gov/frontier/. Accessed 25 May 2021
4. Infiniband Verbs Performance Tests. https://github.com/linux-rdma/perftest
5. Radeon Open Compute (ROCm) Platform. https://rocmdocs.amd.com
6. RLLNL and HPE to partner with AMD on El Capitan, projected as world's fastest supercomputer. https://www.llnl.gov/news/llnl-and-hpe-partner-amd-el-capitan-projected-worlds-fastest-supercomputer. Accessed 25 May 2021
7. Unified Communication X. http://www.openucx.org/. Accessed 25 May 2021
8. Cai, Z., et al.: Synthesizing optimal collective algorithms (2020)
9. Chu, C.H., Khorassani, K.S., Zhou, Q., Subramoni, H., Panda, D.K.: Dynamic kernel fusion for bulk non-contiguous data transfer on gpu clusters. In: 2020 IEEE International Conference on Cluster Computing (CLUSTER), pp. 130–141 (2020). https://doi.org/10.1109/CLUSTER49012.2020.00023

10. Dongarra, J., Heroux, M.A., Luszczek, P.: High-performance conjugate-gradient benchmark: a new metric for ranking high-performance computing systems. Int. J. High Perform. Comput. Appl. **30**(1), 3–10 (2016)

11. Gabriel, E., et al.: Open MPI: goals, concept, and design of a next generation MPI implementation. In: Proceedings. 11th European PVM/MPI Users' Group Meeting, Budapest, Hungary, pp. 97–104, September 2004

12. Hashmi, J.M., Chu, C.H., Chakraborty, S., Bayatpour, M., Subramoni, H., Panda, D.K.: FALCON-X: zero-copy MPI derived datatype processing on modern CPU and GPU architectures. J. Parallel Distrib. Comput. **144**, 1–13 (2020). https://doi.org/10.1016/j.jpdc.2020.05.008.   http://www.sciencedirect.com/science/article/pii/S0743731520302872

13. Khorassani, K.S., Chu, C.H., Subramoni, H., Panda, D.K.: Performance evaluation of MPI libraries on GPU-enabled OpenPOWER architectures: early experiences. In: International Workshop on OpenPOWER for HPC (IWOPH 19) at the 2019 ISC High Performance Conference (2018)

14. Kuznetsov, E., Stegailov, V.: Porting CUDA-based molecular dynamics algorithms to AMD ROCm platform using HIP framework: performance analysis. In: Voevodin, V., Sobolev, S. (eds.) RuSCDays 2019. CCIS, vol. 1129, pp. 121–130. Springer, Cham (2019). https://doi.org/10.1007/978-3-030-36592-9_11

15. Leiserson, C.E., et al.: There's plenty of room at the top: what will drive computer performance after Moore's law? Science 368(6495) (2020). https://doi.org/10.1126/science.aam9744. https://science.sciencemag.org/content/368/6495/eaam9744

16. Panda, D.K., Subramoni, H., Chu, C.H., Bayatpour, M.: The MVAPICH project: transforming research into high-performance MPI library for HPC community. J. Comput. Sci. 101208 (2020). https://doi.org/10.1016/j.jocs.2020.101208. http://www.sciencedirect.com/science/article/pii/S1877750320305093

17. Potluri, S., Wang, H., Bureddy, D., Singh, A.K., Rosales, C., Panda, D.K.: Optimizing MPI communication on multi-GPU systems using CUDA inter-process communication. In: 2012 IEEE 26th International Parallel and Distributed Processing Symposium Workshops PhD Forum, pp. 1848–1857 (2012). https://doi.org/10.1109/IPDPSW.2012.228

18. Potluri, S., Hamidouche, K., Venkatesh, A., Bureddy, D., Panda, D.K.: Efficient inter-node MPI communication using GPUDirect RDMA for InfiniBand clusters With NVIDIA GPUs. In: 2013 42nd International Conference on Parallel Processing (ICPP), pp. 80–89. IEEE (2013)

19. Sharkawi, S.S., Chochia, G.A.: Communication protocol optimization for enhanced GPU performance. IBM J. Res. Dev. **64**(3/4), 9:1–9:9 (2020)

20. Shi, R., et al.: Designing efficient small message transfer mechanism for inter-node MPI communication on InfiniBand GPU clusters. In: 2014 21st International Conference on High Performance Computing (HiPC), pp. 1–10, December 2014

21. Subramoni, H., Chakraborty, S., Panda, D.K.: Designing dynamic and adaptive MPI point-to-point communication protocols for efficient overlap of computation and communication. In: Kunkel, J.M., Yokota, R., Balaji, P., Keyes, D. (eds.) ISC 2017. LNCS, vol. 10266, pp. 334–354. Springer, Cham (2017). https://doi.org/10.1007/978-3-319-58667-0_18

22. Tsai, Y.M., Cojean, T., Ribizel, T., Anzt, H.: Preparing ginkgo for AMD GPUS - a testimonial on porting CUDA code to HIP (2020)

23. Wang, H., Potluri, S., Bureddy, D., Rosales, C., Panda, D.K.: GPU-aware MPI on RDMA-enabled clusters: design, implementation and evaluation. IEEE Trans. Parallel Distrib. Syst. **25**(10), 2595–2605 (2014). https://doi.org/10.1109/TPDS.2013.222

A Tunable Implementation
of Quality-of-Service Classes
for HPC Networks

Kevin A. Brown[1(✉)], Neil McGlohon[2], Sudheer Chunduri[1], Eric Borch[3],
Robert B. Ross[1], Christopher D. Carothers[2], and Kevin Harms[1]

[1] Argonne National Laboratory, Lemont, USA
kabrown@anl.gov
[2] Rensselaer Polytechnic Institute, Troy, USA
[3] Hewlett Packard Enterprise, Houston, USA

Abstract. High-performance computer (HPC) networks are often
shared by communication traffic from multiple applications with varying
communication characteristics and resource requirements. These applications contend for shared network buffers and channels, potentially resulting in significant performance variations and slowdown of critical communication operations such as low-latency MPI collectives. In order to
ensure predictable communication performance, network resources must
be allocated relative to the communication requirements of applications.
Quality of Service (QoS) solutions can regulate the allocation of
resources by defining traffic classes with specified resource allocations
and assigning applications to these classes, thus improving application
performance predictability. However, it is difficult to accomplish facility-
level goals of ensuring efficient application communication when constrained to a limited number of classes.
We propose a practical QoS implementation for large-scale, low-
diameter networks, such as the dragonfly topology, using flexible bandwidth shaping along with traffic prioritization to reduce the impact of
interference on communication performance. Our design gives facilities
more control over tuning QoS class to meet application- and site-specific
performance guarantees. The results show that our solution effectively
eliminates the slowdown of high-priority traffic due to interference with
lower-priority traffic, significantly reducing run-to-run variability. We
also demonstrate how port counters can be used to detect when a job-to-
class assignment is inappropriate for a given system and when a workload
is exceeding the bandwidth limits of its class.

Keywords: Interconnect network · 1D dragonfly topology · QoS ·
Traffic class

1 Introduction

Most high-performance computer (HPC) systems are shared by multiple applications with varying communication characteristics and bandwidth/latency

© UChicago Argonne, LLC, Operator of Argonne National Laboratory 2021
B. L. Chamberlain et al. (Eds.): ISC High Performance 2021, LNCS 12728, pp. 137–156, 2021.
https://doi.org/10.1007/978-3-030-78713-4_8

requirements. The interconnection networks of large HPC systems use high-speed switches to route application traffic across the system. These applications compete for bandwidth and can oversubscribe the links when the available bandwidth is less than the total required by the competing traffic flows.

Heavy traffic flows on low-diameter networks, such as fat tree and dragonlfy, have been shown to unfairly monopolize link bandwidth when each flow is given equally unregulated access to the network channels [20]. Without access constraints, network contention becomes an issue that can result in reduced or delayed network access for different applications. This may severely harm the performance of certain types of application traffic. For example, this situation can lead to significant performance degradation for latency-sensitive communication traffic, such as small message MPI collectives, while potentially posing negligible impact on more latency-tolerant patterns such as checkpointing [1].

HPC networks use a variety of techniques to deliver high system throughput and good application performance. Adaptive routing can be employed to improve communication performance by re-routing packets around high-traffic areas of the network, balancing traffic load across network links [20]. Congestion management is aimed at diagnosing and treating network congestion by temporarily reducing the rate at which packets are injected into the network, when necessary, to reduce the total number of packets queued in network buffers [19]. However, adaptive routing and congestion management techniques cannot allocate network resources, such as buffers and channel bandwidth, to specific applications or classes of traffic based on their respective performance targets. Quality-of-service (QoS), on the other hand, can differentiate how resources are allocated to different types of traffic to better manage resource contention and interference on heavily loaded networks [6].

Numerous studies exist on QoS for wireless networks, data centers, and the internet [15]. However, these solutions and supporting hardware are typically designed to throttle injection at the source or to drop packets in transit when the flow does not conform to QoS policies. Unfortunately, for HPC, throttling is not ideal unless the overall network is congested and dropping packets increases latency and reduces overall system throughput since dropped packets need to be retransmitted.

QoS solutions for HPC differentiate between different types of traffic by placing them in different network-defined traffic classes. Each traffic class is allocated separate network buffers and a guaranteed fraction of the channel bandwidth, based on the performance requirements of the traffic assigned to the class [13]. A small number of traffic classes are usually shared by multiple applications since it is impractical to define a separate class for each of the myriad of traffic patterns. The effectiveness of the QoS solutions therefore depends on how accurately the classes can be tuned to consistently guarantee an appropriate fraction of the resources to their assigned workload, even when the resource availability varies rapidly as in typical production systems.

Studies up until now have mainly focused on priority-driven QoS or QoS based mainly on simple, course-grained bandwidth allocations [16,18,22]. Such solutions do not have the flexibility to effectively configure classes that account for the variations in workloads, interference patterns, and site-specific priorities in HPC facilities. There is need for a QoS solution that can simultaneously balance the needs of multiple competing applications and reallocate bandwidth in a controlled manner as requirements change. However, in addition to the lack of appropriate solutions, there is also limited knowledge available on how to precisely evaluate the suitability of class configurations for HPC workloads with multiple distinct classes of traffic.

Our work aims to address these issues with the contributions as follows:

- We describe a practical method of implementing QoS classes on large-scale, low-diameter networks to enable traffic differentiation, prioritization, and shaping. Our solution allows for better control of bandwidth allocations when traffic load varies by employing two rate limiters per QoS class: one that sets an assured amount of bandwidth, and one that sets a maximum amount of bandwidth at its priority level;
- We propose a scheme for configuring and deploying QoS classes in production to match the varying application performance requirements of mixed workloads on production HPC systems; and
- We evaluate the ability of our scheme to satisfy the relative performance goals of multiple traffic flows sharing a large-scale 1D dragonfly network.

Our solution successfully regulates the traffic flows of dynamic communication workloads to more consistently meet the performance targets of the respective flows. The two rate limiters enable us to tune classes so as to better match the performance targets of dynamic workloads compared to prior work with single rate QoS solutions.

2   Background and Related Work

2.1   Communication Characteristics and Performance Targets

Communication operations can be characterized as being either *latency-bound* or *bandwidth-bound*. Latency-bound transfers have low injection rates, or offered loads, and the resulting communication time depends on individual packet latencies. Small message MPI collectives, such as MPI_Allreduce, are implemented using algorithms that rely on structured communication to minimize message count and data volume. However, long tail latencies can disrupt the structure of the communication and thus severely degrading collective performance. On the other hand, bandwidth-bound operations move relatively large amounts of data through the network, and the overall communication time depends on the throughput instead of individual packet latencies. Bulk data I/O transfers are examples of bandwidth-bound operations.

To meet their respective performance targets, different types of traffic need access to the network resource in different manners. Keeping packet latencies low in latency-bounded flows requires reducing the time spent queuing in the network by providing higher priority to network channels. Bandwidth-bounded flows, however, require high injection rates or longer access to the shared channels in order to move a large amount of data through the network.

HPC facilities may further classify some traffic as having higher priority than others based on site-specific goals. For example, facility administrators may deem that certain latency-sensitive collective operations such as MPI_Allreduce should not be impeded and instead receive highest priority access to network resources, regardless of the source application. In contrast, they may decide that other types of traffic – such as network-monitoring data – can be delayed if the traffic does not require any performance guarantees.

2.2   Managing Contention for Shared Channels on HPC Networks

Contention for shared resources such as channel bandwidth causes interference to communication performance. Interference over the network significantly degrades the performance of many HPC applications that are characterized by latency-sensitive collective communication patterns [7,8]. The main cause of significant slowdown due to interference is increased queuing delays resulting from head-of-line (HoL) blocking, i.e. when fast-draining messages get stuck behind slow-draining messages in shared buffers on congested ports [22].

Adaptive Routing and Congestion Management. Interconnect congestion can be classified into two categories: *intermediate* and *endpoint* congestion [3]. Intermediate congestion occurs when multiple input ports on a router try to use the same router output port, causing packets to get backed up in the buffers of the router. Endpoint congestion occurs due to application incasts – traffic from multiple source endpoints target the same destination endpoint, overwhelming the endpoint's ability to accept all the incoming traffic. Adaptive routing can effectively address intermediate congestion by routing incoming packets to different fabric output ports to avoid oversubscribing any single output port. However, adaptive routing is ineffective against endpoint congestion because there are no alternative paths to the endpoint at the destination switch. With endpoint congestion, as traffic backs up from the target endpoint, adaptive routing will spread incoming traffic to less busy paths and potentially cause traffic to get backed up on those paths across the network as well. Congestion management schemes that appropriately abate the incast flows are essential for handling endpoint congestion. These solutions strive to curtail the injection volume at the congestion-causing sources based on how many packets can be consumed at the endpoints [19].

2.3   QoS Solutions for HPC

QoS mechanisms are not designed to address endpoint or intermediate congestion. QoS is used to decide which packet to send based on priority and bandwidth specifications. This is complementary to both adaptive routing, which determines the path a packet should take, and congestion management, which determines if a packet should be injected into the network based on the state of congestion in the network.

Several QoS solutions have been proposed [13,16,18,22] for low-diameter networks like dragonfly and fat-tree networks, which are very susceptible to inter-application interference [20]. These solutions use separate buffers for each traffic class in order to prevent HoL blocking across classes and reduce packet latencies. Most of these vary the arbitration priority in some manner to reduce packet latencies, or regulate the bandwidth allocation to different flows, or both. Savoie et al. [18] proposed grouping application traffic flows into separate QoS classes and used only priority as a constraint on the QoS classes. However, Jakanaovic et al. [13] noted that this approach has the potential to degrade overall system performance since a bandwidth-intensive workload in the high-priority class can cause prolonged starvation of other workloads. The bandwidth consumption of the high-priority class should be constrained to prevent unintended starvation.

Wilke and Kenny [22] proposed using four different traffic classes with 25% of the bandwidth allocated to each class. Their solution includes two classes that use minimal routing in order to reduce the number of required buffers – minimal routing requires less buffers than adaptive routing [14]. This limits the flexibility of their solution since two of the four classes cannot be re-purposed to carry bandwidth-intensive traffic if the facility requires this.

Mubarak et al. [16] demonstrated that managing the bandwidth allocated to traffic classes may guarantee that important applications can perform well despite interference from lower-priority jobs. They proposed each class using a single rate limiter that must be tuned relative to the other class in order to assure a fraction of the bandwidth. That is, increasing the bandwidth allocated to one class will reduce the bandwidth available to other classes. Unfortunately, their allocations must be tuned to a fixed set of traffic loads while the load on the network usually varies. It is non-trivial to define a static configuration for all classes that consistently match the performance requirements of their assigned workloads given the variability in available resource.

In deploying QoS classes on production systems, multiple studies [16,18,22] have proposed grouping application traffic flows into a few QoS classes to reduce the number of classes in required[1]. The different flows need to be grouped based on performance requirements and characteristics, and their assigned classes must now be tuned to match their collective requirements.

3   Design of a Tunable QoS Solution

An ideal QoS solution should be able to simultaneously (i) ensure low packet latencies for latency-bound traffic, (ii) guarantee high bandwidth for bandwidth-bound traffic, (iii) prevent unintended starvation, and (iv) provide these assur-

---

[1] Switch hardware can only support a limited number of actives classes due to resource limitations.

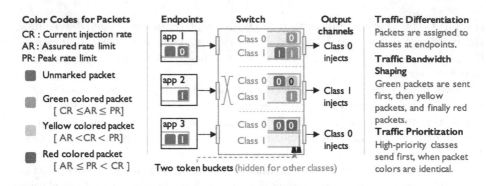

Fig. 1. Illustration of our QoS solution design. Packets are assigned to classes at compute node endpoints, placed in the appropriate class buffers on switches, and then are colored and compete for access to output channels based on the QoS policy. (Color figure online)

ances while network load varies. Since throughput and/or packet latencies affect a traffic flow's ability to meet its relative performance targets, QoS mechanisms should allow for regulating resources that affect the resulting packet latency and bandwidth available to traffic flows. Per-class buffers and priority-based arbitration can be used to prevent HoL blocking and expedite packet forwarding, thereby reducing packet latencies. Bandwidth guarantees (or assured injection rates) can be defined on each class to ensure a fraction of channel bandwidth is available to traffic using that class when channels are oversubscribed, thereby preventing starvation. Importantly, QoS should also manage the reallocation of bandwidth when traffic load changes such that more important flows get priority access to bandwidth released by other flows. This provides more useful resource partitioning for dynamic workloads.

3.1   Flexible Traffic Shaping Using Two Rate Limits

In a production system, network bandwidth usage varies dynamically as the traffic load changes. However, most QoS solutions use only a single assured rate limit to allocate bandwidth and cannot accommodate changing load requirements. When flows reduce their injection rates, their *unused* bandwidth is left unregulated for other traffic to consume, regardless of their importance. Controlling how unused bandwidth gets reallocated to specific workloads can improve the performance of important flows. By using an additional *peak rate* limit, we can give priority access to a portion of the unused bandwidth.

We propose a QoS mechanism that can be more easily tuned to satisfy the needs of HPC workloads and reallocate unused bandwidth more efficiently compared to other solutions. This solution allows for configuring an arbitrary number of traffic classes[2] with independent buffers and unique relative priorities to enable traffic prioritization. To achieve bandwidth shaping, each class is configurable with two rate limits: an *assured rate (AR) limit* and a *peak rate (PR) limit*, where $AR \leq PR \leq 100\%$, based on the Two Rate Three Color Marking design [21] for metering packet streams. The AR provides guaranteed bandwidth allocations and $\sum_{i=1}^{n} AR_i \leq 100\%$, where n is the number of classes. PR controls how excess/unused bandwidth is reallocated for controlled traffic shaping as the load changes. In our design, as illustrated in Fig. 1, packets at the front of switch port buffers are marked as either green, yellow, or red, depending on the current injection rate of its respective class. A packet is marked as red if the class exceeds its PR (and hence AR); it is marked as yellow if only the AR (but not PR) has been exceeded; or it is marked as green if its class does not exceed its AR (thus not PR either). Marking is done at each injection cycle for the purpose of output port arbitration, and stalled packets are re-marked based on the new injection rate in subsequent cycles. The packet content is unchanged and marking information is not communicated downstream.

Output port arbitration is priority-based within the constraints of the classes' rate limits. That is, green packets are sent first from higher priority classes; otherwise, yellow packets are sent in a similar priority order when there are no green packets to send be sent. If neither green nor yellow packets can be sent, a red packet will be chosen from any class by round-robin – priorities are ignored and each class has an equal chance of getting access to the output port. Note that flow control can stop any class from sending if downstream buffers are unavailable, in which case a packet from another class is sent.

We use token buckets, to meter each of the two rate limits per class [21]. Tokens accumulate in each bucket at the rate of the limit it meters, i.e., the assured rate bucket will accumulate tokens at the assured rate limit defined on the class, etc. Whenever a green or yellow packet is sent from a class, a token is removed from each of the two buckets with available tokens. No token can be removed when a red packet is sent because the peak rate limit has been exceeded, at which point both buckets are empty. Empty buckets means the traffic has completely consumed the bandwidth allocated to the class.

3.2   Defining QoS Classes for HPC Traffic

QoS classes for HPC traffic should be configured based on the traffic flow they are assigned. Additionally, systems should use the minimum number of classes required for their workloads to prevent resource fragmentation. Classes have strict priorities relative to each other, so we first consider the traffic flow's priority relative to that of other flows when deciding traffic-to-class assignments. When all other factors are equal, the priority will determine which flow progresses first and achieves lower latency. Inline with industry standards and recommendations [9,17], we argue that the following traffic classes and class assignments

---

[2] The number of traffic classes that can be configured on a given switch will be limited by how many class buffers and rate limiting counters are supported by that switch hardware.

are relevant for the majority of workloads on shared HPC systems and can be efficiently supported by our solution:

Low-Latency Class: Guarantees low packet latencies. This class has the highest arbitration priority to reduce queuing delays and a low assured rate limit to prevent starving other classes.

Suitable Traffic: important traffic that is primarily latency-bound and does not require high throughput, such as small message collectives.

Bulk Data Class: Guarantees high communication throughput. This class is typically allocated bandwidth commensurate with the I/O throughput of the system and the importance of I/O performance to the system workloads.

Suitable Traffic: traffic that moves a lot of data at once, requires high throughput and is not latency-sensitive, such as bulk I/O transfers to network file systems.

Scavenger Class: Guarantees minimal progression of traffic and minimal interference to other classes. This class has the lowest priority and a low assured rate limit to prevent it from impacting the performance of traffic in other classes.

Suitable Traffic: traffic that can be temporarily ignored without significant impact to overall productivity and user experience, such as scraping network counters.

Best-Effort Class: Guarantees best-effort progress of traffic with mixed latency-sensitivity and bandwidth requirements. This class is given a relatively high priority and allocated sufficiently high injection rates based on the high volume of data transferred by its combined expected workload.

Suitable Traffic: traffic that does not strongly map to any other class. Most application traffic will use this class.

Our QoS solution supports these and other class definitions by tuning the dual rate limits and relative arbitration priority on each class. For example, a system may need to support streaming real-time data, in which case such streams may require a high-priority class with the highest bandwidth allocation. One main requirement of an effective traffic-class assignment is that traffic sharing the same class are not adversarial to each other in terms of latency and bandwidth.

The following section demonstrates how traffic shaping with our dual-rate solution provides more consistent communication performance with dynamic workloads than other single-rate QoS solutions. We also show how QoS classes with dual-rate limits can be more easily tuned to simultaneous satisfy multiple performance targets and regulate diverse traffic loads.

4   Evaluation of QoS Solution

4.1   CODES Simulation Toolkit

To collect the data evaluated in this work, we use the CODES HPC interconnection network simulator [5] since HPC hardware does not yet support dual-rate

QoS. CODES is a Parallel Discrete Event Simulation (PDES) toolkit built on top of the Rensselaer Optimistic Simulation System (ROSS) [2] PDES engine. CODES allows for fine-grained, link-level simulations of packets moving across high-performance networks. Additionally, these simulations allow for testing and evaluation of different mechanisms such as adaptive routing algorithms, congestion management, and, as demonstrated in this work, QoS techniques. We implemented our QoS solution in CODES based on the design outlined in the previous section.

4.2 Network Setup

We simulate a tapered 1D dragonfly network with 8320 node endpoints. The network interconnect consists of 1040 routers with 16 routers per group. Each router has eight terminal channels, 15 local channels, and four global channels. The ratio of terminal channels to global channels results in a 2:1 taper of the global network bandwidth, similar to systems such as Theta, Edison, Malbec, and Shandy [10], which increases the potential for contention among competing traffic flows. We use 25 GB/s injection bandwidth for all channels, 10 ns delay for terminal and local channels, and 100 ns delay for global channels. The simulated router delay is 300 ns and the network packet size is set to 160 bytes. These taper and delay configurations are representative real-world dragonfly systems [10]. We use a progressive-adaptive routing algorithm for the network and a random job-to-node allocation scheme. Studies show that this random node allocation strategy improves job throughput for dragonfly systems [23] such as the ones listed above.

4.3 Workload Setup

We use the uniform random traffic (UR) pattern to generate interference on our network because other synthetic patterns, such as random-permutation, can cause congestion hotspots [3] for which QoS is not the appropriate solution. Additionally, unlike real application traffic, this synthetic traffic pattern (i) provides more precise control for managing when and how the traffic load changes and (ii) is less sensitive to the topology, routing, and congestion management capabilities of the systems. This allows us to succinctly capture the difference in traffic shaping capabilities of the dual-rate scheme versus the single-rate scheme.

The UR jobs use 640 B messages and vary the injection load by varying the delay between injecting successive messages, representative of loads recorded on a production HPC system [11]. These small messages allow us to minimize local incasts and evenly spread load across the system. We also use a Scalable Workload Model (SWM) [12] of MPI_Allreduce – a common operation on HPC systems [4] – to simulate latency-sensitive traffic. SWMs are skeletons of applications and benchmarks that capture the communication patterns of the workload that they model. Each allreduce SWM job performs at least 15 calls to

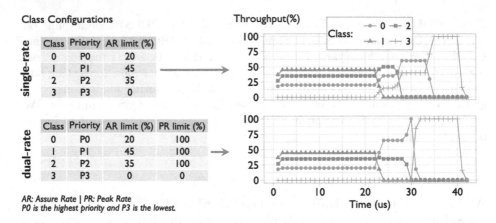

Fig. 2. Partitioning a single port bandwidth between four classes using single-rate and dual-rate QoS solutions. The injection rate in each class 100% of the bandwidth. The peak rate limit on the dual-rate QoS classes ensure that unused bandwidth is reallocated to the highest-priority class when the traffic load changes as the flow in class 1 completes around 23 μs.

MPI_Allreduce, reducing 8 bytes of data across all ranks of the job and requiring very low bandwidth. Our early evaluation survey of different load levels and message sizes produced similar results to experiments presented in this paper.

4.4   Bandwidth Shaping for Dynamic Workloads

The workloads on large production systems often exhibit variations in traffic load as applications start and stop communication operations and vary the volume or frequency sending traffic.

Reallocating Unused Bandwidth with Dual Rate Limits: When a QoS class has an assured bandwidth allocation, it is guaranteed a fraction of the bandwidth of all channels in the system. If traffic in this class does not use all of its allocation on a channel, the *unused* portion of the allocation can be consumed by flows from other classes. Controlling how the unused bandwidth gets consumed can improve the performance of more important flows over less important ones.

To demonstrate that our dual-rate solution allows for controlling the reallocation of unused bandwidth, we simulate four traffic flows sharing the bandwidth of a 16 B/ns channel. Each flow attempts to use 100% of the injection bandwidth to stream 1000 packets over the shared channel. The port is configured with four traffic classes (0, 1, 2, and 3), with one flow assigned to each class. Classes are assured a fraction of the link bandwidth relative to a designated minimum required rate of its assigned flow. The flow in class 3 is designated as having little importance and should not interfere with the other flows; therefore,

Table 1. Configuration for workload with variations in traffic load. UR jobs inject uniform random traffic.

Job	Nodes	QoS class	Initial rate (%)	New rate (%)
all_reduce32_1	32	0 - low latency	<0.08	–
all_reduce32_2	32	0 - low latency	<0.08	–
all_reduce256_1	256	0 - low latency	<0.08	–
all_reduce256_2	256	0 - low latency	<0.08	–
UR-LL	64	0 - low latency	3	–
UR-BE	4160	1 - best effort	50	85
UR-IO	1760	2 - bulk data	80	20
UR-S	1760	3 - scavenger	20	60

class 3 is assured none of the link bandwidth. We compare our QoS solution – which uses two rate limits – to another design that uses a single-rate limit [16].

The class configurations and results for both QoS solutions are shown in Fig. 2. For **single-rate QoS**, classes 0, 1, and 2 are able to share the port's bandwidth at their respective assured rates of 20%, 45%, and 35% from the start of the run. Class 3 is starved and unable to send because it is not assured a fraction of the bandwidth and the port is fully utilized by the other flows. As traffic in classes 1 and 2 complete after 22 μs, the remaining active flows equally share the *unused* bandwidth that becomes available. The flow in class 3 is able to compete for – and consume – a fraction of the unused bandwidth, partially blocking the higher-priority flow in class 0. However, **dual-rate QoS** uses peak rate limits to regulate access to the used bandwidth based on class priority, up until the class's peak rate limit. Our dual-rate solution could also be tuned to reallocate excess bandwidth to other classes besides class 0 by reducing the peak rate limit of class 0.

Maintaining Performance Despite Changing Network Loads: Properly tuned QoS classes should maintain the relative performance targets of their assigned traffic flows regardless of changes in the network load. If a flow requires more than its allocation and unused (or unallocated) bandwidth becomes available, the class should (i) be able to use the available bandwidth if it has sufficiently high priority or (ii) be blocked by another class if the other class is carrying more important traffic as done in the previous experiment.

To demonstrate the effects of system-wide network load variations on performance predictability, we evaluate a workload comprised of eight jobs with multiple changes in traffic load over time. Table 1 describes the jobs and their class assignments. Four allreduce jobs of two different job sizes and a uniform random (UR) job are placed in the low-latency class. The other classes are each assigned one UR jobs with different injection load intensities. The class configurations and UR job injection loads were selected to reflect their class's expected

Injection Rate Variations				
Class	Initial	T1	T2	T3
0	3	-	-	-
1	50	-	85	-
2	80	20	-	-
3	20	-	-	60

Dual-rate Classes			
Class	Priority	Assured %	Peak %
0	P0	5	10
1	P1	30	80
2	P2	20	60
3	P3	5	20

Single-rate Classes		
Class	Priority %	Assured %
0	P0	10
1	P1	50
2	P2	35
3	P3	5

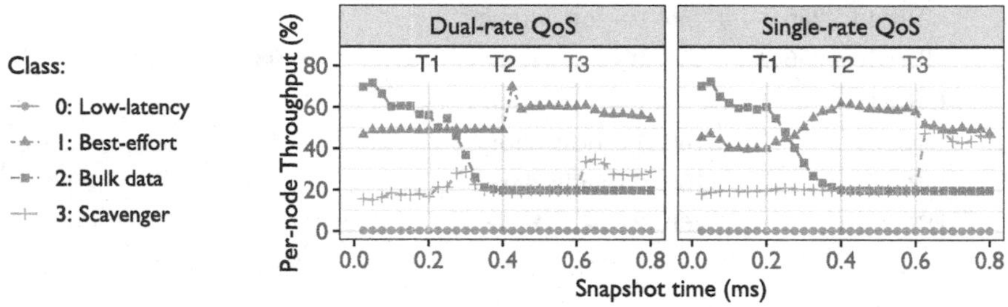

Class:

- 0: Low-latency
- 1: Best-effort
- 2: Bulk data
- 3: Scavenger

Fig. 3. Change in class throughput over time as the injection rates vary at times T1, T2, and T3, as indicated in the *Injection Rate Variations* table.

workloads that were discussed in Sect. 3. That is, the *low-latency class* will guarantee low packet latencies for traffic with a light injection load; the *best-effort class* will carry most application traffic and should guarantee high throughput; the *bulk data* class will carry I/O data and should have sufficiently high bandwidth without interfering with the low latency and best effort classes; and the *scavenger class* should ensure progress of its traffic while causing minimal interference to other flows. Details of the class configurations will be discussed in the following subsection. We create these classes for both dual-rate and single-rate QoS schemes to study each scheme's ability to maintain performance predictability as the traffic load varies. Figure 3 shows the class configurations and the resulting injection throughput during the run. The plots report the average per-node throughput of traffic in each class for both QoS schemes. If traffic flows from two classes that never share a channel, there will be no interference and both flows can theoretically be injected at 100% of the peak node injection rate simultaneously. However, on large systems, flows from multiple classes will contend for shared channels and potentially reduce the throughput that each flow can sustain. The QoS solutions manage this contention to improve workload throughput.

The results in Fig. 3 show that dual-rate QoS classes guarantee consistently high throughput for class 1 (best effort) traffic throughout the experiment. The flow in class 1 maintains its initially desired 50% rate until its injection rate is increased to 85% at 0.4 ms (T2 in the plot), exceeding the peak rate limit of 80% for class 1. From that point, it could only sustain a 60% injection rate due to the heavy load on the network causing the excess packets to be stalled and reducing the *effective* available global bandwidth. The increased network load and stalls caused ≈8% more packets to be routed non-minimally in class

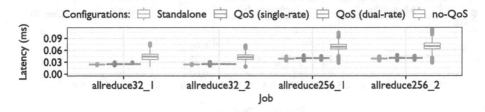

Fig. 4. Distribution of MPI_AllReduce operation latency across the ranks of each allreduce jobs. We achieve near baseline (Standalone) latencies when allreduce jobs use the low latency class of the dual-rate and single-rate QoS configurations.

1 between 0.4 ms and 0.8 ms. Non-minimally routed packets take two global hops on dragonfly networks, and the additional hop reduces the effective global bandwidth [14]. With single-rate QoS, class 1 could sustain only a 40% injection rate even though it desires 50% and it is assured 50% of the system bandwidth. This flow is able to increase its throughput after the load from class 2 is reduced at 0.2 ms (T1). The flow in class 2 has high throughput at start of the simulation when class 1 was not very loaded. After its load is reduced to 20%, which is within its assured rates for both solutions, it sustains this throughput for the rest of the run.

At 0.6 ms (T3) when the load in class 3 increases to 60%, the dual-rate solution is able to prevent traffic in class 3 from severely affecting the flow in class 1. The peak rate for class 1 was set to 80%, allowing this class to claim more of the unused bandwidth and reduce the interference from class 3: class 3 is only able to use more than it's assured rate after the other classes have exceeded their peak rates. On the other hand, the single-rate solution assured 50% of the bandwidth to class 1, which is now carrying 85% load, resulting in both class 1 and class 3 competing for the available bandwidth. Single-rate QoS shapes traffic as required only when the load distribution among the classes matches the class configurations, as shown between times T2 and T3 on the single-rate QoS plot in the figure. Otherwise, network load and interference from lower-priority classes can degrade performance. The dual-rate solution is able to provide more consistent throughput for class 1 regardless of load changes from other workloads in the network.

While maintaining high throughout for traffic in class 1 (best-effort), dual-rate QoS is also able to meet the latency targets of the allreduce jobs in the low-latency class. Figure 4 shows the MPI_Allreduce performance when using the dual-rate and single-rate QoS configurations, with both cases yielding near *Standalone* performance – where each allreduce job is ran on an idle system without background traffic. Performance is much worse in the *no-QoS* case when allreduce jobs run concurrently with the UR jobs without using separate QoS classes, i.e., traffic from all jobs share a single class. These results confirm that the dual-rate solution can also facilitate performance repeatability for low-latency traffic despite variations in network load.

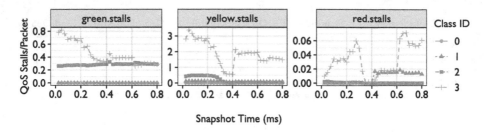

Fig. 5. Breakdown of system-wide QoS stalls per class as the traffic load changes. At 0.2 ms, load in class 2 is reduced; at 0.4 ms, load in class 1 is increased; at 0.6 ms, load in class 3 is increased. Figure 3 show the injection load and class configuration details.

Monitoring QoS Stalls to Understand Class Configuration and Behavior: Class configurations should be tuned to prevent some flows from being unintentionally delayed while simultaneously ensuring other flows are appropriately stalled. However, dynamic workloads present a challenge since they do not have static injection rates to properly guide bandwidth allocations. With dual rate limits per class, each class can be tuned to support a range of traffic loads. Additionally, monitoring how packets get stalled by classes expose how traffic is shaped and the appropriateness of the class configuration for the workloads.

As discussed in Sect. 3.2, traffic in a class is shaped by marking its packet red if the class exceeds its peak rate, yellow if only the assured rate is exceeded, or green if neither rate has been exceeded. Our solution reports three types of stalls based on these colors to expose traffic shaping:

Green Stall: The class is blocked from injecting if it has a green packet *and* a higher priority class also has a green packet ready to inject.

Yellow Stall: The class is blocked from injecting if has a yellow packet *and* either (i) a higher-priority class has a yellow packet ready to inject or (ii) any other class has a green packet ready to inject.

Red Stall: The class is blocked from injecting if has a red packet *and* either (i) another class has a green or yellow packet ready to inject or (ii) it loses to another class in round-robin arbitration.

Figure 5 reports the per-packet stall rates of each stall type over all switch-to-switch channels for the traffic described in Fig. 3. A value of 1 QoS stall/packet means that one packet was stalled for each injected packet, increasing packet latency and potentially reducing class throughput. By analyzing the type of stalls, we can determine which rate limit caused the stall and how its tuning may affect traffic shaping.

Classes 0 and 1 experience overall low QoS stall rates, confirming that their overalls flows were not being delayed. The assured rate limit of class 0 is slightly above the low injection rate of its assigned traffic, guaranteeing sufficient bandwidth to progress quickly, and the peak rate limit is high enough to accommodate momentary bursts. Class 1 is mostly stalled after its injection rate exceeds its

Table 2. Configuration for workload with mission critical traffic along with traditional HPC workload. UR jobs inject uniform random traffic.

Job	Nodes	Class	Injection rate (%)
UR-MC	**832**	**0 - mission critical**	**80**
allreduce512	256	1 - low latency	0.8
allreduce512	256	1 - low latency	0.8
UR-LL	512	1 - low latency	4
UR-BE	4160	2 - best effort	80
UR-IO	1760	3 - bulk data	90
UR-S	512	4 - scavenger	5

peak rate at 0.4 ms. Stalled packets block minimal routing paths, causing the increased use of non-minimal routing paths with extra global hops to reduce the effective available global bandwidth as mentioned earlier.

The relatively high green and yellow stall rates for class 2 confirm that its flow was regulated to limit its effect on class 1 or class 0, as intended. The yellow stall rate of class 2 is reduced when its injection rate drops to match its assured rate at 0.2 ms. The relatively low network load between 0.2 ms - 0.4 ms allowed the throughout of class 3 to be increased, signalled by the eventual reduction in its rate of yellow and red stalls. However, the initial spike in class 3 red stalls from 0.2 ms - 0.3 ms is due to the previously blocked packets being streamed into the network, causing the class to exceed its 20% peak bandwidth allocation. Overall, class 3 has the highest stall rates because it has the lowest priority and a low bandwidth allocation, and is prevented from unduly affecting more important flows.

The changes in the stall rates indicate how traffic shaping is being triggered by the composition of the network load. Having appropriately configured these HPC-oriented QoS classes to control the reallocation of bandwidth to the higher-priority flows, the stalls confirm that traffic is being shaped as intended.

4.5   Supporting Specially Defined QoS Classes

Workload configurations and requirements vary across HPC centers. While we contend that the traffic class configurations defined in Sect. 3.2 should be appropriate for most HPC workloads, centers may also need to define other classes for special workloads. When these special workloads run along the traditional HPC workloads, the QoS mechanism must satisfy the relative performance targets of both sets of workloads. We demonstrate how our QoS solution can support the creation of a site-specific *mission critical* class to carry traffic that must never be delayed by other HPC workloads. The mission critical class is assigned the highest arbitration priority and assured 100% of the system bandwidth to minimize the delay from traffic in other classes. With dual-rate QoS, other classes can be configured with peak rate limits to provide priority-ordered access to

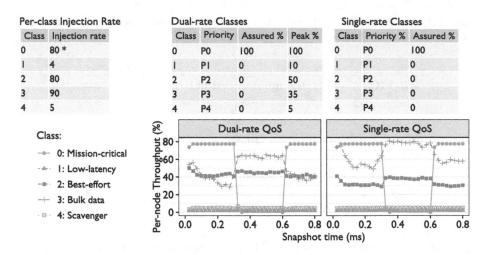

Fig. 6. Change in class throughput over time as mission critical traffic is transferred. *The mission-critical job suspends sending traffic at 0.3 ms and resumes at 0.6 ms. Workload and traffic-to-class assignments details are provided in Table 2. Traffic in class 2 (best effort) is able to sustain higher throughput with the dual-rate solution, even when the mission critical traffic is present.

unused bandwidth, respecting the relative importance of the different types of HPC traffic. However, defining the mission critical class with single-rate QoS does not allow for any regulation of HPC traffic.

We ran the workload setup in Table 2 using both single-rate and dual rate-QoS. Figure 6 shows the class configurations and throughput results for both QoS solutions. With the dual-rate solution, we ensure that class 2 has priority access to 50% of the unused bandwidth, allowing it to sustain high throughput despite heavy interference from traffic in class 3. For the single-rate QoS classes, however, the traffic in class 3 is unregulated and reduces the throughput of the higher priority class 2 traffic.

We allocate peak bandwidths to reduce the likelihood of a class being blocked when the mission critical traffic is not occupying a channel. These rates could be tuned differently depending on the goals of the system administrator. The assured and peak rate limits in our dual-rate QoS solution can be tuned independently to satisfy the performance requirements of traffic using the class while respecting the performance targets of traffic in other classes.

While it is possible to create a single-rate QoS solution using peak rates instead of assured rates, it would still be challenging to tune such a solution for dynamic workloads, as highlighted with these results. Using only a peak rate, the dual-rate QoS classes were unable to increase the allocation of bandwidth available to class 2 when the mission critical job was not injecting. Furthermore, the aggregate peak rate allocations can exceed the link bandwidth, meaning allocations are not guaranteed and lower-priority classes can be starved.

5   Discussion

5.1   Tuning Class Configurations to Match Workload Requirements

Proper QoS tuning requires accurately matching class configurations to their expected traffic load, which requires accurate knowledge of the system's expected workloads and performance targets. Our QoS solution regulates network resource allocation under varying traffic load using dual rate limits. For the assured rate limits, we recommend starting with the minimum required rate needed to attain acceptable throughput and/or latency for traffic assigned to the class. Peak rate limits can be set to the maximum expected traffic load while being mindful of the requirements of other classes. These limits can then be tuned using the QoS stall metrics as guides. Increases in yellow and red stall rates are indicators that constraints rate limit constraints are being applied since these packets get stalled only when the assured/peak rate has been exceeded. Additionally, green stall rates are indicators of priority constraints being applied priority since packets are marked green when the class has not exceeded its assured rate. The acceptable stall rates for a configuration will depend on the workload and the desired traffic shaping outcome. QoS stall rates can therefore be used to flag inappropriate traffic-to-class assignment when unexpected shaping is observed. High stall rates indicate that the traffic has exceeded its class's expected load and will experience increased packet latencies as well as potentially reducing the effective available global bandwidth.

5.2   Production Deployment

Our QoS design can be deployed on any interconnect architecture that supports network traffic classes with independent switch buffers and programmable output port arbitration, as most modern architectures do. Hence, this solution can also be used on other low-diameter topologies such as fat-tree, hyper-x, Slim Fly, and megafly, similar to other solutions [16,22]. While comparison of the different topologies is not the focus of this work, our solution will still provide more flexible control of network resources than the other solutions across the different topologies. Furthermore, being able to tune classes using stall counters will ease the integration of QoS in HPC centers.

The network drivers will provide APIs for assigning different messages to QoS classes. Communication libraries like MPI or parallel I/O libraries can be extended to utilize these APIs and automatically assign messages to different classes based on pre-defined message size/rate thresholds. Such an approach would be transparent to system users while allowing administrators to define system-wide configurations, preventing inappropriate traffic-to-class assignment. Another approach is for the user to choose class assignments for the different operations within their applications. Otherwise, a combination of the these two approaches may also be used when rolling out the QoS solution.

6   Conclusions

HPC networks often run multiple applications with differing communication patterns that compete for network resources. Because different applications may be running at any given time, network contention can result in large run-to-run performance variations for communication-sensitive applications.

Our QoS proposal classifies application traffic into one of several QoS classes, based on performance requirements, and effectively allocates resources among these classes. Each class's arbitration priority, assured bandwidth limit, and peak bandwidth limit can be tuned to match the traffic load assigned to the class. Using this solution, we can define a limited number of QoS classes – *Low-latency*, *Best-effort*, *Bulk data*, and *Scavenger* – to effectively support the diverse traffic loads on HPC systems. Our solution can ensure consistent, low-latency performance for latency-sensitive traffic, achieving near-baseline performance for MPI_Allreduce operations. It also provides the ability to maintain the high throughput required by a best-effort class, securing sufficient bandwidth for applications in order to guarantee overall system throughput.

Our solution's flexibility in provisioning multiple QoS classes with explicit, tunable assured and peak rate limits allows individual HPC sites to tailor class settings to their needs. The dual-rate limits support controlled bandwidth reallocation as traffic load changes, ensuring relative performance targets can be more effectively met in dynamic environments. Furthermore, the use of QoS stall metrics can isolate adversarial traffic-to-class assignments and help tune the configuration, deployment, and management of QoS in production. Future work will consider how to automatically assign and, and potentially reassign, traffic to classes while the workload in running. We will also investigate the interaction of our dual-rate QoS with different adaptive routing and congestion management solutions.

Acknowledgement. This work was supported by the Argonne Leadership Computing Facility, which is a DOE Office of Science User Facility supported under Contract DE-AC02-06CH11357, and by the Exascale Computing Project – learn more at https://www.exascaleproject.org/. We also gratefully acknowledge the computing resources provided and operated by the Joint Laboratory for System Evaluation (JLSE) at Argonne National Laboratory.

References

1. Brown, K.A., Jain, N., Matsuoka, S., Schulz, M., Bhatele, A.: Interference between I/O and MPI traffic on fat-tree networks. In: Proceedings of the 47th International Conference on Parallel Processing, ICPP 2018, pp. 1–10. Association for Computing Machinery, New York, August 2018
2. Carothers, C.D., Bauer, D., Pearce, S.: ROSS: a high-performance, low memory, modular time warp system. In: Proceedings Fourteenth Workshop on Parallel and Distributed Simulation, pp. 53–60 (2000)

3. Chunduri, S., et al.: GPCNeT: designing a benchmark suite for inducing and measuring contention in HPC networks. In: Proceedings of the International Conference for High Performance Computing, Networking, Storage and Analysis. SC 2019. Association for Computing Machinery, New York (2019)
4. Chunduri, S., Parker, S., Balaji, P., Harms, K., Kumaran, K.: Characterization of MPI usage on a production supercomputer. In: Proceedings of the International Conference for High Performance Computing, Networking, Storage, and Analysis. SC 2018. IEEE Press (2018)
5. Cope, J., Liu, N., Lang, S., Carns, P., Carothers, C., Ross, R.: CODES: enabling co-design of multilayer exascale storage architectures (2011)
6. Dordal, P.L.: An Introduction to Computer Networks, August 2020
7. Grant, R.E., Pedretti, K.T., Gentile, A.: Overtime: a tool for analyzing performance variation due to network interference. In: Proceedings of the 3rd Workshop on Exascale MPI, ExaMPI 2015, pp. 1–10. Association for Computing Machinery, New York, November 2015
8. Groves, T., Gu, Y., Wright, N.J.: Understanding performance variability on the aries dragonfly network. In: 2017 IEEE International Conference on Cluster Computing (CLUSTER), pp. 809–813, September 2017. iSSN 2168-9253
9. Hewlett Packard Enterprise: Shasta Software Workshop (2019). https://cug. org/proceedings/cug2019_proceedings/includes/files/inv113s1-file1.pdf. Accessed 19 Oct 2020
10. Hewlett Packard Enterprise: Measuring Network Performance to Better Manage IT. Technical White Paper a50002193ENW, August 2020
11. Jha, S., Brandt, J., Gentile, A., Kalbarczyk, Z., Iyer, R.: Characterizing supercomputer traffic networks through link-level analysis. In: 2018 IEEE International Conference on Cluster Computing (CLUSTER), pp. 562–570, September 2018. https://doi.org/10.1109/CLUSTER.2018.00072, iSSN: 2168-9253
12. John Thompson: Scalable Workload Models for System Simulations (2014). https://hpc.pnl.gov//modsim/2014/Presentations/Thompson.pdf. Accessed 19 Oct 2020
13. Jokanovic, A., Sancho, J.C., Labarta, J., Rodriguez, G., Minkenberg, C.: Effective quality-of-service policy for capacity high-performance computing systems. In: 2012 IEEE 14th International Conference on High Performance Computing and Communication 2012 IEEE 9th International Conference on Embedded Software and Systems, pp. 598–607, June 2012. https://doi.org/10.1109/HPCC.2012.86
14. Kim, J., Dally, W.J., Scott, S., Abts, D.: Technology-driven, highly-scalable dragonfly topology. In: Proceedings - International Symposium on Computer Architecture, pp. 77–88 (2008)
15. Li, F., Niaki, A.A., Choffnes, D., Gill, P., Mislove, A.: A large-scale analysis of deployed traffic differentiation practices. In: Proceedings of the ACM Special Interest Group on Data Communication, Beijing China, pp. 130–144. ACM, August 2019
16. Mubarak, M., et al.: Evaluating quality of service traffic classes on the Megafly network. In: Weiland, M., Juckeland, G., Trinitis, C., Sadayappan, P. (eds.) ISC High Performance 2019. LNCS, vol. 11501, pp. 3–20. Springer, Cham (2019). https://doi.org/10.1007/978-3-030-20656-7_1
17. OFI Working Group: Libfabric Programmer's manual (2020). https://ofiwg.github.io/libfabric/master/man/fi_endpoint.3.html. Accessed 19 Oct 2020
18. Savoie, L., Lowenthal, D.K., de Supinski, B.R., Mohror, K., Jain, N.: Mitigating inter-job interference via process-level quality-of-service. In: 2019 IEEE International Conference on Cluster Computing (CLUSTER), pp. 1–5 (2019)

19. Sensi, D.D., Girolamo, S.D., McMahon, K.H., Roweth, D., Hoefler, T.: An in-depth analysis of the slingshot interconnect. In: Proceedings of the International Conference for High Performance Computing, Networking, Storage and Analysis (SC20), November 2020
20. Smith, S.A., et al.: Mitigating inter-job interference using adaptive flow-aware routing. In: SC18: International Conference for High Performance Computing, Networking, Storage and Analysis, pp. 346–360, November 2018
21. Society, T.I.: A Two Rate Three Color Marker (1999). https://tools.ietf.org/html/rfc2698. Accessed 01 June 2020
22. Wilke, J., Kenny, J.: Opportunities and limitations of quality-of-service in message passing applications on adaptively routed dragonfly and fat tree networks. In: 2020 IEEE International Conference on Cluster Computing (CLUSTER) (2020)
23. Zhang, Y., Tuncer, O., Kaplan, F., Olcoz, K., Leung, V.J., Coskun, A.K.: Level-spread: a new job allocation policy for dragonfly networks. In: 2018 IEEE International Parallel and Distributed Processing Symposium (IPDPS), pp. 1123–1132 (2018)

Scalability of Streaming Anomaly Detection in an Unbounded Key Space Using Migrating Threads

Brian A. Page[(✉)] and Peter M. Kogge

University of Notre Dame, Notre Dame, IN 46556, USA
{bpage1,kogge}@nd.edu

Abstract. Applications where streams of data are passed through large data structures are becoming of increasing importance. For instance network intrusion detection and cyber security as a whole rely on real time analysis of network traffic. Unfortunately, when implemented on conventional architectures such applications become horribly inefficient, especially when attempts are made to scale up performance via some sort of parallelism. An earlier paper discussed an implementation of the Firehose streaming benchmark that assumed only a bounded number of keys and datums. This paper discusses a significantly more complex (and more realistic) variant that analyzes continuously streaming samples from an unbounded range of keys. We utilize a novel migrating thread architecture in which threads may migrate as needed through a single system wide shared memory space, thereby avoiding conventional inefficiencies. As with the earlier paper, results are promising, with both far better scaling and increased performance over previously reported implementations, on a platform with considerably less intrinsic hardware computational resources.

Keywords: Streaming · Emerging architectures · Scalability · Communication overhead

1 Introduction

Applications where streams of data are passed through large data structures are of increasing importance. Examples include cyber-security, social networks, interactive messaging, and e-commerce.

Unfortunately, when implemented on conventional architectures such applications become horribly inefficient, especially when attempts are made to scale up performance via some sort of parallelism. Quoting from the website for a benchmark for one such application [1]: "Streaming data arrives continuously and in volumes and rates that are ever increasing. Timely processing of streaming data is computationally challenging due to limited resources. These include limited CPU operations that can be performed on a datum before the next one

© Springer Nature Switzerland AG 2021
B. L. Chamberlain et al. (Eds.): ISC High Performance 2021, LNCS 12728, pp. 157–175, 2021.
https://doi.org/10.1007/978-3-030-78713-4_9

arrives, limited memory for storing state information about the stream, limited disk storage for the data itself so that the datums may only be seen once, and limited budgets for energy consumption or CPU/memory/disk resources." Particular areas with significant interest in streaming include graphs and big data [2–4,10,11,15]. Studies of streaming in particular include [5,13], with a small but growing suite of software support packages [7,17,18].

A benchmark with these characteristics for which at least some comparative data is called Firehose [6,9,12]. The benchmark is notionally a stand-in for streaming applications where information from different incoming internet packets (called "datums") must be aggregated in some way so that different kinds of "events" can be recognized, and potential "anomalies" be detected. The performance metric is "datums/s:" how many such datums can be pushed through the system per second without dropping things. Much of the data reported on the Firehose website[1] demonstrates a variety of issues with scaling it to use multiple cores. The problem with today's architectures is that very often the software cost of handing off a piece of data to another core for the next step of processing very often wildly exceeds the cost of performing the desired operations, especially when because of the size or structure of the data structures, that core is in a different node.

An earlier study [16] investigated the scalability of streaming in a bounded key space using the Lucata[2] migrating thread architecture. In that study we were able to achieve vastly superior throughput when analyzing datums as per the Firehose benchmark specification, but with some caveats with regard to implementation. Unfortunately variant 1 was only designed as a simple test of anomaly detection and has little relevance to real world streaming applications. Fortunately variant 2 of the Firehose streaming benchmark performs anomaly detection on an unbounded key space and therefore has direct application to many existing applications.

The main contributions of this paper are:

– An implementation of Firehose variant 2 on an early version of the Lucata migrating thread architecture.
– An MPI based implementation using a producer/consumer model similar to our Lucata implementation.
– An analysis and comparison between migrating threads and conventional architectures for our conventional and migrating thread implementations as well as previously reported results.

2   Background

2.1   Firehose Streaming Benchmark

Firehose resembles a cyber-security like streaming function where incoming IP packets are to be monitored. When some number of packets with the same

---

[1] https://firehose.sandia.gov.
[2] Lucata formerly EMU Solutions Inc.

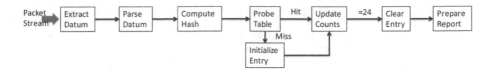

Fig. 1. The firehose data flow.

IP address have been detected, the payload fields are examined for potential anomalies, and if detected, a report issued. Figure 1 diagrams the notional flow. The IP address in each incoming packet is used to probe a very large hash table, and when a match is found, data from the packet's payload is merged into the entry, and a match count incremented. When 24 packets have been found, the aggregated payload is analyzed. An "atypical" outcome results in the IP address being flagged.

The benchmark has three versions. The first two assume incoming packets have three fields formatted as ASCII strings. The first, the *key*, is an IP address that when converted from ASCII represents a 64-bit unsigned integer. The second, the *payload*, is a value of "1" or "0." The third is a *truth flag* that indicates if this packet is part of an "anomaly" sequence. This field is only used when the implementation makes a call to verify if the call was correct. The datum stream associated with a key may have two distributions of payload values. In the normal case, the payload is chosen equally randomly from a "1" or a "0". In the anomalous case, the payload values are biased toward "0."

For the first two versions, the key field is used to look for matches in a giant hash table. At each match, a "match count" field is incremented in the table entry. In addition if the payload is a "1," a separate payload count is incremented. When the match count reaches 24, the payload field is tested. If it is 4 or less, an anomaly report is generated. No IP matches in the hash table causes a new hash entry to be created.

The first benchmark variant is primarily for testing, and the data generator ensures that there will never be more than 128K unique key values. The second is similar in that at one time there will not be more than 128K unique keys, but it has no constraint in the total number of unique keys over time. This version is oriented towards demonstrating handling a never-ending stream of data. Releasing the constraint of a fixed number of key values means that the hash table must be capable of "aging out" entries that are "too old" when new entries must be created and there is no space. The third version is a more complex two-phase process described in the website.

Figure 2 diagrams scaling data extracted from various Firehose references, with Table 1 summarizing the major characteristics of the microprocessors used in them. The curves for small core counts represent scaling data for multi-threaded implementations of both Variant 1 and 2 as taken from the Firehose website. The system the Variant 1 data was measured on was a dual socket node where each socket was an Intel X5690 six-core processor. This data shows relatively poor scaling, with 7 cores providing 10 million datums per sec, less than

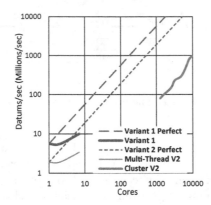

Fig. 2. Reported scaling numbers (mostly from variant 2).

twice that of a single core (5.6 million datums/s). The discrepancy is most likely due to a combination of coherency traffic and the need for expensive guaranteed atomic memory operations when the hash table entries are to be updated.

The Variant 2 data has two parts: data from the same system as the Variant 1, and data from a multi-node dual 6-core socket Cray CS-300 using Intel E5-2670 processors [6]. The former achieves 1.9 million datums/s on one core. The latter curve shows good weak scaling, but at an equivalent performance level per core of 0.6-0.1 million datums/s per core. This is up to 30× less than what perfect scaling from one core would have brought. The reason for the huge loss in efficiency per core is the software stack needed to handle the queuing and streaming of data from one physical node to another.

Table 1. Processor characteristics.

		Intel Xeon 5960	Intel E5-2670	AMD EPYC 7451	Lucata Chick Node Card
Cores		6	8	24	8
Core clock		3.46 GHz	2.6 GHz	2.66 GHz	0.175 GHz
Memory channels		3	4	8	8
Per channel	Bandwidth	10.7 GB/s	12.8 GB/s	21.33 GB/s	1.6 GB/s
	Access rate	0.166 G/s	0.2 G/s	0.26 G/s	0.2 G/s
Total per module	Bandwidth	32 GB/s	51.2 GB/s	170.6 GB/s	12.8 GB/s
	Access rate	0.5 G/s	0.8 G/s	2.08 G/s	1.6 G/s

2.2 Migrating Thread Architecture

A migrating thread architecture [14] is one where the underlying hardware, not software, moves the state of a thread as required during execution. Figure 3 diagrams such an architecture as implemented by Lucata Solutions [8]. The basic unit, a **nodelet**, is a memory module, its controller and some number of multi-threaded cores. All the memory in the collection of nodelets reside in

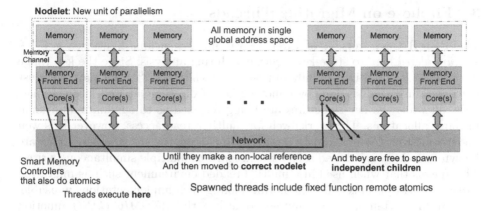

Fig. 3. The migrating thread architecture.

a common address space. A network connects all nodelets. A thread runs in a multi-threaded **"GC core"** until it makes a memory reference that is not contained in that nodelet's memory. The hardware then puts the thread to sleep, packages it, and moves it over the network to the correct nodelet, where it is unpacked and restarted. A thread can spawn independent child threads. Also, the memory controller contains hardware to implement atomic operations as close to memory as possible. Finally, very lightweight threads can be spawned to perform remote memory operations without moving the parent.

The current prototype used in this study is housed at Georgia Tech's CRNCH center[3]. It has up to 64 nodelets, each with 8 GB of memory and one 175 MHz multi-threaded core. These nodelets are packaged 8 to a **node board** which supports a RapidIO-based network. A dual core POWER microprocessor (called an **SC**) on each node board runs Linux, manages a local SSD, and launches migrating threads into the system. The nodelet logic on each board is implemented in an FPGA. The last row of Table 1 summarizes the characteristics of a node board. A larger system is in development.

In comparison to either of the two microprocessors used in the reference data, the aggregate compute cycles (number cores times clock rate) of the nodelet cores on a node card is 1/14'th of either the other two. The actual comparison is probably lower than this as the nodelet cores are single issue and both the Intel cores are multi-issue. The node board aggregate memory bandwidth is about 1/3 to 1/4'th the others, but, because of the memory channel design used in the nodelets, the ability of a node board to handle different independent memory accesses is between 2× to 3× higher that of either microprocessor.

The programming tool chain is based on Cilk, C with a prefix to function calls to spawn new threads, a sync primitive to wait for a set of children to complete, and a parallel *forall* to have a set of independent threads cooperate on a loop. Supported intrinsics include a rich set of atomic operations.

---

[3] https://crnch.gatech.edu/rogues-Lucata.

3   Firehose on Migrating Threads

The PHISH/C++ version of Firehose variant 2 benchmark utilizes a C++ *std::unordered_map* to store key structures during analysis. Since the key range in variant 2 is potentially infinite in practice (technically 2^{64}) the map size must be constrained. This is done by removing keys from the map and inserting new ones, all while the key structures are being recycled as to eliminate additional memory allocations. This works well for multiple read access, however it is well understood that C++ STL data structures including the *std::unordered_map* are known to lack native thread safety with regard to multiple simultaneous writes. This means that when used in a multi-threaded environment such as migrating threads disastrous effects are the norm, making such implementations unusable.

Our first attempt we attempted to utilize the *ATOMIC_CAS()* function as a method for obtaining mutexes in order to lock certain key structs while updating them. However this is not possible as in order to acquire any element in a map in a thread safe manner, requires at least two steps, $find(key)$ which returns an iterator to the map entry for key, and then finally $ATOMIC\_CAS(iterator.second \rightarrow lock, 1, 0)$ to acquire the lock. Notionally it may be possible to skip the step in which the iterator to the map node in question is found by maintaining an iterator to it at all times via some other method, however there are a number of functions performed on a map data structure which can invalidate iterators points to the map's nodes.

Algorithm 1 Multithreaded FireHose v2 - Datum Conversion and Assignment:

C = number of consumers
P = number of producers
N = nodelet count
i = datum currently being generated (initially 0)
D = number of datums generated per nodelet
$cDat$ = num datums assigned to consumer
$usage$ = num datums being assigned which finished assignment
$nDatums$ = array storing all datums generated on the nodelet
$datums$ = array storing datums assigned to consumers
$done$ = num of producers that have finished

```
 1: procedure GENERATEDATUMS()
 2:     i = ATOMIC_ADDM(d, 1)
 3:     while i < D do
 4:         str_to_int64(nDatums[datId], κ, φ, β)
 5:         t ← i%C
 6:         n ← t%P/N
 7:         dcDat ← ATOMIC_ADDM(cDat[n][t], 1)
 8:         datums[n][t][dcDat * 2] = κ
 9:         datums[n][t][(dcDat * 2) + 1] = φ
10:         datums[n][t][(dcDat * 2) + 2] = β
11:         ATOMIC_ADD(usage[n][tid], 1)
12:     end while
13:     ATOMIC_ADD(done, 1)
```

Since the Lucata migrating thread architecture is massively multithreaded by design our version of Firehose variant 2 uses two thread pools **producer** and **consumer**. Producers perform the ascii to integer conversion for datums generated on their nodelet. Consumers perform analysis on the converted datums after having been assigned them via a producer.

3.1   Datum Conversion and Assignment: Producers

Immediately after being spawned producer threads will begin to acquire and convert datum strings containing the key, payload, and bias flag components into 64bit unsigned integers. In Algorithm 1 we can see that the team of P producer threads iterate over the same shared set of datums which were generated locally on the nodelet during the initialization phase. All producers iterate through the while loop on Line 3 until all datums have been evaluated once.

After string conversion the producer determines which consumer to assign the current datum to, as well as on which nodelet that consumer "lives". Once the destination nodelet and consumer id have been determined, the datum must be placed into the remote (if applicable) consumers' datum queue. However since this system can have hundreds of producers pushing datums to any arbitrary consumer the possibility of race conditions are possible if not handled correctly. To rectify this on Line 7 we atomically increment the counter of assigned datums belonging to the destination consumer thread by 1 and store the result. This is done using the *ATOMIC_ADDM()* instruction which allows for a single atomic add operation to any address, triggering a thread migration if necessary to move the calling thread to the nodelet governing the destination address, and returning the result. This allows us to increment the assignment counter, while also insuring that the value returned is unique. With this unique value, in *dcDat*, the producer knows where it can safely place the key, payload, and bias flag values for the datum it is currently working on. All three values are adjacent in memory as can be seen in Lines 8–10.

After assignment has completed the producer must be able to alert the consumer that it is now o.k. to proceed with consumption of the newly assigned datum (Line 11). Lastly once all datums on the nodelet have been converted and assigned to consumers, each producer will atomically increment the *done* counter which is used by the consumers to know when they may exit their work loop.

3.2   Anomaly Detection: Consumers

While consumers are spawned at the same time as producer threads, consumers do not have any initial work allotment to analyze and must wait for datum assignments from producers. Consumers have three major components, a datum vector into which producers assign datums, a state table, and a list of recently seen keys. Consumers use a private hash table for maintaining the state of datums they have been assigned and are the only thread which is allowed to interact with it. Eliminating simultaneous access to the hash table in this manner also eliminates the thread safety issues discussed earlier. Each consumer hash table is of the same size therefore giving each consumer the same probability of being assigned any arbitrary key with the per consumer key coverage being equal to $1/C$.

Algorithm 2 FireHose v2 - Datum Analysis:

P = number of producers
i = thread id
$curDatum$ = datum currently being evaluated (initially 0)
$cDat$ = num datums assigned to consumer
$datums$ = array storing all datums assigned to consumers
κ = key value for current datum
ϕ = payload value for current datum
β = bias flag for current datum
$list$ = list containing keys present in the active set
$state$ = map containing payload and hit counts active set
$hits$ = observed key occurrences
$done$ = num of producers that have finished

```
 1: procedure ANALYZEDATUMS(i)
 2:     ATOMIC_ADD(curDatum, 1)
 3:     while true do
 4:         if curDatum < cDat then
 5:             κ ← datums[i][curDatum].key
 6:             φ ← datums[i][curDatum].payload
 7:             β ← datums[i][curDatum].bias
 8:             if !exists(state[i][κ]) then
 9:                 if !state[i].full() then
10:                     state[i].insert(κ)
11:                 else
12:                     ptr ← list[i].head
13:                     state[i].erase(list[i].head)
14:                 state[i].insert(κ, ptr)
15:                 state[i][κ].pSum = 1
16:                 state[i][κ].hits = 1
17:                 list[i].prepend(κ)
18:             else
19:                 list[i].move2front(κ)
20:                 state[i][κ].pSum+ = φ
21:                 state[i][κ].hits = 1
22:                 if state[i][κ].hits = 24 then
23:                     events++
24:                     if state[i][κ].pSum < 4 then
25:                         if β = true then truePositives++
26:                         else falsePositives++
27:                     else if β = true then falseNegatives++
28:                     else trueNegatives++
29:                 ATOMIC_ADD(curDatum, 1)
30:         if curDatum >= cDat and done = P then
31:             break
32:     end while
```

By segmenting the global key range for assignment to consumers we were able to use the STL *std::unordered_map* data structure. Unordered maps maintain $<key, value>$ pairs in which the keys must be unique and the value can be any datatype. Aside from the datums's key itself we must also keep track of how many times the key has been seen. For this we utilize a *Key* struct which maintains the key value itself, as well as the occurrence counter.

While we could instantiate and use *Key* structures as the value field for elements within an *std::unordered_map* it increases insertion and deletion costs due to the various constructor and or destructor calls which much occur. These operations mean many more instructions which do not directly relate to useful computation. Instead we generate an array of *Key* structs during initialization so that we do not have to allocate any new memory during datum evaluation. When a datum's key is inserted into the hashtable a pointer to an unused *Key* struct is used as the value field in the $<key, value>$ pair. After the initialization phase no new *Key* structs will be created, just overwritten and reused, thereby maintaining a constant memory footprint.

Algorithm 2 shows the computation procedure for an arbitrary consumer thread. Every consumer thread enters the while loop checks to see if the datum id it is attempting to analyze can be used during this iteration. This check is necessary as we do not want to read a datum which is currently being written by a producer thread.

If a consumer has been assigned datums which have not been analyzed yet then the consumer will proceed with the next datum in its datum vector. It will then check if the current datum's key has exists in the hash map (Line 8). If the key does not exist in its local table it is added and given initial payload and hit counter values of 1. Additionally when a key is being evaluated for the first time its key is added to the beginning of the *lru_list* which will be used to remove old keys once the hash table becomes full.

Should a key already be present in the hash map we enter the else block on Line 18 in which we acquire the existing hash map entry for the current key, update its payload and hit counter values, and move the key to the front of *lru_list* to signify it was recently seen. As a consumer updates existing keys it now becomes possible that an anomaly has occurred. Line 22 checks the hit counter for the current key to see if it is equal to some threshold which in the case of the Firehose specification is 24 and If it is triggers an event. The event evaluation process is identical to that of variant 1 in which the payload sum is tested against a threshold value, 4 in the case of the benchmark spec, and subsequently is the bias flag is true of false. The use of the bias flag is also consistent in that truth indicates that the event should have occurred, and false being that the event should not have occurred. After the datum and any accompanying anomaly detection has finished the consumer increments its *curDatum* counter and store the result for use as the datum id to evaluate during the next loop iteration.

While producers have a finite run-time, i.e. they iterate through all datums and then stop, consumers do not. Datum assignment to a consumer occurs based on the datums key value, meaning that the exact number of datums to be assigned to any arbitrary consumer, the order in which they are to be assigned, or when during program execution such assignment will occur are all unknown at run-time. Therefore consumers must not only constantly check if they have been assigned any new datums, but also if it no longer possible to be assigned additional datums. The test on Line 30 performs this check and if true breaks out of the while loop otherwise the consumer begins the next loop iteration until all possible computation has been completed.

3.3   Maintaining Hash Map Size: LRU List

As discussed previously the potential key range for Firehose variant 2 is quite large 2^{64} and while these values may fit into memory on some systems, the accompanying state table data used for anomaly detection will not. A Least Recently Used or LRU list is used to indicate which keys are likely safe for deletion. This works for streaming applications since a stream of packets are often temporally related, meaning that after some arbitrary amount of time after a packet or datum has been received, it is unlikely that another packet/datum with the same key will be seen again. This behavior is also duplicated in the dataset generator used by the Firehose streaming benchmark variations allowing us to remove keys after this threshold with high confidence that its remove will not affect anomaly detection accuracy.

For simplicity our LRU key list utilizes a doubly linked list data structure. Each consumer maintains a private LRU list to use with datums it is assigned. In order to maintain *when* a key was last seen in relation to the rest of the data stream, *Key* structs have several additional fields. First we maintain a pointer to the key's hash map entry which allows for direct access for the purpose of performing erase operations without needing to search the map for the given key. Previous and Next Pointers for facilitating the doubly linked list structure.

The least recently used order is easy to maintain and update. When a key is seen, the key is located or inserted into the hash map. The *Key* for that hash map element has its counter updated. Pointers for the doubly linked list are updated so that the current *Key* struct is placed at the tail end of the list. In doing so we know that the head of the list is always the key which was seen the longest time ago and is therefore the most valid for recycling out of the hash map for use when inserting a newly observed key.

4   Conventional Implementation Using MPI

In addition to our Lucata implementation we developed an MPI based version for comparison on conventional architectures. Our MPI version uses the producer and consumer concept employed for the Lucata design, however rather than having separate teams of threads existing within each process we chose to have each process perform one of the two tasks. This was done primarily out of simplicity as this format allows us to scale the number of processes across a test system without worrying about the precise hardware characteristics of any particular node.

Producer processes generate a set of datums from which they will decode the address and payload values prior to sending the converted values to the consumer process governing the appropriate range of address hashes for the address. *MPI_Isend* is used to perform datum assignment to a consumer in an asynchronous fashion.

Consumer processes continually probe their message buffers for messages containing assigned datums to work over. When a consumer receives a datum from an arbitrary producer, it analyze the address and payload value in exactly the same way as the Lucata implementation. This continues until all datums have been converted, assigned, and analyzed by their respective processes.

We do acknowledge that increasing the number of MPI processes will increase communication based overhead, however since we are using asynchronous writes to the consumer processes via *MPI_Isend* producers can assign datums to a consumer without the consumer having to acknowledge their receipt. This is the same behavior as in the Lucata version. Additionally since each process will be allocated on its own dedicated core, unlike the Lucata system on which 8 producer threads and 16 consumer threads execute together on a single core (nodelet), we expect to see little performance degradation from the lack of multithreading.

5 Communication Overhead

In practice both shared and distributed memory systems require communication, or the transfer of data between processing elements, in order to perform useful work. Shared memory machines may rely on excessive cache invalidation and update traffic to maintain valid memory state, while distributed systems still overwhelmingly use some form of message passing such as MPI. The time required to perform the cache coherency operations, or send and receive messages between processes is time that could have otherwise been spent performing computation.

Communication overhead impact performance in vastly different ways depending on the scaling method being employed. Weak scaling for instance can cause an increase in the computational load of the entire application by increasing problem size proportional to system size. This also simultaneously increases communications requirements, but very often the increase in system size provides the needed resources, especially if the communications per node remains relatively fixed, as it does for many weak scaling problems.

Some applications are capable of overlapping computation and communication such that the impact of communication on performance is reduced. These methods require sufficient computational requirements well in excess of all communication needs to see optimal performance. Network interconnect or bus latencies and bandwidth play enormous roles in the perceived cost of each message or update being performed, as well as the total overall cost of all such operations.

As shown in Sect. 3 our migrating thread implementation of the Firehose variant 2 splits datum string conversion and datum analysis portions of the benchmark. Two disjoint thread pools perform the producer and consumer algorithms simultaneously and there fore create an overlapped computation and communication pattern. While a consumer is processing datums against its local hash table, producers throughout the entire system may be assigning it new datums to work over. Therefore the communication associated with thread the thread migrations and memory copies required to perform the communication inherent to this design is overlapped and indistinguishable from the overall runtime as long as enough datums are assigned to any arbitrary nodelet.

6   Experimental Setup

6.1   Program Execution

As described in Sect. 2.2 the Lucata migrating thread system we evaluated consists of 8 node cards, each containing 8 nodelets and a dual-core SC capable of performing higher level OS functions. It is possible to configure the system in *singlenode* or *multinode* setups allowing the use of one or between 2 and 8 node cards respectively. We utilize multinode setup for our strong scaling experiments.

Nodelets are designed to consist of several light weight cores capable of many operations, yet are not as robust as the heavyweight cores used on the SC on each node card. Because of this, there is no way for a programmer to directly interact with a nodelet from the command line. Instead applications must be executed by using the *Lucata_handler_and_loader* command line utility which loads the programs into memory of for all 8 nodelets. This enables threads executing on the GC cores of a nodelet to continue program instruction execution without having to rely on an SC to update its program counter or instruction queue.

When an application is run, a single thread is spawned on nodelet 0 which begins instruction execution as per the program's design. In order to use additional threads we must spawn them as needed via *cilk_spawn* or the use of remote atomic operations. In our case threads are spawned in the same way for both Algorithms 1 and 2. Prior to evaluation of datums on any nodelet we spawn a single thread on each nodelet. These threads then spawn any number of additional threads locally. At this point every nodelet has a local thread pool with which to perform datum evaluation. The number of threads generated on each nodelet does not need to be the same, however only 64 threads may execute concurrently on any nodelet, with additional threads placed into an execution queue.

Threads proceed to migrate throughout the system as described in Sect. 3 until all datums on a nodelet have been exhausted. Once all datums on a nodelet have been evaluated they exit and return control back to the original calling thread. In our case after evaluation has completed all threads execute and control return to the original thread spawned on $n0$, where statistical information is gathered and output. This final migrating thread then signals the SC that execution has completed.

6.2   Dataset Generation and Placement

In our previous study we opted to ignore the conversion of datums in their raw ascii form and instead assumed a post-conversion state for testing. In this study we perform analysis of the post-conversion datums and evaluate performance, as well as performing tests in which ascii keys are stored after generation then converted into usable values during the timed portion of the tests.

In the post-conversion case space is allocated for *datumCount* number of datums on every nodelet utilized. Here we are performing weak scaling tests and therefore hold the number of datums per nodelet constant for each series of tests, starting at 2^{10} packets per nodelet and ending at 2^{16} packets per nodelet, increasing by powers of 2. Packets consist of 2^6 individual datums, therefore the range of datums per nodelet is 2^{16} to 2^{22}.

Unlike the power law distribution used for key generation in variant 1, variant 2 utilizes an active set generator. In the active set generator, an "active" set of 128K possible keys is used to generate datums. While the active set is always 128K, the exact key values contained within that active set change over time. This creates an "aging key" behavior in which keys may only be generated within a certain window. We incorporated the Firehose benchmark active set generator directly into our implementations to insure correctness.

During the initialization phase nodelet 0 spawns a thread remotely on each remote nodelet. Each thread is then given a distinct seed value which is used to generate randomized datum key values thereby ensuring that each thread does not generate identical keys. By generating keys in this fashion we are simulating the behavior of n number of generators, or 1 per nodelet, each with their own active sets. Keys are stored locally on the nodelet they were generated on in preparation for ascii conversion.

6.3   Scaling Tests

For our weak scaling tests we vary the number of nodelets from between 1 and 64 in powers of 2, as well as the number of threads spawned on each nodelet. Since our implementation has 2 distinct thread pools, datum conversion and datum analysis, we also vary the number of threads in each pool in order to investigate the impact of variable on performance. For datum conversion as well as datum processing we use thread counts between 1 and 32 in powers of 2. For the reference case we utilize a single nodelet with a single thread in each thread pool. The upper limit of our tests is 64 nodelets with 64 total threads each, generating a total of 4096 concurrent threads.

Generation and placement of datums in their ascii form onto their associated nodelet, occurs during the un-timed initialization phase. Run time measurements are started before the recursive spawn which generates worker threads in each team on each nodelet. A *cilk_sync* prevents further program execution until all nodelets have completed, upon which the stop time is measured and total run-time determined. The time required by the asynchronous updates to statistic counters is included, as discussed in the benchmark specification.

7   Evaluation

7.1   Throughput Scalability

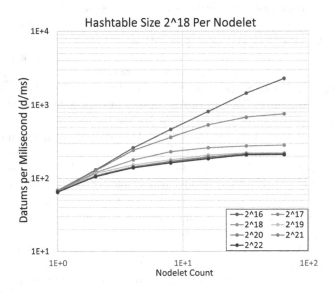

Fig. 4. Throughput scalability on Lucata using a per nodelet hash table size of 2^{18} maximum elements. Each line shows the throughput per millisecond observed for the given datum per nodelet

We performed tests using a wide range of system configurations in which the number of producers and consumers was varied. For all input sizes and nodelet counts peak performance was obtained using 8 producers and 16 consumers. Because of this, the remainder of this section will discuss performance results for the use of 8 producers and 16 consumers per nodelet.

Figure 4 shows throughput, in datums per millisecond (ms) we observed in our tests for each nodelet and datum per nodelet counts. We found that the best throughput was achieved when each nodelet was assigned only 2^{16} datums, in which **near perfect throughput scalability was achieved**. This was to be expected as the systems cores and memory channels are likely not close the saturation at this point.

For comparison the reported results for Firehose on one Xeon X5690 core delivered 1.9M datums/s. and a distributed memory implementation using and 7 cores of the same type delivered only 3.4M datums/s. This represents an unimpressive throughput gain of 1.8× for 7 cores. This is significant as the 7 core *PHISH/C++ 1/4/2* version which runs as a distributed memory parallel program via MPI is similar to our migrating thread based implementation. The Phish/C++ runs 7 processes as follows: One process reads packets, 4 processes

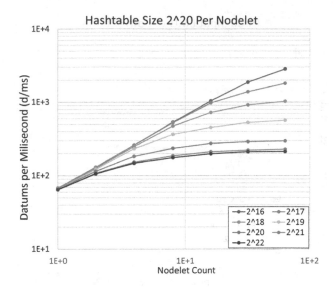

Fig. 5. Throughput scalability on Lucata using a per nodelet hash table size of 2^{20} maximum elements.

re-bundle them by hashing the keys, and the remaining 2 processes perform the analytic computation, each on a subset of the key space.

Additionally the MPI only version we implemented on the AMD Epyc based cluster achieved throughput of up 1.36M datums/s with 1 producer and 0.65M datums/s average with 64 producers, for a scaling factor of 0.6×. The initial throughput of the conventional system is between 1 and 2 orders of magnitude higher than the Lucata system. However as the system size is increased along with the total number of datums to be analyzed we can see from Fig. 6 that the conventional system begins to stagnate and decline as increased communication overhead associated with a greater number of off node MPI messages takes its toll on performance. This is if course something that may be rectified or lessened by further development allowing for a more optimized hybrid MPI/OpenMP implementation, which is something we will be taking a look at in the future.

In theory the time required to analyze any arbitrary datum should remain constant. There are two reasons why this implementation may see variance here. First the Lucata system is cacheless and insures that every read from main memory performs an actual 8 byte read rather than hitting an closer and lower latency cache as in conventional systems. Yet this does not mean that writes back to main memory suffer the same penalties. In fact 64-bit writes back memory are done by performing remote store operations directly in hardware and are very efficient. This means that we can store results in memory in an asynchronous manner which allows the executing thread to continue without having to wait for an acknowledgement of write-back completion by the memory controller.

Secondly is a difference in execution time for a datum depending on whether the hash table is full at the time of insertion. This is due to the use of the LRU

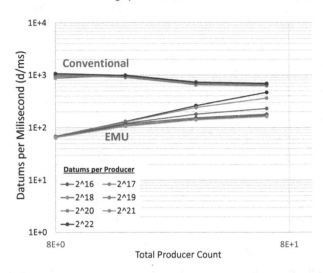

Fig. 6. Throughput comparison for conventional MPI implementation and Lucata migrating threads. Hash table size is 2^{18}. Starting at 8 producers (to match Lucata tests)

mechanism for maintaining a constant hash table size. Naturally the point at which this key insertion cost becomes worst case will occur depends on the hash table size chosen.

To illustrate this we increased hash table size assigned to each nodelet was set to 2^{20} elements. Figure 5 shows observed throughput for tests with an increased hash table size of 2^{20} elements per nodelet. As can be seen the overall behavior remains the same with lower datum per nodelet counts achieving good scalability, and larger datum counts flattening out quickly. Of particular interest is the demarcation point between good and flattening scalability. With the smaller hash table size all but three datum counts were tightly grouped at the bottom of the chart and experienced the same stagnating behavior. This behavior was expected however interestingly we saw that while even the largest datum counts obtained improved throughput it was minuscule compared to the smaller hash table tests.

7.2   Overlapped Datum Conversion and Analysis

Overlapping of communication and computation is a well known technique and is capable of providing increased performance. In nearly every case the efficacy of such overlapping requires the computational cost to exceed that of communication. The Lucata architecture is cacheless with no data cache to speak of for improving performance on data accesses with good locality. In fact during profiling we saw that the Lucata version requires nearly 2× the number of memory access operations as the conventional implementation (if we ignore MPI based buffer swaps per messages). Additionally a producer requires roughly 2800 instructions per datum conversion, while a consumer takes over 1.68 times as many instructions (over 4700) to analyze a datum.

The processing cores on the Lucata system posses a 16 stage pipeline so saturation without migration or stalling should occur around 16 threads per nodelet. This indicates that the increased thread counts at which saturation occurs due to an increase in an overlap of these "in-flight" threads which are migrating and those currently in the pipeline. In short by increasing the thread counts in both the producer and consumer pools we insure that the processing elements are always performing useful work despite higher memory access counts.

The migration of a producer to a remote nodelet for assigning its datum constitutes the communication overhead required by this algorithm. In contrast the PHISH/C++ implementation which used MPI for inter-process communication in Lucata thread migration overhead is overlapped with useful computation on both the source and destination nodelets. Lastly our MPI implementation has only one thread per process and therefore has a singular function. Despite this good overlapping is gained by the conventional system since its producer do not have a migrate and can utilize their core during nearly 100% of their execution for converting datums.

In other words with our design the Lucata system suffers when too many producers migrate to the same nodelet, as they may starve out the consumers local to that nodelet until they have completed their assignment. The exact performance impact is of course highly dependent on the keys being evaluated, how threads are scheduled for execution, and the number of hardware threads and memory channels present. Yet it is likely that given the right workload partitioning the impact on performance should be kept to a minimum as we have seen in our tests.

8   Conclusion

The results of this experiment seem to imply that the migrating thread architecture has much better scalability than the previous reported data. Additionally it achieves good scalability despite the nodelet cores possessing much lower computational power. Unfortunately it is difficult to draw direct comparisons considering the dramatic difference in architectural design. The experimental version of the Lucata cores run at just 0.175 GHz which is roughly 1/15 that of the previously reported systems clock rate. If we take the single node throughput of the Lucata system which was just 65,000 datums per second and adjust proportionally for CR alone then the throughput increases to 0.99M datums/s.

Additionally modern conventional cores are designed to be dual or even quad instruction issue wheres the Lucata Gossamer cores are single issue. This may provide at least 2× improvement in throughput in future hardware iterations bring it above that of the previously reported results. Lastly we attempted to compare the systems on a per unit hardware basis by comparing the number of datums per second per memory channel. Unfortunately however the raw timing data for the original Firehose study is not available. We hope to perform larger scale Firehose benchmark tests from which we can make more substantial comparisons. Another recent with compared Lucata to conventional systems for a machine learning algorithm operating on sparse data sets reported non-zeros per millisecond per memory channel values for the Lucata system up to 1.78× that of the conventional AMD Epyc 7451 used in our Firehose variant 2 study.

Unlike our previous study on Firehose variant 1 this study performed the ASCII key conversion as well as allowing threads to migrate throughout the system in order to assign keys to remote nodelets. This lead to a much more complete implementation of variant 2 of the Firehose streaming benchmark on the migrating thread architecture. It is not hard to imagine that the performance would be at least similar even with the ASCII keys if the nodelet cores were replaced with ASIC versions running 10× or faster than the current FPGA.

In looking at the implementation the gains seem to come from a variety of aspects of the migrating thread architecture. First is the lack of cache coherency traffic and the need for complex routines to perform atomic updates to the hash table, either locally or remotely. Second is the multi-threading that allows the memory channels of each nodelet to be fully utilized, regardless of the non-memory computations needed for each datum. Last but not least is the avoidance of explicit messaging software needed to communicate between physically separate nodes.

The next generation of the Lucata architecture is already in production and boasts substantially higher core per node counts as well as a much richer set of remote atomic operations with which greater thread migration and asynchronous performance might arise. Near-term future work will focus on larger scale tests on a system with greater than 8 nodes (64 nodelets) in order to see if scalability observed here continues as expected. Additionally we intend to develop a version of the code in which only a select number of nodelets perform ASCII key conversion with all datum analysis occurring on a separate set of consumer nodelets, such that producer threads do not interfere with consumer threads during analysis.

References

1. Firehose benchmarks. http://firehose.sandia.gov/
2. Bader, D.A., et al.: STINGER: spatio-temporal interaction networks and graphs (STING) extensible representation. Technical report, Georgia Institute of Technology (2009)
3. Bar-Yossef, Z., Kumar, R., Sivakumar, D.: Reductions in streaming algorithms, with an application to counting triangles in graphs. In: Proceedings of the Thirteenth Annual ACM-SIAM Symposium on Discrete Algorithms, SODA 2002, pp. 623–632. Society for Industrial and Applied Mathematics, Philadelphia (2002). http://dl.acm.org/citation.cfm?id=545381.545464

4. Becchetti, L., Boldi, P., Castillo, C., Gionis, A.: Efficient semi-streaming algorithms for local triangle counting in massive graphs. In: Proceedings of the 14th ACM SIGKDD International Conference on Knowledge Discovery and Data Mining, KDD 2008, pp. 16–24. ACM, New York (2008). https://doi.org/10.1145/1401890.1401898
5. Bernstein, P.A., Goodman, N.: Timestamp-based algorithms for concurrency control in distributed database systems. In: Proceedings of the Sixth International Conference on Very Large Data Bases, VLDB 1980, vol. 6, pp. 285–300. VLDB Endowment (1980). http://dl.acm.org/citation.cfm?id=1286887.1286918
6. Berry, J., Porter, A.: Stateful streaming in distributed memory supercomputers. In: Chesapeake Large Scale Data Analytics Conference (2016)
7. Carbone, P., Katsifodimos, A., Ewen, S., Markl, V., Haridi, S., Tzoumas, K.: Apache Flink: stream and batch processing in a single engine. In: Bulletin of the Technical Committee on Data Engineering, December 2015
8. Dysart, T., et al.: Highly scalable near memory processing with migrating threads on the emu system architecture, November 2016. https://doi.org/10.1109/IA3.2016.7
9. Eaton, J.: FireHose, PageRank, and nvGRAPH: GPU accelerated analytics. In: Chesapeake Large Scale Data Analytics Conference (2016)
10. Ediger, D., Jiang, K., Riedy, J., Bader, D.: Massive streaming data analytics: a case study with clustering coefficients, pp. 1–8, May 2010. https://doi.org/10.1109/IPDPSW.2010.5470687
11. Feigenbaum, J., Kannan, S., McGregor, A., Suri, S., Zhang, J.: On graph problems in a semi-streaming model. Theor. Comput. Sci. **348**(2), 207–216 (2005). https://doi.org/10.1016/j.tcs.2005.09.013
12. FIREHOUSE, S.B., with WATERSLIDE, E.: Karl Anderson. In: Chesapeake Large Scale Data Analytics Conference (2016)
13. Kogge, P.M., Butcher, N., Page, B.: Introducing streaming into linear algebra-based sparse graph algorithms, July 2019
14. Kogge, P.: Of piglets and threadlets: architectures for self-contained, mobile, memory programming. In: Innovative Architecture for Future Generation High-Performance Processors and Systems, pp. 130–138, January 2004. https://doi.org/10.1109/IWIA.2004.10005
15. McGregor, A.: Graph stream algorithms: a survey. SIGMOD Rec. **43**(1), 9–20 (2014). https://doi.org/10.1145/2627692.2627694
16. Page, B.A., Kogge, P.M.: Scalability of streaming on migrating threads. In: High Performance Extreme Computing (HPEC), September 2020
17. Plimpton, S.J., Shead, T.: Streaming data analytics via message passing with application to graph algorithms. J. Parallel Distrib. Comput. **74**(8) (2014). https://doi.org/10.1016/j.jpdc.2014.04.001
18. Riedy, J., Bader, D.: Stinger: multi-threaded graph streaming, May 2014

HTA: A Scalable High-Throughput Accelerator for Irregular HPC Workloads

Pouya Fotouhi(✉), Marjan Fariborz, Roberto Proietti,
Jason Lowe-Power, Venkatesh Akella, and S. J. Ben Yoo

University of California Davis, Davis, CA 95616, USA
{pfotouhi,mfariborz,rproietti,jlowepower,akella,sbyoo}@ucdavis.edu

Abstract. We propose a new architecture called HTA for high through-put irregular HPC applications with little data reuse. HTA reduces the contention within the memory system with the help of a partitioned memory controller that is amenable for 2.5D implementation using Silicon Photonics. In terms of scalability, HTA supports 4× higher number of compute units compared to the state-of-the-art GPU systems. Our simulation-based evaluation on a representative set of HPC benchmarks shows that the proposed design reduces the queuing latency by 10% to 30%, and improves the variability in memory access latency by 10% to 60%. Our results show that the HTA improves the L1 miss penalty by 2.3× to 5× over GPUs. When compared to a multi-GPU system with the same number of compute units, our simulation results show that the HTA can provide up to 2× speedup.

1 Introduction

The advent of exponentially-growing data-intensive applications across several domains has created a category of throughput-oriented workloads. This class of *irregular* applications impose new challenges for computer architects as their data sets are increasingly sparse and they exhibit poor locality in memory accesses. Unlike traditional compute-intensive applications, computing solutions designed for irregular applications should focus on reducing the latency and energy overheads of inevitable data movements.

The computing community has been utilizing GPUs as data-parallel accelerators given their massive throughput offerings. Though GPUs have proved to be effective as high throughput accelerators for many regular applications, we explore *specializing* data-parallel accelerators for efficient execution of *irregular* data-parallel workloads. These applications exhibit random memory access patterns, essentially making any shared component an architectural bottleneck limiting the obtainable throughput. Our main insight in designing HTA is to reduce the *contention* within the memory system and reduce the energy and performance cost of data movement.

This work was supported in part by ARO award W911NF1910470.

B. L. Chamberlain et al. (Eds.): ISC High Performance 2021, LNCS 12728, pp. 176–194, 2021.
https://doi.org/10.1007/978-3-030-78713-4_10

On the scalability front, as we reach the end of transistor scaling, we cannot simply rely on increasing the number of compute units on a single die to scale. An alternative approach is to design processors utilizing multiple "chiplets" [13]. Chiplets assembled using advanced packaging technologies, such as multi-chip-modules (MCMs), can offer a scalable design compared to one large monolithic chip. However, the inter-chiplet communication and its energy efficiency are known as the dominant factors towards performance and scalability due to significant power penalties brought by MCM designs [4]. We propose to address this challenge by taking advantage of recent advances in 2.5D/3D packaging with Silicon Photonics, which offers advantages of significantly lower energy per bit and scalability to much larger interposers than what today's reticle size limits allow. For example, recently TSMC and Broadcom announced $1700\,mm^2$ interposer [36] which is twice the size of the maximum reticle size by proposing to stitch together multiple interposers together.

In this paper, we present the design, evaluation, and 2.5D/3D packaging solution of the high-throughput scalable accelerator architecture called **HTA**. HTA's memory architecture exploits a partitioned memory controller (PMC) and all-to-all SiPh interconnects replacing conventional cross-bar based systems to support nearly-contention-free, high-throughput, and scalable data movement between the compute cores and the main memory. The partitioned memory controller reduces the queuing latency by 10% to 30% which translate to 5% to 26% reduction on overall memory access latency. In addition, addressing the contention in the memory controller reduces the variations in access latency by 10% to 60% in terms of 95th percentile latency. Furthermore, HTA improves the performance of the memory system and reduces L1 misses penalty by 2.3× to 5×. Evaluating our design at scale shows 1.5× speedup on average for HTA compared to a multi-GPU system for the same number of compute units.

The rest of the paper is organized as follows. Section 2 presents challenges towards scaling the memory system in the state-of-the-art data-parallel accelerators. Section 2.1 describes the architecture of partitioned memory controller, utilizing an interconnect fabric described in Sect. 2.2. Section 2.4 presents HTA architecture which builds on top of the proposed memory system. Through simulations with the methodology described in Sect. 3, the performance of partitioned controller and the proposed HTA architecture are evaluated in Sect. 4. Section 5 presents he related work, followed by the conclusions in Sect. 6.

2 HTA - Background, Rationale, and Design

GPUs are the de facto choice for high throughput accelerators in the HPC domain. The left side of Fig. 1 shows an overview of state-of-the-art GPUs. We identify four key challenges to the architecture shown in Fig. 1 when it comes to scaling irregular applications.

1) Crossbar Radix: Increasing the number of core clusters requires increasing the radix of the electrical crossbar between the cores and the L2 caches as current systems implement a mostly uniform L2 architecture. In addition to

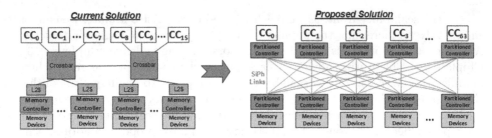

Fig. 1. (left) Overview of baseline memory system where different core clusters (CCs) share a crossbar, a single read/write queue per channel, and a last level cache. (right) Proposed memory system addresses the contention by providing dedicated queues for each core cluster to send memory request to every channel through an all-to-all interconnect.

the power and area overheads of the crossbar, it imposes a trade-off between latency and bandwidth: to increase the bisection bandwidth there must be more layers in the crossbar increasing both latency and area.

2) Overheads of Data Movement: Moving the data through multiple levels of memory hierarchy adds to memory access latency and results in increased energy consumption. This challenge becomes more important as physical distance between different levels increases in multi-chip module systems. In fact, the performance and energy overheads of data movements are known to be the main limiting factor towards scalability of multichip modules systems [4].

3) Bandwidth to Memory: Scaling the number of compute units in the system increases the demand for bandwidth to memory. Already limited by the latency-bandwidth trade-off due to the crossbar design, the number of available pins (between the compute dies and memory) add another constraint on bandwidth, especially in chiplet-based designs.

4) Variability in Memory Latency: Memory requests from different processing units share many deep queues including the crossbar, an L2 bank, the memory controller queues, DRAM bus, and DRAM banks. The contention from different compute units at these components increases the queuing delay which leads to variations in access latency and adds to the complexity of the scheduling for the memory controller and GPU cores.

Recent design trends from NVIDIA and AMD have taken steps to address these challenges. These solutions are inspired by similar techniques used in CPUs, and as a result, they do not address the underlying problem (i.e., contention) especially as we go towards scaling these systems. For instance, on a single GPU, NVIDIA's Ampere architecture [26] increases the number of compute units by 50% (from 84 in Volta to 128 in Ampere). To maintain a reasonable radix for the crossbar, the crossbar in is partitioned into two pieces. However, this approach introduces non-uniform latency and bandwidth to the memory, increasing the programming complexity on these systems. AMD's RDNA architecture [1] reduces the radix of the crossbar by adding a L1 cache which filters requests from all Compute Units (CUs) within a core cluster. While this approach simplifies the crossbar design, and reduces the pressure on the globally shared L2 cache, it adds to variability in memory access latency and only helps workloads which have regular memory access patterns or temporal reuse. AMD's CDNA architecture [2] eliminates the L1 cache along with the fixed-functions logic dedicated for graphics application to free up area and power for adding more CUs. However, the crossbar (and subsequently the L2 cache) is divided into two slices to achieve a reasonable radix for the state-of-the-art electrical interconnect technologies. Similar to NVIDIA's design, this approach increases the programming complexity by introducing non-uniformity in both latency and bandwidth, and further increases the variability in memory access latency.

The *main idea* underlying our proposal for HTA is to eliminate the contention in the memory subsystem as much as possible. We focus on three sources of contention: the on-chip crossbar, the globally shared L2 cache, and the memory controller queues. Our proposal makes the following **contributions** towards addressing the sources of contention in data-parallel accelerators.

(a) To reduce the contention at the request queues, we partition the memory controller into two parts: core-side controller with dedicated queues per core cluster (CC), and memory-side controller in charge of scheduling and issuing DRAM commands. This reduces the contention on read/write queues by offering dedicated queues for each core cluster and reduces queuing latency by avoiding the head-of-line blocking in scheduling. We will discuss the architecture and scheduling of proposed memory controller in Sect. 2.1

(b) The contention at the crossconnect is reduced by providing direct point-to-point links. However, implementing such a topology using electrical links would be extremely challenging due to bandwidth, energy, and routing limitations. To that end, and to reduce the overhead of data movements, we leverage an efficient all-to-all passive optical fabric (called Arrayed Waveguide Grating Router or AWGR) enabled by silicon photonics by taking advantage of 2.5D packaging. Describing the key enabling technology for our architecture, the details of proposed interconnect and packaging solutions are presented in Sect. 2.2 and Sect. 2.3 respectively.

(c) We utilize the partitioned memory controller design, and propose HTA in Sect. 2.4, which benefits from a scalable unified memory architecture and avoid NUMA challenges.

2.1 Partitioned Memory Controller

In this section, we present the details of our proposed Partitioned Memory Controller (PMC) which consists of two parts: the compute-side memory controller (CMC) and the memory-side memory controller (MMC). For the discussions and evaluations presented in this paper, we target HBM as the DRAM device, but the core idea of our proposal is agnostic to DRAM micro-architecture and can be applied to other DRAM technologies (e.g., GDDR, DDR, etc.) in a similar

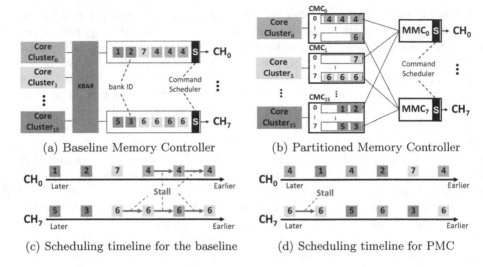

(a) Baseline Memory Controller   (b) Partitioned Memory Controller

(c) Scheduling timeline for the baseline   (d) Scheduling timeline for PMC

Fig. 2. Working example of PMC, showing how the head-of-line blocking is addressed compared to the baseline. The stalls are avoided by scheduling requests from different core clusters, and is limited only to the conflicting requests within a core cluster.

fashion as we focus only on the memory controller design and require no changes to DRAM core architecture (see Sect. 2.3 for details).

Figure 2b presents an overall view of the components within PMC. The key idea is to eliminate the contention on request queues and improve bank utilization by avoiding stalls due to bank conflicts between requests from different core clusters. With dedicated set of queues per channel for each core cluster, the variation in the memory access latency will be limited to unavoidable conflicting patterns from a single core cluster.

While dedicated queues eliminate the contention, the memory controller still needs to have a single scheduler per bank as point of reference for DRAM timings. Thus, we *partition* the memory controller into two parts. We keep the *front-end* (containing dedicated read/write queues) on the accelerator side, and move the *back-end* (including scheduling logic, and command queues) to the memory side.

Our design requires an all-to-all interconnect between the front-end and the back-end. Section 2.2 describes how a multi-wavelength routing device called AWGR can be used to replace the long-latency electrical crossbar while offering high-throughput contention-free communication.

Compute-Side Memory Controller (CMC). As Fig. 2b illustrates, we keep read and write queues on the processor side, with dedicated read and write queues for each channel. The idea is to limit the contention only to requests from the CUs within a single core cluster, and not all core clusters within the system. These queues are the result of breaking down the single shared read/write queue in the baseline memory controller shown in Fig. 2a into per core cluster queues.

Requests from L1 caches in each core cluster are routed to proper queues according to the address mapping scheme, similar to how corresponding L2 banks are selected for each request in the baseline architecture. Each Compute-side Memory Controller (CMC) has dedicated links to communicate with the Memory-side Memory Controller (MMC) for a given channel.

Memory-Side Memory Controller (MMC). Figure 2b shows two channels of our proposed memory controller, and connectivity between MMC and read/write queues from different CMCs. The scheduler looks at requests from all core clusters regardless of their queue occupancy. Therefore, the scheduler can continue servicing memory requests even when one requester has several conflicting requests issued within a short period of time—a common case in high-throughput accelerators illustrated in Fig. 2.

At each cycle, all CMCs send a copy of the request at the head of their queues. Then, an MMC selects a request to serve, it broadcasts back the requester ID (i.e., the winner) and the bank number to all CMCs. Thus, other requesters with requests for the same bank at the head of their queues can wait until the response is provided. Requests from different requesters (i.e., core clusters) are serviced in a round-robin fashion with an FR-FCFS scheduling policy similar to the baseline.

Figure 2 illustrates how the partitioned memory controller can address the head-of-line blocking problem. One core cluster (CC_0) is sending several conflicting requests (going to the same bank) to the first channel (CH_0). This results in several stalls during the scheduling. However, these stalls can be avoided by addressing non-conflicting requests from other CCs between the conflicting requests. PMC achieves this by allowing the MMC to select from dedicated queues for each channel within each CMC. Current systems use deep associative queues to avoid these stalls by finding requests to different banks within the queue. However, one CC can fill the queue with conflicting requests in a short period of time. This leaves the scheduler with no other options to choose from, even using the most sophisticated logic-intensive associative queues, and results in unnecessary back pressure applied to the whole system.

We should note that the processor's total queue size remains unchanged for each core cluster. We are essentially breaking down a large shared queue into n (*i.e.*, number of channels) smaller dedicated queues. The overhead of this is approach is limited to a small fraction to replicate the logic needed for maintaining those queues. On the memory side, there will be a small overhead for the added queues and we envision this logic to be implemented on the logic layer in 3D staked memories.

2.2   Interconnect

To address the contention at the crossconnect, our design utilizes a point-to-point connectivity between the core clusters and memory controllers. Besides addressing the contention, our proposed architecture requires an all-to-all connectivity between CMCs and MMCs. This connectivity allows for our scheduling policy to make local decisions at the MMC and updating CMCs through broadcasting.

As discuss earlier, designing a scalable high-throughput accelerator requires addressing the cost of data movements. Disaggregating the monolithic chip into multiple smaller chiplets allows for more input/output interfaces for each core cluster. However, chiplet electrical interconnection suffers from high distance-dependent signal loss and limited I/O bandwidth [5]. Therefore, interconnecting many non-adjacent chiplets require multi-hop networks with repeaters, incurring large latency and energy overheads. These challenges can be overcome by silicon photonic technology: reducing latency with almost distance-independent communication energy and providing high pin bandwidth density through wavelength-division multiplexing (WDM) [25]. In the following sections, we present a summary on the principle of operation for optical links used in our design, and discuss the details about our proposed interconnect fabric and packaging solution.

Silicon Photonics. Integrated optical interconnects, enabled by silicon photonics, offer properties that can be exploited to address the performance and energy overheads of data movements in high-throughput accelerators.

An external WDM laser (in form of an optical frequency comb source or individual lasers) generates the optical signal at the required wavelengths, which are then coupled from a fiber into on-chip waveguides. On-chip modulators encode bits onto wavelengths (one modulator for each wavelength). Then, the modulated wavelengths traverse the waveguides and are filtered out and converted back into the electrical domain by on-chip photodetectors. In terms of latency, electrical-to-optical (EO) and optical-to-electrical (OE) signal conversions are done at one cycle and incur no additional latency to the transmission line.

Arrayed Waveguide Grating Router. One interesting property of WDM technology (aside from its bandwidth benefits), is that it allows connecting a single node to multiple receiver nodes by leveraging wavelength-selective routing devices. This method allows implementing an all-to-all network without a large number of point-to-point ports.

Among different SiPh wavelength routing devices that have been demonstrated [5], we utilize the Arrayed Waveguide Grating Router (AWGR) with a footprint of $\sim 1 \, \text{mm}^2$ [31] to provide contention-less point-to-point connectivity between all chiplets. AWGR is a *passive* SiPh fabric which provides all-to-all connectivity between any input and any output port. Several studies explored AWGRs as a uniquely compact solution for all-to-all interconnection with lower loss and crosstalk compared with other SiPh devices providing similar connectivity [14,17,40]. The reader can refer to the following articles for what concerns the physics, design principle, and scalability of AWGRs [15,29,41].

2.3   Packaging

Figure 3 presents an overview of the packaging approach we use in our design. We adopt a previously proposed technique for intra-package communication [9,14,38] which can be applied to our memory controller design.

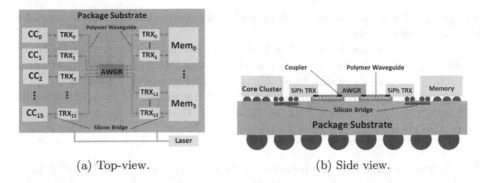

(a) Top-view.   (b) Side view.

Fig. 3. Example of proposed packaging solution, where compute and memory dies are optically-interconnected through an AWGR using SiPh transceivers with transceiver-chiplets and Si bridges on an organic substrate.

This approach considers developing dedicated SiPh transceiver chiplets connected to their respective (compute or memory) dies.

The advantage of this design decision is that it can be leveraged to provide support for off-the-shelf memory devices (e.g., HBM, GDDR, etc.) by choosing the proper command scheduler in MMCs. By integrating the MMC and SiPh TRx (on the memory side) on the same die, no extra logic is required on memory dies, and MMCs can be designed to work with existing PHY interfaces - with minimal distance for data movements on electrical wires.

The dedicated SiPh transceiver chiplets connected to their respective dies on one side through Si bridges and to AWGR (the fabric providing all-to-all connectivity) through polymer waveguides (PWGs). These polymer waveguides are integrated on top of the organic package substrate and provide inter-chiplet optical connectivity. The reader can refer to the work of Dangel et al. [11,12] for the details on the overall integration process for polymer waveguides.

Combining SiPh and Si bridges, our proposal utilizes each interconnection technology where it is the most efficient: SiPh for long-distance cross-package interconnect between chiplets and Si bridges for short-distance electrical interconnect between the TRXs and the memory controller.

SiPh manufacturing processes exploits well established CMOS processes, and photonic integrated circuit design kits (PDKs) have seen significant growth in the past ten years, resulting in cost-effective SiPh integration [39]. The reader can refer to [14,20] for more detailed cost analyses and roadmap.

2.4 HTA Architecture

We discussed the challenges in scaling the memory architecture for today's high-throughput accelerator and how our proposed memory architecture addresses them. In this section we build on top of the proposed memory system, and introduce a high-throughput accelerator (HTA) architecture which takes the advantage of low-latency all-to-all optical fabric and allows elimination of the shared last level cache.

Elimination of last-level caches provide significant advantages in terms of dedicating more area for compute, reducing access latency, and improving predictability in memory access time. The photonic interconnect used in our proposal provides us higher bandwidth at a lower energy per bit cost to make the underlying design tradeoffs such as eliminating the last level caches feasible, especially for irregular workloads with poor locality.

Implications on Core Architecture. Memory accesses in GPUs takes hundreds of cycles to be serviced, and this latency can drastically change during the application execution as different compute units compete for receiving their data through shared memory channels. GPU architects have addressed this issue by increasing the number of contexts executed simultaneously on GPUs. However, this design choice comes with several challenges:

Context Scheduler: Allowing execution of multiple contexts at the same time requires dedicated logic to maintain, track, the state for each of them. Moreover, based on the state of contexts, additional logic is required to perform scheduling with proper arbitration and decoding units involved.

Physical Register Files: GPUs rely on large register files to store data required for computation. Providing support for tens of contexts to be executed simultaneously translates in larger register files, scaling almost linearly with the number of contexts supported.

Both area and power dedicated to the operations discussed above are obstacles towards achieving scalability for high-throughput accelerators. Our proposed memory architecture mitigates these overheads by lowering the access latency and improving the predictability in memory access. The evaluation of these opportunities for micro architectural improvements requires substantial work in terms of modeling, and we leave them for the future work.

Scalability of HTA. One of the main benefits of SiPh interconnects is their distance-independent energy consumption and performance. Combining this with the benefits of packaging solution discussed in Sect. 2.3 allows HTA to scale.

Considering the area saving from eliminating L2 cache (occupying ∼50% of chip area), a single package instance of HTA can support 4× more compute units. Moreover, multiple packages can be utilized to scale further, and realize a scalable high-throughput accelerator with a unified address space without considerable energy and performance overheads.

The major component in HTA that needs to scale with the system is the AWGR. In this paper, we study HTA with 64 and 256 CUs which can be realized using 16×16 and 64×64 AWGR respectively. Scaling above 256 CUs requires AWGR with more than 64 ports. While 512×512 AWGR has been demonstrated [8], the main challenge for implementing AWGRs with high port counts (i.e., >64) is the optical crosstalk. However, the new Thin-CLOS architecture successfully demonstrated by Proietti et al. [29] can utilize multiples of smaller AWGRs (lower port count) in parallel to provide the same functionality of a larger AWGR at lower crosstalk. While these solutions have larger footprints, the area overhead might be negligible in large accelerators with more than 256 CUs.

The bandwidth between any input-output pair in AWGR is limited to the information that can be carried out by a single modulated wavelength. If the bandwidth requirements exceed what a single wavelength offers, there are two alternative options. The first one is to leverage multiple free spectral ranges (FSRs) of an AWGR [16,17], and virtually create a parallel channel of communication. The second one is to use spatial-division multiplexing (SDM), i.e., integrating and transmitting data through parallel AWGRs (either planar or 3D-stacked [32]). Multi-FSR strategy requires a broader laser spectrum and higher laser power to compensate for higher crosstalk inside the AWGR and to guarantee the required minimum optical power at the receiver. The SDM approach has similar laser power requirements but does not need a broader laser spectrum. However, it needs a larger die area or more SiPh layers, as well as more optical IO pins.

3   Methodology

3.1   System Comparisons

To evaluate our proposed HTA architecture, we compare it against a system similar to AMD's RDNA architecture with details of the memory hierarchy shown in Fig. 1. CUs within a core cluster have private caches ("L0") and share the L1 cache, which centralizes all caching functions within each cluster [1]. L1 caches are connected to a globally shared L2 cache through a long-latency crossbar interconnect, resulting in ~100 cycles hit latency for L2 [21]. Therefore, for our simulations, we modelled the electrical crossbar with a latency of 50 cycles in each direction.

Within the memory controller of a given channel, all requests from different CUs share a read and a write queue. In each cycle, the scheduler performs an associative search and issues commands for requests in a First-Ready First-Come-First-Served (FR-FCFS [30]) fashion. For our evaluations, we refer to this design as the baseline memory controller. While we use AMD's RDNA memory hierarchy as our baseline, the challenges in scaling the memory hierarchy of GPUs are common in NVIDIA's systems and our proposal can be applied there similarly.

One example of HTA can host 64 CUs by utilizing a 16 × 16 AWGR to interconnect eight compute chiplets (each with four CUs) to four stacks of HBM2 memory. SiPh links use WDM with 16 wavelengths and perform modulation/demodulation at 32 Gbps. On the compute side, each compute chiplet uses one SiPh WDM TRX with 64 GB/s bandwidth in each direction, making a

Table 1. Simulation parameters

Compute cluster			
Number of CUs	64	CUs per CC	4
Memory hierarchy			
L0 V\$	16 kB (per CU)	L0 I\$	32 kB (per CC)
L0 K\$	16 kB (per CC)	L1 \$	64 kB (per CC)
L2 \$	2 MB (8 banks)	DRAM	4 GB HBM2 [22]

total of 16 SiPh TRXs for CMCs. On the memory side, four SiPh WDM TRXs can match the 256 GB/s bandwidth of a single stack of HBM2 which results in a total of 16 SiPh TRXs for MMCs.

3.2 Simulations

Performance. To model our target systems we use MGPUSim [34] which models the Graphics Core Next 3 (GCN3) ISA. We extended the simulator to model a three level cache hierarchy. We integrated the timing model from DRAM-Sim3 [22] after extending it to model our proposed partitioned memory controller design discussed in Sect. 2. We utilize MGPUSim for collecting the traces on the memory system, and piped those traces on detailed timing model on DRAMSim.

For the performance of the interconnect technologies used in this paper, we used latency reporting in the previous work [14,21]. The details of the modeled system in the simulator for different components are listed in Table 1. It should be noted that the trace-based evaluation approach limits our reporting to the performance of the memory system, and does not allow us to obtain execution times for the two systems under comparison. However, since a significant portion of the pipeline stalls are due to memory accesses, the performance of the memory system would be a reasonable candidate for our evaluation. To this end, we will look at the penalty of L1 misses when comparing the baseline with PMC in Sect. 4.

For evaluating our proposal we used benchmarks from AMD's Accelerated Parallel Processing (APP) Software Development Kit (SDK), Hetero-Mark suite [33], and Scalable Heterogeneous Computing (SHOC) suite [10].

Among those supported by MGPUSim, we chose different benchmarks with different memory behaviours to evaluate our proposal under different scenarios. Breadth-first Search *bfs* and Page Rank *pr* represent applications with irregular memory access patterns (i.e., poor locality). AES-256 Encryption (*aes*), Fast Fourier Transform (*fft*), and FIR Filter (*fir*) represent typical compute intense HPC applications with considerable amount of data reuse (i.e., medium locality). Simple Convolution (*conv*) implementation used for this work divides the image into sub-images to maximize data reuse (i.e., high locality).

4   Evaluation

In this section, we present the evaluation results on three aspects of our proposal.

First, we look at the performance of the proposed memory controller design compared to the baseline memory controller discussed in Sect. 2. This analysis is done under the same cache hierarchy. In these experiments, we look at the average DRAM access latency in both designs, as well as 95th percentile latency as a measure of divergence in the access latency. Second, we evaluate HTA design against the baseline GPU architecture. In this set of analyses, we evaluate our memory controller design combined with a new cache hierarchy, and model a system like the one shown on right in Fig. 1. We report the average miss penalty for L1 caches in the form of Average Memory Access Time (AMAT) for L1 misses. Third, we evaluate our proposal at scale by comparing the performance of HTA with 256 CUs against a multi-GPU system with 4× 64CU GPUs.

4.1   Evaluation of Partitioned Memory Controller

As our first step in evaluating our proposed architecture, we compare the performance of the partitioned memory controller against the baseline memory controller, both using the same cache organization. To emphasize on the importance of the enabling technology used in our design, an implementation of PMC using electrical links (PMC-E) is evaluated.

PMC design reduces access latency divergence by avoiding head-of-line blocking in scheduling. In the baseline design where all requesters share a single queue, if one requester sends a stream of requests over a short window (a common case in data-parallel accelerators), requests from other requesters are blocked until DRAM manages to return pending requests. PMC avoids this by having dedicated queues for each requester and directly applies the back-pressure to the original requester and not the whole system. Figure 4b shows the 95th percentile in access latency, indicating a significant reduction in memory latency variation for PMC over the baseline memory controller. Depending on the access pattern in each workload, the 95th percentile in access latency is improved by 10% to 60%. The benefits gained through scheduling are strong enough to result in improved tail latency even for the electrical implementation of the PMC which suffers from high-latency links.

Besides improving the predictability in access latency, PMC improves the access latency by increasing parallelism in bank accesses within the DRAM. Figure 4a depicts the average memory latency for the baseline memory controller and the proposed PMC. PMC achieves a lower average access latency by avoiding a portion of bank conflicts in the memory requests. If one requester sends several conflicting requests, those would limit bank activations in the baseline design, while in PMC, the scheduler can schedule requests from other requesters. Therefore, the queuing portion of memory access is reduced by 10% to 30% depending on the access pattern exhibited by each workload.

Both PMC-E and PMC take advantage of the scheduling scheme offered by PMC and avoid head-of-line blocking which translates to improvements in tail

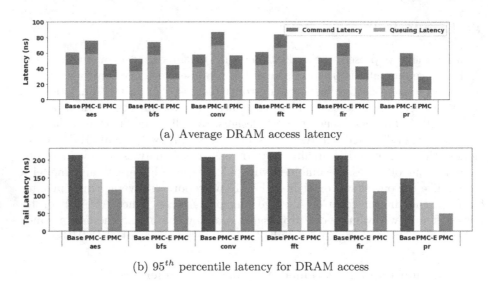

(a) Average DRAM access latency

(b) 95th percentile latency for DRAM access

Fig. 4. DRAM performance for the baseline memory controller (base) compared to a system utilizing partitioned memory controller with implemented with electrical and SiPh links (PMC-E and PMC, respectively). (a) In terms of access latency, PMC improves the queuing latency by 10% to 30% resulting in 5% to 26% reduction on overall access latency compared to the baseline memory controller. (b) The 95th percentile latency for DRAM access is improved by 10% to 60% by reducing contention at read and write queues within the memory controller.

latency. This is purely due to the scheduling scheme in PMC, and it is independent of the technology used to implement the point-to-point fabric. However, as described in Sect. 2.1, the PMC design makes the crossbar latency part of the memory access. Therefore, the latency overhead imposed by the interconnect used in PMC is a critical part of this design. While the PMC design improves the average access latency by 10%–30% (*i.e.*, 5–20 ns), these improvements can be masked when using a long-latency crossbar (*e.g.*, 50 ns). As illustrated in Fig. 4b, the implementation of PMC using electrical links (PMC-E) improves the tail latency. However, as shown in Fig. 4a, the average access latency is significantly increased as the result of long-latency electrical links used in this design. This analysis shows the importance of interconnect technology used for our proposal, making SiPh and AWGR the key enablers for this design.

4.2   Evaluation of HTA

As the next step, we investigate the performance of proposed HTA system which allows for elimination of the last level cache against the baseline GPU described in Sect. 3, along with a GPU with 40 MB of last level cache. In order to analyse different architectural differences between HTA and the baseline, we present evaluate two middle point between the two systems. First, we modeled a system

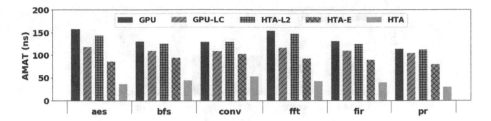

Fig. 5. Average Memory Access Time (AMAT) for L1 misses. The baseline (GPU) is compared to a GPU with 40 MB of last level cache (GPU-LC), a similar system using PMC (HTA-L2), an implementation of HTA using electrical links (HTA-E), and ultimately the proposed HTA. HTA improves the average L1 miss penalty by 2.3× to 5× compared to the baseline GPU architecture by avoiding data transfers over a high-latency crossbar.

similar to the baseline which utilizes the PMC under the same cache organization (labeled HTA-L2). Moreover, we modeled HTA implemented using electrical interconnects to separate the architectural changes from the benefits gained purely from SiPh technology (labeled HTA-E).

As we discussed earlier in Sect. 3, our trace-based evaluation does not allow us to report runtime numbers. Thus, we choose to report the overall performance of the memory system. Figure 5 presents the L1 miss penalty, as a measure of performance of the memory system for both architectures under investigation. Average miss penalty for L1 caches is calculated in the form of AMAT for L1 misses.

As the third bar (HTA-L2) in Fig. 5 shows, DRAM access latency improvements gained from PMC result in 10–15% reduction in L1 miss penalty. However, the latency-intensive (50 cycles) consult with the last level cache is hiding most of the benefits achieved. With L2 caches eliminated in HTA, all L1 misses are directly added to the CMCs, where requests are transferred over the all-to-all fabric to the MMCs.

Even the HTA system using electrical links (with 50 cycles of latency between CMCs and MMCs) significantly reduces the L1 miss penalty. Taking advantage of low-latency (3 cycles) interconnect fabric enabled by SiPh, HTA reduces the latency cost of L1 misses by 2.3× to 5×.

Reductions on the average miss penalty for L1 caches are mostly obtained through improvements on the 95th percentile in access latency, emphasizing the importance of variations in memory access latency in the overall performance of the memory system for high-throughput accelerators.

The second bar (GPU-LC) represents a GPU with a large (*i.e.*, 40 MB) last-level cache, similar to the architectural approach taken by NVIDIA [26], lowering the AMAT by reducing the traffic to DRAM. This approach benefits workloads with high locality. However, as can be seen in Fig. 5, it will only achieve a small fraction of improvements offered by HTA for irregular HPC workloads with sparse data accesses.

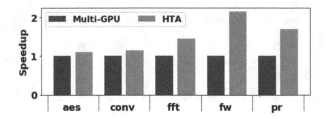

Fig. 6. The speedup of HTA with 256 CUs compared to a multi-GPU system with 4 GPUs each with 64 CUs. The overhead of data movements in multi-GPU setup result in a speedup of up to 2× for HTA.

4.3   Comparison with Multi-GPU Systems

A key motivation for our HTA design is to achieve scalability. Utilizing a 64×64 AWGR, HTA can deliver an accelerator with 256 CUs. The state-of-the-art GPU systems can achieve this scale only by combining multiple GPUs.

For the last part in evaluating HTA, we compared its performance against a multi-GPU system with the same number of compute units (256 CUs). It should be noted that not all the benchmarks provided support for multi-GPU execution, and we only had a few options to run this experiment. Also, we should note that the speedups reported in Fig. 6 are mainly a lower-bound for what the HTA can achieve. As of today, MGPUSim lacks a memory controller with timing details, and DRAM responses are satisfied at a flat latency. That is the main limiting factor for us to evaluate PMC in terms of execution time. However, to show the potential benefits of a scalable system enabled by HTA, we modeled a system with the average DRAM access latency measured in DRAMSim for the baseline controller and PMC. This approach does not take into account the benefits of lower variations in memory access achieved by PMC, and does not reveal the full performance potential of HTA.

According to the evaluation results shown in Fig. 6, HTA can achieve 1.5× speedup on average compared to a multi-GPU system. This improvement is mainly achieved in HTA by avoiding the cross-GPU communication and scheduling overheads in a multi-GPU system.

One interesting observation here is the overhead of a multi-GPU system for different workloads. As can be seen in Fig. 6, applications like *aes* or *conv* with smaller data sharing between their kernels experience less overhead (∼10%) in the multi-GPU system. On the other hand, applications with more inter-kernel data dependencies such as Page Rank (*pr*), *fft*, and Floyd Warshal (*fw*) require more data movements between kernels (running on different GPUs), and result in larger slowdowns (up to 2×) in a multi-GPU setup. These variations depend on both architecture and workload, and impose several barriers in utilizing multi-GPU systems. HTA allows the programmers to migrate their applications to a scalable platform, and avoids considerable performance overheads especially for applications with significant data sharing across different compute units.

5   Related Work

Several studies have looked at the scalability of GPUs. Vijayaraghavan et al. illustrated the roadmap for exascale computing, and suggested aggressive use of chiplet technologies and die-stacking to meet a scalable system design [37]. MCM-GPU [3] argues that GPU scalability can be achieved by partitioning the GPU dies into GPU modules and reducing the cross GPU traffic. Pal et al. took a different approach, and looked at the design space of wafer-scale GPUs [28], where pre-manufactured GPU dies are directly bonded on to a silicon wafer which includes the interconnection fabric on it. Arunkumar et al. [4] created a framework for quantifying the scaling efficiency in terms of both performance and energy which, based on their analysis, lack of inter GPU module bandwidth increases the GPU idle time which increases the energy consumption in the system. As Arunkumar et al. pointed out, the performance and energy overheads of data movements are the main limiting factor towards scalability in GPUs. Many researchers looked at this problem from different viewpoints. Milic et al. [24] proposed a NUMA-aware multi-socket GPU architecture that reduces the traffic on the interconnects. They minimized the NUMA effects by dynamically optimizing the interconnect and the cache management policy in each phase of the application. In MGPUSIM [34] a new memory management policy is introduced in multi-GPU systems which can improve the data placement dynamically with the goal of reducing inter-node communications. We believe that the performance and energy overheads of data movements in GPUs should fundamentally be addressed. Considering how the memory system is designed for the state-of-the-art accelerators, this goal can only be achieved through co-designing the memory system and interconnect fabric. Another limiting factors in high-throughput accelerators is the memory access latency, both in terms of the absolute value and its variations. Lowering the memory access latency would decrease the idle time, improving performance and energy efficiency. Chatterjee et al. improved the performance of the memory systems in GPUs by proposing a new memory controller that can reduce the DRAM latency divergence within the warps [7]. Bojnordi et al. proposed a programmable memory controller along with added instructions to the ISA to improve request scheduling and bank utilization on DDR memories [6]. Hashemi et al. aimed to reduce the pressure on the memory system and proposed adding more logic to the memory controller to execute cache inefficient instructions near DRAM by dynamically identify such instructions at the processor [18]. Liu et al. improved the memory access mapping by using the window-based entropy mapping [23]. This technique reduces the virtual to physical address mapping overhead by quantifying the entropy of each address bit across all memory requests. Hussain et al. looked at the access pattern within irregular memory access, and reduced the DRAM latency by caching different patterns and scheduling memory accesses accordingly [19]. Oh et al. [27] improved the bandwidth utilization in HBM by load balancing across all channels, and decreased the stall time by effectively increasing the request queue. Tian et al. proposed an adaptive technique for bypassing caches [35] which can improve performance and energy efficiency in GPUs, especially for workloads with poor cache utilization. We found all of the aforementioned related work on the memory controller design applicable to our design, providing several valuable pointers for the future directions.

6   Conclusion

In this paper, we proposed a novel partitioned memory controller (PMC) to reduce the contention in memory system of high-throughput accelerators. Utilizing the PMC design along with a scalable all-to-all optical fabric, we proposed a new high-throughput accelerator. Our simulation results show improvements for PMC on DRAM access latency and memory access divergence, and reduced miss penalty in L1 caches. Our chiplet-based design combines our novel PMC design and SiPh technology to support 4× more compute units.

Given the lack of publicly available area/power models of state-of-the-art GPUs, it is difficult to do a fair and accurate comparison of HTA with GPUs in terms of power and area. However, we can present a qualitative analysis. In terms of power consumption, SiPh links used in this work require 1.65–0.66 pJ/bit depending on the technology node used ranging from 65 nm to 14 nm. In terms of area overheads, PMC design does not add any logic for queuing as dedicated queues are result of breaking down the single shared queue in the baseline controller. Moreover, the SiPh components used in our design (the AWGR, and SiPh TRXs) have small footprints compared to size of the processor dies (less than 0.01% for typical compute dies [15]).

In this work we have assumed that the compute units in the HTA are similar to that of a GPU. However the proposed HTA architecture can apply to many different types of processors and accelerators. The combination of the significantly lower memory latency and more deterministic memory access time enables unexplored areas for micro-architecture design of advanced computing units and accelerators. This will form our future work.

References

1. AMD: Introducing RDNA architecture (2019). https://www.amd.com/system/files/documents/rdna-whitepaper.pdf. Accessed 10 Dec 2020
2. AMD: Introducing AMD CDNA architecture (2020). https://www.amd.com/system/files/documents/amd-cdna-whitepaper.pdf. Accessed 12 Dec 2020
3. Arunkumar, A., et al.: MCM-GPU: multi-chip-module GPUs for continued performance scalability. ACM SIGARCH Comput. Archit. News 45(2), 320–332 (2017)
4. Arunkumar, A., et al.: Understanding the future of energy efficiency in multi-module GPUs. In: 2019 IEEE International Symposium on High Performance Computer Architecture (HPCA), pp. 519–532. IEEE (2019)
5. Bergman, K., et al.: Photonic Network-on-Chip Design. Springer, New York (2014). https://doi.org/10.1007/978-1-4419-9335-9
6. Bojnordi, M.N., Ipek, E.: PARDIS: a programmable memory controller for the DDRx interfacing standards. In: 2012 39th Annual International Symposium on Computer Architecture (ISCA), pp. 13–24 (2012)

7. Chatterjee, N., et al.: Managing DRAM latency divergence in irregular GPGPU applications. In: SC 2014: Proceedings of the International Conference for High Performance Computing, Networking, Storage and Analysis, pp. 128–139. IEEE (2014)
8. Cheung, S., et al.: Ultra-compact silicon photonic 512 × 512 25 GHZ arrayed waveguide grating router. IEEE J. Sel. Top. Quantum Electron. **20**(4), 310–316 (2013)
9. Cutress, I.: Intel launches stratix-10-TX leveraging EMIB with 58G transceivers. https://www.anandtech.com/show/12477/intel-launches-stratix-10-tx-leveraging-emib-with-58g-transceivers-. Accessed 28 Nov 2020
10. Danalis, A., et al.: The scalable heterogeneous computing (SHOC) benchmark suite. In: Proceedings of the 3rd Workshop on General-Purpose Computation on Graphics Processing Units, pp. 63–74 (2010)
11. Dangel, R., et al.: Polymer waveguides for electro-optical integration in data centers and high-performance computers. Opt. Express **23**(4), 4736–4750 (2015)
12. Dangel, R., et al.: Polymer waveguides enabling scalable low-loss adiabatic optical coupling for silicon photonics. IEEE J. Sel. Top. Quantum Electron. **24**(4), 1–11 (2018)
13. Das, S.: It's time for disaggregated silicon! (2018). https://www.netronome.com/blog/its-time-disaggregated-silicon/. Accessed 28 Nov 2020
14. Fotouhi, P., et al.: Enabling scalable chiplet-based uniform memory architectures with silicon photonics. In: Proceedings of the International Symposium on Memory Systems, pp. 222–334 (2019)
15. Fotouhi, P., et al.: Enabling scalable disintegrated computing systems with AWGR-based 2.5 D interconnection networks. IEEE/OSA J. Opt. Commun. Netw. **11**(7), 333–346 (2019)
16. Grani, P., et al.: Bit-parallel all-to-all and flexible AWGR-based optical interconnects. In: Optical Fiber Communication Conference, pp. M3K-4. Optical Society of America (2017)
17. Grani, P., et al.: Design and evaluation of AWGR-based photonic NoC architectures for 2.5 D integrated high performance computing systems. In: 2017 IEEE International Symposium on High Performance Computer Architecture (HPCA), pp. 289–300. IEEE (2017)
18. Hashemi, M., et al.: Accelerating dependent cache misses with an enhanced memory controller. In: 2016 ACM/IEEE 43rd Annual International Symposium on Computer Architecture (ISCA), pp. 444–455 (2016)
19. Hussain, T., et al.: Advanced pattern based memory controller for FPGA based HPC applications. In: 2014 International Conference on High Performance Computing Simulation (HPCS), pp. 287–294 (2014)
20. Jeppix: Cost roadmap. https://www.jeppix.eu/wp-content/uploads/2020/04/JePPIXRoadmap2012.pdf. Accessed 28 Nov 2020
21. Jia, Z., et al.: Dissecting the NVIDIA volta GPU architecture via microbenchmarking. arXiv preprint arXiv:1804.06826 (2018)
22. Li, S., et al.: DRAMsim3: a cycle-accurate, thermal-capable DRAM simulator. IEEE Comput. Archit. Lett. **19**(2), 106–109 (2020)
23. Liu, Y., et al.: Get out of the valley: power-efficient address mapping for GPUs. In: 2018 ACM/IEEE 45th Annual International Symposium on Computer Architecture (ISCA), pp. 166–179. IEEE (2018)
24. Milic, U., et al.: Beyond the socket: NUMA-aware GPUs. In: Proceedings of the 50th Annual IEEE/ACM International Symposium on Microarchitecture, pp. 123–135 (2017)

25. Miller, D.A.: Device requirements for optical interconnects to silicon chips. Proc. IEEE **97**(7), 1166–1185 (2009)

26. NVIDIA: A100 tensor core GPU architecture. https://www.nvidia.com/content/dam/en-zz/Solutions/Data-Center/nvidia-ampere-architecture-whitepaper.pdf. Accessed 31 Nov 2020

27. Oh, B., et al.: A load balancing technique for memory channels. In: Proceedings of the International Symposium on Memory Systems, pp. 55–66 (2018)

28. Pal, S., et al.: Architecting waferscale processors - a GPU case study. In: 2019 IEEE International Symposium on High Performance Computer Architecture (HPCA), pp. 250–263 (2019)

29. Proietti, R., et al.: Experimental demonstration of a 64-port wavelength routing thin-CLOS system for data center switching architectures. J. Opt. Commun. Netw. **10**(7), B49–B57 (2018)

30. Rixner, S., et al.: Memory access scheduling. ACM SIGARCH Comput. Archit. News **28**(2), 128–138 (2000)

31. Shang, K., et al.: Low-loss compact silicon nitride arrayed waveguide gratings for photonic integrated circuits. IEEE Photonics J. **9**(5), 1–5 (2017)

32. Su, T., et al.: Interferometric imaging using Si_3N_4 photonic integrated circuits for a SPIDER imager. Opt. Express **26**(10), 12801–12812 (2018)

33. Sun, Y., et al.: Hetero-mark, a benchmark suite for CPU-GPU collaborative computing. In: 2016 IEEE International Symposium on Workload Characterization (IISWC), pp. 1–10. IEEE (2016)

34. Sun, Y., et al.: MGPUsim: enabling multi-GPU performance modeling and optimization. In: Proceedings of the 46th International Symposium on Computer Architecture, pp. 197–209 (2019)

35. Tian, Y., et al.: Adaptive GPU cache bypassing. In: Proceedings of the 8th Workshop on General Purpose Processing Using GPUS, pp. 25–35 (2015)

36. TSMC: Enhancing the CoWoS platform (2020). https://pr.tsmc.com/english/news/2026. Accessed 14 Dec 2020

37. Vijayaraghavan, T., et al.: Design and analysis of an APU for exascale computing. In: 2017 IEEE International Symposium on High Performance Computer Architecture (HPCA), pp. 85–96 (2017)

38. Wade, M., et al.: TeraPHY: a chiplet technology for low-power, high-bandwidth in-package optical I/O. IEEE Micro **40**(2), 63–71 (2020)

39. Wang, J., Long, Y.: On-chip silicon photonic signaling and processing: a review. Sci. Bull. **63**(19), 1267–1310 (2018)

40. Werner, S., et al.: Towards energy-efficient high-throughput photonic NoCs for 2.5 D integrated systems: a case for AWGRs. In: 2018 Twelfth IEEE/ACM International Symposium on Networks-on-Chip (NOCS), pp. 1–8. IEEE (2018)

41. Zhang, Y., et al.: Foundry-enabled scalable all-to-all optical interconnects using silicon nitride arrayed waveguide router interposers and silicon photonic transceivers. IEEE J. Sel. Top. Quantum Electron. **25**(5), 1–9 (2019)

Proctor: A Semi-Supervised Performance Anomaly Diagnosis Framework for Production HPC Systems

Burak Aksar[1]([✉])(iD), Yijia Zhang[1], Emre Ates[1], Benjamin Schwaller[2],
Omar Aaziz[2], Vitus J. Leung[2], Jim Brandt[2], Manuel Egele[1],
and Ayse K. Coskun[1]

[1] Boston University, Boston, MA 02215, USA
{baksar,zhangyj,ates,megele,acoskun}@bu.edu
[2] Sandia National Laboratories, Albuquerque, NM 87123, USA
{bschwal,oaaziz,vjleung,brandt}@sandia.gov

Abstract. Performance variation diagnosis in High-Performance Computing (HPC) systems is a challenging problem due to the size and complexity of the systems. Application performance variation leads to premature termination of jobs, decreased energy efficiency, or wasted computing resources. Manual root-cause analysis of performance variation based on system telemetry has become an increasingly time-intensive process as it relies on human experts and the size of telemetry data has grown. Recent methods use supervised machine learning models to automatically diagnose previously encountered performance anomalies in compute nodes. However, supervised machine learning models require large labeled data sets for training. This labeled data requirement is restrictive for many real-world application domains, including HPC systems, because collecting labeled data is challenging and time-consuming, especially considering anomalies that sparsely occur.

This paper proposes a novel *semi-supervised framework* that diagnoses previously encountered performance anomalies in HPC systems using a limited number of labeled data points, which is more suitable for production system deployment. Our framework first learns performance anomalies' characteristics by using historical telemetry data in an unsupervised fashion. In the following process, we leverage supervised classifiers to identify anomaly types. While most semi-supervised approaches do not typically use anomalous samples, our framework takes advantage of a few labeled anomalous samples to *classify* anomaly types. We evaluate our framework on a production HPC system and on a testbed HPC cluster. We show that our proposed framework achieves 60% F1-score on average, outperforming state-of-the-art supervised methods by 11%, and maintains an average 0.06% anomaly miss rate.

Keywords: Anomaly diagnosis · Semi-supervised learning · High performance computing

© Springer Nature Switzerland AG 2021
B. L. Chamberlain et al. (Eds.): ISC High Performance 2021, LNCS 12728, pp. 195–214, 2021.
https://doi.org/10.1007/978-3-030-78713-4_11

1   Introduction

Modern High-Performance Computing (HPC) systems are massive systems that perform many complex operations concurrently and they are critical for many science and engineering applications. Considering these systems' user demands and complexity, applications even with the same input deck are subject to substantial performance variations, such as running time changes of 100% or higher [12,30]. Hidden hardware problems, shared resource contention [12,18], fluctuating CPU frequency [39], orphan processes [16], and memory-related problems (e.g., memory leak) [2] are some common *anomalies* that cause performance variations. Some of the anomalies even force executing programs to terminate prematurely [16]. These performance variations may trigger sub-optimal scheduling and waste computing power, resulting in degraded overall computing efficiency and user dissatisfaction.

System administrators typically assess system health and identify the root causes of performance variations by gathering and inspecting telemetry data. Considering billions of telemetry data points are generated daily [1], manual analysis of system logs or resource usage data is not feasible due to being highly error-prone and time-consuming. Automated analytics, especially in the diagnosis of *anomalies*, are promising because they can reduce the mitigation time of problems, leading to the prevention of wasted computing power. Although various statistical and machine learning-based techniques have been proposed to detect anomalies in HPC systems (e.g., [13,14,27,45]), one main drawback is that they require a human operator to understand the root causes (i.e., diagnose anomalies) and label anomalous data. Tuncer et al.'s recent method performs automated anomaly diagnosis using supervised machine learning successfully when labeled healthy and anomalous data is available [43]. A common disadvantage of such fully supervised approaches is that they require a large set of *labeled* data that corresponds to the normal/anomalous state of a compute node.

Borghesi et al.'s recent method is semi-supervised and focuses on detecting anomalous runs, but without the ability to diagnose root causes for performance anomalies since they only use normal data samples in training [14,15]. Especially in production HPC systems, a large amount of telemetry data is available, but data labels are scarce. Thus, frameworks that are able to work with a limited amount of labeled data while identifying the root cause of performance anomalies would significantly improve the performance of production HPC systems.

In this paper, we propose *Proctor*, a semi-supervised performance anomaly diagnosis framework, which detects and identifies performance anomalies in compute nodes using a significantly smaller amount of labeled data compared to supervised baselines; hence, Proctor is more suitable for HPC production deployment. Proctor utilizes resource usage characteristics of applications collected by monitoring frameworks to train machine learning models. We evaluate the effectiveness of *Proctor* on a production HPC system and on an HPC testbed using multiple real applications and benchmark suites with synthetic anomalies. Our specific contributions are as follows:

- A novel semi-supervised framework that, once trained, automatically detects and diagnoses known anomalies that contribute to performance variations. We argue that our proposed framework is more suitable for deployment into production HPC systems than previous works as it requires substantially less labeled data.[1]
- Demonstration of the efficacy of our framework on a production HPC system and a testbed HPC cluster. We show that *Proctor* achieves 60% F1-score on average and outperforms supervised baselines by 11% in F1-score while maintaining an average 0.06% anomaly miss rate.

The rest of the paper starts with an overview of the related work. Section 3 describes the technical details of the proposed framework, Sect. 4 explains our experimental methodology, Sect. 5 presents our results, and we conclude in Sect. 6.

2   Related Work and Background

Detection of anomalies in high-dimensional data is a fundamental research topic with numerous applications in the real world. Some example application fields include, but are not limited to, medical anomaly detection [37,44], HPC telemetry data analysis [13,14,43], and sensor networks anomaly detection [32].

2.1   Anomaly Detection and Autoencoders

Machine learning is widely used in anomaly detection, with a variety of supervised, semi-supervised, or unsupervised approaches. Supervised models require normal and anomalous samples to classify anomaly types. In contrast to supervised methods, semi-supervised anomaly detection (SSAD) methods use labeled *normal* samples to identify anomalies. A common SSAD technique is to use autoencoders trained with normal data [33,40]. An autoencoder is an artificial neural network (ANN) composed of three main sequential layers: the input layer, the *code* layer, and the output (or reconstruction) layer. Autoencoders do not require class/label information since all layers are operating in an unsupervised paradigm [25]. An autoencoder with more than one hidden layer is known as a deep autoencoder and is shown in Fig. 1. A deep autoencoder learns to reconstruct the input data through a pair of encoder and decoder mappings, which are composed of hidden layers, as follows:

$$\overline{X} = D(E(X)), \tag{1}$$

where X is the input data, E is an encoder mapping from the input data to the code layer, D is a decoder mapping from the code layer to the output layer, and $\overline{X}$ is the reconstructed version of the input data. During the training stage, the model learns to reconstruct input data by minimizing the *reconstruction*

---

[1] Our implementation is available at: https://github.com/peaclab/Proctor.

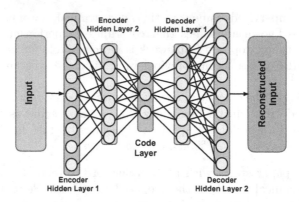

Fig. 1. A generic representation of an autoencoder with multiple hidden layers. The autoencoder learns to reconstruct the input data by learning the weights in the hidden layers.

error, which is one way of measuring how well an autoencoder learned. During the testing stage, an autoencoder classifies a sample as anomalous if the sample's reconstruction error is higher than the predetermined threshold. Stacked autoencoders integrate multiple autoencoders together, where the *code* layer of one autoencoder serves as the input of the other autoencoder. Deep architectures and stacked autoencoders have been shown to produce more abstract representations, improving the classification accuracy [11,17,24]. To perform classification with autoencoders, researchers use encoded features as inputs to supervised machine learning models such as support vector machines (SVM), logistic regression (LR), or neural networks [28,31].

In this work, we use autoencoders as unsupervised feature extractors, along with supervised classifiers to diagnose performance variations in HPC systems.

2.2 Machine Learning for HPC Monitoring Analytics

Due to the complexity of HPC systems and the size of the telemetry data (e.g., billions of data points per day), HPC centers have been investing in research on machine-learning-based approaches to automate performance anomaly analysis [26,39]. Ates et al. design a random forest (RF) based framework for application classification on compute nodes [6]. Klinkenberg et al. define a supervised learning system that extracts statistical features and uses an RF classifier to detect important node failures before they occur [27]. Baseman et al. apply a technique named *classifier-adjusted density estimation* to HPC sensor data [9]. Using density estimation, they learn to generate synthetic samples. Then, both real and synthetically generated data is used to train an RF classifier and assign an "anomalousness" score to each data point to detect performance anomalies.

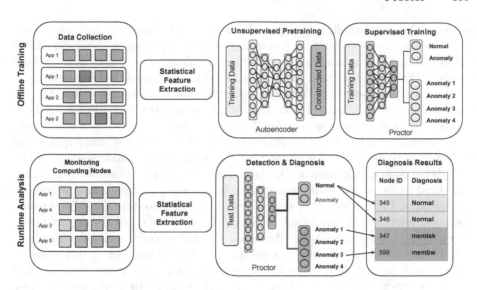

Fig. 2. The high-level architecture of *Proctor*. We collect telemetry data from normal and anomalous application runs and apply statistical feature extraction to convert raw time series into a suitable format for our autoencoder-based framework. We train an autoencoder with unlabeled normal and anomalous samples during the unsupervised pretraining stage to learn high-level characteristics. Then, we train classifiers with a few labeled samples to diagnose anomalies. At runtime, we feed the trained model with telemetry data and classify anomalies on compute nodes.

Borghesi et al. use a simple autoencoder structure trained on only normal data instances and perform reconstruction-error-based anomaly detection in compute nodes [15]. For anomaly diagnosis, which is classifying different types of performance anomalies as opposed to solely detecting anomalies, the most relevant work is Tuncer et al.'s method, where they apply statistical feature extraction along with a feature selection process to diagnose different anomaly types such as memory leak, CPU contention, and others [43].

Existing methods either detect anomalies in a fully supervised way [43] or they use semi-/unsupervised methods but only detect anomalies [9,14] without diagnosing/classifying their root cause. Our work is distinct from related work because our proposed framework is the first to *detect* and *diagnose* performance anomalies in a semi-supervised way using substantially less labeled data compared to supervised approaches.

3   Our Proposed Framework: PROCTOR

Our main objective is to detect whether a compute node in a system exhibits anomalous behavior (i.e., causing performance variability), and if it does, we aim to classify the *type* of anomaly (e.g., memory leak or contention in a specific subsystem) in an application-agnostic fashion. We focus on anomalies that cause performance variability, where applications execute without terminating/crashing. Such anomalies are often more challenging to detect and diagnose compared to faults that lead to errors in programs or premature termination.

We propose a semi-supervised anomaly diagnosis framework called *Proctor* based on an autoencoder, followed by a classification layer that diagnoses performance variations on compute nodes. Figure 2 shows an overview of our framework. We collect telemetry data from compute nodes while running applications with and without anomalies. Note that our framework is independent of the underlying monitoring framework. After that, we extract the raw time series' statistical features and train an autoencoder to learn a representation (encoding) of normal and anomalous samples in an unsupervised manner. In *Proctor*, a sample refers to the entire set of telemetry data collected during an application run on a compute node. Based on the autoencoder's encoder mapping output and using some labeled normal and anomalous samples, we train supervised classifiers that are able to diagnose anomalies. At runtime, Proctor then applies the trained model on collected telemetry samples to detect and diagnose performance anomalies. We next explain these steps in detail.

3.1   Feature Extraction

We implement Tuncer et al.'s easy-to-compute statistical features [42] to convert multivariate time series data into a suitable format for *Proctor*. Some features are simple order statistics (e.g., 25th, 75th, and 90th percentiles, and standard deviation), and some of them are useful for time series clustering such as skewness and kurtosis. This step reduces the overhead that would be caused by using raw time series metrics generated from thousands of compute nodes. The statistical feature extraction methodology is independent of the monitoring framework and can be used across different HPC monitoring tools such as Lightweight Distributed Metric Service (LDMS) [1], Ganglia [20] or Examon [10].

3.2   Unsupervised Pretraining

We implement two different autoencoder topologies, deep autoencoders and stacked autoencoders [31], and compare their efficacy to make a selection. Deep autoencoders and stacked autoencoders serve as effective pretraining methods due to their unsupervised nature for classification tasks when many unlabeled samples are available [3, 21].

In the autoencoder, our training objective is to learn the weights for the encoder and decoder layers so that the reconstructed input is as close to the original input as possible. In other words, the goal is to minimize the difference between X and $\overline{X}$ by performing the following optimization [46]:

$$\min_{D,E} \; ||X - D(E(X))||. \tag{2}$$

We train the autoencoder via backpropagation, which is a way of updating the weights and biases of the layers to perform the optimization in Eq. (2).

We use deep autoencoders in the rest of this paper as they provide higher prediction accuracy in our results compared to stacked autoencoders.

3.3   Supervised Training

For anomaly diagnosis, we implement two different supervised training methods that differentiate anomaly types and choose the best performing one in the evaluation. The first one is *fine-tuning*. We freeze the pre-trained autoencoder's weights and add another fully-connected neural network layer after the encoder part. After that, we retrain the new network to classify the anomaly types as shown in the supervised training part of Fig. 2.

The second method uses the encoded features directly as input to traditional supervised machine-learning models such as LR, RF, and SVM. In our experiments, the second method provides higher accuracy so we only train the supervised models with the encoded data in the rest of the paper.

3.4   Detection and Diagnosis at Runtime

At runtime, Proctor collects telemetry data from compute nodes using a monitoring framework and applies statistical feature extraction. Then, we use the model trained on these features for diagnosis. As described earlier, *Proctor* has a *two-level classification* process. In the first level, *Proctor* decides whether a sample is normal or anomalous. If it is anomalous, we feed the sample to the diagnosis layer to identify the anomaly type.

4   Experimental Methodology

We run controlled experiments on two different HPC systems by running synthetic anomalies with a set of HPC applications. We also describe the implementation details of two baseline methods for anomaly detection and diagnosis, and compare Proctor against these baselines. This section describes the monitoring framework that collects system telemetry data, data sets for anomaly diagnosis, HPC applications, and performance anomalies we use to evaluate our proposed *Proctor* framework.

4.1   HPC Systems and Applications

We conduct experiments on a testbed system, Volta, and on a production HPC system, Eclipse. We run both benchmarks and real applications to evaluate the performance of *Proctor* against baselines.

Volta is a Cray XC30m testbed supercomputer located at Sandia National Laboratories. Volta consists of 52 compute nodes, organized in 13 fully connected switches with four nodes per switch. Each node has 64 GB of memory and two sockets, each with an Intel Xeon E5-2695 v2 CPU with 12 2-way hyper-threaded cores. To cover a representative set of HPC applications in Volta, we use NAS Parallel Benchmarks (NPB) [8] and Mantevo Benchmark Suite [23]. The Mantevo Suite was developed by Sandia National Laboratories for performance and scaling experiments. In addition, we use the Kripke application, which is a proxy application that simulates particle transportation [29]. We list all applications used in our experiments in Table 1. We run each application across 4 or 32 compute nodes for 10–15 min using different application input decks.

Eclipse is a production HPC system located at Sandia National Laboratories. Eclipse consists of 1488 compute nodes, and it is capable of 1.8 petaflops. Each node has 128 GB memory and two sockets, each with 18 E5-2695 v4 CPU cores. In the experiments on Eclipse, we use six applications, LAMMPS, HACC, sw4, ExaMiniMD, SWFFT, and sw4lite. Among them, there are three real applications: LAMMPS, a molecular dynamics simulation with a focus on materials modeling [36]; HACC, an extreme-scale cosmological simulation [22]; sw4, a popular 3D seismic model [35]. The other three, ExaMiniMD, SWFFT, and sw4lite, are proxy applications from the ECP Proxy Apps Suite [19]. We list all applications used in our experiments in Table 2. We run each application on 4 nodes for 20–45 min.

Table 1. Applications we run on Volta for data collection.

Benchmark	Application	Description
NAS	BT	Block tri-diagonal solver
	CG	Conjugate gradient
	FT	3D Fast Fourier Transform
	LU	Gauss-Seidel solver
	MG	Multi-grid on meshes
	SP	Scalar penta-diagonal solver
Mantevo	MINIMD	Molecular dynamics
	CoMD	Molecular dynamics
	MINIGHOST	Partial differential equations
	MINIAMR	Stencil calculation
Other	KRIPKE	Particle transport

4.2   Monitoring Framework

We use LDMS to collect telemetry data from different subsystems. LDMS is a low overhead monitoring framework for HPC systems with a high sampling rate. LDMS collects data simultaneously for each subsystem component (e.g., memory-related metrics, network counters, etc.) across the whole system [38]. At every second, LDMS collects hundreds of metrics per node in the categories as described below:

- Memory (e.g., currently free, active, inactive memory)
- CPU (e.g., per-core and overall idle time, I/O wait time)
- Network (e.g., received/transmitted packets, average packet size, link status)
- Shared File System (e.g., open, read, write counts)
- Cray performance counters (e.g., power consumption, write-back counters)
- Virtual Memory (e.g., free, active and inactive pages).

LDMS is deployed on both systems and it constantly monitors the health of the systems [1,38]. We collect 806 metrics and 721 metrics from Eclipse and Volta, respectively. We fill out any missing metric values using linear interpolation and calculate the difference of cumulative counter values since we are interested in the change. We also exclude the first and last 60 s of the collected time series for each application to avoid any fluctuations during the initialization and termination phases.

Table 2. Applications we run on Eclipse for data collection.

Benchmark	Application	Description
Real Applications	LAMMPS	Molecular dynamics
	HACC	Cosmological simulation
	sw4	Seismic modeling
ECP Proxy Suite	ExaMiniMD	Molecular dynamics
	SWFFT	3D Fast Fourier Transform
	sw4lite	Numerical kernel optimizations

4.3 Synthetic Anomalies

To learn individual anomaly signatures and detect them at runtime, *Proctor* needs a few labeled samples that exhibit anomalous characteristics. To systematically train and test our framework, we use synthetic anomalies from the HPC Performance Anomaly Suite (HPAS) [7] to mimic anomalous behavior during an application run. HPAS is an open-source performance anomaly suite to reproduce performance variations. Synthetic anomalies in HPAS, target five major subsystems: CPU, cache, memory, network, and shared storage. We inject anomalies with multiple configurations to mimic different performance variation levels, as listed in Table 3. While running a multi-node application, we run a synthetic anomaly on a single node in Volta, and we run a synthetic anomaly on every node that the application uses in Eclipse. Each compute node data is labeled with an anomaly type if an anomaly is injected, otherwise labeled as normal.

Table 3. A list of the HPAS anomalies used in our experiments.

Anomaly type	Anomaly behavior	Configuration
CPU intensive process	Arithmetic operations	−u 100%, 80%
Cache contention	Cache read & Write	−c L1, L2/−m 1, 2
Memory bandwidth contention	Uncached memory write	−s 4K, 8K, 32K
Memory leakage	Increasingly allocate & Fill memory	−s 1,3,10 M/−p 0.2,0.4,1

4.4   Baselines

We implement two baseline methods to compare against *Proctor*. The first one is the framework proposed by Tuncer et al. [43] (referred to as RF-Tuncer), which uses statistical feature extraction and a fully supervised RF classifier. The second one is the autoencoder-based anomaly detection approach proposed by Borghesi et al. [14] (referred to as AE-Borghesi).

RF-Tuncer [43] uses statistical feature extraction and feature selection strategies and combines them with an RF classifier to diagnose anomaly types [43]. They use LDMS to collect different metrics (e.g., memory metrics, CPU metrics) while applications run with and without anomalies at every second. They label each node with the injected anomaly type during the application run. Application runs without injected anomalies are labeled "normal". During an offline training phase, they train supervised models and test the saved models at runtime after statistical feature extraction and feature selection are applied.

AE-Borghesi [15] trains an autoencoder with only *normal* samples and detects anomalies according to a statistically determined threshold. It is important to note that their method is limited to anomaly detection instead of classifying anomaly types. *Proctor* can also detect anomalies by slightly modifying the network in the supervised training stage. Borghesi et al. use the *Examon* [4] data collection infrastructure to monitor the D.A.V.I.D.E [10] HPC system which has 45 compute nodes. Examon collects up to 170 metrics with 5s and 10s granularity for Intelligent Platform Management Interface (IPMI) and Open-POWER POWER8 on-chip controller (OCC) metrics, respectively. They use coarse-grained aggregated telemetry data with a 5-min aggregation time window. To mimic their data collection schema, we apply the same aggregation technique. The authors inject three anomalous policies that change CPU frequency, clock speed, and power consumption to mimic anomalous behavior (e.g., *powersave* sets the CPU frequency to the lowest available). They train an autoencoder with only normal data (i.e., intervals without anomaly injection) and select a threshold to detect anomalies. To select this threshold, they vary the percentiles of the reconstruction error observed in the training data and select the value that gives the best F1-score in the validation data. At runtime, if a sample has a higher reconstruction error than the threshold, it is labeled as anomalous.

4.5 Implementation Details

Proctor: We implement our framework in Tensorflow. We create a hyperparameter space using the following values and search the space to find the best values for the autoencoder:

1. Batch size: 32, 64, 128, and 256
2. Number of neurons in hidden a layer: 200, 500, 1000, 2000
3. Number of hidden layers: 1, 2, 3, 5
4. Number of epochs: 50, 100, 300, 500, 1000, 5000
5. Optimizer: Adam, Adadelta, SGD
6. Dropout: 0, 0.1, 0.2, 0.3.

After finding the best parameters for the autoencoder, we stack them to experiment with stacked autoencoders. For the supervised training stage, we experiment with a neural network, an SVM, and an LR. All classifiers are trained using the *one-versus-rest* strategy, which creates an individual classifier for each class. For the neural networks, we use *Adam* optimizer and minimize *Categorical Cross-Entropy* loss.

The final structure of *Proctor* includes a deep autoencoder with 2000 neurons in the code layer and uses SVM and LR for the supervised training part. Stacked autoencoders perform similarly to deep autoencoders, but we choose deep autoencoders because of their lower false alarm rate. We use the *Adadelta* optimizer, which enforces a monotonically decreasing learning rate and minimizes *Mean Squared Error* during the training with a 20% validation split. We also set *EarlyStopping* callback, which stops when the chosen performance measure stops improving.

AE-Borghesi: We adopted the following network topology according to the descriptions of Borghesi et al. [15]:

1. An input layer,
2. A dense *code* layer with a number of neurons ten times larger than input neurons with *Rectified Linear Units* [34] activation and an *L1 norm* [5] regularizer,
3. An output layer with a number of neurons equal to input features with *Linear* activations.

We train the AE-Borghesi model with the *Adam* optimizer, which finds individual learning rates for each parameter by minimizing the *Mean Absolute Error* for 100 epochs with a batch size of 32. We conduct a hyparameter search for the number of neurons in the code layer so as not to put AE-Borghesi at a disadvantage. We also implement their approach with *Dropout* [41] layers as the authors suggested [14]. However, our implementation with dropout layers gives slightly worse results than the original topology, so we only present the best results.

RF-Tuncer: We implement feature extraction and feature selection using *scipy-stats* module. We choose the best performing classifier, RF, and set the number of decision trees to 100 after hyperparameter search. For RF, we use *scikit-learn* implementation.

5   Evaluation

In this section, we first explain the metrics and data sets we use in our evaluation. Then, we compare the anomaly detection and diagnosis results of our framework against the baselines. We also evaluate the performance in cases when a previously unseen anomaly type exists in the test data.

5.1   Performance Metrics

We report our evaluation results with 5-fold stratified cross-validation for each experimental scenario and observe the F1-score, anomaly miss rate (i.e., false negative rate), and false alarm rate (i.e., false positive rate) for different percentages of labeled data. F1-score is the harmonic mean of precision and recall and it is widely used in multiclass classification problems. We calculate the macro average F1-score, which does not take label imbalance into account, hence treating all classes equally. Note that this is important in imbalanced data sets where the number of normal data points is in the overwhelming majority compared to anomalous data points. To assess anomaly detection performance (i.e., distinguishing between normal versus anomalous) of the models, we use the false alarm rate which indicates the percentage of normal runs identified as one of the anomaly types, and the anomaly miss rate, which indicates the percentage of anomalous runs (any anomaly) identified as normal. To improve confidence in our results, we run each classifier ten times and average the results.

$$False\ Alarm\ Rate = \frac{False\ Positives}{False\ Positives + True\ Negatives} \tag{3}$$

$$Anomaly\ Miss\ Rate = \frac{False\ Negatives}{False\ Negatives + True\ Positives} \tag{4}$$

5.2   Data Set Preparation

We devise three experimental scenarios to evaluate the performance of *Proctor*, AE-Borghesi, and RF-Tuncer. While preparing data sets for the proposed experimental scenarios, we use 5-fold stratified cross-validation, and we ensure that any training or testing data set contains every application and anomaly type. The Eclipse data set has 1526 normal samples and 2304 anomalous samples, where each anomaly type is equally represented among the anomalous samples. We use 611 normal samples and 68–70 anomalous samples in training, representing an anomaly ratio of 10% (i.e., anomaly ratio is the number of anomalous runs divided by all runs). This anomaly ratio mimics a production system scenario where anomalous runs are rare compared to normal runs. The Volta data set has 18980 normal samples and 1932 anomalous samples. We use 5694 normal samples and 618–620 anomalous samples in training, representing an anomaly ratio of 10%. In both data sets, samples that are not used during training are placed in the testing data set. We fit a *MinMax* scaler to the training data set, where each feature value is scaled between 0 and 1, and then use the same scaler in the testing data set.

For the supervised training part (only for *Proctor* and RF-Tuncer), we mimic a case where labeled data are accumulating over time, i.e., we start from having only a few labeled data (e.g., 1–2 labeled example per class) and increase the number of labeled data gradually. Chosen labeled data percentages are the following: 2%, 3%, 4%, 5%, 6%, 8%, 10% for Eclipse, and 0.1%, 0.15%, 0.2%, 0.25%, 0.30%, 0.35% for Volta data sets. Chosen labeled data percentages are different due to the size of the data sets. In the Eclipse data set, when the labeled data percentage is 10%, it corresponds to approximately 65 labeled samples in total; in the Volta data set, when the labeled data percentage is 0.35%, it corresponds to approximately 25 labeled samples in total.

5.3   Anomaly Detection Results

The main goal in anomaly detection is to compare *Proctor*'s performance with AE-Borghesi and RF-Tuncer for anomaly detection across different labeled data percentages. For the anomaly detection task, all anomalies are labeled with the same label (i.e., without diagnosing the type of anomaly) regardless of their types. In the unsupervised pretraining part, *Proctor* uses the whole training data set without any supervision (i.e., data are unlabeled). In the supervised training part, we train RF-Tuncer and *Proctor* with the selected labeled data and evaluate their performance in the same testing data set. Then, we repeat the same procedure for each predetermined labeled percentage value.

We train AE-Borghesi by using normal data in the training data set. It is important to note that AE-Borghesi does not have a supervised training part like *Proctor* and RF-Tuncer. We choose the 63th percentile of the mean absolute reconstruction error as a threshold since it achieves the best F1-score in the validation data in our experiments. This threshold is used to classify whether a run is anomalous or not.

As shown in Fig. 3, *Proctor* outperforms the baselines in F1-score and anomaly miss rate for most cases even with very few labeled data points. Both *Proctor* and RF-Tuncer perform similarly in terms of the false alarm rate. *Proctor* outperforms RF-Tuncer by 50% on average in the anomaly miss rate.

Due to the simple thresholding used in AE-Borghesi, as well as the existence of multiple anomaly types in our data sets, AE-Borghesi performs poorly compared to others. In addition, AE-Borghesi needs to be trained with only normal data points, so a system administrator or subject matter expert needs to ensure that system health status is normal to train AE-Borghesi. On the other hand, *Proctor* can be directly deployed and continuously trained with available telemetry data regardless of the system's health status. After training *Proctor* with unlabeled telemetry data, when a subject matter expert labels some anomalous events, these labeled data can be used in the supervised training part of *Proctor*.

5.4   Anomaly Diagnosis Results

The main goal in anomaly diagnosis analysis is to compare *Proctor*'s classification F1-score with RF-Tuncer for anomaly diagnosis across different percentages of available labeled data. In the unsupervised pretraining part, *Proctor* uses the whole training data without any supervision. In the supervised training part, we train RF-Tuncer and *Proctor* using a percentage of the labeled data and evaluate their performance in a constant testing data set. We repeat the process for each labeled data percentage value.

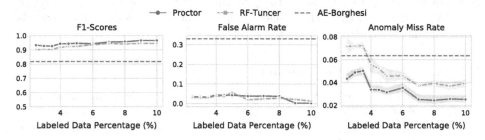

Fig. 3. Comparison of the anomaly detection performance of *Proctor* with AE-Borghesi and RF-Tuncer using the Eclipse data set. *Proctor* performs better than the baselines in F1-score and anomaly miss rate, while maintaining a similar false alarm rate with RF-Tuncer.

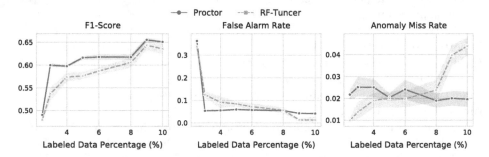

Fig. 4. Comparison of the anomaly diagnosis performance of *Proctor* with RF-Tuncer using the Eclipse data set. Proctor performs better in F1-score and false alarm rate while maintaining a stable anomaly miss rate.

Figure 4 shows the macro average F1-scores for our method and RF-Tuncer for the Eclipse data set. *Proctor* outperforms RF-Tuncer by 4.5% on average (and up to 11%) while maintaining a low false alarm rate and anomaly miss rate. RF-Tuncer performs slightly better in terms of anomaly miss rate when the labeled data percentage is less than 5%. However, the anomaly miss rate of RF-Tuncer increases when the labeled data percentage increases, whereas the anomaly miss rate of *Proctor* is stable and keeps below 2.5%.

Figure 5 shows the macro average F1-scores for *Proctor* and RF-Tuncer for the Volta data set. In terms of the F1-score, *Proctor* outperforms RF-Tuncer by 25% on average (and up to 50%) and maintains similar alarm and miss rates to RF-Tuncer. *Proctor* outperforms RF-Tuncer for most of the cases in terms of all categories until we have approximately 20 labeled data samples in total. After this point, the fully supervised RF-Tuncer method has sufficient labeled anomalous data for training to achieve accurate predictions. RF-Tuncer achieves a similar F1-score to *Proctor* faster in the Volta data set compared to the Eclipse data set. The main reason behind this is less complex application characteristics in the Volta data set.

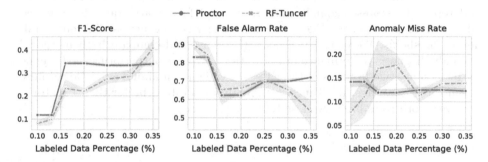

Fig. 5. Comparison of the anomaly diagnosis performance of *Proctor* with RF-Tuncer using the Volta data set. *Proctor* outperforms RF-Tuncer for most of the cases across all categories.

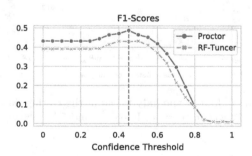

Fig. 6. Choosing a threshold that gives the highest F1-score by sweeping confidence thresholds.

5.5   Impact of Previously Unseen Anomalies

Our primary goal in this scenario is to evaluate the performance of *Proctor* and RF-Tuncer when there are unknown (i.e., previously unseen) anomalies in the testing data set. Since a variety of performance anomalies exists in the production environment, it is common to observe anomalies other than those used during training. We follow the same unsupervised pretraining and supervised training approaches described above, except for one difference: we remove a selected unknown anomaly type from the training set during the supervised training stage and keep the other anomalies. After training, we first test the model on the same training data, this time including the removed anomaly, to determine a confidence threshold. We vary the threshold and choose a threshold value that provides the highest F1-score, and then, evaluate the trained model on a testing data set that consists of all anomalies. We label the sample as *unknown* if the model's highest confidence score for normal and anomalous classes is lower than the selected threshold. RF-Tuncer uses a multiclass RF, and it requires all classes to exist in the training data set; thus, not to put RF-Tuncer at a disadvantage, we apply a *one-versus-rest* strategy to their RF classifier as well.

We experiment on Eclipse data with all labeled data percentages in Sect. 5.2 and report F1-scores, anomaly miss rates, and false alarm rates for selected labeled data percentages. Figure 6 shows the F1-score across different confidence thresholds. We choose 0.45 as a threshold and compare both methods' anomaly diagnosis performance in Fig.7. Here, *Proctor* outperforms the baseline by 10% on average in terms of the F1-score while maintaining a 66% lower false alarm rate on average. RF-Tuncer's anomaly miss rate is better than Proctor's, however, both rates are very close to zero.

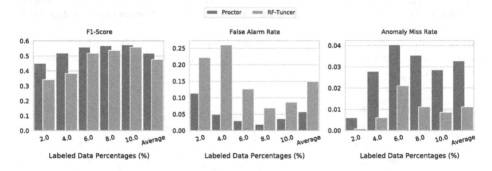

Fig. 7. When there are unknown anomaly types in the testing data set, *Proctor* performs better than RF-Tuncer in terms of F1-score and false alarm rate.

6   Conclusion

Performance variation in HPC systems degrades user satisfaction, reduces the efficiency of resource utilization, and wastes computing power. Considering the growing size and complexity of HPC systems, automated performance anomaly diagnosis has become increasingly crucial for robust and efficient service. However, existing automated methods rely on large labeled data sets for training. This paper proposed *Proctor*, a semi-supervised performance anomaly detection and diagnosis framework for limited labeled data scenarios in production systems. We evaluated our framework using data collected from two different HPC systems, including a production HPC system. We demonstrated that our approach is superior to state-of-the-art approaches in terms of F1-score, anomaly miss rate, and false alarm rate when only a limited set of labeled data is available. We also showed that *Proctor* is robust in presence of previously unseen anomalies and it successfully labeled them as "unknown" in our experiments.

As a next step, we will focus on deploying our framework into a production HPC machine and integrating a user/system administrator feedback system that allows us to label suspicious application runs for continuous model improvement. Furthermore, we will focus on generative machine learning models to synthetically generate anomalous application runs to achieve a higher diagnosis performance with our proposed framework.

Acknowledgment. This work has been partially funded by Sandia National Laboratories. Sandia National Laboratories is a multimission laboratory managed and operated by National Technology and Engineering Solutions of Sandia, LLC., a wholly owned subsidiary of Honeywell International, Inc., for the U.S. Department of Energy's National Nuclear Security Administration under Contract DE-NA0003525. This paper describes objective technical results and analysis. Any subjective views or opinions that might be expressed in the paper do not necessarily represent the views of the U.S. Department of Energy or the United States Government.

References

1. Agelastos, A., Allan, B., Brandt, J., et al.: The lightweight distributed metric service: a scalable infrastructure for continuous monitoring of large scale computing systems and applications. In: SC 2014: Proceedings of the International Conference for High Performance Computing, Networking, Storage and Analysis, pp. 154–165 (2014)
2. Agelastos, A., Allan, B., Brandt, J., et al.: Toward rapid understanding of production HPC applications and systems. In: IEEE International Conference on Cluster Computing, pp. 464–473 (2015)
3. Agrawal, P., Girshick, R., Malik, J.: Analyzing the performance of multilayer neural networks for object recognition. In: Fleet, D., Pajdla, T., Schiele, B., Tuytelaars, T. (eds.) ECCV 2014. LNCS, vol. 8695, pp. 329–344. Springer, Cham (2014). https://doi.org/10.1007/978-3-319-10584-0_22
4. Ahmad, W.A., Bartolini, A., Beneventi, F., et al.: Design of an energy aware petaflops class high performance cluster based on power architecture. In: IEEE International Parallel and Distributed Processing Symposium Workshops (IPDPSW), pp. 964–973 (2017)
5. Alain, G., Bengio, Y.: What regularized auto-encoders learn from the data-generating distribution. J. Mach. Learn. Res. **15**(1), 3563–3593 (2014)

6. Ates, E., et al.: Taxonomist: application detection through rich monitoring data. In: Aldinucci, M., Padovani, L., Torquati, M. (eds.) Euro-Par 2018. LNCS, vol. 11014, pp. 92–105. Springer, Cham (2018). https://doi.org/10.1007/978-3-319-96983-1_7

7. Ates, E., Zhang, Y., Aksar, B., et al.: HPAS: an HPC performance anomaly suite for reproducing performance variations. In: ACM Proceedings of the 48th International Conference on Parallel Processing, pp. 1–10, August 2019

8. Bailey, D.H., Barszcz, E., Barton, J.T., et al.: The NAS parallel benchmarks summary and preliminary results. In: Supercomputing 1991: Proceedings of the 1991 ACM/IEEE Conference on Supercomputing, pp. 158–165 (1991)

9. Baseman, E., Blanchard, S., DeBardeleben, N., Bonnie, A., Morrow, A.: Interpretable anomaly detection for monitoring of high performance computing systems. In: Outlier Definition, Detection, and Description on Demand Workshop at ACM SIGKDD, San Francisco, August 2016 (2016)

10. Beneventi, F., Bartolini, A., Cavazzoni, C., Benini, L.: Continuous learning of HPC infrastructure models using big data analytics and in-memory processing tools. In: Design, Automation Test in Europe Conference Exhibition (DATE), pp. 1038–1043 (2017)

11. Bengio, Y.: Learning Deep Architectures for AI. Now Publishers Inc., New York (2009)

12. Bhatele, A., Mohror, K., Langer, S.H., Isaacs, K.E.: There goes the neighborhood: performance degradation due to nearby jobs. In: SC 2013: IEEE Proceedings of the International Conference on High Performance Computing, Networking, Storage and Analysis, pp. 1–12 (2013)

13. Bodik, P., Goldszmidt, M., Fox, A., Woodard, D.B., Andersen, H.: Fingerprinting the datacenter: automated classification of performance crises. In: Proceedings of the 5th European Conference on Computer Systems, pp. 111–124 (2010)

14. Borghesi, A., Bartolini, A., Lombardi, M., Milano, M., Benini, L.: A semisupervised autoencoder-based approach for anomaly detection in high performance computing systems. Eng. Appl. Artif. Intell. **85**, 634–644 (2019)

15. Borghesi, A., Bartolini, A., Lombardi, M., et al.: Anomaly detection using autoencoders in high performance computing systems. In: Proceedings of the AAAI Conference on Artificial Intelligence, vol. 33, pp. 9428–9433, July 2019. arXiv: 1811.05269

16. Brandt, J., Chen, F., et al.: Quantifying effectiveness of failure prediction and response in HPC systems: methodology and example. In: IEEE International Conference on Dependable Systems and Networks Workshops (DSN-W), pp. 2–7 (2010)

17. Ciregan, D., Meier, U., Schmidhuber, J.: Multi-column deep neural networks for image classification. In: IEEE Conference on Computer Vision and Pattern Recognition, pp. 3642–3649 (2012)

18. Dorier, M., Antoniu, G., Ross, R., et al.: CALCioM: mitigating I/O interference in HPC systems through cross-application coordination. In: IEEE 28th International Parallel and Distributed Processing Symposium, pp. 155–164 (2014)

19. Exascale proxy applications. https://proxyapps.exascaleproject.org/

20. Ganglia monitoring system. http://ganglia.info/

21. Girshick, R., Donahue, J., Darrell, T., Malik, J.: Rich feature hierarchies for accurate object detection and semantic segmentation. In: Proceedings of the IEEE Conference on Computer Vision and Pattern Recognition, pp. 580–587 (2014)

22. Habib, S., Morozov, V., Frontiere, N., Finkel, H., Pope, A., Heitmann, K.: HACC: extreme scaling and performance across diverse architectures. In: SC 2013: Proceedings of the International Conference on High Performance Computing, Networking, Storage and Analysis, pp. 1–10. IEEE (2013)

23. Heroux, M.A., et al.: Improving performance via mini-applications. Sandia National Laboratories, Technical report, SAND2009-5574 3 (2009)
24. Hinton, G.E., Osindero, S., Teh, Y.W.: A fast learning algorithm for deep belief nets. Neural Comput. **18**(7), 1527–1554 (2006)
25. Hinton, G.E., Zemel, R.S.: Autoencoders, minimum description length and Helmholtz free energy. In: Proceedings of the 6th International Conference on Neural Information Processing Systems. NIPS 1993, pp. 3–10. Morgan Kaufmann Publishers Inc., San Francisco (1993)
26. Ibidunmoye, O., Hernández-Rodriguez, F., Elmroth, E.: Performance anomaly detection and bottleneck identification. ACM Comput. Surv. (CSUR) **48**(1), 1–35 (2015)
27. Klinkenberg, J., Terboven, C., Lankes, S., Müller, M.S.: Data mining-based analysis of HPC center operations. In: IEEE International Conference on Cluster Computing, pp. 766–773 (2017)
28. Kunang, Y.N., Nurmaini, S., Stiawan, D., Zarkasi, A., Jasmir, F.: Automatic features extraction using autoencoder in intrusion detection system. In: IEEE International Conference on Electrical Engineering and Computer Science (ICECOS), pp. 219–224 (2018)
29. Kunen, A.J., Bailey, T.S., Brown, P.N.: KRIPKE-a massively parallel transport mini-app. Technical report, Lawrence Livermore National Lab. (LLNL), Livermore, CA (United States) (2015)
30. Leung, V.J., Bender, M.A., Bunde, D.P., Phillips, C.A.: Algorithmic support for commodity-based parallel computing systems. Technical report, Sandia National Laboratories (2003)
31. Liu, G., Bao, H., Han, B.: A stacked autoencoder-based deep neural network for achieving gearbox fault diagnosis. Math. Probl. Eng. (2018)
32. Luo, T., Nagarajan, S.G.: Distributed anomaly detection using autoencoder neural networks in WSN for IoT. In: IEEE International Conference on Communications (ICC), pp. 1–6 (2018)
33. Minhas, M.S., Zelek, J.: Semi-supervised anomaly detection using autoencoders. arXiv:2001.03674 [cs, eess, stat], January 2020. http://arxiv.org/abs/2001.03674
34. Nair, V., Hinton, G.E.: Rectified linear units improve restricted Boltzmann machines. In: ICML (2010)
35. Petersson, N., Sjögreen, B.: Sw4 v1.1 [software] (2014). https://doi.org/http://doi.org/10.5281/zenodo.571844
36. Plimpton, S.: Fast parallel algorithms for short-range molecular dynamics. J. Comput. Phys. **117**(1), 1–19 (1995)
37. Sato, D., Hanaoka, S., Nomura, Y., et al.: A primitive study on unsupervised anomaly detection with an autoencoder in emergency head CT volumes. In: Medical Imaging: Computer-Aided Diagnosis, vol. 10575, p. 105751P. International Society for Optics and Photonics (2018)
38. Schwaller, B., Tucker, N., Tucker, T., Allan, B., Brandt, J.: HPC system data pipeline to enable meaningful insights through analysis-driven visualizations. In: IEEE International Conference on Cluster Computing, pp. 433–441, September 2020
39. Snir, M., Carlson, B., et al.: Addressing failures in exascale computing. Int. J. High Perf. Comput. Appl. **28**(2), 129–173 (2014)
40. Song, H., Jiang, Z., et al.: A hybrid semi-supervised anomaly detection model for high-dimensional data. Comput. Intell. Neurosci. (2017)

41. Srivastava, N., Hinton, G., Krizhevsky, A., Sutskever, I., Salakhutdinov, R.: Dropout: a simple way to prevent neural networks from overfitting. J. Mach. Learn. Res. **15**(1), 1929–1958 (2014)
42. Tuncer, O., et al.: Diagnosing performance variations in HPC applications using machine learning. In: Kunkel, J.M., Yokota, R., Balaji, P., Keyes, D. (eds.) ISC 2017. LNCS, vol. 10266, pp. 355–373. Springer, Cham (2017). https://doi.org/10.1007/978-3-319-58667-0_19
43. Tuncer, O., Ates, E., Zhang, Y., et al.: Online diagnosis of performance variation in HPC systems using machine learning. IEEE Trans. Parallel Distrib. Syst. **30**(4), 883–896 (2018)
44. Wang, K., et al.: Research on healthy anomaly detection model based on deep learning from multiple time-series physiological signals. Sci. Program. (2016)
45. Yu, L., Lan, Z.: A scalable, non-parametric method for detecting performance anomaly in large scale computing. IEEE Trans. Parallel Distrib. Syst. **27**(7), 1902–1914 (2015)
46. Zhou, C., Paffenroth, R.C.: Anomaly detection with robust deep autoencoders. In: Proceedings of the 23rd ACM SIGKDD International Conference on Knowledge Discovery and Data Mining, pp. 665–674 (2017)

HPC Algorithms and Applications

COSTA: Communication-Optimal Shuffle and Transpose Algorithm with Process Relabeling

Marko Kabić[1,2]($\boxtimes$), Simon Pintarelli[1,2], Anton Kozhevnikov[1,2], and Joost VandeVondele[1,2]

[1] ETH Zürich, Zurich, Switzerland
[2] Swiss National Supercomputing Centre (CSCS), Lugano, Switzerland
marko.kabic@cscs.ch

Abstract. Communication-avoiding algorithms for Linear Algebra have become increasingly popular, in particular for distributed memory architectures. In practice, these algorithms assume that the data is already distributed in a specific way, thus making data reshuffling a key to use them. For performance reasons, a straightforward all-to-all exchange must be avoided.

Here, we show that process relabeling (i.e. permuting processes in the final layout) can be used to obtain communication optimality for data reshuffling, and that it can be efficiently found by solving a Linear Assignment Problem (Maximum Weight Bipartite Perfect Matching). Based on this, we have developed a Communication-Optimal Shuffle and Transpose Algorithm (COSTA): this highly-optimised algorithm implements $A = \alpha \cdot \mathrm{op}(B) + \beta \cdot A$, $\mathrm{op} \in \{\text{transpose}, \text{conjugate-transpose}, \text{identity}\}$ on distributed systems, where A, B are matrices with potentially different (distributed) layouts and α, β are scalars. COSTA can take advantage of the communication-optimal process relabeling even for heterogeneous network topologies, where latency and bandwidth differ among nodes. Moreover, our algorithm can be easily generalized to even more generic problems, making it suitable for distributed Machine Learning applications. The implementation not only outperforms the best available ScaLAPACK redistribute and transpose routines multiple times, but is also able to deal with more general matrix layouts, in particular it is not limited to block-cyclic layouts. Finally, we use COSTA to integrate a communication-optimal matrix multiplication algorithm into the CP2K quantum chemistry simulation package. This way, we show that COSTA can be used to unlock the full potential of recent Linear Algebra algorithms in applications by facilitating interoperability between algorithms with a wide range of data layouts, in addition to bringing significant redistribution speedups.

Keywords: COSTA · Communication-optimal · Redistribution · Transpose · Perfect matching · Linear assignment · Random-phase approximation (RPA) · CP2K · Linear algebra

B. L. Chamberlain et al. (Eds.): ISC High Performance 2021, LNCS 12728, pp. 217–236, 2021.
https://doi.org/10.1007/978-3-030-78713-4_12

1   Introduction

Communication-avoiding algorithms for Linear Algebra have become increasingly popular recently, in particular for distributed memory architectures. In practice, these algorithms usually assume the data is already distributed in a specific way. For example, COSMA [16], a communication-optimal matrix multiplication algorithm, natively uses a specialised blocked data layout which depends on matrix shapes and the available resources. Similarly, CARMA [7] is a recursive communication-avoiding algorithm which requires a block-recursive data layout also depending on matrix shapes and the available resources. On the other hand, most of the software packages for scientific applications like CP2K [15] use ScaLAPACK API [4] which assumes a block-cyclic matrix layout. Hence, the data redistribution (i.e. reshuffling) becomes necessary in order to integrate and use these efficient algorithms within the well-established software packages. Performing an all-to-all communication would violate the communication-optimality of these algorithms and must be avoided for performance reasons.

Another example where the data reshuffling is needed is to achieve the optimal performance of existing ScaLAPACK routines. It is known that the performance of ScaLAPACK highly depends on the block size which determines the matrix layout. The optimal block size depends on the target machine and the computational kernel being used [8]. Therefore, the data reshuffling might be needed to achieve the optimal block size on a specific system. ScaLAPACK provides the routine pxgemr2d for data reshuffling [19], but it is limited to block-cyclic layouts.

Here we present COSTA: an algorithm that resolves all these problems: 1) it minimizes the communication-cost of data reshuffling by process relabeling in the target layout 2) it can handle arbitrary grid-like matrix layouts which are not necessarily block-cyclic. Moreover, both row-major and col-major ordering of blocks is supported; 3) it can also transform the data while reshuffling (e.g. transpose or multiply by a scalar). 4) efficiently utilizes the overlap of communication and computation (i.e. the transformation); 5) provides the batched version, which can transform multiple layouts at once, while significantly reducing the latency. COSTA stands for Communication-Optimal (Re-)Shuffle and Transpose Algorithm and refers to the matrix operation that the algorithm implements: $A \leftarrow \alpha \cdot \mathrm{op}(B) + \beta \cdot A$, where $\mathrm{op} \in \{\mathrm{transpose}, \mathrm{conjugate\text{-}transpose}, \mathrm{identity}\}$, A, B are distributed matrices and α, β scalars.

The idea of relabeling processes in order to reduce the communication-cost has already been studied in [10]. However, their model has the following limitations: 1) it implicitly assumes all data pieces (i.e. items) are of the same size; 2) each data piece is assumed to belong to a single process; 3) data transformation (e.g. transpose, or multiplication by a scalar) during reshuffling is not considered; 4) the model does not take into account the data locality, e.g. how the local data is stored in the memory; 5) the latency and the bandwidth of all processes is assumed to be the same.

In this paper, our contribution is twofold. First, we develop a generalization of the model presented in [10] for finding the Communication-Optimal Process

Relabeling that resolves the above-mentioned limitations and is not limited to Linear-Algebra applications. Then, using this model we develop the COSTA algorithm that resolves the limitations of ScaLAPACK `pxgemr2d` and `pxtran` routines and outperforms them even when no process relabeling is used.

2   Preliminaries and Notation

For an arbitrary set $s = \{b_0, b_1, \ldots, b_{n-1}\}$, $|s| = n$ denotes its size. For a Cartesian product between two sets s_1 and s_2 we write $s_1 \times s_2$. We define the range as $[n] := \{0, 1, \ldots, n - 1\}$. A square matrix X of dimension n is denoted by $X = [[x_{ij}]]_{i,j \in [n]}$ or equivalently $X = [[x_{ij}]]_{0 \le i,j < n}$. We might treat a matrix as a set of its entries, in particular, we might write $x_{ij} \in X$ for $i, j \in [n]$.

A graph $G = (V, E)$ has vertices V and edges $E \subseteq (V \times V)$. A weighted graph is a graph in which each edge is assigned some weight. A bipartite graph with partitions U and V is a graph $G = (U \cup V, E)$ where $E \subseteq U \times V$. If $V = \{v_0, v_1, \ldots v_{n-1}\}$ and V', V'' are two identical copies of V, e.g. $V' = \{v'_0, v'_1, \ldots, v'_{n-1}\}$ and $V'' = \{v''_0, v''_1, \ldots, v''_{n-1}\}$, then we abuse the notation and write $G = (V, V, E)$ to denote the bipartite graph $G = (V', V'', E)$. Moreover, for an edge in this graph, we write (v_i, v_j) instead of (v'_i, v''_j). In a bipartite graph $G = (U, V, E)$, we define the set of all left neighbors of some vertex $v \in V$ as $\mathcal{N}_G^L(v) := \{u \in U : (u, v) \in E\}$ and similarly the set of all right neighbors of some vertex $u \in U$ as $\mathcal{N}_G^R(u) := \{v \in V : (u, v) \in E\}$. Two edges are *adjacent* if they have a common vertex. A matching $M \subseteq E$ is a subset of non-adjacent edges. The weight of the matching is the sum of weights of its edges. A perfect matching of G is a matching that covers every vertex of G.

Machine Model. We assume a distributed memory setting with multiple processes, each having its own private memory. Our model best corresponds to the MPI parallel computing model, where our term *process* corresponds to an MPI rank. We use the term *process* instead of *processor* to avoid the confusion arising when MPI is run on many-core architectures with different process affinity bindings. *Local data* of some process, is the data residing in its private memory, whereas *global data* is the union of local data across all processes. All data, that is not local to some rank is called *remote*. We say that each process *owns* its local data.

Data Package, Block and Volume. Let p_i and p_j be two arbitrary processes and let $s = \{b_0, b_1, \ldots, b_{|s|}\}$ be a set of all data that should be sent from p_i to p_j. Each data piece b might contain the information about its memory layout (e.g. if it is stored as a 2D block), data locality (e.g. stride, padding, alignment), memory ordering (e.g. row- or column-major) and similar. Each $b \in s$ is called a *block* and s a *package*. A *block volume* $V(b)$ is the size of block b in bytes and similarly, a *package volume* $V(s)$ is the sum of all block volumes it contains: $V(s) = \sum_{b \in s} V(b)$.

3   Communication Cost Function

The communication cost $w(p_i, p_j, s)$ represents the cost of sending the package $s = \{b_0, b_1, \ldots, b_{|s|}\}$ from process p_i to process p_j. Formally, if $P = \{p_0, p_1, \ldots, p_{n-1}\}$ is the set of all processes and S the set of all packages that are to be exchanged, then the communication cost function is defined as a function $w : P \times P \times S \mapsto \mathbb{R}$. Specifically, $w(p_i, p_j, \varnothing) = 0$ for any $p_i, p_j \in P$.

For an arbitrary $p_i, p_j \in P$ and $s \in S$, in its simplest form, w can be defined as follows:

$$w(p_i, p_j, s) = \begin{cases} V(s), & p_i \neq p_j \\ 0, & \text{otherwise} \end{cases} \tag{1}$$

This cost function considers all local communication free, whereas a remote communication cost is equal to the data volume. We will refer to this communication cost as *locally-free-volume-based* cost.

Alternatively, the cost function can also include the following factors:

- **Network Topology:** w can take into account the physical topology e.g. using some of the bandwidth-latency models [12]. If $L(p_i, p_j)$ is the latency cost between p_i and p_j, and $B(p_i, p_j)$ be the bandwidth cost per data unit, w could be defined as $w(p_i, p_j, s) = L(p_i, p_j) + B(p_i, p_j) \cdot V(s)$.
- **Transformation cost:** if the data also needs to be transformed on-the-fly, while being sent, e.g. the data should be transposed or multiplied by a scalar, then the cost of this transformation can also be included. For example, w can be defined as $w(p_i, p_j, s) = c \cdot \sum_{b \in s} I_T(b) \cdot |b|$, where $I_T(\cdot)$ is an indicator function if the piece of data b should be transformed (e.g. multiplied by a scalar or transposed) while being sent from p_i to p_j and c is a constant that determines the complexity of the transformation to be applied to b.
- **Data Locality:** the way how each piece of data $b \in s$ is stored in the memory can also be taken into account. For example, if b is a 2D block, then w can take into account its stride, padding, alignment and similar.

3.1   Communication Graph

A communication graph describes the communication pattern, i.e., which data the processes are going to exchange.

Let $P = \{p_0, p_1, \ldots, p_{n-1}\}$ be the set of all processes and $S = [[S_{ij}]]_{0 \leq i,j < n}$ be the set of all packages that are to be exchanged, where S_{ij} corresponds to the package to be sent from p_i to p_j.

We can represent this communication pattern with an undirected, bipartite graph (P, P, E) with two identical partitions P and the set of edges E, defined as follows:

$$E = \{(p_i, p_j) : (p_i, p_j) \in (P \times P) \wedge S_{ij} \neq \varnothing\}$$

We now formally define a *communication graph* as an ordered tuple:

$$G = (P, E, S) \tag{2}$$

If $w : P \times P \times S$ is a communication-cost function, then under w, each edge $(p_i, p_j) \in E$ has weight $w(p_i, p_j, S_{ij})$. In the same manner, the *total communication cost* of graph G, denoted by $W(G)$, is defined as the sum of the weights of all edges:

$$W(G) = \sum_{(p_i, p_j) \in E} w(p_i, p_j, S_{ij}). \tag{3}$$

4 Communication-Optimal Process Relabeling (COPR)

In this section, we first formally define the COPR and then show that it can be formulated as a well-known Linear Assignment Problem (LAP). Then, we discuss the current state-of-the-art algorithms to solve the LAP that can also be used to find the COPR.

4.1 The Formal Definition

Let $G = (P, E, S)$ be a communication graph (see Eq. (2)) on processes P, with edges E and data set $S = [[S_{ij}]]_{0 \leq i, j < n}$.

In order to reduce the total communication cost $W(G)$, as defined in Equation (3), we want to relabel the processes. Relabeling p_j to p_i makes their communication become local, hence potentially reducing the communication cost. We will first formally define these terms and then aim to find the process relabeling that minimizes the total communication cost.

Definition 1 *(Process Relabeling). Let $P = \{p_0, p_1, \ldots, p_{n-1}\}$ be a set of processes. A process relabeling σ is a permutation of indices $[n]$, implicitly mapping each p_i to $p_{\sigma(i)}$.*

Applying a process relabeling σ to graph G under communication-cost function w yields the relabeled communication graph G_σ which we define as follows.

Definition 2 *(Relabeled Graph). Let $G = (P, E, S)$ be a communication graph and σ be a process relabeling of P. The relabeled graph G_σ is a communication graph $G_\sigma = (P, E', S')$, where:*

$$E' = \big\{ (p_i, p_{\sigma(j)}) : (p_i, p_j) \in E \big\}$$
$$S'_{i, \sigma(j)} = S_{ij} , \text{ for each } (p_i, p_j) \in E.$$

Remark 1. Observe that the initial graph G is isomorphic to G_{id} where $id(\cdot)$ is the identity permutation $id(i) = i$ for all $i \in [n]$.

We say that graph G_σ is *induced* by σ relabeling. Note that after relabelling $j \to \sigma(j)$, the processes p_i still has to send S_{ij} to $p_{\sigma(j)}$, as before relabelling. If the communication between p_i and $p_{\sigma(j)}$ is faster than between i and j, this relabeling might reduce the communication cost.

Finally, we define the communication-optimal process relabeling (COPR) as the relabeling which yields the graph G_σ with minimal cost.

Definition 3 *(COPR). Let $G = (P, E, S)$ be a communication graph and $w :$ $P \times P \times S \mapsto \mathbb{R}$ be a communication cost function. A communication-optimal process relabeling σ_{opt} w.r.t. the cost function w is defined as:*

$$\sigma_{opt} = \arg\min_{\sigma} W(G_\sigma)$$

4.2   COPR as Linear Assignment Problem

In this section we show how finding the communication-optimal process relabeling (COPR) from Definition 3 can be reduced to solving the Linear Assignment Problem (LAP) [3]. The LAP consists of finding the assignment, i.e. a bijection $\phi : A \mapsto B$ between two equally-sized sets A and B ($|A| = |B|$) that optimizes the objective function of the form:

$$\sum_{a \in A} c(a, \phi(a)) \tag{4}$$

A minimization LAP can be easily turned into the maximization version: it suffices to either change the sign of the objective function or subtract all the costs from the maximum cost. The latter technique is often used in practice, since some implementations of LAP algorithms assume all costs are non-negative. We refer the reader to [3,9] for more details on LAP. Observe that finding the COPR directly by Definition 3 includes finding the process relabeling σ that induces the relabeled graph G_σ with minimal cost $W(G_\sigma)$. This is not directly an instance of LAP because the graph structure depends on σ. However, we will show that it can be reduced to LAP by first defining the relabeling gain, then proving that maximizing the relabeling gain yields the COPR and finally using this relabeling gain to formulate the problem of finding the COPR as a Linear Program corresponding to LAP.

Definition 4 *(Relabeling Gain). Let $G = (P, E, S)$ be a communication graph, w a communication cost function, σ an arbitrary process relabeling and let G_σ be the relabeled graph induced by σ. The relabeling gain $\delta : P \times P \mapsto \mathbb{R}$ for some $p_x, p_y \in P$ describes the gain of relabeling $p_x \xrightarrow{\sigma} p_y$ and is defined as:*

$$\delta(p_x, p_y) = \sum_{p_i \in \mathcal{N}_G^L(p_x)} (\underbrace{w(p_i, p_x, S_{i,x})}_{before\ relabeling} - \underbrace{w(p_i, p_y, S_{i,x})}_{after\ relabeling}) \tag{5}$$

The total relabeling gain is defined as the sum of relabeling gains for each process:

$$\Delta_\sigma = \sum_{p_j \in P} \delta(p_j, p_{\sigma(j)})$$

Remark 2. If w is the *locally-free-volume-based* cost function defined in Eq. (1), then it is easy to see that:

$$\delta(p_x, p_y) = V(S_{y,x}) - V(S_{x,x}),$$

which intuitively means that by relabeling $p_x \xrightarrow{\sigma} p_y$, we gained $S_{y,x}$ as it became a local exchange (which costs 0 under w) but we lost $S_{x,x}$ which after relabeling requires a remote communication.

In the following Lemma we prove that the total relabeling gain is equal to the total weight difference between G and G_σ, i.e. before and after the process relabeling.

Lemma 1. *Let $G = (P, E, S)$ a communication graph, w a communication cost function and σ an arbitrary process relabeling. If $G_\sigma = (P, E', S')$ is the relabeled graph induced by σ and Δ_σ the total relabeling gain, then the following holds:*

$$\Delta_\sigma = W(G) - W(G_\sigma)$$

Proof. By Eq. (3) and Definition 2, for $W(G_\sigma)$ we have:

$$W(G_\sigma) = \sum_{(p_i,p_j)\in E'} w(p_i, p_j, S'_{ij}) = \sum_{(p_i,p_j)\in E} w(p_i, p_{\sigma(j)}, S_{ij})$$

$$= \sum_{p_j\in P} \sum_{p_i\in\mathcal{N}_G^L(p_j)} w(p_i, p_{\sigma(j)}, S_{ij}) \tag{6}$$

Similarly, for $W(G)$, we have:

$$W(G) = \sum_{p_j\in P} \sum_{p_i\in\mathcal{N}_G^L(p_j)} w(p_i, p_j, S_{ij}) \tag{7}$$

Subtracting Eqs. (7) and (6), by Definition 4, we get:

$$W(G) - W(G_\sigma) = \sum_{p_j\in P} \underbrace{\sum_{p_i\in\mathcal{N}_G^L(p_j)} (w(p_i, p_j, S_{ij}) - w(p_i, p_{\sigma(j)}, S_{ij}))}_{=\delta(p_j,\sigma(p_j))} = \Delta_\sigma.$$

Next, we show that the COPR can also be obtained by maximizing the total relabeling gain.

Lemma 2. *Let $G = (P, E, S)$ be a communication graph and $w : P \times P \times S \mapsto \mathbb{R}$ a communication cost function. A communication-optimal process relabeling σ_{opt} with respect to the communication function w is given by:*

$$\sigma_{opt} = \arg\max_\sigma \Delta_\sigma$$

Proof. By Lemma 1, we have:

$$\arg\max_{\sigma} \Delta_\sigma = \arg\max_{\sigma}(W(G) - W(G_\sigma)).$$

Observe that $W(G)$ does not depend on σ and is therefore constant with respect to σ. Hence, we can write:

$$\arg\max_{\sigma}(W(G) - W(G_\sigma)) = \arg\max_{\sigma}(-W(G_\sigma)) = \arg\min_{\sigma} W(G_\sigma) = \sigma_{opt},$$

where the last equality follows from Definition 3.

Finally, we prove that finding the COPR can be reduced to the following Linear Program (LP) that corresponds to the Linear Assignment Problem (LAP).

Theorem 1. *Let $P = \{p_0, \ldots, p_{n-1}\}$ be a set of processes, $G = (P, E, S)$ a communication graph, $w : P \times P \times S \mapsto \mathbb{R}$ a communication cost function and $\delta : P \times P \mapsto \mathbb{R}$ a relabeling gain. Let x_{ij}^* $(i, j = 0, 1, \ldots n)$ be the optimal solution to the following Linear Program:*

$$maximize \sum_{(p_i, p_j) \in P \times P} \delta(p_i, p_j) x_{ij} \tag{8}$$

subject to:

$$\sum_{p_i \in P} x_{ij} = 1 \qquad\qquad j = 0, \ldots, n-1 \tag{9}$$

$$\sum_{p_j \in P} x_{ij} = 1 \qquad\qquad i = 0, \ldots, n-1 \tag{10}$$

$$x_{ij} \geq 0 \qquad\qquad i, j = 0, \ldots, n-1. \tag{11}$$

The communication-optimal process relabeling (COPR) σ_{opt} is given by:

$$\sigma_{opt}(i) = j \Leftrightarrow x_{ij}^* = 1 \text{ for all } i, j = 0, \ldots, n-1$$

Proof. This LP corresponds to the Linear Assignment Problem [3]. Due to Birkhoff [2] (also reformulated as Theorem 1.1 in [9]), we can assume $x_{ij} \in \{0, 1\}$, as this condition can be relaxed to $x_{ij} \geq 0$ in this case. The conditions (9) and (10) ensure the induced process relabeling is a bijection. Therefore, each feasible solution of this LP is a matrix representation of the permutation it induces.

The stated LP is always feasible, because $x_{ij} = 1 \Leftrightarrow i = j$ for all $i, j \in [n]$, corresponding to the identity permutation, is always a feasible solution. Let x'_{ij} be an arbitrary feasible solution of the LP and let σ be the permutation induced by x'_{ij}. Since $x'_{ij} \in \{0, 1\}$ and $x'_{ij} = 1 \Leftrightarrow \sigma(i) = j$, the objective function becomes:

$$\sum_{(p_i, p_j) \in P \times P} \delta(p_i, p_j) x'_{ij} = \sum_{p_i \in P} \delta(p_i, p_{\sigma(i)}) = \Delta_\sigma \tag{12}$$

By Lemma 2, maximizing the total relabeling gain Δ_σ yields the communication optimal process relabeling σ_{opt} which finalizes the proof.

Since the Linear Assignment Problem can also be formulated in terms of Graph Matchings [9], we also provide the equivalent reformulation of Theorem 1 in terms of the *Maximum Weight Bipartite Perfect Matching* problem.

Theorem 2. *Let* $P = \{p_0, \ldots, p_{n-1}\}$ *be a set of processes,* $G = (P, E, S)$ *a communication graph,* $w : P \times P \times S \mapsto \mathbb{R}$ *a communication cost function and* $\delta : P \times P \mapsto \mathbb{R}$ *a relabeling gain. Let* $G_\delta = (P, P, E_\delta)$ *be a complete bipartite graph with edges* $E_\delta = P \times P$, *where each edge* $(p_i, p_j) \in E_\delta$ *is assigned weight* $\delta(p_i, p_j)$. *If* $M \in E_\delta$ *is a Maximum Weight Perfect Matching of graph* G_δ, *the communication-optimal process relabeling (COPR)* σ_{opt} *of* G *is given by:*

$$\sigma_{opt}(i) = j \Leftrightarrow (p_i, p_j) \in M \tag{13}$$

Proof. This is just a reformulation of Theorem 1 where each feasible solution $x'_{ij}, i, j \in [n]$ of the LP from Theorem 1 can also be viewed as a matching of G_δ. The relation between $x'_{ij}(i, j \in [n])$, the corresponding relabeling σ and the corresponding matching M is given by:

$$x'_{ij} = 1 \Leftrightarrow \sigma(i) = j \Leftrightarrow (p_i, p_j) \in M.$$

Remark 3. The graph G_δ admits a Perfect Matching because $M = \{(p_i, p_i) : p_i \in P\}$ is always a valid Perfect Matching.

4.3   COPR Algorithm

In Theorem 1 it is shown how finding the COPR can be reduced to the Linear Program that corresponds to the Linear Assignment Problem (LAP). A reformulation of this LAP in terms of Maximum Weight Bipartite Perfect Matching (MWBPM) yields Theorem 2. In addition, the LAP can also be formulated in terms of Network Flows, in which case it is reduced to the *Maximum Flow of Optimal Cost* problem [9].

An example of the matching-based algorithm for finding the COPR that follows from Theorem 2 is shown in Algorithm 1. The complexity of this algorithm depends on the complexity of 1) computing the weights, i.e. costs 2) solving a LAP (Line 6). Let $|P| = n$ be the number of processes.

The weights are computed in Lines 3–5. If all data volumes $V(S_{ij}), i, j \in [n]$ are precomputed, then the for-loop computing all $\delta(p_i, p_j)$ by Eq. (5) serially takes $O(n^3)$. On distributed architectures, this reduces to $O(n^2)$. Furthermore, for simpler cost functions like locally-free-volume-based cost from Eq. (1), computing $\delta(p_i, p_j)$ is constant (see Remark 2), which further reduces the total complexity down to $O(n)$. The complexity is therefore dominated by the complexity of solving the LAP.

The LAP solver is invoked in Line 6. One of the most famous LAP algorithms is the Hungarian (KuhnMunkres) Algorithm [14,18] with complexity $O(n^3)$, which is optimal for dense graphs that we are dealing with (note that the graph G_δ from Theorem 2 is a *complete* bipartite graph). This algorithm has also been GPU-accelerated [17] and there is also a distributed version with a multi-gpu support [5]. Other interesting LAP algorithms include a fast matching-based randomized algorithm [20] and a recently developed, distributed, approximation algorithm [1] that achieves great speedups while finding near-optimal solutions.

Algorithm 1. Finding the COPR

Require:

   Process Set: $P = \{p_0, p_1, \ldots, p_{n-1}\}$

   Data Set: $S = [[S_{ij}]]_{0 \le i,j < n}$ ▷ S_{ij} := package to be sent $p_i \mapsto p_j$

   Communication-cost function: w ▷ $w(p_i, p_j, S_{ij})$:= cost of sending $p_i \xrightarrow{S_{ij}} p_j$

Ensure:

   Comm-Optimal Process Relabeling (COPR): $\sigma_{opt} : [n] \mapsto [n]$ ▷ $p_i \to p_{\sigma_{opt}(i)}$

1: **procedure** FINDCOPR$(P, S, w) \to \sigma_{opt}$

2:    $\sigma_{opt} = \mathbf{0}_n$ ▷ COPR as an array of size n

3:    $weights = \mathbf{0}_{n \times n}$ ▷ adjacency matrix of G_δ from Theorem 2

4:    **for** $(p_i, p_j) \in P \times P$ **do**   ▷ G_δ is a complete bipartite graph

5:        $weights[i][j] = \delta(p_i, p_j)$ ▷ $\delta(\cdot, \cdot)$ defined in Eq. (5)

6:    $M = \text{MWBPM}(n, weights)$ ▷ Max Weight Bipartite Perfect Matching(G_δ)

7:    **for** $(i, j) \in M$ **do**

8:        $\sigma_{opt}[i] = j$ ▷ $M \mapsto \sigma_{opt}$ as in Eq. (13)

9:    **return** σ_{opt}

---

5   COSTA: Comm-Optimal Shuffle and Transpose Alg.

COSTA uses the communication-optimal process relabeling (COPR) to implement the routine:

$$A = \alpha \cdot \text{op}(B) + \beta \cdot A, \quad \text{op} \in \{\text{transpose}, \text{conjugate-transpose}, \text{identity}\} \quad (14)$$

on distributed systems, where A, B are matrices with potentially different layouts and α, β are scalars. Since this routine, in a distributed setting, includes the data reshuffling (i.e. redistribution) across processes while potentially transposing the data, we call this routine: *Shuffle and Transpose*. It encapsulates the functionality of two ScaLAPACK routines: `pxtran(u)` for matrix transpose and `pxgemr2d` for data redistribution.

   Matrix Layout: describes how the matrix is distributed among processes. The way how a matrix A is partitioned is given by two sorted arrays: row-splits R_A and column-splits C_A where block b_{ij} contains the rows in range $[R_A(i), R_A(i+1))$ and the columns in range $[C_A(j), C_A(j+1))$. The row-splits and columns-splits together define the grid $\text{Grid}_A = (R_A, C_A)$. The owner of a block b from this grid is given by $\text{Owners}_A(b) \in P$, where P is the set of processes holding A. The layout of a matrix A is hence an ordered tuple $L(A) = (\text{Grid}_A, P, \text{Owners}_A)$.

Grid Overlay: given two grids $\text{Grid}_A = (R_A, C_A)$ and $\text{Grid}_B = (R_B, C_B)$ we define the Grid Overlay $\text{Grid}_{A,B} = (R_A \cup R_B, C_A \cup C_B)$ as the grid obtained by overlaying both grids. It is easy to see that each block $b_{A,B} \in \text{Grid}_{A,B}$ is covered by one and only one block $b_A \in \text{Grid}_A$ and one and only one block $b_B \in \text{Grid}_B$. We therefore define $\text{cover}_A(b_{A,B}) = b_A$ and $\text{cover}_B(b_{A,B}) = b_B$.

Data Reshuffling: given matrices A and B with same dimensions, but different layouts $L(A)$ and $L(B)$ on processes $P = \{p_0, p_1, \ldots, p_{|P|}\}$, we want to copy the values of B into the layout of A. In a distributed setting, this includes communication of matrix pieces. In order to be able to use Algorithm 1 for obtaining the communication-optimal process relabeling (COPR) σ_{opt} for this problem, we have to construct the set of packages $S = [[S_{ij}]_{0 \leq i,j < |P|}$ where S_{ij} contains all blocks that should be sent from process p_i to p_j. We show how to obtain the COPR for this problem in Algorithm 2.

Algorithm 2. COPR for (Matrix) Data Reshuffling

Require:
    Matrix Layout $L(A) = (\text{Grid}_A, P, \text{Owners}_A)$
    Matrix Layout $L(B) = (\text{Grid}_B, P, \text{Owners}_B)$
    Communication-Cost Function w
Ensure:
    Set of data packages: $S = [[S_{ij}]]_{0 \leq i,j < |P|}$ ▷ package S_{ij} to be sent from p_i to p_j
    COPR: σ_{opt} for copying B into the layout of A   ▷ σ_{opt} relabeling: $p_i \rightarrow p_{\sigma_{opt}(i)}$
1: **procedure** FINDCOPRFORMATRICES$(L(A), L(B), w) \rightarrow (S, \sigma_{opt})$
2:     $S = [[S_{ij}]]_{0 \leq i,j < |P|} = \varnothing_{|P| \times |P|}$ ▷ set of data packages: initialize all $S_{ij} = \varnothing$
3:     **for** $b \in \text{Grid}_{A,B}$ **do**   ▷ iterate over the Grid Overlay
4:         $p_i = \text{Owners}_A(\text{cover}_A(b))$ ▷ owner of the block which covers b in $L(A)$
5:         $p_j = \text{Owners}_B(\text{cover}_B(b))$ ▷ owner of the block which covers b in $L(B)$
6:         $S_{ij} = S_{ij} \cup \{b\}$ ▷ add block b to the right package
7:     $\sigma_{opt} = FindCOPR(P, S, w)$ ▷ Algorithm 1
8:     **return** (S, σ_{opt})

Scale and Transpose/Conjugate: observe that the routine from Eq. (14) includes the possibility to scale the matrices (multiply by a scalar), transpose/conjugate or take a submatrix. Let $L(A)$ and $L(B)$ be two different matrix layouts. In the previous paragraph we discussed the case when matrix B should be copied to the layout of matrix A without any transformation. Here, we discuss the cases when B should also be transformed. If only a submatrix of B should be taken, then we can first truncate the corresponding row-splits and column-splits in Grid_B and then apply the Algorithm 2 to obtain the COPR. If B should also be transposed/conjugated or scaled before being copied to A, then the cost of this transformation can be taken into account in the communication-cost function w (see Sect. 3). Practically, the transformation can be performed in one of the following ways:

- transform before sending: each process can first transform the data locally in temporary send buffers, and then send it.
- transform after receiving: each process can transform the data upon receipt in temporary receive buffers. This approach is better in asynchronous settings because the data transformation can be overlapped with communication of other packages.

We chose to transform upon receipt, since we are using asynchronous communication.

Communication-Cost Function: the communication cost function can be arbitrary. In practice, we use the simple locally-free-volume-based cost function defined in Eq. (1).

Finally, taking into account these insights, we present COSTA in Algorithm 3.

Algorithm 3. COSTA: Comm-Optimal Shuffle and Transpose Algorithm

---
Require:
    Matrix A with Layout $L(A) = (\text{Grid}_A, P, \text{Owners}_A)$
    Matrix B with Layout $L(B) = (\text{Grid}_B, P, \text{Owners}_B)$
    Scalars α, β
    Operator op $\in \{\text{transpose}, \text{conjugate-transpose}, \text{identity}\}$
    Comm-Cost Function (optional) w ▷ by default, defined by Eq. (1)
    Process id: $p_{id} \in P$
Ensure:
    Performs $A = \alpha \cdot \text{op}(B) + \beta \cdot A$
1: **procedure** COSTA$(A, L(A), B, L(B), \alpha, \beta, op)$
2:    $(S, \sigma_{opt}) = \text{FindCOPRforMatrices}(L(A), L(B), w)$ ▷ Algorithm 2
3:    **for** $p_j \in P$ **do**
4:       send asynchronously $S_{id,j}$ to $p_{\sigma(j)}$ ▷ send local data to relabeled processes
5:    **for** package $\in \{0, 1, \ldots, |P|\}$ **do**
6:       receive from any $p_i \in P$ in a temp. recv buffer
7:       scale, transpose or conjugate the received package $S_{i,id}$ if needed

---

6   Implementation Details

COSTA (Algorithm 3) is implemented using the hybrid MPI+OpenMP parallelization model. The code is publicly available under the BSD-3 Clause Licence at [11]. It has the following features: 1) provides the ScaLAPACK wrappers for `pxgemr2d` and `pxtran`; 2) supports arbitrary grid-like matrix layouts (not limited to block-cyclic). It also support both row- and col-major ordering of matrices, unlike ScaLAPACK; 3) can use the COPR to minimize the communication; 4) supports batched transformation, i.e., multiple pairs of matrix layouts can be transformed in the same communication round; 5) supports arbitrary data types using C++ templates.

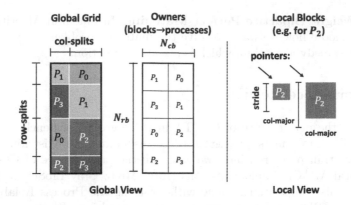

Fig. 1. COSTA Matrix Descriptor: a global view contains a grid (defined by row-splits and col-splits) and the owners matrix mapping blocks to processes. A local view is a list of blocks, each containing a pointer, a stride, dimensions and the ordering type (row- or col-major).

Matrix Layout Descriptor. Following the theoretical definition of a matrix layout from Sect. 5, in practice we use a more detailed matrix descriptor depicted in Fig. 1, that also takes into account block strides and whether the blocks are stored in row- or col-major order. This makes the COSTA layout descriptor more general than the block-cyclic descriptor used by ScaLAPACK.

Implementation. After $S = [[S_{ij}]]$ is computed in Line 2, each process has a list of blocks it should send and a list of blocks it should receive. Each process first copies all blocks into a temporary send buffer using OpenMP, such that all blocks to be sent to the same target are packed together into a single, contiguous package in the send buffer. These packages are then sent using the non-blocking `MPI_Isend` such that only a single package (containing multiple blocks) is sent to each receiving process, which significantly reduces the latency costs.

Overlap of Communication and Computation. Upon receipt of a package with `MPI_Waitany`, blocks within this package are unpacked and the transformation (transpose, conjugate-transpose or multiplication by a scalar) is performed using OpenMP, while other packages are still being communicated in the background, thus enabling the overlap of communication and computation. A cache-friendly, multi-threaded kernel for matrix transposition is provided. Moreover, the blocks that are local in both the initial and the final layouts are not copied to temporary send/receive buffers, but are handled separately with OpenMP, to avoid unnecessary data copies to and from temporary buffers and potentially additional copies that MPI might perform. The handling of these blocks is also overlapped with MPI communication.

Batched Transformation. If multiple pairs of layouts are to be transformed together, then the procedure is the same, except that now a package contains blocks that might belong to different layouts. Still, all the blocks to be sent to the same process are packed together and sent within a single message, thus reducing the latency costs even further.

Max Weight Bipartite Perfect Matching. In Line 6 in Algorithm 1 we are free to choose how we want to solve the matching problem. In practice, we use a simple greedy algorithm, which is a 2-approximation.

7   Performance Results

We evaluate the performance of COSTA in three groups of benchmarks: first, since COSTA implements `pxgemr2d` (data-reshuffling, i.e. distributed copy) and `pxtran` (transpose) routines, we compare the performance of COSTA vs. available ScaLAPACK implementations (Intel MKL, Cray LibSci) in isolation (Sect. 7.1). This comparison is done without using the Process Relabeling, as ScaLAPACK API does not support it. In the second part (Sect. 7.2), we measure how much communication-volume can be reduced by using the process relabeling. In the final benchmark (Sect. 7.3), we run COSTA within a real-world application and analyse its performance, as well as the communication-volume reduction.

Hardware Details: all the experiments are performed on Piz Daint Supercomputer of Swiss National Supercomputing Centre (CSCS) which consists of two partitions: the CPU partition with 1813 nodes (Cray XC40 compute nodes, Intel Xeon E5, 2×18 cores, 64-128 GB RAM) and the GPU partition with 5704 nodes (Cray XC50 compute nodes, Intel Xeon E5, 12 cores, 64 GB RAM + NVIDIA P100 16 GB GPU).

Software Details: in the benchmarks, we used Cray-MPICH v7.7, Intel MKL v19.1, Cray LibSci and Cray LibSci-Acc v20.06, CP2K v7.1, COSMA v2.3 and COSTA v1.0. All the libraries were compiled with a GCC v10.1 compiler available on the Piz Daint Supercomputer.

7.1   COSTA vs. ScaLAPACK

We compare the performance of COSTA, Intel MKL and Cray LibSci for the following routines: `pdgemr2d` (distributed copy, i.e. reshuffling) and `pdtran` (transpose). To this end, we use the ScaLAPACK wrappers that COSTA provides (see Sect. 6).

It is known that ScaLAPACK performance often varies drastically for different block sizes which determine the matrix distributions (i.e. layouts) and the optimal block size depends on the target machine [8]. Scientific applications usually have a default block size (e.g. in [13], it is 32×32) and reaching the optimal block size (which is 128×128, for our applications) requires data reshuffling and potentially a transpose operation. Inspired by this example, we run the following benchmark: we vary the matrix size from 100–200 (square-case) and for each size we transform the matrix from 32×32 to 128×128 block size, using the pdgemr2d routine and the same for the pdtran (transpose) routine.

We also include the batched version of COSTA for comparison. The batched version amortizes the latency costs since multiple layouts are transformed within the same communication round. This is often useful for operations like matrix multiplication which involves 3 matrices and each of them might potentially need to be transformed, as is the case in the COSMA algorithm [16]. To account for this scenario, we also ran the batched version of COSTA on each test-case from this benchmark with one difference: instead of transforming a single instance of each test case, we let the batched version transform 3 identical instances of each test-case and report the amortized cost per test-case instance.

This benchmark is run on 128 dual-socket CPU nodes (2×18 cores) of Piz Daint Supercomputer using 2 MPI ranks per node, 18 threads per rank and 16×16 process grid. Each experiment was repeated 5 times and the best time is reported in Fig. 2. We observed similar performance with other matrix shapes (including rectangular matrices) and other process grids, so here we present just the square-matrices case.

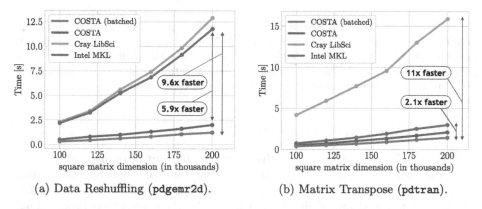

(a) Data Reshuffling (`pdgemr2d`).   (b) Matrix Transpose (`pdtran`).

Fig. 2. The performance comparison of ScaLAPACK routines for data reshuffling (left) and matrix transpose (right) by different algorithms (see Sect. 7.1). Reported times for COSTA (batched) are amortized over 3 identical instances of a test-case.

7.2   Process Relabeling

We measured how much communication-volume is reduced when redistributing (reshuffling) a matrix between two block-cyclic layouts. The matrix size was $10^5 \times 10^5$ and the process grid was 10×10. The process grid was row-major for the initial layout and column-major for the final layout. The target layout had block size fixed at 10^4. The block size of the initial layout was varied from 1 up to 10^4 and for each block size the communication-volume was computed before and after relabeling. Based on this we computed the communication-volume reduction (in percent) due to process relabeling, that is shown in Fig. 3. When both layouts have the same block size ($= 10^4$), then they only differ in the block assignment to processes, in which case the process relabeling is able to completely eliminate the communication.

Comm-Vol [%] reduced by Process Relabeling

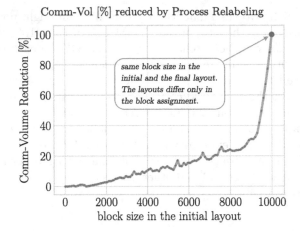

Fig. 3. The initial layout of the matrix (i.e. the block size) was varied, whereas the final layout was fixed with a block size of 10^4. The process grid was fixed to 10×10 in both layouts. When the initial and target layouts have the same blocks (and hence the same grids), process relabeling makes all communication local, thus eliminating the need for remote communication (the red dot). (Color figure online)

7.3   Real-World Application: RPA Simulations

In Random Phase Approximation (RPA) [6] simulations, a major part of computation consists of many large tall-and-skinny matrix multiplications with matrix transposition. For a system size N (the number of atoms), the matrices to be multiplied are of size $O(N^2) \times O(N)$, where $O(N^2)$ is proportional to (occupied orbitals · virtual orbitals) and $O(N)$ is proportional to the number of auxiliary basis functions. Concretely, for simulating 128 water molecules, the matrix sizes are depicted in Fig. 5. This multiplication is repeated many times and takes $\approx 80\%$ of the total simulation time on 128 dual-socket CPU nodes of Piz Daint. Therefore, an efficient matrix-multiplication routine is essential for this benchmark. Recently, a communication-optimal matrix-multiplication algorithm COSMA [16] has been developed which offers significant speedups for all matrix shapes. However, COSMA natively uses a specialized blocked matrix layout which depends on matrix dimensions and the number of available processors. Moreover, as shown in Fig. 5, one of the matrices (matrix A) also has to be transposed during the reshuffling. On the other hand, the CP2K [15] software package, which implements the RPA method, assumes a block-cyclic (ScaLA-PACK) layout. Since COSMA layout is not block-cyclic, existing ScaLAPACK routines for reshuffling and transpose cannnot be used.

We used COSTA with Process Relabeling to integrate COSMA into CP2K and compare its performance to Intel MKL, Cray LibSci (CPU) and Cray Lib-Sci (GPU). We simulate 128 water molecules with the RPA method on 128, 256, 512 and 1024 GPU nodes of Piz Daint Supercomputer. The total matrix-multiplication time as well as the total simulation time are reported in Fig. 4.

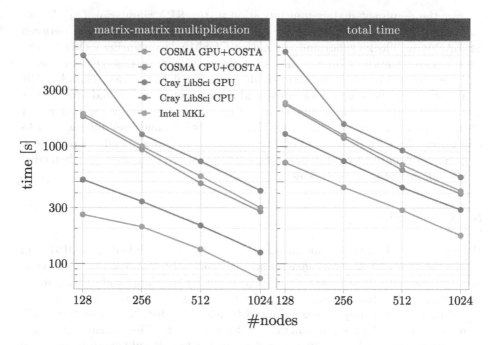

Fig. 4. The RPA simulation of 128 water molecules using different matrix-multiplication backends. We used COSTA with Process Relabeling to redistribute and transpose matrices between ScaLAPACK (block-cyclic) and the native COSMA layout in each matrix-multiplication call. COSMA + COSTA outperform alternative libraries on both CPU and GPU. COSTA accounts for roughly 10% of the total runtime of COSMA+COSTA in these cases.

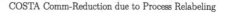

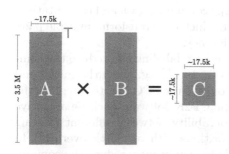

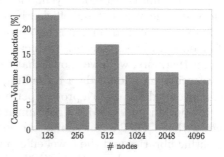

Fig. 5. The computationally dominant matrix multiplication in the RPA simulation that is performed many times throughout the simulation. The exact size of A and B is $3,473,408 \times 17,408$.

Fig. 6. The communication volume reduction due to process relabeling in COSTA during the transformation of matrices (left) between the ScaLA-PACK (block-cyclic) and the native COSMA layouts.

For the dominant matrix multiplication in the RPA simulation (Fig. 5), we computed the total communication volume for transforming matrices between ScaLAPACK (block-cyclic) and the native COSMA layout using COSTA. The total communication volume with and without process relabeling is measured and the percentual volume reduction is shown in Fig. 6. In this case, ScaLAPACK is always using the same block sizes (and same layouts) for A and B, whereas matrix C is distributed only on a subset of processes (the ones in the upper part of the rectangular process grid). COSMA on the other hand uses different blocks and layouts for each matrix and all matrices are distributed on all the processes. This makes it hard to predict how this interplay of different layouts is behaving as the number of nodes increases.

8   Conclusion

We have shown how the communication-optimal process relabeling (COPR) can efficiently be found in a very general setting where the network topology, data-locality, data transformation cost (e.g. transposing the data) and other parameters can all be taken into account through a cost-function. The theoretical contribution of this paper is not limited to matrix redistribution or transposition, but can also be used in general, e.g. for tensors. Besides transposition, any other operation can be performed on the local data – it suffices to include the operation cost into the cost function of the COPR algorithm (Algorithm 1).

We developed COSTA: a highly-efficient algorithm with process relabeling for performing matrix shuffle and transpose routine (Eq. (14)). The experiments have shown that COSTA outperforms ScaLAPACK multiple times even when no process relabeling is used. COSTA provides ScaLAPACK wrappers for `pxgemr2d` and `pxtran` routines making the integration into scientific libraries straightforward. In addition, COSTA can also deal with arbitrary grid-like matrix layouts and is not limited to block-cyclic layouts and supports both row- and column-major storage of blocks and efficiently overlaps communication and computation. Moreover, a batched version is also provided, which can transform multiple pairs of layouts, while significantly reducing the latency.

Furthermore, we have shown that the process relabeling can reduce the communication volume for data reshuffling even by 100%, e.g. when the initial and final layouts differ up to a process permutation. We used COSTA to integrate the highly-optimized COSMA algorithm into the CP2K software package and have shown that COSTA can enable the interoperability between different existing scientific libraries and the novel efficient algorithms with very little overhead. In practice, we have shown that COSTA is able to significantly reduce the communication cost also in real world applications where initial and final layouts are both changing in different ways.

References

1. Azad, A., Buluç, A., Li, X.S., Wang, X., Langguth, J.: A distributed-memory algorithm for computing a heavy-weight perfect matching on bipartite graphs. SIAM J. Sci. Comput. **42**(4), C143–C168 (2020)
2. Birkhoff, G.: Tres observaciones sabre el algebra lineal. Univ. Nac. Tucumán Rev. Ser. A **5**, 147–151 (1946)
3. Burkard, R., Dell'Amico, M., Martello, S.: Assignment Problems: Revised Reprint. SIAM (2012)
4. Choi, J., Dongarra, J.J., Pozo, R., Walker, D.W.: Scalapack: a scalable linear algebra library for distributed memory concurrent computers. In: The Fourth Symposium on the Frontiers of Massively Parallel Computation, pp. 120–121. IEEE Computer Society (1992)
5. Date, K., Nagi, R.: GPU-accelerated Hungarian algorithms for the linear assignment problem. Parallel Comput. **57**, 52–72 (2016). https://doi.org/10.1016/j.parco.2016.05.012, http://www.sciencedirect.com/science/article/pii/S016781911 630045X
6. Del Ben, M., Schütt, O., Wentz, T., Messmer, P., Hutter, J., VandeVondele, J.: Enabling simulation at the fifth rung of DFT: large scale RPA calculations with excellent time to solution. Comput. Phys. Commun. **187**, 120–129 (2015). https://doi.org/10.1016/j.cpc.2014.10.021, http://www.sciencedirect.com/science/article/pii/S0010465514003671
7. Demmel, J., et al.: Communication-optimal parallel recursive rectangular matrix multiplication. In: 2013 IEEE 27th International Symposium on Parallel and Distributed Processing, pp. 261–272. IEEE (2013)
8. Dongarra, J.J., Walker, D.W.: Software libraries for linear algebra computations on high performance computers. SIAM Rev. **37**(2), 151–180 (1995). https://doi.org/10.1137/1037042
9. Du, D., Pardalos, P.M.: Handbook of Combinatorial Optimization, vol. 4. Springer Science & Business Media, Boston (1998). https://doi.org/10.1007/978-1-4613-0303-9
10. Herrmann, J., Bosilca, G., Hérault, T., Marchal, L., Robert, Y., Dongarra, J.: Assessing the cost of redistribution followed by a computational kernel: complexity and performance results. Parallel Comput. **52**, 22–41 (2016)
11. Kabic, M., Pintarelli, S., Kozhevnikov, A., VandeVondele, J.: COSTA: communication-optimal shuffle and transpose algorithm (2020). https://github.com/eth-cscs/COSTA
12. Kielmann, T., Gorlatch, S.: Bandwidth-Latency models (BSP, LogP). In: Paduda, D. (ed.) Encyclopedia of Parallel Computing, pp. 107–112. Springer, Boston (2011). https://doi.org/10.1007/978-0-387-09766-4_189
13. Kozhevnikov, A., Schulthess, T.: Sirius library for electronic structure (2013). https://github.com/electronic-structure/SIRIUS
14. Kuhn, H.W.: The Hungarian method for the assignment problem. Naval Res. Logistics Q. **2**(1–2), 83–97 (1955)
15. Kühne, T.D., et al.: Cp2k: an electronic structure and molecular dynamics software package-quickstep: efficient and accurate electronic structure calculations. J. Chem. Phys. **152**(19), 194103 (2020)

16. Kwasniewski, G., Kabić, M., Besta, M., VandeVondele, J., Solcà, R., Hoefler, T.: Red-blue pebbling revisited: near optimal parallel matrix-matrix multiplication. In: Proceedings of the International Conference for High Performance Computing, Networking, Storage and Analysis, New York. SC 2019. Association for Computing Machinery (2019). https://doi.org/10.1145/3295500.3356181
17. Lopes, P.A., Yadav, S.S., Ilic, A., Patra, S.K.: Fast block distributed CUDA implementation of the Hungarian algorithm. J. Parallel Distrib. Comput. **130**, 50–62 (2019). https://doi.org/10.1016/j.jpdc.2019.03.014, http://www.sciencedirect.com/science/article/pii/S0743731519302254
18. Munkres, J.: Algorithms for the assignment and transportation problems. J. Soc. Ind. Appl. Math. **5**(1), 32–38 (1957)
19. Prylli, L., Tourancheau, B.: Efficient block cyclic data redistribution. In: Bougé, L., Fraigniaud, P., Mignotte, A., Robert, Y. (eds.) Euro-Par 1996. LNCS, vol. 1123, pp. 155–164. Springer, Heidelberg (1996). https://doi.org/10.1007/3-540-61626-8_20
20. Schwartz, J., Steger, A., Weißl, A.: Fast algorithms for weighted bipartite matching. In: Nikoletseas, S.E. (ed.) WEA 2005. LNCS, vol. 3503, pp. 476–487. Springer, Heidelberg (2005). https://doi.org/10.1007/11427186_41

Enabling AI-Accelerated Multiscale Modeling of Thrombogenesis at Millisecond and Molecular Resolutions on Supercomputers

Yicong Zhu[1], Peng Zhang[1], Changnian Han[1], Guojing Cong[2], and Yuefan Deng[1(✉)]

[1] Department of Applied Mathematics and Statistics,
Stony Brook University, Stony Brook, NY, USA
{yicong.zhu,peng.zhang,changnian.han,yuefan.deng}@stonybrook.edu
[2] Oak Ridge National Laboratory, Oak Ridge, TN, USA
congg@ornl.gov

Abstract. We report the first congruent integration of HPC, AI, and multiscale modeling (MSM) for solving a mainstream biomechanical problem of thrombogenesis involving 6 million particles at record molecular-scale resolutions in space and at simulation rates of milliseconds per day. The two supercomputers, the IBM Summit-like AiMOS and our University's SeaWulf, are used for scalability analysis of, and production runs with, the LAMMPS with our customization and AI augmentation and they attained optimal simulation speeds of 3,077 μs/day and 266 μs/day respectively. The long-time and large scales simulations enable the first study of the integrated platelet flowing, flipping, aggregating dynamics in one dynamically-coupled production run. The platelets' angular and translational speeds, membrane particles' speeds, and the membrane stress distributions are presented for the analysis of platelets' aggregations.

Keywords: Multiscale modeling · AI · High-performance computing · Platelet aggregation

1 Introduction

Multiscale modelling (MSM), a powerful tool to mitigate over- or under-modeling of the multi spatial-temporal scales problems occurred in multi-component systems, generates massive data at many varying resolutions [1]. The MSM itself and the massive data thus generated require integrated analysis by the latest development of machine learning (ML) methodologies. These simulation and analysis of the integrated MSM and ML require so much computing resources that only the fastest supercomputers can handle [2]. Our work focuses on the challenges of understanding one main cause of cardiovascular diseases or stroke, i.e., the thrombogenesis. With two supercomputers of fairly different architectures, our modeling has reached an unprecedented temporal and spatial scales and resolutions: reaching milliseconds in simulated time and molecular resolutions in structure details.

© Springer Nature Switzerland AG 2021
B. L. Chamberlain et al. (Eds.): ISC High Performance 2021, LNCS 12728, pp. 237–254, 2021.
https://doi.org/10.1007/978-3-030-78713-4_13

Cardiovascular diseases (CVDs) were confirmed as the number one cause of death worldwide by WHO, which accounted for nearly 17.8 million deaths globally in 2017, an increase of 21% compared to 2007. Thrombosis formation is the most dominant cause of the related death, including stroke, atherosclerosis and infarction [3]. Due to the stenotic flow patterns occurring in implanted devices, the elevated shear stress exacerbates the platelet activation and thrombosis formation [4]. During the recent COVID-19 pandemic, platelet-rich thrombi was discovered in the pulmonary, hepatic, renal, and cardiac microvasculature, resulting in multiple organs dysfunction and deaths [5, 6]. Thrombosis formation is a complex physiological process, ranging over multiple spatial and temporal scales involving several important modules, such as fluid mechanics, coagulation cascade, cell mechanics, platelet adhesion, activation and aggregation, and receptor-ligand binding [7].

To understand the mechanism at such multiple spatiotemporal scales and multi-component biochemical system, we developed a novel MSM framework to exploit its multiscale nature and the efficient algorithms for utilizing available computing resources. The MSM framework simulates the high-resolution details of the blood clotting and thrombosis generation through platelet-platelet interactions and mechanotransduction induced by blood flow [8]. The MSM simulator embedded in our customized LAMMPS package was also enhanced by an AI-guided multiple time stepping algorithm (AI-MTS) we proposed recently [9]. By overcoming the potential computing resources waste caused by the conventional standard time stepping algorithms, the AI-MTS intelligently selects the timestep sizes by adapting to the real-time biophysical states of the underlying simulations.

Integrating the MSM with the AI-MTS algorithms and implementing them in the multi-CPU and multi-GPU supercomputers with diverse architectures, we boost the simulation performance and enable the large time scale simulation of thermogenesis in molecular resolution. During these simulations, the mechanics and dynamics characteristics of platelets were collected and analyzed. We present rotational and translational speed of platelets, velocity magnitude mapping of platelet membrane, and shear flow conditions around platelets. Furthermore, the localized stress mapping on the platelet surface membrane and subcellular mechanotransduction between platelet membranes will also be analyzed.

In summary, the main contributions are as follows.

(1) The first congruent integration of HPC, AI, and multiscale modeling to help advance understanding of a critical application in biomedicine: thrombogenesis.
(2) Significant reduction in simulation time from 1 week to 14 h resulting from our implementation of the integrated framework in the heterogeneous hardware architectures.
(3) Achievement of a record simulated time scales (milliseconds) and spatial resolutions (molecular level) for a complex application by methodically meshing a high sophisticated software framework on the supercomputers and demonstrated that such real-world simulations are, for the first time, feasibility with currently available HPC resources.

(4) Potential insights for antiplatelet drug design and therapy, resulting from our *in silico* data of the molecular features such as binding and flow-induced stress response to fluid-platelet interface.

The remainder of the paper is organized as follows. In Sect. 2, we review recent molecular dynamics simulation work and thrombosis related simulation study. In Sect. 3, we describe the MSM framework and AI-MTS algorithm and the two supercomputers with which, also, the two *in silico* experiments we conducted. Sects. 4, 5, and 6 present the relevant physiological results, the analysis of scalabilities on the supercomputers, and the discussions, respectively.

2 Related Work

The all-atom molecular dynamics (MD) simulation, as a technique widely used in numerical simulation, can simulate and describe the behavior of molecules at atomic level. As an important track in numeric simulation, the implementation of MD could help reveal the biomolecular phenomenon at microscopic scale which is hard to obtain from *in vitro* or *in vivo* experiments in biology, chemistry or medicine fields [10]. However, restricted by the computation costs, such MD simulations could be challenging tasks to build at long timescales, i.e., millisecond scale.

Many efforts have been made in recent years to further extend the simulation timescales with high speed by designing specialized hardware or developing new MD packages/algorithms. Shaw *et al.* [11] designed Anton machine, a special-purpose parallel supercomputer for MD simulation with 512 processing cores, achieves simulation speed of several microseconds per day for 10,000 to 500,000 atom chemical systems. Furthermore, the second-generation Anton machine, Anton 2 [12], which was devoted to efficient fine-grained operation, improved its performance at a rate of 85 μs/day for 23,558-atom system. Yang *et al.* [13] designed the first full-scale FPGA-based simulation engine, which has the state-of-arts simulation rate at 630 ns/day on a 23.5K DFHR dataset. Zhang *et al.* [14] redesign GROMACS, a popular MD application, on SW26010 to further utilize the Sunway TaihuLight, the 4th ranked supercomputers worldwide. The SW_GROMACS achieved more than 60 times speedup for the calculation of the short-range interaction. In SC'20, Jia *et al.* [15] reported a ML-based simulation protocol, DeePMD, which could be easily accelerated with GPU on Summit supercomputer. The new scheme made the performance record of simulating ab initio molecular dynamics for 127 million atoms at more than 1 ns per day.

In thrombosis growth computational study, complex components including blood flow, blood cells, receptors and ligands are interfaced interactively at multiple scales [16]. Long simulation is needed in order to observe meaningful dynamic progress at molecular details. However, applications mentioned above are hard to be extended to such a complex system. These applications are designed for homogeneous systems and a single scale is too expensive to capture multiscale dynamics of thrombosis formation.

Many related computational studies on thrombosis were introduced in recent decades. They could be categorized as four methods: (1) Immersed boundary (IB) methods [17]; (2) discrete particle-based methods, such as DPD or SCEs [18–20] (3) continuum MSM [21, 22]; (4) molecular dynamics models [23]. However, in these studies, the continuum MSM failed to capture the binding phenomenon in molecular level, while all-atom molecular simulation focused on the local phenomenon in nanoscale. The computation capability of such MD is hard to capture the whole platelet interactions and aggregation process in millisecond scales. For instance, Shiozaki *et al.* studied the equilibrated states for 1 ns.

We developed MSM that integrates the DPD-CGMD methods to model the dynamics of platelets in shear blood flow compared to the traditional CFD and MD scheme [8, 24, 25]. The MSM framework together with the AI-MTS algorithm enable simulating thrombogenesis for longer timescales to study their properties at molecular scales.

3 The Methods

3.1 The Multiscale Model

Given the multiscale nature of the bio-medical system, we employ our previous studies on multiscale model to simulate the dynamics and mechanics of platelets in blood flow. Platelet, in quiescent state, is of discoid shape with diameter 2–4 μm and it consists of three main zones: the peripheral, structural and organelle. In order to depict the resting model at cellular scale and simulate its characteristic under shear stress, we developed a CGMD nano-to-micro model of human platelets as a discoid shaped spheroid with dimensions $4 \times 4 \times 1$ μm^3. Each platelet consists of 140,303 particles [24]. The dissipative particle dynamics (DPD) method is applied to simulate the hydrodynamics of blood plasma in vessels. A hybrid force field is introduced to describe the spatial interface between platelet membrane and flow system [8].

An aggregation force field is developed and validated by Gupta *et al.* [25] to simulate the αIIbβ3-fibrinogen binding, including a harmonic term to mimic the short range binding between receptors and ligands and a Morse term to mimic the long-medium range effect of aggregation.

$$U_{\text{total}} = U_{\text{bonded}} + U_{\text{nonbonded}} \tag{1}$$

$$U_{\text{bonded}} = \sum_{\text{bonds}} \frac{f^A}{2r_0}(r - r_0)^2 \tag{2}$$

$$U_{\text{nonbonded}} = \sum_{\text{neighbors}} D_0\left(e^{-2\alpha(r-r_0)} - 2e^{-\alpha(r-r_0)}\right) \tag{3}$$

where r is the distance between two particles and r_0 is the equilibrium bond length, D_0 is the well depth, α is the scaling factor, $\boldsymbol{r}_{ij} = \boldsymbol{r}_i - \boldsymbol{r}_j$, $r_{ij} = |\boldsymbol{r}_{ij}|$, $\boldsymbol{e}_{ij} = \boldsymbol{r}_{ij}/r_{ij}$, f^A is the force coefficient. Differentiating the potential, we obtain the hybrid force field as below,

$$\boldsymbol{F}_{ij} = \left(2\alpha D_0\left(e^{-2\alpha(r_{ij}-r_0)} - e^{-\alpha(r_{ij}-r_0)}\right) + f^A\left(1 - \frac{r_{ij}}{r_0}\right)\right)\boldsymbol{e}_{ij} \tag{4}$$

The equilibrium bond length of αIIbβ3-fibrinogen binding r_0 is 67.5 nm. The parameters D_0, α, f^A are determined by validating the aggregation force field with the *in vitro* experiments, where D_0 is 10.0, α is 1.0 and f^A is 10.0 in DPD units.

3.2 AI-MTS

When simulating the thrombogenesis involving multi components with temporal scales from picosecond to millisecond and spatial scales from nanometer to millimeter, we must reform the conventional standard time stepping algorithms (STS) to treat these vastly different scales without waste of computing resources for redundant computations [26]. Recently, A novel data-driven AI-MTS algorithm is introduced to overcome such problem by adjusting Δt accommodating with underlying biophysical dynamics. An optimal Δt will be predicted by the AI inference pipeline and carried back to the MSM simulator. It has accelerated the mainstream STS algorithm by 4000 times while preserving accuracy to above 97%, when measuring the velocities and kinetic energies of the platelets during their rotation and translation [9, 27].

Time stepping algorithm is based on the scheme of the velocity Verlet integrator, using the time discretization to integrate the governing equations with a timestep Δt,

$$\mathbf{v}\left(t + \frac{\Delta t}{2}\right) = \mathbf{v}(t) + \frac{\Delta t}{2m} \cdot \mathbf{F}[x(t)],$$

$$\mathbf{x}(t + \Delta t) = \mathbf{x}(t) + \mathbf{v}\left(t + \frac{\Delta t}{2}\right),$$

$$\mathbf{v}(t + \Delta t) = \mathbf{v}\left(t + \frac{\Delta t}{2}\right) + \frac{\Delta t}{2m} \cdot \mathbf{F}[x(t + \Delta t)]. \tag{5}$$

Specifically, in the AI-MTS mechanism, the whole simulation system is decomposed into subsystems according to the different scales of biology components. Small (large) Δt's are applied for subsystems at bottom (top) levels. In our thrombogenesis simulation, two subsystems, the fluid subsystem at the mesoscopic scale and the platelet subsystem at microscopic scale are introduced. AI-MTS learns the platelets' states by analyzing the time series of states, extracted from the MSM simulator, such as angular velocity, kinetic energies, and the surrounding flow speed. We predict the adaptive timestep sizes and number of jumps by a deep learning framework consisting of (a) a 2-stage denoising by moving average and wavelet transform filters to cleanse high-frequency noise in raw data and (b) two RNN-based AEs to extract latent features. The MSM uses three sets of timesteps: two static timesteps for the fluid and fluid-platelet interface, and variable Δt's for platelets, determined by AI-MTS on-the-fly.

The 3-level integration procedure (Table 1) in AI-MTS involves communication, force computation, and AI-interface. For each, we summarized the level of integration for different components, as well as its implementation on the heterogeneous supercomputers with CPU and GPU complexes.

3.3 Numerical Experiments

We applied MSM to simulate the multiple platelets recruitment through αIIbβ3-fibrinogen binding near the vessel wall. Figure 1 summarizes the setup of the two numerical experiments we conducted: (1) Exp(3+3), (2) Exp(3+4). Exp(3+3) are in a microchannel of length 39.1 μm, width 16 μm, and height 16 μm, consists of

Table 1. Overview of the AI-MTS algorithm for MSM.

AI-MTS Algorithm	Component	CPU[a]	GPU[b]	AI[c]
Repeat:				
Integration of half-step v	Fluid	√		
Neighbor list construction and communication			√	
Integration of half-step v	Fluid-Platelet	√		
Integration of half-step v	Platelet	√		
Integration of full-step x	All Particles	√		
Communication		√		
Compute non-bonded pair forces	Platelet		√	
Compute bonded forces	Platelet	√		
Communication		√		
Integration of half-step v	Platelet	√		
Compute non-bonded pair forces	Fluid-Platelet		√	
Communication		√		
Integration of half-step v	Fluid-Platelet	√		
Compute non-bonded pair forces	Fluid		√	
Communication		√		
Integration of half-step v	Fluid	√		
AI inference for platelet timestep sizes regulation		√		√
Integration parameters update		√		
Until simulation ends				

[a] Computation & communication carried on CPU. [b] Computation carried on GPU in hybrid CPU-GPU architecture. [c] AI inference.

six platelets: 3 flowing platelets driven by flow are rotating and translocating towards the 3-platelet aggregates (blood clot) on the wall. We assume the bottom two adhered platelets are captured by the wall via GPIba-vWF binding and have no movement. The top platelet is aggregated by the two bottom platelets via αIIbβ3-Fg binding. Another experiment, Exp(3+4), consists of seven platelets in the same simulation box. Compared with Exp(3+3), we increase the volume of blood clots by putting one more platelet on top of the blood clot. Each platelet has 67,004 αIIbβ3 receptors, while the receptor density on the platelet membrane is 2,342 particles/μm^2. The simulation results of platelets and flow conditions will be further compared and discussed in Sect. 4. Figure 1 shows details of our models, including single platelet structure, platelet-platelet interaction and experiments' settings. Both models use the same parameter set as presented in Table 2.

Periodic boundary conditions are employed in x and z dimensions. A x-direction force $g_x = 0.006$ is added on all fluid particles in the two experiments to produce typical viscous flow, Poiseuille shear flow, in our micro simulation box. The number density for fluid particles is 3.0, while the fluid density of blood plasma is 1060 kg/m^3. The no slip boundary condition on the wall in y dimension is performed. The αIIbβ3 receptors on the platelet membrane associated with Fibrinogen in the shear flow will initial the platelet aggregation. We continue running the simulation system and collect the platelet properties, fluid profiles in molecular resolution for milliseconds.

We customized LAMMPS with corresponding algorithms for DPD-CGMD hybrid potential [8] and platelet aggregation force potential [25]. The AI-enhanced MTS algorithm, learning the optimal Δt during platelet-fluid interaction simulation by adapting to the multiple scales of physics, further accelerates our simulations. The simulation performance is to be analyzed in terms of the five components defined in Table 3 for future discussions. For force calculations, `Pair` indicates the non-bonded force calculation while `Bond` indicates the bonded force calculation. In parallel computing, LAMMPS partitions the global simulation domain into small 3d subdomains, which requires neighbor list construction during simulation. This related work is assigned to `Neigh`. Specifically, the non-bonded force calculation `Pair` and neighbor list construction `Neigh` could be carried on GPUs to further improve the simulation speed on hybrid CPU-GPU architectures. In addition, `Comm` represents inter-processor communication of particles and their properties, and `Modify` means integration computations.

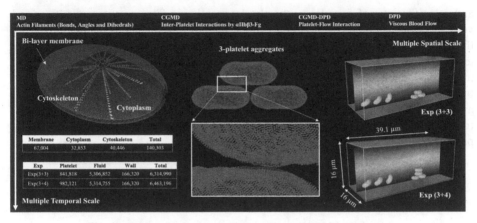

Fig. 1. Schematic model representation and MSM framework.

Table 2. Reference units and parameters of the simulation system.

Terms	Symbol, formula	Model values	SI values	SI units
Length	σ	1	1.778×10^{-7}	m
Time	t	1	2.083×10^{-6}	s
Mass	m	1	1.985×10^{-18}	kg
Force	$m\sigma/t^2$	1	8.151×10^{-14}	N
Energy	$m\sigma^2/t^2$	1	1.446×10^{-20}	J
Velocity	σ/t	1	8.533×10^{-2}	m/s

3.4 The Measures

In order to quantify and interpret the massive data of platelets and fluid particles obtained in our long timescale simulations, we first introduce measures including the stress tensor

Table 3. Definitions of components used in implementation.

Components	Definitions
Pair	Non-bonded force computations
Bond	Bonded force computations: bonds, angles, dihedrals, impropers
Neigh	Neighbor list construction
Comm	Inter-processor communication of particles and their properties
Modify	Time integration computations

and velocity vector of particles on the platelet membrane. The instantaneous stress and velocity of platelet membrane particles only reflect the instantaneous fluctuation during the simulation process and are not applicable for direct use. Therefore, we need to apply temporal and spatial averaging of these files and obtain more meaningful magnitude and trend. Specifically, we use three steps to calculate the magnitude of stress distribution on platelets membrane from stress tensor: 1) Convert tensor into scalar value; 2) Temporal averaging; 3) Spatial averaging. The window size for temporal averaging is for 25,000 timesteps (10 μs), the cutoff threshold for spatial averaging is 1.2. For a membrane particle p at time t, we compute the magnitude of stress

$$\hat{\tau}(p, t) = \frac{1}{\sqrt{3}} \sqrt{\tau_{xx}^2 + \tau_{yy}^2 + \tau_{zz}^2 - \tau_{xx}\tau_{yy} - \tau_{xx}\tau_{zz} - \tau_{yy}\tau_{zz} + 3\left(\tau_{xy}^2 + \tau_{yz}^2 + \tau_{xz}^2\right)} \quad (6)$$

3.5 The Supercomputers

The multiscale fluid-platelet experiments are implemented on the two supercomputers: the AiMOS and SeaWulf.

AiMOS, ranking 29th on the November 2020 TOP500 list, consists of 252 compute nodes each containing 2 IBM POWER 9 processors at 3.15 GHz. Each POWER 9 processor has 256 GB DDR4 memory of 135 GB/s peak bandwidth and has 20 cores with 4 hardware threads per core. Combined, the two POWER 9 CPUs on an AiMOS node can perform 0.97 TFLOP/s in double precision. The CPU to GPU ratio is 1:3 in one socket, so each node also has one 6x NVIDIA Tesla V100 GPUs with 32 GB of memory via a 900 GB/s bus, providing 7.5 TFLOP/s per GPU in double precision. The nodes are interconnected with the Mellanox EDR InfiniBand [28].

SeaWulf is a cluster consisting of 164 compute nodes. One compute node has two Intel Xeon E5-2683v3 processors of 14 cores each. Each node has 128 GB DDR4 memory of 133 GB/s combined memory bandwidth, and operates at 0.89 TFLOP/s. The nodes are interconnected via the Connect-IB FDR InfiniBand.

4 The *in Silico* Experiment Results

After the flow system warm-up for approximately 600 μs, the velocity profile was fully developed as a parabolic Poiseuille flow with the mean velocity 6 cm/s and the platelet dynamics and mechanics became measurable. The MSM framework and AI-MTS algorithm enabled us to observe the continuous platelet phenomenon in molecular resolution for a large system consisting of more than 6 million particles that interact at different scales. We observed the platelets' flowing, flipping, and aggregations, and each platelet trajectory, for milliseconds.

4.1 Platelet Dynamics

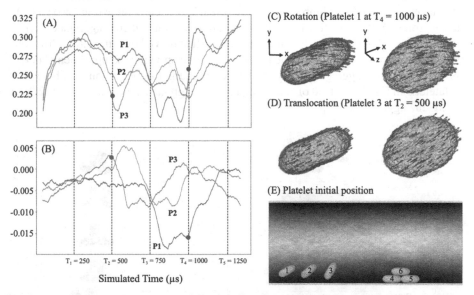

Fig. 2. The motion details of three platelets: P1(blue), P2(yellow), P3(green). (A) Translational speed. (B) Angular speed. (C) Rotation of Platelet 1. (D) Translocation of Platelet 3. Times of highlighted observations: $T_1 = 250$ μs, $T_2 = 500$ μs, $T_3 = 750$ μs, $T_4 = 1000$ μs, $T_5 = 1250$ μs. (Color figure online)

Translational and Angular Speed. Platelets are numbered in setup for tracking (Fig. 2E). Driven by blood flow, three flowing platelets start rotation and translocation towards the 3-platelet aggregates which were located on the right side of the simulation box. We document their translocating and angular speed every 1 μs and notice each platelet as a rigid body has its own unique trajectory. After time averaging, we present each platelet continuous movement of Exp(3+3) for more than 1250 μs, as shown in Fig. 2. Initially, all three flowing platelets start to accelerate pushed by the blood flow in the first 250 μs (Fig. 2A). In the meantime, due to shear stress induced by flow, all three platelets start rotation (Fig. 2B). Each platelet maintains its regular movement, translocation plus rotation, until approaching the adhered 3-platelet aggregates. The flow conditions around the aggregates is quite different from its normal state. At $T_2 = 500$ μs when platelet 3 gets close to the aggregates, "stack up" pattern (Fig. 2D) forms. At T_4 = 1000 μs when platelet 1 finishes its "climbing" and sliding down rapidly under the downward flow (Fig. 2C).

Platelet Membrane Jiggling. By tracking for milliseconds, we noticed that the platelets' motions, individually and collectively, are highly dependent on their surrounding flow conditions, epitomizing the lasting argument that large-scale simulation is able to, and is needed to, better understand the platelet dynamics in the process of aggregation and thrombosis formations. We calculated the average velocity magnitude of each platelet membrane particle as a function of time and, in Fig. 3, We select 5 special timesteps from our two setup experiments to analyze their motions. Combined with Fig. 2, the three stages, "regular" – "climb up" – "slide down" are clearly shown in Exp(3+3). It takes around 500 μs for flowing platelets to approach the adhered aggregates. After another 500 μs, flowing platelets "climb up" and "slide down" over the clots. However, Exp(3+4) shows different phenomena compared to the previous setup. When platelets approach the bigger aggregates, they experience the larger deceleration (see blue area on Platelet 3 in Fig. 3). Instead of "climbing up" the aggregates, the Platelets 3 & 2 "roll around" the aggregates.

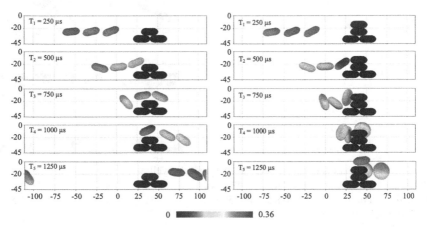

Fig. 3. Speed distributions on platelet membrane for the two experiments at $T_1 = 250$ μs, $T_2 = 500$ μs, $T_3 = 750$ μs, $T_4 = 1000$ μs, $T_5 = 1250$ μs.

Platelet Membrane Stress. Our millisecond simulation helps better understand how platelets are dynamically influenced by blood flow through mechanotransduction during thrombogenesis. We render the stress tensor of each platelet particle we collected into a stress scalar. After temporal and spatial averaging, we described in Sect. 3.4, the stress distribution map on platelets' membranes are presented in Fig. 4. We observe all platelets have high stress spots on the periphery of their membrane compared to their center part. This is the evidence that how platelet membranes respond to hemodynamics stresses, and this phenomenon may be the trigger of platelet activation. Researchers observed the platelet pseudopodia grow from the periphery of platelets [29].

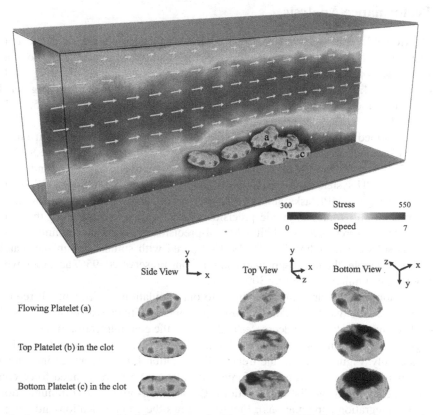

Fig. 4. Average stress on platelet membrane for $T_2 = 500$ µs. DPD fluids velocity were shown at the simulation slice box with z from -1 to 1. Space average cutoff for stress spatial averaging is 1.2.

4.2 Blood Flow

Like the platelet particles, the more than 5 million fluid particles are also updated at every time step to allow us to simulate the fluid-platelet interface details at molecular level. Specifically, we present the snapshot of our simulation experiment Exp(3+3), and discuss how blood flow leads to platelet distinguish behavior and how it adapted to forming blood clot.

For fluid particles within a slice of our simulation box, we collect their velocity vectors. After calculating the speed of each particle, we perform spatial average to obtain the velocity vector field as shown in Fig. 4, from which we noticed expected velocity patterns at various regions, of the simulation box, including the upper side without the platelet-aggregates and the bottom side with the adhered aggregates. The red spots at the periphery of the platelet membrane indicate the high stress induced by the viscous linear shear stress flow.

5   Performance Analysis

Using affordable computational costs within reasonable simulating time, we could observe and analyze the molecular level mechanics and dynamic details of the whole thrombogenesis process, including platelet flipping, flowing and aggregating as discussed in Sect. 4. We tested the performance of two supercomputers of our big benchmark simulation experiment, Exp(3+3), and the results are shown in Figs. 5, 6, 7, 8 and Table 4.

We performed strong scalability tests of the same problem size, scaling from 4 to 192 nodes. We conducted two CPU-only systems on AiMOS-C (POWER9) and SeaWulf (Xeon E5), using 36 and 28 MPI tasks per node, respectively. We also conducted a hybrid CPU-GPU system with mixed precision for GPUs on AiMOS-G (POWER9 + 6x V100) using 36 MPI tasks and 6 GPUs per node, where mixed precision stands for computing pair forces in single precision (32 bits) then accumulating them into double-precision force vectors (64 bits). Mixed-precision is a technique commonly used in various software including LAMMPS. Compared with simulations in the platelet dynamics in double, the mixed-precision simulations preserve 90–95% accuracy while improving the simulation speed by 30%–50%.

Space domain decomposition is applied to our simulation experiments. It requires each node to communicate with its six closest neighbors. With increasing the nodes, the per-node communication load decreases and so does the communication time.

Figure 5 presents the simulation speed in µs/day for SeaWulf, AiMOS-C, AiMOS-G, respectively. Figure 6 shows the trends of simulation time percentage in terms of five components: Pair (non-bonded force computations), Bond (bonded force computations), Neigh (neigh list construction), Comm (inter-processor communication), Modify (integration computations). Figure 7 shows the communication and computation time reduction while increasing nodes. Figure 8 summarizes the feasibility and efficiency of our MSM framework plus AI-MTS algorithm, which achieve a reduction in simulating time from 1 week to 14 h for the 1.75-ms simulation. Based on the performance results of our simulation on two heterogeneous supercomputers, we have five main conclusions.

(1)   Figure 5 shows the computing speed in µs/day for three tested systems. A common practice to benchmark large scale simulations, following the Golden Bell wining report Anton-2 [12], is µs/day. Both AiMOS-C and AiMOS-G show scalability, and significantly faster than SeaWulf that exhibits linear scalability.

(2) GPUs play a key role in accelerating the computations, resulting in a speedup of 2.7–12.2 over CPU-only implementation (Fig. 5). In order to improve simulation performance, the non-bonded pair force computations are carried on the GPUs. Since the neighbor list construction occupies a large amount of computing time on CPUs, we port it to GPUs to further accelerate the simulation. GPU uses multithread to construct the neighbor list in parallel. The workload percentage in terms of five components on AiMOS-C and AiMOS-G are compared in Fig. 6. We could find out how the workload weighted and scaled on varying architectures with different numbers of nodes. For the CPU-only system, `Modify` and `Neigh` cost 98% simulating time on CPUs. For the hybrid system, `Modify` still dominates the simulating time. `Pair` measures the GPU operating time under the hybrid system, including neighbor list construction and non-bonded pair force computations. As a result, `Pair` and `Modify` together consumes over 90% simulating time.

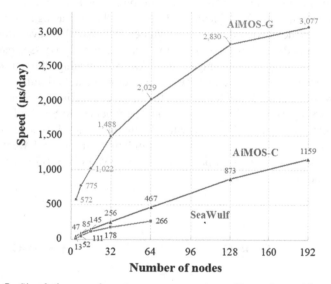

Fig. 5. Simulation speeds on two supercomputers with varying architectures.

(3) With increasing nodes, computation and communication time decreased. We sum up the `Pair, Bond, Modify` as computation time, and sum up `Neigh` and `Comm` as communication time. As shown in Fig. 7, the decreasing trend of AiMOS-C differs from the AiMOS-G. The computation load and communication load are proportional to the volume and the surface area of a single subdomain, respectively. The increasing number of nodes will reduce the size of the subdomain, resulting in the decrease of computation and communication time. For AiMOS-G, since we use GPU to build up the neighbor list, the communication time is significantly saved.

(4) Parallel efficiency is influenced by the load imbalance for tightly coupled MSM. The load imbalance is caused by the computational complexity of multi-physics

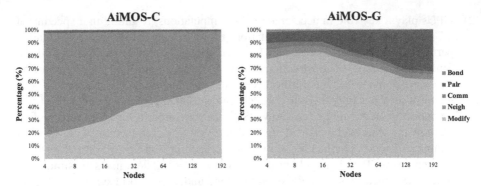

Fig. 6. Profiling of MSM on AiMOS with and without GPUs.

governing functions, multiple timestep sizes, domain decompositions, and hardware architectures. Using AiMOS as an example, when applying the space domain decomposition method from 4 nodes to 192 nodes, the increasing number of subdomains reduces the maximum particle count per processor. However, the imbalance factor, which is defined as the ratio of the maximum per processor particle count among all processors to the averaged value, keeps increasing all the time (Table 4).

(5) We enabled the large-scale platelet-mediated thrombogenesis simulation on AiMOS and SeaWulf, by using MSM framework to improve modeling efficiency and applying AI-MTS algorithm to improve simulating efficiency. At SeaWulf, we achieved the best performance as 266 μs/day with 64 compute nodes. Moreover, with mixed-precision GPUs, we further reduced the simulating time from 1 week (SeaWulf) to 14 h (AiMOS-G). The best performance of AiMOS is 3,077 μs/day with 192 compute nodes.

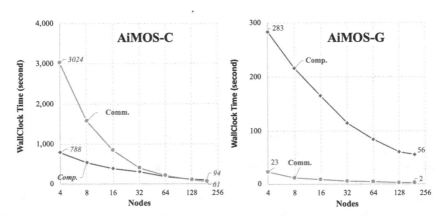

Fig. 7. Ratios of computation to communication for AiMOS.

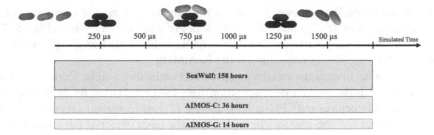

Fig. 8. Comparison of simulation efficiencies of SeaWulf and AiMOS.

Table 4. Details of the space domain decomposition.

Node	MPI processors	Decomposition (x × y × z)	Max count	Avg count	Imbalance factor
4	144	$9 \times 4 \times 4$	168,796	43,854	3.8
8	288	$12 \times 6 \times 4$	115,224	21,927	5.3
16	576	$16 \times 6 \times 6$	84,544	10,964	7.7
32	1,152	$18 \times 8 \times 8$	58,465	5,482	10.7
64	2,304	$24 \times 12 \times 8$	33,592	2,741	12.3
128	4,608	$32 \times 12 \times 12$	21,720	1,370	15.8
192	6,912	$36 \times 16 \times 12$	16,921	914	18.5

6 Discussions and Future Work

We completed *in silico* experiments on two supercomputers to quantitatively understand the thrombogenesis through αIIbβ3-fibrinogen bonds between multiple platelets under linear viscous shear flow using a multiscale model at millisecond scale. This study has (1) expanded the simulated system size from the published studies and enabled a more integrated experiment of multiple platelets in blood vessel with 6M particles; (2) augmented our previous studies to consider more biomechanically realistic phenomena for capturing, for the first time, the integrated platelet flowing, flipping, aggregating dynamics in one dynamically-coupled production run; and (3) extended the simulated time enabled by our new framework to observe more meaningful and clinically relevant dynamics. All of these molecular level results are observed separately and validated with *in vitro* experiments in our previous simulation study [8, 24, 25], demonstrating the accuracy of this study. In addition, related antiplatelet drug therapy needs those detailed results and analysis of shear-induced platelet aggregation phenomena [30].

Supercomputers enable larger-scale MSM for biology applications. However, to start simulating such a complex biology event with multiple spatial and temporal scales, a tremendous amount of computation resources is needed. Compared to previous approaches, we proposed the MSM framework and developed the AI-MTS algorithm to efficiently use the powerful and invaluable computing resources provided by top supercomputers. We achieved (1) record performance for such a complex multi-component system of 3,077 μs/day using 192 nodes of AiMOS (252 cores) (Figs. 5–7); (2) reduced simulating time from 1 week (SeaWulf) to 14 h (AiMOS-G); (3) obtained strong scalability to 76% of computing nodes in AiMOS.

Further studies to improve simulation speed and scalability will be focused on load balancing by adaptive domain decomposition for MSM simulation by exploiting the system-level architectures and CPU-multithreading. (1) Load imbalance is caused by the intrinsic nature of our application where particles, the main object of our calculations, distribute irregularly in space and time with fairly short time scales. Specifically, the particle densities for the two major components of the simulated system, the platelet itself and the surrounding fluid, can differ by 30 times. Therefore, as discussed in Sect. 5, the space domain decomposition is a natural cause of huge load imbalance. New particle decomposition with which each computing unit is allotted equal number of particles can alleviate a substantial amount of load imbalance and thus boost overall simulation performance. This new approach, quite cumbersome to implement, has its own flaws. A need to dynamically redistribute the particles to adapt to the model dynamics of platelet flowing, flipping and aggregating posts new challenges. Our next tasks are to and adiabatically adjust the particle assignment by learning the underlying dynamics. In addition, the computational complexity of different force fields in MSM and the varied calculation needs of multiple timestep sizes introduced by AI-MTS are needed to be considered as well. (2) Multithreading will be fused into the customized LAMMPS package to optimize the intra-node communication and accelerate the integrations on CPUs.

Our simulation may lead to applications in thrombosis, cardiovascular diseases and COVID-19 study. For instance, to better understand how platelet aggregation as a multistep adhesion will be influenced by different blood flow conditions, we could adjust the shear rate of fluid systems driven by the pressure. Many receptor-ligand bonds play important roles during hemostasis and thrombosis generation processes. Adding GPIba-vWF binding to our current study, together with αIIbβ3-Fg bonds we used, will better describe the whole progress of platelet margination, adhesion and aggregation in thrombosis formation. Compared to the current rigid-body platelet model, deformable platelets induced by lower shear stress have bigger contact area and higher rate of bond formation [25]. If we release the rigid constraint, a more realistic representation of platelet-platelet interactions could be obtained. Nevertheless, to study large sizes of thrombosis formation located in human blood, which consists of hundreds of or thousands of platelets, requires more computing resources and much more efficient algorithms in the future.

Acknowledgement. The project is supported by the SUNY-IBM Consortium Award, IPDyna: Intelligent Platelet Dynamics, FP00004096 (PI: Y. Deng, Co-PI: P. Zhang). The simulations were conducted on the AiMOS at Rensselaer Polytechnic Institute and the SeaWulf at Stony Brook University.

References

1. Hodak, H.: The nobel prize in chemistry 2013 for the development of multiscale models of complex chemical systems: a tribute to Martin Karplus, Michael Levitt and Arieh Warshel. J. Mol. Biol. **426**(1), 1–3 (2014). https://doi.org/10.1016/j.jmb.2013.10.037. ISSN 0022-2836
2. Alber, M., et al.: Integrating machine learning and multiscale modeling—perspectives, challenges, and opportunities in the biological, biomedical, and behavioral sciences. NPJ. Digit. Med. **2**, 1–11 (2019)
3. Virani, S.S., et al.: Heart disease and stroke statistics—2020 update: a report from the American Heart Association. Circulation E139-E596 (2020)
4. Bluestein, D., Yin, W., Affeld, K., Jesty, J.: Flow-induced platelet activation in a mechanical heart valve. J. Heart Valve Dis. **13**, 501–508 (2004)
5. Poor, H.D., et al.: COVID-19 critical illness pathophysiology driven by diffuse pulmonary thrombi and pulmonary endothelial dysfunction responsive to thrombolysis. Clin. Transl. Med. **10**, e44 (2020)
6. Rapkiewicz, A.V., et al.: Megakaryocytes and platelet-fibrin thrombi characterize multi-organ thrombosis at autopsy in COVID-19: a case series. EClinicalMedicine **24**, 100434 (2020)
7. Wang, W., King, M.R.: Multiscale modeling of platelet adhesion and thrombus growth. Ann. Biomed. Eng. **40**, 2345–2354 (2012)
8. Zhang, P., Gao, C., Zhang, N., Slepian, M.J., Deng, Y., Bluestein, D.: Multiscale particle-based modeling of flowing platelets in blood plasma using dissipative particle dynamics and coarse grained molecular dynamics. Cell. Mol. Bioeng. **7**, 552–574 (2014)
9. Han, C., Zhang, P., Bluestein, D., Cong, G., Deng, Y.: Artificial intelligence for accelerating time integrations in multiscale modeling. J. Comput. Phys. **427**, 110053 (2021)
10. Dror, R.O., Dirks, R.M., Grossman, J., Xu, H., Shaw, D.E.: Biomolecular simulation: a computational microscope for molecular biology. Annu. Rev. Biophys. **41**, 429–452 (2012)
11. Shaw, D.E., et al.: Anton, a special-purpose machine for molecular dynamics simulation. Commun. ACM **51**, 91–97 (2008)
12. Shaw, D.E., et al.: Anton 2: raising the bar for performance and programmability in a special-purpose molecular dynamics supercomputer. In: SC 2014: Proceedings of the International Conference for High Performance Computing, Networking, Storage and Analysis, pp. 41–53 (2014)
13. Yang, C., et al.: Fully integrated FPGA molecular dynamics simulations. In: Proceedings of the International Conference for High Performance Computing, Networking, Storage and Analysis, pp. 1–31 (2019)
14. Zhang, T.: SW_GROMACS: accelerate GROMACS on sunway TaihuLight. In: Proceedings of the International Conference for High Performance Computing, Networking, Storage and Analysis, pp. 1–14 (2019)
15. Jia, W., et al.: Pushing the limit of molecular dynamics with ab initio accuracy to 100 million atoms with machine learning. In: Proceedings of the International Conference for High Performance Computing, Networking, Storage and Analysis, pp. 1–14 (2020)
16. Jackson, S.P.: The growing complexity of platelet aggregation. Blood **109**, 5087–5095 (2007)
17. Fogelson, A.L., Guy, R.D.: Immersed-boundary-type models of intravascular platelet aggregation. Comput. Methods Appl. Mech. Eng. **197**, 2087–2104 (2008)
18. Sweet, C.R., Chatterjee, S., Xu, Z., Bisordi, K., Rosen, E.D., Alber, M.: Modelling platelet–blood flow interaction using the subcellular element Langevin method. J. R. Soc. Interface **8**, 1760–1771 (2011)
19. Grinberg, L., et al.: A new computational paradigm in multiscale simulations: application to brain blood flow. In: Proceedings of 2011 International Conference for High Performance Computing, Networking, Storage and Analysis, pp. 1–5 (2011)

20. Wu, Z., Xu, Z., Kim, O., Alber, M.: Three-dimensional multi-scale model of deformable platelets adhesion to vessel wall in blood flow. Philos. Trans. Royal Soc. A Math. Phys. Eng. Sci. **372**, 20130380 (2014)
21. Mody, N.A., King, M.R.: Platelet adhesive dynamics. Part I: characterization of platelet hydrodynamic collisions and wall effects. Biophys. J. **95**, 2539–2555 (2008)
22. Mody, N.A., King, M.R.: Platelet adhesive dynamics. Part II: high shear-induced transient aggregation via GPIbα-vWF-GPIbα bridging. Biophys. J. **95**, 2556–2574 (2008)
23. Shiozaki, S., Takagi, S., Goto, S.: Prediction of molecular interaction between platelet glycoprotein Ibα and von Willebrand factor using molecular dynamics simulations. J. Atheroscl. Thrombosis 32458 (2015)
24. Zhang, P., Zhang, L., Slepian, M.J., Deng, Y., Bluestein, D.: A multiscale biomechanical model of platelets: Correlating with in-vitro results. J. Biomech. **50**, 26–33 (2017)
25. Gupta, P., Zhang, P., Sheriff, J., Bluestein, D., Deng, Y.: A multiscale model for recruitment aggregation of platelets by correlating with in vitro results. Cell. Mol. Bioeng. **12**, 327–343 (2019)
26. Zhang, P., Zhang, N., Deng, Y., Bluestein, D.: A multiple time stepping algorithm for efficient multiscale modeling of platelets flowing in blood plasma. J. Comput. Phys. **284**, 668–686 (2015)
27. Han, C., Zhang, P., Deng, Y.: AI-guided adaptive multiscale modeling of platelet dynamics. In: ACM Student Research Competition Poster of the International Conference for High Performance Computing, Networking, Storage and Analysis (2020)
28. Hanson, W.A.: The CORAL supercomputer systems. IBM J. Res. Dev. **64**, 1:1–1:10 (2019)
29. Sheriff, J., Bluestein, D.: Platelet dynamics in blood flow. In: Dynamics of Blood Cell Suspensions in Microflows, pp. 215–256. CRC Press (2019)
30. Slepian, M.J., et al.: Shear-mediated platelet activation in the free flow: perspectives on the emerging spectrum of cell mechanobiological mechanisms mediating cardiovascular implant thrombosis. J. Biomech. **50**, 20–25 (2017)

Evaluation of the NEC Vector Engine for Legacy CFD Codes

Keith Obenschain[1]([✉]), Yu Yu Khine[1], Raghunandan Mathur[2], Gopal Patnaik[3], and Robert Rosenberg[1]

[1] U.S. Naval Research Laboratory, Washington DC 20375, USA
keith.obenschain@nrl.navy.mil
[2] NEC Corporation India (US Branch), Santa Clara, CA 95054, USA
[3] Syntek Technologies, Fairfax, VA 22031, USA

Abstract. Many codes that are still in production use trace their origins to code developed during the vector supercomputing era from the 1970's to 1990's. The recently released NEC Vector Engine (VE) provides an opportunity to exploit this vector heritage. The VE can provide state-of-the-art performance without a complete rewrite of a well-validated codebase. Programs do not require an additional level of abstraction to use the capabilities of the VE. Given the time and cost required to port or rewrite codes, this is an attractive solution. Further tuning as described in this paper can realize maximum performance.

The goal was to assess how the NEC VE's performance and ease of use compare with that of existing CPU architectures (e.g. AMD, Intel) using a legacy Computational Fluid Dynamics (CFD) solver, FDL3DI written in Fortran. FDL3DI was originally vectorized and optimized for efficient operation on vector processing machines. The NEC VE's architecture, high memory bandwidth and ability to compile Fortran was the primary motivation for this evaluation.

Through profiling and modifying the key compute kernels using typical vector and NEC VE specific optimizations, the code was successfully able to utilize the vector engine hardware with minimal modification of the code. Scalar code developed later in FDL3DI's lifetime was substituted with vector friendly implementations. With optimizations, this vector architecture was found to be 3× faster for main-memory bound problems with the CPU architectures competitive for smaller problem sizes. This performance using standard well-known techniques is considered to be a key benefit of this architecture.

Keywords: Vectorization · CFD · Optimization

1 Introduction

Many codes that are still in production use trace their origins to code developed during the vector supercomputing era from the 1970's to 1990's. Many of those codes are still in use with vector friendly constructs in their codebase. The recently released NEC

© Springer Nature Switzerland AG 2021
B. L. Chamberlain et al. (Eds.): ISC High Performance 2021, LNCS 12728, pp. 255–271, 2021.
https://doi.org/10.1007/978-3-030-78713-4_14

Vector Engine (VE) provides an opportunity to exploit this vector heritage. The VE can potentially provide state of the art performance without a complete rewrite of a well-validated codebase. Given the time and cost required to port or rewrite codes, this is an attractive solution.

For this project, the goal was to assess how the NEC Vector Engine's performance and ease of use compare with that of existing CPU architectures (e.g. AMD, Intel) using a legacy Computational Fluid Dynamics (CFD) solver, FDL3DI written in Fortran. FDL3DI was originally vectorized and optimized for efficient operation on vector processing machines. The NEC Vector Engine's architecture, high memory bandwidth and ability to compile Fortran was the primary motivation for this evaluation.

1.1 NEC Vector Architecture

NEC has been a major provider in the supercomputing domain for over 37 years and starting from the early 1980s, NEC has developed a product line of vector computers. Among the earliest HPC systems developed by NEC in 1983 was the SX-2, a prominent machine of its time that used high-performance vector pipelines for computing multiple data over a single instruction in parallel. NEC's SX-6, better known as The Earth Simulator, later secured the top position on the Top500 list of super-computers from the year 2002 to 2004. Over evolving computing trends from specialized to commodity hardware, and from large-memory symmetric multiprocessor systems to massively parallel distributed systems, NEC has evolved to implement the same vector processors on a PCI-e card known as NEC Vector Engine [1].

NEC Vector Engine is a PCIe card implementation of NEC's traditional vector architecture with a large HBM2 memory on chip with 48 GB capacity and a high memory bandwidth of 1.22 TB/s connected to 8 large vector processor cores as shown in Fig. 1(a). In Fig. 1(b) each processor core has 64 specialized vector registers that can store vectors as large as 512 single-precision elements long that can deliver up to 2.15 Teraflops of performance for double precision elements (4.30 Teraflops for single precision elements). An arbitrary vector up to 256 double-precision elements in length can thus be scheduled through a single vector instruction. It is ideal to process 256 elements since a fully utilized vector register provides better scheduling per instruction and allows the Vector Processing Unit to keep the vector pipeline filled. As the vector processor processes an instruction, the vector processed elements are available for other instructions to begin work.

The VE PCIe card is hosted on an x86-based host machine named Vector Host (VH), where the VH and VE can together provide a scalar-vector hybrid framework for delivering the best performance by selecting the right architecture for the right workload. Figure 2 shows the default offload mechanism, where the load module is launched on the VH, but the entire application is offloaded on to the VE with no PCIe communication required during the entire execution of the application. The benchmarks and codes examined in this study were run with this default offload mechanism.

The Linux based Vector Host system (VH) runs VEOS [2], a software that controls the VE and provides OS functionality for programs that run on VE. This program controls VE program loading, system call handling, VE process management, VE memory management, signal handling, OS commands such as `gdb`, `ps`, `free`, `top`, `sar`, etc.

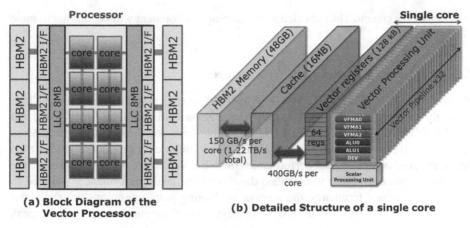

Fig. 1. Architecture of NEC Vector Engine

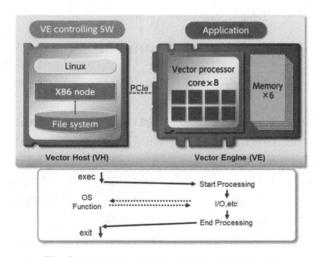

Fig. 2. Vector Host-Vector Engine hybrid model

The native compilers and toolkits support standard C/C++ and Fortran programming paradigms thereby eliminating the need to refactor the code to make it run on the VE. For ease of the user, the NEC compilers automatically find relevant loops and array operations that can be vectorized and generate corresponding vector instructions that help execute that operation on the vector processor. It can also apply automatic loop transformations and subtle tweaks in the code for best performance. The programming environment is diverse where frameworks such as MPI and OpenMP can co-exist in the same program which the compiler further vectorizes to provide an ideal parallel processing environment. The available NEC Numeric Library Collection [3] allows users to create advanced scientific computation programs without requiring awareness of complex numerical algorithms, greatly improving the productivity of numerical simulation program development. The provided programming environment will be familiar to most HPC developers.

1.2   Comparison with Reference Architectures

We compare the NEC Vector Engine Type 10B (VE) to two other platforms using CPUs typically deployed in HPC environments - Intel Xeon Platinum 8260 (Intel Xeon) and the AMD EPYC 7702 (AMD EPYC). The Intel Xeon and AMD EPYC processors selected are representative of processors FDL3DI would use for production runs. Based on purely peak computational performance, the NEC Vector Engine should provide the best performance. In order to calculate the theoretical peak performance, we need to know the processor frequency, the number of floating-point operations per cycle and the number of cores per CPU. Table 1 displays this information along with the peak performance in GFLOPS.

Table 1.   Architectures evaluated [1, 4–6].

	Intel Xeon Platinum 8260	AMD EPYC 7702	NEC Vector Engine Type 10B
Cores per device	24	64	8
Device per node	2	2	2
Memory per device	512 GB	128 GB	48 GB
Memory technology	DDR4-2933	DDR4-3200	HBM2
Memory channels	6 channels	8 channels	6 modules
Memory bandwidth	141 GB/s	204.8 GB/s	1.2 TB/s
LLC cache per device	35.75 MB	256 MB	16 MB
Process technology	14 nm Intel	7 nm TSMC	16 nm TSMC
Theoretical double-precision GFLOPS per device	1766 GFLOPS	2048 GFLOPS	2150 GFLOPS
Clock frequency	2.3 GHz	2.0 GHz	1.4 GHz

Note: Device refers to a processor on AMD EPYC and Intel Xeon architectures

Each Intel Xeon core implements the AVX512 instruction set (ISA) that can pack eight double precision (DP) floating-point values into one 512-bit register. When executing AVX512 instructions, the Intel Xeon core's two AVX512-FMA units can produce a total of 32 double-precision (DP) floating point operations per cycle. The AMD EPYC core uses the AVX2 ISA that can pack four DP floating-point values into one 256-bit register. The AMD EPYC core's two AVX2-FMA units yield 16 DP FLOPS per cycle. The NEC Vector Engine Vector Pipeline Unit (VPU) has 32 pipes each capable of 6 FLOPS for a total of 192 FLOPS per cycle. The core counts for the architectures vary, with the NEC only having 8 cores versus 64 for the AMD EPYC. The end result is the theoretical double-precision performance is fairly close. For memory bandwidth, there are two features that stand out. The VE is one of the first platforms to employ HBM2 and as we see below, it is the VE's memory bandwidth which distinguishes its overall performance. The other is the AMD EPYC that has a significantly larger last level cache than the VE and Intel Xeon.

1.3 Benchmark Studies

NEC demonstrated that the STREAM and DGEMM benchmark [1] results on the VE show the significant advantage of the HBM2 memory system over the Intel and NVIDIA systems. We corroborated the results of these benchmarks on our local systems and also employed two other simple benchmarks. These benchmarks, where the computation is expressed in a few memory-bound computational loops, also reflect the advantages of the VE memory system. The Intel compiler was used throughout for both the AMD and Intel platforms with the appropriate compiler optimization flags.

In Fig. 3, we display the results for one of these benchmarks, HEATX, which solves the 3D heat equation on a cubic domain [7]. The code's main loop consists of averaging a point in the cube with its six face neighbors. Like many CFD codes, it is memory bandwidth limited. In the plot, we can see the Intel Xeon and AMD EPYC systems perform better for smaller problems, but as the vector length of problem grows beyond 256 elements and the available memory caches, the VE has the better performance.

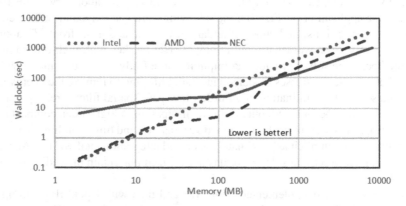

Fig. 3. HEATX benchmark on Intel, AMD, and NEC systems

In Fig. 4, we display the results for the second of these benchmarks, FAST3D, a typical CFD code which uses the Flux Corrected Transport (FCT) algorithm to solve a bursting diaphragm problem in 3D [8]. The code scans the domain volume, line by line, in each direction, segmenting each line by boundary conditions, gathering the elements into a 1D array and then applying the FCT algorithm to that array in a multiple vectorizable loops. Here again, we see a cross over in performance for vector lengths greater than 256.

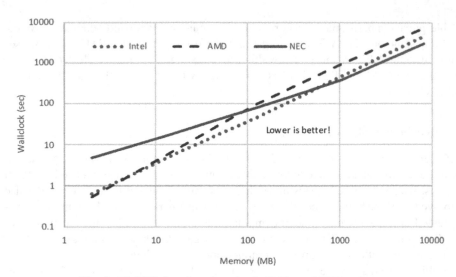

Fig. 4. FAST3D benchmark on Intel, AMD, and NEC systems

2 FDL3DI

FDL3DI is an extensively validated high-order Navier-Stokes solver utilizing curvilinear grids and was developed at United States Air Force Research Laboratory in the 1990's [9, 10]. Some applications of FDL3DI include wing-vortex aerodynamics, flow control for laminar flow airfoils, and shock/boundary layer interaction in front of canonical shapes. The solver can work with multiblock overset meshes with high-order interpolation methods. The solver provides an implicit Large Eddy Simulation mode with the effect of sub-grid scale stresses modeled via spatial filtering to remove the energy at the unresolved scales. Discriminating, high-order, low-pass spatial filters are implemented that regularize the procedure without excessive dissipation. A high-order, compact finite-difference approach is employed for spatial discretization and time marching is achieved through an iterative, implicit approximately-factored integration method [11]. At boundary points, higher-order one sided formulas are utilized that retain the tridiagonal form of the scheme.

The solver was first implemented with MPI and then with OpenMP resulting in a hybrid code and offers linear scaling up to thousands of processors. FDL3DI has been optimized to run on various architectures including SGI, Cray, HP, Intel and AMD processors. For example, FDL3DI has undergone optimization for the Intel Xeon Phi to specifically support AVX-512 instructions. The compiler options used in this comparison for Intel and AMD were selected to enable AVX-512 and AVX2, respectively. However, there is no GPU implementation for FDL3DI. Recent updates include Fortran 90 with MPI I/O, robust hole-cutting and scheme adaption for overset grid, and algorithmic enhancements via filter compact delta formulation.

2.1 Problem Description

We considered a classical flow past a cylinder test case with freestream Mach number of 6 with zero angle of attack. The DUCROS type sensor described in [12] is activated in the simulations to capture sharp discontinuities such as shocks. Figure 5 shows the Mach number at one second after impulsive start. The flow, from left to right, comes to a halt at cylinder surface and travels around the cylinder with maximum Mach number of 10 in the downstream region.

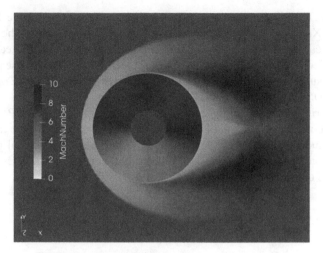

Fig. 5. Mach number representation of the test case

We studied three problem sizes as described in Table 2 below.

Table 2. Problem sizes for FDL3DI studies.

Problem size	Block size	Maximum vector length
128^3	64	68
256^3	128	132
480^3	240	244

We ran the cases using 8 MPI ranks with 2 OpenMP threads on NEC Vector Engine. Each MPI rank is assigned a single domain. A choice of domain decomposition is possible in FDL3DI. The size of the domains is determined by the complexity of the geometry and to match the hardware capabilities of the processors. The choice of 2 OpenMP threads per rank gave the best performance. For 8 MPI ranks, each problem dimension is divided by two so the maximum vector length is one-half of the problem dimension plus additional guard cells. In our cases, the small and large cases have the maximum vector length of 68 and 244, respectively. The reason behind choosing the

480^3 case is that the maximum vector length for this problem is 244 elements, which almost completely fills the VE's 256 double precision vector register allowing the VPU to efficiently schedule work. For a problem size of 512^3, the vector length is 260, which is slightly larger than the VE's vector register. This results in a situation where the first 256 elements fully utilize a vector register, but the remainder (4 elements) only uses a fraction of a vector register, resulting in an overall inefficient scheduling of a VPU.

2.2 Initial Performance Observation

The original FDL3DI code was compiled without modifications on the NEC Vector Engine, Intel Xeon, and AMD EPYC systems. The performance of the unmodified FDL3DI code can be seen in Fig. 6. The performance results are normalized by the 128^3 case on Intel Xeon system. Timings were taken for steps 101–150 for these performance studies. The results were obtained on the Intel Xeon system with AVX-512 optimizations while the AMD EPYC was run with AVX2 optimizations.

With this original version of the code, the large cache on the AMD EPYC processor makes it very competitive for smaller problem sizes. As the problem size increases, the faster HBM2 memory on the NEC starts to come into play. This initial performance analysis prompted a closer look at performance bottlenecks on the VE and initiated several months of optimization.

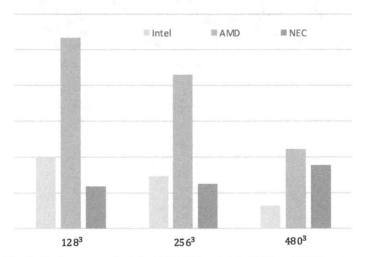

Fig. 6. Performance of original FDL3DI on Intel, AMD and NEC systems

2.3 Optimization Process for FDL3DI

Figure 7 depicts the optimization process for FDL3DI. First, the most time-consuming routines in the code were identified by profiling of the code. Once they were determined, reproducers were generated that represent portions of the parent code without any proprietary information so that the reproducers could be distributed if necessary. Next, the reproducers were optimized in consultation with NEC to improve their performance on the NEC Vector Engine. Once the performance of the reproducer was improved the modifications were incorporated into the FDL3DI code. The optimized version of code was verified to ensure that the results were not affected by the modifications. The process was repeated for each of the most time-consuming routines in FDL3DI.

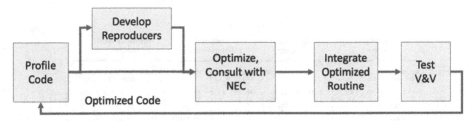

Fig. 7. Workflow of optimization process for FDL3DI

2.4 Performance Analysis Using the NEC Toolchain

Compiler Listing. Figure 8 shows several examples of the optimization diagnostics from the NEC compilers. The NEC compilers provide annotated listings with the source lines for each procedure together with information on the vector and parallel status of loops and array expressions, the status of inline expansion, etc.

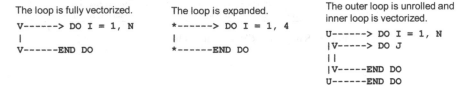

Fig. 8. Examples of NEC's compiler listings with annotations

NEC Profiler – FTRACE. A user can obtain performance information for the overall program, each function as well as user specified regions with the NEC profiler FTRACE [13]. FTRACE is used to obtain information such as the CPU usage and vectorization aspects. The user just needs to compile and link a program with –ftrace to an executable file for performance measurement. At the end of execution, one or more analysis information files are generated in the working directory where the program is executed. In case of non-MPI programs, a single analysis information file is created, while in the case of MPI programs, analysis information files are created for each MPI process. The FRACE utility can combine these files into a single report.

FTRACE profiler outputs analysis lists from hardware performance counters on the VE at the runtime up to the granularity of a subroutine. The user can control the use of sets of performance counters by several environment variables to suit the requirement. Figure 9 shows an FTRACE report that provides performance information for each subroutine. The report can show performance for user defined regions within a subroutine by manually defining the region of interest. Parameters like vector operation ratio, average vector length, cache hits and misses, bytes-per-flops, etc. provide a strong base to estimate the program's performance and how well it can utilize the underlying hardware.

	FTRACE			
	Execution time	Operation counts	Vector information	Memory and cache
FREQUENCY	EXCLUSIVE TIME[sec](%)	AVER.TIME [msec]	MOPS MFLOPS	V.OP AVER. VECTOR L1CACHE RATIO V.LEN TIME MISS	CPU PORT VLD-LLC PROC.NAME CONF HIT E.%

FREQUENCY	EXCLUSIVE TIME[sec](%)	AVER.TIME [msec]	MOPS	MFLOPS	V.OP RATIO	AVER. V.LEN	VECTOR TIME	L1CACHE MISS	CPU PORT CONF	VLD-LLC HIT E.%	PROC.NAME
1012	49.093(24.0)	48.511	23317.2	14001.4	96.97	83.2	42.132	5.511	0.000	80.32	funcA
160640	37.475(18.3)	0.233	17874.6	9985.9	95.22	52.2	34.223	1.973	2.166	96.84	funcB
160640	30.515(14.9)	0.190	22141.8	12263.7	95.50	52.8	29.272	0.191	2.544	93.23	funcC
160640	23.434(11.5)	0.146	44919.9	22923.2	97.75	98.5	21.869	0.741	4.590	97.82	funcD
160640	22.462(11.0)	0.140	42924.5	21989.6	97.73	99.4	20.951	1.212	4.590	96.91	funcE
53562928	15.371(7.5)	0.000	1819.0	742.2	0.00	0.0	0.000	1.253	0.000	0.00	funcG
8	14.266(7.0)	1783.201	1077.3	55.7	0.00	0.0	0.000	4.480	0.000	0.00	funcH
642560	5.641(2.8)	0.009	487.7	0.2	46.45	35.1	1.833	1.609	0.007	91.68	funcF
2032	2.477(1.2)	1.219	667.1	0.0	89.97	28.5	2.218	0.041	0.015	70.42	funcI
8	1.971(1.0)	246.398	21586.7	7823.4	96.21	79.6	1.650	0.271	0.000	2.58	funcJ
54851346	204.569(100.0)	0.004	22508.5	12210.7	95.64	76.5	154.524	17.740	13.916	90.29	total
62248	37.709(18.4)	0.606	2200.2	1026.4	0.00	0.0	0.000	0.532	0.000	20.00	loop#1
2032	4.834(2.4)	2.379	415.8	0.0	28.61	6.3	4.098	0.246	0.000	0.00	loop#2
...											

User specified regions

```
#include <ftrace.h>
...
(void) ftrace_region_begin("loop#1") // outside region begin

for (i = 0; i < n; i++)
{
    ...
}

(void) ftrace_region_begin("loop#2") // inside region begin
for (j = 0; j < n; j++)
{
    ...
}
(void) ftrace_region_end("loop#2")   // inside region end
(void) ftrace_region_end("loop#1")   // outside region end
```

Fig. 9. Sample FTRACE analysis tool report

2.5 Optimization Techniques

Vectorization of Computationally Intensive Kernels. The computational performance of the NEC Vector Engine arises from its vector processing capability. Therefore, it is critical that all computationally intensive kernels in the code are vectorized and any scalar portions be extremely limited. FDL3DI was first developed in the era of the early vector computers and has still retained its vector-friendly structure and the vast majority of the inner loops vectorize.

The FTRACE utility, however, identified two routines in the top ten that showed very little vector usage. This was determined by comparing the vector time to the exclusive time as given by the FTRACE output (see Fig. 9 above for an example). The two routines in question had essentially no vector time and so were investigated further. The annotated listing of these routines confirmed that loops therein were not vectorized. In one routine, an OpenMP directive was used to collapse all three levels of a triply-nested loop, which prevented vectorization of the innermost loop (this is a feature/limitation of the NEC

Fortran compiler). So, with a minor change, this loop was vectorized. With some other rearrangements, the remaining loops in this routine also were vectorized.

The other routine made use of do-while loop structures. This style of loop structure does not vectorize, but still works well on the scalar processors on the Intel Xeon and AMD EPYC, but not on the relatively weak scalar processor of the NEC Vector Engine. The do-while loop structure had to be replaced with a canonical do loop which does vectorize. This did involve some restructuring and the introduction of some additional computations. However, the increase in performance of the vectorized version outweighs the cost of the additional computations.

Memory Optimization with Vector Registers. The NEC compilers identify statements that can be vectorized, and the participating arrays are automatically assigned to vector registers. For computation, the arrays are loaded from and stored to these vector registers in each iteration of the loop. However, the compilers provide additional support for manual assignment of vector registers to specific arrays within the scope of a subroutine by using the compiler directive:

$$!NEC\$ \ vreg \ (array-name)$$

The compiler directive vreg [14] declares that arrays in a list are allocated to vector registers instead of memory (similar to register qualifier from old C standards). The compiler translates all references of vreg assigned arrays within a subroutine to reference of vector register instead of load/store from memory. During code generation, the compiler prioritizes the assignment of a vector register to the specified array. If a vector register is not available for use, the vectorized data would spill-out to the memory but the compiler prepares instruction sequences such that this spill-out is minimized. The advantage of using vreg is that it avoids the vector store instruction which is the compiler's default method of automatically storing the same array. There are 64 vector registers available per core and vreg directive can utilize up to 57.

In the FDL3DI program, most loops are automatically optimized and vectorized by the compiler. Figure 10 shows one such code snippet with an automatically tuned loop structure. Compiler listings provide helpful indicators that inform which loops have been automatically optimized and vectorized. There is however a significant amount of memory reuse in between each iteration and these memory-bound loops involve additional memory latency due to several loads and stores. A fine-tuning approach for such loops is to reduce the memory latency by using the vreg compiler directive.

Figure 10 shows the modifications performed on the code snippet for optimization. The program is modified to prepare participating arrays that are the same size as one vector register. The vreg directive is used to assign these arrays to dedicated vector registers. The outer loop is blocked at 256 elements such that the fetches within each iteration comply with the size of a vector register for the functionality to work. The key here is to retain the vreg arrays on the vector registers between iterations of the outer loop, and that is managed by modifying the source. The same computation from the original loop block now works faster with dedicated vector registers while avoiding redundant load-store latencies. The indicators from compiler listings help identify each statement that utilizes these dedicated registers.

Compiler automatically unrolls the outer loop.

Compiler automatically vectorizes inner loop.

Vector registers are used for the computation with vector loads and stores in each iteration.

Compiler directive that assigns specific arrays to vector registers.

Block the outermost loop at 256 elements to ensure absolute usage of the vector registers.

Arrays assigned to dedicated vector registers.

The computation utilizes dedicated vector registers avoiding load-store latency.

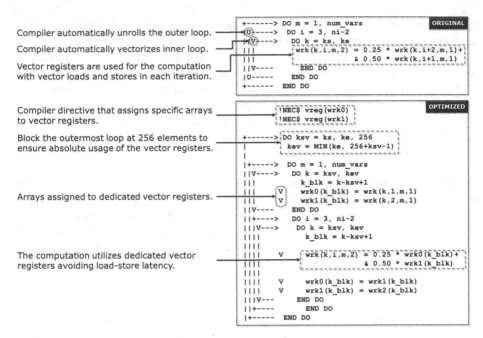

Fig. 10. Code optimization using `vreg` directive

Long Vectors Through Loop Collapse. The last technique is loop collapsing. If the inner loop has a length that is less than the vector register length 256, then it may be possible to combine the inner and outer loops for a vector length significantly longer than 256. We could change the arrays throughout the entire code to arrays with the first two dimensions combined, but it is simpler to use one-dimensional pointers to the original arrays for just the current subroutine.

In Fig. 11, we create a one-dimensional pointer to the original multiple dimensioned array. Normally, a pointer and its target array must have the same rank, but Fortran 2008 allows this if the `contiguous` specifier is added. Thus, if we convert the original allocatable array to a pointer with the `contiguous` specifier, the pointer association will be permitted. It is possible to mask off elements that should not be stored and still retain the vectorization status of the loop [15].

3   FDL3DI Performance with Optimization

The result of the current optimizations is depicted in Fig. 12. For all problem sizes there were significant increases in the performance of the NEC Vector Engine. For the 480^3 problem size, the performance on the VE was approximately a factor of three faster after optimization. For smaller problem sizes, the use of `vreg`, loop unrolling, and the vectorization of time-consuming scalar loops made the VE competitive against architectures with a large amount of cache due to better use of available memory bandwidth and better utilization of the VPU. The code optimized for the VE was also run on the

Declaration of multidimensional allocatable work array.

First two dimensions of the array are traversed using nested loops.

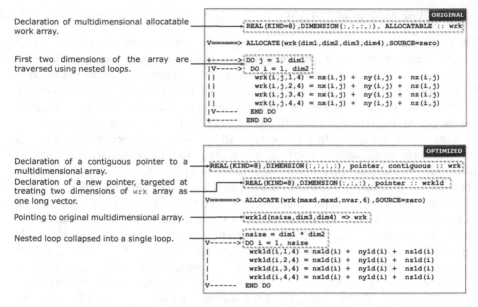

Declaration of a contiguous pointer to a multidimensional array.

Declaration of a new pointer, targeted at treating two dimensions of `wrk` array as one long vector.

Pointing to original multidimensional array.

Nested loop collapsed into a single loop.

Fig. 11. Code optimization using loop collapse

AMD EPYC and Intel Xeon. The performance on these two architectures was roughly the same compared to the original codebase.

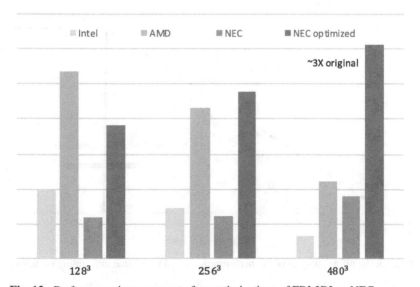

Fig. 12. Performance improvement after optimizations of FDL3DI on NEC system

3.1   Roofline Analysis of FDL3DI

The roofline model [16] is an effective way to quickly visualize performance with respect to key system bottlenecks, i.e., processor performance and off-chip memory traffic and to determine potential benefit and prioritization of optimizations. The model ties together floating-point performance, arithmetic intensity (FLOP/byte), and memory performance in a two-dimensional graph. The roofline sets an upper bound on performance of a routine depending on the routine's arithmetic intensity. Peak floating- point performance and memory bandwidth can be found experimentally or using hardware specifications (as presented here) to determine the performance limits, or roofline, as denoted by the dashed line in Fig. 13. Measured performance in GFLOPS and the arithmetic intensity are easily obtained for each routine in FDL3DI using the FTRACE profiling utility.

In the roofline model, a procedure is considered bandwidth-bound if it is under the sloped portion of the roofline (left of the solid vertical line) and compute-bound when under the flat portion of the roofline (to the right of the solid vertical line). The circle and square symbols represent the top 15 time-consuming routines for the 128^3 and 480^3 cases, respectively. For FDL3DI the arithmetic intensity is low, and all its procedures are bandwidth bound. Low arithmetic intensity is typical of the majority of CFD codes in use today, especially those based on finite volumes or finite elements. Discontinuous Galerkin techniques coming into use have higher arithmetic intensity and are more suited to the machine balance of modern hardware.

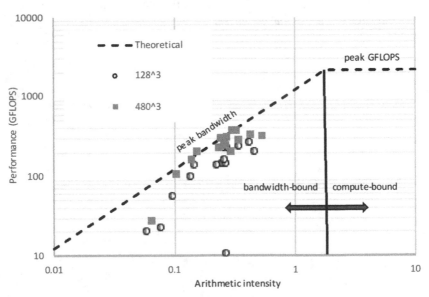

Fig. 13. Roofline analysis of the performance of 15 most time-consuming routines

The large 480^3 problem performs near the peak bandwidth line, so it is efficiently using the vector engine and is limited only by the available memory bandwidth. To further improve performance, one would have to change the algorithms employed to have higher arithmetic intensity or find ways to raise the effective memory bandwidth, e.g., increase the use of vector registers. For the smaller 128^3 problem, the vector units are only partially filled in routines without loop collapse, resulting in lower performance for those routines.

This roofline analysis helps instruct optimization of the FDL3DI code. From this analysis, the NEC Vector Engine has more than adequate floating-point capability for the algorithms in FDL3DI. As the code is memory bound, efforts must be focused on reducing memory traffic to the HBM memory. To improve performance of larger problem sizes, memory bandwidth is the key, but for smaller sizes, the number of memory references also plays a role. Techniques such as the use of vreg and loop collapse are critical in improving memory utilization.

4 Conclusions/Future Work

We were able to compile and run FDL3DI without modification on the NEC Vector Engine and begin optimization immediately. Typically, the introduction of a novel architecture requires a complete refactoring of a code. With optimization, FDL3DI runs efficiently on the NEC Vector Engine and for larger problems sizes it outperforms the other architectures evaluated. FDL3DI has targeted different architectures throughout its lifetime. Some newer portions of the code written for scalar architectures needed to be vectorized for performance on the VE. The techniques and methodologies we employed are well known and understood. This should be considered to be a benefit given the novelty of the hardware. The optimization introduces some additional complexity; the good news for the optimization effort is that the current developers of FDL3DI can still comprehend the VE optimized code. In general, optimization is required to take full advantage of the architecture.

The NEC Vector Engine achieves its best performance when a vector register is fully utilized. The VE's 256-element double precision vector register is longer than equivalent registers on other vector architectures, so even previously vector friendly codes need to be examined/profiled with tools such as FTRACE to identify any performance issues.

From our evaluation, the NEC Vector Engine is suited for CFD codes with low arithmetic intensity, where the primary bottleneck is main-memory bandwidth. The optimization techniques in this paper can make the VE more competitive for codes that are cache friendly or have relatively short vectors.

Our work will continue with scaling efforts past two NEC Vector Engines. The scaling tests will be run with at least eight VEs to understand how bottlenecks change with larger problems. In addition, we will be looking at a development version of FDL3DI. The improvements to FDL3DI's algorithms and implementation could change the performance characteristics and from an initial evaluation appear to be promising. We need to examine how performance changes with different numbers of OpenMP threads and if any optimizations to improve the hybrid MPI/OpenMP implementation are required.

Aside from FDL3DI, we will be evaluating the NEC Vector Engine's performance for other codes such as public-domain mini-apps [17] and for machine learning applications. We made significant progress using the FTRACE profiler, but there are limitations compared to profilers available on other architectures. We are anxious to determine if profilers such as Tau [18] that have initial support for the NEC Vector Engine give us additional insight into FDL3DI.

Acknowledgements. This project is co-sponsored by the U.S. Department of Defense Foreign Comparative Testing Program within the Office of the Undersecretary of Defense for Research & Engineering, the DoD High Performance Computing Modernization Program, and by the Office of Naval Research through the Naval Research Laboratory 6.1 Materials Science Task Area. The collaboration with NEC was conducted via the NRL CRADA-20-716. The authors would like to thank the NEC consultants and supporting hardware and software teams who helped us understand and address any issues with the platform. Finally, we would like to thank Dr. D. Garmann at the U.S. Air Force Research Laboratory for his guidance on the FDL3DI code.

References

1. Komatsu, K., et al.: Performance evaluation of a vector supercomputer SX-Aurora TSUBASA. In: IEEE Conference Proceedings, USA, pp. 685–696 (2018)
2. VEOS high level design. https://veos-sxarr-nec.github.io/doc/VEOS_high_level_design.pdf
3. NEC Numeric Library Collection User's Guide. https://www.hpc.nec/documents/sdk/SDK_NLC/UsersGuide/main/en/index.html
4. AMD 7702 Datasheet, April 2020. https://www.amd.com/system/files/documents/AMD-EPYC-7002-Series-Datasheet.pdf
5. Intel 8160 Datasheet. https://ark.intel.com/content/www/us/en/ark/products/192474/intel-xeon-platinum-8260-processor-35-75m-cache-2-40-ghz.html
6. Second Generation Intel® Xeon® Scalable Processors Specification Update, October 2020. https://www.intel.com/content/dam/www/public/us/en/documents/specification-updates/xeon-scalable-spec-update.pdf
7. Quinn, M.J.: Parallel Programming in C with MPI and OpenMP. McGraw-Hill Education (2004)
8. Boris, J.P., Landsberg, A.M., Oran, E.S., Gardner, J.H.: LCPFCT - a flux-corrected transport algorithm for solving generalized continuity equations. NRL Memorandum Report 93-7192 (1993)
9. Gaitonde, D., Visbal, M.: High-order schemes for Navier-Stokes equations: algorithm and implementation into FDL3DI. Technical report AFRL-VA-WP-TR-1998-3060, Air Force Research Laboratory, Wright-Patterson AFB (1998)
10. Garmann, D.J., Visbal, M.R.: AFRL contributions to the third international workshop on high-order CFD methods. In: Third International Workshop on High-Order CFD Methods (2015)
11. Gordnier, R.E., Visbal, M.R.: Numerical simulation of delta-wing roll. Aerosp. Sci. Technol. **6**, 347–357 (1998)
12. Ducros, F., et al.: Large-eddy simulation of the shock/turbulence interaction. J. Comput. Phys. **152**, 517–549 (1999)
13. PROGINF/FTRACE User's Guide. https://www.hpc.nec/documents/sdk/pdfs/g2at03e-PROGINF_FTRACE_User_Guide_en.pdf
14. Fortran Compiler User's Guide. https://www.hpc.nec/documents/sdk/pdfs/g2af02e-FortranUsersGuide-020.pdf
15. SX-Aurora TSUBASA Performance Tuning Guide. https://www.hpc.nec/documents/guide/pdfs/AuroraVE_TuningGuide.pdf

16. Williams, S., Waterman, A., Patterson, D.: Roofline: an insightful visual performance model for multicore architectures. Commun. ACM. **52**(4), 65–76 (2009). https://doi.org/10.1145/1498765.1498785.ISSN0001-0782
17. Mantevo Project, Mantevo Organization (2020). https://mantevo.github.io/
18. Department of Computer and Information Science, University of Oregon Advanced Computing Laboratory, LANL, NM Research Centre Julich, ZAM, Germany, 24 July 2020. https://www.cs.uoregon.edu/research/tau/tau-referenceguide.pdf

Distributed Sparse Block Grids on GPUs

Pietro Incardona[1,2,3], Tommaso Bianucci[2,3] (ID),
and Ivo F. Sbalzarini[1,2,3,4,5](✉) (ID)

[1] Technische Universität Dresden, Faculty of Computer Science, Dresden, Germany
[2] Max Planck Institute of Molecular Cell Biology and Genetics, Dresden, Germany
{incardon,bianucci,ivos}@mpi-cbg.de
[3] Center for Systems Biology Dresden, Dresden, Germany
[4] Cluster of Excellence Physics of Life, TU Dresden, Dresden, Germany
[5] Center for Scalable Data Analytics and Artificial Intelligence, Dresden, Germany

Abstract. We present a design and implementation of distributed sparse block grids that transparently scale from a single CPU to multi-GPU clusters. We support dynamic sparse grids as, e.g., occur in computer graphics with complex deforming geometries and in multi-resolution numerical simulations. We present the data structures and algorithms of our approach, focusing on the optimizations required to render them computationally efficient on CPUs and GPUs alike. We provide a scalable implementation in the OpenFPM software library for HPC. We benchmark our implementation on up to 16 Nvidia GTX 1080 GPUs and up to 64 Nvidia A100 GPUs showing state-of-the-art scalability (68% to 96% parallel efficiency) on three benchmark problems. On a single GPU, our implementation is 14 to 140-fold faster than on a multi-core CPU.

Keywords: Sparse grid · Block grid · CUDA · GPU · Distributed data

1 Introduction

Sparse volumetric data structures are frequently used in scientific computing and computer graphics for problems involving complex or time-varying geometries. Examples include hierarchical data structures for implicit geometry representation [7,9,10,14,15], multi-resolution methods [3,4], wavelet-adaptive methods [5], and narrow-band formulations of level-set methods [1,6]. Designing and implementing efficient dynamic sparse volumetric data structures, however, is challenging on massively parallel architectures, as race conditions occur when thousands of threads independently access the data. These challenges amplify for implementations of sparse volumetric data structures on distributed-memory parallel computer clusters, on Graphics Processing Units (GPUs), and on clusters of multiple GPUs. Consequently, it remains unclear how to best implement scalable, dynamic, sparse volume data structures on clusters of multiple GPUs.

Here, we provide reusable containers for sparse block grids distributed over multiple CPUs or GPUs. We provide both CPU and GPU implementations of

B. L. Chamberlain et al. (Eds.): ISC High Performance 2021, LNCS 12728, pp. 272–290, 2021.
https://doi.org/10.1007/978-3-030-78713-4_15

scalable, runtime-adaptive distributed sparse grids in C++ and CUDA. We analyze the design choices and their performance consequences when implementing such volumetric data structures on distributed GPU clusters. Based on this, we provide suggestions for a memory- and compute-efficient design, describing both its external interface and its internal architecture. The interface is designed to transparently abstract the internal implementation, providing flexibility for future improvements and portability.

We also provide a scalable software implementation of the proposed sparse block grid data structures. Our implementation is integrated into the open-source parallel computing framework OpenFPM [11], providing a fully templated C++ implementation that relies on the OpenFPM infrastructure for memory management, memory layout abstraction, CUDA kernels, and interconnect communication. We use this implementation to benchmark the performance and scalability of the proposed design.

2   Single-GPU Sparse Block Grids

We first describe a design of sparse block grids for a single GPU. The description is independent of the specifics of particular hardware or a particular programming language. It is based on fundamental primitives commonly used for dynamic algorithms on GPUs. These primitives can be found in many accelerator libraries and GPU languages, rendering our design reasonably portable. Here, we use the primitives provided by a combination of the two libraries CUB [13] and moderngpu [2]. The following primitives constitute the basic building blocks for our sparse block grid design:

- scan: Given a vector, the scan operation produces a vector of all partial cumulative sums; for example, scan([1,6,9,10]) = [0,1,7,16,26].
- merge: Two sorted vectors are merged into one sorted vector with duplicate entries appearing twice; for example, merge([1,6,7,10,26], [0,3,7]) = [0,1,6,7,7,10,26].
- sort: A vector is sorted in ascending order; for example, sort([1,10,2,6]) = [1,2,6,10].

Sparse grids are grid data structures where points/nodes can be dynamically inserted and removed at runtime. A simplified view is to see a sparse grid as a hash map, where the key is the grid index (i.e., the discrete position in the grid) and the value is the data stored at that grid point. An empty sparse grid does not allocate any memory for the grid data, but only for the access and bookkeeping data structures. This is in contrast to a dense grid, or array, where all memory is allocated when the grid is instantiated. The usual get function is present in both sparse and dense grids to access an (allocated) grid point. Sparse grids have an additional insert function to newly allocate grid nodes.

Another important difference between dense and sparse grids is how they are traversed or iterated over. In dense grids all nodes are always allocated, and iterators usually proceed to neighboring nodes until all nodes have been visited. In sparse grids, iterators can visit all allocated nodes, or any subset of allocated and unallocated nodes. Apart from specific limitations of a numerical method, this interface allows for easy conversion of dense-grid codes to spare-grid codes, which is useful for comparative benchmarking. The changes required are: (1) inserting all existing nodes at the start and (2) changing the iterator to an all-node sparse-grid iterator.

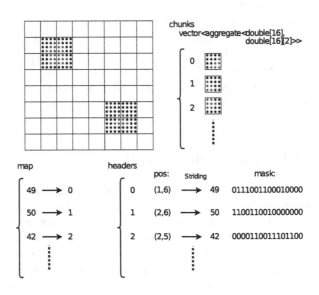

Fig. 1. Data structures of a sparse block grid illustrated in 2D for a grid of size 32×32 subdivided into chunks of size 4×4 (top left). Red points are in use, black points are empty. A chunk is allocated as soon as at least one point is inserted within that chunk. Only chunks containing at least one inserted point are explicitly shown in the figure. All allocated chunks are stored in a vector of aggregates (top right). In the example, each chunk contains $4 \times 4 = 16$ grid points each storing a scalar `double` and a 2-array `double[2]`, hence each chunk is an `aggregate<double[16],double[16][2]>`. For each chunk, the headers (bottom right) store its Cartesian and linear position in the grid (according to the selected grid ordering) and a bit mask (here 16 bits) indicating which points in the chunk are allocated/inserted (points within a chunk are ordered bottom-left to top-right). The map (bottom left) converts linear position in the grid of chunks (grid of square blocks) to chunk ID (Color figure online).

In most applications, the inserted nodes are not randomly scattered in a sparse grid, but concentrate in dense sub-regions. Sparse block grids exploit this to reduce neighborhood access time. Instead of storing each inserted node individually, they store a list of blocks of nodes. A common approach is to divide the grid into regular blocks of equal size, set at compile time, and to allocate a whole block as soon as at least one node is inserted within it. These grid blocks are called *chunks* to differentiate from GPU thread blocks. Each chunk of a sparse block grid is identified by a globally unique *chunk ID*. This requires a few bookkeeping data structures as illustrated in Fig. 1:

- **chunks**: A vector that stores the chunks' data. The chunks are stored in aggregates or tuples representing the different data types stored on the grid. The **chunks** vector can potentially retain empty chunks for anticipated reuse.
- **headers**: An array storing for each chunk in the **chunks** array its position in the grid (both in Cartesian coordinates and as a linear stride) and a mask indicating which nodes in the chunk are allocated/inserted.
- **map**: A map converting the linear stride position of a chunk to its chunk ID.

The map can be implemented using different data structures (unordered map, tree, sorted array, hash map). In this paper, we use sorted arrays on GPUs and hash maps on CPUs, because hash maps are not performant on GPUs while optimized GPU primitives for sorted arrays exist. The position of each chunk in the grid is converted from the Cartesian grid coordinate to a linear stride using a particular grid ordering. Space-filling curves, like the Morton Z-curve, are popular choices for cache efficiency. In our C++ implementation in OpenFPM, the specific grid ordering to be used is specified as a template parameter. This linearizes the position of each chunk to a single integer. For the benchmarks presented here, we always use Z-Morton ordering.

A key challenge on GPUs is to dynamically insert points. In our design, we use a three-phase strategy: First, we *collect*, in parallel, all chunks to be inserted. This leads to a list that potentially contains duplicates. Second, we create *correspondence groups* between new and existing chunks. A correspondence group is a set of chunks that are either duplicated in the insert list, or already exist. Third, correspondence groups are *merged* in parallel.

In the first phase, we *collect* all changes. This requires two buffers, one for the IDs of the chunks to be added, and one for their grid data. Rather than keeping a memory reservation for each thread, we reserve space for a block of threads together. This reduces memory allocation overhead as well as the total amount of memory required for the insert buffers. The insert buffers are allocated before running the GPU kernel that executes the insertions.

Merging based on *correspondence groups* is done by a **flush** operation, as shown in Algorithm 1. An step-by-step example of this algorithm is provided in in Fig. 2. The algorithm requires a *merge operator* to be specified. Consider the example that two insertions with values 3 and 4 target the same existing grid point already containing the value 5. The merge operator specifies how the data is reduced. Common choices are: **max** (result in the example is 5), **min** (result 3), or **sum** (result 12). The specific choice is provided as a parameter, as it depends on the computational problem to be solved using the sparse block grid. Data reduction and copying of the result is done at the very end, since moving chunks is expensive. Until that point, the flush algorithm only works on index maps of required data transfers, executing them jointly only in the end.

3   Multi-GPU Distributed Sparse Block Grids

In order to distribute a sparse block grid over multiple GPUs connected by a communication network, we decompose the grid into rectangular (cuboidal in

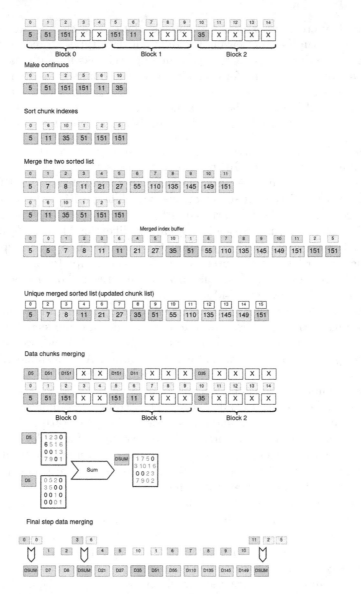

Fig. 2. Step-by-step example of the `flush` operation from Algorithm 1. Yellow boxes show positions of the chunks in the original array. Red boxes are the corresponding chunk IDs with "X" marking nonexistent chunks for alignment. Curly braces indicate how chunks are grouped in GPU thread blocks (here five chunks per thread block) for parallel execution. Green boxes are the positions of existing data in the pre-existing chunks. Purple boxes indicate chunk IDs that require data merging. Boxes labeled Di represent the data contained in the chunk with ID i. The example in the penultimate row shows how D5 is merged using the `sum` operator, creating a new chunk DSUM containing the element-wise sums of the data from the two input chunks. Black numbers indicate unused grid points containing invalid data, while magenta numbers indicate valid data on allocated/inserted points. The green and yellow arrays are used to track *how* to merge the data in the final step. These temporary maps avoid moving data chunks when determining correspondence groups (Color figure online).

Algorithm 1. The `flush` operation

Input: IDs of chunks to be inserted and their data; merge oprator

1: Prune unallocated chunks from the list (i.e., make the list of chunks contiguous).
2: Sort the insert chunk IDs.
3: From the sorted IDs, construct the set of unique IDs (because they are sorted, duplicates are neighbors). Construct a list of all segments that need to be merged and keep track of the merged IDs.
4: Merge the list of existing chunk IDs with the list of unique IDs to be inserted.
5: From this merged list, construct the set of unique IDs. This is the list of sorted chunk IDs for the updated grid.
6: Merge the insert data buffer into the sparse block grid using the merged list to construct the final data buffer with the data merged using the merge operator.

3D) *patches* that are then distributed across the different GPUs. Each patch contains exactly one sparse grid container. We do not require or assume patch boundaries to align with chunk boundaries. This allows for patches to be determined using any cuboidal domain decomposition method for grids, independent of the chunks. Our benchmarks show that runtimes with aligned patch-chunk boundaries are similar than with non-aligned boundaries, since the map-flush kernel is not a bottleneck. We therefore choose to implement the general case.

To allow for data exchange between patches, each individual patch is extended by a *ghost layer* of user-defined width (typically 1 to 3 grid points, depending on the numerical method to be used on the grid). Ghost layers exist only between immediately adjacent neighbors in the domain decomposition. Each overlap intersection between a ghost layer and a neighboring patch defines a *ghost box*. Allocated chunks and grid points covered by these ghost boxes are to be communicated between the involved processes.

The communication is divided into three phases: In the first phase, we identify overlaps between ghost layers and neighboring patches, hence defining the ghost boxes, and we serialize the data contained in the ghost boxes into a send buffer. In the second phase, we perform the actual network communication between the different processes or GPUs. In the third phase, we unpack the data from the received buffers into the destination sparse grid blocks.

3.1 Packing and Serialization

Data packing and serialization consists of two parts: (1) the size and structure of the buffer required to pack the grid data is determined; (2) the data are packed into that send buffer. To determine the size and structure of the send buffer, our design uses a queue paradigm where pack requests are first queued, then the queue is consolidated, and finally the buffer size is determined. This requires three functions: `packReset`, `packRequest`, and `packCalculate`. The first function clears the queue, starting a new serialization. The second function queues a request to pack data, accepting a ghost box as input argument. The third function consolidates the queue and determines the required send buffer in the form of the following buffer skeleton:

1 The number of chunks to pack;
2 The starting point and size in the send buffer for each ghost box to be packed;
3 A vector containing the chunk ID of each chunk to be packed;
4 A vector containing the number of points to be packed for each chunk;
5 An array of properties (data types of the grid data) to be packed for each point using an SoA memory layout;
6 An array of offsets (`short int`) for each grid point in each chunk to be packed;
7 An array of `char` with a mask for each point.

The mask (point 7) is used to indicate additional flag properties. In our current implementation, bit 0 indicates whether a point in the chunk is inserted/allocated. Bit 1 indicates whether a point is a border point, i.e., has at least one unallocated point in its neighborhood. The remaining six bits of the mask are unused at the time of writing.

After determining the send buffer and allocating it in each process, we pack the grid data for inter-process communication. This step involves the two functions `pack` and `packFinalize`. The `pack` function constructs a queue of requests to serialize grid data into the send buffer according to the information in the seven data structures listed above. It does not actually copy any data yet. This is done by `packFinalize` after all offsets and chunk pointers have been determined. Packing is never done twice, and only one CUDA kernel is launched for each patch of the domain decomposition.

Figure 3 illustrates an example of this process. In the example, one patch (dashed blue box) overlaps with six chunks with IDs given in the green-shaded boxes. As illustrated, the patch boundary does not (have to) align with chunk boundaries. The send buffer for the red ghost box is shown on the right, illustrating how the data are serialized in memory. This is independently done for each ghost box in parallel. Before sending, the information is compressed to only contain the data elements selected by the user via template parameters, and only for the inserted/allocated grid nodes.

Phase two is straightforward. Once the send buffers have been constructed on each process or GPU, they are communicated over the interconnect. This is done using asynchronous MPI communication with CUDA support to transparently and asynchronously perform the point-to-point communications of the packed send buffers between pairs of processes or GPUs.

3.2 Unpacking and Deserialization

In phase three, the receiving processes unpack the buffers. Similar to packing, unpacking also uses a queue paradigm. This means that all unpacking requests are first queued, then merged, and finally executed jointly. This requires additional care, since the chunk boundaries of the sending and receiving sides are not required to align. An example of this is illustrated in Fig. 4A in 2D for the blue patch from Fig. 3 overlapping with a yellow patch from a neighboring process in an unaligned way. The corresponding ghost boxes are shown as shaded areas for

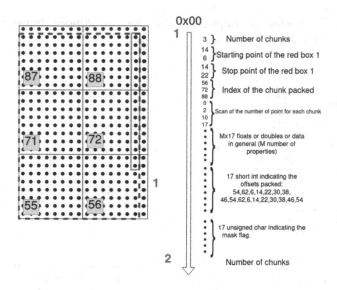

Fig. 3. Example illustrating the send buffer contents for a ghost box. A single patch (dashed blue box) overlapping with six chunks (black squares, chunk IDs in green-shaded boxes) is shown. The red rectangle is the ghost box to be packed. The memory layout and corresponding contents of the buffer for this ghost box are shown on the right with memory address increasing from top to bottom. (Color figure online)

a ghost layer width of one grid point. The yellow shaded area corresponds to the ghost box used as an example in Fig. 3.

An incoming chunk can overlap with up to four (in 2D) or eight (in 3D) chunks of the destination grid upon unpacking. We therefore construct per-patch maps to translate between the two sparse block grids. Each map is of the same size as one chunk and is valid for all incoming chunks from the same patch. It stores for each point in a chunk a number from 0 to 3 (2D) or from 0 to 7 (3D), indicating the overlapping chunks of the destination grid that point maps to. In addition, the map also stores for each point its offset in the destination chunk. This is illustrated in Fig. 4B, where the square in the center (left panel) is an incoming chunk, and color in the right panel indicates the four areas of overlap with the different chunks of the destination grid. The corresponding offsets of the points in the destination grid are given by the numbers of the same color. These maps enable on-the-fly conversion of the packed information in the received buffer of each chunk to the chunk layout of the destination grid.

Using these maps, we construct for each incoming chunk a list of destination chunks it overlaps with. In 2D, the lists are ordered {bottom-left, bottom-right, top-left, top-right}, similarly in 3D. Therefore, chunk 56 in Fig. 4A will have the list $(X, X, X, 0)$, where X indicates no overlap. Similarly, incoming chunk 72 intersects $(X, 0, X, 30)$, and chunk 88 intersects $(X, 30, X, 60)$. This is done in parallel for each incoming chunk. Each thread takes a chunk ID based on where the information should be unpacked, and map conversion is performed in the

GPU kernel. Nonexistent overlaps (X in the lists) are skipped, but remain in the lists for better memory alignment.

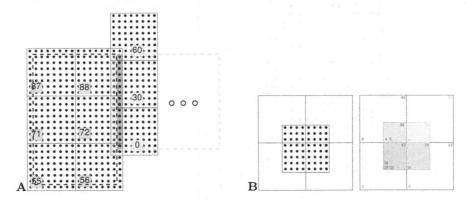

Fig. 4. A: Example of two patches (blue and yellow dashed boxes) from neighboring processes/GPUs with unaligned grid chunks (chunk IDs in the colored boxes). The two patches do not overlap. Their respective ghost boxes with the other patch are shown as shaded regions of same color for a ghost layer width of one grid point. **B**: Example of a chunk map between two grids. The incoming chunk (square in the center with grid points shown as dots) overlaps with four chunks of the destination grid (empty squares). Each chunk contains 8×8 grid points indexed from 0 (bottom-left) to 63 (top-right). The map is visualized in the right panel. Each point in the map stores the "color" (a number from 0 to 3) of the destination chunk as shown by the shaded areas. In addition, the offset of each incoming point in the respective destination chunk is stored as shown by the numbers of the same color. (Color figure online)

Once map conversion is done, the grid data are unpacked into the receiving patches using the pre-computed maps. For the yellow patch from Fig. 4A, the `unpack` operation is illustrated in Fig. 5. We use the `flush` operation from Algorithm 1 to construct the "merged index buffer" and the "unique merged sorted list" from Fig. 2. Using the chunk maps (purple boxes in Fig. 5) and a map between the destination chunk IDs and the position in the merged index buffer ("unique merged sorted list" in the `flush` algorithm), a GPU kernel is launched that merges the correct part of the incoming data buffer into the destination grid. Merge conflicts cannot occur for `ghost_get`.

The index and chunk maps are only recomputed if grid points have been added or removed between two communications. Otherwise the maps are reused, thus accelerating communication. Therefore, each process keeps track of its maps and stores them. Any external call to the `flush` operation (Algorithm 1) invalidates the maps, as it indicates a potential change to the grid structure. Invalid maps are recomputed upon the next `pack`/`unpack` operation.

4   Implementation in OpenFPM

We implement the design, algorithms, and data structures described so far in the open-source OpenFPM parallel computing library [11]. The open frame-

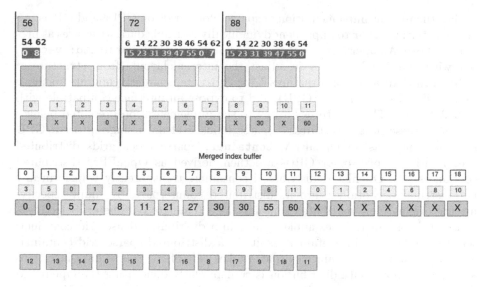

Fig. 5. Illustration of the unpack operation for the example from Fig. 4. Green boxes contain the IDs of the incoming chunks in the received buffer. The grid point offsets of the incoming chunks are given as black numbers below. The corresponding mapped grid point indices in the destination grid are given in the gray boxes. They have been converted using the map illustrated in Fig. 4B. The colors of the numbers and boxes below indicate the different destination chunks (bottom-left: red, bottom-right: green, top-left: blue, top-right: yellow). In 2D, each incoming chunk has up to 4 destination chunks. The corresponding destination chunk IDs are given in the red boxes below with the yellow boxes just above them a running index. An X indicates a nonexistent overlap (see main text). The merged index buffer is then constructed using the flush operation from Algorithm 1. Finally, the final map (purple array at the bottom) is constructed by running a GPU kernel on the merged index buffer. In the example, the first three Xs map to positions 12, 13, and 14 in the merged index buffer. The next 0 maps to position 0 in the merged index buffer, the (X, 0, X, 30) maps to positions (15, 1, 16, 8) in the merged index buffer, and so on. (Color figure online)

work for particles and meshes (OpenFPM) is a fully templated C++ library that facilitates implementation of scalable parallel codes on CPUs and GPUs. OpenFPM uses template meta programming (TMP) to generate data-type and hardware specific implementations at compile time and to abstract memory layout and communication of data structures. OpenFPM consists of multiple layers of abstraction: based on memory allocators and memory-layouting abstractions, OpenFPM implements single-core data structures. Using data-decomposition and network communication abstractions, these are then composited into multi-core and distributed-memory data structures. Finally, a library of frequently used numerical solvers is implemented using these data structures. Transparent in-situ visualization of simulation results [8] completes the framework.

For the present implementation of sparse block grids on CPUs and GPUs, we use `openfpm::vector` to implement dynamically resizable data structures as presented above. An `openfpm::vector` is a C++ structure similar to `std::vector`, but with additional features to adjust the internal layout (from structure of arrays (SoA) to array of structures (AoS)), to transparently migrate memory from host (CPU) to device (GPU), and to expose an interface compatible with CUDA kernels. These features are key to the implementation presented below.

Using these data structures, a sparse block grid on a single process/GPU is implemented as an OpenFPM `container`. Sparse block grids distributed over multiple processes or GPUs are then derived as OpenFPM distributed containers [11]. OpenFPM distributed containers transparently transform any non-distributed container into its distributed counterpart, by simply specifying the original non-distributed container as a template parameter. Selecting a dense grid container, for example, results in a distributed dense grid container; selecting a sparse grid container results in a distributed sparse grid container. Simply specifying a container as sparse takes care of the sparse data insertions and the iterators. Data distribution is transparently done using the OpenFPM domain decomposition primitives [11]. Network communication within a distributed container is abstracted by the OpenFPM communication primitive `ghost_get`, which can send and receive arbitrary Byte strings and is data-type agnostic [11]. This matches well with the present serialization/deserialization approach to inter-process communication for arbitrary grid data types.

4.1   Optimizing CPU Performance

We optimize the CPU performance of our OpenFPM implementation so that it can be used as a fair baseline to compare performance on GPUs. Given the type of benchmarks we consider here, we optimize for performance of discrete convolution operations on the CPU. On the CPU, we use an SoA memory layout for `openfpm::vector`, implement all maps as hash maps, and use Z-Morton linearization for the chunk locations. We also perform explicit in-core vectorization using the Vc library [12].

The Z-Morton chunk ordering is chosen because led to the highest L3 cache hit rate. Using a profiler, we measured that this linearization improves the L3 cache hit rate by 30% and reduces the overall runtime by 15% compared to the standard row-major ordering. Profiling also revealed that pre-fetching the data into temporary blocks, as we do on the GPU, is not optimal on the CPU. Assuming the temporary block is small enough to fit into L1 cache, the data would travel memory→register→L1 for loading the block, L1→register→L1 for computation, and L1→register→memory to store the block. Omitting the temporary block and directly transferring memory→register→memory turns out to be significantly faster on the CPU, and we thus do this. This is because it needs far fewer assembly-level instructions and avoids the latency of L1 cache access.

We also take special care of chunk boundaries, where a single vectorized load is not possible because the data are not contiguous in memory. These load operations are therefore transparently split into two distinct vectorized loads on the CPU. As this would be cumbersome to program manually, we provide an interface where the computation can be specified with a C++ lambda function.

5   Benchmark Results

We benchmark the performance of the presented design as transparently implemented in the OpenFPM library [11]. We compare GPU performance against the optimized CPU implementation (see Sect. 4.1) in OpenFPM and against the state-of-the-art sparse volumetric code OpenVDB [14]. We first show benchmarks on a single GPU before moving to clusters of multiple GPUs of two different architectures.

5.1   Single-GPU Performance

We first benchmark our OpenFPM C++/CUDA implementation of the present distributed sparse block grid design on a single GPU and on a single CPU. This allows comparing CPU and GPU performance, quantifying the overhead introduced by the bookkeeping data structures and by partially occupied chunks, and comparing with the performance of the state-of-the-art sparse block grid implementation in OpenVDB [14].

To quantify the bookkeeping overhead, we compare with a plain-array implementation for a case where the grid is actually dense. For this, we implement a finite-difference solver for the Gray-Scott reaction-diffusion system on a regular Cartesian grid in 3D with periodic boundaries in all directions, as previously considered [11]. The regular Cartesian grid is fully occupied with float two-vectors. We implement both a version with plain C++ arrays and a version using the present sparse grid implementation. Analyzing the machine code the compiler produced, we ensured that SIMD instruction were generated in both cases. Comparing the runtimes of the two code variants on an Intel i7-8700 CPU with clock frequency locked at 3.2 GHz, we measure that the plain-array implementation is 32% faster than the sparse-grid variant (see Table 1). In order to assess which part of this is due to the mask required in the sparse grid (i.e., due to keeping track of which grid nodes are inserted), we also measure a version of the sparse grid code with all mask handling removed ("NM"). The code is then 22% slower than the plain-array implementation, indicating that mask handling accounts for about one third of the overhead. The rest of the overhead stems from increased code complexity, chunk layouting, and from the operations required to construct the index maps.

We also benchmark the same code on multiple cores of the Intel i7-8700 CPU (see Table 2). Comparing with times for computation only (i.e., without any communication), the slowdown beyond 4 cores can be attributed to memory contention, as expected from the dual-channel architecture of the benchmark machine (measured memory bandwidth counting all access: 21.6 GB/s (1 core) to 59.6 GB/s (6 cores)).

Table 1. Runtime in seconds required to compute one time step of the Gray-Scott simulation on a regular Cartesian 256^3 grid of `float`. We compare plain-array and sparse block grid implementations on a single CPU/GPU. Removing the mask handling in the sparse block grid code ("NM") quantifies its overhead. On the GPU, the sparse block grid code is between 14 and 146 times faster than on the CPU (*Extrapolated).

Plain array	Sparse block grid			
CPU	CPU	CPU NM	GTX 1080	A100
0.063	0.083	0.077	0.0024	0.00058*

Table 2. Runtime in seconds required to compute one time step (averaged over 200 time steps) of the Gray-Scott benchmark on a regular Cartesian 512^3 grid of `float` using the present sparse block grid implementation on multiple CPU cores. We compare the full code with the time spent in computation, i.e., without communication.

Number of CPU cores	1	2	4	6
Complete code	0.910	0.575	0.360	0.380
Computation only	0.800	0.490	0.300	0.290

When running the sparse block grid code on a single Nvidia GTX 1080 GPU, the runtime reduces by a factor of about 35 compared to the single-thread CPU implementation on the 3.2 GHz Intel i7-8700 (see Table 1) and by a factor of about 14 compared to using 4 CPU cores, which is the optimal performance of the CPU (see Table 2). On a single Nvidia A100 GPU, runtime is about $4.16\times$ less (extrapolated from the multi-GPU benchmarks below) than on a single GTX 1080 and thus between 56 (for 4 CPU cores) and 146 (for 1 CPU core) times faster than on the CPU. Since the grid in this benchmark is dense, all chunks of the sparse block grid are fully occupied, leading to the best thread efficiency on the GPU. We define the *density* of a sparse block grid as the average (over all allocated chunks) occupancy of the chunks, i.e., the average fraction of grid points in each existing chunk that are allocated/inserted. The lower the density, the lower we expect the thread efficiency of our GPU implementation to be. This is confirmed in the measurements reported in Table 3 for a 512^3 grid of `float` values on a single GTX 1080. The thread efficiency is normalized at density 1.0 and from there, reduces approximately linearly with the density. This is expected because in our implementation the density of a chunk directly determines the fraction of busy versus idle threads in each GPU thread block (cf. Fig. 2).

We further compare our implementation with the widely used OpenVDB [14] library for sparse volumetric data structures. In this comparison, we measure the time to insert and fill all 512^3 grid points of an initially empty sparse grid. The points are inserted sequentially from $(0, 0, 0)$ to $(511, 511, 511)$. On the GPU the entire procedure described in Sect. 2 is measured, consisting of: (1) resetting and creating the insert queue, (2) collecting the insertions, and (3) flushing them. To test for retention of internal data structures and memory-allocation overhead, we

Table 3. Thread efficiency (ratio between GPU threads that do work vs. the total number of GPU threads) on one GTX 1080 GPU for inserting new grid points and for evaluating a 3D 7-point finite-difference stencil at different grid densities. The grid density is the average (over all chunks) fraction of grid points that are allocated/inserted. Efficiencies are computed relative to density 1, where all chunks are fully occupied. Measurements were done on a 512^3 grid of `float`.

Density	1.00	0.50	0.25	0.10
Insert	100%	59%	36%	15%
Stencil	100%	62%	45%	24%

Table 4. Runtime in seconds for inserting 512^3 points of a sparse block grid in sequential order. We compare the present OpenFPM implementation on the CPU and on two different GPUs with the CPU implementation in OpenVDB [14] over multiple cycles of insertions. Inserting points in OpenVDB is done using the function `setValue`.

Insertion cycle	1st	2nd	$3^{rd}+$
OpenFPM CPU	0.803	0.295	0.295
OpenFPM GPU (GTX 1080)	0.34	0.17	0.012
OpenFPM GPU (GTX 1650)	0.30	0.19	0.037
OpenVDB (`setValue`)	0.86	0.68	0.68

repeat multiple cycles of inserting all points, removing all points again, inserting them again, etc. The results are given in Table 4 for the first, second, and all subsequent cycles. As expected, the first cycle is always the slowest, because all queues and buffers are initially allocated. This overhead is independent of the speed of the GPU used, as can be seen by comparing the Nvidia GTX 1080 with the lower-tier GTX 1650 Ti. The higher speed of the GTX 1080 only shows after three or more cycles. The table also shows that two cycles are required on either GPU to retain all buffers, whereas on the CPU they are retained after the first cycle. Once all buffers are allocated, the OpenFPM implementation of the present sparse block grid design is about a factor of two faster than OpenVDB on the same CPU. We attribute this to the fact that OpenVDB traverses a tree when it accesses a node, whereas our code converts linear coordinates to block IDs using a hash map.

5.2   Multi-GPU Performance

We benchmark the distributed performance and scalability of the present sparse block grid implementation on two HPC systems with multiple GPUs. Benchmarks using Nvidia GTX 1080 GPUs were run on the *furiosa* computer of the Max Planck Institute of Molecular Cell Biology and Genetics (MPI-CBG), which has 20 nodes each containing two Nvidia GTX 1080 GPUs and two Intel Xeon E5-2698 v4 CPUs at 2.2 GHz. Nodes are connected by 40 Gb/s Infiniband.

Table 5. Runtime in seconds for 5000 time steps of the sparse block grid Gray-Scott simulation on dense Cartesian grids of different grid sizes and floating-point precisions as indicated, run on different numbers and types of GPUs as both strong and weak scaling. Parallel efficiencies are given in parentheses.

#GPUs	GTX 1080 (strong)		A100 (weak, `float`)
	`float` 512^3	`double` 384^3	$768^3 \ldots 3072^3$
1	99.14 (1.00)	78.92 (1.00)	72.50 (1.00)
2	60.20 (0.82)	50.02 (0.79)	-
4	41.40 (0.60)	35.70 (0.55)	-
8	27.16 (0.46)	25.50 (0.39)	76.60 (0.95)
16	33.44 (0.19)	31.85 (0.15)	196.0 (0.37)
32	-	-	238.6 (0.30)
64	-	-	240.0 (0.30)

We measured the bandwidth between a GPU and a CPU in the same node and across nodes to both be around 5.5 GB/s (measured using `osu_bibw` from MVAPICH OSU micro-benchmarks). Benchmarks using the Nvidia A100 GPUs were run on the *taurus* computer of TU Dresden, which has 32 nodes with 8 Nvidia A100-SXM4 GPUs each and two AMD EPYC 7352 CPUs at 2.3 GHz. Within each node of this cluster, the GPUs are connected by NVLink (measured bandwidth 986 GB/s) and across nodes by 200 Gb/s Infiniband (measured 18.2 GB/s). At the time of writing, the system was being installed with 8 nodes operational.

For all benchmarks, we gave MPI direct GPU memory buffer space. We used OpenMPI 4.0.4 CUDA-aware with UCX, no other MPI implementation. For the GTX 1080, the `gdr` plugin was not installed, but it was for the A100. In both cases, `nv_peer_mem` for GPU-direct RDMA was disabled because it was not supported by the combination of Nvidia and Mellanox drivers on the machines.

In the first benchmark, we measure the performance of the sparse block grid Gray-Scott simulation on different numbers of GPUs for dense Cartesian grids with periodic boundary conditions in all dimensions, so communication is representative of larger setups. Each simulation performs 5000 time steps with ghost layer (width 1) communication as detailed in Sect. 3 after each time step. A simulation result is visualized in Fig. 6A. The results on 1 to 64 GPUs are given in Table 5. All GPUs in a cluster node are used before expanding to the next node. Using single-precision arithmetics on 16 GPUs for a 512^3 grid, network communication accounts for 72% of the total runtime. We confirm this by profiling the time spent in the different communication operations of our implementation. The results in Table 6 quantify the increasing communication overhead for the strong scaling. We also measure the sustained bandwidth on the interconnect of the GTX 1080 cluster. Using 2 GPUs in the same node, we measure 7.2 GB/s. This reduces to 4.4 GB/s when using 4 GPUs in two nodes,

Table 6. Time in seconds spent in communication operations for 5000 time steps of the Gray-Scott simulation for a 512^3 Cartesian grid of `float` on GTX 1080 GPUs.

Number of GPUs	1	2	4	8	16
Packing	0.01	1.93	1.38	0.90	0.73
Send-Receive	0.03	8.05	13.3	13.1	24.8
Unpacking	0.007	2.31	1.68	1.26	1.16

Table 7. Runtime in seconds for 5000 time steps of the Gray-Scott simulation in a complex-shaped domain represented on sparse block grids of different sizes and precisions on different numbers and types of GPUs. Parallel efficiencies are in parentheses.

#GPUs	GTX 1080 (strong) double 968^3	A100 (weak, `float`) $1024^3 \dots 4096^3$
1	200.2 (1.00)	26.32 (1.00)
2	105.3 (0.95)	–
4	59.21 (0.85)	–
8	36.81 (0.68)	27.60 (0.96)
16	–	33.92 (0.78)
32	–	36.72 (0.72)
64	–	38.60 (0.68)

3.4 GB/s on 8 GPUs, and 1.2 GB/s on 16 GPUs. This reduction is due to the number of MPI messages increasing with the size of each message decreasing.

In the second benchmark, we use our OpenFPM implementation to simulate the Gray-Scott system in a complex-shaped domain represented by a sparse block grid with density 0.854. A visualization is shown in Fig. 6B. On the boundary of the complex-shaped domain we impose no-flux Neumann boundary conditions using the method of images. Because there are no periodic boundaries, and the domain decomposition cuts perpendicular to the thin cylinders connecting the spheres, less communication is required. On 8 GTX 1080 GPUs, the communication overhead is now 30%, whereas it was 48% in the Cartesian case. Together with the increased computational intensity of the stencil kernel (because of the method of images), this results in the improved scalability shown in Table 7.

In the third benchmark, we simulate a dynamic, time-varying geometry. The simulation considers a spherical shell in a cubic domain of edge length 2.5 as shown in Fig. 6C. The cube is discretized by a 512^3 grid. As simulated time progresses, the shell expands from initially an internal radius of 0.2 and an external radius of 0.4 to a final internal radius of 0.82 and external radius of 1.02. In each of the 100 simulation time steps, i.e., after each expansion of the shell, the sparse block grid is re-adapted to the evolving geometry, followed by a `flush` operation. The measured runtimes for the complete simulation are given in Table 8 for different numbers of GPUs. We (unnecessarily) perform two ghost

Table 8. Runtime in seconds for all 100 simulation steps of the expanding spherical shell simulation on a 512^3 `float` sparse grid on different numbers of GTX 1080 GPUs (strong scaling).

#GPUs	1	2	4	8
	2.8	4.0	3.9	3.8

Table 9. Time in milliseconds to complete each communication function once for thee dynamic grid case from Table 8.

#GPUs	1	2	4	8
ghost_get 1	0.0	11.7	13.8	13.4
ghost_get 2	0.0	1.2	3.0	3.4
flush	14	7.5	4.2	2.7

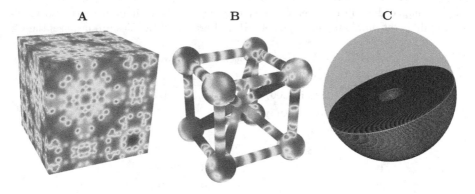

Fig. 6. Visualizations of the simulations used in the three benchmarks. **A**: Gray-Scott reaction-diffusion simulation at time $t = 3000$ on a dense Cartesian grid computed with second-order central finite differences in space and explicit Euler time-stepping. **B**: The same simulation in a complex-shaped domain at time $t = 10\,000$. **C**: Growing spherical shell with final outer radius shown. For visualization, the sphere is culled by its mid-plane.

layer communications in each simulation step in order to show the performance difference between the first one that determines all maps and the second one that reuses them (see Table 9). Times are given for the last simulation step, when the spherical shell is the largest, as this has the maximum communication overhead. Because in this benchmark there is no computation on the grid, performance is entirely limited by communication. While the `flush` operation scales well, the first `ghost_get` is the bottleneck, as expected. The second `ghost_get` has a much smaller runtime than the first one, because it reuses the maps (see Sect. 3). As expected for a strong scaling, the communication overhead increases when distributing the constant grid size over an increasing number of GPUs.

6   Related Work

Libraries that implement sparse volumetric grids include the Academy Software Foundations's OpenVDB [14], Nvidia's GVDB [9], and AMReX [16]. These libraries have been very successful in applications ranging from computer graphics to numerical simulations. OpenVDB provides efficient CPU implementations with SIMD support in C++ and CUDA-based GPU acceleration in the recent (August 2020) NanoVDB extension contributed by Nvidia. GVDB offers native GPU acceleration, but is limited to a single GPU. Moreover, the volumetric data in GVDB is always constructed or geometrically modified on the CPU, incurring a high host-device data transfer overhead. Ghost layers in GVDB are present at the chunk level, which is not the case in our implementation where they are only at the patch level. AMReX provides block-structured adaptive meshes with MPI parallelism and CUDA GPU support for some parts.

7   Conclusions

We have presented a generic sparse block grid design for distributed-memory CPU and multi-GPU environments. While the algorithms and data structures presented here are independent of a specific implementation, we provided a concrete C++/CUDA implementation in the OpenFPM parallel computing middleware [11], which allowed us to empirically measure performance.

The performance measurements have shown from 14-fold to about 140-fold speedups when using an Nvidia GTX 1080 or A100 GPU instead of all cores of an Intel i7 CPU. They also showed that the overhead introduced by the sparse block grid data structures when used on an actually dense grid is about 32% (over plan arrays) with approximately one third accounted for by the sparsity mask handling. Benchmarks on computer clusters with multiple Nvidia GTX 1080 or A100 GPUs have shown scalability up to 64 GPUs with parallel efficiencies ranging from 68% to 96% for sparse problems, depending on problem size, floating-point precision, and the GPU model used.

Despite these encouraging results, the current software implementation in OpenFPM has a number of limitations. The most important one is that it only supports Nvidia GPUs at the moment. The algorithms and data structures, however, are generic, and an implementation for AMD GPUs using HIP-clang is currently underway. Another limitation is that the `flush` operation is currently implemented using double-buffering. This requires twice the memory, effectively halving the usable VRAM. This could be addressed in the future by exploiting the new capability added in CUDA 10.2 to remap physical device memory into a different virtual address space. This could be used to remap the old buffer into the new buffer without creating a new one. The potentially required reordering of chunk IDs could be handled with an additional, smaller map. Finally, our current implementation does not use advanced GPU features like multi-DMA and RDMA over Infiniband. Ideally, the MPI library would leverage such extensions internally. Of these, RDMA seems particularly promising. Multi-DMA is probably not too useful for our implementation, since we stay on the device to minimize host-device transfers.

Notwithstanding these limitations, our implementation in OpenFPM is fully usable, flexible to use advanced GPU features in the future, and provides templated distributed C++ containers with an intuitive programming interface. The implementation runs on both CPU and GPU clusters and transparently encapsulates much of the complexity of distributed sparse block grids.

Our implementation is available as open source from http://openfpm.mpi-cbg.de and from https://github.com/mosaic-group.

Acknowledgments. The authors are grateful to the Centre for Information Services and High Performance Computing (ZIH) of TU Dresden and to the Scientific Computing Facility of MPI-CBG for providing their facilities for the benchmarks. This work was supported by the Federal Ministry of Education and Research (Bundesministerium für Bildung und Forschung, BMBF) under funding codes 01/S18026A-F (competence center for Big Data and AI "ScaDS.AI Dresden/Leipzig") and 031L0160 (project "SPlaT-DM – computer simulation platform for topology-driven morphogenesis").

References

1. Adalsteinsson, D., Sethian, J.A.: The fast construction of extension velocities in level set methods. J. Comput. Phys. **148**, 2–22 (1999)
2. Sean Baxter. moderngpu 2.0 (2016)
3. Bayati, B., Chatelain, P., Koumoutsakos, P.: Adaptive mesh refinement for stochastic reaction-diffusion processes. J. Chem. Phys. **230**(1), 13–26 (2011)
4. Bergdorf, M., Cottet, G.-H., Koumoutsakos, P.: Multilevel adaptive particle methods for convection-diffusion equations. Multiscale Model. Simul. **4**(1), 328–357 (2005)
5. Bergdorf, M., Koumoutsakos, P.: A Lagrangian particle-wavelet method. Multiscale Model. Simul. **5**(3), 980–995 (2006)
6. Bergdorf, M., Sbalzarini, I.F., Koumoutsakos, P.: A Lagrangian particle method for reaction-diffusion systems on deforming surfaces. J. Math. Biol. **61**, 649–663 (2010)
7. Brun, E., Guittet, A., Gibou, F.: A local level-set method using a hash table data structure. J. Comput. Phys. **231**(6), 2528–2536 (2012)
8. Gupta, A., Incardona, P., Aydin, A.D., Gumhold, S., Gunther, U., Sbalzarini, I F.: An architecture for interactive in situ visualization and its transparent implementation in OpenFPM. In: In Situ Infrastructures for Enabling Extreme-Scale Analysis and Visualization (ISAV'20), pp. 20–26. ACM, New York (2020)
9. Hoetzlein. R.K.: GVDB: raytracing sparse voxel database structures on the GPU. In: Eurographics/ACM SIGGRAPH Symposium on High Performance Graphics (2016)
10. Houston, B., Nielsen, M.B., Batty, C., Nilsson, O., Museth, K.: Hierarchical RLE level set: a compact and versatile deformable surface representation. ACM Trans. Graph. **25**(1), 151–175 (2006)
11. Incardona, P., Leo, A., Zaluzhnyi, Y., Ramaswamy, R., Sbalzarini, I.F.: OpenFPM: a scalable open framework for particle and particle-mesh codes on parallel computers. Comput. Phys. Commun. **241**, 155–177 (2019)
12. Kretz, M., Lindenstruth, V.: Vc: A C++ library for explicit vectorization. Softw. Pract. Exper. **42**(11), 1409–1430 (2012)
13. Merrill, D.: CUDA UnBound (CUB) library (2015)
14. Museth, K.: VDB: high-resolution sparse volumes with dynamic topology. ACM Trans. Graph. **32**(3), 27 (2013)
15. Setaluri, R., Aanjaneya, M., Bauer, S., Sifakis. E.: SPGrid: a sparse paged grid structure applied to adaptive smoke simulation. ACM Trans. Graph. **33**(6), 205 (2014)
16. Zhang, W., et al.: AMReX: a framework for block-structured adaptive mesh refinement. J. Open Source Softw. **4**(37), 1370–1370 (2019)

iPUG: Accelerating Breadth-First Graph Traversals Using Manycore Graphcore IPUs

Luk Burchard[1,3]([⊠]) [iD], Johannes Moe[1,2] [iD], Daniel Thilo Schroeder[3,4] [iD],
Konstantin Pogorelov[1] [iD], and Johannes Langguth[1,5] [iD]

[1] Simula Research Laboratory, Fornebu, Norway
{konstantin,langguth}@simula.no
[2] University of Oslo, Oslo, Norway
johanom@ifi.uio.no
[3] Technical University Berlin, Berlin, Germany
l.burchard@campus.tu-berlin.de
[4] Simula Metropolitan Center for Digital Engineering, Oslo, Norway
daniels@simula.no
[5] BI Norwegian Business School, Oslo, Norway

Abstract. The Graphcore Intelligence Processing Unit (IPU) is a newly developed processor type whose architecture does not rely on the traditional caching hierarchies. Developed to meet the need for more and more data-centric applications, such as machine learning, IPUs combine a dedicated portion of SRAM with each of its numerous cores, resulting in high memory bandwidth at the price of capacity. The proximity of processor cores and memory makes the IPU a promising field of experimentation for graph algorithms since it is the unpredictable, irregular memory accesses that lead to performance losses in traditional processors with pre-caching.

This paper aims to test the IPU's suitability for algorithms with hard-to-predict memory accesses by implementing a breadth-first search (BFS) that complies with the Graph500 specifications. Precisely because of its apparent simplicity, BFS is an established benchmark that is not only subroutine for a variety of more complex graph algorithms, but also allows comparability across a wide range of architectures.

We benchmark our IPU code on a wide range of instances and compare its performance to state-of-the-art CPU and GPU codes. The results indicate that the IPU delivers speedups of up to 4× over the fastest competing result on an NVIDIA V100 GPU, with typical speedups of about 1.5× on most test instances.

Keywords: IPU · Graph500 · BFS · Performance optimization

1 Introduction

In their Turing lecture 2018, John Hennessy and David Patterson announced a *"new golden age for computer architecture"* [18]. They based the statement

© Springer Nature Switzerland AG 2021
B. L. Chamberlain et al. (Eds.): ISC High Performance 2021, LNCS 12728, pp. 291–309, 2021.
https://doi.org/10.1007/978-3-030-78713-4_16

on the fact that due to the slower performance gains made by general purpose processors today, domain-specific architectures becomes more and more viable. Indeed, a large number of startups that develop specialized processors, usually for AI applications, have appeared in the recent years.

One of these companies is Graphcore, who presented their first processor, called the Colossus GC2, in 2018. It is targeted at machine intelligence applications and referred to as an intelligence processing unit (IPU). Similar to GPUs, the IPU offers a high number of low precision FLOPS that come from a large number of compute cores. However, unlike the GPU, which focuses on single instruction multiple data (SIMD) processing, the IPU offers true multiple instruction multiple data (MIMD). Furthermore, instead of DRAM with a cache hierarchy, it uses SRAM as its main memory. In theory, this design makes the IPU uniquely suited for highly irregular workloads such as graph algorithms. The goal of this paper is to test whether these architectural advantages result in measurable performance benefits.

To this end, we implement an IPU-based breadth-first search (BFS), following the specifications of the Graph500 [28] benchmark. Introduced in 2010, Graph500 collects BFS performance results for a wide range of hardware platforms and instance sizes making it by far the most studied parallel graph problem, which gives us a wide range of meaningful comparison points. The Graph500 uses a Kronecker graphs generator similar to R-MAT [11]. Results are denoted in traversed edges per second (TEPS). In addition, we use a test set of Yang et al. [32], which consists of matrices from the SuiteSparse [22] matrix collection.

We consider our work primarily as a building block for multi-IPU BFS and other, more sophisticated graph algorithms that use BFS repeatedly. These include graph centralities and other algorithms used in the analysis of social networks, graph matchings, and similar algorithms.

While the IPU's large number of independent compute cores, fast interconnect between these cores, and fast SRAM memory make it a very attractive platform for graph algorithms, we face two major challenges when using the IPU in this manner. First, the device was designed for machine intelligence applications, and the provided data structures and architecture design reflect that. While the cores are MIMD capable, there is no special support for irregular data structures such as graphs. Furthermore, all communication between the IPU cores must be declared at compile time. Naturally, this is a major challenge for computations such as BFS or other graph algorithms that determine communication patterns based on decisions done at run-time. Second, since the main IPU memory is SRAM, it is very limited, which puts a strict limit on the size of the graphs that can be processed by a single IPU.

To tackle the former limitation, the code creates its own mapping of the graph to the compute cores. We also control memory alignment explicitly, as well as the spawning of worker threads on the compute cores. Via temporal multithreading, the memory access latency can be hidden such that the individual threads do not experience latency. Naturally, the latter cannot be overcome via software. Thus, our paper makes the following contributions:

1. We present the first implementation of a graph algorithm on the new Graphcore IPU architecture whose features promise outstanding performance for such problems.
2. We give a detailed discussion of the challenges that need to be overcome to run efficient graph algorithms on the IPU. We expect that these techniques are applicable to a wide range of other graph algorithms as well.
3. We present performance comparison experiments using state-of-the-art CPU and GPU codes and hardware. The results show that our IPU implementation (which we refer to as iPUG) compares favorably to all tested alternatives.

The remainder of the paper is organized as follows: we introduce the IPU in Sect. 2 and discuss related BFS work on other architectures in Sect. 3. We present our IPU implementation in Sect. 4 and our experiments in Sects. 5 and 6. In Sects. 7 and 8 we discuss the implications of these results and conclude the paper.

2   IPU Hardware

2.1   Architecture

The Colossus GC2 IPU has 1216 *tiles*, each tile having a compute core and its own local memory of 256 KiB. Thus, the IPU has a total of 304 MiB of memory. The tile layout is illustrated in Fig. 1. The memory of the tiles is implemented in SRAM and is thus part of the chip. Naturally, this offers a far higher bandwidth (45 TB/s, aggregate) and lower latency (6 clock cycles) than DRAM. The tiles themselves are organized into *islands* consisting of four tiles, and the islands are grouped into *columns* of 19 islands each. The GC2 IPU has 16 such columns. The cores run at a default frequency of 1.6 GHz, but they can be clocked down to 1.3 GHz for thermal or electrical reasons, such as the PCIe slot not being able to provide the required power. A single GC2 IPU has 150W TDP. The PCIe version hosts two IPUs per card for a total of 300W TDP, which requires additional cables, similar to powerful GPUs. A rack-mounted IPU-POD with four socketed GC2 IPUs is also available. In this version all IPUs run at 1.6 GHz. For an in-depth discussion of the architectural details including microbenchmarks, we refer the reader to Jia et al. [20]. In 2020, Graphcore presented an GC200 IPU with more tiles and more memory per tile, but the device was not available for development at the time of this writing.

2.2   Programming Model

IPU programming follows the classical dataflow model. Programs are assembled by composing a logical execution graph at compile time. It consists of alternating layers of state and computation vertices. The state is exclusively organized in multidimensional arrays called tensors, which are symbolically represented at compile time and have pre-determined dimensions. Such a structure makes it ideally suited for Tensorflow [1] applications.

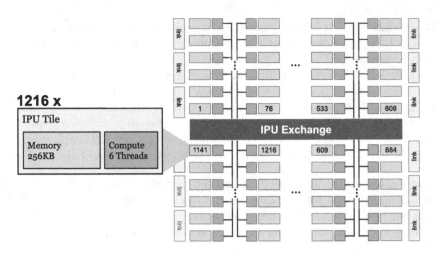

Fig. 1. Tile layout on the IPU processor. Source: Graphcore.

Each computation vertex is associated with a *codelet*, i.e. a piece of code that prescribes the computation to occur in the vertex. Multiple codelets at the same layer of the graph can be executed in parallel as long as they do not write to the same part of a tensor, and all codelets must be executed before progressing to the next layer of the computation graph. At the end of such a compute step, data is exchanged among the cores to ensure a consistent state, thereby creating a bulk-synchronous parallel (BSP) [30] superstep structure. The rationale for this structure is that due to bandwidth contention, overlapping memory-bound computation and communication is difficult and sometimes impossible [25]. Furthermore, it provides a clear computation structure and obviates the need for message buffers and thus additional memory on the chip, making communication very efficient. On the other hand, this brings about that all communication must be planned at compile time. This poses a challenge when communicating sparse data, which is necessary in graph algorithms such as BFS.

3   Background

3.1   Related Work

BFS and DFS are the most fundamental ways of traversing graphs. For sequential execution, the BFS algorithm is essentially defined by the data structure used to store the graph, as its fundamental operation is to iterate over the edges of a given vertex. However, parallel implementation of BFS, particularly on distributed memory systems, is far more complicated. Consequently, there are far more possibilities for algorithm design and performance optimization.

While parallel BFS has been studied earlier [15], the topic gained widespread interest in the previous decade on distributed memory computers [16,34], on shared memory [5,23], and on GPU systems [17]. The establishment of the

Graph500 benchmark [28] in 2010 marks a turning point, since it encouraged direct comparability of results. This increased activity on the topic further, resulting in a large number of publications on that topic [10,12,13,19,33]. Furthermore, BFS implementations for GPUs have also received considerable attention in the recent years [14,27,31,32]. In addition to the parallel implementation, algorithmic improvements have been presented in the last decade. Possibly the most important among those was the introduction of direction optimizing searches [7]. At the same time, efficient parallel algorithms for BFS and DFS were also developed in the context of other graph problems, such as parallel matching algorithms [4,24,26].

3.2   Graph Algorithms in the Language of Linear Algebra

Among the approaches developed for parallel graph processing, we focus on the linear algebra based formulation [9] of BFS. This is a natural fit since the IPU is designed for machine learning applications, and is thus geared towards linear algebra.

A graph $G = (V, E)$, $|V| = n$, $|E| = m$ can be represented as an adjacency matrix $A \in R^{n \times n}$ with $a_{ij} = 1$ if $(i, j) \in E$ and 0 if $(i, j) \notin E$. Each row in the adjacency matrix encodes the outgoing edges of a vertex. In practice the input graphs are always sparse. We can use the sparsity, and only store the non-zero values of the matrix in a compressed format. For our implementation, we choose the CSC format where the number of values non-zero and their positions are stored for each column. This encoding allows for fast iteration through the column but prohibits quick A_{ij} lookups as we may need to scan through a whole column.

We can formulate a BFS search step by performing a multiplication of an adjacency matrix A with a vector x. We initialize the frontier vector x with the index of the source node s with $x(s) = 1$. We can perform a step $A^T x_1 = x_2$ which yields the next frontier. Further we can union all previous frontiers into an array to mark the already visited nodes $v_k = x_1 + \ldots + x_k$, where $v_k(i) \neq 0$ if node i was visited during step k. We can choose A and a further x to be represented by an efficient sparse data structure.

The advantage of this representation is that it allows the use of highly optimized sparse linear algebra primitives to accelerate graph algorithms. It provides a high level view for understanding and comparing communication patterns. It is important to note that most applications in scientific computing and machine learning exhibit sparse matrix dense vector (SpMV) communication, which means that the same communication pattern repeats over multiple rounds. On the other hand, graph algorithms such as BFS exhibit sparse matrix sparse vector (SpMSpV) communication where only some of the vertices or matrix rows/columns are active in each round, thus creating a new communication pattern each time.

4   BFS Implementation on IPU

The distributed memory model of the Graphcore IPU forces us to partition our input problem beforehand; to do so, we divide the input graph and assign one part to each tile. During the following BFS steps, new tile memory needs to be allocated in order to store the previous step's output. Thus, the decomposition of the graphs for the IPU is similar to BFS implementations for distributed memory systems rather than GPUs. The graph decomposition remains static during the algorithm and no additional data is loaded during the entire BFS kernel.

4.1   Parallel BFS

Splitting a subset of vertices with their outgoing edges is called 1D partitioning because of the row-wise split in the adjacency matrix. Since input, output, and vertex data must be stored in the tile memory, load-balancing becomes challenging, especially in the case of graphs with vertices of high degree. Furthermore, 1D partitioning requires allocating $\mathcal{O}(n)$ bytes for input and output on each tile, making it an inappropriate partitioning strategy, even for small graphs.

In contrast to 1D, the 2D decomposition splits the adjacency matrix into a chessboard-like $p_x \times p_y$ pattern. Thus, an adjacency matrix A is decomposed into p square partitions $A_{1,1} \ldots A_{x,y}$. Each such partition is mapped to an individual physical tile on the IPU. In this scenario, each partition is only responsible for a subset of the outgoing edges of each vertex. Therefore, no single partition has the global state of their vertices and thus the partitions that own a vertex need to communicate their partial results to arrive at a single global state. Our 2D data decomposition is very similar to that used for distributed memory systems [8,34], and we also permute the vertices randomly. Unlike the 1D partitioning, in 2D we need to allocate only $\mathcal{O}(n/\sqrt{p})$ bytes for communication with other tiles.

4.2   Parallel Top-Down

Algorithm 1 shows the parallel top-down, 2D, bulk synchronous parallel (BSP) algorithm. As writing IPU does not require explicit declaration of communication between the tiles, we describe it as a mapping of input and output tensor data regions. In the current implementation all partitions are square, and thus the notation v_c represents an n/p_x sized vector with starting offset $p_x * (1 - c)$. A processor $P_{i,j}$ receives inputs from the frontier queue Q_j and produces the new partial outputs represented by a bitmap matrix $SA_{i,j}$ working on the partition $A_{i,j}$. SA is called the intermediate status array. In order to process one BFS level, our algorithm requires two separate communication steps, each of which requires a synchronization barrier before proceeding to the next step.

1. Local Expansion: Each processor $P_{i,j}$ receives a Q_j part of the frontier queue and uses it to create a new intermediate status array $SA_{i,j}$.

Algorithm 1: Topdown BFS algorithms, adopted from [8] and the linear algebraic version [10]

---

input : A 2D partitioned adjacency sparse matrix A, a source vertex s, vertex count n, partition count p

output: A vector b containing the parent for each explored i as $b(i)$.

$p_x = p_y \leftarrow \sqrt{p}$

$Q \leftarrow \{s\}, SA(:,:) \leftarrow 0, b(:) \leftarrow 0$

for *all processors* $P_{i,j}$ *in parallel* **do**

    while $Q \neq \emptyset$ **do**

        $frontier \leftarrow Q_i$ ▷ **Done through mapping and exchange**

        for $vertex \in frontier$ **do**

            for $neighbour \in adj(A_{i,j}, vertex)$ **do**

                $SA(i : neighbour) \leftarrow true$

            end

        end

        Global BSP Barrier   ▷ **End ComputeSet**

        $Q \leftarrow \emptyset$

        $activations \leftarrow SA(i * p_y + j : i * p_y + j + 1, :)$ ▷ **Like AllGather**

        for $v \in b$ **do**

            if $v \neq visited$ **then**

                for $incoming \in activations(row, :)$ **do**

                    if $any(incoming)$ **then**

                        $b(row) \leftarrow visited$

                        $Q \leftarrow Q \cup \{row\}$

                    end

                end

            end

        end

        Global BSP Barrier   ▷ **End ComputeSet**

    end

end

---

2. Intermediate Status Array Reduction: A reduction that uses the parent array (i.e., Algorithm 1) to check all partial results of a vertex to determine if a new parent was found. This step uses all partitions along the row j of size n/p to reduce into the new frontier queue Q_j.

All communication during the local expansion happens column-wise, where the input frontier Q is sent to all rows in their respective parts, as shown in Fig. 2. During the reduction phase all communication happens row-wise as all data comes from the partial results of the row to be reduced. In general, the communication before the local discovery is simpler, since we have a one-to-many communication in contrast to the reduction phase where a many-to-many communication pattern is required.

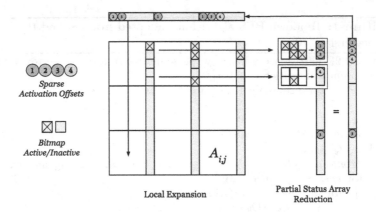

Fig. 2. Layout of the 2D decomposition. We map each partition to a physical processor tile. Each tile also receives a copy of the sparse input frontier, along the first dimension, indicated with colored balls as activated vertices normalized to local offsets on each tile. In the reduction phase processor tiles receive the output status array of the local expansion and merge these into a new sparse frontier vector of the next BFS level.

4.3 Mapping Data and Compute

Mapping and allocating data is an important part of the implementation as the compiler does not automate or abstract data and operation placement away from the developer. Thus it is necessary to specify a complete mapping of each tensor partition to each target tile. The same applies when placing vertices of the compute graph on the IPU: each vertex is assigned to a tile. If the necessary data is already present on a tile, then no additional overhead is introduced. However, due to the fast communication between the tiles, this overhead is relatively small when mapping data and compute on a single IPU. Moreover, any unnecessary communication leads to additional allocations of landing zones for data that is transferred between the tiles. This is crucial due to the limited memory on the IPU, which means that suboptimal allocations can cause a computation to fail due to lack of memory.

4.4 Challenges of IPU Graph Implementations

Memory Alignment. Traditionally memory alignment is done by the compiler via padding. Such padding can align the values on cache line boundaries, which ensures that they can be accessed or written efficiently. However, when working with *Poplar* compute graphs, aligning data is not trivial and needs to be done explicitly through the size and splits of a data section. Without manual data alignment, the *popc* IPU compiler allocates rearrangement buffers on the tiles, which costs additional memory. When working with large tensors, the rearrangement buffers tend to grow quickly, thus rendering feasible graph instances infeasible.

Memory Management. Each compute-and-data section of the compute graph is statically mapped to a tile during compile time. It is not possible to change the location of a data regions to a different tile during runtime and the compute graph does not allow for recursion. Thus, memory space and offsets needed to receive, transfer, and compute vertices can be determined during compilation. Therefore, allocating more memory than available on a single tile leads to an *out of memory* error during compile time. With 256 KB of addressable space the per-tile memory is very small compared to traditional memory systems, making memory management a primary concern.

Like traditional compilers, Graphcore's *popc* compiler has dead code elimination [3]. Hence, we call tensors that will not be eliminated *Always Live* variables. These variables need to be allocated during the whole lifetime of the program. Variables that are not *Always live* may get optimized away at some point in the program. For our program, the lifetime of variables connected to the expansion phase is related to the reduction phase and vice versa. Table 1 gives an overview over the variables allocated by our algorithm. The factor of two for the input data is due to the fact that we also need to store the input of the previous round.

Table 1. Per tile memory allocated by the BFS algorithm. nz_{max} represents the largest number of nonzeroes among all partitions. If a variable is always live it can not be optimized away by the compiler and is always present in an allocation.

Use	Type	Size	Always live
Expansion input	int16	$2n/p_x$	False
Expansion output	int32	n/p_y	False
Matrix	int16	$(n/p + 1) + nz_{max}$	True
Backpointers	int32	n/p	True
Reduction input	int32	$2n/p_x$	False
Reduction output	int16	n/p_y	False

4.5 Optimizations

Removal of Isolated Vertices. The Kronecker graph generator used to generate the graphs for the Graph500 benchmark produces isolated vertices. The greater the generated graph's scale, the larger the ratio of isolated vertices in the generated graph. For our input sizes, we observe 26% isolated vertices at scale 15, which increase to 36% at scale 19. Other papers report a ratio of up to 74% [29] for scale 42 graphs.

For BFS, as well as many other graph algorithms, isolate vertices are completely irrelevant. By filtering these vertices while reading the graph we can reduce the dimension of the generated matrix by 1.6× in linear time, accessing every vertex exactly once. This makes it almost possible to run a scale 20 Kronecker graph on the IPU and further reduces the space needed to store the CSC matrix. By reducing the dimension of the matrix the status array and frontier are also reduced by an additional factor of 2×, thus saving communication and computation time.

First Reduction Optimization. Our algorithm is required to iterate over all partitions in a row to find an activation if the parent for this row has not been found at the current level. The number of these iterations gets smaller the more vertices have already been flagged as found. Thus, when processing the first BFS level, this number is highest. For a single GC2 IPU we are required to check 34 partition outputs. However, in the first pass, we know that no vertices have been flagged as visited yet and that all possible activations can only come from partitions that get the frontier input section containing the single source vertex. Therefore, we can replace the first reduction with an algorithm saving $\mathcal{O}((p_x - 1)/p_x)$ time which is equivalent to skipping 97% of the instructions at the first level. Thus, instead of first checking the visited array and iterating over all incoming partitions we directly iterate over the incoming intermediate frontier from the partition responsible for handling the source vertex. If an activation was found we can simply insert it without the possibility of overwriting any information as we are in the first reduction phase.

Utilizing Threads. Similar to GPUs, the IPU allows scheduling multiple threads per core on a tile to hide latencies and fill the processor's pipeline more efficiently. Unlike modern CPUs, which use *simultaneous multithreading*, the IPU architecture leverages a barrel processor design with *temporal multithreading* of up to six hardware threads. A feature of barrel processors is that each execution context has a constant instruction scheduling time as it alternates between active threads in a round-robin fashion. When six threads are executed in this manner, the memory access latency of six cycles can be hidden effectively. The *Poplar* SDK allows us to spawn a compute vertex into a supervisor mode, which is a restricted administrative context thought to be the entry point for starting and orchestrating the six worker contexts. The supervisor can further synchronize context flows into a single sequential point.

Our algorithm utilizes a sparse frontier vector generated in the reduction phase. We cannot write an interleaved value into the frontier immediately after finding it during the reduction, as no atomic instructions are available. To synchronize an unknown amount of value insertions we leverage a prefix sum often found in parallel algorithms on GPUs. Instead of computing and immediately inserting vertices into the output frontier queue, we split the algorithm into three parts: parallel flagging of frontier vertices in a temporary bitmap vector, synchronized prefix-sum calculation for the worker contexts, and parallel writes from the bitmap into the output queue vector adhering to worker regions using the prefix-sum.

5 Experimental Setup

We have implemented iPUG in under 2000 lines of code, including the code required to read and process Matrix Market files. We compile our project with the *Poplar* 1.3.6 SDK and *popc* running on a single GC2 IPU.

Based on the guidelines of the Graph 500 benchmark, we split our measurements into two kernels: (1) the reading, preparing, and loading of the graph onto the device, and (2) the BFS graph traversal itself. Since our goal is to evaluate BFS performance on the IPU architecture, we concentrate on the second kernel. We begin measuring time of the second kernel t when the search key is loaded onto the device. We stop measuring when the final BFS round terminates.

Following the codes we aim to compare our results with [27,32], we count TEPS from both sides for undirected edges. As per Graph 500 specification, we ignore isolated search keys. Thus, since all our test instances are connected with the exception of isolated vertices, we always report TEPS $:= m/t$ where m is the number of non-zero entries in the adjacency matrix that connect visited edges. Due to limitations in some of the codes, we report the arithmetic rather than the harmonic or geometric mean over the prescribed 64 searches.

We do not perform any special operations in the first kernel such as sorting vertices or finding vertices with special properties. However, we are filtering self-loops and vertices of degree zero from the graph while converting it into the CSC format required by our 2D decomposition algorithm. In the 2D decomposition algorithm we are splitting the matrix into square n/p_x by n/p_y sized parts. We always use a square processor grid, i.e. $p_x = p_y$. Since the number of cores on the GC2 IPU is 1216, the largest smaller square number is 1156, and thus $p_x = p_y$ = 34. The remaining 60 cores do not take part in the computation.

To measure the runtime of the second kernel executed on the IPU, we measure the start and end cycle counter of the IPU and divide the difference by the tile frequency returned by the Poplar SDK. We run our experiments on an IPU-POD system. It does not have the power limitations of the PCIe version and is thus running at the full 1.6 GHz. As most runs only take microseconds, thermal throttling is no concern either. For each run we randomly generate 64 keys that have at least one edge connected to it in the input graph. We run the second kernel with all given keys and take the mean.

Test Instances. We use both Graph500 instances as well as graphs derived from SuiteSparse [22] matrices. The matrices were selected to match a published test set [32] after removing all instances that are too large to run on the IPU. Table 2 lists all the instances along with their size and diameter. The sources of the graph come from the following groups:

- **kron_(n)_(e)** are Kronecker graphs with 2^n vertices and edge factors **e**. The edge factor is the average number of edges per vertex. Graphs with larger values of **e** typically show higher TEPS as work is being amortized over a larger number of edges. Graphs generated by the Graph500 benchmark specification have **e** = 16 and can be used to compare implementations to other published Graph500 results. All graphs were generated with R-MAT parameters $A = 0.57$, $B = 0.19$, $C = 0.19$, and $D = 0.05$. Note that we filter isolated vertices. Thus, the number of vertices in the BFS is always lower than 2^n.

- **kron_g500-logn(n)** are Kronecker graphs from the 10th DIMACS implementation challenge. Despite the SuiteSparse name these graphs are not conform to the Graph500 benchmark, as they have an edge factor of 48, but they use the same R-MAT parameters as the Graph500 instances.
- **G43** represents a 1% sparse uniformly random matrix.
- **coAuthorsDBLP** and **coPapersDBLP** are academic research interaction and cooperation networks.
- **Journals** represent co-readerships in magazines.
- **delaunay_(n)** are planar graphs from the 10th DIMACS implementation challenge. They are generated by the triangulation of points in a flat area, with size 2^n.
- **loc-Gowalla** represents friendships of a social network based on location data retrieved from the SNAP suite.
- **ship_003** represents a 3D mesh of a structural problem by the DNVS group.

Comparison Platforms. As the Graphcore IPU is a completely new architecture, it is crucial to assess its performance in comparison to established processors. For comparison with the GPU we use two state of the art codes: **Enterprise** created by Hang Liu and H. Howie Huang [27] and **Gunrock** by Yangzihao Wang et al. [13,31]. The Gunrock[1] and Enterprise[2] code were both run on an NVIDIA Tesla V100-SXM3 with 32 GB of memory compiled with nvcc 10.1 and clang 11.0.0. Like the IPU, the V100 runs at 1.6 GHz.

As the performance benefits of the GPU over the CPU are well established, we consider this the primary point of comparison. However, we also study CPU performance. For that purpose, we use the Graph 500 BFS reference (Ref) implementation [28] which relies on MPI, a sophisticated MPI/OpenMP implementation provided by Yasui et al. [33] from Tokyo Institute of Technology (TITech), and the BFS implementation from the GAP benchmark suite [6]. The latter has the advantage that it reads the Matrix Market format. We thus use it for comparison on SuiteSparse matrices outside of the Graph 500.

We run all three codes on two dual-socket CPU platforms, an AMD Epyc 7601 with 64 total cores and an Intel Xeon Gold 6130 with 32 total cores. Since the CPUs are not the focus of this paper, we refer the reader to online resources[3,4] or the manufacturer's documentation for more information about their technical specifications. The codes are compiled with gcc 6.1.2 and run with MPICH 3.3.

---

[1] Git commit: 5ee3df5, Online: https://github.com/gunrock/gunrock.
[2] Git commit: 426846f, Online: https://github.com/iHeartGraph/Enterprise.
[3] https://en.wikichip.org/wiki/amd/epyc/7302p.
[4] https://en.wikichip.org/wiki/intel/xeon_gold/6130.

Table 2. Overview of the test instances. All graphs are undirected. Thus their adjacency lists contain twice as many entries as the number of edges. The diameter represents the longest path found during the BFS runs. Datasets marked with (†) conform to the Graph500 benchmark specification.

SuiteSparse				Generated			
Name	Diam	Vertices	Edges	Name	Diam	Vertices	Edges
G43	4	1K	10K	kron19_16†	8	356K	8M
coAuthorsDBLP	24	300K	978K	kron19_16.2†	8	356K	8M
Journals	2	124	6K	kron19_16.3†	7	356K	8M
coPapersDBLP	23	540K	15M	kron18_16†	8	197K	4M
loc-Gowalla	16	197K	950K	kron17_16†	7	118K	2M
ship_003	58	122K	4M	kron16_16†	8	66K	1M
delaunay_n12	36	4K	12K	kron15_16†	6	33K	524K
delaunay_n13	49	8K	25K	kron19_48	7	432K	25M
delaunay_n14	65	16K	49K	kron19_32	8	393K	16M
delaunay_n15	87	33K	98K	kron18_128	6	236K	34M
delaunay_n16	119	66K	197K	kron18_96	6	236K	25M
delaunay_n17	167	131K	393K	kron18_64	7	236K	17M
delaunay_n18	228	262K	786K	kron18_32	7	236K	8M
kron_g500-logn16	6	66K	2M	kron16_32	7	66K	2M
kron_g500-logn17	6	118K	5M	kron15_32	6	33K	1M
kron_g500-logn18	6	236K	11M	kron17_32	7	118K	4M
kron_g500-logn19	7	432K	22M				

6   Experimental Results

6.1   Performance Comparison Experiment

Our experimental results are collected in Figs. 3 and 4. They show the performance of iPUG on the IPU compared to the GPU codes on the V100 and GAP on the Intel Xeon, along with the speedup of the IPU compared to the fastest alternative. iPUG shows the highest speedups for very small instances. This is understandable since the CPU and GPU codes are not designed for such instances. However, on the largest and thus most relevant Kronecker instances that fit in IPU memory, we still observe a speedup of about 1.5×.

For the Suitesparse graphs, we observe 3× speedups for smaller and 1.5× speedups for the larger *DBLP* instances over Gunrock, which is the best alternative here. An exception are the larger and thus higher diameter *delaunay* graphs which exhibit little parallelism. On average there are far fewer vertices in the frontier each round than the IPU has threads, thus making the wide parallelism inefficient. As a result, the CPU performs better than both IPU and GPU, although the difference between CPU and IPU is small. The only instance

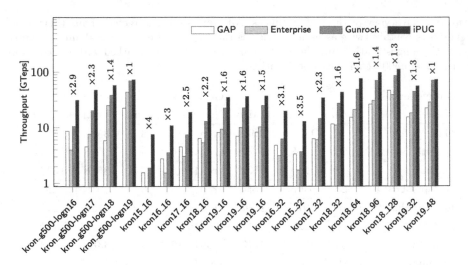

Fig. 3. Performance of iPUG compared to CPU and GPU for the Kronecker graphs.

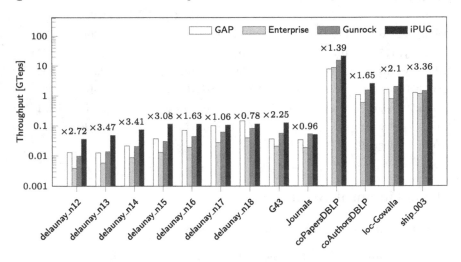

Fig. 4. Performance of iPUG compared to CPU and GPU for the Suiteparse instances.

where the GPU exceeds IPU performance is the very small and dense *Journals*, and even there the difference is very small.

6.2   Graph 500 Scaling Experiment

In an additional experiment, we show the performance of the IPU in context of the scaling behaviour of other BFS implementations. Results are shown in Fig. 5. We observe that the CPU type has little influence for all three codes. On the other hand, the TiTech code is almost an order of magnitude faster than

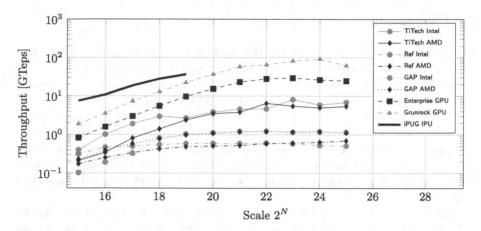

Fig. 5. Performance of Graph500 Kron-N-16 graphs by scale on all tested codes and architectures.

GAP and the reference code, reaching almost 10 GTEPS. The CPU codes seem to reach maximum performance at Scale 22.

The GPU implementations are consistently faster, with Gunrock reaching almost 100 GTEPS at Scale 24. It also maintains a consistent and substantial lead over Enterprise. Furthermore, while iPUG starts with a large advantage at Scale 15, the gap closes to $1.5\times$ at Scale 19. Thus, due to the limitations in IPU memory, it is not possible to say at which scale maximum IPU performance will be attained, and whether it would be faster than Gunrock on the V100. Since the larger instances have a higher fraction of isolated vertices, and removing such vertices has a substantial effect on IPU performance, it is possible that the IPU would maintain its lead if it had more memory.

An important insight from these results is that implementations may affect performance more than the hardware platform. This effect is certainly visible for the CPUs. Furthermore, GPUs were initially not widely considered a suitable architecture for BFS, but steady algorithmic advances have made GPUs highly competitive for the specific problem of BFS on Kronecker graphs.

In addition to direction optimization [7], sophisticated GPU codes explicitly cache the status of high degree vertices in shared memory during the backwards search phase, as suggested for the Enterprise BFS code [27]. This obviates the need for about 80% of all status queries, thereby improving performance dramatically. However, the technique is far less effective for other types of graphs. Furthermore, it creates a point of performance which depends on the size of the programmer-controlled shared memory. For both GPU codes, performance seems to decrease when going towards Scale 25. Naturally, the IPU cannot replicate this technique since it lacks a memory hierarchy in which such caching could take place.

7 Discussion

We have tested our BFS code on the IPU and achieved speedups between 0.96×
and 4× over the fastest GPU code, with a typical speedup of 1.5× for the
largest feasible Kronecker graphs. The GPU results could certainly be improved
by running on an NVIDIA Ampere A100 or AMD Instinct MI100 GPU, while
the IPU results will benefit from the larger memory and increased core count of
the M2000 IPU once it becomes widely available. However, the M2000 IPU does
not provide a large increase in memory bandwidth or clock frequency, which
means that the latest hardware generation could close the current gap between
GPU and IPU to some extent. Even so, we expect that the IPU will maintain a
lead for most instances.

Furthermore, based on the memory bandwidth of the IPU, it is conceivable that a far higher performance is possible. During the first few years after
its inception, the Graph500 [28] performance results increased massively, but
improvements have slowed down substantially thereafter. While we have considered several optimizations on the IPU, we are far from having exhausted its
possibilities. We were not able to show performance improvements via direction
optimizing search, although in principle such algorithmic improvements can be
applied on the IPU. Thus, it is likely that faster Graph500 results will appear
in the future.

Naturally, the small memory of the IPU limits its application to real-world
problems. Furthermore, it is debatable whether it is fair to compare an SRAM
based device to a DRAM based processor since the IPU is essentially running out
of what would be cache on a CPU. However, our results indicate that the CPU
does not experience a similar speedup when running on the smallest instances
which certainly fit inside the L3 cache of the Intel Xeon or AMD Epyc. This is
consistent with an observation from the 2018 Turing lecture [18], which points
out that programmer controlled scratchpad memory offers significant performance advantages compared to transparent general-purpose caches. In case of
the IPU, no additional programming complexity is incurred by this, since the
memory hierarchy only has a single level.

8 Conclusion

We have implemented the first BFS code on the Graphcore IPU and thus presented the first benchmark results of a graph algorithm on that platform. The
results typically show 1.5× speedups over the fastest competing GPU and CPU
codes, thus demonstrating the potential of this new architecture for graph algorithms. The main limitation to its usefulness is the small memory of the IPU.
This means that it is more suited to algorithms with higher time complexities such as matching, betweenness centrality, or even NP-hard optimization
problems. Furthermore, kernelization techniques [2,21] will become even more
valuable if they allow shrinking problems to the point of fitting into IPU memory. However, the main challenge in future work will be to scale graph problems

to multiple IPUs in order to overcome the memory limitations. While the IPU programming model extends transparently to multiple IPUs, it is likely that substantial optimizations will be needed to scale up its performance. Consequently, future work will focus on scaling BFS to multiple IPUs, as well as use the current code as a basis to implement more sophisticated graph algorithms.

References

1. Abadi, M., et al.: Tensorflow: a system for large-scale machine learning. In: 12th USENIX Symposium on Operating Systems Design and Implementation (OSDI 2016), pp. 265–283 (2016)
2. Abu-Khzam, F.N., Collins, R.L., Fellows, M.R., Langston, M.A., Suters, W.H., Symons, C.T.: Kernelization algorithms for the vertex cover problem (2017)
3. Aho, A.V., Sethi, R., Ullman, J.D.: Compilers, Principles, Techniques, and Tools. Addison-Wesley Pub. Co., Boston (1986)
4. Azad, A., Buluç, A.: Distributed-memory algorithms for maximum cardinality matching in bipartite graphs. In: 2016 IEEE International Parallel and Distributed Processing Symposium (IPDPS), pp. 32–42. IEEE (2016)
5. Bader, D.A., Madduri, K.: Designing multithreaded algorithms for breadth-first search and ST-connectivity on the cray MTA-2. In: 2006 International Conference on Parallel Processing (ICPP 2006), pp. 523–530. IEEE (2006)
6. Beamer, S., Asanović, K., Patterson, D.: The gap benchmark suite. arXiv preprint arXiv:1508.03619 (2015)
7. Beamer, S., Asanovic, K., Patterson, D., Beamer, S., Patterson, D.: Searching for a parent instead of fighting over children: a fast breadth-first search implementation for graph500. EECS Department, University of California, Berkeley, Technical report UCB/EECS-2011-117 (2011)
8. Buluç, A., Beamer, S., Madduri, K., Asanovic, K., Patterson, D.: Distributed-memory breadth-first search on massive graphs. arXiv preprint arXiv:1705.04590 (2017)
9. Buluç, A., Gilbert, J.R.: The combinatorial BLAS: design, implementation, and applications. Int. J. High Perf. Comput. Appl. **25**(4), 496–509 (2011)
10. Buluç, A., Madduri, K.: Parallel breadth-first search on distributed memory systems. In: Proceedings of 2011 International Conference for High Performance Computing, Networking, Storage and Analysis, pp. 1–12 (2011)
11. Chakrabarti, D., Zhan, Y., Faloutsos, C.: R-MAT: a recursive model for graph mining. In: Proceedings of the 2004 SIAM International Conference on Data Mining, pp. 442–446. SIAM (2004)
12. Checconi, F., Petrini, F.: Traversing trillions of edges in real time: graph exploration on large-scale parallel machines. In: 2014 IEEE 28th International Parallel and Distributed Processing Symposium, pp. 425–434. IEEE (2014)
13. Chenglong, Z., Huawei, C., Guobo, W., Qinfen, H., Yang, Z., Xiaochun, Y., Dongrui, F.: Efficient optimization of graph computing on high-throughput computer. J. Comput. Res. Dev. **57**(6), 1152 (2020)
14. Gaihre, A., Wu, Z., Yao, F., Liu, H.: XBFS: exploring runtime optimizations for breadth-first search on GPUs. In: Proceedings of the 28th International Symposium on High-Performance Parallel and Distributed Computing, pp. 121–131 (2019)

15. Ghosh, R.K., Bhattacharjee, G.: Parallel breadth-first search algorithms for trees and graphs. Int. J. Comput. Math. **15**(1–4), 255–268 (1984)
16. Gregor, D., Lumsdaine, A.: Lifting sequential graph algorithms for distributed-memory parallel computation. ACM SIGPLAN Not. **40**(10), 423–437 (2005)
17. Harish, P., Narayanan, P.J.: Accelerating large graph algorithms on the GPU using CUDA. In: Aluru, S., Parashar, M., Badrinath, R., Prasanna, V.K. (eds.) HiPC 2007. LNCS, vol. 4873, pp. 197–208. Springer, Heidelberg (2007). https://doi.org/10.1007/978-3-540-77220-0_21
18. Hennessy, J.L., Patterson, D.A.: A new golden age for computer architecture. Commun. ACM **62**(2), 48–60 (2019)
19. Hong, S., Oguntebi, T., Olukotun, K.: Efficient parallel graph exploration on multicore CPU and GPU. In: 2011 International Conference on Parallel Architectures and Compilation Techniques, pp. 78–88. IEEE (2011)
20. Jia, Z., Tillman, B., Maggioni, M., Scarpazza, D.P.: Dissecting the graphcore ipu architecture via microbenchmarking. arXiv preprint arXiv:1912.03413 (2019)
21. Kaya, K., Langguth, J., Panagiotas, I., Uçar, B.: Karp-Sipser based kernels for bipartite graph matching. In: 2020 Proceedings of the Twenty-Second Workshop on Algorithm Engineering and Experiments (ALENEX), pp. 134–145. SIAM (2020)
22. Kolodziej, S.P., et al.: The suitesparse matrix collection website interface. J. Open Source Softw. **4**(35), 1244 (2019)
23. Korf, R.E., Schultze, P.: Large-scale parallel breadth-first search. In: AAAI, vol. 5, pp. 1380–1385 (2005)
24. Langguth, J., Azad, A., Halappanavar, M., Manne, F.: On parallel push-relabel based algorithms for bipartite maximum matching. Parallel Comput. **40**(7), 289–308 (2014)
25. Langguth, J., Cai, X., Sourouri, M.: Memory bandwidth contention: communication vs computation tradeoffs in supercomputers with multicore architectures. In: 2018 IEEE 24th International Conference on Parallel and Distributed Systems (ICPADS), pp. 497–506. IEEE (2018)
26. Langguth, J., Patwary, M.M.A., Manne, F.: Parallel algorithms for bipartite matching problems on distributed memory computers. Parallel Comput. **37**(12), 820–845 (2011)
27. Liu, H., Huang, H.H.: Enterprise: breadth-first graph traversal on GPUs. In: Proceedings of the International Conference for High Performance Computing, Networking, Storage and Analysis, pp. 1–12 (2015)
28. Murphy, R.C., Wheeler, K.B., Barrett, B.W., Ang, J.A.: Introducing the graph 500. Cray Users Group (CUG) **19**, 45–74 (2010)
29. Seshadhri, C., Pinar, A., Kolda, T.G.: An in-depth analysis of stochastic Kronecker graphs. J. ACM (JACM) **60**(2), 1–32 (2013)
30. Valiant, L.G.: A bridging model for parallel computation. Commun. ACM **33**(8), 103–111 (1990)
31. Wang, Y., Davidson, A., Pan, Y., Wu, Y., Riffel, A., Owens, J.D.: Gunrock: a high-performance graph processing library on the GPU. In: Proceedings of the 21st ACM SIGPLAN Symposium on Principles and Practice of Parallel Programming, pp. 1–12 (2016)
32. Yang, C., Buluc, A., Owens, J.D.: GraphBLAST: a high-performance linear algebra-based graph framework on the GPU (2020)

33. Yasui, Y., Fujisawa, K., Goto, K.: NUMA-optimized parallel breadth-first search on multicore single-node system. In: 2013 IEEE International Conference on Big Data, pp. 394–402. IEEE (2013)
34. Yoo, A., Chow, E., Henderson, K., McLendon, W., Hendrickson, B., Catalyurek, U.: A scalable distributed parallel breadth-first search algorithm on BlueGene/L. In: SC 2005: Proceedings of the 2005 ACM/IEEE Conference on Supercomputing, p. 25. IEEE, November 2005. https://doi.org/10.1109/SC.2005.4

Performance Modeling, Evaluation, and Analysis

Optimizing GPU-Enhanced HPC System and Cloud Procurements for Scientific Workloads

Richard Todd Evans$^{(\boxtimes)}$ ⓘ, Matthew Cawood, Stephen Lien Harrellⓘ,
Lei Huang, Si Liuⓘ, Chun-Yaung Lu, Amit Ruhelaⓘ, Yinzhi Wangⓘ,
and Zhao Zhangⓘ

Texas Advanced Computing Center, University of Texas at Austin,
Austin, TX 78727, USA
rtevans@tacc.utexas.edu

Abstract. Modern GPUs are capable of sustaining floating point operation rates and memory bandwidths that exceed those of most currently available CPUs, making them attractive options for the acceleration of scientific and machine learning (ML) workloads. However, many applications are either not GPU-enabled or only partially GPU-enabled. In addition, some applications leverage the additional GPU flops and memory bandwidth more effectively than others, and derive greater performance benefits from GPU acceleration. Combining these performance considerations with the significant hardware cost of GPU-enhancement, it is possible to derive an estimate for the optimal ratio of CPU and GPU architectures to use when designing a system procurement to support a given workload.

We describe a methodology to calculate this optimal ratio and demonstrate it using a proxy workload comprised of benchmarks from nine GPU-enabled applications. The scaling behavior of each application on each platform is combined with relative costs of hardware to minimize a cost-per-run and compute the most cost-effective architecture and scale on which this application should be run. This information is then used to estimate the optimal ratio of architectures for the procurement. We perform this evaluation considering three different computational platforms: NVIDIA's DGX A100 server with 8 A100s, IBM's AC922 servers with 4 V100s, and Dell's PowerEdge servers with Intel 8280 Xeon Cascade Lake-SP processors. We intend for the methodology described here to aid in HPC system design for computing service providers and assist in optimizing HPC cloud procurements.

Keywords: Accelerators · Cloud · Benchmarking

1 Introduction

In this work, we describe a model that quantifies the cost versus benefits of adopting various architectures such as GPUs in a HPC procurement and how it

© Springer Nature Switzerland AG 2021
B. L. Chamberlain et al. (Eds.): ISC High Performance 2021, LNCS 12728, pp. 313–331, 2021.
https://doi.org/10.1007/978-3-030-78713-4_17

can be used to optimize the ratio of architectures supporting a given workload. When designing a HPC system, the cost can be quantified in terms of hardware procurement and depreciation along with operations and maintenance requirements, while in a cloud procurement the cost is dictated by the vendor. With our cost model, the cost differences of running on various architectures can be quantified, allowing the determination of the optimal architecture on which to run an application. The costs of deviations from the optimum can also be explored. An additional output of this model is the calculation of the most cost-effective CPU or GPU device count used to run a particular component of the workload. This model is architecture agnostic and readily applicable to comparing different CPU-only and network architectures in addition to the GPU-focused analysis of this work.

The momentum to leverage GPU devices for compute capacity is based on the trend for many modern GPUs to provide higher floating point operation rates (FLOPS) and sustained memory bandwidths (MBW) than most CPUs. GPUs achieve this higher capability through a combination of highly parallel execution units and High Bandwidth Memory (HBM). The additional FLOPS and MBW can translate into additional performance for an application that has been suitably modified, or *ported*, to take advantage of a particular GPU architecture. While GPUs are an added cost, they provide the opportunity to accelerate performance. However, it is ambiguous for many workloads whether this added cost is worthwhile: the ability to harness the GPUs' compute capacity depends on an application's implementation and scale at which it is run.

To address this ambiguity, we construct a model that represents the cost of an application run (or unit of simulation time). The model can incorporate whatever costs are relevant to a system designer or cloud procurer, although we anticipate hardware procurement and depreciation, porting to new architectures, and operations and maintenance to make up the bulk of the cost. Operations and maintenance costs include a variety of factors such as power consumption, software and hardware maintenance, and labor costs. Of course in the case of a cloud provider, some of these costs are already incorporated into their prices.

We will demonstrate our cost model on a proxy workload of eight scientific application benchmarks and one machine learning benchmark. We will run these 9 application benchmarks on three different architectural platforms at multiple scales. This data will be used to determine the optimal architecture and device count at which to run those benchmarks and be used to design a hypothetical HPC system or cloud procurement.

2   Cost Model Based HPC Procurement

Our goal is to build a model that allows us to determine the most cost-effective ratio of CPU and GPU architectures that will compose a hypothetical system, whether that system is an on-site HPC system or cloud procurement. In this approach the CPU and GPU architectures are chosen from a fixed set of pre-existing architectures to support a pre-defined workload. We will show that to accomplish this goal, an optimal architecture can be found for each component of the workload by combining scaling behavior and time-to-solution data with costs of hardware, operations and maintenance or offered cloud provider rates. The diversity of many modern HPC workloads suggests a large number of workload components would have to be considered. In practice though, it is often the case that a proxy workload, composed of a small number of application benchmarks chosen to be representative of the intended workload, is used when designing a procurement. Additional application benchmarks can always be included until the proxy workload is realistic enough to satisfy service providers or funding agencies requirements. Multiple, well-defined scientific application benchmarks will be used as the proxy workload for our approach in the following.

2.1   Methodology

Our approach to optimizing the ratio of architectures from which to design an HPC procurement begins with determining the fraction of the cost of the procurement, ω^a, that is to support each component of the intended workload. a is a superscript indexing each component of the proxy workload (application benchmark in our case) and $\sum_a \omega^a = 1$. The optimal architecture i, out of a fixed set of architectures we are considering, should then be chosen for each application, and the fraction of the cost of the system devoted to that workload assigned that architecture. Here the overall cost of the system is fixed - only the proportion of its cost devoted to each architecture is permitted to change.

We then construct a model for the cost of a unit of simulation time (e.g. an iteration, nanoseconds-per-day, time-to-solution), which we henceforth refer to as a run. This cost model should account for the cost of *compute-time* and *research-time*. The definition of compute-time cost will differ for every service provider, but we anticipate it to be estimated from a combination of power, labor, maintenance contracts, network, storage, and architecture costs - hardware, operations and maintenance. Certain funding bodies, such as the National Science Foundation (NSF), often provide fixed awards separately for the hardware procurement and the operations and maintenance of a system, enabling straightforward estimates for compute-time costs. In the case of cloud providers, they offer specific rates for compute-time, making this estimation trivial. The cost of research-time is less concrete, although value is clearly generated from research otherwise it wouldn't be performed. We discuss the cost of research-time later in this section.

We can combine these considerations into a cost-per-run model for each application a on architecture i as

$$c_i^a(n) = \alpha_i^a n_i^a t_i^a(n) + \beta_i^a t_i^a(n) = \alpha_i^a(n_i^a t_{s,i}^a + t_{p,i}) + \beta_i^a(t_{s,i}^a + t_{p,i}^a/n_i^a), \qquad (1)$$

where a and i index the application and architecture used for the run respectively. n_i^a is the number of devices used for the run and $t_i^a(n)$ is the runtime at that device count. In Eq. 1 we have used a form of Amdahl's law to express $t_i^a(n)$ as a function of devices used

$$t_i^a(n) = t_{s,i}^a + \frac{t_{p,i}^a}{n_i^a}, \qquad (2)$$

where the model is based on strong scaling behavior. $t_{s,i}^a$ and $t_{p,i}^a$ in Eq. 2 are the portions of time taken up by work that is strictly serial and parallelizable respectively when running in a serial fashion. The first term in Eq. 1 is the cost in compute-time of a run and the second term is the cost in research-time of a run. The first coefficient, α_i^a, has units of dollars (or some other definition of value) per device per unit time and as previously stated can be straightforwardly estimated. We parameterize α_i^a as $\alpha_i^a = \kappa_i^a/T$, where T is the overall service time of the system. κ_i^a will generally differ across architectures and may differ across applications because certain applications consume more power or require more software maintenance than others on different architectures.

β_i^a is more difficult to estimate, although it should have units of dollars per unit time and we can parameterize it as $\beta_i^a = \gamma_i^a/\tau$, where γ_i^a that is the total research value produced by application a on architecture i over time period τ. From the perspective of an agency funding both the system and the research, γ_i^a could be estimated from the amount of funding of the research project running application a that is related to computation (making it independent of the architecture). In any case, demanding that $\gamma_i^a \geq \kappa_i^a$, i.e. research output per unit time is at least as valuable as compute-time consumed, ensures the investment in the computational resource is worthwhile.

Finding the minimum cost-per-run in terms of device count ($\frac{dc_i^a}{dn_i^a} = 0$) then results in

$$n_i^a = \sqrt{\frac{\gamma_i^a T t_{p,i}^a}{\kappa_i^a \tau t_{s,i}^a}} \tag{3}$$

Assuming τ is the lifetime of the procurement $\tau = T$, since we are optimizing for a constant workload, we have an optimal device count per run of

$$n_i^a = \sqrt{\frac{\gamma_i^a t_{p,i}^a}{\kappa_i t_{s,i}^a}} = \sqrt{\frac{\gamma_i^a p_i^a}{\kappa_i^a (1 - p_i^a)}}. \tag{4}$$

Here p_i^a is the fraction of work in a run that can be parallelized. This equation indicates that for fixed p_i^a, increasing the value placed on research-time leads to a higher optimal device usage, while increasing the cost per compute-time (higher hardware costs, higher power costs etc.) results in lower optimal device usage. Simultaneously, a higher fraction of the work capable of running in parallel results in higher device counts preferred and vice versa for a higher fraction of serial work. Of course, $n_i^a \geq 1$ and $n_i^a < N_i$, where N_i is the number of devices of architecture i that a HPC procurement will have. Note that n_i^a is independent of the overall time required to complete a run.

We can now determine the cost-per-run for each architecture at the optimal device count for architecture i and application a to be

$$c_i^a = \frac{1}{T} \left(\sqrt{\gamma_i^a t_{s,i}^a} + \sqrt{\kappa_i^a t_{p,i}^a} \right)^2. \tag{5}$$

$t_{s,i}^a$ and $t_{p,i}^a$, measured from scaling data, will in general differ across architectures and applications. If we insist that the research-time is as important as the compute-time in Eq. 1 then $\gamma_i^a = \kappa_i^a$ and we have

$$c_i^a = \frac{\kappa_i^a}{T} \left(\sqrt{t_{s,i}^a} + \sqrt{t_{p,i}^a} \right)^2. \tag{6}$$

This is a plausible value for γ_i^a in many circumstances - otherwise we would be left with the conclusion that the value of the research we extract from the system is less than or more than the value we put in. If the value is less than what we extract than we shouldn't procure the system at all, while if it is more than we should be able to use the proceeds to add more devices which would produce more proceeds and so on. This argument ignores the obvious impracticality in an academic setting of converting research proceeds to hardware, but in a commercial setting this approach would common sense up to the scale where other costs or supply and demand effects start to dominate. We use this estimate for γ_i^a and therefore Eq. 6 throughout the rest of this paper. Service providers that value the research-time of some components of the workload more than others, or value research-time more than compute-time due to funding arrangements and priorities, may choose different estimates for γ_i^a customized to their requirements.

The derivation of Eq. 6 assumes Amdahl's law governs the strong scaling behavior at the device counts where we made our performance measurements and where we make our recommendations. Amdahl's law is an idealized approximation of behavior which may not be reasonably accurate at all device counts, as it assumes synchronization and communication overheads are constant with device count. Measurements made at device counts where it is not approximately applicable should be discarded. Recommendations made for device counts beyond where we have data should be verified by collecting additional data at or above those device counts and ensuring Amdahl's law is still approximately valid. We leave the estimation of errors due to the approximations made in Amdahl's law to future work, addressing the two extremes where it breaks down - superlinear speedup and slowdown - below.

If measurements were made at device counts where superlinear speedup was in effect then $n_i^a t_i^a(n)$ and $t_i^a(n)$ are decreasing with increasing device count and therefore the cost in Eq. 2 is decreasing with device count - we are not at a cost minimum. Superlinear scaling will subside at some device count (if not, then the most cost-effective device count to run at will be the maximum possible), where a new reference device count for speed-up should be chosen. For device counts after this reference point, Amdahl's law should govern speedup and hence Eq. 6 should be applicable. If measurements were made at device counts where increasing device count causes a slowdown, then $n_i^a t_i^a(n)$ and $t_i^a(n)$ are increasing with increasing device count and we are not at a cost minimum. Data at these device counts and higher can be discarded from the model because their range will not contain a cost minimum. Naturally, if speedup declines for device counts greater than one then using one device is the most cost-effective.

Finally we note that weak-scaling is not relevant to our cost model. The model is intended to minimize the costs for fixed problem sizes from a predetermined set of benchmark applications. Non-trivial weak scaling solves a different benchmark problem at each device count. Even if the same physical problem is being solved, the resolution or fidelity must be increased to maintain a constant amount of work per device. The requirements for simulation fidelity are governed by the science or use case requirements, and thus would be input into the model.

Using our estimate of $\gamma_i^a = \kappa_i^a$, all of the terms in Eq. 6 are either measured in scaling studies or known from system requirements and costs. The length of service time, T, for the system is important for the overall cost of a run but not for choosing the optimal architecture. At this point we compute c_i^a for each architecture under consideration and choose the lowest cost one that will support application a. Once we have chosen the optimal architecture for each application we can determine the number of devices of that architecture the system procurement should have to support that application

$$N_i^a = \frac{w^a C}{\kappa_i^a}, \tag{7}$$

where C is to total budget for the procurement. As stated at the start of this section, w^a is the fraction of the cost of the system we devote to supporting application a. The exact value of c_i^a is not critical for the determination of an optimal architecture, only the relative values across architectures and applications. We note an outcome of our model is that we are able to recommend optimal device counts at which to run applications. We are also able to quantitatively explore the cost effects of deviations from the optimal procurement configuration.

Equation 7 assumes the flexibility to choose arbitrary fractions of architectures from our set under consideration. Hence a heterogeneous setup of possibly independent systems could be the recommendation. This may or may not be reasonable depending on the architectures being compared, the size of the procurement, the man-power available to maintain possibly disparate software stacks (which should be accounted for in the cost κ_i^a), and whether the procurement is of hardware or from the cloud. If the architectures under consideration have similar software stacks and maintenance requirements (e.g. different models of the same processor family) then it may be straightforward to use Eq. 7 in a procurement. If the procurement and HPC center are large enough to justify multiple, possibly independent systems, then Eq. 7 may be reasonable, assuming additional costs due to heterogeneity such as system setup, infrastructure and operations are accounted for in κ_i^a. Finally, if it is a cloud procurement then Eq. 7 is likely reasonable, again assuming costs for the various software setup and maintenance required have been accounted for in κ_i^a.

If there are factors that require the procurement to have a homogeneous architecture (small procurement, labor restrictions, vendor requirements etc.) then we can use the model to choose the most cost-effective architecture to support the workload. This will require us to compute the relative costs of the architectures under consideration. We begin by computing the normalized cost-per-run for each application a on architecture i, $\hat{c}_i^a$, at the optimal node count, Eq. 6, by dividing the cost-per-run by the sum of the cost-per-run of each architecture under consideration

$$\hat{c}_i^a = \frac{c_i^a}{\sum_j c_j^a}. \tag{8}$$

Using the normalized cost allows us to compare the relative cost of different applications by removing any dependence on how we defined a run. We can then compute the total normalized cost C_i for each architecture i as:

$$\hat{C}_i = \sum_a w^a \hat{c}_i^a \tag{9}$$

The architecture i with the lowest normalized cost computed in Eq. 9 should be chosen for procurement. This approach assumes that we value the relative cost of each application across architectures equally. Indeed, we have already accounted for how much the cost of each application is to be weighted when we determined the fraction of the cost of the procurement to devoted to the each application, w^a.

2.2   Demonstration on a Proxy Scientific Workload

We will demonstrate the methodology described in Sect. 2.1 on a hypothetical workload composed of eight widely used scientific applications and one ML framework. The application and software versions used to compile and run each benchmark are summarized in Table 1. Descriptions of each application and benchmark case will be detailed in Sect. 4. We use the benchmark case for each application as a proxy for the various execution modes of that application. We note that while some execution modes of an application may be GPU-enabled and others may not, it is up to the service provider or funding agency to define applications and execution modes of those applications that are a sufficiently representative proxy workload for a prospective system procurement.

We ran the benchmark problems on the three architectures shown in Table 2 at multiple device counts. We measured values for $t_{s,i}^a$ and $t_{p,i}^a$ by fitting these scaling results to Amdahl's Law, excluding device counts where Amdahl's Law was not applicable (e.g. super-linear scaling regimes where cache containment effects are evident). Here we define scaling in terms of the number of servers in the case of CPU-only architectures (labeled clx), and the number of GPUs in the case of GPU-enabled architectures (labeled $v100$ and $a100$). While the GPUs may be collocated on the same server, they are considered separate devices for purposes of scaling. We note that many definitions of a device are possible - core, socket, server, GPU. So long as they are properly reflected in the values assigned to the κ_i^a and scale according to Amdahl's law the exact definition should not be critical.

In Table 2, The DGX A100 platform, labeled as $a100$, is a single server with two AMD EPYC 7742 64-core processors and eight NVIDIA A100 GPUs connected via NVLINK. The AC922 platform, labeled as $v100$, consists of up to two of IBM AC922 (8335-GTH) servers with two 40-core Power9's and four V100's per server connected via NVLINK. The two servers are connected via Infiniband EDR. The Dell C6420 PowerEdge platform, labeled clx, has multiple servers

Table 1. Application versions [V] and compilers [C] used for each application and platform (*architecture*), and benchmark cases.

Application	PowerEdge (*clx*)	AC922 (*v100*)	DGX A100 (*a100*)	Benchmark case
MILC	[V] 7.8.1 [C] Intel 19.1.1, Intel MPI 19.0.7	[V] 7.8.1 [C] GCC 9.1.0, CUDA 10.2, MVAPICH2 GDR 2.3.4	[V] 7.8.1 [C] GCC 9.1.0, CUDA 10.1, Intel MPI 19.0.7	APEX 36 × 36 × 36 × 72
NAMD	[V] 2.14 [C] Intel 19.1.1, Intel MPI 19.0.7	[V] 2.14 [C] xl16.1.1, CUDA 10.2, Spectrum MPI 10.3.0	[V] 2.14 [C] GCC 9.1.0, CUDA 10.1, Intel MPI 19.0.7	Tobacco Mosaic Virus, 1.2M atoms, 2 fs, 30000 timesteps
AMBER	[V] A20u6, AT20u10 [C] Intel 19.0.5, Intel MPI 19.0.5	[V] A20u6, AT20u10 [C] GCC 7.3.0, CUDA 10.2, MVAPICH2 GDR 2.3.4	[V] A20u6, AT20u10 [C] GCC 9.1.0, CUDA 11.0, MVAPICH2-X 2.3	STMV_NPT_4 fs
SPECFEM3D_GLOB	[V] 7.0.2 [C] Intel 19.1.1, Intel MPI 19.0.7	[V] 7.0.2 [C] xl16.1.1, CUDA 10.2, Spectrum MPI 10.3.0	[V] 7.0.2 [C] Intel19.1.1, Cuda 11.0, MVAPICH2-x/2.3	Regional forward simulation, s362ani model, 1 × 224 × 256 spectral elements
PyTorch	[V] [C]	[V] [C] GCC 7.3.0, CUDA 10.2, NCCL-2.5.6	[V] [C] CUDA 11, NCCL-2.7.8	ResNet-50
VPIC	[V] 2.0 beta [C] Intel 19.1.1, Intel MPI 19.0.7, Kokkos 3.2.0	[V] 2.0 beta [C] GCC 7.3, MVAPICH2-gdr 2.3.4, CUDA 10.2, Kokkos 3.2.0	[V] 2.0 beta [C] GCC 9.1.0, MVAPICH2-x 2.3, CUDA 11.0, Kokkos 3.2.0	lpi_head_single_new _diag_for_Bird-GC Dim 1 × 56 × 3584 PPC: 448
WRF	[V] 3.8.1 [C] Intel 19.1.1, Intel MPI 19.0.7	NA	Precompiled AceCASTv1.1	conus 3 km: 1500 × 1500 × 50
GROMACS	[V] 2020.4 [C] Intel 19.1.1, Intel MPI 19.0.7, FFTW3 3.3.8	[V] 2020.4 [C] GCC 7.3.0, built-in thread-MPI, CUDA 10.2	[V] 2020.4 [C] GCC 9.1.0, built-in thread-MPI, CUDA 11.0	benchPEP: 12M atoms
LAMMPS	[V] stable_29Oct2020 [C] GCC 9.1.0, Intel MPI 19.0.7	[V] stable_29Oct2020 [c] GCC 7.3.0, OpenMPI 3.1.2, CUDA 10.2	[V] stable_29Oct2020 [C] GCC 9.1.0, MVAPICH2-x/2.3, CUDA 11.0	InP.snap: 50 × 50 × 50, 1M atoms

each containing two Intel Xeon 8280 Cascade Lake-SP 56-core processors. These CPU-only servers are connected by Infiniband HDR-100.

The estimates we use for κ_i^a are also shown in Table 2. κ_i^a is meant to be an estimate for the holistic cost per device, where we reiterate a device is defined to be an entire server in the case of *clx* and an individual GPU in the case of the *a100* and *v100* architectures. The holistic cost should include the infrastructure that supports the device such as the host server and fabric. To avoid any ambiguity regarding pricing and vendor concerns, here we simply estimate κ_i^a to be one dollar per GFLOP of peak performance of the device. We also add the appropriate fraction of the host server CPUs' GFLOPS to the *a100* and *v100* κ_i^a estimates (1/8 and 1/4 respectively). These price estimates are for demonstration purposes only and for a real-world analysis these estimates should be substituted with the actual negotiated vendor rates. Numerous other costs should also be carefully included for the most accurate estimate for κ_i^a; however, we ignore those as they doesn't hinder the demonstration of the model. We leave

Table 2. Architectures considered in this evaluation.

Label	Platform	Interconnect	CPU	GPU	κ_i
$a100$	NVIDIA DGX A100	NVLINK	2 AMD 7742	8 A100	10400
$v100$	IBM AC922 (8335-GTH)	NVLINK/IB EDR	2 IBM Power9	4 V100	7700
clx	Dell C6420 PowerEdge	IB HDR	2 Intel 8280	NA	4800

the careful inclusion of those considerations for future work. Note that $\kappa_i^a \rightarrow \kappa_i$ is the same for every application with our approximations.

Once we have estimates for κ_i and our measurements for $t_{s,i}^a$ and $t_{p,i}^a$ we can compute the most cost-effective device counts and the cost-per-run for each application on each architecture. We then assign the lowest cost architecture as the one that will be used to support an application, and determine the fraction of nodes on the prospective system that should be made up of that architecture.

3   Prior Work

There is a vast body of work comparing application and benchmark performance on various architectures of which we only provide a sampling. The majority of published benchmarking work is focused upon either one specific algorithm [1], one specific architecture [2,3] or both [4]. While these approaches are crucial for optimizing scientific codes and the acceptance of HPC systems, they add little to determining a cost-optimized mix of architectures for a variety of applications.

Performance measurements of applications are the standard approach to evaluate architectures' effectiveness. Performance comparisons between architectures are often used in Service Providers' proposals to justify system designs and are also published by vendors to distinguish their products from their competitors'. Additionally, metrics have been devised to account for performance portability or the ability to run efficiently on multiple platforms [5]. While this metric may be an analog for cost between multiple architectures for a single code base, it excludes the application heterogeneity that one might see on an HPC batch system. These evaluations do not, in general, systematically account for hardware cost differences and cost-effectiveness of disparate applications, with unique runtime characteristics, running on disparate architectures.

When benchmark performance comparisons across architectures are restricted to a discrete set of device counts, it can be straightforward to evaluate the relative cost-effectiveness of the architectures. For example, NVIDIA presents the performances of a number of applications on multiple architectures on the NVIDIA HPC Application Performance website [6]. NVIDIA uses a Node Replacement Factor (NRF) metric to measure how many CPU-only servers it takes to equal the performance of a certain number of GPU's for a particular application benchmark. While this type of study could be straightforwardly extended to include a cost-effective comparison, it is not presented on their site. They also make no attempt to capture the value of time-to-solution differences across architectures and scales. Due to the different scaling behavior of each application benchmark on each architecture, an architecture that is most cost-effective at one time-to-solution (and device count) may no longer be at another time-to-solution (and device count).

One of the closest works to what we present in this paper for GPU usage is demonstrated for GROMACS [7]. In this research, the authors attempt to find the GPU architecture that provides the greatest MD trajectory (ns/day) within a fixed budget for the GROMACS application [8]. They evaluate a wide variety of architectures and runtime configurations in order to find the most cost-effective architecture. They do not, however, perform the necessary scaling studies or have a cost model to determine optimal device counts to run the application.

We conclude from the lack of prior work that the model presented in this paper is a novel approach to analyzing cost-effectiveness of applications and hardware. The recommendations our model produce have no doubt been arrived at countless times through practical experience; however, it provides a systematic approach to exploring and optimizing the cost versus benefit of using various architectures to support scientific applications.

4   Demonstration and Results

In this section we demonstrate our methodology on a proxy workload made up of commonly used scientific applications. We describe the applications and benchmark cases in detail. We then present performance and scaling results for each application on the three architectures shown in Table 2, with comments on observed performance behavior and noting where particular benchmark runs were treated uniquely. In general, we aimed to run each benchmark on 1, 2, 4, and 8 devices but deviated from this where necessary. Finally, we apply the cost-model described in Sect. 2.1 to this proxy workload and compute the optimal ratio of architectures for our hypothetical HPC procurement.

4.1   Description of Proxy Workload

Amber. Amber is a collection of packages to perform and analyze Molecular Dynamics (MD) simulations [9]. The Satellite Tobacco Mosaic Virus (STMV) NPT Ensemble dataset containing 1,067,095 atoms was used for this investigation. The skin_permit feature was used to implement the 'leaky pair lists' optimization. One MPI rank per core was used for CPU runs, while one rank per card was used for GPU runs. Amber is known to be well optimized but scale inefficiently on GPUs. Therefore we only include scaling data up to two GPUs. Performance is reported in ns/day.

GROMACS. GROMACS is a publicly available parallel MD package that is extensively used for studying biological functions at the atomic level [7]. In this benchmark, we simulate an aqueous peptide system comprising over 12 million atoms that was previously used to study peptide aggregation [10]. The input file was obtained from the Max Planck Institute for Biophysical Chemistry website [11]. The CPU benchmark runs used 56 MPI tasks per node, whereas in the GPU runs, combinations of settings (GPU = 1, 2, 4, 8 per node, MPI tasks = 1, 2, 4, 8 per node, OpenMP threads = 8, 16 per MPI task) were used to find out the best performance scenario. The Verlet cut-off scheme is used and the value of the parameter nstlist was tuned to optimize the performance for each case (CPU: 80, GPU: 300–500). For GPU runs, the computations of long-range non-bonded interactions, short-range non-bonded interactions, and bonded interactions were offloaded to GPUs. Performance is reported in ns/day.

LAMMPS. LAMMPS is an open-source classical MD code developed at Sandia National Laboratories [12]. In this work, the LAMMPS Kokkos package [13], built with CUDA support, is used to run MD simulations across multiple GPUs. Here we use the SNAP potential, a new generation of machine-learned interatomic potential which has demonstrated *ab initio* level of accuracy in MD simulations [14]. We evaluated the performance under various CPU/GPU configurations using the SNAP example, InP [15], shipped with the LAMMPS package. The dimensions of the system were set to $50 \times 50 \times 50$ (1,000,000 atoms). The CPU runs used 56 MPI ranks per node and the scaling data were obtained from the simulations (100 MD steps with timestep = 0.5 fs) ran on 1, 2, 4, and 8 nodes. The GPU runs used 1, 2, 4, and 8 MPI ranks with 1 GPU per MPI rank and with the command options newton on and neigh half. The default domain decomposition setting was applied for all the CPU and GPU cases. Performance is reported in ns/day.

MILC. MILC is an open-source application for performing Lattice Quantum Chromodynamics (QCD) calculations [16]. MILC is GPU-enabled through the CUDA-based QUDA library [17]. The benchmark used here is the $36 \times 36 \times 36 \times 72$ APEX case [18] and evolves the lattice gauge field through 2 trajectories using a hybrid Monte-Carlo method. Scaling fits to the runs were performed on 18, 27, 54 and 81 servers for the *clx* architecture in order to avoid the super-linear scaling regime. Scaling fits to *v100* architecture were similarly performed on 4 and 8 GPUs to avoid the super-linear scaling regime. Fits to the *a100* architecture results were done on 1, 2, 4 and 8 devices as no super-linear scaling was observed. Performance is reported in overall runtime.

NAMD. NAMD is a parallel MD code for high performance simulation of large molecular systems used by many research teams around the world and the 2002 Gordon Bell Prize winner [19]. This study uses the STMV (2 fs timestep, 12A cutoff + PME every 3 steps) NAMD benchmark with modified input. The STMV benchmark is a 1,066,628-atom molecular dynamics simulation of Satellite Tobacco Mosaic Virus. Performance is reported in ns/day.

PyTorch. PyTorch is a popular machine learning framework. We used its implementation of the ResNet-50 deep learning application with the ImageNet dataset for our benchmark case. The benchmark case uses stochastic gradient descent (SGD) or its variants such as momentum SGD and LAMB [20]. ResNet-50 is an image classification neural network that composes 49 convolutional layers in five convolution groups [21] with 23 million trainable parameters. The ResNet-50 network was trained with the ImageNet dataset for 90 epochs. We use the open source implementation as it converges to the 75.9% MLPerf baseline [22,23]. Performance is reported in images/s.

SPECFEM3D_GLOBE. SPECFEM3D_GLOBE is an open-source package that simulates three-dimensional global and regional seismic wave propagation using the spectral element method [24]. Here, we use a small-scale regional simulation from the benchmark data set published by NVIDIA as our benchmark [25]. The internal mesher of SPECFEM3D_GLOBE breaks the globe into 6 chunks with a cubed-sphere mapping, and each chunk is further subdivided into slices along the two sides of a chunk. Our regional simulation is done on one chunk only. To accommodate the factor of 7 in the core count on the *clx* architecture, we define the number of slices to be 224 × 256. Certain numbers of domains defined by the slices were then assigned to each MPI rank. The GPU runs were done with one MPI rank per GPU. The CPU runs were done with one MPI rank per core. We measure the performance with the average time per step of the last 300 steps of the simulation and simply refer to this as the runtime.

VPIC. The Vector Particle-in-Cell (VPIC) application is a first principles particle-in-cell plasma physics model that tracks particles and electromagnetic fields in a structured grid [26,27]. Traditionally, VPIC has been hand-optimized using CPU intrinsics to achieve high performance. This application is known to scale well on many CPU platforms - up to 2 million MPI ranks with 7 trillion particles [28]. In this paper we will use a VPIC 2.0 beta which is based on the Kokkos [13] performance portability framework [29] in order to compare performance across CPUs and GPUs. The Kokkos OpenMP and CUDA backends are used to perform the benchmarking runs. This version of the VPIC 2.0 beta release has not undergone any targeted optimization efforts or platform specific tuning, although optimized versions are forthcoming. In this study a 2D dataset is used that has been created as a baseline to exercise all of the features of VPIC on CPUs and GPUs. The dataset was designed to run within one 16 GB GPU and contains 3.7 million particles. Performance is reported as overall runtime.

WRF. The Weather Research Forecasting (WRF) model is a mesoscale model designed for operational forecasts and atmospheric research [30]. The WRF model serves a wide range of meteorological applications with different scales. AceCAST-WRF/WRFg is a proprietary GPU-enabled version of WRF developed by TempoQuest, Inc. (TQI), which supports 23 physics options and some nesting functionality [31]. The benchmark case comes from NCAR's NWSC-3 North America benchmark [32]. The mesh grid is 1500 × 1500 with 50 vertical levels. The benchmark run is configured with the following physical parameterization: mp_physics = 8, cu_physics = 0, ra_lw_physics = 4, ra_sw_physics = 4. The simulation is implemented with a 10 s time step for an hour. This WRF case is implemented with the WRF 3.8.1 distributed-memory version on the *clx* architecture and AceCAST 1.1 on the *a100* architecture. We have not been able to run the AceCAST 1.1 version on the *v100* architecture due to the availability of the required binaries. Performance is reported as overall runtime.

4.2 Scaling and Cost Optimization of Proxy Workload

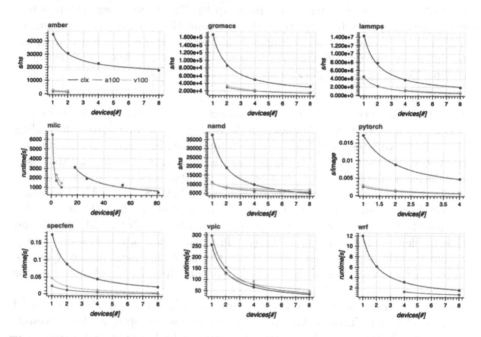

Fig. 1. The scaling curves on all three architectures for each application are shown. The *clx* results are shown in blue, the *a100* results in green, and the *v100* results in yellow. Measured data is displayed as dots and the fits to that data as curves. There was no *v100* data available for WRF. (Color figure online)

Scaling. The scaling behavior on all three architectures for each application is shown in Fig. 1. The device count used for a run is shown on the x-axis, and the performance on the y-axis. For Amber, GROMACS, LAMMPS, and NAMD we report seconds per nanosecond of simulation time (s/ns) and for PyTorch seconds per image processed ($s/image$), as these applications' performances are traditionally reported in terms of these units. We report runtime for the MILC, SPECFEM, VPIC, and WRF benchmarks.

While the runs on the *clx* architecture may demonstrate better scaling behavior for many benchmarks, the absolute performance is generally superior on the GPUs, with VPIC as the notable exception. In fact, the scaling behavior of the VPIC beta on the CPUs and GPUs is remarkably similar. Upon further examination, due to the fact that the initialization is not yet optimized for GPUs, approximately 30% of the total runtime is spent in this stage on GPUs and less than 1% of time on CPUs which results in this scaling outcome. The CPU-only and GPU code paths are nearly identical at the code-base level. We expect the upcoming optimization of GPU initialization to improve the runtime of VPIC.

The speedup when using GPUs is 2–3× at most device counts for most of the application benchmarks, with the *a100* results always faster than the *v100* results (except for VPIC). Amber appears to display the greatest benefits from GPU-acceleration, with speedups of up to 27×. In all cases, the absolute performance disparity between the CPU-only and GPU-enhanced architectures decreases with increasing device count. It is because of this, combined with the cost differences of the different architectures that it is not clear which architecture provides the greatest performance for cost.

Cost. The cost to run each application on each architecture across device counts is shown in Fig. 2. Our measurements for $t_{s,i}^a$ and $t_{p,i}^a$, determined from the scaling studies, and estimates for κ_i^a and $\gamma_i^a = \kappa_i^a$ from Table 2 are used here. The service period T of the system used in these plots is for 1 year. The exact value used for T does not change the most cost-effective architecture because it is the same for all architectures. For Amber, GROMACS, LAMMPS, and NAMD we show the cost in units of dollars per nanosecond of simulation time ($/ns$) and for PyTorch show dollars per image ($/image$). For MILC, SPECFEM, VPIC, and WRF we show cost in dollars per run ($). The distinction in units used is purely for convenience and does not affect the outcome of the methodology - we are comparing the cost of the same unit of simulation time across architectures for each application.

The optimal architecture and device count on which each application should be run is shown in Table 3. We rounded to the nearest optimal device count, as the methodology treats device counts continuously. We note that non-integer device counts may be informative if the granularity of resources able to be allocated to an application is less than used in the scaling study. The cost difference from rounding to the nearest integer values of device is in any case easily determined from the cost curves in Fig. 2.

For our benchmarks and cost estimates, the *v100* architecture is optimal for five of the applications: GROMACS, LAMMPS, MILC, NAMD, and PyTorch. The *a100* is optimal for Amber, SPECFEM, and WRF (WRF was not run on the *v100* architecture though). VPIC is the only application which is optimal to run on *clx*. A benefit of the model shown in Fig. 2 is the ability to judge how far off from optimal a particular device configuration may be for an application benchmark. For instance, although *v100* is optimal for MILC, it is only 6% cheaper than using *a100* when comparing costs at optimal device counts. In two

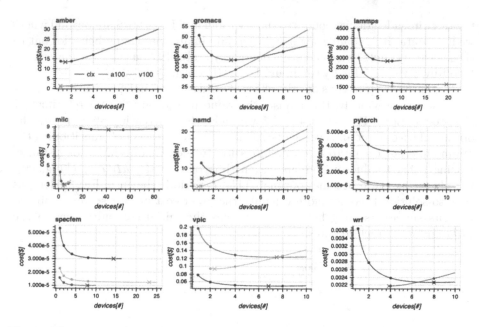

Fig. 2. The estimated cost to run on all three architectures for each application are shown. The *clx* results are shown in blue, the *a100* results in green, and the *v100* results in yellow. Measured data is displayed as dots and the fits to that data as curves of the same color. There was no *v100* data available for WRF. The optimal device count (minimum cost) at which to run each application on each architecture is indicated by an × of the corresponding architecture's color. (Color figure online)

Table 3. Optimal architecture and device count to use for each application benchmark.

Application	Architecture	Device #
Amber	*a100*	1
GROMACS	*v100*	2
LAMMPS	*v100*	16
MILC	*v100*	3
NAMD	*v100*	1
PyTorch	*v100*	9
SPECFEM	*a100*	8
VPIC	*clx*	7
WRF	*a100*	4

other instances, using four *v100*s to run PyTorch is only 6% more expensive than using the optimal device count of nine, and using eight GPUs to run LAMMPS instead of the optimal count is only 2% more expensive. Differences of this magnitude are unlikely to manifest in significant cost distinctions in practical settings. This consideration is particularly relevant to our demonstration, where the recommended device counts to run PyTorch and LAMMPS are beyond where we have data. If Amdahl's law failed to approximate the scaling behavior out to those device counts, we could still confidently state that our cost estimates may be off by 6% or 2% for PyTorch and LAMMPS respectively.

It is interesting to consider the effect of adjusting γ_i^a independently of κ_i. As we've stated previously, this adjusts the value placed on the research-time (or time-to-solution). From Eqs. 4 and 5 we know that increasing γ_i^a increases the optimal device count and overall cost. This can have the effect of transitioning the minimum cost-per-run to a new architecture. In the case of NAMD for instance, placing a fixed value on the simulation time of 10× the $a100$ κ_i ($104,000), the clx architecture becomes optimal. This scenario is shown in Fig. 3. Here, as time-to-solution becomes more valuable, the lower cost per clx server combined with its superior scaling behavior overcomes the initial cost advantage of the $v100$ and $a100$ architectures.

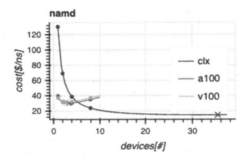

Fig. 3. The estimated cost to run on all three architectures for NAMD are shown. Here γ_i^a has been fixed to 10× the $a100$ κ_i cost, driving the optimal device count higher and transitioning the optimal architecture to clx.

Finally, for completeness, we compute the number of devices an optimal system procurement should have when each application is equally supported, i.e. $w^a = \frac{1}{9}$, $\forall a$. The fraction of the cost devoted to each architecture in an optimal procurement is: 25% $a100$, 57% $v100$, and 18% clx. If we assume a 10 million dollar budget for the procurement, the device count for each architecture should be: 240 $a100$, 740 $v100$, and 375 clx devices or 30 DGX A100, 185 IBM AC922, and 375 PowerEdge servers. We note that in a practical procurement, the costs of maintaining heterogeneous architectures should be incorporated into the compute-time cost κ_i^a from the start of the analysis. These may be significant costs, as in this demonstration where three different vendors and several different software stacks are part of the recommended procurement. For example, if additional staff must be assigned or hired to support an architecture the site is not familiar with, or port codes to a new architecture, those costs should be included in κ_i^a. If the architecture choices consisted instead of a single vendor with a software stack familiar to a site, offering different processor families, then the additional costs would probably be minimal.

If the system must have a homogeneous architecture than we would compute the normalized costs for each application and use Eq. 9 to evaluate the most cost-effective architecture option. In our demonstration the normalized costs for supporting our proxy workload on each architecture are: $C_{clx} = 4.6$, $C_{v100} = 2.3$, and $C_{a100} = 2.6$. Thus, a system composed of 1299 $v100$s would be optimal for our demonstration. Again, the percentage cost of choosing an architecture different from the optimal can be evaluated.

5   Conclusion

We have presented a methodology for optimizing the ratio of architectures that make up a system procurement to support a specified workload. Our approach is based on optimizing a cost model for individual runs of applications, where the cost has a compute-time and a research-time component. Using measured scaling data, an optimal device count on which to run and cost-per-run is computed for each architecture and application. The lowest cost architecture for each application is then chosen to support it. The HPC system procurement is finally constructed using these optimal architectures along with the fraction of procurement cost devoted to each application and overall procurement budget. The methodology allows for integrating additional information regarding cost, such as power consumption or labor, in a systematic manner. Effects of cost assumptions or modifications can be quantitatively explored using the model. The approach is hardware agnostic, and could readily be applied to comparing CPU-only and network architectures.

We demonstrated this methodology on a proxy scientific workload of eight scientific application benchmarks and one machine learning benchmark, comparing three different architectures. Various approximations for cost were used, with their effects noted. The cost model enabled a quantitative examination of the effects of deviating from the optimal system configurations. Finally, we report the optimal ratio of architectures from which to compose a hypothetical HPC system procurement to support the proxy workload.

This work should enable a more systematic approach to HPC system and cloud procurements than the empirically-based approach that is typically employed by service providers. A need for such an approach has grown with the rise of expensive but computationally capable GPU-enabled servers and cloud services. This need will be even further accentuated with the arrival of ML-focused co-processors and more exotic architectures. We hope this work can assist HPC service and cloud providers design more cost-effective HPC system procurements and better support their stakeholders.

References

1. Stegailov, V.V., Orekhov, N.D., Smirnov, G.S.: HPC hardware efficiency for quantum and classical molecular dynamics. In: Malyshkin, V. (ed.) PaCT 2015. LNCS, vol. 9251, pp. 469–473. Springer, Cham (2015). https://doi.org/10.1007/978-3-319-21909-7_45

2. Bauer, G., Hoefler, T., Kramer, W., Fiedler, B.: Analyses and modeling of applications used to demonstrate sustained petascale performance on Blue Waters. Cray User Group, May 2012
3. Evans, R.T.: Application performance in the frontera acceptance process. In: 2020 ACM SIGHPC SYSPROS Workshop (2020)
4. Tsai, Y.M., Cojean, T., Anzt, H.: Evaluating the performance of NVIDIA's a100 Ampere GPU for sparse linear algebra computations (2020)
5. Pennycook, S., Sewall, J., Lee, V.: Implications of a metric for performance portability. Future Gener. Comput. Syst. **92**, 947–958 (2019)
6. NVIDIA: NVIDIA HPC application performance. https://developer.nvidia.com/hpc-application-performance. Accessed 17 May 2021
7. GROMACS (2020). http://www.gromacs.org. Accessed 17 May 2021
8. Kutzner, C., Páll, S., Fechner, M., Esztermann, A., de Groot, B.L., Grubmüller, H.: More bang for your buck: improved use of GPU nodes for GROMACS 2018 (2019)
9. Case, D.A.: AMBER 2020. University of California, San Francisco (2020)
10. Matthes, D., Gapsys, V., de Groot, B.L.: Driving forces and structural determinants of steric zipper peptide oligomer formation elucidated by atomistic simulations. J. Mol. Biol. **421**(2–3), 390–416 (2012)
11. Kutzner, C.: A free GROMACS benchmark set. https://www.mpibpc.mpg.de/grubmueller/bench. Accessed 17 May 2021
12. Plimpton, S.: Fast parallel algorithms for short-range molecular dynamics. J. Comput. Phys. **117**(1), 1–19 (1995). http://www.sciencedirect.com/science/article/pii/S002199918571039X
13. Edwards, H.C., Trott, C.R., Sunderland, D.: Kokkos: enabling manycore performance portability through polymorphic memory access patterns. J. Parallel Distrib. Comput. **74**(12), 3202–3216 (2014)
14. Thompson, A., Swiler, L., Trott, C., Foiles, S., Tucker, G.: Spectral neighbor analysis method for automated generation of quantum-accurate interatomic potentials. J. Comput. Phys. **285**, 316–330 (2015)
15. Cusentino, M.A., Wood, M.A., Thompson, A.P.: Explicit multielement extension of the spectral neighbor analysis potential for chemically complex systems. J. Phys. Chem. A **124**(26), 5456–5464 (2020)
16. The MIMD Lattice Computation (MILC) Collaboration (2020). http://www.physics.utah.edu/detar/milc. Accessed 17 May 2021
17. Clark, M., Babich, R., Barros, K., Brower, R., Rebbi, C.: Solving lattice QCD systems of equations using mixed precision solvers on GPUs. Comput. Phys. Commun. **181**(9), 1517–1528 (2010)
18. NERSC (2020). https://github.com/lattice/quda/wiki/Running-the-NERSC-MILC-Benchmarks. Accessed 17 May 2021
19. Phillips, J.C., et al.: Scalable molecular dynamics with NAMD. J. Comput. Chem. **26**(16), 1781–1802 (2005)
20. You, Y., Hseu, J., Ying, C., Demmel, J., Keutzer, K., Hsieh, C.J.: Large-batch training for LSTM and beyond. In: Proceedings of the International Conference for High Performance Computing, Networking, Storage and Analysis, SC 2019. Association for Computing Machinery, New York (2019)
21. He, K., Zhang, X., Ren, S., Sun, J.: Deep residual learning for image recognition. In: IEEE Conference on Computer Vision and Pattern Recognition, pp. 770–778 (2016)

22. Pauloski, J.G., Zhang, Z., Huang, L., Xu, W., Foster, I.T.: Convolutional neural network training with distributed K-FAC. In: Proceedings of the International Conference for High Performance Computing, Networking, Storage and Analysis, pp. 1–14 (2020)

23. MLCommons. https://www.mlperf.org. Accessed 17 May 2021

24. Komatitsch, D., Tromp, J.: Introduction to the spectral element method for three-dimensional seismic wave propagation. Geophys. J. Int. **139**(3), 806–822 (1999)

25. NVIDIA: SPECFEM3d globe GPU & software configurations from NVIDIA data center. https://www.nvidia.com/en-sg/data-center/gpu-accelerated-applications/specfem3d-globe/. Accessed 17 May 2021

26. Bowers, K.J., Albright, B.J., Yin, L., Bergen, B., Kwan, T.J.T.: Ultrahigh performance three-dimensional electromagnetic relativistic kinetic plasma simulation. Phys. Plasmas **15**(5), 055703 (2008)

27. Bowers, K.J., et al.: Advances in petascale kinetic plasma simulation with VPIC and Roadrunner. In: Journal of Physics: Conference Series, vol. 180, p. 012055, July 2009

28. Byna, S., Sisneros, R., Chadalavada, K., Koziol, Q.: Tuning parallel I/O on blue waters for writing 10 trillion particles. In: Cray User Group (CUG) 2015. Citeseer, April 2015

29. Harrell, S.L., et al.: Effective performance portability. In: 2018 IEEE/ACM International Workshop on Performance, Portability and Productivity in HPC (P3HPC), pp. 24–36 (2018)

30. Skamarock, W., et al.: A description of the advanced research WRF. NCAR Technical Notes (2018). https://opensky.ucar.edu/islandora/object/technotes:500

31. TQI: WRFg - GPU Accelerated WRF. https://wrfg.net/. Accessed 17 May 2021

32. The National Center for Atmospheric Research: CISL High-Performance Computing (HPC) Benchmarks (2010). https://www2.cisl.ucar.edu/hpc_benchmarking

A Performance Analysis of Modern Parallel Programming Models Using a Compute-Bound Application

Andrei Poenaru$^{(\boxtimes)}$ ⓘ, Wei-Chen Lin, and Simon McIntosh-Smith$^{(\boxtimes)}$ ⓘ

Department of Computer Science, University of Bristol, Bristol, UK
{andrei.poenaru,cssnmis}@bristol.ac.uk

Abstract. Performance portability is becoming more-and-more important as next-generation high performance computing systems grow increasingly diverse and heterogeneous. Several new approaches to parallel programming, such as SYCL and Kokkos, have been developed in recent years to tackle this challenge. While several studies have been published evaluating these new programming models, they have tended to focus on memory-bandwidth bound applications. In this paper we analyse the performance of what appear to be the most promising modern parallel programming models, on a diverse range of contemporary high-performance hardware, using a compute-bound molecular docking mini-app.

We present miniBUDE, a mini-app for BUDE, the Bristol University Docking Engine, a real application routinely used for drug discovery. We benchmark miniBUDE on real-world inputs for the full-scale application in order to follow its performance profile closely in the mini-app. We implement the mini-app in different programming models targeting both CPUs and GPUs, including SYCL and Kokkos, two of the more promising and widely used modern parallel programming models. We then present an analysis of the performance of each implementation, which we compare to highly optimised baselines set using established programming models such as OpenMP, OpenCL, and CUDA. Our study includes a wide variety of modern hardware platforms covering CPUs based on ×86 and Arm architectures, as well as GPUs.

We found that, with the emerging parallel programming models, we could achieve performance comparable to that of the established models, and that a higher-level framework such as SYCL can achieve OpenMP levels of performance while aiding productivity. We identify a set of key challenges and pitfalls to take into account when adopting these emerging programming models, some of which are implementation-specific effects and not fundamental design errors that would prevent further adoption. Finally, we discuss our findings in the wider context of performance-portable compute-bound workloads.

Keywords: Programming models · Performance portability · Performance analysis · Compute-bound benchmark

B. L. Chamberlain et al. (Eds.): ISC High Performance 2021, LNCS 12728, pp. 332–350, 2021.
https://doi.org/10.1007/978-3-030-78713-4_18

1   Introduction

In High-Performance Computing (HPC), the majority of programs utilise established, long-running parallel programming frameworks. OpenMP and MPI are widely adopted [1], generally on top of the C and Fortran programming languages, and other frameworks are sometimes used in more specific situations, such as task-based parallelism libraries, C++-native applications, or programming models that can target GPUs [2].

Recent developments in parallel programming frameworks—be it frameworks developed from scratch, such as Kokkos, or additions and improvements to existing ones, such as tasking and offload support in OpenMP 4.5 and later—have all shared a number of common goals: performant support for a wide range of hardware platforms, interoperability with modern versions of the C++ language, and a focus on programmers' productivity. These goals have organically arisen as a result of the shortcomings in established programming models, and together contribute to the wider endeavour in the field of HPC towards achieving *performance portability* [3].

In order to support both GPU and CPU platforms, high-level programming frameworks manage underlying data structures automatically: the programmer expresses what data needs to be computed on, and the framework arranges it in a format suitable for the target hardware. Because this process is desirable but not always optimal, it is one of the key focuses of previous analyses of high-level parallel programming models [4]. However, the portability and productivity advantages alone brought by these frameworks may be enough to also justify their usage on applications that are not memory-bandwidth-bound, provided that they can deliver performance comparable to established frameworks.

One suitable application for such heterogeneous frameworks is the Bristol University Docking Engine (BUDE), a molecular docking code that is heavily compute-bound [5]. BUDE is routinely used for *in silico* drug discovery, and out of a need to support both CPUs and GPUs, it is comprised of two parallel implementations: an OpenMP version for CPUs and an OpenCL version for GPUs. In this paper, we used a mini-app created from the core computation kernel for BUDE to analyse the performance of emerging parallel programming models compared to that of traditional models.

This paper makes the following contributions:

- Highly optimised implementations of the miniBUDE mini-app in six parallel programming models: OpenMP (for CPU and offload), OpenCL, CUDA, OpenACC, Kokkos, and SYCL;
- An analysis of the performance of each implementation on contemporary high-performance processors from Intel, AMD, Fujitsu, Marvell, and NVIDIA;
- A discussion of the lessons learned from developing the miniBUDE benchmark, and their implications for other compute-bound workloads and the wider HPC field.

2   Background

2.1   High-Performance Molecular Docking

BUDE is an application for *in silico* molecular docking, a computational technique for predicting the structure of a complex formed between two molecules and estimating the strength of their interaction [5]. Docking is computationally challenging because of the many different ways in which two molecules may be arranged together to form a complex (three translational and three rotational degrees of freedom). Indeed, interacting all patches of the surface of one protein molecule with all patches of a second molecule requires on the order of 10^7 trials, each one of which is a computationally expensive operation [6].

The application includes several modes of operation, of which the most commonly used—and the most computationally intensive—is *virtual screening*. In this mode, molecules of drug candidates, known as *ligands*, are generated using a genetic algorithm and are bonded to a *target* protein molecule. BUDE uses a tuned empirical free-energy forcefield to predict the binding energy of the ligand with the target. There are many ways in which this bonding could occur, so a variety of positions and rotations of the ligand relative to the protein are attempted; these are known as *poses*. For each pose, the energy, i. e. the strength, of the bond is evaluated.

2.2   Modern Parallel Programming Models

In the previous decade, low-level programming models that offered the programmer great control over the hardware saw a rise in their usage. Their appeal of low overhead and extensive tuning options made them popular with Graphics Processing Units (GPU) programmers [7], but over the years the HPC community has learned the cost these frameworks incur: they require extensive knowledge of the hardware, and they steer towards over-optimisations for one target, up to the point where a significant fraction of the code needs to be rewritten when moving to a new system [8–10]. The latter observation is particularly relevant in the context of the upcoming exascale systems Frontier, El Capitan, Aurora, and Perlmutter, which together utilise combinations of CPUs from two vendors and GPUs from three vendors [11,12]. It is, thus, not feasible to use platform- or vendor-specific programming models, and a portable approach is needed.

In moving to new programming models, the C++ language has particular appeal: it can achieve the same zero-overhead performance compared to C and Fortran, but it also offers modern features to write more expressive and safer code. Programmers writing parallel C++ hope to outweigh any lost performance with time gained through easier-to-write and easier-to-debug code. This is the core selling point of modern parallel programming frameworks [13].

Two modern, single-source frameworks with a focus on performance, portability, and productivity have emerged: Kokkos [14] and SYCL [15]. Kokkos is a new framework developed natively for C++, while SYCL builds on previous OpenCL toolchains and integrates them with modern C++ code. Both of these frameworks can generate machine code for both CPUs and GPUs without any change to the high-level source code.

These frameworks solve the same problem in different ways. Kokkos is distributed as source code that needs to be integrated into the application's build process. This means that every application using Kokkos needs to build Kokkos itself—a relatively quick process—but it also avoids the pitfalls of system-wide libraries; a C++ compiler is all that is needed to compile a Kokkos application.

In contrast, SYCL applications rely on a SYCL compiler. At the time of writing, there are three major SYCL compilers: Data-Parallel C++ (DPC++) [16], ComputeCpp [17], and hipSYCL [18]. Each implementation can use different backends: DPC++ can use OpenCL, CUDA, or Intel's Level Zero; ComputeCpp relies on OpenCL; and hipSYCL supports OpenMP to target CPUs, CUDA to target NVIDIA GPUs, and ROCm to target AMD GPUs.

2.3   Performance Portability

In recent years, the HPC community has made efforts to understand how to quantify performance portability. Although some formal metrics have been developed and are commonly applied in portability studies [19], the results are not always trivial to interpret correctly [20]. One attempt to solve this challenge relies on carefully designed visualisations [21].

Portability is a common concern for developers—and users—of modern programming models. These make it more feasible to target several kinds of compute devices simultaneously, which has led to a diverse landscape of architectures being investigated in contemporary HPC research. As such, significant attention to portability and programmer productivity is also given in recent studies that evaluate the applicability of novel parallel frameworks [22,23].

3   Evaluation Methodology

3.1   A BUDE Mini-App

We have implemented a mini-app for BUDE virtual-screening runs, with kernels written in a range of widely used parallel programming models. The baseline implementation is written in OpenCL and is virtually identical to the core kernel of the full-scale BUDE application. There is a CUDA port with minimal changes, a CPU OpenMP version that restructures the computation in the OpenCL kernel to make it easier for compilers to vectorise, and similar implementations for GPUs using OpenACC and OpenMP `target` offload. We chose SYCL and Kokkos for implementations in novel programming models because of their relative popularity and compatibility with a wide range of platforms, covering both CPUs and GPU.

The focus of the mini-app is on the core computation, and so most of the plumbing around it, such as flexible I/O and custom file formats, has been removed. Instead of using a genetic algorithm to generate ligands, a procedure which takes negligible time in a full-scale BUDE run, the mini-app uses pre-generated

Table 1. Hardware platforms used for evaluation.

Platform	Abbrev.	Type	Cores	Clock speed	Peak SP performance
Intel Skylake 8176	SKL	CPU	2 × 28	2.1 GHz	5,734 GFLOP/s
Intel Cascade Lake 6230	CXL	CPU	2 × 20	2.1 GHz	4,096 GFLOP/s
AMD Rome 7742	Rome	CPU	2 × 64	2.25 GHz	9,216 GFLOP/s
Marvell ThunderX2	TX2	CPU	2 × 32	2.5 GHz	2,560 GFLOP/s
Fujitsu A64FX	A64FX	CPU	48	1.8 GHz	5,530 GFLOP/s
NVIDIA V100	—	GPU	80	1.13 GHz	15,700 GFLOP/s
AMD Radeon VII	—	GPU	60	1.4 GHz	13,800 GFLOP/s
Intel Iris Pro 580	—	GPU	72	0.95 GHz	1,094 GFLOP/s

molecules obtained from the full BUDE application. The main advantages of this approach are that it simplifies the mini-app logic, it makes the results easier to reproduce, and it allows for a built-in validation procedure by comparing mini-app output against reference output from the full application. Thus, the mini-app simply reads in a protein and a ligand, computes the bonding energies over a user-defined number of poses, and compares them against a reference set. To enable custom-length benchmarks, the mini-app can run several iterations of the same ligand–protein combination instead of requiring a new ligand each time. The result is a benchmark consisting of a few hundred lines of code for each implementation, which is easy to understand, feasible to profile and analyse, has built-in validation, requires no external libraries, and with a performance profile that maintains the same important characteristics of the full application.

3.2   Performance Analysis

We analysed the performance of our mini-app on a range of modern HPC platforms; Table 1 shows the systems used and their specifications. Where several compilers could be used for the same programming model, we tested all the options and picked the best-performing one in each case. We used aggressive compiler optimisation flags to the level of `-march=native -Ofast`. Table 2 lists the compilers used, the parallel programming frameworks supported by each, and any platform targetting restrictions they have.

We collected performance data using industry-standard tools. On CPU platforms, we accessed hardware counters through the built-in Linux `perf` tool, and collected application-level profiles with Cray Perftools; on GPUs, we used the NVIDIA CUDA profiler and the OpenCL Intercept Layer. We obtained peak memory bandwidth figures using BabelStream [24] and the University of Bristol's HPC Group's cache-bandwidth measurement tool [25].

We used two input decks to benchmark the application: a small input set, consisting of 26 ligands, and a large set, with 2672 ligands. The former takes around 0.5 s to run on a contemporary dual-socket-CPU HPC system, while the latter takes around 1.5 min. In both cases, we ran 8 iterations of the algorithm and we computed 2^{16} poses per iteration. We utilised all the available cores on

Table 2. Compilers used and their programming model and target platform support.

Compiler	CPUs	GPUs		Frameworks
AOCC 2.3	X			m k s
AOMP 11.0		M		m
Arm Compiler 21.0	R			m k s
ComputeCpp 2.1.1	X	I		m k s
Cray Compiler 10.0	R X	N	a[1]	m k s
Fujitsu Compiler 4.3	R			m k s
GCC 10.3	R X	M N	a	l m k s
Intel ICX 2019	X			m k[2] s
Intel DPC++ 2021.1	X	N		m k s
LLVM 11.0	R X	N		m k s
NVCC 10.2		N	c	
PGI 19.10		N	a	

CPUs: **ARM**, **X**86; GPUs: **AMD**, **NVIDIA**, **INTEL**
Frameworks: **c**uda, opena**c**c, open**c**l, open**m**p, **k**okkos, **s**ycl

[1] Version 9.0 only; [2] With the experimental INTEL_GEN backend.

each platform, using a single thread per core on all the CPU platforms; where available, using more than a single thread per core did not improve performance. A warm-up iteration was always run before the timers were started.

There was very little run time variability in miniBUDE. Even on the small input set, when individual iterations take less than 100 ms, variance was only fractions of a percent. This was true for both CPU and GPU implementations, as long as care is taken to bind threads correctly, especially when two interacting systems are present, e.g. OpenMP's OMP_PROC_BIND and Cray's aprun. There was one exception to this observation, which we addressed in Sect. 5.

4   Results and Performance Analysis

4.1   CPUs

OpenMP. The OpenMP implementation was written in plain C, without any higher-level framework, and was optimised for CPU platforms. We expected thisversion to incur the least overhead and thus perform fastest on the CPU. As we will see in this section, OpenMP did offer the best performance on CPUs in most cases, but higher-level implementations were sometimes able to match it.

Parallelism is exposed through OpenMP at two levels: poses are distributed between threads, and the calculations for each pose take advantage of each thread's SIMD lanes. Thread-level parallelism is achieved by dividing the poses into groups and then distributing the groups over threads; this creates an execution model similar to OpenCL workgroups, where each thread iterates over its assigned poses. The size of the group of poses is specified as a compile-time parameter.

We found that the group size had significant impact on the performance of the OpenMP implementation of miniBUDE. On each platform, this parameter should be at least as large as the native vector length, such that all the SIMD lanes are utilised for computation, but we found that most platforms achieved the best performance at group sizes several times larger than the native vector length. This happened because compilers were able to fully unroll the inner thread loops. As such, the group size is not only a vectorisation factor, but also an unroll factor, and higher values allowed platforms to fully exploit their out-of-order resources by interleaving several (unrolled) loop iterations. Furthermore, a small part of the arithmetic can be factored out and computed only once per work group, resulting in additional computation time savings. Figure 1 shows the impact of the group size parameter on performance for each platform.

The other defining factor for the performance of the OpenMP implementation is vectorisation. In order to maintain portability, no architecture-specific intrinsics are used; we rely on compiler auto-vectorisation. The code is structured such that vectorisation is required at the innermost level, which allowed all compilers tested to vectorise the main computation. The Cray and Intel compilers successfully vectorised *all* the loops in the code, while GCC and the Arm compiler did not understand the structure of one `do-while` loop and so did not vectorise it. This last loop, however, is not critical for performance.

The compilers further differed in their instruction choice and scheduling. On the Intel platforms, only the Cray compiler generated 512-bit vector code by default. Because this code is compute-heavy, long vectors greatly benefit performance, and forcing the Intel and GNU compilers to generate 512-bit operations—instead of their 256-bit default—significantly reduced the run time. In addition, the Intel and Cray compilers automatically interleaved the loop bodies, thus overlapping arithmetic and memory operations from different iterations.

On the other hand, GCC only unrolled the loops, without interleaving, and so instructions for each iteration were scheduled sequentially. This lowered the achieved performance on the platforms with fewer out-of-order resources, such as the A64FX, which performed slower than a ThunderX2, even though the former has 4× the vector width of the latter. The Fujitsu compiler, which has a good cost model of the A64FX and performs aggressive software pipelining and division optimisation, generates the fastest code in this case. Figure 2 shows the performance of the OpenMP implementation on the CPU platforms across the compilers tested.

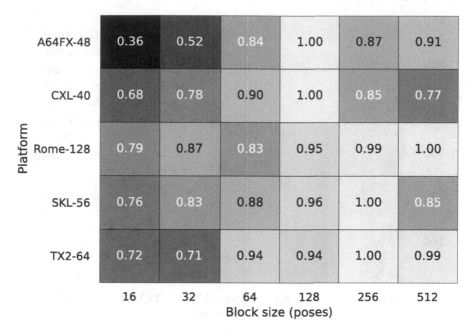

Fig. 1. Performance of the OpenMP implementation at different group sizes, normalised to the best result on each platform. Platforms are labelled using the abbreviations in Table 1 and the number of cores. Higher numbers, shown here in brighter colours, correspond to higher performance.

Figure 3 shows a roofline chart of the Cascade Lake platform. The OpenMP implementation of miniBUDE has an operational intensity of 0.3 and achieved a performance of 2301 GFLOP/s, which represents 56.2% of the platform's peak. The application sits directly below the arithmetic roof and above the memory bandwidth bound, confirming the code is compute-bound. For the purposes of the roofline model, FLOPs and memory traffic (assuming caching as per the cache-aware roofline model) were manually counted in the application's source code and corroborated using hardware counters.

Kokkos. The Kokkos implementation is a direct port of the OpenMP version, with parallelism expressed via the idiomatic `Kokkos::parallel_for` function. We retained the group size parameter to investigate the effects of unrolling, and we found that it had the same effect as in the case of OpenMP, and the same values were optimal on each platform. Like the OpenMP version, Kokkos does not offer built-in types for vectors and functions to use with them. From a productivity standpoint, it may be preferable for the framework and runtime to provide optimised versions of common math types and functions, so that compilers can better optimise code with the correct constraints. This is especially important for parallel frameworks that can target different backends—as Kokkos

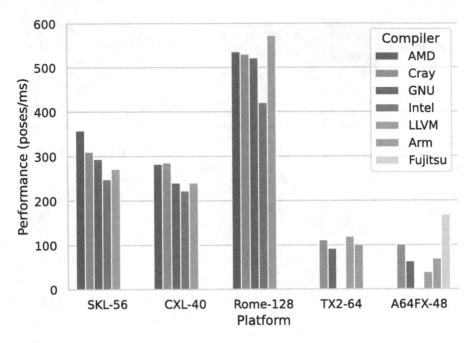

Fig. 2. Performance of the OpenMP implementation across systems and compilers. Higher numbers represent faster execution.

does—where each platform can have its own unique requirements, e. g. alignment on specific boundaries.

Kokkos was able to provide complete platform support in our study by virtue of being able to utilise many different programming frameworks as backends. Because a C++ compiler is the only requirement to build a Kokkos application, and because Kokkos itself is built as part of the same process, we can compare the relative performance on the platforms studied when using different compilers. Figure 4 shows a performance comparison on each CPU platform, where Kokkos uses the OpenMP backend, normalised to the fastest result. The results shows a strong correlation compared to the OpenMP implementation results described in Sect. 4.1, which shows Kokkos is using OpenMP efficiently on all the architectures.

SYCL. The SYCL implementation was written in idiomatic SYCL 1.2.1. The kernel is a direct port of the OpenCL version, utilising workgroup-based parallelism (`sycl::nd_range`) with few changes required. We retained the existing GPU-friendly optimisations from the OpenCL kernel where data is first copied to local memory via OpenCL's `async_work_group_copy`. Due to SYCL's roots in OpenCL, the APIs used for implementing these operations are identical both in name and semantics. We were even able to retain the use of 3d vector types which corresponds to the `cl_vec3` in OpenCL.

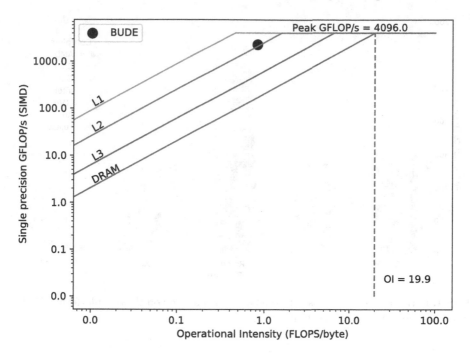

Fig. 3. Cache-aware roofline for the Cascade Lake platform showing the achieved performance for miniBUDE.

For comparison, we also implemented a separate kernel that is closer to the OpenMP implementation, where parallelism is achieved with flat `parallel_for` calls based on `sycl::range`. Although in theory plain `range` may be easier to map onto the hardware than `nd_range`, we found the performance difference between the two implementations to be negligible (below 2%).

Figure 5 shows the performance of all SYCL implementations on the platforms tested where at least two implementations were supported. On each platform, performance is normalised to the fastest implementation. For hipSYCL on the x86-based platforms, we tried all the compilers available and picked the one that produced the fastest binary, which was Cray on both Cascade Lake and Rome. The Skylake platform is missing from these results because an incorrect interaction between the Intel OpenCL driver installed on the system and the Cray `aprun` launcher resulted in all threads being pinned to a single core, effectively invalidating the results obtained with the two implementations that reply on OpenCL, OneAPI and ComputeCpp. On the V100 and the Radeon VII, hipSYCL is the only usable SYCL implementation.

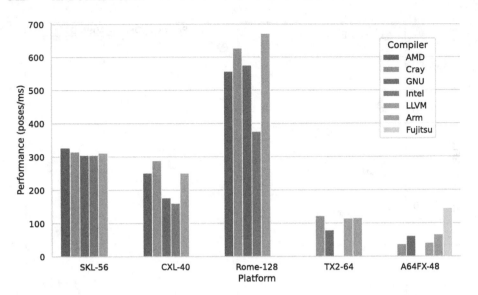

Fig. 4. Performance of Kokkos with the OpenMP backend on the test platforms. Higher numbers represent faster execution.

4.2 GPUs

Low-Level: OpenCL and CUDA. The OpenCL implementation is a close representation of the main kernel in the full-scale application, with the modifications presented in Sect. 3.1; the CUDA implementation is a direct port of the OpenCL version. The two versions performed similarly on the NVIDIA V100 GPU: the CUDA implementation was 18% faster than the OpenCL code, on both the small and the large input decks. The performance difference was evenly spread across the execution of the program: all the kernels were slightly slower when using OpenCL. Memory transfers are not timed for the purposes of the benchmark, and they take negligible time (<1% of the total run time). All of the benchmarks were run on CUDA Toolkit 10.2 running on NVIDIA driver version 440.64, so the difference likely came from more optimisation on the CUDA side of the NVIDIA library.

Both versions also ran on the AMD Radeon VII, converting the CUDA version through HIP, but OpenCL was 1.6× faster on this platform. Since the kernel code for both implementations was very similar, we attributed the performance difference to inefficiencies in AMD's HIP compiler. CUDA and HIP cannot be used on the Intel GPU.

Directives-Based: OpenMP Offload and OpenACC. The directive-based GPU implementations run the same kernel code in the OpenCL implementation, but expressed in the same C file as the host application and without any of the explicit OpenCL platform set-up and clean-up code. This is a significant advantage for productivity: given host code, only three `pragma` directives are

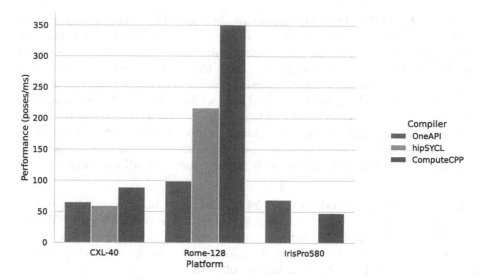

Fig. 5. Relative performance of SYCL implementations, on the platforms where more than one was available. Higher numbers represent faster execution.

used to transfer the data to the GPU and generate GPU kernel code. The main difference from the OpenCL version is that the global and local sizes aren't set by the programmer, but are controlled by the runtime. To control the amount of computation per workgroup, the directives-based implementations include a macro to control loop unrolling, similarly to the CPU OpenMP implementation.

The implementations achieved virtually identical performance on the V100. This was expected, because the same CUDA-based backend is used to generate code for both frameworks. Compiler support, however, differs between the two: the OpenMP code can use the latest versions of the Cray and GNU compilers, but the OpenACC version could only be compiled with an older version of the Cray compiler (9.0). The GNU and PGI compilers produced non-working code for OpenACC, and newer versions of CCE have dropped support for it.

On the V100, the directives-based approach showed about 0.4× the performance of the optimised CUDA code. This is the combined result of inefficiencies we identified in two places: 1) high register usage in the kernels generated by the compiler limits the maximum achievable GPU occupancy; 2) lower performance of library functions. This difference is higher than what has been observed in previous studies [4], and is likely exacerbated by the heavily compute-bound nature of miniBUDE.

On the Radeon, OpenACC can be compiled with GNU, but the resulting code was two orders of magnitude slower than OpenMP, which in turn only reached 0.3× the performance of the fastest model, OpenCL. The low-level nature of OpenCL allowed the code to map very well onto the target hardware, a performance which the GNU offload maths libraries could not match.

On the Intel GPU, OpenMP `target` reached only $0.2 - 0.3\times$ the performance of the fastest model, which in this case was SYCL. Although SYCL uses the same drivers as OpenCL on this platform, in this case the OneAPI compiler was better able to extract performance from the hardware when starting from higher-level, more expressive programming model. The OpenCL implementation was developed with HPC GPUs in mind, and while with code changes specific to the Intel GPU architecture it should be possible to reach the same performance with a low-level OpenCL implementation, this result highlights the productivity benefit of the higher-level programming model when targetting several platforms simultaneously, as long as the model is well-supported on all the targets.

High-Level: Kokkos and SYCL. Kokkos and SYCL both run on all the GPUs studied, but only one implementation, hipSYCL, runs on AMD and NVIDIA. The code run on the GPU platforms was unchanged from the version run on CPUs, not even to define different parallelism, as was the case when moving from CPU OpenMP to OpenMP `target` offload.

Figure 6 shows the results on the GPU platforms for all programming models studied. The three GPUs each target different segments: the V100 is a top-end HPC GPU, the Radeon VII is a high-end consumer GPU, and the Iris Pro is a mobile chip designed for a very constrained power and transistor budget. A direct performance comparison between such different platforms is not useful; instead, we present programming model performance normalised to the fastest result on each platform. In absolute figures, the best result on the V100 (CUDA) was twice as fast than the best on the Radeon VII (OpenCL) and $14\times$ faster than the best Iris Pro 580 result (OneAPI SYCL).

5   Towards Portable High-Performance Code

Section 4 has analysed the performance of the miniBUDE implementations on the platforms studied, but the implications of these results are further-reaching. Figure 7 aggregates the performance results over all the platforms and programming models and highlights that no programming model can currently achieve optimal performance on *all* platforms.

This effect is more pronounced on GPUs: each of the three platforms studied achieved the highest performance using a *different* programming model, and they relied on parameter tuning to do so. This immediately imposes a penalty when moving to a new platform, at which point at the very least tuning needs to be redone. In the worse case, low-level frameworks can trap users into code so specific to one platform that a major rewrite is needed when changing targets. However, OpenCL was the fastest model on the Radeon VII and a close second on the other two GPUs studied, suggesting that is may still be the best choice for good performance portability.

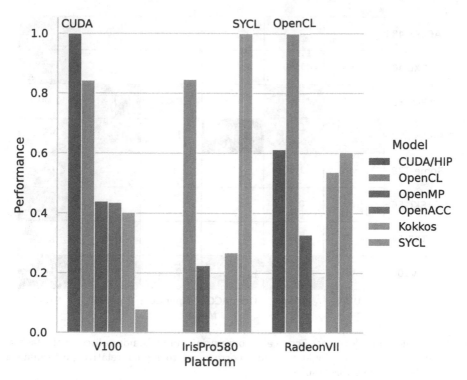

Fig. 6. Performance of the GPU implementations, normalized to the fastest result on each platform. The fastest model on each platform is labelled explicitly.

Higher-level programming models avoid this issue of over-specialisation of the code, instead relying on being able to translate the high-level code to efficient machine code as part of the framework. Kokkos is a good example of this: on the CPU platforms it achieves performance close to that of OpenMP, and both frameworks require similarly small amounts of framework-specific code, which consists mostly of loop annotations. The same Kokkos code is able to run on both CPUs and GPUs, and on the platforms studied it again achieved performance similar to that of OpenMP, but *without any source changes*; with OpenMP, a *different* version of the code was written for GPUs. Kokkos was the only framework that was able to support all CPU and GPU platforms in one package.

The SYCL landscape is rapidly evolving, and indeed the new SYCL 2020 standard—which is already being adopted by the three main implementations— brings much-needed productivity improvements such as built-in reduction support and alignment with the newer C++17 standard [26]. However, at the time of writing there are still rough edges to the current SYCL compilers, mainly around platform support fragmentation. First, support for non-GPU or non-x86 platforms is experimental, or even missing from some implementations. Even for GPUs, there is no single implementation that works across all the hardware from the major vendors.

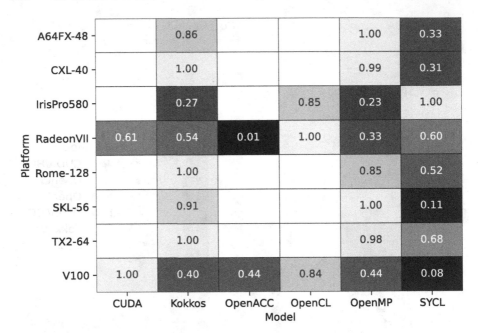

Fig. 7. Achieved performance across all programming models, normalised to the fastest result on each platform. Lighter colours correspond to higher relative performance; blank cells are impossible results.

The open-source hipSYCL implementation is the most portable of the set, being able to run on CPUs, as well as on NVIDIA and AMD GPUs. Both ComputeCpp and OneAPI provide experimental NVIDIA GPU support, but there are still blocking issues such as missing built-in function implementations, which prevent miniBUDE from compiling. Finally, running SYCL on Intel GPUs requires Intel's OpenCL-based ComputeRuntime, but only ComputeCpp and OneAPI support this mode of operation.

The situation on CPUs is similarly complicated. For x86-based platforms, both ComputeCpp and OneAPI run on top of the Intel OpenCL runtime, similar to the situation on Intel GPUs. The OpenCL runtime achieves parallelism via Intel's OneAPI Threading Building Blocks (OneTBB), which provides an optimised abstraction for managing logical threads. Such runtime approaches limit the extent of SYCL implementations to what the underlying runtime supports, from platform coverage to features it can provide; this currently prevents the use of ComputeCpp or OneAPI on Arm-based platforms.

On the other hand, hipSYCL translates SYCL abstractions to OpenMP code, which can then take advantage of existing compiler optimisations natively. This approach results in wide platform support for hipSYCL, but it also means, in principle, that parallelism abstractions are mapped to straightforward OpenMP equivalents. In practice, we found that performance was lower with hipSYCL compared to Kokkos or plain OpenMP, and code changes such as using different parallelism abstractions made little difference for miniBUDE. On platforms not explicitly supported by hipSYCL, as was the case of the A64FX at the time of writing, the additional layer of abstraction also prevented optimal code from being generated, despite having used the correct C++ compiler target flag.

Portability between CPUs and GPUs remains a concern, as SYCL has inherited the same set of problems seen when running OpenCL on the CPU: it is problematic to map workgroup-based parallelism onto a CPU intuitively and efficiently, and it suffers from unexpected setup costs compared to the OpenMP implementation. To work around potentially inefficient mapping, we implemented a compile-time tuning parameter to adjust the amount of work performed by each workgroup, though we found no common setting that provided the best performance on all platforms. On platforms that use Intel's OpenCL runtime, i. e. ComputeCpp and OneAPI, we found the kernel runtime to have large variations, and no functionality was provided to address or mitigate this. In particular, investigations revealed that initialisation of the SYCL context—the queue—took upwards of 800 ms in certain cases, even for a simple benchmark that itself ran in half that time.

We also discovered that when running several iterations of a benchmark back-to-back, the first run was usually up to 2× slower than subsequent runs. It was essential to implement a "warm-up" run, which is completely discarded, before starting the timer on the benchmark. Once the warm-up run was completed, the remaining iterations showed consistent run times, as with the other programming models. Both ComputeCpp and OneAPI compile SYCL kernels ahead-of-time, and neither give any indication why initialisation imposes such a large overhead; it is most likely an interaction with the underlying driver. Implementations that do not use the Intel OpenCL runtime, e. g. hipSYCL, did not incur this performance penalty.

6   Future Work

This study opens the path to additional work on the full-scale BUDE application. Instead of maintaining separate implementations in OpenCL for GPUs and OpenMP for CPUs, the code could incorporate a framework like SYCL or Kokkos to reduce divergence. Of course, embracing a new programming model for a scientific application is bound to encounter additional challenges, but in solving those the boundary of performance portability will be pushed further. A higher-level language undoubtedly benefits the ease of maintaining an application, but the higher the price that needs to be paid in terms of performance, the less eager developers are be to adopt it. A targeted investigation using the full application, one with more focus on productivity and software development practices, could reveal if this trade-off would be beneficial for BUDE.

In addition, Kokkos is constantly expanding its support for existing programming models as parallelism backends, thus further increasing its reach on platforms: a SYCL backend is being added, while the existing—but experimental—OpenMP target and HIP backends begin to mature. A future study could revisit the performance of hand-tuned, low-level kernels versus implementations using future Kokkos versions.

7   Reproducibility

The source code for all the miniBUDE implementations used in this study, as well as build and run instructions and benchmark input cases, can be found online[1]. A set of scripts is also provided to build and run the benchmark on the platforms used in this study[2].

8   Conclusion

In this paper we have explored performance portability through the lens of a simple, yet realistic, compute-bound benchmark. We have implemented the benchmark in several programming models, including low- and high-level, both well-established and up-and-coming. We have shown that modern programming models can perform on-par with traditional ones, and with constant work done to improve them, their platform support continues to grow.

On the other hand, we have seen that true performance portability is still out of reach: no single version of the code achieved the best performance—or a high fraction of it—on all the platforms studied. Even for a small kernel, platform-specific optimisations and empirical tuning of parameters accounted for more than 30% of the performance and that was enough to differentiate the best-performing implementation from the rest. On GPUs, low-level APIs continue to provide the highest possible performance, and on CPUs, the still-immature driver and implementation ecosystem around SYCL presents an obstacle to the wide adoption of this programming model as a true cross-platform, cross-architecture framework. Of the frameworks studied, Kokkos emerged as a reliable choice, with its lightweight, optimised implementation, and OpenMP remains in a strong position due to it widespread support, although different code paths are still needed for optimal CPU and GPU implementations at the time of writing.

Acknowledgement. The authors would like to thank Si Hammond at Sandia National Laboratories for providing short-notice results for the A64FX platform. Thank you to James Price and Matt Martineau for their original contributions towards optimised OpenMP, OpenCL, and CUDA implementations of the BUDE kernel. This study would not have been possible without previous work by the developers of the Bristol University Docking Engine: Richard Sessions, Deborah Shoemark, and Amaurys Avila Ibarra.

This work used the Isambard UK National Tier-2 HPC Service (https://gw4.ac.uk/isambard/) operated by GW4 and the UK Met Office, and funded by EPSRC (EP/T022078/1). Access to the Cray XC50 supercomputer Swan was kindly provided

---

[1] https://github.com/UoB-HPC/miniBUDE.
[2] https://github.com/UoB-HPC/performance-portability/tree/2021-benchmarking/benchmarking/2021/bude.

through the Cray Marketing Partner Network. Work in this study was carried out using the HPC Zoo, a research cluster run by the University of Bristol HPC Group (https://uob-hpc.github.io/zoo/).

References

1. Laguna, I., et al.: A large-scale study of MPI usage in open-source HPC applications. In: Proceedings of the International Conference for High Performance Computing, Networking, Storage and Analysis, SC 2019. Association for Computing Machinery, Denver (2019). https://doi.org/10.1145/3295500.3356176. ISBN 9781450362290
2. Bernholdt, D.E., et al.: A survey of MPI usage in the US exascale computing project. Concurr. Comput. Pract. Exp. **32**(3), e4851 (2020)
3. Deakin, T., et al.: Performance portability across diverse computer architectures. In: 2019 IEEE/ACM International Workshop on Performance, Portability and Productivity in HPC (P3HPC). IEEE, Denver, pp. 1–13, November 2019. https://doi.org/10.1109/P3HPC49587.2019.00006. ISBN 978-1-72816-003-0
4. Deakin, T., et al.: Tracking performance portability on the yellow brick road to exascale. In: 2020 IEEE/ACM International Workshop on Performance, Portability and Productivity in HPC (P3HPC), Atlanta, GA, USA, p. 13. In press
5. McIntosh-Smith, S., et al.: High performance in silico virtual drug screening on many-core processors. Int. J. High Perf. Comput. Appl. **29**(2), 119–134 (2015). https://doi.org/10.1177/1094342014528252
6. Cherfils, J., Janin, J.: Protein docking algorithms: simulating molecular recognition. Current Opinion Struct. Biol. **3**(2), 265–269 (1993). https://doi.org/10.1016/S0959-440X(05)80162-9. ISSN 0959-440X
7. Fuchs, A., Wentzla, D.: The accelerator wall: limits of chip specialization. In: 2019 IEEE International Symposium on High Performance Computer Architecture (HPCA), pp. 1–14 (2019). https://doi.org/10.1109/HPCA.2019.00023
8. Price, J., McIntosh-Smith, S.: Exploiting auto-tuning to analyze and improve performance portability on many-core architectures. In: Kunkel, J.M., Yokota, R., Taufer, M., Shalf, J. (eds.) ISC High Performance 2017. LNCS, vol. 10524, pp. 538–556. Springer, Cham (2017). https://doi.org/10.1007/978-3-319-67630-2_38
9. Katz, M.P., et al.: Preparing nuclear astrophysics for exascale. In: The International Conference for High Performance Computing, Networking, Storage, and Analysis (SC 2020), Atlanta, GA, USA, November 2020, in press
10. Siegel, A.: ECP: lessons learned in porting complex applications to accelerator-based systems. Presentation, Atlanta, GA, USA (2020)
11. Heroux, M.A., et al.: ECP software technology capability assessment report-public. Technical report, NNSA, p. 200 (2020)
12. Lambert, J., et al.: CCAMP: an integrated translation and optimization framework for OpenACC and OpenMP. In: The International Conference for High Performance Computing, Networking, Storage, and Analysis (SC 2020), Atlanta, GA, USA, November 2020, in press
13. Mills, R.T., et al.: Toward performance-portable PETSc for GPU-based exascale systems. In: arXiv preprint arXiv:2011.00715 (2020)
14. Carter Edwards, H., Trott, C.R.: Kokkos: enabling performance portability across manycore architectures. In: Extreme Scaling Workshop (XSW 2013). IEEE, pp. 18–24 (2013)

15. Hammond, J.R., Kinsner, M., Brodman, J.: A comparative analysis of Kokkos and SYCL as heterogeneous, parallel programming models for C++ applications. In: Proceedings of the International Workshop on OpenCL, IWOCL 2019. Association for Computing Machinery, Boston (2019). https://doi.org/10.1145/3318170.3318193. ISBN 9781450362306

16. Intel: Intel® oneAPI: A Unied X-Architecture Programming Model (2020). https://software.intel.com/content/www/us/en/develop/tools/oneapi.html. Accessed 16 Dec 2020

17. Codeplay Software: ComputeCPP. https://developer.codeplay.com/products/computecpp/ce/home. Accessed 16 Dec 2020

18. Alpay, A., Heuveline, V.: SYCL beyond OpenCL: the architecture, current state and future direction of HipSYCL. In: Proceedings of the International Workshop on OpenCL. Association for Computing Machinery, Munich (2020). https://doi.org/10.1145/3388333.3388658. ISBN 9781450375313

19. Harrell, S.L., et al.: Effective performance portability. In: 2018 IEEE/ACM International Workshop on Performance, Portability and Productivity in HPC (P3HPC), pp. 24–36 (2018). https://doi.org/10.1109/P3HPC.2018.00006

20. Pennycook, S.J., Sewall, J.D., Lee, V.W.: Implications of a metric for performance portability. Future Gener. Comput. Syst. **92**, 947–958 (2019). https://doi.org/10.1016/j.future.2017.08.007. ISSN 0167–739X

21. Sewall, J., et al.: Interpreting and visualizing performance portability metrics. In: 2020 IEEE/ACM International Workshop on Performance, Portability and Productivity in HPC (P3HPC), Atlanta, GA, USA (2020, in Press)

22. Deakin, T., McIntosh-Smith, S.: Evaluating the performance of HPCStyle SYCL applications. In: Proceedings of the International Workshop on OpenCL, IWOCL 2020. Association for Computing Machinery, Munich (2020). https://doi.org/10.1145/3388333.3388643. ISBN 9781450375313

23. Lin, W.-C., Deakin, T., McIntosh-Smith, S.: On measuring the maturity of SYCL implementations by tracking historical performance improvements. In: Proceedings of the International Workshop on OpenCL, IWOCL 2020. Association for Computing Machinery (2021, in Press)

24. Deakin, T., Price, J., Martineau, M., McIntosh-Smith, S.: GPU-STREAM v2.0: benchmarking the achievable memory bandwidth of many-core processors across diverse parallel programming models. In: Taufer, M., Mohr, B., Kunkel, J.M. (eds.) ISC High Performance 2016. LNCS, vol. 9945, pp. 489–507. Springer, Cham (2016). https://doi.org/10.1007/978-3-319-46079-6_34

25. Martineau, M., Atkinson, P., McIntosh-Smith, S.: Benchmarking the NVIDIA V100 GPU and tensor cores. In: Mencagli, G., et al. (eds.) Euro-Par 2018. LNCS, vol. 11339, pp. 444–455. Springer, Cham (2019). https://doi.org/10.1007/978-3-030-10549-5_35

26. Reyes, R., et al.: SYCL 2020: more than meets the eye. In: Proceedings of the International Workshop on OpenCL, IWOCL 2020. Association for Computing Machinery, Munich (2020). https://doi.org/10.1145/3388333.3388649. ISBN 9781450375313

Analytic Modeling of Idle Waves in Parallel Programs: Communication, Cluster Topology, and Noise Impact

Ayesha Afzal[1,2]([envelope]), Georg Hager[1], and Gerhard Wellein[1,2]

[1] Erlangen National High Performance Computing Center, 91058 Erlangen, Germany
{ayesha.afzal,georg.hager,gerhard.wellein}@fau.de
[2] Department of Computer Science, University of Erlangen-Nürnberg,
91058 Erlangen, Germany

Abstract. Most distributed-memory bulk-synchronous parallel programs in HPC assume that compute resources are available continuously and homogeneously across the allocated set of compute nodes. However, long one-off delays on individual processes can cause global disturbances, so-called idle waves, by rippling through the system. This process is mainly governed by the communication topology of the underlying parallel code. This paper makes significant contributions to the understanding of idle wave dynamics. We study the propagation mechanisms of idle waves across the processes of MPI-parallel programs. We present a validated analytic model for their propagation velocity with respect to communication parameters and topology, with a special emphasis on sparse communication patterns. We study the interaction of idle waves with MPI collectives and show that, depending on the implementation, a collective may be permeable to the wave. Finally we analyze two mechanisms of idle wave decay: topological decay, which is rooted in differences in communication characteristics among parts of the system, and noise-induced decay, which is caused by system or application noise. We show that noise-induced decay is largely independent of noise characteristics but depends only on the overall noise power. An analytic expression for idle wave decay rate with respect to noise power is derived. For model validation we use microbenchmarks and stencil algorithms on three different supercomputing platforms.

1 Introduction

1.1 Idle Waves in Barrier-Free Bulk-Synchronous Parallel Programs

Parallel programs with alternating computation and communication phases and without explicit synchronization are ubiquitous in high performance computing. In theory, when running on a clean, undisturbed system and lacking any load imbalance or other irregularities, such applications should exhibit a regular lockstep pattern. In practice, however, a variety of perturbations prevent this: system and network noise, application imbalance, and delays caused by one-off events such as administrative jobs, message re-transmits, I/O, etc. Among all

© Springer Nature Switzerland AG 2021
B. L. Chamberlain et al. (Eds.): ISC High Performance 2021, LNCS 12728, pp. 351–371, 2021.
https://doi.org/10.1007/978-3-030-78713-4_19

of these, long one-off events have the most immediate impact on the regular compute-communicate pattern. They cause periods of idleness in the process where they originated, but via inter-process dependencies they "ripple" through the system and can thus impact all other processes as well. In massively parallel programs, delays can occur anytime, impeding the performance of the application. On the other hand, idle waves may also initiate desynchronization among processes, which is not necessarily disadvantageous since it can lead to automatic communication overlap [3].

The speed and overall characteristics of idle wave propagation have been the subject of some scrutiny [3,4,12], but a thorough analytical understanding of their dynamics with respect to the communication topology of the underlying parallel code is still lacking. There is also no investigation so far of the interaction of idle waves with global operations such as reductions, and how the system's hardware topology and the particular characteristics of system noise impact the decay of idle waves. These topics will be covered by the present work. We restrict ourselves to *process-scalable* scenarios, i.e., where multiple MPI processes running on a hardware contention domain (such as a memory interface or a shared out-level cache) do not feel scalability loss due to hardware bottlenecks.

1.2 Related Work

Noise has been studied for almost two decades. A large part of the work focuses on sources of noise outside of the control of the application and explores the influence of noise on collective operations [6,9,13]. However, it lacks coverage of pair-wise communication and the interaction of noise with idle periods, which are common in distributed-memory parallel codes. Gamell et al. [7] noted the emergence of idle periods in the context of failure recovery and failure masking of stencil codes. Markidis et al. [12] used a LogGOPS simulator [9] to study idle waves and postulated a linear wave equation to describe wave propagation.

Afzal et al. [1–4] were the first to investigate the dynamics of idle waves, (de)synchronization processes, and computational wavefront formation in parallel programs with core-bound and memory-bound code, showing that nonlinear processes dominate there. Our work builds on theirs to significantly extend it for analytic modeling with further influence factors, such as communication topology, communication concurrency, system topology and noise structure.

Significant prior work exists on the characterization of noise and the influence of noise characteristics on performance of systems. Ferreira et al. [6] noted that HPC applications with collectives can often absorb substantial amounts of high-frequency noise, but tend to be affected by low-frequency noise. Agarwal et al. [5] found noise properties to matter for the scalability of collectives, comparing different distributions (exponential, heavy tail, Bernoulli). Hoefler et al. [10] used their LogGOPS-based simulator and studied both point-to-point (P2P) and collective operations. They found that application scalability is mostly determined by the noise pattern and not the noise intensity. In the context of idle wave propagation and decay, the present work finds that the noise intensity is the main influence factor rather that its detailed statistics.

Table 1. Key hardware and software specifications of systems.

	Systems	Emmy[a]	SuperMUC-NG	Hawk
Micro-architecture	Processor	Intel Xeon Ivy Bridge EP	Intel Xeon Skylake SP	AMD EPYC Rome
	Processor Model	E5-2660 v2	Platinum 8174	7742
	Base clock speed	2.2 GHz	3.10 GHz (2.3 GHz used*)	2.25 GHz
	Physical cores per node	20	48	128
	Numa domains per node	2	2	8
	LLC size	25 MB	33 MB	256 MB = 16 × 16 MB / CCX (4C)
	Memory per node (type)	64 GB (DDR3)	96 GB (DDR4)	4 TB =16 × 256 GB (DDR4)
Network	Node interconnect	QDR InfiniBand	Omni-Path	HDR InfiniBand
	Interconnect topology	Fat-tree	Fat-tree	Enhanced 9D-Hypercube
	Raw bandwidth p. lnk n. dir	40 Gbits^{-1}	100 Gbits^{-1}	200 Gbits^{-1}
Software	Compiler	Intel C++ v2019.5.281	Intel C++ v2019.4.243	Intel C++ v2020.0.166
	Optimization flags	-O3 -xHost	-O3 -qopt-zmm-usage=high	-O3 -xHost
	SIMD	-xCORE-AVX2	-xCORE-AVX512	-mavx2
	Message passing library	Intel MPI v2019u5	Intel MPI v2019u4	Intel MPI v2019u6
	Operating system	CentOS Linux v7.7.1908	SUSE Linux ENT. Server 12 SP3	CentOS Linux 8.1.1911
Tool	ITAC	v2019u4	v2019	v2020

[a] https://anleitungen.rrze.fau.de/hpc/emmy-cluster.
*A power cap is applied on SuperMUC-NG, i.e., the CPUs run by default on a lower than maximum clock speed (2.3 GHz instead of 3.10 GHz).

1.3 Contribution

This work makes the following novel contributions:

- We analytically predict the propagation velocity of idle waves in scalable code with respect to (i) communication topology, i.e., the distance and number of neighbors in point-to-point communication, and (ii) communication concurrency, i.e., how many point-to-point communications are grouped and subject to completion via MPI_Waitall.
- The analytical model is validated with measurements on real systems and applied to microbenchmarks with synthetic communication topologies and a realistic scenario from the context of stencil codes with Cartesian domain decomposition.
- We show that not all MPI collective routines eliminate a traveling idle wave; some may even be almost permeable to it, depending on their implementation.
- We show that idle wave decay can also be initiated by the system topology via heterogeneities in point-to-point communication characteristics between MPI processes.
- We show analytically that the decay rate (and thus the survival time until running out) of an idle wave under the influence of noise is largely independent of the particular noise characteristics and depends only on the overall noise power. This prediction is validated with experiments.

Overview. This paper is organized as follows: Sect. 2 provides details about our experimental environment and methodology. In Sect. 3, we first introduce some important terms to categorize execution and communication in distributed-memory parallel programs and then develop and validate an analytical model of delay propagation. Section 4 covers the interaction of idle waves with collective primitives. An analysis of idle wave decay with respect to noise and system topology is conducted in Sect. 5. Finally, Sect. 6 concludes the paper and gives an outlook to future work.

2   Test Bed and Experimental Methods

The three clusters listed in Table 1 were used to conduct various experiments and validate our analytical models.

Process-core affinity was enforced using the I_MPI_PIN_PROCESSOR_LIST environment variable. We ignored the simultaneous multithreading (SMT) feature and used only physical cores. The clock frequency was always fixed to the base value of the respective CPUs (or to 2.3 GHZ in case of SuperMUC-NG because of the power capping mechanism). On Emmy, experiments with up to 120 nodes were conducted on a set of nodes connected to seven 36-port leaf switches in order to achieve homogeneous communication characteristics. A similar strategy was not possible on the other systems. Open-chain boundary conditions were employed unless specified otherwise. Communication delays for non-blocking calls were measured by the time spent in the MPI_Wait or MPI_Waitall function. We used Intel Trace Analyzer and Collector (ITAC)[1] for timeline visualization and the C++ high-resolution Chrono clock for timing measurements. For tuning of the Intel MPI collectives implementations, we used the Intel MPI *autotuner*[2]; the configuration space is defined by I_MPI_ADJUST_<opname>[3].

We run barrier-free bulk-synchronous MPI-parallel micro-benchmarks with configurable latency-bound communication and compute-bound workload. This results in process scalability, i.e., there is no contention on memory interfaces, shared caches, or network interfaces. The code loops over back-to-back divide instructions (vdivpd), which have low but constant throughput. The message size was set to 1024 B, which is well within the default eager limit of the MPI implementation. For more realistic workloads we chose a 3D Jacobi stencil and sparse matrix-vector multiplication (SpMV) with the High Performance Conjugate Gradient (HPCG)[4] matrix. Further characterization will be addressed in Sect. 3. One-off idle periods were generated by massively extending one computational phase via doing extra work on one arbitrary MPI process, usually rank 5. Since we use only MPI_COMM_WORLD communicator, so "rank" is a unique identifier for a process.

All experiments described in this paper were conducted on all three benchmark systems. However, we show the results for all of them only if there are relevant differences.

---

[1] https://software.intel.com/en-us/trace-analyzer.
[2] http://tiny.cc/intel-autotuning.
[3] http://tiny.cc/intel-i-mpi-adjust-family.
[4] https://www.hpcg-benchmark.org/.

3   Idle Wave Propagation Velocity for Scalable Code

In this section we first categorize the execution and communication characteristics of parallel applications. Later, we investigate how they influence the idle wave velocity and construct an analytic model for the latter.

3.1   Execution Characteristics

HPC workloads have a wide spectrum of requirements regarding code execution towards resources of the parallel computing platform. The most straightforward categorization is whether the workload is sensitive to certain resource bottlenecks, such as memory bandwidth. Since we restrict ourselves to scalable code here, we run the traditionally memory-bound algorithms such as stencil updates or SpMV with one MPI process per contention domain (typically a ccNUMA node). This is not a problem for the microbenchmarks since we deliberately choose an in-core workload there.

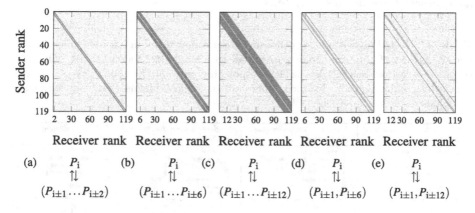

Fig. 1. Compact and non-compact communication topologies with bidirectional open chain characteristics. P_i sends (receives) data to (from) $P_{i\pm1}$ (a) to $P_{i\pm2}$ (b) to $P_{i\pm6}$ (c) to $P_{i\pm12}$, (d) and $P_{i\pm6}$ (e) and $P_{i\pm12}$.

3.2   Categorization of Communication Characteristics

Here we briefly describe the different communication characteristics under investigation. We start by assuming a "P2P-homogeneous" situation where all processes (except boundary processes in case of open boundary conditions) have the same communication partners and characteristics. We will later lift this restriction and cover more general patterns.

Communication Topology. Communication topology is a consequence of the physical problem underlying the numerical method and of the algorithm (discretization, geometry). It boils down to the question "which other processes does rank i communicate with?" and is characterized by a *topology matrix* (see Fig. 1 for examples of *compact* and *noncompact* topologies).

In a compact topology, each process communicates with a dense, continuous array of neighbors with distances $d = \pm 1, \pm 2, ..., \pm j$. The topology matrix comprises a dense band around the main diagonal. In a noncompact topology, each process communicates with processes that are not arranged as a continuous block, e.g., $d = \pm 1, \pm j$. In both variants, the topology matrix can be symmetric or asymmetric.

For example, sparse matrices emerging from numerical algorithms with high locality lead to compact communication structures, while stencil-like discretizations on Cartesian grids lead to noncompact structures with far-outlying sub-diagonals. Figures 1(a)–(c) depict symmetric cases with 4, 12, and 24 neighbors, respectively (2, 6 and 12 distinct processes per direction) for every process, while there are always four neighbors (two distinct processes per direction) for both noncompact cases in Figs. 1(d)–(e).

Table 2. Selected algorithms for communication concurrency in our MPI microbenchmarks. Arrows of the same color correspond to a single `MPI_Waitall` call. "One distance" means that one `MPI_Waitall` is responsible only for the send/recv pair of one particular communication distance, while "all distances" means that it encompasses all distances in one dimension.

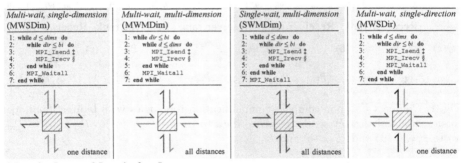

‡ P_i send to $P_{i+dir \times d}$;   § P_i receive from $P_{i-dir \times d}$

Communication Concurrency. When a process communicates with others, it is often a deliberate choice of the developer which communications are grouped together and later finished using `MPI_Waitall` ("split-waits"). However, since interprocess dependencies have an impact on idle wave propagation, such details are relevant. Of course, beyond user-defined communication concurrency, there could still be nonconcurrency "under the hood," depending on the internals of the MPI implementation.

Here we restrict ourselves to a manageable subset of options that nevertheless cover a substantial range of patterns. We assume that all P2P communication is nonblocking. Table 2 shows the four variants covered here in a 2D Cartesian setting according to the number of split-waits: *multi-wait, single-dimension* (MWSDim), *multi-wait, multi-dimension* (MWMDim), *single-wait, multi-dimension* (SWMDim), and *multi-wait, single-direction* (MWSDir). The iteration space of loops in Table 2 is defined as the outer (d) loop goes over the Cartesian dimensions (i.e., x and y here) and the inner (dir) loop goes over the two directions per dimension (i.e., positive and negative). For each direction (e.g., positive x), the communication is effectively a linear shift pattern; the pairing of send and receive operations per MPI_Waitall ensures that no deadlocks will occur. The third and fourth option are corner cases with minimum and maximum number of MPI_Waitalls.

More Complex Patterns. Beyond the simple patterns described above, we will also cover more general *P2P heterogeneous* communication scenarios, where subsets of processes have different communication properties, such as in stencil codes or sparse-matrix algorithms. Figure 4 shows an example with compact long-range and short-range communication, which could emerge from a sparse-matrix problem with "fat" and "skinny" regions of the matrix. Finally, we will discuss implementation alternatives of collective communication primitives.

3.3   Analytical Model of Idle Wave Propagation

The propagation speed of an idle wave is the speed, in ranks per second, with which it ripples through the system. Previous studies of idle wave mechanisms on silent systems [3,4] characterized the influence of execution time, communication time, communication characteristics (e.g., uni- vs. bidirectional communication patterns and eager vs. rendezvous protocols), and the number of active multi-threaded or single-threaded MPI processes on a contended or noncontended domain. However, the scope of that work was restricted to a fixed P2P communication pattern (fourth column in Table 2 – MWSDir). Here we extend the analysis to more general patterns, which show a much richer phenomenology. We restrict ourselves to open boundary conditions across the MPI processes. This is not a severe limitation since it only affects the survival time and not the propagation speed of the wave.

Corner Cases. Minimum. idle wave speed, v_{silent}^{min}, (and thus maximum survival time) is observed with simple direct next-neighbor communication ($d = 1$). If T_{exec} and T_{comm} are execution and communication times of one iteration of the bulk-synchronous program, then the idle wave speed is

$$v_{silent}^{min} = 1 \left[\frac{ranks}{iter} \right] \times \frac{1}{T_{exec} + T_{comm}} \left[\frac{iter}{s} \right]. \tag{1}$$

In this case, the wave survives until it runs into system boundaries [4], i.e., for at most as many time steps as there are MPI processes. Barrier-like, i.e., long-distance synchronizing communication leads to *maximum* wave speed, $v_{\text{silent}}^{\max}$, and the wave dying out quickly in a minimum of one time step. Thus, in this case,

$$v_{\text{silent}}^{\max} = \alpha \left[\frac{\text{ranks}}{\text{iter}} \right] \times \frac{1}{T_{\text{exec}} + T_{\text{comm}}} \left[\frac{\text{iter}}{\text{s}} \right], \tag{2}$$

where square brackets denote the dimensions of the quantities written to the left of them. For instance, "$\frac{\text{ranks}}{\text{iter}}$" means the number of processes traversed by iteration of the code, which is the dimension of alpha in Eq. 2. Also, α depends on the rank r_{inject} where the idle wave originated and the total number of MPI processes $\text{size}_{\text{comm}}$:

$$\alpha = \max \left(\text{size}_{\text{comm}} - r_{\text{inject}} - 1, r_{\text{inject}} - 1 \right). \tag{3}$$

Multi-neighbor Communication. Away from the extreme cases, we have to distinguish between compact and noncompact multi-neighbor communication patterns, but the basic mechanisms are the same. The propagation speed of the idle wave can be analytically modeled as

$$v_{\text{silent}} = \kappa \cdot v_{\text{silent}}^{\min} \left[\frac{\text{ranks}}{\text{s}} \right], \tag{4}$$

Where dimensionless κ is the distance in processes traveled by the wave in one time step and depends on communication concurrency and topology:

$$\kappa = \begin{cases} \displaystyle\sum_{k=1}^{j} k = \frac{j(j+1)}{2} & \text{if compact MWSDim/MWSDir/blocking} \\ \displaystyle\sum_{k=1,j} k = j + 1 & \text{if non-compact MWSDim/MWSDir/blocking} \\ j & \text{if MWMDim/SWMDim} \end{cases} \cdot \tag{5}$$

Here, j is the longest-distance communication partner of a process. Summation bounds are $1, 2, 3, \ldots, j$ in the first case and two terms only (1 and j) in the second case. Modifications to these expressions may apply for complex communication topologies; we will discuss them in the validation section.

3.4   Experimental Validation

In this section, we first validate the analytical model via measurements using synthetic benchmarks on a real system. Thereafter, we apply the model to a 3D a stencil code with Cartesian domain decomposition. Since stencil codes are commonly memory-bound, we run a single thread per ccNUMA domain only in order to maintain resource scalability. Since the phenomenology matches across all three clusters (Table 1), we show results only for the Emmy system.

Microbenchmarks. Figures 2 and 3 (top row) show traces of the propagation of injected one-off idle phases (extra work at rank 5, dark blue) and its dependency on communication concurrency and communication topology, using the variants shown in Table 2. In these experiments, we used an execution phase of $T_{\text{exec}} = 13\,\text{ms}$ (light blue) and a data volume of 1 KiB per message. The insets show close-ups of parts of the wave. In the second row, a quantitative timeline of the number of MPI processes executing MPI library code (i.e., waiting or communicating) is displayed. In these settings, the natural system noise is weak enough to not cause decay of the idle wave until it runs into the system boundary. The experimental values of κ can be inferred from the timescales on the x-axis of rank-time graphs or from the zoomed-in insets to ease the interpretation.

Compact Communication. In Fig. 2, the observed propagation speed of the idle waves is independent of the number of split-waits, as expected. Higher speeds are observed when (i) the overall communication distance goes up, i.e., with growing number of communication partners, and (ii) the number of dimensions spanned within each `MPI_Waitall` (communication concurrency). In Fig. 2(a), where $P_i \rightleftarrows (P_{i\pm1}, P_{i\pm2})$, higher speed results in (a1) with $\kappa = \sum_{k=1}^{2} k = 3$ due to the MWSDim concurrency pattern, while in (a2) we have $\kappa = j = 2$ for the other patterns. The data confirms the model in (4) and (5). In addition to zoom-in inserts, the κ values can also be inferred from the gradient of the idle time visible in the timelines, i.e., the higher speed in (a1) via the idle wave ending soon at 2.2 s compared to 2.4 s in (a2).

In Fig. 2(b) and (c), the number of communication partners per direction is increased to six and twelve, respectively, with expected consequences: In (b1) we

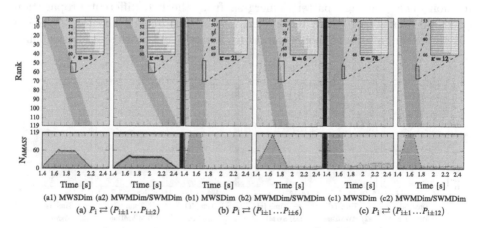

(a1) MWSDim (a2) MWMDim/SWMDim   (b1) MWSDim (b2) MWMDim/SWMDim   (c1) MWSDim (c2) MWMDim/SWMDim

(a) $P_i \rightleftarrows (P_{i\pm1}\ldots P_{i\pm2})$ (b) $P_i \rightleftarrows (P_{i\pm1}\ldots P_{i\pm6})$ (c) $P_i \rightleftarrows (P_{i\pm1}\ldots P_{i\pm12})$

Fig. 2. Top row: idle wave propagation for 60 iterations in a core-bound microbenchmark for an injected delay at rank 5 (see text for details) and compact communication patterns with different numbers of communication partners: (a) two, (b) six, and (c) twelve partners per direction. The quantitative N_{AMASS} timelines in the second row of panels show the fraction of MPI processes executing MPI library code (orange) versus the number of processes in user code (blue). (Color figure online)

have $\kappa = \sum_{k=1}^{6} k = 21$, and in (b2) $\kappa = j = 6$. In (c1), we get $\kappa = \sum_{k=1}^{12} k = 78$, confirming intuitively our prediction that survival time in the high-speed limit is equal to $T_{\text{exec}} + T_{\text{comm}}$. Finally, in (c2) we get $\kappa = j = 12$.

The second row in Fig. 2 shows that slower wave propagation causes a more even spread of waiting times and thus resource utilization across processes. A rising/constant/falling slope indicates an oncoming/traveling/leaving wave. Although our particular scenarios have been designed to show no resource bottlenecks, these utilization shapes will be significant in case of memory-bound execution or bandwidth-contended communication [3]. An exploration of these mechanisms is left for future work.

Noncompact Communication. Topology matrices with noncompact characteristics (Figs. 1(d)–(e)) entail a more complex phenomenology of idle wave propagation. The presence of "gaps" leads to multiple waves propagating at different speeds, with the added complication that each "hop" of a faster wave sparks local idle waves wherever it hits (see Fig. 3). These secondary waves propagate and annihilate each other eventually (more specifically, after $j/2$ hops), and what remains is the fast wave emerging from the longest-distance communication. The speed of this residual wave is faster with (i) a larger number of split-waits, (ii) a smaller number of communication dimensions spanned by each MPI_Waitall, and evidently (iii) a larger longest communication distance j. The interpretation of timelines provides a visual aid for verification, e.g., the idle wave ends sooner on the x-axis for the same number of split-waits in (a1) and (a2) compared to the larger numbers of split-waits in (a3).

With respect to communication concurrency, there is a fundamental difference between multiple split-waits and one wait-for-all in non-compact communication. The "zig-zag" pattern emerging from the two different propagation speeds prevails in case of SWMDim (one wait-for-all) but dies out for MWSDim and MWMDim after a couple of iterations. This decay is entirely a consequence

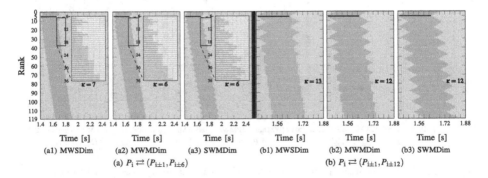

Fig. 3. Idle wave propagation in a core-bound microbenchmark for an injected delay at rank 5 (see text for details) and noncompact communication patterns with two communication partners per direction at different distances on Emmy: (a) $P_i \rightleftarrows (P_{i\pm1}, P_{i\pm6})$ for 60 iterations and (b) $P_i \rightleftarrows (P_{i\pm1}, P_{i\pm12})$ for 20 iterations. (Color figure online)

of the communication concurrency and has nothing to do with the other mechanisms of idle wave decay, such as noise and communication inhomogeneity (see Sect. 5). The propagation of the "envelope wave" is untouched by this effect.

This phenomenon is shown in Fig. 3 (a1, b1, a2, b2), where the zig-zag pattern dissolves eventually, and the residual wave exhibits (a1) $\kappa = \sum_{k=1,6} k = 7$, (a2) $\kappa = j = 6$, (b1) $\kappa = \sum_{k=1,6} k = 13$, and (b2) $\kappa = j = 12$. The number of time steps required for the zig-zag to even out depends on the propagation speed. In case of a single MPI_Waitall, however (a3, b3), the pattern prevails. The envelope travels with (a3) $\kappa = j = 6$ and (b3) $\kappa = j = 12$.

The results from these microbenchmarks show that our model is able to describe the basic phenomenology of idle wave propagation on a silent system in the parameter space under consideration. In the following we cover some more general patterns.

Heterogeneous Communication. From the basic propagation model and its validation on simple communication patterns we can now advance to more complex scenarios. In Fig. 4, we use a compact topology matrix that is "fatter" for the middle 40 processes, mimicking an heterogeneous situation that may, e.g., emerge with some sparse matrix problems (Fig. 4(a)). Since the idle wave speed emerges from local properties of the topology matrix, we expect a "refraction effect," where the wave travels faster within the fat region of the matrix. Indeed, this is exactly what is observed (see Fig. 4(b)), and the quantitative model of propagation speed holds for the different regions: We have $\kappa = 12$ in the middle and $\kappa = 3$ elsewhere.

Blocking Communication and Eager vs. Rendezvous Mode. Instead of grouped nonblocking point-to-point calls, a popular choice is MPI_Sendrecv for a pair of in- and outgoing messages along the same direction. This is

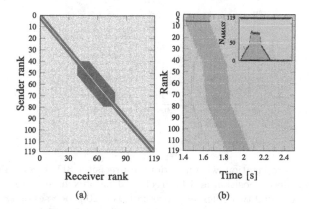

(a)   (b)

Fig. 4. Idle wave propagation with heterogeneous compact communication charactersitics (60 iterations) on Emmy. (a) Topology matrix: P_i sends (receives) 1 KiB to (from) $P_{i\pm1},\ldots,P_{i\pm3}$ for processes near boundaries and to (from) $P_{i\pm1},\ldots,P_{i\pm12}$ for 40 inner processes. (b) Idle wave propagation for SWMDim concurrency.

identical to the MWSDir case in Table 2, so the phenomenology shown in
Figs. 2 (a1, b1, c1) and Figs. 3 (a1,b1) applies. Similarly one can employ a
MPI_Irecv/MPI_Send/MPI_Wait sequence within the innermost loop. In all these
cases, the wave propagation speed doubles in rendezvous mode, where synchronization between sender and receiver is implied. However, the difference between
eager and rendezvous mode does not impact the other variants beyond MWSDir.

Stencil Smoother with Halo Exchange. Figure 5 shows an idle wave
experiment with a double-precision Jacobi smoother using Cartesian domain
decomposition and two different process grids ($4 \times 5 \times 6$ vs. $2 \times 6 \times$
10; inner dimension goes first). Here we used MWSDir concurrency via
MPI_Irecv/MPI_Send/MPI_Wait per direction. The message sizes are such that
the rendezvous mode applies. As expected from the model, the longest-distance
communication determines the overall wave speed, i.e., it is lower in case (b)
where the topology matrix is narrower.

The communication topology is more intricate here than in the microbenchmark studies covered so far. It turns out that all connections apart from the
longest-distance one can be summarized by averaging over their respective dis-

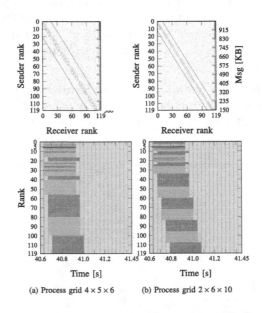

(a) Process grid $4 \times 5 \times 6$ (b) Process grid $2 \times 6 \times 10$

Fig. 5. Idle wave propagation within a double-precision 3D Jacobi algorithm with
Cartesian domain decomposition and bidirectional halo exchange (15 iterations) at a
problem size of 1200^3 and two different process grids (120 processes on Emmy) with open
boundary conditions. Top row: topology matrices color-coded with communication volume. Bottom row: timelines of idle wave progression. Orange color shows idleness in
MPI_Wait, while pink color indicates waiting time in MPI_Send. See text for communication grouping. Single-message communication volumes are (a) 576 kB, 480 kB, 384 kB
and (b) 960 kB, 576 kB, 192 kB per dimension. (Color figure online)

tances and taking the largest smaller integer (floor function) when calculating the κ factor. For the case in Fig. 5(a), this leads to $\kappa = 2 + 20 = 22$, so the propagation speed is $22 \times 2 = 44$ times larger than $v_{\text{silent}}^{\min}$. For Fig. 5(b), we have $\kappa = 0 + 12 = 12$ and thus 24 times $v_{\text{silent}}^{\min}$. Both predictions are confirmed by the data after the initial slow, short-distance waves have died out.

SpMV with Halo Exchange. The High Performance Conjugate Gradient (HPCG) benchmark is popular for ranking supercomputers beyond the ubiquitous LINPACK. Here we choose to discuss idle wave propagation during multiple back-to-back sparse matrix-vector multiplications using the HPCG matrix, which emerges from a sparse linear system using a 27-point stencil in 3D. Communication is largely symmetric, except for boundaries. The number of communication partners varies between 7 (corners) and 26 (interior processes), and MWSDir concurrency applies just like in the stencil example. The per-process problem size is small enough for eager mode, but communication time is a relevant contribution to the overall runtime.

Figure 6 shows idle wave propagation through three different process grids with $2 \times 4 \times 5 = 40$, $4 \times 3 \times 5 = 60$, and $4 \times 5 \times 5 = 100$ processes, respectively (inner dimension goes first). The decomposition is indicated in the captions of Figs. 6(a)–(c). In case (a) we get $\kappa = 8$, for (b) we get $\kappa = 12$, and for (c) we get $\kappa = 24$.

4 Idle Waves Interacting with MPI Collectives

Few MPI programs use point-to-point communications only. Concerning idle wave propagation, the question arises which collective routines may be permeable to a traveling wave. In practice, the elimination or the survival of the wave may be desirable depending on the context; for instance, it was shown that idle waves can lead to automatic communication-computation overlap in desynchronized bottleneck-bound programs [3].

The effects we discuss here for collective communications are certainly heavily dependent on the details of the MPI implementation, the communication buffer size, and possibly other parameters, so it is impossible to give a comprehensive overview. We thus restrict ourselves to Intel MPI on one of the three benchmark systems (Emmy). The results are summarized in Fig. 7 and discussed below.

Globally Synchronizing Primitives. Examples of necessarily synchronizing collectives are MPI_Allreduce, MPI_Alltoall, MPI_Allgather, MPI_Barrier, etc. These destroy propagating idle waves completely (see Figure 7(a)). The default Intel implementations of MPI_Scatter and MPI_Bcast are also synchronizing. If the *autotuner mode* is enabled by setting I_MPI_TUNING_AUTO_SYNC=1 (disabled by default), an internal barrier is called on every tuning iteration. This, of course, completely eradicates an idle wave on *any* collective call.

Global Non-synchronizing Primitives. Figure 7(b) shows an idle wave colliding with the default Intel implementation of MPI_Reduce. Reductions are not

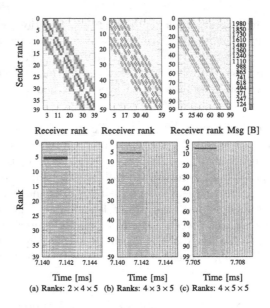

Fig. 6. Idle wave propagation in sparse matrix-vector multiplication (SpMV) using the HPCG matrix with a problem size of 16^3 per process and bidirectional halo exchange (15 iterations) on Emmy and three different process grids (a)–(c). Top row: topology matrices with color-coded communication volumes. Bottom row: Timelines of idle wave progression. Message sizes are 8 B, 128 B, and 2.05 kB per dimension (symmetry across main diagonals).

necessarily synchronizing, and indeed the idle wave can pass the collective, which appears like a global, compact communication block through which the wave travels with maximum speed (see the discussion of inhomogeneous communication above).

If the survival of idle waves is desirable, one option is to avoid synchronizing collectives if the performance implications are noncritical. In Fig. 7(c), we show that the default MPI_Gather implementation is completely permeable to the wave.

Implementation Variants. MPI implementations usually provide tuning knobs to optimize the internal implementation of collectives in order to better adapt it to the application. The process of finding the optimal parameter settings can also be automated [11,14]. With Intel MPI, the I_MPI_ADJUST_<opname> environment variable can be set to a value that selects a particular implementation variant for the <opname> collective. Eleven documented settings are available in case of MPI_Reduce. Figure 7(c), although it depicts a gather operation, is also applicable to MPI_Reduce with I_MPI_ADJUST_REDUCE set to 2 or a value between 4 and 7. Finally, Fig. 7(d) illustrates how the interaction of the idle wave with MPI_Reduce changes for I_MPI_ADJUST_REDUCE set to 3 (topology-aware Shumilin's algorithm).

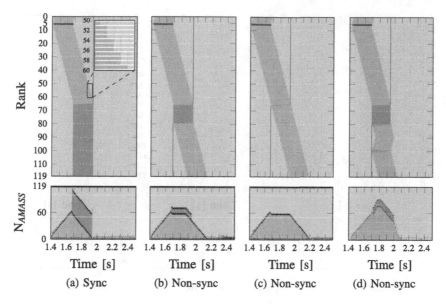

Fig. 7. Transparency of collective routines for idle waves on Emmy. (a) Default Intel MPI implementation of MPI_Allreduce/MPI_Alltoall/MPI_Allgather/MPI_Scatter/MPI_Bcast/MPI_Barrier/I_MPI_ADJUST_REDUCE=1/any collective with I_MPI_TUNING_AUTO_SYNC=1, (b) default MPI_Reduce or with I_MPI_ADJUST_REDUCE=8-11, (c) default MPI_Gather/MPI_Reduce with I_MPI_ADJUST_REDUCE=2,4-7, (d) MPI_Reduce with I_MPI_ADJUST_REDUCE=3. Collective calls are injected at rank 5 in the 20th iteration and the root (where applicable) is rank 0. The message size is 1024 B, and MPI_SUM is used for all operations. Green color indicates the time spent by MPI processes in the collective routines. (Color figure online)

Another option is to override the default shared-memory node-level implementation of collectives and substitute it with a standard point-to-point variant. For instance, setting I_MPI_COLL_INTRANODE=pt2pt (insted of the default shm) modifies the reduction behavior from Fig. 7(b) to Fig. 7(c).

In general, our results show that it is possible to implement collectives that are permeable to idle waves. Thus, the existence of collectives in a program does not make idle waves a non-issue and extends their relevance beyond collective-free algorithms.

5 Idle Wave Decay

The decay of traveling idle waves is a well-known phenomenon [12], and the underlying microscopic mechanism via interaction with short idle periods ("noise") is well understood [4]. There are, however, two questions that have not been addressed so far: (i) Does the system topology lead to idle wave decay also for resource-scalable parallel programs?, and (ii) Which characteristics of

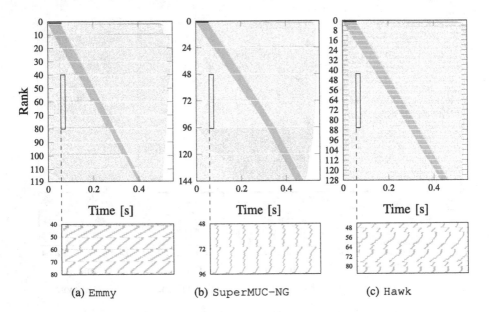

Fig. 8. Topological idle wave decay on the benchmark systems running one process per core (scalable workload) using nonblocking MPI distance-1 communication topology (i.e., $P_i \rightleftarrows P_{i\pm1}$) for 120 iterations. We chose $T_{\text{exec}} = 2.7\,\text{ms}$ (white color) and injected extra work of 58 ms (blue color) at rank 0. The message size was 1 MB. (a) 12 domains (sockets), 120 processes (b) 5 domains (sockets), 120 processes, (c) 30 domains (CCX), 120 processes. Topological boundaries exist at every 10, 24, and 4 cores on Emmy, SuperMUC-NG and Hawk, respectively. (Color figure online)

the system noise have an impact on the decay rate of the idle wave? Here we answer both.

5.1 Topological Decay

It has been shown that the system topology, specifically a memory bandwidth bottleneck, can cause idle wave decay without the presence of system noise [3]. For the resource-scalable codes considered here this mechanism does not apply, but there is more to system topology than memory bottlenecks. The three benchmark systems we use here have quite different features in this respect, even within a single node: Hawk has 16 cores (4 × 4 CCX) per ccNUMA domain, 4 ccNUMA domains per socket, and 2 sockets per node. SuperMUC-NG has 24 cores per ccNUMA domain, 1 ccNUMA domain per socket, and 2 sockets per node. Emmy has 10 cores per ccNUMA domain, 1 ccNUMA domain per socket, and 2 sockets per node. The inherent topological boundaries cause communication heterogeneities, which create structured noise as small variations in communication time (intranode vs. internode) propagate and interact with the idle wave to cause visible kinks. This is demonstrated in Fig. 8 for the three benchmark clusters, running one MPI process per ccNUMA domain. The kinks at the topological

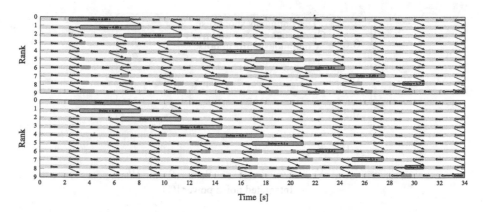

Fig. 9. Experiment comparing the average decay rate of an idle wave (initial duration 4850 ms) for two different noise characteristics (top vs. bottom). In both cases, the integrated noise power is 9.1% of the total area below the idle wave, i.e., 13 s of 142 s, but the distribution of the fine-grained noise is different. However, the overall average decay rate is the same (480 ms/rank), as is the wave survival time (34 s).

boundaries are best seen in the second row. The "large-scale effect" is seen in the top row, where the idle wave takes a "hit" at every topological boundary (white horizontal lines). For 120 iterations, we measured an average decay rate of 149 μs/rank on SuperMUC-NG, 203 μs/rank on Hawk, and 346 μs/rank on Emmy. Although one might expect Hawk to show the strongest topology effects due to its intricate node structure, it is not only the number of hierarchy levels but also the actual communication inhomogeneity that determines the decay effect. In Fig. 8, all 128 processes were run on a single node of Hawk, so the internode boundary is missing there.

In order to substantiate the claim that this decay emerges from system topology and communication heterogeneities, we repeated all experiments with *round-robin placement* [8] of MPI processes across nodes. In this way, node-level differences in communication characteristics are all but eliminated since all interprocess boundaries are internode boundaries. Indeed, the decay observed with standard placement (consecutive cores on a node map to consecutive MPI processes, SMT ignored) vanishes under these conditions.

5.2   Noise-Induced Decay

For the purpose of this work, we define "noise" as any (per-process) deviation from a fixed, repeatable, lockstep-type compute-communicate pattern. In this sense, strong one-off delays are also noise, but in this section we specifically consider noise that is considerably more fine grained. One of the unsolved questions in previous work about idle wave decay, specifically with resource-scalable code, is whether the detailed statistical properties of the fine-grained noise or just the integrated noise power impact the rate of decay. In order to exert full control over

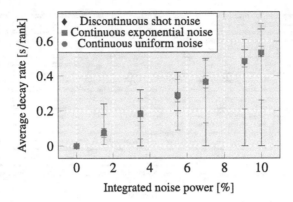

Fig. 10. Decay rate (min/max/median at sixteen cross-process transitions) of an idle period in s/rank, comparing three different noise patterns (see [4]) on the InfiniBand Emmy (18 processes, one per node, single leaf switch). The x-axis shows integrated noise power with respect to overall integrated runtime of 142 s.

all noise characteristics, we conduct experiments with artificial noise injections that are orders of magnitude stronger than natural noise. Due to the fundamental scale invariance of these mechanisms, the conclusions must also hold for realistic scenarios.

How idle waves interact with each other in a nonlinear way has been analyzed in previous work [4]; noise-induced decay is just a variant of this process. Noise "eats away" at the trailing edge of the wave, so a small idle period (i.e., a part of the noise) of duration T_{noise} that collides with the idle wave shortens the latter by an amount of exactly T_{noise}. This process is cumulative, which leads to the immediate conclusion that multiple interactions $\{T^i_{\text{noise}}\}$ diminish the idle wave by $\eta = \sum_i T^i_{\text{noise}}$. Noise statistics is of minor importance for the average decay rate. It will only impact the "smoothness" of the decay. Figure 9 illustrates this fact by comparing the decay of the same idle wave under two widely different noise characteristics with identical integrated "noise power" η. All non-labeled orange boxes are noise. In the top figure, the noise "particles" are more evenly distributed than in the bottom figure, which shows more like a "burst"-type noise with longer duration for each "particle" and a higher frequency of particles. Although the details of the decay are different, the survival time and hence the average decay rate of the wave is the same in both cases. This holds as long as the noise is fine-grained enough to not annihilate the idle wave in one fell swoop at an early stage. Note that previous research [5,6,10] only studied the influence of noise statistics on application and global operations scalability. Our observable is idle wave decay rate, which is largely robust against noise statistics.

Experimental Validation. To better validate this hypothesis, we measured the decay rate of an idle wave under three different noise characteristics with the same noise power. That is, how much shorter the delay gets per "hop."

Fig. 10 shows results for 18 processes (one per node) on one leaf switch of Emmy to rule out topological effects. Apart from this detail, the setting is similar to Fig. 9. The microscopic shape of the decay is influenced by the statistics: Shot noise, i.e., random but strong, sparse noise injections of a single duration, lead to discontinuous decay and strong variations in decay rate (diamonds in Fig. 10). On the other hand, exponential (squares) and uniform (circles) noise characteristics, where noise injections show a whole spectrum of durations, and the variation in decay rates is much weaker. The shape of an idle wave is always roughly a wedge. The variations come because of the way the decay is measured across hops: we take individual data points by looking at different points along the edges of the wedge. The min and max whiskers denote points where the decay – at a certain point on the timeline – was particularly weak or strong. These variations are stronger with shot noise than with fine-grained noise because the edge is more "jagged" with shot noise. The median of measured decay rates, however, only depends on the noise power.

6 Summary and Future Work

We have presented an analytical model of idle wave propagation speed based on communication topology and concurrency characteristics of resource-scalable MPI programs. The model was validated against simple microbenchmarks, a 3D stencil smoother, and sparse matrix-vector multiplication with the HPCG matrix. We have also shown that MPI collective routines can be permeable to idle waves depending on the type and implementation of the collective, which extends the relevance of idle wave phenomena beyond bulk-synchronous algorithms without collective communication. In light of the fact that the presence of idle waves is not necessarily detrimental for performance, this result can be quite relevant to the performance analysis of highly scalable codes. Furthermore, we have uncovered the relevance of system topology for idle wave decay: The presence of heterogeneous communication characteristics emerging from the hierarchical structure of modern compute nodes leads to fine-grained noise even on very silent systems that causes the decay of idle waves. Finally, we have shown that it is the noise power, and not its detailed statistical properties, that govern the noise-induced decay rate. All these findings contribute significantly to the understanding of the idle wave phenomenon on multicore clusters.

Beyond their theoretical significance, our findings point to optimization strategies a developer can apply to a parallel code that is subject to idle waves: if a program can benefit from the idle wave via better resource utilization [3], the slowest velocity may be best, otherwise the highest. This can be achieved by a change in communication scheme, for instance, by bringing non-zeros closer to the diagonal in spMV via some reordering techniques. While, in programs with non-contended processes, slower idle waves can absorb some noise better with non-linear interaction to reduce the runtime penalty on noisy systems [4].

Future work will include the extension of the analysis to programs that are not resource scalable, i.e., that are limited by node-level or network-level bottlenecks. There is also the open question which wave and noise phenomena can be described by effective models that abstract away from the details of the cluster hardware. Finally, we will develop a capable MPI simulation tool that can take node-level characteristics into account and will allow for more extensive experimental studies and architectural exploration.

Acknowledgments. This work was supported by KONWIHR, the Bavarian Competence Network for Scientific High Performance Computing in Bavaria, under project name "OMI4papps," and by the BMBF under projects "Metacca" and "SeASiTe." We are indebted to LRZ Garching and to HLRS Stuttgart for granting CPU hours on their "SuperMUC-NG" and "Hawk" systems.

References

1. Afzal, A., et al.: An analytic performance model for overlapping execution of memory-bound loop kernels on multicore CPUs. In arXiv (2020). arXiv:2011.00243 [cs.DC]. Submitted
2. Afzal, A., et al.: Delay flow mechanisms on clusters. Poster at EuroMPI 2019, 10–13 September 2019, Zurich, Switzerland. https://hpc.fau.de/files/2019/09/EuroMPI2019_AHW-Poster.pdf
3. Afzal, A., Hager, G., Wellein, G.: Desynchronization and wave pattern formation in mpi-parallel and hybrid memory-bound programs. In: Sadayappan, P., Chamberlain, B.L., Juckeland, G., Ltaief, H. (eds.) ISC High Performance 2020. LNCS, vol. 12151, pp. 391–411. Springer, Cham (2020). https://doi.org/10.1007/978-3-030-50743-5_20
4. Afzal, A., et al.: Propagation and decay of injected one-off delays on clusters: a case study. In 2019 IEEE International Conference on Cluster Computing, CLUSTER 2019, Albuquerque, NM, USA, 23–26 September 2019, pp. 1–10 (2019). https://doi.org/10.1109/CLUSTER.2019.8890995
5. Agarwal, S., Garg, R., Vishnoi, N.K.: The impact of noise on the scaling of collectives: a theoretical approach. In: Bader, D.A., Parashar, M., Sridhar, V., Prasanna, V.K. (eds.) HiPC 2005. LNCS, vol. 3769, pp. 280–289. Springer, Heidelberg (2005). https://doi.org/10.1007/11602569_31
6. Ferreira, K.B., et al.: Characterizing application sensitivity to OS interference using kernel-level noise injection. In: Proceedings of the 2008 ACM/IEEE Conference on Supercomputing, p. 19. IEEE Press (2008). https://doi.org/10.1109/SC.2008.5219920
7. Gamell, M., et al.: Local recovery and failure masking for stencil-based applications at extreme scales. In: SC 2015: Proceedings of the International Conference for High Performance Computing, Networking, Storage and Analysis, pp. 1–12, November 2015. https://doi.org/10.1145/2807591.2807672
8. Hager, A.G., et al.: Introduction to High Performance Computing for Scientists and Engineers. CRC Press (2010). ISBN: 978-1-4398-1192-4
9. Hoefler, T., et al.: LogGOPSim - simulating large-scale applications in the log- GOPS model. In: Proceedings of the 19th ACM International Symposium on High Performance Distributed Computing (2010). https://doi.org/10.1145/1851476.1851564
10. Hoefler, T., et al.: Characterizing the influence of system noise on large-scale applications by simulation. In: Proceedings of the 2010 ACM/IEEE International Conference for High Performance Computing, Networking, Storage and Analysis, pp. 1–11. IEEE Computer Society (2010). https://doi.org/10.1109/SC.2010.12

11. Hunold, S., et al.: Predicting MPI collective communication performance using machine learning. In: 2020 IEEE International Conference on Cluster Computing CLUSTER. IEEE (2020). https://doi.org/10.1109/CLUSTER49012.2020.00036
12. Markidis, S., et al.: Idle waves in high-performance computing. Phys. Rev. E **91**(1) (2015). https://doi.org/10.1103/PhysRevE.91.013306
13. Nataraj, A., et al.: The ghost in the machine: observing the effects of kernel operation on parallel application performance. In: Proceedings of the 2007 ACM/IEEE Conference on Supercomputing (2007). https://doi.org/10.1145/1362622.1362662
14. Vadhiyar, S.S., et al.: Automatically tuned collective communications. In: SC 2000: Proceedings of the 2000 ACM/IEEE Conference on Supercomputing, pp. 3–3. IEEE (2000). https://doi.org/10.1109/SC.2000.10024

Performance of the Supercomputer Fugaku for Breadth-First Search in Graph500 Benchmark

Masahiro Nakao[1]([✉]) [iD], Koji Ueno[2], Katsuki Fujisawa[3], Yuetsu Kodama[1], and Mitsuhisa Sato[1]

[1] RIKEN Center for Computational Science, 7-1-26 Minatojima-minami-machi, Chuo-ku, Kobe, Hyogo 650-0047, Japan
{masahiro.nakao,yuetsu.kodama,msato}@riken.jp
[2] Fixstars Corporation, 1-11-1 Osaki, Shinagawa-ku, Tokyo 141-0032, Japan
[3] Institute of Mathematics for Industry, Kyushu University, 744 Motooka, Nishi-ku, Fukuoka 819-0395, Japan
fujisawa@imi.kyushu-u.ac.jp
https://www.r-ccs.riken.jp, https://www.fixstars.com,
https://www.imi.kyushu-u.ac.jp

Abstract. In this paper, we present the performance of the supercomputer Fugaku for breadth-first search (BFS) problem in the Graph500 benchmark, which is known as a ranking benchmark used to evaluate large-scale graph processing performance on supercomputer systems. Fugaku is a huge-scale Japanese exascale supercomputer that consists of 158,976 nodes connected by the Tofu interconnect D (TofuD). We have developed a BFS implementation that can extract the performance of Fugaku. We also optimize the number of processes per node, one-to-one communication, performance power ratio, and process mapping in the six-dimensional mesh/torus topology of TofuD. We evaluate the BFS performance for a large-scale graph consisting of about 2.2 trillion vertices and 35.2 trillion edges using the whole Fugaku system, and achieve 102,955 giga-traversed edges per second (GTEPS), resulting in the first position of Graph500 BFS ranking in November 2020. This performance is 3.3 times higher than that of Fugaku's previous system, the K computer.

Keywords: Breadth-first search · Performance evaluation · Graph500

1 Introduction

There is an increasing demand for computer systems capable of converting large-scale real-world data into a graph, which is a data structure representing relationships between elements with vertices and edges, and processing it at high speed. The graph processing is used in various fields for the analysis of connections between social network users, the optimization of very large scale integration

The original version of this chapter was revised: an incorrect value was given for the number of giga-traversed edges per second (GTEPS). The correction to this chapter is available at https://doi.org/10.1007/978-3-030-78713-4_25

B. L. Chamberlain et al. (Eds.): ISC High Performance 2021, LNCS 12728, pp. 372–390, 2021.
https://doi.org/10.1007/978-3-030-78713-4_20

Table 1. Specifications of the supercomputer Fugaku and the K computer

Name	Supercomputer Fugaku	The K computer
CPU	A64FX, 48+2/4cores, 2.0/2.2 GHz,	SPARC64 VIIIfx, 8cores, 2.0 GHz,
	3,072/3,379 GFlops (double precision)	128 GFlops (double precision)
Memory	HBM2, 32 GB, 1,024 GB/s	DDR3 SDRAM, 16 GB, 64 GB/s
Network	TofuD, 0.49 to 0.54 μs (Latency)	Tofu, 0.91 to 1.15 μs (Latency)
	6.8 GB/s (Bandwidth)	5.0 GB/s (Bandwidth)
Nodes	158,976	82,944

(VLSI) layouts and road networks, whole-brain simulation, Internet of Things
(IoT), search engines, drug discovery, gene analysis, and so on [7,11,16,17]. In
such cases, the number of vertices can exceed 1 trillion, and the number of edges
can be several tens of times the number of vertices.

Against this background, Graph500, a project for evaluating large-scale graph
processing performance, has been ongoing since 2010 and released new listings of the top-performing systems twice-yearly (June and November) [1,12].
In Graph500, a scale-free graph called Kronecker graph [8] is used. The term
scale-free describes a property in which some vertices are connected to many
other vertices while numerous others are connected to only a few vertices. Social
network data are known to have a similar property. The Graph500 benchmark
consists of breadth-first search (BFS) and single-source shortest path (SSSP).
This paper focuses on BFS, which is a crucial algorithm used in the strongly
connected component decomposition and centrality analysis of graphs.

The K computer [6] was ranked first in Graph500 for nine consecutive terms
until June 2019, and it was removed from Graph500 following the decommissioning of the K computer. And then, the supercomputer Fugaku (Fugaku) [10],
which is the successor of the K computer, has been ranked first since June 2020.
This paper describes the BFS algorithm used for the Graph500 submission and
the experimental evaluation results conducted on Fugaku.

The remainder of this paper is structured as follows. Section 2 provides an
overview of Fugaku. Section 3 describes the Hybrid-BFS algorithm commonly
used in Graph500. Section 4 introduces the BFS algorithm based on the Hybrid-
BFS. Section 5 describes how we tune the performance of BFS. Section 6 discusses
the evaluation of BFS on Fugaku. Section 7 summarizes this paper and discusses
our future work.

2   The Supercomputer Fugaku

Fugaku is a supercomputer installed at the RIKEN Center for Computational
Science in Japan, and is scheduled to commence operation in 2021. Table 1 shows
the specification of Fugaku. Each node has a single Fujitsu A64FX processor
(A64FX) [10]. Figure 1 shows the block diagram of A64FX. Fugaku consists of
"compute node" and "compute node with IO node". While the "compute node"
performs calculations, the "compute node with IO node" performs both calculations and input/output processings. A64FX has 48 compute cores, while the

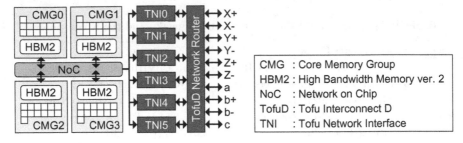

Fig. 1. A64FX processor [20]

"compute node" and "compute node with IO node" use two and four assistant cores, respectively. The assistant core deals with interruptions caused by OS, communications, and so on. The clock frequency of the A64FX core can be set to either 2.0 GHz or 2.2 GHz for each job depending on the user's preferences. The peak performance of double precision is 3,072 GFlops at 2.0 GHz and 3,379 GFlops at 2.2 GHz. A64FX consists of four Core Memory Groups (CMGs), each of which has 12 compute cores, a single assistant core, and an 8 GB High Bandwidth Memory ver. 2 (HBM2). The four CMGs are connected via a Network on Chip (NoC). The Fugaku interconnect uses Tofu Interconnect D (TofuD) [20]. The topology of TofuD is a six-dimensional mesh/torus in which the node position is specified by $XYZabc$ axes. Since the size of Fugaku is $(X, Y, Z, a, b, c) = (24, 23, 24, 2, 3, 2)$, the total number of nodes is 158,976. Also, A64FX has ten ports for TofuD, each $XYZb$ axis uses two ports, and each ac axis uses one port because ac axes consist of two nodes. The latency (8 bytes put communication) of Fugaku is 0.49 to 0.54 µs [20]. A64FX has six Tofu Network Interfaces (TNIs) and can communicate at 6.8 GB/s in six directions simultaneously. Thus, the injection bandwidth of each node is 40.8 GB/s.

Table 1 also shows the specification of the K computer for comparison. The peak performance of A64FX at 2.2 GHz is 26.4 times, the memory capacity is twice, and the memory bandwidth is 16.0 times that of the K computer. The network interconnect used in the K computer is Tofu Interconnect (Tofu) [19], which is the predecessor of TofuD. While its topology is the same as TofuD, the size of the K computer is $(X, Y, Z, a, b, c) = (24, 18, 16, 2, 3, 2)$. Since the total number of nodes is 82,944, the number of nodes in Fugaku is 1.9 times that of the K computer. The latency of Fugaku is about half and the network bandwidth of Fugaku is 1.4 times that of the K computer. Since the K computer had four TNIs in each node, the injection bandwidth is 20.0 GB/s. Thus, the injection bandwidth of Fugaku is 2.0 times that of the K computer.

3   Hybrid-BFS for Large-Scale System

3.1   Algorithm for Shared Memory System

Figure 2 shows an overview of Hybrid-BFS [13] where BFS is executed while switching between the conventional search method called "top-down approach"

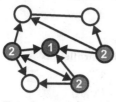

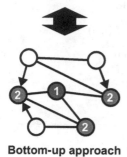

Top-down approach

Bottom-up approach

Fig. 2. Overview of Hybrid-BFS

Algorithm 1: Hybrid-BFS

```
1  hybrid-bfs(vertices, source, nbr)
2      frontier ← {source}
3      next ← {}
4      parents ← [-1,-1,...,-1]
5      while frontier ≠ {} do
6      |   if next-direction(...) = top-down then
7      |   |   top-down(vertices, frontier, next, parents, nbr)
8      |   else
9      |   |   bottom-up(vertices, frontier, next, parents, nbr)
10     |   frontier ← next
11     |   next ← {}
12     return parents
13
14 top-down(vertices, frontier, next, parents, nbr)
15     for v ∈ frontier do
16     |   for n ∈ nbr[v] do
17     |   |   if parents[n] = -1 then
18     |   |   |   parents[n] ← v
19     |   |   |   next ← next ∪ {n}
20
21 bottom-up(vertices, frontier, next, parents, nbr)
22     for v ∈ vertices do
23     |   if parents[v] = -1 then
24     |   |   for n ∈ nbr[v] do
25     |   |   |   if n ∈ frontier then
26     |   |   |   |   parents[v] ← n
27     |   |   |   |   next ← next ∪ {v}
28     |   |   |   |   break
```

and another search method called "bottom-up approach". The current starting points are ②, looking for unsearched adjacencies. The issue with the top-down approach is that current start points must check all adjacencies. Since most adjacencies have been searched (the first start point ① and current start points ② have been searched), redundant checks occur frequently. Therefore, in the bottom-up approach, the search is performed in the opposite direction to the top-down approach, in which the current start points ② are searched from the unsearched vertices (○ in the figure). The advantage of the bottom-up approach is that if even one of the current start points ② is found, the check can be terminated, reducing redundant checks.

Algorithm 1 shows the pseudo-code of the Hybrid-BFS. In line 2, the first starting point (*source*) is substituted for the visited points set (*frontier*). In line 3, the next visitation point set (*next*) is initialized as an empty set. In line 4, BFS tree (*parents*) for the final output, is initialized. Note that the substitution of "−1" for *parents* means that a vertex has not yet been visited.

The top-down approach in the function **top-down()** first checks whether the vertices adjacent to *frontier* have been visited (lines 15–17). Note that *nbr* (*neighbors*) is an adjacent set of vertices. If unvisited, the connection source of an unvisited vertex is assigned to *parents* (line 18). Additionally, the unvisited vertices are added to *next* without duplication (line 19). In the top-down approach, vertices in *frontier* are used as the starting points in searches for unvisited

$$
\begin{matrix}
A_{1,1} & A_{1,2} & \cdots & A_{1,C} \\
A_{2,1} & A_{2,2} & \cdots & A_{2,C} \\
\vdots & \vdots & \ddots & \vdots \\
A_{R,1} & A_{R,2} & \cdots & A_{R,C}
\end{matrix}
$$

Fig. 3. Distribution of adjacency matrix

Algorithm 2: Parallel top-down approach

```
1  parallel-top-down(...)
2     f ← {source}
3     n ← {}
4     π ← [-1,-1,...,-1]
5     for all processes P(i,j) in parallel do
6     |  while f ≠ {} do
7     |  |  transpose-vector(f_{i,j})
8     |  |  f_i ← allgatherv(f_{i,j}, P(:,j))
9     |  |  t_{i,j} ← {}
10    |  |  for u ∈ f_i do
11    |  |  |  for v ∈ A_{i,j}(:,u) do
12    |  |  |  |  t_{i,j} ← t_{i,j} ∪ (u,v)
13    |  |  t_{i,j} ← alltoallv(t_{i,j}, P(i,:))
14    |  |  for (u,v) ∈ t_{i,j} do
15    |  |  |  if π_{i,j}(v) = -1 then
16    |  |  |  |  π_{i,j}(v) ← u
17    |  |  |  |  n_{i,j} ← n_{i.j} ∪ v
18    |  |  f ← n
19    |  |  n ← {}
20    return π
```

vertices adjacent to them. In contrast, in the bottom-up approach of the function **bottom-up()**, all unvisited vertices are used as the starting points and the searches determine whether the vertices adjacent to them belong to *frontier* (lines 22–25). When a vertex belonging to *frontier* is found, it is assigned to *parents* and its starting point is added to *next* without duplication (lines 26–27).

The advantage of the bottom-up approach is that when one vertex belonging to *frontier* is found, the search for that starting vertex can be terminated (line 28), thus reducing the redundant checks seen in the top-down approach. However, since the bottom-up approach requires checking whether all vertices have been visited, the top-down approach is faster when *frontier* is small. Therefore, the Hybrid-BFS uses the top-down approach when *frontier* is small, and the bottom-up approach when *frontier* is large. Although we have omitted the full details here, the **next-direction()** function in line 6 dynamically decides whether to switch between the top-down and bottom-up approaches.

3.2 Algorithm for Distributed Memory System

To handle large graphs, the parallel Hybrid-BFS has been proposed [14]. In the parallel Hybrid-BFS, the adjacency matrix A is assigned to the processes divided into two dimensions (R rows and C columns) as shown in Fig. 3. A process $P(i,j)$ has information on a partial adjacency matrix $A_{i,j}$. Algorithms 2 and 3 show the pseudo-codes for the parallel top-down and bottom-up approaches, respectively. The parallel Hybrid-BFS is executed by switching the approaches, as well as the Hybrid-BFS in Algorithm 1. The f, n, and π correspond to *frontier*, *next*, and *parents*, respectively. The t is a sparse vector for temporarily holding two

Algorithm 3: Parallel bottom-up approach

```
1  parallel-bottom-up(...)
2      f ← {source}
3      c ← {source}
4      n ← {}
5      π ← [-1,-1,...,-1]
6      for all processes P(i, j) in parallel do
7      |  while f ≠ {} do
8      |  |  transpose-vector(f_{i,j})
9      |  |  f_i ← allgatherv(f_{i,j}, P(:, j))
10     |  |  for s in 0 .. C-1 do
11     |  |  |  t_{i,j} ← {}
12     |  |  |  for u ∈ c_{i,j} do
13     |  |  |  |  for v ∈ A_{i,j}(u, :) do
14     |  |  |  |  |  if v ∈ f_i then
15     |  |  |  |  |  |  t_{i,j} ← t_{i,j} ∪ (u, v)
16     |  |  |  |  |  |  c_{i,j} ← 1
17     |  |  |  |  |  |  break
18     |  |  |  t_{i,j} ← sendrecv(t_{i,j}, P(i, j+s), P(i, j-s))
19     |  |  |  for (v, u) ∈ t_{i,j} do
20     |  |  |  |  π_{i,j}(v) ← u
21     |  |  |  |  n_{i,j} ← n_{i,j} ∪ v
22     |  |  |  c_{i,j} ← sendrecv(c_{i,j}, P(i, j+1), P(i, j-1))
23     |  |  f ← n
24     |  |  n ← {}
25     return π
```

row-starts	0 2 2 2 2 2 2 3 4
dst	4 5 3 1

Compressed Sparse Row (CSR)

row-starts	0 2 3 4
bitmap	1 0 0 0 0 0 1 1
offset	0 1 3
dst	4 5 3 1

Bitmap-based CSR (BCSR)

Fig. 4. Compressed formats

adjacent vertices (u and v). The c is a bitmap of checked vertices, while the f and n are sparse vectors for the top-down approach and bitmaps for the bottom-up approach, respectively. The π is a dense vector in both approaches.

In Algorithm 2, in lines 7–8, the f is shared in the column process. In lines 9–13, information about the f and the adjacent vertices is exchanged in the row process. In lines 14–17, the π and n are created. In Algorithm 3, lines 8–9 are the same as lines 7–8 of Algorithm 2, except for the data structure of the f. The **for** statement in lines 10–22 is divided into C sub-steps. The reason is to reduce the number of vertices to be searched for in each process by periodically updating c in the row process in line 22, thereby improving the overall speed. In lines 10–18, the information on unvisited vertices adjacent to the f is exchanged in the row process. In lines 19–21, the π and n are created.

4   Improvement to Hybrid-BFS

This section introduces the BFS algorithm for Fugaku, which is also adopted in the K computer [9]. Since the algorithm is an improved version of the Hybrid-BFS described in Sect. 3, this section describes only the changes.

Table 2. Memory consumption in CSR and BCSR

	CSR		BCSR	
	Order	Actual	Order	Actual
row-starts	$n'C$	2048 MB	$n'p$	190 MB
bitmap	–	–	$n'C/64$	32 MB
offset	–	–	$n'C/64$	32 MB
dst	$n'd$	1020 MB	$n'd$	1020 MB
Total	$n'(C+d)$	3068 MB	$n'(\frac{C}{32}+p+d)$	1274 MB

4.1 Bitmap-Based Representation for Adjacency Matrix

When using a conventional compressed sparse row (CSR) as a format for storing an adjacency matrix, the array *dst*, which holds the output vertex number, and the offset array *row-starts* of the edge vertex numbers are used. For efficient edge information retrieval, the smaller *row-starts* size is desirable. However, the size of *row-starts* is proportional to C in the case of a two-dimensional division of R rows and C columns.

To resolve the issue, Bitmap-based CSR (BCSR) is proposed, which can extract edge information more efficiently and with less memory than CSR. BCSR provides the following features: (1) Compress the *row-starts* in CSR so that only the edge start position of a vertex with one or more edges is retained. (2) Use the *bitmap*, which is an array of bits per vertex that indicates whether each vertex has at least one edge. (3) Use the array *offset* to efficiently calculate the vertex number of an edge source. The position of *row-starts* at a vertex is the number of bits standing from the beginning of the *bitmap* to the bit corresponding to the vertex. To efficiently calculate the number of standing bits in *bitmap*, the cumulative total of bits is stored at *offset* in advance, word by word.

Figure 4 shows examples of CSR and BCSR when the edge list is $\{(0, 4),$ $(0, 5), (6, 3), (7, 1)\}$ where each word is assumed to be 4 bits for the sake of explanation. The *row-starts* in CSR is represented in BCSR as three arrays: *row-starts*, *bitmap*, and *offset*. Next, Table 2 shows a comparison of the amount of memory where one word is set to 64 bits. Here, n' is the number of vertices per node, d is the degree, and p is the probability of having one or more edges in a row from a partial adjacency matrix of a process. Table 2 also shows the actual memory usage using a Kronecker graph used in Graph500 with 16 billion vertices and 256 billion edges when the two-dimensional division of $R \times C = 64$ $\times$ 32. This result indicates that BCSR is more memory-efficient than CSR.

4.2 Sorting of Vertex Number

Bit positions in the bitmap are generally in vertex number order. A Kronecker graph has vertices with large and small degrees, and the vertices with larger degrees are accessed more frequently. Thus, the memory locality can be improved

$$
\begin{array}{cccc}
A_{1,1}^{(1)} & A_{1,2}^{(1)} & \cdots & A_{1,C}^{(1)} \\
A_{2,1}^{(1)} & A_{2,2}^{(1)} & \cdots & A_{2,C}^{(1)} \\
\vdots & \vdots & \ddots & \vdots \\
A_{R,1}^{(1)} & A_{R,2}^{(1)} & \cdots & A_{R,C}^{(1)} \\
A_{1,1}^{(2)} & A_{1,2}^{(2)} & \cdots & A_{1,C}^{(2)} \\
\vdots & \vdots & \ddots & \vdots \\
A_{R,1}^{(C)} & A_{R,2}^{(C)} & & A_{R,C}^{(C)}
\end{array}
$$

Fig. 5. Distribution of adjacency matrix by Yoo [4]

Algorithm 4: Simple thread parallelization

1 **top-down-sender-naive**$(f_i, A_{i,j})$
2 **for** $u \in f_i$ **in parallel do**
3 | **for** $v \in A_{i,j}(:,u)$ **do**
4 | | $k \leftarrow$ **owner**(v)
5 | | $t_{i,j,k} \leftarrow t_{i,j,k} \cup (u,v)$

Algorithm 5: Proposed thread parallelization

1 **top-down-sender-load-balanced**$(f_i, A_{i,j})$
2 **for** $u \in f_i$ **in parallel do**
3 | **for** $k \in P(i,:)$ **do**
4 | | $(v_0, v_1) \leftarrow$ **edge-range**$(A_{i,j}(:,u), k)$
5 | | $r_{i,j,k} \leftarrow r_{i,j,k} \cup (u, v_0, v_1)$
6 **for** $k \in P(i,:)$ **in parallel do**
7 | **for** $(u, v_0, v_1) \in r_{i,j,k}$ **do**
8 | | **for** $v \in A_{i,j}(v_0:v_1, u)$ **do**
9 | | | $t_{i,j,k} \leftarrow t_{i,j,k} \cup (u,v)$

by arranging the bit positions in degree order. In the algorithm, vertex numbers are reassigned in degree order within the process. Note that *parents* is created in degree order with the technique. Thus, it prepares a new array that holds the original vertex numbers and is used for writing to *parents*.

4.3 Yoo's Distribution of Adjacency Matrix

When applying the distribution shown in Fig. 3 to the adjacency matrix, communication in **transpose-vector()** is required to transpose *frontier* shown in line 7 of Algorithm 2 and line 8 of Algorithm 3. By applying the distribution proposed by Yoo [4], the communications can be removed. Figure 5 shows the distribution. The distribution in the rows is the same as Fig. 3, while the distribution in the columns is $R \times C$ block-cyclic distribution.

4.4 Load Balancing in Top-Down Approach

Algorithm 4 shows a simple example of thread implementation in lines 10–12 of Algorithm 2. In line 2, it is threaded by the input source vertices in *frontier*. In line 3, $A_{i,j}(:,u)$ is an edge list whose edge input source is u. In line 4, the **owner**(v) function returns the process in charge of the output destination vertex v. In line 5, the adjacent vertex information is stored. Although the technique is simple, a large load imbalance between threads may occur because the degree of a Kronecker graph differs significantly depending on the vertex.

To resolve this load imbalance, it is threaded by the output destination vertices. Algorithm 5 shows the technique which uses two thread-parallelized **for** statements. The first **for** statement stores the information of the output destination vertices for each process in charge, and the second **for** statement stores the set of adjacent vertices. The function **edge-range**$(A_{i,j}(:,u), k)$ in line 4 returns the range of the edge list for which the process in charge is k.

Algorithm 6: Proposed bottom-up approach

```
1  parallel-bottom-up(...)
2    f ← {source}
3    c ← {source}
4    n ← {}
5    π ← [-1,-1,...,-1]
6    for all processes P(i, j) in parallel do
7    |  while f ≠ {} do
8    |  |  f_i ← allgatherv(f_{i,j}, P(:, j))
9    |  |  for s in 0 .. C-1 do
10   |  |  |  t_{i,j} ← {}
11   |  |  |  for u ∈ c_{i,j} do
12   |  |  |  |  for v ∈ A_{i,j}(u, :) do
13   |  |  |  |  |  if v ∈ f_i then
14   |  |  |  |  |  |  t_{i,j} ← t_{i,j} ∪ (u, v)
15   |  |  |  |  |  |  c_{i,j} ← 1
16   |  |  |  |  |  |  break
17   |  |  |  c_{i,j} ← sendrecv(c_{i,j}, P(i, j+1), P(i, j-1))
18   |  |  |  t_{i,j} ← alltoallv(t_{i,j}, P(i, :))
19   |  |  |  for (v, u) ∈ t_{i,j} do
20   |  |  |  |  π_{i,j}(v) ← u
21   |  |  |  |  n_{i,j} ← n_{i,j} ∪ v
22   |  |  f ← n
23   |  |  n ← {}
24   return π
```

Table 3. Communication costs

Approach	Pattern	Times	Words
Top-down	allgatherv	$O(1)$	nR
	alltoallv	$O(1)$	$4m$
Bottom-up	allgatherv	$O(1)$	$s_b n R/64$
	sendrecv	$O(C)$	$s_b n C/64$
	alltoallv	$O(1)$	$2n$

In Algorithm 4, an adjacent vertex is not stored in the communication buffer, but in a temporary buffer in line 5. The reason is that the data need to be contiguous for communication but the number of elements to be sent to each process cannot be known in advance. In contrast, in Algorithm 5, the number of vertices passed to each process in the first **for** statement can be counted. Therefore, in line 9, the adjacent vertices are used for communication without the temporary buffer. However, the disadvantage of the technique is that the amount of information in r is larger than that in t. When searching for vertices whose degree is relatively small compared to the number of destination processes, the amount of data written to r is larger than that to t, which is inefficient. Accordingly, the techniques in Algorithm 4 and Algorithm 5 are switched depending on the degree of each vertex and the number of destination processes.

4.5   Communication in Bottom-Up Approach

Use of Collective Communication. In the **sendrecv** communication in line 18 of Algorithm 3, point-to-point communication is performed within the row process group. As a result of preliminary experiments in a large-scale environment, it was found that the communication efficiency deteriorates when such unscheduled communications occur frequently. Therefore, by using **alltoallv** communication instead of the **sendrecv** communication, data are exchanged collectively, as shown in line 18 of Algorithm 6. Additionally, as described in Sect. 4.3, the **transpose-vector()** function is removed in Algorithm 6.

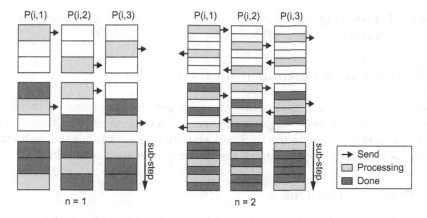

Fig. 6. Overlapping communication with computation

Switching Data Structure by Vertex Concentration. Table 3 shows the communication costs of BFS. The third column shows the order of the communications required to perform one approach. The fourth column shows the communication size required to perform one BFS, assuming that the approach is not switched. Here, one word is 64 bits, n is the number of vertices, R and C are the sizes of each dimension of the process grid, m is the number of edges, and s_b is the number of times the bottom-up approach is performed. Additionally, for the sake of formula simplification, $(C-1)/C \approx 1$ is set and one-word communications are excluded. In the bottom-up approach, the one-step communication sizes of **allgatherv** and **sendrecv** increase in proportion to R and C, respectively. Note that **allgatherv** in the top-down approach uses a sparse vector and is executed only when $frontier$ is small, so there is no problem.

To reduce the communication size of the **allgatherv** and **sendrecv** in the bottom-up approach, a technique is used to select a bitmap or sparse vector according to the vertex concentration of the data automatically. When a sparse vector is used for each communication, the communication size of **allgatherv** is proportional to the number of vertices in $frontier$, and the communication size of **sendrecv** is proportional to the number of the unvisited vertices. In other words, when the number of vertices is smaller than $n/64$, the communication size of each can be reduced by using the sparse vector.

Overlapping Communication with Calculation. To proceed with communication and calculation simultaneously in lines 9–17 of Algorithm 6, the sub-step in line 9 increases from C to $n \times C$. Our implementation uses $n = 4$. In addition, to effectively use torus topology networks such as TofuD, the **sendrecv** communication in line 17 is performed simultaneously in two directions. Figure 6 shows its concept when $C = 3$. In the case of $n = 2$, communication to the right side, calculation process, and communication to the left side can be performed simultaneously. Note that $P(i,1)$ and $P(i,3)$ are directly connected in a torus topology. For reducing the communication waiting time, the processing order of the receiving process is the receiving order, not the loop order.

5   Performance Optimization for Fugaku

This section reports how to optimize the BFS performance using up to 16,384 nodes, while the next Sect. 6 reports the final evaluation using more nodes. Note that these sections evaluate the BFS performance on Fugaku, but the evaluation results are not guaranteed to match the results at the start of sharing.

5.1   Graph500 Benchmark

The number of vertices in a graph used in Graph500 is a power of two and is expressed as 2^{SCALE}. The number of edges is 16 times the number of vertices. The BFS performance unit is a traversed edges per second (TEPS) [1]. According to the Graph500 regulation [1], 64 vertices are randomly selected as the start points, after which BFS processing is performed on each. The harmonic mean of all 64 BFS performance values is set as the evaluation performance value. Since 64 times is excessive for the performance optimization performed in this section, the harmonic mean of 16 times in BFS is used as the performance value. In the next Sect. 6, the harmonic mean value produce by 64 BFS repetitions is used.

5.2   Setting Parameters

In the evaluations, a graph size per node is set at $SCALE = 24$ and is measured with weak scaling. In Fugaku, users can specify one- to three-dimensional logical process layouts (job shapes). Since BFS uses the $R \times C$ two-dimensional process grid, we specify the two-dimensional job shape. In this case, each process is assigned to a node so that it has a physically two-dimensional torus topology. Please note that due to Fugaku's job scheduler, if the number of nodes used is 384 or less, it may not become the torus physically. Thus, in this experiment, 384 or more nodes will be used. Table 3 indicates that the communication size becomes smaller when the values of R and C are close. Note that if $R = C$ cannot be set, $R > C$ is desirable. Thus, if the number of processes is a square number, R and C should be set to the same value. If not a square number, R should be set to be larger and the difference between R and C should be set to be as small as possible. For example, if the number of processes is 8, then $(R, C) = (4, 2)$.

5.3   Optimization of the Number of Processes per Node

This section examines the optimum number of processes assigned to one node. The evaluation uses 1, 2, or 4 processes per node (denoted 1 ppn, 2 ppn, and 4 ppn, respectively) because A64FX has four CMGs shown in Fig. 1. The number of threads in each process is 48, 24, or 12.

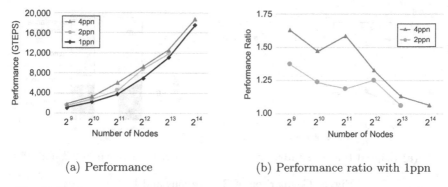

(a) Performance   (b) Performance ratio with 1ppn

Fig. 7. Performance and performance ratio for each process with weak scaling

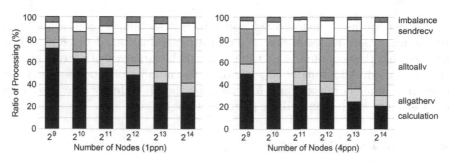

Fig. 8. Processing time ratio of Fig. 7

Figure 7a shows the performance results for each number of processes per node and Fig. 7b shows the relative performance of 2 ppn and 4 ppn when the result of 1 ppn is 1.0. The result of 16,384 ($=2^{14}$) nodes for 2 ppn could not be measured due to a system malfunction. The results of 16,384 nodes for 1 ppn and 4 ppn are 17,560 GTEPS and 18,738 GTEPS, respectively. Figure 7 indicates that the performance is higher in the order of 4 ppn, 2 ppn, and 1 ppn, but the performance difference becomes smaller as the number of nodes increases. One of the reasons for this performance difference is that at 1 ppn and 2 ppn, each thread frequently gets data across the CMGs in the process. In addition, 4 ppn has a smaller data size per process, so the cache hit rate is higher. According to the profiler provided by Fugaku, the number of L2 misses in the case of 4 ppn was about half that in the case of 1 ppn.

Figure 8 shows the time ratio of each BFS process for 1 ppn and 4 ppn. The **calculation** is the local processing, while **allgatherv**, **alltoallv**, and **sendrecv** are the communication times listed in Table 3. Additionally, **imbalance** is the synchronization waiting time when barrier synchronization is performed at the end of the approach. Figure 8 indicates that the communication time ratio for 1 ppn is smaller than that for 4 ppn. The reason is considered to be that the number of communication partners of 1 ppn is less than that of 4 ppn.

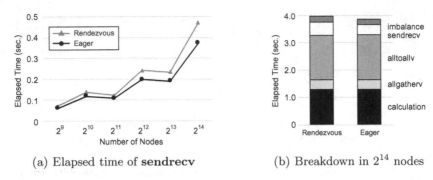

(a) Elapsed time of **sendrecv**   (b) Breakdown in 2^{14} nodes

Fig. 9. Comparison of Rendezvous and Eager

Although we used up to 16,384 nodes in this section, we will report evaluations using more nodes in Sect. 6. From an examination of Fig. 8, it can be predicted that the communication time ratio will be larger when a larger number of nodes is used. Additionally, in general, as the number of processes increases, the amount of memory consumed internally by the MPI library increases. Thus, the subsequent evaluations will be performed for 1 ppn.

5.4 Use of Eager Method

In the point-to-point communication of most MPI implementations, the Eager and Rendezvous methods are implemented. The Eager method sends a message via a buffer regardless of the state of the receiving process. In contrast, the Rendezvous method does not send a message until the receiving process is ready. Since the Eager method is suitable for small message communication, most MPI implementations switch the Eager and Rendezvous methods automatically depending on message size.

As shown in Table 3 and Fig. 6, point-to-point communication is performed in **sendrecv**. In the previous evaluation described in Sect. 5.3, we found that the Rendezvous method was used for all **sendrecv** communications. Here, it should be noted that the Fujitsu MPI library provided by Fugaku can change the switching threshold between the Eager and Rendezvous methods by setting a parameter in the "mpiexec" command. If the node on Fugaku has sufficient memory, the Eager method usage rate can be increased using the parameter. In this experiment, the threshold is set to 512,000 bytes.

This section evaluates the performance when the Eager method is used for all **sendrecv** communications. Figure 9 shows the results. For comparison purposes, Fig. 9 also shows the results for 1ppn in Sect. 5.3 as the "Rendezvous" item. Figure 9a shows the communication time of **sendrecv**, and Fig. 9b shows the breakdown when using 16,384 nodes. These results show that BFS performance is improved by using the Eager method. The result of 16,384 nodes using the Eager method is 17,964 GTEPS. In Fig. 9a, the reason for the staircase shape of the measured value is its relationship to the value of C, shown in Table 3. For example, the values of (R, C) when using 2^{12}, 2^{13}, and 2^{14} nodes are (64, 64), (128, 64), and (128, 128), respectively.

In the subsequent evaluations, the switching threshold will be adjusted so that all **sendrecv** communications will use the Eager method.

5.5   Power Management

As mentioned in Sect. 2, the clock frequency of the A64FX core can be specified as either 2.0 or 2.2 GHz for each job. While the operation at 2.0 GHz is called "Normal mode", that at 2.2 GHz is called "Boost mode". Of course, Boost mode requires more power than Normal mode. To reduce power consumption, "Eco mode" is also available on A64FX. In Eco mode, the two floating-point arithmetic pipelines of A64FX are limited to one, and power control is performed according to the maximum power used at that time. Since BFS does not perform floating-point arithmetic, Eco mode can be expected to reduce power consumption without affecting performance. With that point in mind, this section reports on the performance and power consumption of BFS when using Boost mode and Eco mode. Since the modes are orthogonal settings, the evaluation is performed using the following four combinations:

- **Normal mode:** 2.0 GHz and two floating-point arithmetic pipelines (this mode was used in Sects. 5.3 and 5.4).
- **Boost mode:** 2.2 GHz and two floating-point arithmetic pipelines.
- **Eco mode:** 2.0 GHz and one floating-point arithmetic pipeline.
- **Boost Eco mode:** 2.2 GHz and one floating-point arithmetic pipeline.

There are two power measurement methods used in Fugaku. One is performed by a user (called user method), the other is performed by the facility (called facility method). The user method measures the power in a part of the user program using dedicated APIs on a node-by-node basis, whereas the facility method measures the entire job in rack units (384 nodes are stored in one rack), which means that nodes executing BFS must occupy the rack. In this section, power is measured using the user method. The difference is that the user method measures the direct current (DC) supplied from the power supply unit (PSU), while the facility method measures the 200 V alternating current (AC) supplied to the PSU. In a preliminary evaluation of three racks (1,152 nodes) using Normal mode, the power measured by the user method was found to be 117 kW, while the facility method measurement was 126 kW. The difference between these values is considered to be the AC/DC conversion loss plus the power of the control device in the rack that is not included in the node power [18].

Figure 10a shows the performance ratio of the other modes to that of Normal mode, and Fig. 10b shows the corresponding power efficiency (TEPS/W) ratios. Thus, a value higher than 1.00 indicates performance or power efficiency better than that of Normal mode. Figure 10a indicates that the performance is improved by about 4 to 7 % by setting Boost mode or Boost Eco mode, whereas the performance does not change when Eco mode is set. Figure 10b indicates that

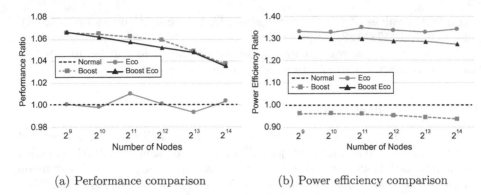

(a) Performance comparison   (b) Power efficiency comparison

Fig. 10. Comparison between modes

the power efficiency is improved by 27 to 35 % by setting Eco mode or Boost Eco mode. From the above results, it can be said that Boost Eco mode is most suitable for BFS because it has both high performance and good power efficiency. In Boost Eco mode, the result for 16,384 nodes is 18,607 GTEPS in performance, 1,408 kW in power consumption, and 13.22 MTEPS/W in power efficiency.

5.6   Six-Dimensional Process Mapping

As described in Sect. 5.2, it is desirable that R and C be close to each other. However, since the maximum size of two-dimensional job shapes supported by the Fugaku job scheduler is $YZc \times Xab$, it is $1{,}104 \times 144$ for the whole system, and the difference between R and C is 7.67 times. Therefore, we perform a process mapping that can set any combination of axes of the TofuD six-dimensional network to R and C. For example, in the case of the whole system, by assigning R to the XY axes and C to the $Zabc$ axes, 552×288 process grid is created. The difference between R and C is 1.92 times.

In the process mapping for C, since the **sendrecv** communication shown in Fig. 6 is suitable for adjacent communication, the mapping should ensure that all the nodes are adjacent. If not, performance will be degraded due to communication collisions. Figure 11 shows an example of assigning the abc axes ($2 \times 3 \times 2$) to C. First, the assigned axis is expanded in two dimensions. The horizontal is the first axis, and the vertical is the remaining axes. Then, all processes are assigned so that they are adjacent to each other. To make the first and last processes (0 and 11) adjacent to each other physically, the topology of the last axis must be either a torus, or the a or c axis because the a and c axes consist of two nodes. Regarding the process mapping for R, it is not necessary to take the above measure because there is no adjacent communication.

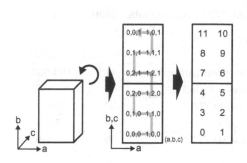

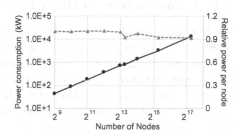

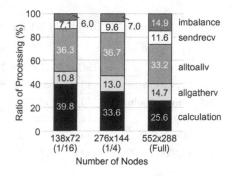

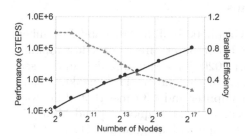

Fig. 11. Process mapping for C **Fig. 12.** Time ratio of processing

Fig. 13. Performance   **Fig. 14.** Power consumption

6   Performance Evaluation on Fugaku

6.1   Performance on Whole Fugaku System

This section evaluates the BFS algorithm on the whole Fugaku system. As described above, we set (R, C) to $(552, 288) = 158{,}976$ nodes, $SCALE = 41$ (a graph with 2^{41} vertices and 2^{45} edges), and Boost Eco mode. For a comparison purpose, we also conducted evaluations using $1/4$ and $1/16$ of Fugaku. We set (R, C) to $(276, 144) = 39{,}744$ nodes and $SCALE = 39$ for $1/4$ system, and (R, C) to $(138, 72) = 9{,}936$ nodes and $SCALE = 37$ for $1/16$ system. Figure 12 shows the time ratio of each process in this evaluation. As the number of nodes increases, the ratio of total communication (**sendrecv** + **alltoallv** + **allgatherv**) and imbalance increase. The performance of each is 102,955 GTEPS for the whole system, 38,749 GTEPS for $1/4$ system, and 13,738 GTEPS for $1/16$ system. In addition, power consumption and power efficiency in the whole system measured by the facility method are 14,961 kW and 6.88 MTEPS/W, respectively.

Figure 13 and Fig. 14 summarize the performance and power consumption results so far; they also show the parallel efficiency and relative power per node with the 2^9-node result set to 1. Note that for power consumption, all results are measured with the user method. As the number of nodes increases, Fig. 13 shows a sharp drop in parallel efficiency, whereas Fig. 14 shows a slight decrease in relative power per node. The reason is considered to be that the communication load becomes large.

Table 4. Graph500 list for June 2019 and November 2020

	June 2019			November 2020		
	NAME	SCALE	GTEPS	NAME	SCALE	GTEPS
1st	**K computer**	40	**31,302**	**Supercomputer Fugaku**	41	**102,955**
2nd	Sunway TaihuLight	40	23,756	Sunway TaihuLight	40	23,756
3rd	Sequoia	41	23,751	TOKI-SORA	36	10,813
4th	Mira	40	14,982	Summit	40	7,666
5th	SuperMUC-NG	39	6,279	SuperMUC-NG	39	6,279

6.2 Comparison with Other Systems

Table 4 shows the first to fifth places of Graph500 in June 2019 and November 2020. In June 2019, the first place was the K computer; this was the last ranking prior to its decommissioning. In November 2020, Fugaku was ranked first based on the performance optimization described in this paper. The Fugaku performance value was 3.3 times that of the K computer and 4.3 times that of Sunway TaihuLight. Between June 2019 and November 2020, Sequoia [5] and Mira [15] were removed from the ranking due to decommissioning, while TOKI-SORA [2] and Summit [3] were newly ranked. TOKI-SORA consists of 5,760 nodes of PRIMEHPC FX1000, which has almost the same specification as Fugaku shown in Table 1, and our implementation is used for the evaluation.

Although omitted in Table 4, in June 2020, Fugaku achieved 70,980 GTEPS in $SCALE = 40$ using 92,160 nodes (60% of Fugaku) and also won the first place. Since this calculation scale is almost the same as the K computer, we will try to compare the two systems. The per-node performance of the K computer and Fugaku at 92,160 nodes is 377 MTEPS (31,302 GTEPS/82,944 nodes) and 770 MTEPS (70,980 GTEPS/92,160 nodes), respectively, so Fugaku has about twice the performance. As shown in Fig. 12, most of the communication time is occupied by collective communication (alltoallv and allgatherv), and the injection bandwidth is important for them. As described in Sect. 2, the difference in injection bandwidth between Fugaku and the K computer is a factor of two. Since the overall performance difference is also twice, we can assume that there is also a 2x difference in local calculation performance, but it is not as great as the specification. For example, the difference in bandwidth is 16.0 times. The reason why Fugaku's local performance is relatively low is that since the measurement is performed with 48 threads per process, there is a lot of memory access across CMGs. The performance modeling of BFS and the CMG-aware locality optimization of A64FX are the future works.

Green Graph500 [1] is a ranking that evaluates the power efficiency performance (TEPS/W) among the systems ranked in Graph500. Green Graph500 is divided into two categories: the BIG DATA category deals with $SCALE \geq 30$, and the SMALL DATA category is for $SCALE \leq 29$. Since $SCALE = 30$ is a relatively small graph size, most top results in the BIG DATA category utilize only one node. Therefore, it can be said that the current Green Graph500 regulations are not suitable for a large-scale system such as Fugaku. As described in Sect. 6.1, BFS on Fugaku uses $SCALE = 41$ and Sequoia was the only machine that ran at the same size in Table 4. Since the power efficiency of Sequoia was 3.72 MTEPS/W, that of Fugaku is 1.9 times better than that of Sequoia.

7   Conclusion and Future Work

This paper presents the performance optimization of BFS in the Graph500 benchmark and evaluations conducted on Fugaku. In the performance evaluation using all Fugaku nodes for a large-scale graph consisting of about 2.2 trillion vertices and 35.2 trillion edges, we achieve 102,955 GTEPS and won the award in Graph500 in November 2020. This performance is 3.3 times that of the K computer, and 4.3 times that of Sunway TaihuLight which is the second place in the Graph500.

Future work will focus on the following: (1) We will optimize our BFS implementation to be aware of the four CMGs in A64FX. For this, NUMA architecture-aware techniques for BFS will be useful [21]. (2) Detailed performance modeling will be necessary to clarify the relationship between hardware and BFS performance. (3) We will develop various graph processing codes including SSSP in the Graph500 benchmark, and utilize Fugaku to perform graph processing of real-world data. (4) From the experiments in this paper, it was found that the communication time became dominant as the number of nodes increased. Future supercomputers for higher performance of BFS will require higher dimensional topologies than TofuD.

Acknowledgments. We would like to express our sincere thanks to Fujitsu engineers of the supercomputer Fugaku for helping us execute the benchmark. We are also grateful to Dr. Yutaka Ishikawa, the project leader of the Flagship 2020 Project. This work is partially funded by the Ministry of Education, Culture, Sports, Science and Technology (MEXT) program for the Development and Improvement for the Next Generation Ultra-High-Speed Computer System, under its Subsidies for Operating the Specific Advanced Large Research Facilities. This work is also partially funded by RIKEN Incentive Research Projects.

References

1. Graph500 and Green Graph500. https://graph500.org
2. Overview of JSS3. https://www.jss.jaxa.jp/en/
3. Summit. https://www.olcf.ornl.gov/olcf-resources/compute-systems/summit/
4. Yoo, A., et al.: A scalable distributed parallel breadth-first search algorithm on BlueGene/L. In: SC 2005: Proceedings of the 2005 ACM/IEEE Conference on Supercomputing, pp. 25–25 (2005). https://doi.org/10.1109/SC.2005.4
5. Barnes Peter, D., et al.: Warp speed: executing time warp on 1,966,080 cores. In: Proceedings of the 1st ACM SIGSIM Conference on Principles of Advanced Discrete Simulation, pp. 327–336 (2013)

6. Miyazaki, H., et al.: Overview of the K computer. Fujitsu Sci. Tech. J. **48**(3), 255–265 (2012)
7. Jakob, J., et al.: Extremely scalable spiking neuronal network simulation code: from laptops to exascale computers. Front. Neuroinform. **12**, 2 (2018)
8. Leskovec, J., et al.: Kronecker graphs: an approach to modeling networks. J. Mach. Learn. Res. **11**(33), 985–1042 (2010)
9. Ueno, K., et al.: Efficient breadth-first search on massively parallel and distributed-memory machines. Data Sci. Eng. **2**, 22–35 (2016)
10. Sato, M., et al.: Co-design for A64FX manycore processor and "Fugaku". In: International Conference for High Performance Computing, Networking, Storage and Analysis, pp. 651–665. IEEE Computer Society, Los Alamitos (2020)
11. Buhlmann, P., et al. (ed.): Handbook of Big Data. Chapman and Hall/CRC, London (2016). https://doi.org/10.1201/b19567
12. Murphy, R.C., et al.: Introducing the graph 500. In: Cray User's Group (2010)
13. Beamer, S., et al.: Direction-optimizing breadth-first search. In: Proceedings of the International Conference on High Performance Computing, Networking, Storage and Analysis, SC 2012, pp. 12:1–12:10. IEEE Computer Society Press, Los Alamitos (2012)
14. Beamer, S., et al.: Distributed memory breadth-first search revisited: enabling bottom-up search. In: IEEE International Symposium on Parallel Distributed Processing, Workshops and Phd Forum, pp. 1618–1627 (2013)
15. Wallace, S., et al.: Measuring power consumption on IBM blue Gene/Q. In: 2013 IEEE International Symposium on Parallel Distributed Processing, Workshops and Phd Forum, pp. 853–859 (2013)
16. Brohee, S., van Helden, J.: Evaluation of clustering algorithms for protein-protein interaction networks. BMC Bioinform. (2006). https://doi.org/10.1186/1471-2105-7-488
17. Da, Y.-F., Zhao, X.-M.: A survey on the computational approaches to identify drug targets in the postgenomic era. BioMed Research International, pp. 1–9 (2015). https://doi.org/10.1155/2015/239654
18. Kodama, Y., et al.: Evaluation of power controls on supercomputer Fugaku. In: Energy Efficient HPC State of the Practice Workshop in conjunction with IEEE Cluster 2020, pp. 484–493 (2020)
19. Ajima, Y., et al.: Tofu: a 6D Mesh/Torus interconnect for exascale computers. Computer **42**(11), 36–40 (2009). https://doi.org/10.1109/MC.2009.370
20. Ajima, Y., et al.: The Tofu interconnect D. In: IEEE International Conference on Cluster Computing, pp. 646–654 (2018)
21. Yasui, Y., et al.: NUMA-optimized parallel breadth-first search on multicore single-node system. In: 2013 IEEE International Conference on Big Data, pp. 394–402 (2013)

Under the Hood of SYCL – An Initial Performance Analysis with An Unstructured-Mesh CFD Application

Istvan Z. Reguly[1,2(✉)], Andrew M. B. Owenson[2], Archie Powell[2], Stephen A. Jarvis[3], and Gihan R. Mudalige[2]

[1] Faculty of Information Technology and Bionics, Pazmany Peter Catholic University, Budapest, Hungary
reguly.istvan@itk.ppke.hu
[2] University of Warwick, Coventry, UK
{a.m.b.owenson,a.powell.3,g.mudalige}@warwick.ac.uk
[3] University of Birmingham, Birmingham, UK
s.a.jarvis@bham.ac.uk

Abstract. As the computing hardware landscape gets more diverse, and the complexity of hardware grows, the need for a general purpose parallel programming model capable of developing (performance) portable codes have become highly attractive. Intel's OneAPI suite, which is based on the SYCL standard aims to fill this gap using a modern C++ API. In this paper, we use SYCL to parallelize MG-CFD, an unstructured-mesh computational fluid dynamics (CFD) code, to explore current performance of SYCL. The code is benchmarked on several modern processor systems from Intel (including CPUs and the latest Xe LP GPU), AMD, ARM and Nvidia, making use of a variety of current SYCL compilers, with a particular focus on OneAPI and how it maps to Intel's CPU and GPU architectures. We compare performance with other parallelizations available in OP2, including SIMD, OpenMP, MPI and CUDA. The results are mixed; the performance of this class of applications, when parallelized with SYCL, highly depends on the target architecture and the compiler, but in many cases comes close to the performance of currently prevalent parallel programming models. However, it still requires different parallelization strategies or code-paths be written for different hardware to obtain the best performance.

1 Introduction

With the switch to multi-core processors in 2004, the underpinning expectation of commercial hardware developers and vendors has been that performance improvements of applications could be maintained at historical rates by exploiting the increasing levels of parallelism in emerging devices. However, a key barrier that has become increasingly significant is the difficulty in programming them. The hardware architectures have become highly complex with massively-parallel and heterogeneous processors, deep and multiple memory hierarchies and complex interconnects. Consequently, extensive parallel programming knowledge is required to fully exploit the potential of these devices.

© Springer Nature Switzerland AG 2021
B. L. Chamberlain et al. (Eds.): ISC High Performance 2021, LNCS 12728, pp. 391–410, 2021.
https://doi.org/10.1007/978-3-030-78713-4_21

A wide range of parallel programming models, extensions and standards have been introduced to address this problem. Over the years these have included proprietary extensions such as CUDA, TBB, Cilk and OpenACC as well as evolving open standards such as OpenMP, OpenCL, and MPI. However, as observed by David Patterson in 2010 [17], industry, academia and stakeholders of HPC have still not been able to provide an acceptable and agile software solution for exploiting the rapidly changing, massively parallel diverse hardware landscape. On the one hand, open standards have been slow to catch up with supporting new hardware, and for many real applications have not provided the best performance achievable from these devices. On the other hand, proprietary solutions have only targeted narrow vendor-specific devices resulting in a proliferation of parallel programming models and technologies. As a result, we have seen and continue to see a golden age of parallel programming software research. A primary target of most such research has been achieving performance portability, where software techniques and methods are developed to enable an application to achieve efficient execution across a wide range of HPC architectures without significant manual modifications.

The most recent addition to the myriad array of parallel programming technologies and software suites is Intel's OneAPI. The need for a single application programming interface (API) to program their divergent hardware products – the currently dominant Xeon multi-core CPUs, recently announced Xe GPUs and Intel's FPGA devices – is driving this development. OneAPI is based on SYCL [2], a C++ abstraction layer for programming parallel systems, initially based on OpenCL, but now decoupled from it [20] to allow for different backends (e.g. CUDA, OpenMP). With the advent of OneAPI and the emerging vendor support for SYCL, it has been touted as one possible open standard for addressing the HPC performance portability problem. As such the objective of the research presented in this paper is to explore the performance of SYCL with a view to evaluate its performance portability, contrasting achieved performance to more established programming models on a range of modern multi-core and many-core devices.

We carry out this work building on the OP2 Domain Specific Language (DSL) [14], which already has wide-ranging capabilities to target modern architectures. OP2 uses source-to-source translation and automatic code generation to produce multiple parallellizations of an application written using the OP2 high-level API. It is currently able to generate parallel code that use SIMD, OpenMP, CUDA and their combinations with MPI together with different optimizations for each version to obtain the best performance from different hardware. In this work we extend these capabilities to also rapidly generate different variants of highly optimized SYCL code and apply it to a recently developed, representative unstructured-mesh CFD application [16] that is written with the OP2 API. We generate SYCL paralleizations for this application, and explore its performance, allowing for a fair and direct comparison of performance, including comparisons with other parallelizations generated through OP2. The work aims to provide a preliminary performance evaluation using current state-of-the-art SYCL. More specifically we make the following contributions:

- We explore how an implementation of the unstructured-mesh parallel motif can be achieved using the SYCL programming model. The main aspect for efficient parallelization is on handling the race-conditions of indirect array increments/updates which we do through coloring and atomics schemes implemented with SYCL.
- The SYCL parallelization is used to develop a new target source generator for OP2. This is used to automatically generate optimized SYCL code for a representative CFD application called MG-CFD. Performance of the SYCL-based MG-CFD parallelization is benchmarked on a range of single-node hardware platforms and compared to the same application parallelized through OP2 using currently established programming models, including SIMD, OpenMP, CUDA and their combinations with MPI.
- Finally, we present a detailed performance analysis of all the parallelizations explored above, contrasting the SYCL implementation with other parallelizations.

The use of an unstructured mesh application, which is characterized by their indirect memory accesses leads to an interesting benchmarking study as such an irregular motif is difficult to parallelize. This we believe will provide a more contrasting evaluation of SYCL, complementing previous work [9] on regular parallel motifs such as structured-mesh applications. Furthermore, the use of OP2's source-to-source translator to automatically produce SYCL parallelizations enables us to rapidly explore the design space and various optimizations without needing to manually modify MG-CFD's 25 loops. We also show that the use of OP2 does not impact the best achievable performance from SYCL for this application. Given the range of modern and emerging multi-core and many-core architectures benchmarked, the different parallelizations explored for each, together with the use of multiple SYCL compilers, makes this study, to our knowledge, the most comprehensive performance investigation into a non-trivial, representative application developed with SYCL to-date.

Details of OP2's performance and portability for existing parallelizations along with the benefits and limitations of such a DSL-based approach have been extensively studied and presented in previous publications [11, 15, 18, 19]. As such we focus on the performance portability of SYCL. As this work uses OP2, we also do not draw conclusions with respect to the usability and maintainability of SYCL, as it is fully hidden from the users of the OP2 library.

The rest of this paper is organized as follows: in Sect. 2 we present an introduction to unstructured mesh applications and the key challenges in parallelizing this class of applications. Next, in Sect. 3 we briefly detail the OP2 API and the target SYCL parallelizations developed for subsequent code-generation through OP2. In Sect. 4 we present empirical performance results of our main benchmark application MG-CFD, parallelized using SYCL, compared to other parallelizations generated with OP2. In Sect. 5 we present a bottleneck analysis of the systems benchmarked and the achievable performance of each parallelization. Finally, conclusions are presented in Sect. 6.

2 Parallelizing Unstructured-Mesh Applications

The key characteristic of the unstructured-mesh motif is the use of explicit connectivity information between elements to specify the mesh topology and consequently to access data defined on neighboring elements [7]. This is in contrast to the use of stencils in structured-mesh applications where the regular geometry of the mesh implicitly provides the connectivity information. As such, iterations over unstructured meshes lead to highly irregular patterns of data accesses over the mesh, due to indirections. For example, computations over the mesh involve iterating over elements of a set (e.g. cell faces), performing the same computations (on different data), accessing/modifying data on the set which they operate on (e.g. fluxes defined on the faces), or using indirections accessing/modifying data defined on other sets (such as data on connected cells). These indirect accesses are particularly difficult to parallelize. For example when parallelizing a loop over mesh edges, then updating data on the two connected nodes will lead to connected edges updating the same nodal data simultaneously, unless explicitly handled by the programmer.

Several strategies exists for handling data races depending on the target hardware and parallel programming model. SIMD vectorization on CPUs parallelize the iterative loop over the mesh elements, stepping through it in strides of the SIMD vector length of the processor. On a processor such as the current generation Intel Xeon – Skylake or Cascade Lake processors, this will be a vector length of 8 with double precision arithmetic. Thus the computation over edges will proceed by computing over 8 edges simultaneously at a time, updating values on the two nodes connected to each edge. One way to handle data races within each step is to implement explicit gather-scatter operations to apply the indirect increments [15]. A gather will stage indirectly-accessed data into a local SIMD-length sized array, then carrying out a computation as SIMD-vector operations on this local data. Finally a scatter will serially apply the increments to the indirectly-accessed data.

For multi-threading on CPUs, the parallelization should make sure that multiple edges assigned to threads do not update the same node simultaneously. With an OpenMP parallelization, one way to avoid data races is to color the edges such than no two edges of the same color update the same node [14]. Coloring can be similarly used for parallelizing on GPUs. Given the larger number of threads executable on GPUs, and the availability of GPU shared memory, different variations of coloring can be used [21]. For distributed-memory parallelizations, such as using MPI, explicitly partitioning the mesh and assigning them to different processors leads to a decomposition of work that only have the potential to overlap at the boundaries of the partitions. An owner-compute model with redundant computation can be used in this case to handle data races [14]. Other strategies published for parallelizing unstructured-mesh applications have included the use of a large temporary array [1] and atomics [21]. Using a large temporary array entails storing the indirect increments for the nodes in a staging array, during the edge loop for example, and then a separate iteration over the nodes to apply the increments from the temporary array on to the nodal data. Atomics on the other hand simply allow for updates to be done one increment at a time with the use of hardware-locks.

3   SYCL Parallelizations with OP2

The best performance we have observed with multi-threading on CPUs and SIMT on GPUs has been through the use of coloring and atomics, respectively. As such, for the

```
 1/* ----- elemental kernel function ---------------*/
 2void res(const double *edge,
 3         double *cell0, double *cell1 ){
 4  //Computations, such as:
 5  cell0 += *edge; *cell1 += *edge;
 6}
 7
 8/* ----- main program ------------------------*/
 9// Declaring the mesh with OP2
10// sets
11op_set edges = op_decl_set(numedge, "edges");
12op_set cells = op_decl_set(numcell, "cells");
13// mppings -connectivity between sets
14op_map edge2cell = op_decl_map(edges, cells,
15                  2, etoc_mapdata,"edge2cell");
16// data on sets
17op_dat p_edge = op_decl_dat(edges,
18                1,"double",edata,"p_edge");
19op_dat p_cell = op_decl_dat(cells,
20                4,"double",cdata,"p_cell");
21
22// OP2 parallel loop declaration
23op_par_loop(res,"res", edges,
24   op_arg_dat(p_edge,-1,OP_ID   ,4,"double",OP_READ),
25   op_arg_dat(p_cell, 0,edge2cell,4,"double",OP_INC ),
26   op_arg_dat(p_cell, 1,edge2cell,4,"double",OP_INC));
```

Fig. 1. Specification of an OP2 parallel loop

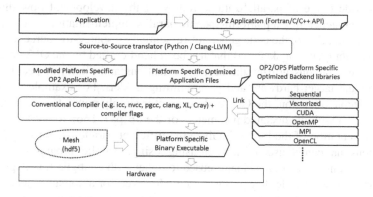

Fig. 2. Developing an application with OP2

SYCL implementation, we solely explore these strategies as appropriate to the target hardware. To ease the development of multiple parallelizations with a range of different optimizations, we use of the OP2 DSL [4, 14].

OP2 allows to define the unstructured-mesh problem in four abstract components: (1) sets (e.g. cells/nodes, faces/edges), (2) data on sets (e.g. node coordinates, edge weights, cell fluxes), (3) explicit connectivity (or mapping) between the sets and (4) operations over sets declared as kernels iterating over each element of the set, accessing indirectly via mappings. A simple example illustrating the OP2 API is presented in Fig. 1. A loop over the set of edges, carrying out computation on each edge defined by the function res, accessing edge data in p_edge directly, and updating the data held on the two adjacent cells, in p_cell, indirectly via the mapping edge2cell. The

```
1 p_par_loop(compute_flux_edge_kernel,
2 "compute_flux_edge_kernel", op_edges,
3 op_arg_dat(vars,0,en,5,"double",OP_READ),
4 op_arg_dat(vars,1,en,5,"double",OP_READ),
5 op_arg_dat(edwgts,-1,OP_ID,3,"double",OP_READ),
6 op_arg_dat(fluxes,0,en,5,"double",OP_INC),
7 op_arg_dat(fluxes,1,en,5,"double",OP_INC));
```

Fig. 3. MG-CFD's compute_flux_edge_kernel loop

op_arg_dat specifies how an op_dat's data is accessed in the loop. Its first argument is the op_dat, followed by (i) its indirection index, (ii) op_map used to access the data indirectly, (iii) parity of the data in the op_dat and (iv) the type of the data. The final argument is the access mode of the data - read only, increment, and others (such as read/write and write only, not shown here). The outer op_par_loop call contains all the necessary information about the computational loop to perform the parallelization. Due to the abstraction, the parallelization depends only on a handful of parameters such as the existence of indirectly-accessed data or reductions in the loop, and the data access modes that lends to optimizations.

Parsing a code written in the above API, OP2's automatic code generator can produce a wide range of parallelizations following the development flow illustrated in Fig. 2. When generating a platform-specific parallel implementation of a loop specified by an op_par_loop, the code generator (essentially a source-to-source translator), selects a base template (or skeleton) that has been hand-crafted by the OP2 developers. Each of these skeletons utilizes the best optimizations and platform-specific configurations for the target hardware and programming models. For example, to produce the CUDA implementation, the OP2 code generator simply populates the appropriate CUDA skeleton with the declared parameters of the op_par_loop to produce the concrete implementation of the loop [6]. Given the different parallelization strategies and optimizations that can be used even when using a single parallel programming model, different skeletons are maintained and reused together with configuration flags for further customizing what code they will generate. However, for a domain scientist developing an unstructured-mesh application, the process of generating a concrete parallel implementation will be automatic.

In this work, we formulate the unstructured-mesh problem using OP2's domain-specific abstraction and then extend its automatic code generation tools to produce an optimized SYCL parallelization. Given the range of hardware and SYCL compilers available, multiple parallelization strategies were investigated to ascertain the best performance. On CPUs, we found that a hierarchical coloring strategy (with 1 work item per workgroup) to apply the indirect increments produced the best performance. On the NVIDIA GPUs benchmarked, the best performance with SYCL was achieved with atomics. However, a SYCL compiler exposing non-standard atomics (fp64) is required to take advantage of the hardware support available on these many-core devices.

```
 1 *Cast OP2 dats, maps and coloring plan as SYCL buffers*/
 2 rg0_buffer = ... ; // vars - indirectly accessed
 3 rg3_buffer = ... ; // fluxes - indirectly accessed
 4 ap0_buffer = ... ; // en - mapping table
 5 rg2_buffer = ... ; // edwgts - directly accessed
 6
 7 ol_reord_buffer = ... ; // coloring array
 8
 9 or ( int col=0; col<Plan->ncolors; col++){//for each color
10   int start = Plan->col_offsets[0][col];
11   int end = Plan->col_offsets[0][col+1];
12   int nblocks = (end - start - 1)/nthread + 1;
13
14   // enqueue arguments and elemental kernel
15   op2_queue->submit([&](cl::sycl::handler& cgh) {
16     ind_arg0 = (*arg0_buffer).. // enqueue vars
17     ind_arg1 = (*arg3_buffer).. // enqueue fluxes
18     opDat0Map = (*map0_buffer).. //enqueue mapping en
19     arg2 = (*arg2_buffer).. // enqueue edwgts
20
21     // enqueue coloring array
22     col_reord = (*col_reord_buffer)..
23     // enqueue any global constants used in the kernel
24     ...
25     //elemental kernel function as lambda - enqueue it
26     auto compute_flux_edge_kernel_gpu = [=](
27         const double *var_a, const double *var_b,
28         const double *edwgts,double *fluxes_a,
29         double *fluxes_b)
30         { .../*body of kernel*/... };
31
32     // setup kernel work items
33     auto kern = [=](cl::sycl::item<1> item) {
34       int tid = item.get_id(0);
35       if (tid + start < end) {
36         int n = col_reord[tid + start];
37         int map0idx; int map1idx;
38
39         // get the indirect index via mapping
40         map0idx = opDat0Map[n+set_size*0];
41         map1idx = opDat0Map[n+set_size*1];
42
43         //user-supplied kernel call
44         compute_flux_edge_kernel_gpu(
45           &ind_arg0[map0idx*5], &ind_arg0[map1idx*5],
46           &arg2[n*3],
47           &ind_arg1[map0idx*5], &ind_arg1[map1idx*5]);
48       }
49     };
50     // execute kernel
51     cgh.parallel_for
52     <class compute_flux_edge_kernel>
53     (cl::sycl::range<1>(nthread * nblocks), kern);
54   }); // end of enqueue arguments and elemental kernel
55
```

Fig. 4. Global coloring parallelization generated by OP2 for the `compute_flux_edge_kernel` loop in MG-CFD

3.1 Coloring

As noted before, coloring can be applied to avoid the data races in unstructured-mesh computations. This parallelization strategy can be generally implemented on any shared memory multi-threaded system, including CPUs and GPUs without any restrictions

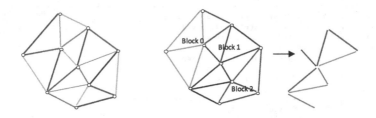

Fig. 5. Coloring strategies in OP2 – global (left) and hierarchical (right)

due to hardware capabilities. Different variations of coloring have been implemented within OP2 as detailed in previous works [21]. Figure 4 details an excerpt of the SYCL code generated by OP2 for the most time-consuming parallel loop `compute_flux_edge _kernel` in MG-CFD. The OP2 API declaration of this loop is listed in Fig. 3. This loop iterates over the set of mesh edges, `op_edges`, indirectly reading DP floating-point data held in the node-indexed array `vars`, using the mapping from edges-to-nodes, `en`; it also directly reads DP floating-point data held on edges from array `edwgts`. The resulting flux contributions are indirectly incremented onto the output node-indexed array `fluxes`, again via the edges-to-nodes mapping.

There are two fundamental coloring schemes and execution strategies, which are illustrated in Fig. 5. The first drawing shows the simplest strategy, *global coloring*, which performs a single level of greedy coloring of set elements (edges) based on a mapping (edges-to-nodes), such that no two edges with the same color share a node. During execution, edges with the same color can now be executed in parallel, with a synchronization between colors. The second strategy, called *hierarchical coloring*, performs two levels of coloring. First, the mesh is split into blocks of edges, and the blocks colored such that no two blocks with the same color share any node. Second, edges within the block are greedily colored. During execution, blocks of the same color can be executed in parallel, and within blocks there is further parallelism, so edges of the same color can be executed in parallel. This hierarchical scheme maps to architectures with hierarchical parallelism, for example blocks map to OpenMP threads or CUDA thread blocks, and intra-block parallelism maps to vector units or CUDA threads. We map this hierarchical scheme to `nd_range` parallel for loops in SYCL.

The SYCL parallelization with global coloring starts by extracting the SYCL typed buffers from OP2's data structures (Fig. 4, lines 1–5). The iteration set, in this case the mesh edges, has been colored by OP2, with coloring information stored in internal struct `Plan`. For SYCL execution, this coloring information is also stored in a SYCL integer buffer. An outer loop over colors initiates parallel execution across edges of the same color (line 9). Edge indices are held in the `col_reord` array, with edges of the same color stored consecutively. The current color determines the loop range `start` to `end`, read from `Plan->col_offsets`, determining which edges of `col_reord` to iterate through for that particular parallel execution.

Similar to the setup required for executing an OpenCL kernel, the arguments for the execution kernel, the kernel itself and any global constants referenced by it are enqueued (lines 15–30). The kernel itself is specified as a lambda function (lines 25–30). Next, the SYCL kernel is set with flat parallelism, so that `nthread*nblocks` work items are launched (lines 51–53). The indirections are resolved by using the edge index n to access the indices held in the mapping table `opDat0Map` (lines 40–41). The elemental kernel is called with these indices, together with the directly accessed data as arguments (lines 44–47).

The advantage of global coloring is its simplicity – it can be easily expressed in any parallel programming environment. The main disadvantage with global coloring is the loss of data-reuse between edges that share a node, as these edges will necessarily have different colors, so reducing temporal locality. A further disadvantage is reduced spatial locality, as elements of the same color are distributed more sparsely in memory.

The hierarchical coloring scheme maps well to GPU architectures, and in principle to CPU threads and vector units as well. However, the OpenMP-based implementations (hipSYCL) have a mismatch between the abstraction and the implementation, leading to poor performance; they need to launch one thread per work item when using two-level parallelism (nd_range), when one thread per work *group* would be best. Intel's OneAPI compilers can optimize and map this better to hardware, yet despite achieving vectorization, as we show in Sect. 4, performance was poor. To address these issues, we implemented a variation of the hierarchical execution scheme in SYCL where each work group consists of a single work item, which then iterates through the edges in that block sequentially. This proved to perform better on all CPU platforms with all compilers. This implementation now matches the execution scheme used by OP2's OpenMP execution scheme. However, it prevents vectorization by construction.

All coloring-based executions add a one-time setup cost to the total runtime for creating the colored execution scheme. For production applications that iterate over many cycles, this setup cost becomes negligible or indeed could be pre-computed if the mesh is known before runtime.

3.2   Atomics

In contrast to coloring, atomics-based parallelizations enable the indirect updates (i.e. increments) to be applied sequentially using hardware atomic operations. The disadvantage is that not all hardware has fast DP implementations of atomics, and that the SYCL 1.2.1 standard does not include them, however hipSYCL has support for them on NVIDIA GPUs. Figure 6 details an excerpt of the SYCL code generated by OP2 for `compute_flux_edge_kernel` loop using atomics targeting the hipSYCL compiler (which has support for DP atomics). This code is similar to the global coloring scheme for much of the setup. The `start` and `end` now points to the full iteration range over the mesh edges. The key difference with atomics is the use of local arrays `arg3_1` and `arg4_1` to hold the indirect increments and apply them using atomics (lines 44–53). This results in an extra 10 floating-point operations per edge. In contrast to coloring schemes, there is no setup cost for coloring plan construction when using atomics.

4   Performance

In this section, we generate SYCL parallelizations with OP2 for MG-CFD [16]. MG-CFD is a 3D unstructured multigrid, finite-volume computational fluid dynamics (CFD)

```
1  *Cast OP2 dats, maps and coloring plan as SYCL buffers*/
2  rg0_buffer = ... ; // vars - indirectly accessed
3  rg3_buffer = ... ; // fluxes - indirectly accessed
4  ap0_buffer = ... ; // en - mapping table
5  rg2_buffer = ... ; // edwgts - directly accessed
6
7  f (end-start>0) {
8   int nblocks = (end-start-1)/nthread+1;
9   // enqueue arguments and elemental kernel
10  op2_queue->submit([&](cl::sycl::handler& cgh) {
11
12     ind_arg0 = (*arg0_buffer).. // enqueue vars
13     ind_arg1 = (*arg3_buffer).. // enqueue fluxes
14     opDat0Map = (*map0_buffer).. //enqueue mapping en
15     arg2 = (*arg2_buffer).. // enqueue edwgts
16     // enqueue any global constants used in the kernel
17     ...
18     //elemental kernel function as lambda
19     auto compute_flux_edge_kernel_gpu = [=](...)
20     { .../*body of kernel*/... };
21
22     // setup kernel work items
23     auto kern = [=](cl::sycl::nd_item<1> item) {
24       //local variables for holding indirect increments
25       double arg3_l[5], arg4_l[5];
26       for ( int d=0; d<5; d++ ){ arg3_l[d] = 0.0;}
27       for ( int d=0; d<5; d++ ){ arg4_l[d] = 0.0;}
28       int tid = item.get_global_linear_id();
29       if (tid + start < end) {
30         int n = tid+start;
31         int map0idx; int map1idx;
32
33         // get the indirect index via mapping
34         map0idx = opDat0Map[n + set_size * 0];
35         map1idx = opDat0Map[n + set_size * 1];
36
37         //elemental kernel call
38         compute_flux_edge_kernel_gpu(
39         &ind_arg0[map0idx*5], &ind_arg0[map1idx*5],
40         &arg2[n*3],
41         arg3_l, arg4_l);
42
43     //apply indirect increments using atomics
44       {cl::sycl::atomic<double> a
45       {cl::sycl::global_ptr<double>
46       {&ind_arg1[0+map0idx*5]}};
47       a.fetch_add(arg3_l[0]);}
48       ...
49       ...
50       {cl::sycl::atomic<double> a
51       {cl::sycl::global_ptr<double>
52       {&ind_arg1[4+map1idx*5]}};
53       a.fetch_add(arg4_l[4]);}
54     }
55   };
56   // execute kernel
57   cgh.parallel_for
58   <class compute_flux_edge_kernel>
59   (cl::sycl::nd_range<1>(nthread*nblocks,nthread),kern);
60  }); //end of enqueue arguments and elemental kernel
61
```

Fig. 6. Atomics-based paralelization generated by OP2 for `compute_flux_edge_kernel` loop in MG-CFD

mini-app for inviscid-flow. Developed by extending the CFD solver in the Rodinia benchmark suite [5,8], it implements a three-dimensional finite-volume discretization of the Euler equations for inviscid, compressible flow over an unstructured grid. It performs a sweep over faces to accumulate fluxes, implemented as a loop over all mesh edges. Multi-grid support is implemented by augmenting the construction of the Euler solver presented in [8] with crude operators to transfer the state of the simulation between the levels of the multi-grid. Initially written as a standalone CPU-only implementation [16], MG-CFD has now been converted to use the OP2 API. It is available as open-source software at [3]. This repository also contains the concrete parallel implementations generated through OP2 for SIMD, OpenMP, CUDA, OpenMP4.0, OpenACC and their combinations with MPI. The branch feature/sycl contains the generated SYCL versions of the application used in our performance investigation.

Our aim is to compare the performance of the SYCL implementations to that of other parallel versions for MG-CFD and explore how similar execution strategies can be expressed using SYCL. For benchmarking we use several systems based on currently prevalent and emerging processor architectures. A summary of the key specifications of these systems are detailed in Table 1 and Table 2.

Table 1. Benchmark systems specifications: GPUs

GPU	NVIDIA V100	NVIDIA A100	AMD Radeon VII	Intel Iris XE MAX
Bus protocol	PCI-e 3.0	SXM4	PCI-e 3.0	PCI-e 4.0
Cores	5120	6912	3840	768
Clock (MHz)	1245–1380	1410	1400–1750	300–1650
TFLOPS/s compute	7	9.7	3.46	2.53 (single)
Bandwidth (GB/s)	900	1600	1024	68
Measured BW (GB/s)	789	1269	668	53.5
Memory size (GB)	16	40	16	4
TDP (W)	250	400	300	25

We use the NVIDIA V100 and AMD Radeon VII GPUs of our local cluster. The A100 GPUs used were in AWS (Amazon Web Services) p4d.24xlarge instances, and the Iris XE MAX (based on XE LP architecture) GPUs were accessed through Intel's DevCloud. To benchmark CPUs, we have evaluated three high-end machines available through AWS instances. The c5d.24xlarge instance has a dual-socket Intel Xeon Cascade Lake Platinum, each with 24 cores and 2 threads per core (SMT-2). The c5a.24xlarge has a single-socket AMD EPYC Rome with 48 physical cores and SMT-2. The c6g.16xlarge has a single-socket AWS Graviton2 ARM with 64 cores. While all of these were virtual machines, these contain some of the latest hardware

Table 2. Benchmark systems specifications: CPUs

System	AWS c5d.24xlarge	AWS c5a.24xlarge	AWS c6g.16xlarge
Node Architecture	Intel Xeon Platinum 8275CL 3.00 GHz (**Cascade Lake**)	AMD EPYC (**Rome**) 7R32 3.20 GHz (custom SKU)	AWS **Graviton2** ARM v8.2 @ 2.5 GHz
Procs × cores	2×24 (2 SMT/core)	1×48 (2 SMT/core)	1×64 (1 thread/core)
CPU Vector Length (ISA)	512 bits (AVX-512)	256 bits (AVX-2)	128 bits (NEON)
Cache Hierarchy	32 KB L1D/core, 1 MB L2/core, 35.75 MB L3/socket	32 KB L1D/core 512 KB L2/core 256 MB L3/socket	64 KB L1D/core 1 MB L2/core 32 MB L3/socket
CPU Main Memory	192 GB	192 GB	128 GB
Measured BW (GB/s)	109.3 (per socket)	131.6	173.6
O/S	Ubuntu 20.04	Ubuntu 20.04	Ubuntu 20.04
TDP per CPU	~240 W	~220W	~100W

Table 3. Compilers and compiler flags

Compiler	Version	Compiler flags
Intel OneAPI Compilers `icc, icpc, dpcpp`	Beta 9 Backend: OpenCL	`-O3 -xHOST -inline-forceinline -restrict -qopenmp|-fsycl`
`nvcc`	CUDA 10.2	`-O3 -restrict` V100 : `-gencode arch=compute_70,code=sm_70` A100 : `-gencode arch=compute_80,code=sm_80`
HipSYCL Compiler `syclcc-clang`	Based on Clang 9 Backend: OpenMP Backend: CUDA Backend: CUDA Backend: HIP	`-O3` All CPUs: `--hipsycl-platform=cpu` V100 : `--hipsycl-gpu-arch=sm_70` A100 : `--hipsycl-gpu-arch=sm_80` Radeon VII : `--hipsycl-gpu-arch=gfx906`
GNU `gcc,g++`	9.3	AMD Rome, AWS Graviton2 `-Ofast -fopenmp`

architectures available, and achieve the same fraction of peak performance as our internal, less powerful, Intel-based bare-metal systems.

Figures 7 and 8 present the runtime of the main time-marching loops of MG-CFD on the above systems, solving a NASA Rotor 37 [10] benchmark mesh consisting of 8 million edges on the finest level. The time to solution of 25 multi-grid cycles are reported here. The time for initial I/O (mesh loading and partitioning) are not included, given that these are a one-off setup cost and depends on other libraries such as HDF5, ParMETIS/PTScotch etc., that are not the subject of this paper. The figure presents

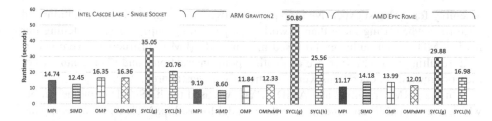

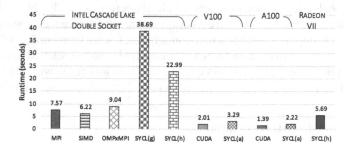

Fig. 7. MG-CFD, Runtime (seconds) on single socket CPUs – 8M edges, 25 MG Cycles

Fig. 8. MG-CFD, Runtime (seconds) on a dual socket CPUs and GPUs - 8M edges, 25 MG Cycles

the runtime of the application without any coloring plan time construction overheads, which was discussed in Sect. 3.1. Given these setup costs are one-off or indeed can be computed a priori if the mesh is known before runtime, we believe the figure provides a fairer comparison between the actual performance of each architecture and parallelization model. Compilers and compiler flags used for each version of the parallelizations are detailed in Table 3.

Reference performance numbers were collected using existing parallelizations in OP2: plain MPI which does not auto-vectorize, an MPI+SIMD version which uses explicit gathers and scatters to enable auto-vectorization, OpenMP that does not auto-vectorize, hybrid MPI+OpenMP, and for NVIDIA GPUs using CUDA with atomics.

4.1 CPU Results

On the Intel Cascade Lake CPU, we used the OneAPI compilers to compile SYCL. The global colouring variant *(g)* uses a flat parallel for loop, however due to poor memory access patterns it performs the worst. To improve memory locality, we utilize the hierarchical execution scheme *(h)* – mapping blocks to threads as done in case of OpenMP, and optionally elements within blocks to vector lanes. The performance reported in Fig. 7 (SYCL(h)) uses the same number of blocks as the OpenMP version and only uses a single work item per workgroup, which mirrors the behavior of our OpenMP execution scheme, and overall runtime is 26% slower. We also evaluated using 8 work items (AVX512 with FP64) and utilized Intel's subgroup extension to perform safe colored updates, however performance further degraded. An examination of the generated assembly for the most expensive loop provides two key insights: (1) computations did vectorize (when using more than 1 work item per workgroup), closely matching our MPI+SIMD variant, although no fused multiply-add (FMA) instructions were generated, resulting in a 32% increase of floating point instructions, and (2) the number of memory movement operations were significantly larger (approx. $2\times$).

On the ARM Graviton2 and AMD EPYC, we used the hipSYCL implementation, which uses OpenMP underneath. For flat parallel loops, hipSYCL will map computations to a flat OpenMP parallel loop, however when using hierarchical parallelism it will launch one thread per work item to guarantee that barriers can be handled correctly. The global coloring execution scheme clearly performs poorly, due to the lack of memory locality. For the hierarchical execution scheme, we used a single work item per workgroup, mirroring the OpenMP execution scheme. On the Graviton2, SYCL performance is $2.16\times$ worse than plain OpenMP – largely due to the relative immaturity of ARM support in Clang (used by hipSYCL) versus GNU g++ (used with flat OpenMP). On the AMD EPYC however, SYCL performs only 21% slower than plain OpenMP.

4.2 NVIDIA and AMD GPU Results

For the comparison with GPUs, we also ran on both sockets of the Intel Cascade Lake CPU, and observed over 95% scaling efficiency for pure MPI and MPI+SIMD, though only 80% for MPI+OpenMP. SYCL however did not improve when running over both sockets due to NUMA issues – OP2 does not yet have an MPI+SYCL backend, which would address this. For both NVIDIA and AMD GPUs, we utilized the automatic *Array-of-Structs $\rightarrow$ Struct-of-Arrays* data layout conversion feature of OP2. On NVIDIA GPUs, we used the atomics versions and compiled with hipSYCL – this showed a $60-64\%$ slowdown compared to the atomics version of CUDA. These differences are likely due to the immaturity of the hipSYCL compiler, resulting in higher register pressure and lower occupancy. The AMD Radeon VII GPU does not have hardware support for double precision atomics, and therefore we utilized the hierarchical coloring execution scheme with 128 work items per workgroup. OP2 does not have support for either HIP or OpenCL, therefore we could not compare this to a reference implementation.

4.3 Intel Iris XE MAX Performance

To further explore OneAPI, we have evaluated the recently released Intel datacenter GPU built on the XE LP (low-power) platform. As the specifications in Table 1 show, this is a GPU in an entirely different class to the others tested. It has a $10-16\times$ lower TDP, and a similarly lower maximum bandwidth (53 GB/s measured), yet a relatively high maximum computational throughput – though it has to be noted that the card does not support double precision. This makes the platform have the highest ratio of FLOPS to bandwidth among all the tested hardware.

We prepared a single precision version of MG-CFD to evaluate performance – without considering the implications on accuracy and convergence at the moment. These

GPUs also do not support single precision atomics, therefore we compared the various colored execution schemes. Intel's GPUs also support the subgroups extension of SYCL, and indeed are vital for good performance. We found the best performing combination is the hierarchical coloring execution scheme with 16 work items per workgroup, and 16 work items per subgroup (i.e. one subgroup per workgroup), and relied on subgroup barriers to perform the colored updates. The automatic AoS $\rightarrow$ SoA data layout conversion did not improve performance on this GPU. The best runtime was 22.4 s – for context, we compared performance to a single-socket Platinum 8256 CPU (4 cores, 51 GB/s STREAM bandwidth), which ran MPI+SIMD in 21.6 s and pure OpenMP in 42.4.

5   Bottleneck Analysis

To gather further insight into the performance profile of the application, we selected the most time-consuming kernel (`compute_flux_edge`), responsible for over 50% of total runtime, to carry out a bottleneck analysis. This kernel operates on edges, for each performing about 150 floating-point instructions, reading 5 values from each node and 3 values from the edge, then indirectly incrementing 5 further values on each node. Due to the indirect accesses it is not a trivially vectorizable kernel, and it is highly sensitive to data reuse. For each platform we collected the relevant compute (GFLOPS/s) and bandwidth (GB/s) measures onto the rooflines of each platform using the Berkeley Empirical Roofline Tool [12] and the STREAM [13] benchmark.

Table 4. Floating point operations per edge with different compilers

	Scalar		SIMD			CUDA
	Intel	ARM/AMD	AVX 512	AVX	ARM	
FLOPs/edge	150	165	216	165	164	323

To calculate the floating-point operation counts (FLOPs) per edge, we inspected the assembly generated for the computation of each edge for different implementations (see Table 4, which shows operations, not instructions). There are over 150 floating point operations per edge (with minor variations between compilers), and 13 of these are `sqrt` and `div` operations. It is important to note here that on CPUs there are specific instructions for division and square root operations (though with much lower throughput than multiply or add), whereas on NVIDIA GPUs these are mapped to a sequence of multiplications and additions – hence the much higher FLOPS per edge for CUDA. Furthermore, depending on the compiler and the instruction set architecture (ISA) used (scalar, AVX or AVX512) we get different FLOP counts; AVX generates precise divisions (single instruction), whereas AVX512 generates approximate reciprocals followed by additional multiply and add operations. With SIMD and hierarchical execution schemes, the SIMD-calculated increments are staged in a local array, then applied sequentially, adding a further 10 add operations per edge. Finally, as reported before, Intel's SYCL version does not use FMA instructions, therefore even though the number of floating point operations is the same, the number of instructions is 32% higher.

The achieved computational throughput of `compute_flux` is shown in Table 5, with the highest fraction of peak achieved on the V100 GPU at 26%. While the maximum throughput is not representative particularly on CPUs due to the long-latency sqrt and division instructions, it is nevertheless clear that operational throughput – particularly for vectorized and GPU versions - is not a bottleneck. On CPU architectures, it is on the ARM platform, where the highest fraction of peak is achieved: 22% with the MPI+SIMD variant.

Table 5. Achieved computational throughput (GFLOPS/sec) of `compute_flux`

	Intel CSX	AMD EPYC	ARM Graviton2	NVIDIA V100	NVIDIA A100	AMD Radeon VII
Peak	**1150**	**1420**	**845**	**6950**	**9540**	**3300**
MPI	101	139	171			
MPI+SIMD	215	104	190			
OpenMP	98	117	138			
SYCL	74	88	67	1140	1269	517
CUDA				1836	2480	

Table 6. Amount of data moved (in GB) from/to off-chip RAM with various parallelizations

MPI	OpenMP hierarchical	SYCL global	SYCL hierarchical	CUDA atomics	AMD SYCL hierarchical
448	778	2856	818	381	1190

To measure the amount of data moved, and to determine the extent to which `compute_flux` is bound by available memory bandwidth, we have created a stripped-down version of the kernel with negligible compute operations, but the same memory accesses, called `unstructured_stream`. Then, we instrumented this `unstructured_stream` kernel using LIKWID [22], and used the MEM performance counter group to determine the amount of data that is read from and written to off-chip DRAM. For the GPU architectures, we used NVIDIA Nsight Compute tool and ROCm's `rocprof` tool to gather the same information. The collected results are shown in Table 6, and it highlights a very important aspect of unstructured mesh computations: the execution method used to avoid race conditions has enormous implications on the amount of data moved, and consecutively performance.

1. MPI – with distributed memory parallelism, each process iterates sequentially over the elements it owns, and the additional cost is in the explicit communications between processes.
2. Hierarchical coloring – when we break the edges into blocks, color them, then execute blocks of the same color in parallel, then by construction there will be no data reuse between blocks, but there will be reuse within blocks. On average 26 colors are required. With OpenMP and SYCL running on the CPU, we use blocks of size 2048; when running on the AMD GPU, we use a block size of 128. Correspondingly, these execution schemes move $1.73 - 2.65\times$ the amount of data compared to MPI.
3. Global coloring – when edges are colored based on potential race conditions, and all edges with the same color are executed in parallel, then there is no data reuse between edges by construction. On average 22.8 colors are required. This approach requires moving the most data; $6.25\times$ the amount compared to MPI.
4. CUDA Atomics – flat parallelism is used, and there is no need for explicit communication between the processes or thread as in the case of MPI. Therefore this approach incurs the least overhead in terms of data movement.

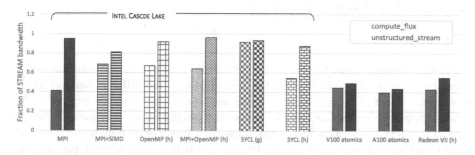

Fig. 9. Fraction of STREAM bandwidth achieved by unstructured_stream and compute_flux

The performance of unstructured_stream can then be directly contrasted with STREAM; in Fig. 9, we show the fraction of peak STREAM bandwidth achieved by both unstructured_stream and compute_flux. It is clear that on the Intel CPU, all parallelizations are bandwidth bound – MPI+SIMD achieves a lower fraction of peak than the others due to the overhead of explicitly packing and unpacking registers. On the GPU platforms, performance is reported to be limited by L1/Texture cache throughput as well as atomics on NVIDIA and block synchronization overhead (required for colored updates) on AMD cards.

When comparing the achieved bandwidth of compute_flux, the performance differences of different parallelizations are seen from a different perspective; how much performance is bottlenecked by data movement, and how much computations are interleaved with data movement. The MPI and MPI+SIMD variants move the same amount of data, VTune reports 99.7% vector capacity usage for the computational body of the SIMD version, while the plain MPI version does not vectorize at all. Despite good vectorization with SIMD, there is poor overlap between computations and data movement, reducing the achieved fraction of STREAM to 69%. When enabling Hyper-threading (which is shown in the results), performance of compute_flux is improved by 17% compared to only using 1 thread per core (but makes no difference for unstructured_stream), which supports the conclusion of poor overlap. This is even more obvious on the non-vectorized MPI version, where the cost of scalar computations reduces the achieved fraction of STREAM of compute_flux to 41%, and is therefore just as much bound by the throughput of scalar operations.

The lack of vectorization is much less impactful on other parallelizations; even though neither OpenMP nor hierarchical SYCL versions vectorize (SYCL's vectorized hierarchical version performs even worse as discussed above), they still achieve over 55% of peak bandwidth – due to having to move $1.7 - 1.8\times$ more data. The lack of overlap between compute and data movement is responsible for the rest of the gap to STREAM. With global coloring, the SYCL implementation does vectorize, yet the cost of data movement dwarfs that of computations.

On the GPUs, only 43–62% of peak bandwidth is achieved by unstructured stream, but compute_flux also achieves 39–44% of peak as well. Computations and data movement is much better overlapped thanks to the massive parallelism, but while unstructured_stream achieves 100% occupancy, compute_flux only has 35%, leading to slightly worse overlap.

6   Conclusion

The results shown indicate that the SYCL API brings comparable performance (within a factor of 1.3-$2.0\times$) overall for both CPUs and GPUs from different vendors in this application. The SYCL ecosystem is rapidly closing the performance gap with other parallel programming models. This is an essential quality of any new parallel API, so the fact that SYCL already achieves this shows that it is a good foundation for Intel's OneAPI software suite. In addition, as the standard is further developed, performance parity with other models is expected as software and hardware vendors optimize.

However, as with other portable parallelization approaches, there is still the need to write different parallelizations within the code to achieve the best runtimes. In the case of this unstructured mesh application, that entailed writing a coloring parallelization for CPUs and Radeon GPUs, and an atomics version for NVIDIA GPUs. Thus, the idea of SYCL abstracting away device-specific code may not be entirely representative of real world use cases. This is especially true for irregular classes of applications, such as unstructured-mesh, as opposed to the more commonly explored regular applications.

If this disparity continues, then it could lead to SYCL being seen as yet another industry standard, being grouped together with existing compute frameworks which offer similar levels of performance portability. For example, OpenMP is a far more mature standard which can also be written for all devices that SYCL currently supports, not to mention code-bases that do not use modern C++ (e.g. Fortran), which then cannot use SYCL. The DSL-based code generator used in this work, OP2, has been able to keep up with such changes by adding new code generators which can produce code based on emerging standards and models. However, for applications which are not based on frameworks and require a rewrite, developers could be hesitant to adopt SYCL for these reasons.

Nevertheless, SYCL is a major step forward, in that it presents a modern, succinct C++ API (in contrast to e.g. OpenCL), capable of targeting an impressively wide set of parallel architectures (in contrast to vendor-specific extensions, e.g. CUDA), that allows fine grained control over parallelism, and is reasonably capable of exposing low-level features of various architectures. Given the improving performance of compilers, we do recommend SYCL to application developers who want a unified parallel programming framework.

As a continuation of this work, we are developing multi-device and distributed memory support with MPI+SYCL in OP2, and we are evaluating performance with a range of further applications already using OP2. We also intend to explore the support for targeting FPGAs using SYCL.

Acknowledgment. This research is supported by Rolls-Royce plc., and by the UK Engineering and Physical Sciences Research Council (EPSRC): (EP/S005072/1 – Strategic Partnership in Computational Science for Advanced Simulation and Modelling of Engineering Systems – ASiMoV). Gihan Mudalige was supported by the Royal Society Industry Fellowship Scheme(INF/R1/1800 12). István Reguly was supported by National Research, Development and Innovation Fund of Hungary, project PD 124905, financed under the PD_17 funding scheme.

References

1. Hydrodynamics Challenge Problem, Lawrence Livermore National Laboratory. Technical Report LLNL-TR-490254
2. C++ Single-source Heterogeneous Programming for OpenCL (2019). https://www.khronos.org/sycl/
3. MG-CFD-OP2 GitHub Repository (2019). https://github.com/warwick-hpsc/MG-CFD-app-OP2
4. OP2 github repository (2019). https://github.com/OP-DSL/OP2-Common
5. Rodinia: Accelerating Compute-Intensive Applications with Accelerators (2019). https://rodinia.cs.virginia.edu/
6. Balogh, G., Mudalige, G., Reguly, I., Antao, S., Bertolli, C.: OP2-Clang: a source-to-source translator using Clang/LLVM LibTooling. In: 2018 IEEE/ACM 5th Workshop on the LLVM Compiler Infrastructure in HPC (LLVM-HPC), pp. 59–70 (2018). https://doi.org/10.1109/LLVM-HPC.2018.8639205
7. Colella, P.: Defining Software Requirements for Scientific Computing (2004). (Presentation)
8. Corrigan, A., Camelli, F., Löhner, R., Wallin, J.: Running unstructured grid CFD solvers on modern graphics hardware. In: 19th AIAA Computational Fluid Dynamics Conference. No. AIAA 2009–4001, June 2009
9. Deakin, T., McIntosh-Smith, S.: Evaluating the performance of HPC-Style SYCL applications. In: Proceedings of the International Workshop on OpenCL. IWOCL 2020, New York. Association for Computing Machinery (2020). https://doi.org/10.1145/3388333.3388643
10. Denton, J.: Lessons from rotor 37. J. Thermal Sci. **6**(1), 1–13 (1997)
11. Giles, M., Mudalige, G., Spencer, B., Bertolli, C., Reguly, I.: Designing OP2 for GPU architectures. J. Parallel Distrib. Comput. **73**(11), 1451–1460 (2013). https://doi.org/10.1016/j.jpdc.2012.07.008, https://www.sciencedirect.com/science/article/pii/S0743731512001694
12. Lo, Y.J., et al.: Roofline model toolkit: a practical tool for architectural and program analysis. In: Jarvis, S.A., Wright, S.A., Hammond, S.D. (eds.) PMBS 2014. LNCS, vol. 8966, pp. 129–148. Springer, Cham (2015). https://doi.org/10.1007/978-3-319-17248-4_7

13. McCalpin, J.D.: Memory bandwidth and machine balance in current high performance computers. In: IEEE Computer Society Technical Committee on Computer Architecture (TCCA) Newsletter, pp. 19–25 (1995)

14. Mudalige, G., Giles, M., Reguly, I., Bertolli, C., Kelly, P.: OP2: An active library framework for solving unstructured mesh-based applications on multi-core and many-core architectures. In: 2012 Innovative Parallel Computing, InPar 2012 (2012). https://doi.org/10.1109/InPar.2012.6339594

15. Mudalige, G., Reguly, I., Giles, M.: Auto-vectorizing a large-scale production unstructured-mesh CFD application. In: Proceedings of the 3rd Workshop on Programming Models for SIMD/Vector Processing, New York, pp. 5:1–5:8. WPMVP 2016. ACM (2016). https://doi.org/10.1145/2870650.2870651

16. Owenson, A., Wright, S., Bunt, R., Ho, Y., Street, M., Jarvis, S.: An unstructured CFD mini-application for the performance prediction of a production CFD code. Concur. Comput. Pract. Exper. **32**, e5443(2019). https://doi.org/10.1002/cpe.5443

17. Patterson, D.: The trouble with multi-core. IEEE Spectrum **47**(7), 28–32 (2010). https://doi.org/10.1109/MSPEC.2010.5491011

18. Reguly, I.Z., et al.: The VOLNA-OP2 tsunami code (version 1.5). Geoscientific Model Dev. **11**(11), 4621–4635 (2018). https://doi.org/10.5194/gmd-11-4621-2018, https://gmd.copernicus.org/articles/11/4621/2018/

19. Reguly, I.Z., et al.: Acceleration of a full-scale industrial CFD application with OP2. IEEE Trans. Parallel Distrib. Syst. **27**(5), 1265–1278 (2016). https://doi.org/10.1109/TPDS.2015.2453972

20. Reyes, R., Brown, G., Burns, R., Wong, M.: SYCL 2020: more than meets the eye. In: Proceedings of the International Workshop on OpenCL. IWOCL 2020, New York. Association for Computing Machinery (2020). https://doi.org/10.1145/3388333.3388649, https://doi.org/10.1145/3388333.3388649

21. Sulyok, A., Balogh, G., Reguly, I., Mudalige, G.: Locality optimized unstructured mesh algorithms on GPUs. J. Parallel Distrib. Comput. **134**, 50–64 (2019). https://doi.org/10.1016/j.jpdc.2019.07.011

22. Treibig, J., Hager, G., Wellein, G.: LIKWID: a lightweight performance-oriented tool suite for x86 multicore environments. In: 2010 39th International Conference on Parallel Processing Workshops, pp. 207–216 (2010). https://doi.org/10.1109/ICPPW.2010.38

Characterizing Containerized HPC Applications Performance at Petascale on CPU and GPU Architectures

Amit Ruhela$^{(\boxtimes)}$, Stephen Lien Harrell, Richard Todd Evans,
Gregory J. Zynda, John Fonner, Matt Vaughn, Tommy Minyard,
and John Cazes

Texas Advanced Computing Center, Austin, TX, USA
{aruhela,sharrell,rtevans,gzynda,
jfonner,vaughn,minyard,cazes}@tacc.utexas.edu

Abstract. Containerization technologies provide a mechanism to encapsulate applications and many of their dependencies, facilitating software portability and reproducibility on HPC systems. However, in order to access many of the architectural features that enable HPC system performance, compatibility between certain components of the container and host is required, resulting in a trade-off between portability and performance. In this work, we discuss our experiences running three state-of-the-art containerization technologies on five leading petascale systems. We present how we build the containers to ensure performance and security and their performance at scale. We ran microbenchmarks at a scale of 6,144 nodes containing 0.35 M MPI processes and baseline the performance of container technologies. We establish the near-native performance and minimal memory overheads by the containerized environments using MILC - a lattice quantum chromodynamics code at 139,968 processes and using VPIC - a 3d electromagnetic relativistic Vector Particle-In-Cell code for modeling kinetic plasmas at 32,768 processes. We demonstrate an on-par performance trend at a large scale on Intel, AMD, and three NVIDIA architectures for both HPC applications.

Keywords: Petascale · HPC · Containerization · Cloud computing · Singularity · Charliecloud · Podman · MILC · VPIC

1 Introduction

Containerization is a powerful tool for scientific software development and portability across systems. It considerably reduces the time to build, test, and deploy applications by encapsulating code and dependencies together, allowing them to run on diverse platforms with minimal additional efforts. HPC infrastructures provide tremendous computing capabilities along with optimized message communication actualized through advanced features like eager communication, shared memory, and Remote Direct Memory Access making them ideal for intensive scientific computation but challenging for software portability. Containers

© Springer Nature Switzerland AG 2021
B. L. Chamberlain et al. (Eds.): ISC High Performance 2021, LNCS 12728, pp. 411–430, 2021.
https://doi.org/10.1007/978-3-030-78713-4_22

provide a promising way to hide system-level complexities, allowing researchers to focus on productive studies that include COVID-19 research, climate modeling, agriculture, healthcare, smart cities, e-commerce, deep learning, etc.

Containerization is a light-weight, low-overhead alternative to full machine virtualization. With Docker's [1] introduction in 2013, containerization gained tremendous popularity. Since then, several containerization techniques have been developed primarily based on chroot, control groups, and Linux namespace features. Table 1 compares four state-of-the-art containerization approaches - Docker, Singularity, Charliecloud, and Podman. Docker is a user-friendly industry-standard containerization approach designed to support stateful microservices. This stateful approach creates security concerns on HPC systems due to its need for root privileges. The security issues combined with a lack of MPI support and resulting scaling limitations make Docker unfit for an HPC environment. Singularity and Charliecloud take different approaches and are designed for HPC users. Once installed with root privileges, Singularity and Charliecloud users can run respective containers without elevated permissions.

Several studies in the past have focused on the performance characterization of containerized workloads [2–7]. These studies, conducted at small problem sizes, indicate near-native performance by container-based techniques. However, none of the prior studies have comprehensively shown the performance, usability, and portability of state-of-the-art container approaches at medium and large scale. This motivates us to study the following two questions: **(1) Does the performance of container-based solutions on HPC clusters match bare-metal runs at varying problem scales? (2) What are the challenges and possible directions to exploit the state-of-the-art container techniques at a massive scale?**

Table 1. Features of Containers

Attribute	Namespaces	Cgroups	User Escalation	Default Network	Root daemon	Keep changes after restart	Suitable for HPC
Docker	✓	✓	✓	Bridge	✓	✗	✗
Singularity	✓	✓	✗	Host	✗	✓	✓
Charliecloud	✓	✗	✗	Host	✗	✓	✓
Podman	✓	✗	✗	Host	✗	✓	✓

1.1 Contributions

To the best of our knowledge, this is the first study investigating the performance of containers at HPC petascale. The main contributions of this paper are:

1. We present the challenges and possible approaches to build HPC clouds with container-based approaches.

2. We present the changes required to adapt containerization approaches to HPC infrastructures.
3. We establish the usability and portability of three user-defined containerization stacks (Singularity, Charliecloud, Podman) at various problem scales.
4. We compared the performance of state-of-the-art containers at a scale of 6,144 HPC nodes containing 344,064 processes with MPI microbenchmarks.
5. We compared the performance of native and container environments with two HPC scientific applications at up to 138,968 processes on 2,592 nodes.
6. We establish the performance of three state-of-the-art containers on five diverse HPC architectures: NVIDIA Quadro RTX 5000, V100, A100, Intel Cascade Lake, and AMD Rome).

The rest of the paper is organized as follows: Sect. 2 presents the prior research works and establishes the novelty and basis of research conducted in this paper. Section 3 presents the background of the Singularity, Charliecloud, and Podman container technologies and describes the benchmarks and applications experimented in this paper. Section 4.1 presents the experimental setups and software configurations. Section 4.2 and Sect. 4.3 provide detailed experimental evaluations with microbenchmarks and HPC scientific applications. Section 5 presents an in-depth discussion on containerization issues and provides recommendations to the users. Finally, the conclusion are presented in Sect. 6.

2   Related Work

The technology landscape of containerization started with the chroot system call in 1979 and was followed by FreeBSD Jails in 2000, the Linux VServer in 2001, Solaris Containers in 2004, Open VZ in 2005, Process Containers in 2006, Linux Containers(LXC) in 2008, Warden in 2011, and Google's Let Me Contain That For You (LMCTFY) in 2013. Containerization then became enormously popular with Docker's introduction in 2013. Since then, tremendous efforts have been made by researchers and industry to develop performant, secure, and portable container techniques for both Cloud and HPC environments.

In an early research paper by Xavier et al. [5] from 2013, the trade-offs between performance and isolation in Linux VServer, OpenVZ, and LXC containers compared with traditional hypervisor-based Xen virtualization are presented. Later, Carlos et al. [4] in 2017 evaluated LXC, Docker, and Singularity's performance through a customized single node HPL-Benchmark and an MPI-based application on a multi-node testbed. They also studied application-level performance using a NAMD benchmark on a single GPU device attached with an eight-core processor. In the same year, Younge et al. [2] compared Singularity's performance on a Cray XC-series supercomputer and Docker on Amazon's Elastic Compute Cloud (EC2) and reported significant overheads in the cloud environment mainly due to the use of Ethernet rather than the Cray Aries interconnect.

In more recent studies, Hu et al. [8] investigated CPU, memory, and network bandwidth of Singularity containers whereas Rudyy et al. [9] explored the scalability and portability aspects of Docker, Singularity, and Shifter in the biological systems using Alya code at 256 nodes. At the benchmarks level on a medium system scale, Torrez et al. [10] demonstrated minimal overheads by Charliecloud, Shifter, and Singularity containers. In another interesting work, Cérin et al. in Ref. [11] proposed a pervasive methodology for containerization of HPC jobs schedulers that shows better management of system resources in an economical way.

Apart from performance studies, Canon et al. in [12] reviewed the challenges and gaps in existing containerized approaches for HPC applications. A survey by Bachiega et al. [13] on recent research and challenges revealed a lack of thorough studies involving containers and their performance in the HPC environment. In light of this research and need, our focus in this paper is to bridge the gap in prior research work to establish the performance, portability, and usability of containers in the HPC environment using both microbenchmarks as well as HPC applications with real workloads. We present rigorous and comprehensive performance evaluations at petascale on five leading Intel, AMD and NVIDIA, architectures.

3   Background

Containerization on HPC infrastructures is challenging due to access privileges and security requirements. Further, batch processing of jobs along with container overheads adds unique challenges to their usability. Portability of containers is restricted by ABI compatibility between the container and host hardware driver libraries along with instruction compatibility with the host architecture (high speed interconnect drivers, GPU drivers, processor ISAs, processor specific compiler optimizations). For non-optimal performance, the container need not utilize specialized drivers and hardware capabilities, and only ISA and ABI portability is required.

3.1   Container Technologies

Out of the available container technologies, we evaluate Charliecloud [14], Singularity [15], and Podman [16] in this work. The goal is not to investigate them comprehensively but to determine the simplicity, usefulness, and performance of a few popular container types at petascale clusters.

Singularity. Singularity is a container platform specifically crafted for HPC systems. Similar to other user space container systems, Singularity bind mounts a container image and changes the apparent root (chroot) to the container. Singularity goes a step further to support the HPC ecosystem by mounting native devices (e.g., GPU, network, IB) and configured filesystem paths while also preserving Linux namespaces and user mapping inside the container. Singularity does not run a daemon service, but must be installed by the root user for privilege escalation. After building images from their own development systems, or on HPC if fakeroot is configured, users can pull images built with Singularity or Docker, and safely run them on shared HPC resources. While images can be stored in the cloud, they exist as single files on a filesystem, allowing them to be shared and managed like all other files.

Charliecloud. Charliecloud is a user defined software stack (UDSS) that exploits user and mount namespaces of Linux to run containers without needing privileged operations and/or daemons. Any packaging software capable of producing a standard Linux filesystem can build container images that can be hosted on private or public repositories (Dockerhub, Gitlab, NVIDIA NGC, etc.). Charliecloud is 800 lines of open source code that demands minimal system control (sysctl) commands [14] to configure on computing facilities, which avoids most security risks.

Podman. Podman is a new native container runtime. It builds and runs OCI-standard containers, but adds several attractive capabilities. Notably, it can run either individual containers or Kubernetes-style pods (orchestrated sets of containers) and it does so more safely and securely than Docker. As opposed to Docker's client/server approach (which requires privileged access), Podman uses a traditional fork/exec model. By leveraging user namespaces, root-level access is not required to run containers, and additional isolation is enforced via UID separation. Podman is an attractive emerging technology since its CLI and user experience is nearly identical to Docker, which could make use of containers on HPC more accessible to end users. However, full use of Podman's rootless capabilities requires advanced kernel features such as version 2 cgroups and user-space FUSE, and is not yet compatible with network filesystems, which limited the extent to which we were able to evaluate it on a production HPC system.

3.2 Microbenchmarks and Applications

We evaluate the performance of all the container technologies at the micro-benchmark level with Intel MPI Benchmarks (IMB) and at the application-level with two well-known HPC scientific applications - MILC and VPIC.

IMB: IMB [17] is a suite of MPI benchmarks that perform performance measurements for point-to-point and global communication operations for a range of message sizes. We use the standard MPI_Bcast Latency benchmark, which measures the one-way latency of the MPI broadcast operation. All experiments are performed at least three times with one Processes per node (PPN) and a full subscription for 10 to 1000 repetitions at various message sizes.

MILC: MIMD Lattice Computation (MILC) [18] is a Quantum Chromodynamics (QCD) code that is used in the study of strong interactions of sub-atomic physics to understand atomic nuclei, the evolution of the early universe, and connections with condensed matter physics. QCD describes the interaction of fundamental matter particles called quarks and force carriers called gluons, which bind to form the composite, hadronic particles, such as protons and neutrons. Lattice QCD (LQCD) is a numerical approach to QCD that approximates space and time by a 4D lattice. Physical quantities are computed by evaluating high-dimensional integrals using Molecular Dynamics and Markov-chain Monte Carlo methods. It's an open-source C89 code that utilizes the Highly-Improved Staggered-Quark (HISQ) formulation of LQCD. All the core components can be offloaded to GPUs through the QUDA library. On CPU architecture (Cluster C), MILC is scaled to run with $72 \times 72 \times 72 \times 144$ lattice at $17\,K$, $35\,K$, $70\,K$, and $140\,K$ processes. On GPU architecture (Cluster A), MILC is run with $36 \times 36 \times 64 \times 64$ lattice on 32, 64, 128, and 256 V100 devices. Performance numbers are reported for time to solve Conjugate gradient, entire computations (Total Time), Linux reported time in seconds, and memory consumption.

VPIC: The Vector Particle-in-Cell (VPIC) model is a particle-in-cell, first principles plasma physics application. It uses a structured grid and compute particles and electromagnetic fields [19,20]. An unreleased VPIC 2.0 beta is used, which has been ported to the Kokkos [21] performance portability framework [22]. The Kokkos OpenMP and CUDA backends are used to perform the benchmarking runs. The dataset used is 2D and uses all features of VPIC. The GPU experiments use 31.1 million particles, and 88 million particles are used for the CPU experiments. Performance is reported as overall runtime in seconds.

NAS BTIO Pseudo Application and HPC IOR Benchmark: NASA's BTIO [23] benchmark solves the Block-Tridiagonal (BT) problem on a three-dimensional array across a square number of compute nodes and periodically writes structured MPI datatypes to a file. Out of four available implementations for writing files on disks, we use BTIO.mpi_io_full that leverage MPI-IO with collective communications. IOR (Interleaved Or Random) [24] is a parameterized parallel IO benchmark which is widely used to validate the performance of parallel storage systems using various interfaces and access patterns.

4   Performance Evaluation

This section describes the experimental setup, provides the results of our experiments and presents an in-depth analysis of performance results. Running experiments on five different clusters ensure the generality of our performance analysis.

We use four distinct approaches to compare containerization overheads. In Sect. 4.2, we start with baselining overheads at the MPI initialization level and then investigate the overheads at the collective communication level using MPI broadcast operation. We then compare the overheads at the container technology level with MPI Alltoall collective operation. Following in Sect. 4.3 we investigate the overheads at the application level with diverse hardware architectures on petascale systems.

4.1 Experimental Setup

Cluster Configurations

Cluster A: IBM OpenPOWER + InfiniBand + V100 [25]: Each node on TACC's Frontera Longhorn system contains dual socket Power-9 processors with 20 physical cores on each socket operating at 2.4 GHz, and contains 256 GB DDR4 and 900 GB of local temporary storage. The interconnect is Mellanox EDR (100 Gb/s) InfiniBand with OFED version 4.5-2.2.9.0. The operating system is RHEL v7.6 with kernel version Linux 4.14.0-115.10.1.el7a.ppc64le. Each node contains four NVIDIA V100 GPUs, each having 16GB GDDR6 memory.

Cluster B: AMD Rome + InfiniBand [26]: Each node on the Purdue Bell system contains dual socket AMD Rome processors with 64 physical cores on each socket operating at 2.0 GHz and contains 256 GB physical memory. The interconnect is Mellanox ConnectX-4 EDR 100 Gb/s InfiniBand (OFED version 5.0-2.1.8.0) and is configured in a fat-tree topology that is 3:1 oversubscribed. The operating system is CentOS Linux v7.8.2003 (kernel version Linux 3.10.0-1127.19.1.el7.x86_64).

Cluster C: Cascade Lake + InfiniBand [25]: Each node on TACC's Frontera primary compute system contains dual socket Intel Xeon Platinum 8280 processors having 28 cores per socket and cores operating at 2.70 GHz speed and contains 192 GB of main memory. The interconnect is composed of Mellanox HDR technology (OFED version 5.1-2.5.8) with full HDR (200 Gbps) connectivity between the switches and HDR-100 (100 Gbps) connectivity to the compute nodes. The computing network is configured in a fat-tree topology with a small oversubscription factor of 11:9. The operating system is CentOS Linux release 7.8.2003 (kernel version Linux 3.10.0-1127.19.1.el7.x86_64).

Cluster D: AMD EPYC + InfiniBand + A100 (DGX-2): AMD EPYC + InfiniBand box consists of 256 cores on dual-socket AMD EPYC 7742 processors operating at 2.25 GHz and contains 8 NVIDIA A100 GPUs. Each node contains 15 TB Gen4 NVME SSD memory, whereas each GPU contains 40 GB of HBM2 memory. Eight single-port Mellanox ConnectX-6 200 Gb/s HDR InfiniBand interconnects available onboard provide 3.2 Tb/s of peak bandwidth from a single system. The operating system is RHEL 7.5 (kernel version Linux 3.10.0-1127.13.1.el7.x86_64), and Mellanox OFED version is 5.0-2.1.8.

Cluster E: Broadwell + InfiniBand + Quadro RTX 5000 [25]: Each node on TACC's Frontera liquid submerged system contains dual socket Intel Xeon E5-2620 v4 processors with 16 physical processors operating at 2.10 GHz frequency and equipped with 192 GB DDR4 and 128 GB SSD memory. The interconnect is Mellanox FDR 56 Gb/s InfiniBand with OFED version 5.0-2.1.8.

The operating system is CentOS Linux v7.8.2003 with kernel version Linux 3.10.0-1127.13.1.el7.x86_64. Four NVIDIA Quadro RTX Turing 5000 GPUs having 16 GB GDDR6 memory on each GPU are installed on each node.

Software Configurations: Containers used in this study come from various sources, but very few of them ran without any modification. Sources include repositories from dockerhub [27,28] and containers built for Cluster C. The software configurations for benchmarks and both applications are listed in Tables 2, 3 and 4.

Table 2. Software configurations - MPI microbenchmarks

Cluster	Compiler	MPI	CUDA	Container platform(s)
Cluster A	GCC 7.3.0	MVAPICH2 GDR 2.3.4	10.2	Singularity 3.5.3
Cluster C	GCC 9.1.0	Intel MPI 19.0.7	-	Charliecloud 0.21 pre
Cluster D	GCC 9.1.0	Intel MPI 19.0.7	10.2	Charliecloud 0.21 pre, Singularity 3.5.3

Table 3. Software configurations - MILC

Cluster	Compiler	MPI	CUDA	Container platform(s)
Cluster A	GCC 7.3.0	MVAPICH2 GDR 2.3.4	10.2	Singularity 3.5.3
Cluster C	GCC 9.1.0	Intel MPI 19.0.7	-	Charliecloud 0.21 pre

Table 4. Software configurations - VPIC

Cluster	Compiler	MPI	CUDA	Container platform(s)
Cluster A	GCC 7.3.0	MVAPICH2-GDR 2.3.4	10.2	Singularity 3.5.3
Cluster B	Intel 19.0.5	Intel MPI 19.0.5	-	Singularity 3.6.1
Cluster C	Intel 19.1.1	Intel MPI 19.0.7	-	Singularity 3.6.3
Cluster E	GCC 8.3.0	MVAPICH2-GDR 2.3.4	10.1	Singularity 3.6.3

4.2   Micro-benchmark Evaluation

We used three MPI benchmarks - MPI_Init, MPI_Bcast and MPI_Alltoall of Intel MPI Benchmarks suite [17] to compare the performance of Singularity and Charliecloud containers with bare metal runs. Each microbenchmark was run at least five times on all the clusters to average out performance variations.

Baseline Performance: We baseline the performance of containerization with bare metal runs with OSU_Init microbenchmark. Figure 1 plots the time to execute MPI_Init operation at a system scale ranging from 3,584 processes (64 Nodes, 56 PPN) to 229,376 processes (4,096 Nodes, 56 PPN). We observe that container setup and teardown overheads in Charliecloud range between 6% and 14% at various system scales.

Collective Communication Performance: We next establish the overheads of containerization with MPI collective operations. Figure 2a plots the latency of MPI_Bcast operation on 6,144 nodes with 1 process per node (PPN) at Cluster C. We observe on par communication performance by Charliecloud container with bare metal runs at all message sizes. The performance numbers indicate that containerization does not incur any performance overheads during runtime, even at a large system scale. To discern setup and teardown overheads of containers with communication collectives, we compare total time to run the MPI Broadcast benchmark at 64, 128, 256, 512, 1 K, 2 K, 4 K, and 6 K nodes in Fig. 2b. We observe overheads less than 5 s to instantiate containers on up to 6,144 nodes at 1 PPN.

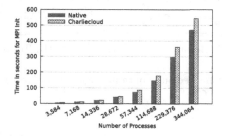

Fig. 1. Baseline performances of containerized and bare metal runs with MPI_Init benchmark on Cluster C

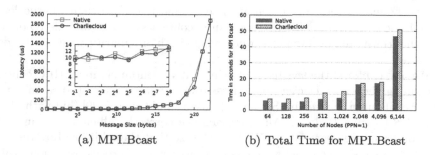

(a) MPI_Bcast   (b) Total Time for MPI_Bcast

Fig. 2. Performance comparison of Charliecloud containers against native runs with 1 PPN on Cluster C

Since most of the applications in HPC intend to utilize the full potential of computing cores, we, therefore, conducted our next level of evaluations at the full subscription of the nodes. Figure 3a shows the performance of broadcast collective algorithm on 4,096 nodes on Cluster C. Processes per node (PPN) was set to 56 in these experiments which fully subscribe to the nodes on Cluster C. For containerized runs, we instantiated 56 containers through MPI job launcher on each node. We observe a similar trend in the performance of Charliecloud container and bare metal runs at all the message sizes. Again, to expose the containerization overheads in Charliecloud, we plot the total time to run the complete benchmark at 64, 128, 256, 512, 1 K, 2 K, and 4 K nodes in Fig. 3b. We observe an additional 66 s of overheads in instantiating the 229,376 containers at 4K nodes. Given the scale at which containers are instantiated, the overheads seem insignificant to run the collective benchmarks.

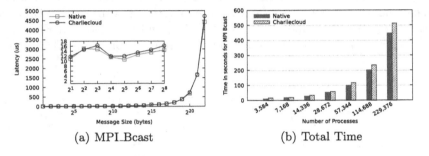

(a) MPI_Bcast   (b) Total Time

Fig. 3. Performance of Charliecloud container against native runs at full subscription of 4,096 nodes on Cluster C

At the microbenchmark level, we further investigate the performances of Charliecloud and Singularity on Cluster D containing NVIDIA A100 devices. Figure 4a shows on par latency numbers for MPI Alltoall benchmark with bare metal, Charliecloud, and Singularity. Figure 4b presents additional attributes of all three runtimes. We observe that user time, CPU%, and Maximum Resident Set Size (MaximumRSS) remain similar for all runtimes; however, Singularity incurs 10% more overheads in container setup and teardown than Charliecloud. From Table 4, we observe higher page faults, context switches, and file IO operations that constitute performance overheads in both Singularity and Charliecloud (Table 5).

We also explored the feasibility of using native containers in an HPC context by running the exact Docker containers from our large-scale studies on a test cluster configured to resemble SkyLake + InfiniBand Cluster [29] (but with Linux kernel 5.8.1) using Podman. All workloads ran correctly, albeit with minor (5–10%) performance degradation. We hypothesize that the additional overhead is due to Podman's use of fuse-overlay fs and further inter-process isolation, which may be resolvable with additional resource tuning. This experiment leaves us optimistic about the future use of native containers on HPC.

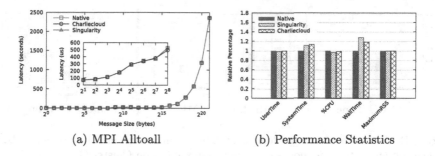

(a) MPI_Alltoall   (b) Performance Statistics

Fig. 4. Performance of singularity and Charliecloud containers against native runs at 256 processes on Cluster D

Table 5. Runtime statistics of alltoall benchmark on Cluster D

Attribute	Bare metal	Singularity	CharlieCloud
Major IO page faults	0	1,031	38
Minor page faults	22,538,0957	232,077,485	230,106,890
Voluntary context switches	30,001	884,644	222,086
Involuntary context switches	107,709	147,361	110,452
File system inputs	0	975,798	8,664
File system outputs	0	0	4,096

4.3   Application Level Evaluation

MILC: MILC was run with Charliecloud on up to 140K processes at Cluster C and Singularity on up to 256 NVIDIA V100 devices at Cluster A. We set the number of trajectories to one and steps per trajectory to 30. Figure 5 plots the time to solve Conjugate Gradient (CG Time) and Linux time (time command) for native and Charliecloud runs. Charliecloud shows less than 10% overheads at various system scales. Small performance differences are racked up by container instantiation overheads, which is nearly 40 s for 0.14 million containers as investigated at the microbenchmark level in Sect. 4.2. In practice, where MILC is allowed to run for multiple trajectories and several steps per trajectory, the instantiation overheads would become insignificant with long running time of the application. Figure 5c plots the memory consumption reported by the MILC application, which is nearly identical for bare metal and container runs.

On IBM Power 9 Cluster A, MILC was run with the QUDA library to offload computation to NVIDIA V100 devices. From Fig. 6, we observe that Singularity incurs less than 4% overheads against bare metal runs. No significant difference in memory consumption was observed at any system size.

Apart from running time and memory usage attributes, we also compare the CPU, device, InfiniBand, NUMA, DRAM, and Lustre parameters and observed

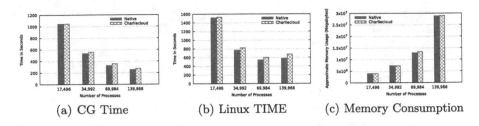

(a) CG Time   (b) Linux TIME   (c) Memory Consumption

Fig. 5. Performance of Charliecloud container against bare metal runs with MILC application on up to 2,592 nodes containing 140K cores on Cluster C

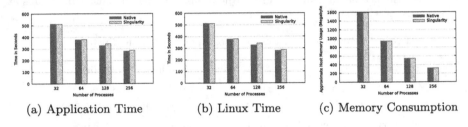

(a) Application Time   (b) Linux Time   (c) Memory Consumption

Fig. 6. Performance of Singularity container with MILC application using up to 256 V100 GPUs on Cluster A

on par performance values for all three runtimes. The plots for these attributes are enormous and can be made available on request to the interested researchers.

VPIC: The VPIC experiment includes four architectures; two CPU architectures, scaled to 32,768 processes as seen in Fig. 8, and two GPU architectures scaled to 256 GPUs as seen in Fig. 7. Each experiment is run five times, and the average of the runs are shown in the respective figures. The software used for each experiment is available in Table 4. At each scaling tier, all runs are done within the same job and consequently use the same nodes, fabric location, etc. This is done to reduce the variation associated with running on different nodes and hence network topologies. The authors note this can create a significant discrepancy between "cold" to "warm" cache runs, as the container image and application software and libraries are loaded on a shared parallel filesystem. Although these outliers show a slowdown in first test run within a job whether the test case is bare metal or containerized, they do not show any change in overhead. To combat this, the "cold cache" outliers are pruned from the averages. Singularity is used as the container platform in order to analyze the overhead of different architectures.

In this experiment, we see in Figs. 7 and 8 that architecture does impact the containerization overhead. On average, the RTX platform discrepancy is .29 s, while V100 is 2.46 at the same scale (Fig. 7). Similarly, on the CPU runs, Rome shows a 3.3 s difference, and Cascade Lake shows the most considerable difference between runs at 13.53 s (Fig. 8). Although this shows a 4× slowdown, even in the worst case, it is unlikely that the containerization overhead will be impactful for any jobs except those at the largest scale or incredibly short run times.

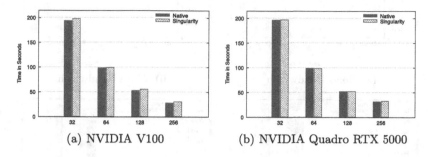

Fig. 7. Performance of singularity containers against bare-metal runs with VPIC on up to 256 GPUs on Cluster A and Cluster E respectively. (smaller is better)

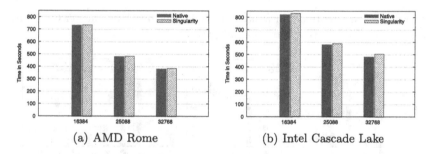

Fig. 8. Performance of singularity containers against bare-metal runs with VPIC up to 32,768 cores on Cluster B and Cluster C respectively. (smaller is better)

4.4   IO Benchmark and Application

Figure 9 compares the read and write bandwidth performance for Charliecloud containers against bare metal runs for the IOR benchmark on Cluster C and Cluster B. Figure 10 compares the performance of Class C, Class D, and Class E subtypes of NAS BT-IO pseudo application at a system size of up to 14 K processes. In both IO testcases, containerized runs demonstrate on par performance to bare metal runs.

4.5   Capacity Workload Performance

We next evaluate the performance of containerized applications for a typical job arrival pattern in the supercomputing centers. Based on findings from priors

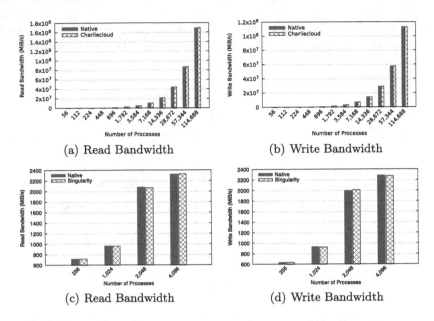

Fig. 9. File read and write performance with IOR benchmark on Cluster C (Figure (a) and (b)) and on Cluster B (Figure (c) and (d))

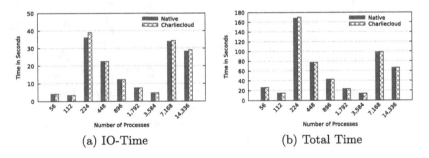

Fig. 10. Performance with NAS BT-IO benchmark (Class C: 56 - 112, Class D: 224 - 3K, Class E: > 7K Processes) on Cluster C

studies [30,31], we design five distinct capacity workloads having 10,000 single-node jobs for a scale down 10-node cluster. The distribution for job duration is set to exponential, having a mean value of one minute and a maximum value of 15 min. Any higher value of job length and problem size favors containerized runs due to fewer jobs executed per unit of time. Figure 11a shows the cumulative distribution of job duration, and Fig. 11b indicate up to 4% overheads with all containerized runs against all bare metal runs.

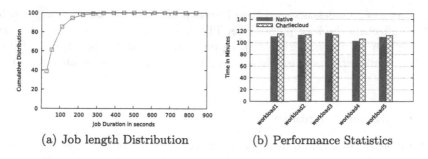

(a) Job length Distribution   (b) Performance Statistics

Fig. 11. Performance of capability jobs on Cluster C with 5 workloads

4.6   Outcomes

Our experiments with microbenchmarks and applications indicate that container solutions are an optimal choice for long-running applications. However, short-lived applications only benefit from containers when their build process is complicated or time-consuming or if computing platforms lack the required functionalities to run the applications. For instance, in jobs at petascale with very short run times, the setup and teardown of containers can be a large percentage of runtime as seen in Sect. 4.2. We also see that architecture differences do impact the overhead on containerization in 4.3.

We also find this claim on the Singularity FAQ [32]: *"So far we have not identified any appreciable regressions of performance (even in parallel applications running across nodes with InfiniBand). There is a small startup cost to create and teardown the container, which has been measured to be anywhere from 10 - 20 thousandths of a second."* The authors find this not true at a large scale as shown in Sect. 4.2 where we can see slowdowns on the order of 10s of seconds.

5   Discussion

5.1   Containerization in the Linux Kernel

All of the container technologies that are featured in this paper use Linux kernel namespaces as their primary tool for creating a container that is fast and efficient. Namespaces are used to partition what a specific process can read and write to. The key to maintaining efficiency is that the kernel does not add a layer of abstraction to implement the namespaces. From the kernel's viewpoint, each namespace process is running in the same way as every other process. The namespace only serves to limit what the process can access. As an example, only directories that are bind-mounted from the host to the container are available to be seen. All other directories are not in a viewable namespace from the view of the container. The root directory of this type of namespace comes from the container itself, and all directories are bind-mounted on that virtual file-system. Inter-process communication (IPC) also plays an important role in separating shared memory namespaces, so base libraries like GLIBC can be switched out without affecting the host namespace. The eight namespaces are mnt, pid, net, ipc, uts, user (in Linux kernel 3.8), cgroup (in 4.6), and time (in 5.6). Details on what container types use the user and cgroup namespaces are available in Table 1.

5.2   Container Portability

Containers are often said to increase the portability of applications and can offer an easy way to share application-stacks. This is true in some cases, such as the need to run on older Linux operating systems where the core user-space libraries, i.e., GLIBC, are not compatible with newer software, or if applications require specific versions of libraries that for technical or political reasons cannot be installed. However, it is clear that container portability is a much murkier issue when working with different MPI implementations, different CUDA versions, and different architectures.

As per documentation [33], Singularity supports MPICH and OpenMPI [34,35] by default. However, the applications that are shown in this paper required MVAPICH2 [36], MVAPICH2-GDR, and Intel MPI [17]. This required the experiments to be run with a unique container for each experiment. For instance, on Cluster E, MVAPICH2-GDR was needed to use the GPUs effectively. However, on Cluster B, MVAPICH2-GDR was not available, and Intel MPI was the default. The complexity of the many containers was also compounded by the binary-incompatibility of the x86 and Power 9 platform. This required a completely different set of containers for the Cluster A experiments.

Additionally, while using CUDA on GPU clusters, Charliecloud containers require NVIDIA container runtimes, which was non-trivial to install without privileged user accesses. GPU containers were then configured by injecting NVIDIA libraries using Charliecloud "ch-fromhost" command. Although MPI benchmarks and VPIC ran successfully on NVIDIA Quadro RTX GPUs on Cluster E, the QUDA library used by the MILC application was not able to offload computations on to the available GPU devices.

Another consideration with container portability is the software ecosystem of the cluster to be run on. Containerization has a different set of security concerns and connection points between user-space applications and the kernel than traditional HPC. This can create misunderstood requirements and misconfigured installations. The authors of this paper encountered these problems during this series of experiments and worked with HPC Systems Administrators to rectify them in order to finish these experiments. From the view of a multi-cluster HPC user, containerization is far from portable.

With the complexity put forth by an experiment like this, the authors conclude that while in some cases containers provide portability, in large-scale multi-cluster situations, containerization does not simplify the work needed to complete the tasks and adds an additional level of complexity to the existing scientific applications.

5.3 Recommendations

In this research work, we investigate containerization aspects that make them a popular choice for Cloud and HPC environments. Some of these are portability, usability, accessibility, packageability, software choice, and performance. While most of them proved to be valid, there are fundamental challenges in specific use cases as detailed in Sects. 5.1 and 5.2. No straightforward solutions exists as some of these concerns are either caused by underlying kernel implementations or purposefully held to preserve system security.

Based on our research work in this paper, we provide the following recommendations to the HPC community on containerization.

1. If the full source code is available for all the libraries needed by an application on the target system, developing portable containers is never an issue.
2. In cases where target libraries are available only in binary format, tools/utilities from containerization technology developers, e.g. "–nv" environment variable in Singularity, "ch-fromhost –nvidia" in Charliecloud, can be leveraged to port applications on the target environment.
3. In all other cases, portability, and performance are not guaranteed from containerization, and application developers/users may have to build complete applications on each target system.
4. There is a trade-off between performance and build complexity for short-lived jobs running at a large scale. For mission-critical works, an additional layer of containerization increases latency as well as uncertainty to the application behavior.
5. For typical applications, containers usage is recommended to exploit massive tuning and optimizations realized within application containers by their developers.
6. Memory consumption is hardly a concern on modern supercomputing platforms as container instances are lightweight, and host resources are shared to the containers. However, on embedded platforms or co-devices, containerization could be avoided to use all available memory for logic and data storage maximally.

6 Conclusion

Recent technological advancements in containerization runtimes have commenced a new trend of HPC software development, which effectively reduces the build and deployment issues caused by complex software dependencies at a small scale. In this work, we presented the challenges in leveraging containerization within HPC systems and showcased the feasibility of three state-of-the-art container technologies. We explored the performance, usability, and portability of container workflows through experiments conducted at petascale on leading HPC platforms across tens of thousands of processes. We conclude that developers, testers, and end-users can leverage containerization on HPC systems in a performant way, at a large scale, to reduce software development and maintenance efforts except for specific usecases involving proprietary libraries or noncompatible architectures and binary formats. The cost of performance at scale is to build support for non-portable libraries into the containers. This addition, however, does not exclude their use in environments that only have generic library support such as shared memory or TCP/IP in communication, CPU in processing devices, and local or unmanaged memory in storage.

Acknowledgment. This work is supported by UT Austin-Portugal Program, a collaboration between the Portuguese Foundation of Science and Technology and the University of Texas at Austin, award UTA18-001217. Authors would also like to thanks Melyssa Fratkin from TACC for providing valuable feedback, and Preston Smith and Xiao Zhu from Purdue for providing an allocation and support for testing on Purdue's Bell cluster.

References

1. Merkel, D.: Docker: Lightweight linux containers for consistent development and deployment. Linux J. 2014(239) (Mar 2014)
2. Younge, A.J., Pedretti, K., Grant, R.E., Brightwell, R.: A tale of two systems: using containers to deploy HPC applications on supercomputers and clouds. In: IEEE International Conference on Cloud Computing Technology and Science (2017)
3. Larsson, T.J., Hunold, S., Versaci, F. (eds.): Euro-Par 2015. LNCS, vol. 9233. Springer, Heidelberg (2015). https://doi.org/10.1007/978-3-662-48096-0
4. Arango Gutierrez, C., Dernat, R., Sanabria, J.: Performance evaluation of container-based virtualization for high performance computing environments. Revista UIS Ingenierías 18 (2017)
5. Xavier, M.G., Neves, M.V., Rossi, F.D., Ferreto, T.C., Lange, T., De Rose, C.A.F.: Performance evaluation of container-based virtualization for high performance computing environments. In: : 2013 21st Euromicro International Conference on Parallel, Distributed, and Network-Based Processing (PDP'21) (2013)
6. Brayford, D., Vallecorsa, S.: Deploying scientific al networks at petaflop scale on secure large scale HPC production systems with containers. In: Proceedings of the Platform for Advanced Scientific Computing Conference (2020)
7. Wang, Y., Evans, R.T., Huang, L.: Performant container support for HPC applications. In: Proceedings of the Practice and Experience in Advanced Research Computing on Rise of the Machines (learning)(PEARC 2019) (2019). https://doi.org/10.1145/3332186.3332226
8. Hu, G., Zhang, Y., Chen, W.: Exploring the performance of singularity for high performance computing scenarios. In: 2019 IEEE 21st International Conference on High Performance Computing and Communications; IEEE 17th International Conference on Smart City; IEEE 5th International Conference on Data Science and Systems (HPCC/SmartCity/DSS) (2019)
9. Rudyy, O., Garcia-Gasulla, M., Mantovani, F., Santiago, A., Sirvent, R., Vázquez, M.: Containers in HPC: a scalability and portability study in production biological simulations. In: 2019 IEEE International Parallel and Distributed Processing Symposium (IPDPS 2019) (2019). https://doi.org/10.1109/IPDPS.2019.00066

10. Torrez, A., Randles, T., Priedhorsky, R.: HPC container runtimes have minimal or no performance impact. In: 2019 IEEE/ACM International Workshop on Containers and New Orchestration Paradigms for Isolated Environments in HPC (CANOPIE-HPC) (2019)
11. Cérin, C., Greneche, N., Menouer, T.: Towards pervasive containerization of HPC job schedulers. In: 2020 IEEE 32nd International Symposium on Computer Architecture and High Performance Computing (SBAC-PAD) (2020)
12. Canon, R.S., Younge, A.: A case for portability and reproducibility of HPC containers. In: 2019 IEEE/ACM International Workshop on Containers and New Orchestration Paradigms for Isolated Environments in HPC (CANOPIE-HPC) (2019)
13. Bachiega, N.G., Souza, P.S.L., Bruschi, S.M., de Souza, S.: Container-based performance evaluation: a survey and challenges. In: 2018 IEEE International Conference on Cloud Engineering (IC2E) (2018)
14. Charliecloud documentation. https://hpc.github.io/charliecloud/install.html
15. Kurtzer, G.M., Sochat, V., Bauer, M.W.: Singularity: Scientific containers for mobility of compute. PLoS ONE **12**(5), e0177459 (2017)
16. Podman. https://podman.io
17. Intel MPI benchmarks. https://github.com/intel/mpi-benchmarks
18. The MIMD Lattice Computation (MILC) Collaboration: http://www.physics.utah.edu/~detar/milc (2020). Accessed 26 May 2021
19. Bowers, K.J., Albright, B.J., Yin, L., Bergen, B., Kwan, T.J.T.: Ultrahigh performance three-dimensional electromagnetic relativistic kinetic plasma simulation. Phys. Plasmas **15**(5), 2840133 (2008)
20. Bowers, K.J., et al.: Advances in petascale kinetic plasma simulation with VPIC and roadrunner. J. Phys. Conf. Ser. **180**, 012055 (2009)
21. Edwards, H.C., Trott, C.R., Sunderland, D.: Kokkos: enabling manycore performance portability through polymorphic memory access patterns. J. Parallel Distrib. Comput. **74**(12), 3202–3216 (2014)
22. Harrell, S.L., et al.: Effective performance portability. In: 2018 IEEE/ACM International Workshop on Performance, Portability and Productivity in HPC (P3HPC), pp. 24–36 (2018)
23. NAS Parallel Benchmarks: https://www.nas.nasa.gov/assets/pdf/techreports/2003/nas-03-002.pdf (2021). Accessed 26 May 2021
24. IOR: https://github.com/hpc/ior (2021). Accessed 26 May 2021
25. Stanzione, D., West, J., Evans, R.T., Minyard, T., Ghattas, O., Panda, D.K.: Frontera: the evolution of leadership computing at the National Science Foundation. In: Practice and Experience in Advanced Research Computing (PEARC 2020), pp. 106–111. Association for Computing Machinery, New York, NY (2020). https://doi.org/10.1145/3311790.3396656
26. McCartney, G., Hacker, T., Yang, B.: Empowering faculty: a campus cyberinfrastructure strategy for research communities. Educ. Rev. (2014)
27. ibmcom/powerai - docker hub. https://hub.docker.com/r/ibmcom/powerai/
28. centos–docker hub. https://hub.docker.com/_/centos
29. Stampede2: https://www.tacc.utexas.edu/systems/stampede2 (2021). Accessed 26 May 2021
30. Chen, X., Lu, C., Pattabiraman, K.: Predicting job completion times using system logs in supercomputing clusters. In: 2013 43rd Annual IEEE/IFIP Conference on Dependable Systems and Networks Workshop (DSN-W) (2013)
31. Amvrosiadis, G., Park, J., Ganger, G., Gibson, G.A., Baseman, E., DeBardeleben, N.: Bigger, longer, fewer: what do cluster jobs look like outside google? Technical Report CMU-PDL-17-104, Carnegie Mellon Univedrsity (2017)

32. Frequently asked questions—singularity. https://singularity.lbl.gov/faq#misc
33. Singularity and MPI applications: https://sylabs.io/guides/3.3/user-guide/mpi.
    html (2021). Accessed 26 May 2021
34. Gabriel, E.: Open MPI: goals, concept, and design of a next generation MPI imple-
    mentation. In: Kranzlmüller, D., Kacsuk, P., Dongarra, J. (eds.) EuroPVM/MPI
    2004. LNCS, vol. 3241, pp. 97–104. Springer, Heidelberg (2004). https://doi.org/
    10.1007/978-3-540-30218-6_19
35. Kurtzer, G.M.: Containers in HPC with singularity (2015)
36. Panda, D.K., Tomko, K., Schulz, K., Majumdar, A.: The MVAPICH project: evo-
    lution and sustainability of an open source production quality MPI Library for
    HPC. In: International Workshop on Sustainable Software for Science: Practice
    and Experiences (2013)

Ubiquitous Performance Analysis

David Boehme$^{(\boxtimes)}$ [ID], Pascal Aschwanden, Olga Pearce, Kenneth Weiss [ID],
and Matthew LeGendre

Lawrence Livermore National Laboratory, Livermore, CA 94550, USA
boehme3@llnl.gov

Abstract. In an effort to guide optimizations and detect performance
regressions, developers of large HPC codes must regularly collect and
analyze application performance profiles across different hardware platforms and in a variety of program configurations. However, traditional
performance profiling tools mostly focus on ad-hoc analysis of individual program runs. *Ubiquitous performance analysis* is a new approach
to automate and simplify the collection, management, and analysis of
large numbers of application performance profiles. In this regime, performance profiling of large HPC codes transitions from a sporadic process
that often requires the help of experts into a routine activity in which
the entire development team can participate. We discuss the design and
implementation of an open source ubiquitous performance analysis software stack with three major components: the Caliper instrumentation
library with a new API to control performance profiling programmatically; Adiak, a library for automatic program metadata capture; and
SPOT, a web-based visualization interface for comparing large sets of
runs. A case study shows how ubiquitous performance analysis has helped
the developers of the Marbl simulation code for over a year with analyzing performance and understanding regressions.

Keywords: Performance · Measurement · Instrumentation · Caliper

1   Introduction

Lawrence Livermore National Laboratory hosts several application teams who
develop and maintain large multi-physics simulation codes. These production
codes are under continuous development, run in a wide variety of configurations, and on complex, heterogeneous HPC systems where frequent hardware
and software updates create a constantly evolving execution environment. To
guide optimizations and detect unexpected performance problems, developers
must proactively monitor the performance of their codes throughout the application lifecycle, both during development and in production. To support this
need, we have developed and deployed software infrastructure to simplify and
automate application-level performance data collection, storage, and analysis.

Traditional HPC performance profiling tools typically focus on analyzing
individual program runs. They employ powerful mechanisms to collect detailed

© Springer Nature Switzerland AG 2021
B. L. Chamberlain et al. (Eds.): ISC High Performance 2021, LNCS 12728, pp. 431–449, 2021.
https://doi.org/10.1007/978-3-030-78713-4_23

data for finding performance bottlenecks, but are often difficult to automate or too intrusive to be used in production runs. With *ubiquitous* performance analysis, we instead aim to collect application performance data whenever possible, and provide a central interface for developers to analyze the collected data. We address several challenges to accomplish this. First, we want to avoid complex measurement setup or postprocessing steps: performance profiling should be available for any user, at any time, and for any run. We therefore integrate a performance profiling library into applications and control measurements programmatically, for example through a command-line option. As we collect data from many runs, the performance analysis focus shifts from analyzing individual program runs to comparing data across runs or across HPC platforms. To facilitate this, we have developed a web interface with novel analysis and visualization tools for analyzing large collections of runs. Finally, to effectively work with such collections, we need descriptive metadata about the program and system configuration for each run. We collect this data automatically with code annotations using a new metadata collection library.

To adopt ubiquitous performance analysis, application developers augment their codes with instrumentation markers, metadata annotations, and initialization code to configure and activate performance profiling. With performance measurement capabilities built into applications, it is easy to enable profiling in production runs or in automated workflows like nightly Continuous Integration (CI) tests. It also simplifies performance profiling for application end users, who may not be familiar with traditional developer-oriented HPC profiling tools. Performance analysts can thus observe real program usage in practice and identify problems due to misconfiguration. Central data storage and access through our analysis web frontend simplifies sharing of performance data across a development team and with other stakeholders. Developers are no longer limited to infrequent ad-hoc profiling of individual runs, but can analyze a complete record of program performance covering many different program configurations over the entire lifespan of the code. Stated simply, ubiquitous performance analysis represents a shift in how we view performance tracking within long-lived HPC codes. It transitions performance analysis from a process that the team performs sporadically, often only with the help of external experts, to a routine activity in which the entire development team can easily, or even unknowingly, participate.

Contributions. Our ubiquitous performance analysis system builds upon the Caliper instrumentation and profiling library [11], whose low runtime overhead affords it to be compiled into HPC applications. In this paper, we introduce additional frontend and backend components to implement a full ubiquitous performance analysis software stack:

- ConfigManager, a profiling control API in Caliper to let applications control performance measurements programmatically;
- Adiak, a library for collecting user-defined metadata; and
- SPOT, a web-based data analysis and visualization interface with novel visualizations to explore large collections of runs.

More importantly, we explain the motivation, key concepts, and design behind the ubiquitous performance analysis approach, and discuss our experiences implementing ubiquitous performance analysis in the LULESH proxy app and the Marbl production code.

2   State of the Art

In this section, we compare our approach to the current state-of-the-art in tools and methodologies for HPC performance analysis.

There is a wide range of community-driven and commercial HPC performance analysis tools covering different measurement methodologies, systems, and use cases. Frameworks like HPCToolkit [7], Score-P [22], TAU [30], and OpenSpeedShop [32] collect detailed per-thread execution profiles or traces for in-depth analyses, such as automatic bottleneck detection [14] or profile analysis [15,24]. Vampir [12] and Paraver [27] visualize large-scale parallel execution and communication traces. Many tools support the collection of CPU, GPU, and on-core hardware counters via PAPI [26] or similar APIs, as well as analysis of communication, multithreading, and GPU usage through the MPI profiling interface, the OpenMP tools interface [13], and NVIDIA's CUPTI API [4]. Generally, these tools are best characterized as *performance debugging tools*, designed around interactive measure-analyze-refine debugging workflows and focused on finding root causes of performance bottlenecks for individual program runs. Measurement setup can be complex. Instrumentation-based tools like Score-P and TAU require the target code to be re-compiled with instrumentation turned on, while sampling-based tools like HPCToolkit require postprocessing steps to map binary addresses to symbol names. The tools use custom profile and trace data formats, and require tool-specific graphical applications for data analysis. Due to the complex measurement setup, usage of performance debugging tools within regular application development and production workflows is often limited, and relegated to expert users with specific performance debugging needs.

Many HPC codes employ some form of built-in *lightweight always-on profiling* to keep track of time spent in major application subsystems or kernels for monitoring and benchmark purposes. Some codes use libraries like GPTL [29], Caliper [11], or TiMemory [23] for this purpose, while others include custom time measurement solutions, typically using small marker functions or macros placed around code regions of interest. Our system can replace custom lightweight timing solutions, and offers rich measurement capabilities that can be activated by the application without complex setup steps.

Performance data management tools such as PerfDMF [16] and PerfTrack [18,19,21] provide the ability to analyze and compare performance data collected from different runs of an application. PerfDMF provides robust, interoperable components for performance data management. PerfDMF is the SQL-based storage backend for PerfExplorer2 [17], a data mining framework with capabilities to correlate performance data and metadata, allowing many types of analyses to compare performance data from multiple experiments (e.g., scaling studies). The PerfTrack performance experiment management tool also uses a SQL database to store profile data from multiple experiments. It includes interfaces to the data store, a GUI for interactive analysis, and modules to automatically collect experiment metadata. The IPM [31] performance monitoring framework gathers MPI function profiles together with environment and application information for cross-run performance comparisons such as scaling studies. Ubiquitous performance analysis builds upon many of the elements developed in these performance data managers. We provide an analysis and visualization web frontend to access data without specialized GUI tools, and a library for collecting user-defined program metadata automatically.

Some *commercial cloud and data center* operators have developed in-house automatic performance analysis solutions for large-scale distributed applications. Among the ones that are known are Alibaba's P-Tracer [25] and Google's Google-Wide Profiling [28] (GWP). P-Tracer samples call-stack traces from applications, while GWP continuously records performance data, including application-level call-stack profiles, across Google data centers. Both P-Tracer and GWP provide web-based query interfaces for data analysis. Unlike our system, P-Tracer and GWP are proprietary, and lack the ability to compare performance based on application-specific metadata (e.g., program configuration).

3   Ubiquitous Performance Analysis

Ubiquitous performance analysis aims to simplify application performance analysis for HPC software development teams, and integrate it better into their software development workflows. This section discusses our approach in detail.

3.1   Overview

The major components of our system are the Caliper instrumentation and profiling library [11], the Adiak metadata collection library [1], and the SPOT web frontend [6]. Application developers integrate Caliper and Adiak into their codes by marking major components (kernels, application phases) with Caliper's annotation macros and exporting program metadata with Adiak. Performance measurements can then be enabled by the application through Caliper's new ConfigManager API. Caliper can perform lightweight always-on time profiling of the annotated code regions, but also collect data for more sophisticated performance analysis experiments. Performance data for an application run is initially written to a file, which can be copied to a directory or imported into a SQL database. Users then analyze the collected performance data in SPOT. Policies for instrumentation, performance measurement, and data collection are defined by the application developers and can be tailored to each code. Performance analysts work together with application developers to define appropriate strategies.

3.2   Code Instrumentation

We primarily rely on manual source-code instrumentation for application profiling, where developers place annotation macros into the source code to mark code regions of interest. Many performance debugging tools use symbol translation or automatic instrumentation approaches which do not require source code modifications for profiling. However, for our purposes, manual instrumentation provides distinct advantages:

- *Control.* Manual instrumentation allows for precise control of measurement granularity. Automatic instrumentation methods easily over- or under-instrument programs, resulting in high measurement overheads or clutter.
- *Interpretability.* Manual annotations describe high-level logical program abstractions such as kernels or phases that developers are familiar with. Automated approaches that rely on compiler-generated identifiers often produce obscure associations, particularly with modern C++ template abstractions.
- *Consistency.* Much of our work involves performance comparisons between different program versions. Identifiers like function names and source line numbers change frequently during development, making comparisons based on such associations difficult. In contrast, the logical program structure expressed in manually instrumented regions typically remains much more stable, allowing for meaningful performance comparisons over long time spans.
- *Reliability.* Many traditional profiling tools rely on binary analysis and the DWARF debugging information to correlate performance metrics to code. This is a common source of complexity and fragility, as not all compilers prioritize correct DWARF information or easily analyzable binary code. By relying on manual instrumentation with tight application integration, we can avoid the traditional attribution complexity and easily integrate our profiling infrastructure with an application's regular testing framework.

The placement of instrumentation annotations follows the logical subdivisions of the code, such as computational kernels and communication or I/O phases. While the one-time setup costs for adding instrumentation annotations could be prohibitive for one-off performance debugging tasks, they are less of a concern for implementing long-term, continuous monitoring strategies. The annotations are not meant to pinpoint specific bottlenecks, but should allow developers to monitor and study the performance evolution of the code. If developers find performance issues in an annotated code region and need more detailed information, they can conduct follow-up experiments with Caliper's complementary sampling-based measurement mechanisms or third-party performance debugging tools to identify root causes.

The Caliper library provides high-level macros to mark functions, loops, or arbitrary code regions in C, C++, and Fortran programs. In addition, many of LLNL's large, long-lived codes already have existing instrumentation for lightweight timing functionality, which we can adapt to invoke Caliper calls instead. Caliper preserves the nesting of stacked regions, and combines annotations from independent components (e.g., libraries), providing complete context information for the combined program across all layers of the software stack. Once in place, the annotations can stay in the code permanently. New annotations can be added incrementally as needed.

3.3   ConfigManager: A Measurement Control API in Caliper

Complementing the instrumentation API, Caliper includes a wide range of profiling capabilities. Essentially, Caliper serves as a built-in profiling tool embedded in the application codes.

We have enhanced Caliper with the ConfigManager API that lets applications control performance profiling activities programmatically. ConfigManager accepts profiling commands in the form of short configuration strings. This configuration string is typically provided by the user as an application configuration file or as a command-line parameter. The configuration specifies an *experiment*, which determines the kind of profiling to be performed, and *options* to customize output or enable additional functionality. Some experiments print human-readable output, while others write machine-readable files for post-mortem analysis in SPOT or other tools. For example, `runtime-report` prints a tree with the time spent in the instrumented regions; `hatchet-region-profile` writes a per-thread region time profile for processing with the Hatchet call-tree analysis library [9]; `event-trace` records a timestamp trace of enter and leave events for the instrumented regions; and `spot` writes a region time profile for analysis with the SPOT web interface. In addition to basic runtime profiling, Caliper provides advanced measurement functionality for specific analyses that can be enabled via runtime options for the selected configuration. Available options include time-series analysis for loops, MPI function profiling, memory high-water mark analysis, I/O profiling, CUDA profiling, hardware-counter access, and top-down analysis for Intel CPUs. Measurements are only enabled on demand, and we take care to avoid interference with production runs or third-party profiling and tracing tools.

The ability to enable complex profiling configurations through a simple application switch greatly simplifies performance measurements, especially for application end users. Some of Caliper's built-in experiments support basic performance debugging tasks: Examples include call-path sampling experiments to capture application details beyond user-defined source code annotations. Caliper also interoperates with other performance tools. For example, we provide adapters that forward Caliper annotations to third-party instrumentation libraries, so that the Caliper-annotated regions are visible in tools like NVIDIA NSight or Intel VTune - a tremendous benefit for developers who regularly use these specialized tools on large codes. In turn, Caliper is available as a backend for the ultra low-overhead TiMemory [23] instrumentation framework.

3.4   Adiak: A Library for Recording Program Metadata

Ubiquitous performance analysis lets users compare performance results from many different application runs. To make meaningful analyses, we need descriptive metadata to capture the provenance of each dataset: for example, it makes little sense to compare the performance of a 1-dimensional test problem against a 3-dimensional multi-physics problem. Metadata helps the user group or filter out datasets when comparing runs. Useful metadata can include environment information such as the machine the program was running on, the launch date and time, or the user running the program; program information such as program version, build date, and compiler vendor and options; and job configuration such as MPI job size and number of threads. In addition, developers often run performance studies based on application-specific input and configuration parameters, such as problem description, problem size or enabled features. We need a customizable solution that can capture these application-specific parameters. We also want to collect this data automatically and avoid manual data input for each run. Therefore, similar to the region annotations for profiling, we record metadata programmatically through an API. We created the Adiak [1] library for this purpose. Adiak records user-defined metadata in the form of key/value pairs. It also includes functionality to fetch common metadata like MPI job size or launch date automatically. The recorded metadata values are stored in the Caliper performance profile datasets.

3.5   SPOT: A Web Interface for Ubiquitous Performance Analysis

Web-based visualization tools are extremely convenient as they do not require the installation of specialized visualization tools. SPOT, our data visualization frontend, is a custom web interface for ubiquitous performance analysis. Compared to traditional profiling tool GUIs, which deep-dive on the performance of individual runs, SPOT analyzes and tracks the performance of many runs over an application's lifetime. At LLNL, SPOT is hosted locally by Livermore Computing (LC) and is available to every LC account holder via LC's web portal. We also provide a containerized version [6] that can be deployed at other sites. SPOT reads data directly from a user-provided directory on a shared filesystem or a database link through a background data-fetching process, which runs as the logged-in user. Thus, filesystem or SQL database permissions ensure that users can only access performance data for which they have appropriate permissions. SPOT provides tools to filter, visualize, and compare performance data, with novel visualizations specifically targeting the analysis of large collections of performance data. Users can create plots to display any of the collected metadata values and performance metrics. They can also open SPOT datasets in Jupyter [5] notebooks directly from the SPOT web page to create custom analysis scripts and visualizations. We discuss specific visualization examples in Sect. 4.4.

3.6   Ubiquitous Data Collection

Caliper provides the spot profiling configuration that produces datasets for analysis with the SPOT web interface. As a baseline, these datasets contain a summary time profile with the total, minimum, maximum, and average time spent in each annotated region across MPI ranks, as well as all recorded metadata for a program run. The datasets are usually quite small, in the order of kilobytes.

For comparisons studies in SPOT, all recorded datasets are copied to a shared directory or a SQL database. Depending on the use case, developers and users can manage these datasets manually, or set up automated workflows for long-term, continuous data collection. They can define and implement data retention or purge policies as needed, otherwise storage requirements grow linearly as datasets are added. The SPOT web frontend has options for limiting the amount of data to be imported, e.g. only the last N days, to maintain scalability.

4   Example: LULESH

In this section, we describe the practical implementation of ubiquitous performance analysis in an HPC code using the Lulesh proxy application [3,20] as an example. As a baseline, we use Lulesh 2.0 with MPI and OpenMP parallelization. We show how the code is prepared for profiling and illustrate the analysis capabilities of our web interface.

4.1   Region Instrumentation with Caliper

Lulesh contains 39 computational functions and 5 communication functions in C++, as well as a number of data initialization and utility functions. In Lulesh, function names and the logical subdivision of code semantics along function boundaries provide a good basis for meaningful performance analysis. We instrumented 17 of its top-level computational functions, the 5 communication functions, and the main loop with Caliper annotation macros. To keep clutter and measurement overhead low, utility functions and very small functions were not instrumented. The `CALI_CXX_MARK_FUNCTION` macro in `LagrangeLeapFrog` in Listing 1.1 demonstrates function annotations in Lulesh. Here, Caliper creates a function region from the location of the macro to the function exit, with the name taken from the compiler-provided `__FUNCTION__` macro.

4.2   Metadata Collection with Adiak

In addition to the function instrumentation, we added Adiak calls in Lulesh to collect run metadata. As shown in Listing 1.1, Adiak provides two types of calls: The first form accesses built-in functionality to collect common information, such as the `adiak::user()` call to record the user name, while the second, generic `adiak::value()` form lets developers provide custom metadata in the form of key-value pairs. Adiak can record a variety of datatypes, including integer and floating-point scalars, strings, tuples, and composite types such as lists.

In Lulesh, we record basic environment information like the user name, machine, launchdate, and MPI job size. In addition, we record the Lulesh problem settings, such as the maximum number of iterations, problem size, number of regions, region costs, and region balance. We also record the user-defined "figure of merit" performance number computed by Lulesh at the end of the run. Note that Listing 1.1 shows only a subset of the Adiak calls.

Listing 1.1. Configuring Caliper and recording metadata in Lulesh

```
void LagrangeLeapFrog(Domain& domain) {
  CALI_CXX_MARK_FUNCTION;
  // (...)
}

int main(int argc, char* argv[]) {
  // (...)
  cali::ConfigManager mgr(opts.caliper_config);
  mgr.start();

  adiak::user();
  adiak::launchdate();
  adiak::value("iterations", opts.its);
  adiak::value("problem_size", opts.nx);
  // (...)

  CALI_MARK_FUNCTION_BEGIN;
  // (...)
  CALI_MARK_FUNCTION_END;

  mgr.flush();
}
```

4.3 Integrating the Caliper ConfigManager API

To enable and control performance measurements in Lulesh, we use the Caliper ConfigManager API. Listing 1.1 shows the relevant steps: First, we create a ConfigManager object and initialize it with a user-provided configuration string. The ConfigManager class parses the configuration string and sets up Caliper's performance measurement and data recording components. Next, we invoke the ConfigManager's start() method to begin profiling based on the given performance measurement configuration. At the end of the program, we invoke the flush() method to stop profiling and write out the recorded performance data.

In Lulesh, users provide the Caliper configuration string via a command-line parameter. As an example, we can enable the runtime-report experiment on the command line to print out an aggregate time profile of the user-annotated regions at the end of the execution. With the profile.mpi option, the experiment also wraps and measures all MPI calls:

```
$ ./lulesh2.0 -P "runtime-report(profile.mpi)"
```

In our experience, controlling performance profiling through application-specific means like configuration files or a command line parameter has proven to be very convenient for users, and we encourage developers to provide this capability when adopting Caliper.

4.4   Data Analysis and Visualization in SPOT

For demonstration purposes, we recorded 1,149 profile datasets with Lulesh using different program configurations. For analysis, users load the SPOT website and point it to a directory or SQL database with the recorded datasets. SPOT then populates the landing page, where users can start their analysis.

Landing Page. The SPOT landing page serves as entry point for performance studies, and lets users filter runs of interest out of potentially thousands of profiling datasets. The landing page is populated with charts that show summary histograms for selected metadata attributes, for example the runs performed by a particular user or runs that invoked a particular physics package. The histogram charts on the landing page are interactive and connected through a crossfilter system [2]. Users can select subsets of data in one or more charts, causing the remaining charts to adapt to include only the selected datasets. This is useful to select specific subsets and to discover correlations between metadata variables.

For our Lulesh example, Fig. 1 shows the distribution of runs with a given compiler, "figure of merit" (FOM), input problem size, and number of threads in the 1,149 Lulesh runs. In Fig. 2, the user applied a crossfilter to select the runs that had the highest figure of merit, which shows that those runs predominately were done with binaries produced by the Intel compiler, input problem size 30, and one thread. The original 1,149 datasets were reduced to 24 entries by the "figure of merit" selection.

Comparison Page. The SPOT comparison page is a powerful tool for comparing performance profiles from multiple application runs. Users can select datasets on the landing page using the crossfilter, and open the comparison page to show the performance for all selected runs in a stacked line graph. Users can also group data using additional metadata flags, for example to compare performance between different compilers or MPI versions. A typical comparison configuration for tracking nightly test performance might show a chart per group of tests (where the tests in a group could be defined by metadata values), the test date on the x-axis, and the sum of walltime performance for every test in the group on the y-axis.

Figure 3 shows the runtime in different instrumented code regions for a set of runs in our Lulesh datasets, ordered by the launchdate of the job and grouped by compiler. The colors in the chart correspond to the different instrumented code regions. Users can select the regions shown in the chart in the region hierarchy overview in the lower left. The bottom part of the comparison page shows detailed information for the dataset selected in the chart with the black bar.

Users can group and order datasets using any of the recorded metadata attributes, providing a great deal of flexibility to conduct a wide variety of analyses. Figure 4 shows an interesting example. Here, we ran additional experiments with Lulesh with 343 MPI processes, using three different MPI implementations (mvapich2 v2.3, OpenMPI 2, and OpenMPI 4) and different problem sizes, with

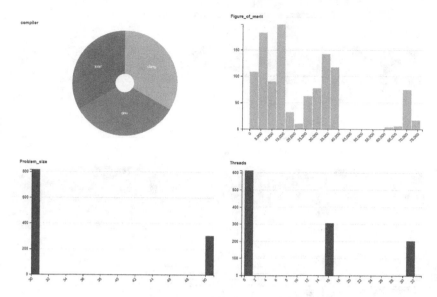

Fig. 1. The SPOT landing page featuring four histogram charts for a set of Lulesh runs. Charts show the numbers of runs with certain metadata values; here: compiler, figure-of-merit (FOM), input problem size, and number of threads.

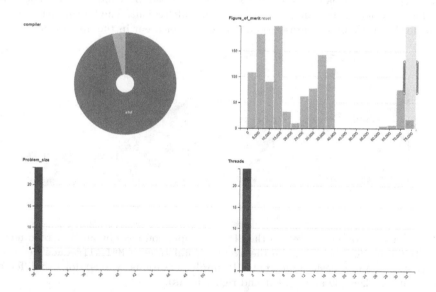

Fig. 2. The landing page charts from Fig. 1 with a crossfilter applied. Selecting runs with highest FOM (top right) shows relationship to compiler (top left), problem size (bottom left), and threads (bottom right).

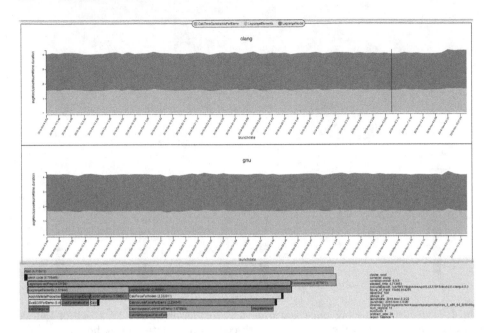

Fig. 3. The SPOT comparison page, here showing runtime (y-axis) for a set of Lulesh runs, ordered by job launch date (x-axis) and grouped by compiler (top and bottom charts). Colors correspond to instrumented code regions. The bottom pane shows details for the highlighted dataset (marked by the black bar in the upper chart).

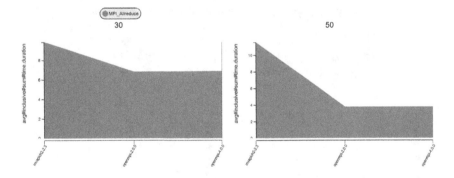

Fig. 4. Users can order datasets in the SPOT comparison page by any recorded meta-data attribute. Here, we compare the average total time in `MPI_Allreduce` per rank (y-axis, seconds) in Lulesh in different MPI implementations (x-axis), for two different input problem sizes (30 and 50; left and right charts).

all other configuration parameters fixed. In the chart, we show average total runtime spent in `MPI_Allreduce`, ordered by MPI version on the x-axis, and grouped by Lulesh problem size. We see that in our tests, OpenMPI outperformed mvapich, especially at large problem sizes.

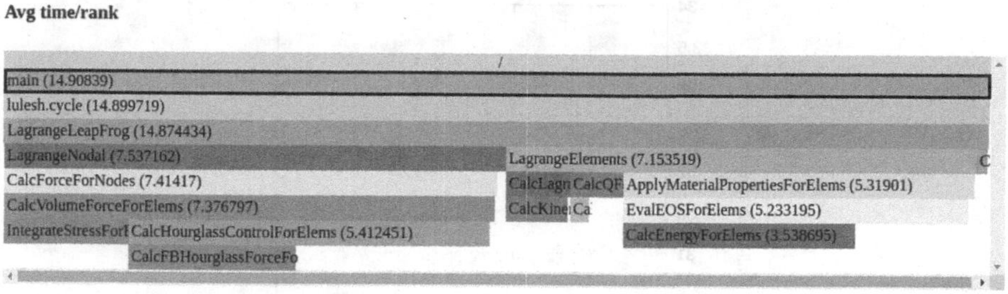

Avg time/rank

Fig. 5. A detailed performance profile view for a single Lulesh dataset in SPOT showing code hierarchy plots for recorded performance metrics (here: average time in seconds per MPI rank) within instrumented code regions.

Detail Views. From the landing page, users can open detail views for individual datasets, such as a flame graph visualization showing the time spent in each annotated regions. Figure 5 shows a flame graph visualization for the time spent in the instrumented code regions for a single Lulesh dataset.

5   Overhead Evaluation

It is critical that measurement activities do not negatively impact program performance. We quantify the measurement overheads in our Lulesh example when recording SPOT data. We compare four different configurations: an uninstrumented executable ("No instrumentation"), the Caliper-instrumented version with no measurements enabled ("No measurement"), recording a basic region time profile for SPOT ("Spot"), and recording region profile for SPOT with MPI function profiling enabled ("Spot+MPI"). Our experiments ran on Quartz, a 2,634-node cluster system at LLNL with Intel OmniPath interconnect, dual 18-core Intel Xeon E5-2695 2.1 GHz processors, and 128 gigabytes of memory per node. We use Caliper v2.3.0 and Adiak v0.1.1. Both Lulesh and Caliper were built with gcc 4.9.3. Caliper was compiled with optimization level -O2, Lulesh with -O3. We ran this experiment on a single allocated node using 8 MPI processes and 4 OpenMP threads per process using the Lulesh default input problem.

We ran each configuration 5 times and report the minimum, maximum, and average runtime with each configuration. Figure 6 shows the results. The runtime of the uninstrumented Lulesh executable was between 32.8 and 33 s, with an average of 32.9 s. The average runtime of the instrumented program is virtually unchanged with 33.0 s. When recording basic region time profiles for SPOT, we see a 1.3% runtime overhead in the instrumented Lulesh. The overhead increases slightly to 2% with MPI profiling turned on. Measurement overhead depends heavily on the instrumentation granularity. For our typical ubiquitous performance analysis use cases, we only instrument high-level program regions; therefore, measurement overheads generally stay low in produc-

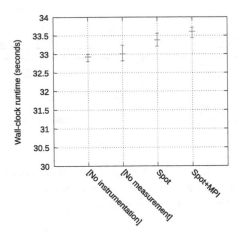

Fig. 6. Caliper instrumentation and measurement overhead in Lulesh with different embedded performance measurement configurations enabled. The bars show the average wall-clock runtime and runtime variation over 5 runs for each configuration.

tion use. In absolute terms, results from the Caliper-provided cali-annotation-perftest benchmark program on our test machine show average costs for a single Caliper instrumentation event (i.e., enter or exit of an instrumented region) of $0.65\,\mu$s in the Spot runtime profiling configuration, and $0.12\,\mu$s with no active profiling configuration.

The data collection step producing the SPOT output file uses Caliper's flexible aggregation mechanism, which offers $O(\log N)$ scalability over N MPI ranks [10]. Otherwise, Caliper performs no inter-process communication during program execution. Because we record only aggregate information, the amount of data stored on each process during execution remains constant, and only depends on the number of instrumented code regions. The resulting profiling datasets for individual program runs are quite small: in our Lulesh example, the dataset size is 10 KiB per run for the basic region time profile and 14 KiB for the time profile with MPI functions.

6   Case Study: Marbl

This section discusses our experience integrating ubiquitous performance analysis into Marbl, a large multi-physics production code that simulates high energy density and focused physics experiments driven by high-explosive magnetic or laser based energy sources.

Integrating Caliper and Adiak into Marbl was relatively easy and took approximately two man-weeks of developer effort, including coding, testing, reviews, and integration. The details of the integration effort were largely similar to the Lulesh example in Sect. 4. One notable addition is that Marbl also exposes its annotations to users in the form of lua functions that can be added at runtime:

- `annotation_begin(name)`
- `annotation_end(name)`
- `annotation_metadata(key,value,category)`.

This allows users (and CI suites) to easily tag and compare the performance for different configurations of a problem.

Unlike many other large LLNL applications, Marbl did not already have built-in timers where we could hook in Caliper annotations. We used HPCToolkit [7] to quickly identify approximately a dozen interesting regions of code that we then annotated, which was enough for Marbl's developers to start using SPOT. The Marbl development team then iteratively refined and added code annotations as they used the tool. A Caliper experiment that counted annotation executions was useful for identifying annotations that were too low-level, such as when an annotation was added in an inner loop and briefly caused a performance regression (seen as a spike from December 20–30 in Fig. 7).

A motivating factor for integrating SPOT into Marbl was to track performance regressions in nightly tests. Marbl's nightly continuous integration (CI) test scripts were modified to drop a Caliper performance file into a persistent directory, which the SPOT web interface uses as a data source. This required only minor changes to the existing CI scripts, specifically, enabling the spot Config-Manager configuration for a subset of test instances designated for performance testing. The nightly tests track performance on CPU and GPU architectures over several different configurations of around ten benchmark problems. Each of the ~80 test runs generates a ~30KiB dataset. Since there were too many tests for a human to look at each test's individual daily performance, we grouped tests by their set of utilized physics packages using Adiak-collected metadata. SPOT's comparison view was set to show each test group's (determined by tests that utilized the same physics packages) aggregate performance over a time period. If a test group shows a performance anomaly, a Marbl developer can then use SPOT to view the performance of individual tests in the group, or the aggregate performance of certain code regions in a test or test group. The SPOT configuration that shows any particular view is reflected in the URL, so Marbl developers can bookmark the test results page or send a particular view to a colleague.

The Marbl development team had other uses for SPOT. During development of a new algorithm they wanted to measure the scaling performance and memory overhead of a region of code. They ran before-and-after versions of the code at various scales and collected the automatically-generated performance files into a directory. By pointing SPOT at that directory and selecting a few options in the comparison view, they were able to easily create before-and-after scaling graphs of that code region. This effort generated a request for more complicated graph types, which eventually led to a SPOT feature to automatically export performance data for sets of runs into a Jupyter notebook, where Python's powerful data analytics tools and graphing infrastructure can be used to slice data into highly-customizable visualizations and graphs (see Sect. 3.5).

Ubiquitous performance analysis has also been instrumental in helping the Marbl development team track and understand the code's performance as they

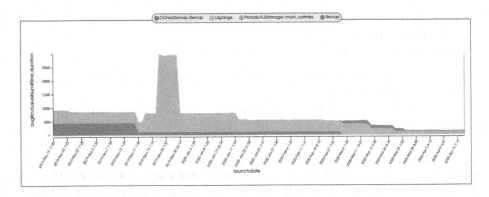

Fig. 7. SPOT performance tracking for Marbl's `Triple-Point-3D` problem on a 4 GPU compute node over the course of several months during its ongoing GPU port. Ubiquitous performance analysis made it easy to detect a performance regression (in late December 2019) and can seamlessly handle changing annotation labels, such as when the "DGFieldRemap::Remap" annotation (pink) was renamed to "Remap" (brown) around March 2020. (Color figure online)

port the codebase to new architectures, an ongoing effort which began in Fall 2019. Figure 7 shows the performance of a 3D Triple-Point hydrodynamics problem on a single IBM Power9 node with 4 NVIDIA Volta GPUs over about a six month period. Automatic performance capture has also helped the team ensure that there have not been performance regressions on other platforms during the porting process. Similarly, ubiquitous performance analysis made it easy to set up Node-to-Node performance scaling studies in Marbl to compare the code's performance across several HPC architectures including Intel- and ARM-based CPU clusters as well as a GPU-based cluster [8]. The integrated Caliper annotations enabled comparisons across different phases of the simulation, custom metadata annotations enabled filtering by scaling study type (e.g. strong-scaling, weak-scaling and throughput scaling) and the Jupyter integration streamlined the process of analyzing and charting the data.

7   Conclusion

Ubiquitous performance analysis seamlessly integrates performance profiling into HPC software development workflows. It facilitates continuous recording, analysis, and comparison of program performance data for long-lived HPC codes. We have created and deployed new software infrastructure to accomplish this goal: the ConfigManager API in Caliper to embed programmatically controlled, always-on profiling capabilities into applications; the Adiak metadata collection library; and the SPOT web interface with novel visualization and analysis tools to explore large collections of performance datasets. Our entire ubiquitous performance analysis stack is developed and released as open source packages [1,6,11].

The Marbl case study shows how ubiquitous performance analysis enables automated performance regression testing and custom cross-platform studies, and greatly simplifies collaborative performance optimization work in large development teams.

At LLNL, we continue to integrate Caliper and SPOT into additional in-house production codes. We also continue to develop new turnkey-style measurement options in the ConfigManager interface with matching visualization tools in SPOT for specific analyses. In that regard, we see the ubiquitous performance analysis software stack as an ideal platform to deploy new performance analysis methodologies. Finally, we recognize that a large amount of long-term performance data can be obtained through automatic data collection, and we expect that this data will enable a wealth of new automated performance analysis approaches based on data mining and machine learning.

Acknowledgment. This work was performed under the auspices of the U.S. Department of Energy by Lawrence Livermore National Laboratory under contract DEAC52-07NA27344 and supported by the Office of Science, Office of Advanced Scientific Computing Research as well as the Advanced Simulation and Computing (ASC) program. The views and opinions of the authors do not necessarily reflect those of the U.S. government or Lawrence Livermore National Security, LLC neither of whom nor any of their employees make any endorsements, express or implied warranties or representations or assume any legal liability or responsibility for the accuracy, completeness, or usefulness of the information contained herein. LLNL-CONF-808977.

References

1. Adiak: Standard interface for collecting HPC run metadata. https://github.com/LLNL/Adiak. Accessed 16 Mar 2020
2. dc.js - dimensional charting javascript library. https://dc-js.github.io/dc.js/. Accessed 7 Apr 2019
3. Livermore Unstructured Lagrangian Explicit Shock Hydrodynamics (LULESH). http://computation.llnl.gov/casc/ShockHydro
4. NVIDIA CUDA Profiling Tools Interface. https://developer.nvidia.com/CUPTI-CTK10_2. Accessed 8 Apr 2020
5. Project jupyter. https://jupyer.org/. Accessed 10 Apr 2019
6. SPOT Container. https://github.com/llnl/spot2_container. Accessed 31 Mar 2021
7. Adhianto, L., et al.: HPCToolkit: tools for performance analysis of optimized parallel programs. Concurrency Comput. Pract. Experience **22**(6), 685–701 (2010)
8. Anderson, R., et al.: The Multiphysics on Advanced Platforms Project. Technical Report LLNL-TR-815869, LLNL (2020). https://doi.org/10.2172/1724326
9. Bhatele, A., Brink, S., Gamblin, T.: Hatchet: Pruning the overgrowth in parallel profiles. In: Proceedings of the International Conference for High Performance Computing, Networking, Storage and Analysis, New York, SC 2019. Association for Computing Machinery (2019). https://doi.org/10.1145/3295500.3356219
10. Böhme, D., Beckingsale, D., Schulz, M.: Flexible data aggregation for performance profiling. In: 2017 IEEE International Conference on Cluster Computing (CLUSTER), pp. 419–428 (2017). https://doi.org/10.1109/CLUSTER.2017.34

11. Böhme, D., et al.: Caliper: performance introspection for HPC software stacks. In: Supercomputing 2016 (SC 2016). Salt Lake City (2016). lLNL-CONF-699263
12. Brunst, H., Hoppe, H.C., Nagel, W.E., Winkler, M.: Performance optimization for large scale computing: the scalable VAMPIR approach. In: Proceedings of the 2001 International Conference on Computational Science (ICCS 2001), San Francisco, pp. 751–760 (2001)
13. Eichenberger, A.E., et al.: OMPT: an OpenMP tools application programming interface for performance analysis. In: Rendell, A.P., Chapman, B.M., Müller, M.S. (eds.) IWOMP 2013. LNCS, vol. 8122, pp. 171–185. Springer, Heidelberg (2013). https://doi.org/10.1007/978-3-642-40698-0_13
14. Geimer, M., Wolf, F., Wylie, B.J.N., Ábrahám, E., Becker, D., Mohr, B.: The Scalasca performance toolset architecture. Concurrency Comput. Pract. Experience **22**(6), 702–719 (2010). https://doi.org/10.1002/cpe.1556, http://apps.fz-juelich.de/jsc-pubsystem/pub-webpages/general/get_attach.php?pubid=142
15. Huck, K.A., Malony, A.D.: PerfExplorer: A performance data mining framework for large-scale parallel computing. In: Proceedings of the 2005 ACM/IEEE conference on Supercomputing. SC 2005. IEEE Computer Society (2005)
16. Huck, K.A., Malony, A.D., Bell, R., Morris, A.: Design and implementation of a parallel performance data management framework. In: 2005 International Conference on Parallel Processing (ICPP 2005), pp. 473–482. IEEE (2005)
17. Huck, K.A., Malony, A.D., Shende, S., Morris, A.: Knowledge support and automation for performance analysis with perfexplorer 2.0. Sci. Program. **16**(2–3), 123–134 (2008)
18. Karavanic, K.L., et al.: Integrating database technology with comparison-based parallel performance diagnosis: the perftrack performance experiment management tool. In: Supercomputing 2005. Proceedings of the ACM/IEEE SC 2005 Conference, p. 39 (2005). https://doi.org/10.1109/SC.2005.36
19. Karavanic, K.L., Miller, B.P.: Experiment management support for performance tuning. In: SC 1997: Proceedings of the 1997 ACM/IEEE Conference on Supercomputing, p. 8. IEEE (1997)
20. Karlin, I., et al.: LULESH programming model and performance ports overview. Technical Report LLNL-TR-608824 (2012)
21. Knapp, R.L., et al.: PerfTrack: scalable application performance diagnosis for linux clusters. In: 8th LCI International Conference on High-Performance Clustered Computing, pp. 15–17. Citeseer (2007)
22. Knüpfer, T., et al.: Score-P: a joint performance measurement run-time infrastructure for Periscope, Scalasca, TAU, and Vampir. In: Brunst, H., Müller, M.S., Nagel, W.E., Resch, M.M. (eds.) Tools for High Performance Computing 2011, pp. 79–91. Springer, Heidelberg (2011). https://doi.org/10.1007/978-3-642-31476-6_7
23. Madsen, J.R., et al.: TiMemory: modular performance analysis for HPC. In: Sadayappan, P., Chamberlain, B.L., Juckeland, G., Ltaief, H. (eds.) ISC High Performance 2020. LNCS, vol. 12151, pp. 434–452. Springer, Cham (2020). https://doi.org/10.1007/978-3-030-50743-5_22
24. Mellor-Crummey, J., Fowler, R., Marin, G.: HPCView: a tool for top-down analysis of node performance. J. Supercomputing **23**, 81–101 (2002)
25. Mi, H., Wang, H., Cai, H., Zhou, Y., Lyu, M.R., Chen, Z.: P-tracer: path-based performance profiling in cloud computing systems. In: 2012 IEEE 36th Annual Computer Software and Applications Conference, pp. 509–514 (2012)
26. Mucci, P.J., Browne, S., Deane, C., Ho, G.: PAPI: a portable interface to hardware performance counters. In: Proceedings Department of Defense HPCMP User Group Conference (1999)

27. Pillet, V., Labarta, J., Cortes, T., Girona, S.: PARAVER: a tool to visualize and analyze parallel code. In: Proceedings of WoTUG-18: Transputer and Occam Developments, pp. 17–31 (1995)

28. Ren, G., Tune, E., Moseley, T., Shi, Y., Rus, S., Hundt, R.: Google-wide profiling: a continuous profiling infrastructure for data centers. IEEE Micro **30**(4), 65–79 (2010)

29. Rosinski, J.M.: GPTL-general purpose timing library (2016)

30. Shende, S., Malony, A.: The TAU parallel performance system. Int. J. High Perform. Comput. Appl. **20**(2), 287–331 (2006)

31. Skinner, D.: Performance monitoring of parallel scientific applications (2005). https://doi.org/10.2172/881368, https://www.osti.gov/biblio/881368

32. The Open|SpeedShop Team: Open|SpeedShop for Linux. http://www.openspeedshop.org

Programming Environments
and Systems Software

Artemis: Automatic Runtime Tuning of Parallel Execution Parameters Using Machine Learning

Chad Wood[1]([✉]), Giorgis Georgakoudis[2], David Beckingsale[2], David Poliakoff[3], Alfredo Gimenez[2], Kevin Huck[1], Allen Malony[1], and Todd Gamblin[2]

[1] University of Oregon, Eugene, OR, USA
{cdw,khuck,malony}@cs.uoregon.edu
[2] Lawrence Livermore National Laboratory, Livermore, CA, USA
{georgakoudis1,beckingsale1,giminez1,gamblin2}@llnl.gov
[3] Sandia National Laboratory, Albequerque, NM, USA
dzpolia@sandia.gov

Abstract. Portable parallel programming models provide the potential for high performance and productivity, however they come with a multitude of runtime parameters that can have significant impact on execution performance. Selecting the optimal set of those parameters is non-trivial, so that HPC applications perform well in different system environments and on different input data sets, without the need of time consuming parameter exploration or major algorithmic adjustments.

We present Artemis, a method for online, feedback-driven, automatic parameter tuning using machine learning that is generalizable and suitable for integration into high-performance codes. Artemis monitors execution at runtime and creates adaptive models for tuning execution parameters, while being minimally invasive in application development and runtime overhead. We demonstrate the effectiveness of Artemis by optimizing the execution times of three HPC proxy applications: Cleverleaf, LULESH, and Kokkos Kernels SpMV. Evaluation shows that Artemis selects the optimal execution policy with over 85% accuracy, has modest monitoring overhead of less than 9%, and increases execution speed by up to 47% despite its runtime overhead.

Keywords: Artemis · HPC · Performance · In situ · Machine learning

1 Introduction

HPC software can contain tens to thousands of parallel code regions, each of which may have independent performance tuning parameters. Optimal choices for these tuning parameters can be specific to a target system architecture, the set of input data to be processed, or the overall shared state of the machine during a job's execution. There are costs associated with discovering and maintaining optimal choices, in a developer's time to manually adjust settings and rebuild

© National Technology & Engineering Solutions of Sandia, LLC 2021
B. L. Chamberlain et al. (Eds.): ISC High Performance 2021, LNCS 12728, pp. 453–472, 2021.
https://doi.org/10.1007/978-3-030-78713-4_24

projects, or the compute time to explore the space of possible configurations to find optimal settings automatically.

The goal of *performance portability* in HPC is for applications to operate optimally across a range of current and future systems without the need for costly code interventions in each new deployment. Given large job scales, increasing software complexity, platform diversity, and hardware performance variability, a performance portability is a challenging problem – with the same inputs, code performance is observed to change between invocations on the same machine and, worse, can be variable even during execution.

Recent work has turned to machine learning techniques to train classification models on code and execution feature vectors that then can be used to make dynamic tuning selection for each kernel of interest [3]. For instance, the Apollo [9] work demonstrated the use of offline machine learning methods to optimize the selection of RAJA [8] kernels at runtime. The RAJA programming methodology provides abstractions that allow code regions to be implemented once but compiled for a variety of architectures, with several execution policies capable of being selected at runtime. Apollo's offline training approach built statistical classifiers that directly selected values for tuning parameters. The classification model could then be embedded in RAJA programs to provide a dynamic, low-overhead, data-driven auto-tuning framework. The decision to do offline training was a trade-off Apollo made to avoid costly online search for autotuning.

Offline machine learning methods are not sufficient for guiding *online optimizations* that deliver general performance portability. There are several reasons for this to be the case: 1. Without knowing what the user is actually doing, combinatorial exploration of all possible settings is difficult to exhaust, even with a decent sampling strategy. A great many different models need to be represented by whatever ends up being deployed, hopefully providing optimal recommendations for every unique combination of architectures, configurations, input decks, and so on. 2. In order to cover all scenarios, the expense of training and re-training will grow. The entire campaign of parameter testing would need to be done with any new code deployment, significant modification, change in configuration, use of new input deck, or increase in job scale. Certainly, moving to a new platform or modification of an existing platform could trigger a new training study. Ideally, the testing should happen at the full scale and duration that the job was intended to be run at once its model was in use, but this is a costly proposition. Ultimately, this suggests that offline training is unable to fully capture enough for model fitness to be reliable over time. 3. Once trained offline, static models are unable to adapt to changes between application invocations or simulation steps in a workflow. Such changes can make even very good models go stale over time. Furthermore, the potential dynamic variations in the execution environment can expose gaps in the model due to the fact that they never occurred during training.

To further motivate the need for online methods, we note the paradigmatic shift in HPC underway in the move to extreme scales and cloud-based computing. Applications are increasingly being developed and deployed where it is accepted as a given that there will be dynamism in their runtime environment. Even within tightly-controlled on-site dedicated clusters, novel *in situ* resources and services are being deployed in support of classic block-synchronous applications, decreasing the emphasis on their synchronous behavior to maximally saturate available computation and I/O resources.

Our current research is motivated by the need to address tuning challenges presented by these performance complexities and realities of new *in situ* development models: the scale of jobs, asynchronous data movement, and dynamic performance characteristics of modern hardware. Instead of working against the general nature of the problem, we propose to embrace it and investigate the productive outcomes of adopting modern (online) training techniques. In the spirit of prior work, we created the *Artemis* continuous tuning framework to analyze code kernels online during application execution. Artemis trains new kernel performance models *in situ*, deploying and evaluating them at runtime, observing each model's recommendations during execution to rate its ongoing fitness.

Our primary research contributions are:

- We present Artemis, an online framework that dynamically tunes the execution of parallel regions by training optimizing models.
- We provide an implementation of a RAJA parallel execution policy that uses Artemis to optimize the execution of `forall` and `collapse` loop pattern.
- We extend Kokkos to use Artemis for tuning CUDA execution on GPUs.
- We evaluate Artemis using three HPC proxy applications: LULESH, Cleverleaf, and Kokkos Kernels SpMV. Results show that Artemis has overhead of less than 9%, and model training and evaluation overhead is in the order of hundreds of microseconds. Artemis selects the optimal policy $\tilde{8}5\%$ of the time, and can provide up to 47% speedup.

2   Background

Parallel programming frameworks have emerged to address the performance portability challenge by providing a "write once, run anywhere" methodology where alternate versions of a code section (called kernels) can be generated to target architectural tuning parameters. In this manner, the programming methodology decouples the specification of a kernel's parallelism from the parameters that govern policies for how to execute the work in different forms. The tuning of the policy choices and execution variants can be done without changing the high-level program.

Parallel frameworks such as RAJA [19] and Kokkos [13,14] use lightweight syntax and standard C++ features for portability and ease of integration into production applications. Related prior work on Apollo [9] focused on developing an autotuning extension for RAJA for input-dependent parameters where the best kernel execution policy depends on information known only at application runtime. However, Apollo's methodology required executions under all runtime scenarios to create an offline static training database, leading to many of the limitations discussed in the introduction. Thus, it is interesting to pursue a new question: is it possible to train a classification model online and apply it during application execution? Of course, this question immediately raises several concerns, mainly having to do with how training data is generated, the overhead of measurement, and the complexity costs of machine learning algorithms.

3   Artemis: Design and Implementation

Artemis is at once a methodology for in situ, ML-based performance auto-tuning and an architecture and operational framework for its implementation. The following captures these aspects as we describe how Artemis actually works. In a nutshell, it is the observation of an application's execution of its tunable parallel code regions, extracting features and performance data with different execution policies, coupled with the training of ML models online to select optimized execution policies per-region and feature set.

3.1   Design

Without loss of generality, Artemis thinks of applications being iterative where a sequence of *steps* are conducted during which parallel regions are being executed. At the end of those steps, the application ends.

If the a parallel region is to be tuned, it must be provide the different execution policy variants it can choose between, and then Artemis must be invoked for that region. In the case of the reference implementations presented here, this can be largely automated.

The *user* of Artemis need not be thought of as the ultimate end-user of an application, but more likely the developer implementing a performance portability framework such as RAJA or Kokkos within some application. By design, our embedding of an Artemis interface into the portability framework layer enables all parallel regions of an application to be automatically decorated with the necessary Artemis API calls, and furnished with a set of common execution policies that come pre-packaged, and may be integrated into any application making use of that performance portability framework. Artemis is designed to be extensible and programmable, so expert users are always going to be able to provide their own execution policy variants, or make use of the Artemis API directly without the benefits of a performance portability layer managing it.

In the common case where an application is making use of performance portability framework as described above, all an end-user will need to do to is to select to enable Artemis functionality at build time, and then at run time they could opt to enable the Artemis tuning capabilities for any given session, which would then exploit the built-in policies that are bundled with the framework. Essentially, this is the end of involvement for the Artemis user.

Within a step, each parallel region executed is done so for a particular policy as determined by the policy model. Artemis controls how the policy model behaves. It could either be controlled to test out different policies during training, thereby allowing performance measurements to be obtained for analysis, or it could select a particular policy determined by the auto-tuned model evaluation. Each application step represents an opportunity for parallel region training or re-training. Within a step, each encounter with an Artemis-guided parallel region allows that region's model to make an optimized policy selection based on immediately-observed local features.

Artemis instruments parallel regions to collect data on their execution and tune them. Marking the beginning of region execution, the user additionally provides a set of *features* that characterize the execution and a set of execution *policies* that are selectable for the execution of this region. After the call marking the beginning of a region, the user calls the Artemis API function that returns the policy to use when executing the region. The region proceeds to execute a refactored variant of itself that corresponds to that policy selection. Finally, the instrumented region calls the Artemis API to mark the end of its execution, and Artemis makes note of the features and performance measurements. Region execution time is the primary measurement of interest, but it is possible to capture other performance data for analysis.

Artemis is implemented as a runtime library that merges with the application to provide region performance/metadata measurement/analysis, ML model training, and auto-tuning optimization. It presently targets parallel MPI programs that use RAJA or Kokkos for on-node parallelization.

3.2   Training and Optimization

The set of user-provided features and policies for each region are the input data to Artemis for ML training and optimization. During training, Artemis explores among the available policies and in particular measures their execution times, which is the optimization target we selected for our experimental evaluation. Artemis keeps per-region records of the feature set, policy, and measured execution time as tuples of (feature set, policy, execution time) to compile the training data and create an optimizing policy selection model. Whenever a region is executed multiple times per step, if different features are captured or policies are explored, each unique combination will have executions times recorded for use in model development.

By design, Artemis exposes an API call to the user to invoke optimization on-demand. Artemis expects the user to invoke the optimization API function after a sensible amount of computation has executed, permitting Artemis to have collected a representative set of measurement records. This can be different for different applications, and depends somewhat on the number of optimization points to be explored when searching the space of available policies. If models are initially trained from an inadequate set of measurements inputs, such that their fitness is insufficient to make reasonably accurate predictions of the measures for an iteration, Artemis will place the deviating regions into a training mode again to gather data on additional policies, so that future models for that region, within the run, will be more robustly informed. Programs with iterative algorithms should typically invoke optimization every time step of execution. When the user invokes the API, Artemis performs the following steps:

1. For every instrumented region it goes through the measurement records and finds the policy with the fastest measured execution for each feature set

to enunciate the optimal pairs of each unique (feature set, policy) combination for this region; 2. In case of multi-process execution, Artemis communicates per-process best policy data between all executing processes to build a unified pool of these pairs and implement *collective training*, 3. From those feature set and policy pairs, it creates the training data to feed to the classification ML model, where the feature set is the feature input to the model and policy is the response; 4. Artemis feeds those data to train the ML model and derive an optimizing policy classifier for each region, that takes as input a feature set and produces as output the optimized selection policy.

When later executions of the instrumented regions query Artemis for the policy to execute, the trained model provides the optimizing policy index. Note that even after training an optimized policy selection model, Artemis continues to collect execution time data for optimized regions to monitor execution and trigger re-training, which we discuss next.

3.3 Validation and Retraining

Artemis includes a *regression* model to trigger re-training, anticipating that time-dependent or data-dependent behavior may change the execution profiles of regions, thus rendering previous optimizing models sub-optimal. Specifically, Artemis creates a regression model to predict execution time given the measurement records. The input features to train this regression model are the features set by instrumentation, including the policy selection, and the response outputs are the measured execution times.

At every invocation of the optimization API call by the user, Artemis compares the measured execution time per region, feature set, and policy to the predicted execution time provided by the regression model. When the measured time exceeds the predicted time over a threshold, Artemis discards the optimizing model and reverts the region to a training regime, trying out different execution policies on region execution to collect new data for training an optimized model. On a later invocation of the optimization API call, Artemis creates the new optimizing classification model and the new regression model for a new cycle of optimization and monitoring.

3.4 Extending RAJA OpenMP Execution

The RAJA [8] programming model was extended to enable Artemis optimization by defining an auto-tuned execution policy for parallel loop programming patterns implemented with OpenMP. Interestingly, much of region instrumentation is hidden by the end-user of RAJA since instrumentation happens inside the RAJA header library. The only refactoring required for a RAJA program is to make on-demand calls to the optimization API of Artemis and use the Artemis-recommended execution policy when defining parallel kernels through the RAJA templated API.

Specifically, we create an Artemis tuning policy for the `forall` programming pattern, which defines a parallel loop region, and for the `Collapse` kernel pattern, which collapses 2-level and 3-level nested to a single parallel loop, fusing the nested iteration spaces. For this implementation, we choose the `forall` and `Collapse` patterns since they are frequently used in applications. Artemis can integrate with other parallel patterns of RAJA, such as scans, OpenMP offloading, and CUDA, which is work-in-progress. The Artemis policy used in our evaluation framework tunes execution by choosing between two policies: either OpenMP or sequential. The choice for those two policies is motivated by prior work [9] concluding that varying additional OpenMP parameters (number of threads, loop scheduling policy) results in sub-optimal tuning. Nevertheless, Artemis is general to tune for additional OpenMP parameters, which can be abstracted as different execution policies to input to the Artemis API. Artemis instrumentation is within the implementation of those patterns, in the RAJA header library.

```
template <typename Iterable, typename Func>
RAJA_INLINE void forall_impl (artemis_exec &,
                              Iterable    &&iter,
                              Func        &&loop_body) {
  static Artemis::Region *region = nullptr;
  if (region == nullptr)
    region = Artemis::create_region(num_policies=2);
  region->begin({ distance(begin(iter), end(iter)) });
  int policy = region->getPolicyIndex();
  switch(policy) {
  case 0: {
    #pragma omp parallel
    { RAJA_EXTRACT_BED_IT(iter);
      #pragma omp for
      for (decltype(distance_it) i = 0; i < distance_it; ++i)
        loop_body(begin_it[i]);
    } } break;
  case 1: {
      RAJA_EXTRACT_BED_IT(iter);
      for (decltype(distance_it) i = 0; i < distance_it; ++i)
        loop_body(begin_it[i]);
    } break; };
  region->end();
}
```

Fig. 1. Using Artemis in the RAJA forall execution pattern.

Listing 1 shows a code excerpt for the instrumentation of the `forall` implementation with Artemis, redacting implementation details for RAJA closure privatization, for brevity of presentation. Note, the code for the `Collapse` kernel is similar. The `forall` implementation instruments the region execution with a call to `region->begin()` providing the number of iterations as the single feature in the feature set. For the `Collapse` implementation, the feature set consists of the iterations of all loop levels, creating a vector of features. Next, the implementation calls `region->getPolicyIndex()` which returns an index selecting the execution policy variant; 0 indicates executing with OpenMP and 1 indicates executing the region sequentially. This policy index is the input to the following `switch-case` statement that selects the execution variant. Lasty, there is a call to `region->end()` to marks the end of region execution.

This pattern of API use is general, and serves as a model for other interfaces and ports of Artemis, such as it's integration with the tuning API of the Kokkos portability framework.

3.5   Enhancing Kokkos CUDA Execution

Besides RAJA OpenMP execution, we integrate Artemis to tune CUDA kernel execution within Kokkos [14]. Specifically, our experiment tuned parameters for the execution of an SpMV kernel computation in CUDA, including the *team size*, which is the outer level of parallelism of thread blocks, the *vector size*, which is the inner level of parallelism of numbers of threads and the *number of rows* of computation assigned to each thread.

3.6   Training Measurement

Initially, when Artemis first encounters an instrumented region, it deploys a *round-robin* strategy to collect training data. This strategy cycles through the set of provided policies, which contains the OpenMP execution policy and the sequential policy in our RAJA implementation, or policies representing combinations of the various kernel launch parameters in the Kokkos integration. When searching, Artemis returns a policy index to explore a particular execution variant. In our implementation, round-robin advances the policy selection index for each region and each set of unique features independently. While searching the space of available policies, the Artemis runtime library records the unique feature set and the measured execution time for each instrumented region.

When Artemis is being used in an MPI application, it is capable of *collective training*, whereby training datasets across the processes are analyzed together.

At the end of an application step, every process issues a collective *allgather* operation to share their training datasets and gather the training datasets of every other process. Each process combines them to create a unified training dataset per region, informed by the rank-offset parallel round-robin searches, to find the best explored policy that minimizes execution time across both the local and peer training data.

3.7   Training Model Analysis and Optimization

Artemis processes the metrics gathered during training to construct the matrix of features to use in model construction. This includes the feature set, the performance responses, and the optimal policies. A Random Forest Classifier (RFC) model is trained per region, implemented using the OpenCV machine learning library. Artemis evaluates this RFC model in later invocations of `region->getPolicyIndex()` of a trained region, to return the optimized execution policy using as input the feature set provided in the arguments of the `region->begin( features )` call. We choose RFC modeling because it has fast evaluation times of $\mathcal{O}(m \log n)$ complexity for m decision trees of n depth in the forest. Fast evaluation is important for reducing the overhead during execution since `region->getPolicyIndex()` is called with every region's execution. For experimentation, we set the depth to 2 levels and the forest size to 10 trees, which has shown to be effective for optimization.

Artemis uses the same measurement data to train a per-region Random Forest Regression (RFR) model that predicts expected execution time. Artemis uses this regression model to detect time-dependent or data-dependent divergence in the execution of a region that invalidates a previously trained RFC optimizing model, indicating that re-training is needed. In the implementation, RFR models train with regression accuracy of $1e-6$, hence micro-second resolution for predicting time, and implement a forest size of 50 trees. RFR evaluation is off the critical path, hence affords the largest forest size, since it is called only on invocations of `Artemis::processMeasurements()`. For time regression analysis, Artemis compares the profiled execution time with the predicted one for all the region's feature sets. If the measured time for a feature set is greater than the predicted one given a threshold, then the model is considered *diverging*. This threshold limits re-trains due to transient perturbations when measuring execution time. We have experimentally found that this threshold value of 2× filters out needless re-trains for the applications under test. Nonetheless, the threshold value is configurable and also re-training can be turned completely off, through environment variables. If the execution of an application region is pathological, such that execution time continuously diverges with the same features, then this region is ineligible for tuning and should be omitted or re-training should be turned off. This is a challenging scenario to naively automate, and future work involves exploring strategies to effectively manage regions that do not have stable performance profiles even when features or loop inputs are held constant.

Artemis counts all diverging feature sets in a region. If they are found to be more than a threshold, more than half feature sets in a region for our implementation, Artemis deems the RFC model invalid and sets up the round-robin search strategy to re-train an optimized model for that region.

Artemis is generalized to support *heterogeneous execution*, where an application deploys to a cluster of heterogeneous machines, or for cases where a heterogeneous workload is specified on the same regions. Differences in machine architectures can be captured as a feature that describes the machine type, e.g., CPU or GPU micro-architecture. Differences in a heterogeneous workload, for the same code region, can be captured as a feature describing the condition causing it, e.g., the MPI rank or an application-designated parameter.

4   Experimentation Setup

The Artemis framework is intended to target environments where performance portability is important. When evaluating Artemis we want to compare its benefits to standard configurations of application and systems that they run on. On the one hand, Artemis is optimizing an application's execution on a machine from some point of reference. If that starts with an already optimized version, there is little likely to be gained. Thus, choosing a "default" version of the application with standard settings is more appropriate to gauge improvement. On the other hand, Artemis is optimizing an application across machines, where different architecture component (e.g., CPU, memory) could lead to different code variants being selected. The application code needs to be developed in such a way that making selection of those code variants is possible without completely rewriting the application. This is the reason for working with RAJA and Kokkos for the experiments discussed below.

4.1   Comparators

The applications used in our study are developed with either RAJA or Kokkos, and we focus our attention on the parallel regions impacted by those portability frameworks. We define the *baseline* in performance comparison to be, for OpenMP, execution with the RAJA OpenMP execution policy using the same thread count for all regions, or in the CUDA case, the expert-tuned and hard-coded settings within the Kokkos Kernels suite. This is the *default mode* of executing these parallel applications. To quantify the instrumentation overhead of Artemis, we create a version of Artemis with this baseline that always selects the fixed default policy when guiding execution of a region, but does not perform any of the collection of performance measurements or online training. We call this the *Artemis-OpenMP* or *Artemis-Expert Heuristic* version. Lastly, we denote as *Artemis* the configuration where Artemis dynamically optimizes execution, using online profiling and machine learning for optimized policy selection and regression monitoring.

Table 1. Applications and their configurations

Application	Inputs	Nodes
LULESH	−r 100 −c 1 *or* 2 *or* 4 *or* 8 −i 100	1
Cleverleaf	Domain: (500, 500), triple point calculation,	1, 2, 4, 8
	4 refinement levels, 25 timesteps,	
	max patch size: 100 ×100 *or* 200 × 200,	
	400 × 400 *or* −1 ×−1(no limit)	
Kokkos Kernels SpMV	Domain: 100 M to 600 M non-zero values	1
	team size: 1–1024, vector size: 1–32	
	rows per thread: 1–4096	

4.2   Applications

We chose three HPC proxy-applications to perform our experiments: LULESH [1, 20] and Cleverleaf [6,10] for OpenMP, and Kokkos Kernels SpMV [24] for CUDA.

Table 1 shows details of the application inputs used and execution configurations. LULESH is configurable to create regions of different computational

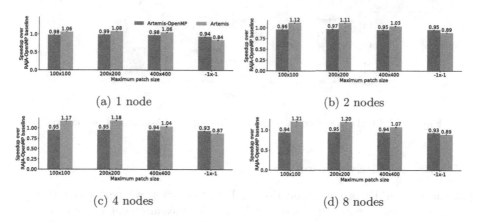

Fig. 2. Cleverleaf, speedup of Artemis-OpenMP and Artemis over the baseline.

cost, to mimic multi-material calculation. Cleverleaf uses adaptive mesh refinement to create a range of problem subdomains, called patches, with varying computational cost. Thus, both data-dependent and input-dependent settings can create regions of different computation. Kokkos Kernels SpMV computes a sparse matrix vector product for very large matrices, allowing for a configurable count of non-zero values.

In the OpenMP codes, Artemis dynamically optimizes each parallel region by selecting OpenMP execution policies only when there is enough work to justify the overhead of parallel execution, otherwise it will elect for sequential execution. LULESH inputs create heterogeneous computation by using a large count of regions (100) that emulate different materials, changing the computational cost of various region subsets by 1, 2, 4, or 8 times the base cost – LULESH adjusts the cost of 45% of the regions to be this multiple and 5% of regions to be 10× this multiple. For Cleverleaf, heterogeneous computation is created by changing the maximum patch size permitted during refinement, ranging from from 100×100, 200×200, 400×400, up to an unlimited maximum by selecting -1×-1. The RAJA LULESH implementation does not support distributed execution with MPI, thus our experiments are single node. Cleverleaf provides support for MPI execution, so we performed experiments on multiple nodes to show Artemis's response to Cleverleaf's strong scaling properties. Kokkos Kernels SpMV experiments used Artemis to explore and select policies representing combinations of Kokkos settings and CUDA kernel launch parameters, across a variety of problem sizes.

4.3 Hardware and Software Platforms

Experiments were run on nodes featuring dual-socket Intel Xeon E5-2695v4 processors for 36 cores and 128 GB of RAM per node and the TOSS3 software stack. We compiled applications and Artemis using GCC version 8.1.0 and MVAPICH2 version 2.3 for MPI support. Artemis used the OpenCV machine learning library version 4.3.0. For Kokkos CUDA we targeted the NVIDIA V100 (Volta) on an IBM Power9 architecture, using CUDA version 10.

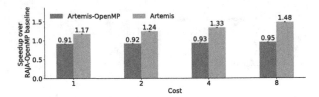

Fig. 3. LULESH, speedup over the baseline of RAJA-OpenMP execution.

4.4 Statistical Evaluation

For each OpenMP proxy application and configuration we performed 10 independent measurements. Unless otherwise noted, measurement counts the total application execution time end-to-end. Confidence intervals shown correspond to a 95% confidence level, calculated using Bootstrapping to avoid assumptions on the sampled population's distribution.

5 Evaluation

Here we provide results and detailed analysis of tuning for OpenMP with RAJA, as well as summary results from applying Artemis to tune Kokkos settings and CUDA kernel launch parameters.

For evaluating the performance of Artemis with OpenMP, we compute the speedup over the baseline of RAJA-OpenMP execution for both Artemis-OpenMP, which always selects OpenMP execution, and the optimizing Artemis, which dynamically chooses between OpenMP or sequential execution for a region, using the machine learning methods we described. Artemis-OpenMP exposes the instrumentation overhead of Artemis, hence the expected slowdown compared to non-instrumented RAJA-OpenMP execution. Figure 2 shows results for Cleverleaf, and Fig. 3 shows results for LULESH. Values on bars show the mean speedup (or slowdown) compared to RAJA-OpenMP execution.

5.1 Instrumentation Overhead

Observing the slowdown of Artemis-OpenMP, the overhead of instrumentation is modest, cumulatively less than 9% across both applications and tested configurations of input and node numbers. This shows that Artemis does not overburden execution and given tuning opportunities, it should recuperate the overhead and provide speedup over non-instrumented RAJA-OpenMP execution.

5.2 Model Training and Evaluation Overhead

The average training time for LULESH is 310 ms, while for Cleverleaf is 150 ms, which is minimal contrasted with the timescale of execution of regions, as we show in later measurements, so Artemis recovers this overhead, effectively

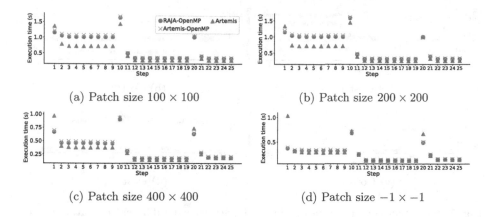

(a) Patch size 100×100

(b) Patch size 200×200

(c) Patch size 400×400

(d) Patch size -1×-1

Fig. 4. Execution time per timestep for Cleverleaf on 8 nodes, varying the maximum patch size. Regridding operation performed after every 10 steps.

tuning and speeding up execution. Moreover, model training (or re-training) is infrequently done as trained models persist during execution. By contrast, model evaluation happens at every execution of a tunable region. Its overhead depends on the forest size and tree depth of the trees in the evaluated forest. Given the limits in forest size (10) and tree depth (2) set in our implementation, see Sect. 3, we measure the time overhead for evaluating the maximum possible forest configuration to be less than 10 microseconds.

5.3   Speedup on Cleverleaf

For Cleverleaf, varying the maximum patch size changes the number and size of computational regions. A smaller size means more regions, hence more parallelism, but also finer-grain decomposition of the computation domain. So, there is greater disparity between regions that lack enough work, hence sequential policy is fastest, and regions with enough parallel work, for which OpenMP execution is fastest. Note, the special value -1×-1 means there is no maximum set and Cleverleaf by default prioritizes decomposing in larger regions. Figure 2 shows results for all node configurations, demonstrating that Artemis consistently speeds up execution for the smaller patch sizes of 100×100 and 200×200, no less than 8%, executing with one node, and up to 21%, executing on 8 nodes. For the larger patch size of 400×400, execution with Artemis is on par with RAJA-OpenMP, successfully recuperating the overhead with marginal gains, within measurement error. For the unlimited patch size of -1×-1, Artemis results in a net slowdown, also compared with Artemis-OpenMP, since there is lack of optimization opportunity, and the training and monitoring overhead inflated execution time.

For further analysis, we show results comparing execution times per timestep for different execution modes. Figure 4 shows results when executing with 8 nodes. Results for other node counts are similar, thus we omit them for brevity.

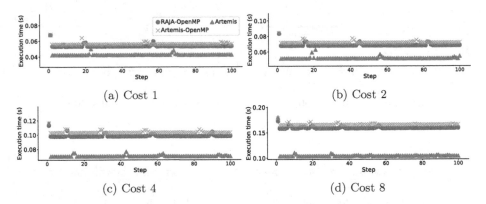

(a) Cost 1   (b) Cost 2

(c) Cost 4   (d) Cost 8

Fig. 5. Execution time per timestep for LULESH, showing different execution modes on one node, varying the cost of computational regions.

Note that Cleverleaf performs a *re-gridding* operation [7] every 10 timesteps that re-shuffles domain decomposition to reduce computation error, thus the spikes in execution time in the 10th and 20th timesteps.

Observing results, Artemis inflates execution time for the first timestep across all patch sizes, since this step includes training for bootstrapping tunable regions. For most of the rest of timesteps, Artemis reduces execution time, by as much as 40% for the least patch size of 100 × 100, compared to the default execution with RAJA-OpenMP. Artemis tuning potential lessens the larger the patch size, since larger regions favor OpenMP execution. Nevertheless, observing Fig. 4d for the largest patch size selection, Artemis correctly selects OpenMP execution and any performance lost is due to the initial training overhead. Notably, Cleverleaf execution with 8 nodes has second to sub-second timesteps, and Artemis is fast enough to optimize execution even at this short time scale. Expectedly, Artemis-OpenMP has slightly higher execution time per timestep compared to RAJA-OpenMP, reflecting instrumentation overhead as seen by the speedup results.

5.4   Effectiveness of Cleverleaf Policy Selection

Cleverleaf instantiates a multitude of regions and each region executes with multiple different feature sets, corresponding to different patch sizes from decomposing the domain and load balancing. So, to highlight Artemis effectiveness we fix the patch size to 100 × 100, which presents the most optimization potential, and pick one region to plot the average execution time of each feature set for the top-20 most frequently executed ones, contrasting OpenMP only execution vs. sequential execution vs. Artemis execution with dynamic policy selection. The region comprises of feature sets corresponding to 2d collapsed loops, so there are two values describing (outer,inner) loop iterations. Depending on the feature set size, OpenMP or sequential is the best. For example, feature set (3,201) executes faster with OpenMP and feature set (55, 2) executes faster sequentially. Observing execution times measured for Artemis, policy recommendations converge to the optimal policy for the majority of feature sets for which the performance difference between the sequential and OpenMP policy selection is more than 20%. Artemis selects the optimal policy in 10 of the 15 such regions.

Further, we find positive results for the accuracy of Artemis in selecting optimal policies. For the initial timestep, Artemis has low accuracy, ranging from 10% to 20%, due to training, without any discernible trend among different patch sizes. However, accuracy significantly improves after this initial, training step to a range of 85% to 95%, showing Artemis is effective in selecting the optimal policy most of the time.

5.5   Strong Scaling with Different Node Counts

Figs. 2a–d show results for increasing node counts. Following the discussion on smaller patch sizes that present optimization opportunities for Artemis, increasing the number of nodes also boosts the speedup achieved by Artemis. Cleverleaf distributes computational regions among different MPI ranks and executes bulk-synchronous, advancing the simulation time step after all MPI ranks have finished processing. Artemis dynamically optimizes execution per rank, thus it reduces execution time on the critical path, with multiplicative effect on the overall execution.

5.6   Speedup on LULESH

Figure 3 shows results for LULESH on a single node due to the limitation of the RAJA version of LULESH supporting only single node execution. For this experiment, the number of regions is kept constant (100) and the cost of computation varies between 1× (default) and 8×, as explained in Sect. 4. Similarly to Cleverleaf, the instrumentation overhead of Artemis, shown by observing the slowdown of Artemis-OpenMP, is within 9% of non-instrumented execution of RAJA-OpenMP.

Regarding speedup of Artemis, it is consistently faster than RAJA-OpenMP. Artemis improves execution time even for the default setting of cost 1× by 16%. Expectedly, increasing the cost creates more computational disparity between LULESH computational regions, thus Artemis achieves higher speedup. For the highest cost value we experiment with, a cost of 8×, Artemis achieves significant speedup of 47% over the RAJA-OpenMP baseline.

For more detailed results, Fig. 5 shows execution time per timestep for all execution modes varying the cost of computational regions. Observations are similar to Cleverleaf, the first timestep under Artemis is slower due to training while the rest of the timesteps execute faster than RAJA-OpenMP. Artemis speeds up the execution of timestep up to 50% compared to RAJA-OpenMP, increasingly so as the cost input increases. Different than Cleverleaf, the resolution of the execution time of LULESH is much more fine-grain, in the range of hundreds of milliseconds. Nonetheless, Artemis effectively optimizes execution even at this time scale, showing that training effectively optimizes policy selection and overcomes any instrumentation overhead.

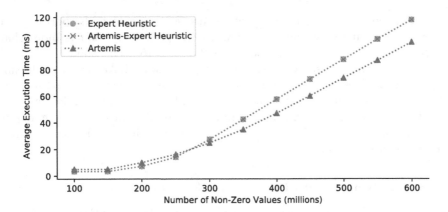

Fig. 6. Artemis improves performance of the Kokkos SpMV kernel up to 16.8% compared to the hardcoded expert heuristic.

5.7   Speedup on Kokkos Kernels SpMV

Figure 6 shows the results of our integration with Kokkos, tuning the parallel team size, vector size, and number of rows assigned to each thread. The x-axis shows scaling the number of non-zero elements y-axis plots the average execution time for 1500 SpMV kernel invocations. *Expert Heuristic* is the existing, hardcoded tuning strategy set by the expert kernel developer, setting those parameters based on the input data and expert knowledge. This heuristic function settles on 1 row per thread, a vector length of 2, and a team size of 256 for inputs shown. *Artemis-Expert Heuristic* exposes the instrumentation overhead of Artemis, by foregoing tuning, instead executing with the same settings of the expert heuristic. The performance of Artemis-Expert Heuristic is on par with execution of Expert Heuristic without Artemis intervening, thus instrumentation overhead is minimal. *Artemis* shows the performance improvement when tuning is enabled. Kokkos provides a range of 664 selectable policies to Artemis for tuning, with parameters team size ranging from 1–1024, vector size from 1–32, and number of rows per thread from 1–4096. Results show that Artemis succesfully navigates the tuning space, and provides increasingly faster performance as the problem size increases, for a maximum of 16.8% performance improvement on the largest input of 600 M non-zero elements.

6   Related Work

Existing tuning frameworks are either application-specific [5,28], programming-model-specific [2,23], hardware-specific [4,15], or feature the need for offline training [9,27], and thus have limited scope. By design, Artemis is a general framework that gives an API to tune at any of those levels, and we show its generality by integrating Artemis with the RAJA programming model, tuning a variety of HPC proxy applications and kernels. The closest to our work is the

Apollo paper by Beckingsale et al. [9], with the important distinction that, rather than exhaustive offline tuning, the Artemis framework performs the search space exploration at runtime.

Empirical techniques directly measure all the possible variants and select the fastest. Established projects like the ATLAS [4,29] and FFTW [15] libraries apply this technique with great success, but it requires the up front cost of finding the best code variant choices for each system. ATF [25,26]presents a generic extensible framework for automated tuning, independent of programming language or domain. Oski [28] performs runtime tuning, optimizing over sparse linear algebra kernels. Orio [17] and OpenTuner [2] are able to facilitate general purpose kernel tuning using empirical techniques to select the best performing configurations for production. ActiveHarmony [18] uses parallel search strategies to perform online tuning, though sweeping large parameter spaces can take significant amounts of time.

Using some form of a model to predict the performance of the code, analytical examples make tuning decisions based on model output. Similarly to Artemis, AutoTuneTMP [23] makes use of C++ template metaprogramming to abstract-away the tuning mechanisms of kernels and facilitate performance portability. It constrains the search space for online training using parameterized kernel definitions. Unlike Artemis's use of RAJA policies that are compiled in alongside the application, AutoTuneTMP uses JIT compilation and dynamic linking at runtime to produce kernel variants, a mechanism which could impose non-trivial overhead in a large large class of HPC codes in production settings. Mira [21] uses static performance analysis to generate and explore performance models offline. Mira's abstract performance models allow it to avoid some of the limitations to offline learning.

A statistical model is built by applying machine learning techniques, and this model is used to make tuning decisions. Sreenivasan et al. [27] demonstrated performance gains using an OpenMP autotuner framework that performs offline tuning using a random forest statistical model of the reduced search space to eliminate exhaustive tuning. HiPerBOt [22] presents an active learning framework that uses Bayesian techniques to maintain optimal outcomes while collapsing the required number of samples for learning.

Other work [11,12,16] has looked into auto-tuning the number of OpenMP threads in multi-program execution. Those approaches look at architectural metrics, such as Instructions-Per-Cycle and memory stalls, to dynamically throttle thread allocation when contention occurs.

7   Conclusion and Future Work

We have presented Artemis, a novel framework that optimizes performance by tuning an application's parallel computational regions online. Artemis provides a powerful API to integrate online tuning in existing applications, by defining tunable regions and execution variants. Artemis automatically adapts to data-dependent or time-dependent changes in execution using decision tree and regression models. We integrated Artemis with RAJA and Kokkos and evaluated online tuning performance on HPC proxy applications: Cleverleaf and LULESH, and a CUDA SpMV kernel. Results show that Artemis is up to 47% faster and its operating overhead is minimal.

Future work includes: 1. using Artemis for tuning of additional GPU-offloaded compute kernels with heterogeneous memory hierarchies. 2. tuning additional parallel execution parameters such as loop tiling and nesting. 3. expanding experimentation to large applications by extending the Artemis codebase and integration with RAJA, Kokkos, and lower level parallel programming models, such as OpenMP, CUDA, and HIP.

Acknowledgment. This work was performed under the auspices of the U.S. Department of Energy by Lawrence Livermore National Laboratory under Contract DE-AC52-07NA27344 (LLNL-CONF-809192). Additional support was provided by a LLNL subcontract to the University of Oregon, No. B631536. This document was prepared as an account of work sponsored by an agency of the United States government. Neither the United States government nor Lawrence Livermore National Security, LLC, nor any of their employees makes any warranty, expressed or implied, or assumes any legal liability or responsibility for the accuracy, completeness, or usefulness of any information, apparatus, product, or process disclosed, or represents that its use would not infringe privately owned rights. Reference herein to any specific commercial product, process, or service by trade name, trademark, manufacturer, or otherwise does not necessarily constitute or imply its endorsement, recommendation, or favoring by the United States government or Lawrence Livermore National Security, LLC. The views and opinions of authors expressed herein do not necessarily state or reflect those of the United States government or Lawrence Livermore National Security, LLC, and shall not be used for advertising or product endorsement purposes.

References

1. Hydrodynamics Challenge Problem, Lawrence Livermore National Laboratory. Tech. Rep. LLNL-TR-490254, Lawrence Livermore National Laboratory
2. Ansel, J., et al.: Opentuner: an extensible framework for program autotuning. In: Proceedings of the 23rd International Conference on Parallel Architectures and Compilation, pp. 303–316 (2014)
3. Balaprakash, P., Dongarra, J., Gamblin, T., Hall, M., Hollingsworth, J.K., Norris, B., Vuduc, R.: Autotuning in high-performance computing applications. Proc. IEEE **106**(11), 2068–2083 (2018)
4. Baldeschwieler, J.E., Blumofe, R.D., Brewer, E.A.: Atlas: an infrastructure for global computing. In: Proceedings of the 7th Workshop on ACM SIGOPS European Workshop: Systems Support for Worldwide Applications, pp. 165–172 (1996)
5. Bari, M.A.S., Chaimov, N., Malik, A.M., Huck, K.A., Chapman, B., Malony, A.D., Sarood, O.: Arcs: adaptive runtime configuration selection for power-constrained openmp applications. In: 2016 IEEE International Conference on Cluster Computing, pp. 461–470. IEEE (2016)
6. Beckingsale, D.A., Gaudin, W.P., Herdman, J.A., Jarvis, S.A.: Resident block-structured adaptive mesh refinement on thousands of graphics processing units. In: 44th International Conference on Parallel Processing, pp. 61–70 (2015)

7. Beckingsale, D., Gaudin, W., Herdman, A., Jarvis, S.: Resident block-structured adaptive mesh refinement on thousands of graphics processing units. In: 2015 44th International Conference on Parallel Processing, pp. 61–70. IEEE (2015)
8. Beckingsale, D.A., Hornung, R.D., Scogland, T.R.W., Vargas, A.: Performance portable C++ programming with RAJA. In: Proceedings of the 24th Symposium on Principles and Practice of Parallel Programming, pp. 455–456 (2019)
9. Beckingsale, D.A., Pearce, O., Laguna, I., Gamblin, T.: Apollo: reusable models for fast, dynamic tuning of input-dependent code. In: 31st IEEE International Parallel & Distributed Processing Symposium, pp. 307–316 (2017)
10. Beckingsale, D.A.: Towards scalable adaptive mesh refinement on future parallel architectures. Ph.D. thesis, University of Warwick (2015)
11. Creech, T., Kotha, A., Barua, R.: Efficient multiprogramming for multicores with scaf. In: 2013 46th Annual IEEE/ACM International Symposium on Microarchitecture (MICRO), pp. 334–345 (2013)
12. Creech, T., Barua, R.: Transparently space sharing a multicore among multiple processes. ACM Trans. Parallel Comput. **3**(3) (Nov 2016). https://doi.org/10.1145/3001910
13. Edwards, H.C., Trott, C.R.: Kokkos: Enabling performance portability across manycore architectures. In: 2013 Extreme Scaling Workshop (xsw 2013), pp. 18–24. IEEE (2013)
14. Edwards, H.C., Trott, C.R., Sunderland, D.: Kokkos: enabling manycore performance portability through polymorphic memory access patterns. J. Parallel Distrib. Comput. **74**(12), 3202–3216 (2014)
15. Frigo, M., Johnson, S.G.: FFTW an adaptive software architecture for the FFT. In: Proceedings of the 1998 IEEE International Conference on Acoustics, Speech and Signal Processing (ICASSP 1998) (Cat. No. 98CH36181). vol. 3, pp. 1381–1384. IEEE (1998)
16. Georgakoudis, G., Vandierendonck, H., Thoman, P., Supinski, B.R.D., Fahringer, T., Nikolopoulos, D.S.: Scalo: scalability-aware parallelism orchestration for multi-threaded workloads. ACM Trans. Archit. Code Optim. **14**(4) (Dec 2017). https://doi.org/10.1145/3158643
17. Hartono, A., Norris, B., Sadayappan, P.: Annotation-based empirical performance tuning using orio. In: 2009 IEEE International Symposium on Parallel & Distributed Processing, pp. 1–11. IEEE (2009)
18. Hollingsworth, J., Tiwari, A.: End-to-end auto-tuning with active harmony. In: Performance Tuning of Scientific Applications, pp. 217–238, CRC Press, Boca Raton (2010)
19. Hornung, R.D., Keasler, J.A.: The RAJA Portability Layer: Overview and Status. Tech. Rep, Lawrence Livermore National Lab (2014)
20. Karlin, I., Keasler, J.A., Neely, R.: Lulesh 2.0 updates and changes. Tech. Rep. LLNL-TR-641973, Lawrence Livermore National Laboratory (August 2013)
21. Meng, K., Norris, B.: Mira: a framework for static performance analysis. In: 2017 IEEE International Conference on Cluster Computing (CLUSTER), pp. 103–113. IEEE (2017)
22. Menon, H., Bhatele, A., Gamblin, T.: Auto-tuning parameter choices in HPC applications using Bayesian optimization. In: 2020 IEEE International Parallel and Distributed Processing Symposium (IPDPS) (2020)
23. Pfander, D., Brunn, M., Pflüger, D.: AutoTuneTmp: auto-tuning in C++ with runtime template metaprogramming. In: 2018 IEEE International Parallel and Distributed Processing Symposium Workshops (IPDPSW), pp. 1123–1132. IEEE (2018)

24. Rajamanickam, S.: Kokkos kernels: Performance portable kernels for sparse/dense linear algebra graph and machine learning kernels. Tech. Rep., Sandia National Lab. (SNL-NM), Albuquerque, NM (United States) (2020)
25. Rasch, A., Gorlatch, S.: ATW a generic directive-based auto-tuning framework. Concurr. Comput. Prac. Exp. **31**, e4423 (2019)
26. Rasch, A., Haidl, M., Gorlatch, S.: AFT: a generic auto-tuning framework. In: 2017 IEEE 19th International Conference on High Performance Computing and Communications; IEEE 15th International Conference on Smart City; IEEE 3rd International Conference on Data Science and Systems (HPCC/SmartCity/DSS), pp. 64–71. IEEE (2017)
27. Sreenivasan, V., Javali, R., Hall, M., Balaprakash, P., Scogland, T.R.W., de Supinski, B.R.: A framework for enabling openMP autotuning. In: Fan, X., de Supinski, B.R., Sinnen, O., Giacaman, N. (eds.) IWOMP 2019. LNCS, vol. 11718, pp. 50–60. Springer, Cham (2019). https://doi.org/10.1007/978-3-030-28596-8_4
28. Vuduc, R., Demmel, J.W., Yelick, K.A.: OSKI: a library of automatically tuned sparse matrix kernels. J. Phys. Conf. Ser. **16**, 521 (2005)
29. Whaley, R.C., Petitet, A., Dongarra, J.J.: Automated empirical optimizations of software and the atlas project. Parallel Comput. **27**(1–2), 3–35 (2001)

Correction to: Performance of the Supercomputer Fugaku for Breadth-First Search in Graph500 Benchmark

Masahiro Nakao⬤, Koji Ueno, Katsuki Fujisawa, Yuetsu Kodama, and Mitsuhisa Sato

Correction to:
Chapter "Performance of the Supercomputer Fugaku for Breadth-First Search in Graph500 Benchmark" in: B. L. Chamberlain et al. (Eds.): *High Performance Computing*, LNCS 12728, https://doi.org/10.1007/978-3-030-78713-4_20

In an older version of this paper, instead of 102,955 giga-traversed edges per second (GTEPS), the value given was 102,956. This has been corrected.

The updated original version of this chapter can be found at
https://doi.org/10.1007/978-3-030-78713-4_20

Author Index

Printed in the United States
by Baker & Taylor Publisher Services

Printed in the United States
by Baker & Taylor Publisher Services